Handbook of Positive Psychology in Schools
Second Edition

Understanding the factors that encourage young people to become active agents in their own learning is critical. Positive psychology is one lens that can be used to investigate the factors that facilitate a student's sense of agency and active school engagement. In the second edition of this groundbreaking handbook, the editors draw together the latest work on the field, identifying major issues and providing a wealth of descriptive knowledge from renowned contributors. Major topics include: the ways that positive emotions, traits, and institutions promote school achievement and healthy social and emotional development; how specific positive-psychological constructs relate to students and schools and support the delivery of school-based services; and the application of positive psychology to educational policy making. With thirteen new chapters, this edition provides a long-needed centerpiece around which the field can continue to grow, incorporating a new focus on international applications of the field.

Michael J. Furlong is a professor in the Department of Counseling, Clinical, and School Psychology at the University of California, Santa Barbara.

Rich Gilman is in the Division of Child and Adolescent Psychiatry at Cincinnati Children's Hospital Medical Center, and Professor in the Department of Pediatrics at the University of Cincinnati Medical School, US.

E. Scott Huebner is Professor in the School Psychology Program in the Department of Psychology at the University of South Carolina.

Educational Psychology Handbook Series
Series Editor: Patricia A. Alexander

Handbook of Positive Psychology in Schools

Second Edition

Edited by
Michael J. Furlong, Rich Gilman,
and E. Scott Huebner

Routledge
Taylor & Francis Group

NEW YORK AND LONDON

Second edition published 2014
by Routledge
711 Third Avenue, New York, NY 10017

and by Routledge
2 Park Square, Milton Park, Abingdon, Oxon OX14 4RN

Routledge is an imprint of the Taylor & Francis Group, an informa business

First edition published in 2009 by Routledge

Library of Congress Cataloging-in-Publication Data
Handbook of positive psychology in schools / [edited by] Michael J. Furlong, Richard Gilman, E. Scott Huebner.—Second edition.
    pages cm.—(Educational psychology handbook series)
  Includes bibliographical references and index.
  1. School psychology—Handbooks, manuals, etc.   2. Positive psychology—Handbooks, manuals, etc.   I. Furlong, Michael J., 1951-editor of compilation.   II. Gilman, Rich, 1968-editor of compilation.   III. Huebner, Eugene Scott, 1953-editor of compilation.
  LB1027.55.H363 2014
  370.15—dc23   2013030519

ISBN: 978-0-415-62185-4 (hbk)
ISBN: 978-0-415-62186-1 (pbk)
ISBN: 978-0-203-10652-5 (ebk)

Typeset in Minion
by Apex CoVantage, LLC

CONTENTS

Section I
Conceptual Foundations

1

TOWARD A SCIENCE AND PRACTICE OF POSITIVE PSYCHOLOGY IN SCHOOLS
A Conceptual Framework

Rich Gilman, Cincinnati Children's Hospital Medical Center, University of Cincinnati Medical School, Cincinnati, Ohio, USA

E. Scott Huebner, Department of Psychology, University of South Carolina, Columbia, South Carolina, USA

Michael J. Furlong, Department of Counseling, Clinical, and School Psychology, University of California Santa Barbara, Santa Barbara, California, USA

Corresponding author:
Rich Gilman, Division of Developmental and Behavioral Pediatrics, Cincinnati Children's Hospital Medical Center, University of Cincinnati, Cincinnati, OH 45229. Phone: (513) 636-8172. E-mail: Richard.Gilman@cchmc.org

INTRODUCTION

There is much agreement that positive youth development takes place in families, peer groups, and out-home contexts, such as schools (Gilman, Huebner, & Buckman, 2008). Nevertheless, investigations of factors that contribute to optimal school experiences in youth have traditionally lagged behind scholarship examining the other two contexts. Research has shown that from the earliest ages, the quality of school experiences plays a contributory role in key developmental and learning milestones such as motivation (van Grinsven & Tillema, 2006), identity development (e.g., Gonzalez, 2009), health outcomes (Forrest, Bevans, Riley, Crespo, & Louis, 2013), and overall academic success (Cohen, McCabe, Michelli, & Pickeral 2009). Further, the quality of experiences during the formative school years dictates, in part, the choices students make as adults. For example, longitudinal studies find that students who report more positive school experiences also report higher levels of mental and physical health as young adults (Reynolds & Ou, 2010; Wickrama & Vazsonyi, 2011), are less likely to engage in risk behaviors such as alcohol use (Locke & Newcomb, 2004), and report that they were better prepared for their future (Lapan, Gysbers, & Sun, 1997).

The limited perspective on factors that contribute to optimal school experiences can be explained, in part, by prevailing legislative mandates, proposals, and training models that often dictate problem-focused approaches (i.e., fixing what is broken) rather than emphasizing practices that seek to advance positive health and/or educational agenda (Froh, Huebner, Youssef, & Conte, 2011; Knoop, 2011; Kristjánsson, 2012). Even a cursory examination of the education literature over the past decade reveals that studies investigating pathology-based constructs such as anxiety, depression, mental illness, and problem behaviors outnumber studies investigating assets such as self-esteem, school satisfaction, hope, and personal values (by a factor of 4:1). This skewed ratio is not specific to education, however. Various literature reviews find that for every article examining positive constructs, far more attention is devoted to studies that explore "what goes wrong" in humans, such as psychological, physical, and educational disorders (Lopez et al., 2006; Myers, 2000).

Such overemphasis presumes that repairing or restoring factors that contribute to psychological distress automatically progresses to optimal development. This presumption has repeatedly been called into question. For example, studies among adults demonstrate that correlates of life quality are distinct from those that contribute to psychopathology (e.g., Fredrickson & Losada, 2005; Keyes, 2005). Thus, the absence of psychopathological symptoms is not necessarily concordant with optimal functioning (e.g., Keyes & Westerhof, 2012). Collectively, these findings provide empirical support to longstanding conceptualizations that mental "health" is more than the absence of problems, distress, and disease (Jahoda, 1958; World Health Organization, 1948) and emphasize the need to understand factors that contribute to well-being in addition to factors that contribute to ill-being.

In reaction to the overemphasis on research and practice related to weakness and problems, "positive psychology" has gained prominence over the last 15 years (Seligman & Csikszentmihalyi, 2000; Sheldon & King, 2001; Snyder & McCullough, 2000). As a general definition, positive psychology ". . . is the scientific study of what goes right in life, from birth to death and all stops in between . . . and takes seriously those things in life that make life most worth living" (Peterson, 2006, p. 4). The phrase *scientific study* is highlighted here to distinguish it from highly influential theories in which principles such as strengths, character, and values are underlined conditions to a life well lived (see Simonton, 2011, for a review). By incorporating rigorous scientific methods into both correlational and experimental designs, positive psychology serves as a lens to empirically examine presumed causes and correlates of optimal human functioning. Further, prior to emerging as a general movement, most efforts to examine positive psychology constructs were conducted in isolation and within disciplines (e.g., counseling psychology, theology, economics), thus hindering knowledge and insights that would contribute to a collective understanding of human strengths and capacities. Positive psychology has served as an important focal point for like-minded researchers and has connected heretofore islands of scholarship that have led to important and provocative findings (Ingram & Snyder, 2006; King, 2011).

Although not exclusive, most of these studies have been based on adult or gerontological samples. However, efforts have been made over the past 20 years to examine the good life in children for at least two reasons. First, similar to what has been reported in adults, "mental illness" and "mental health" are distinct (although not orthogonal) constructs in youth. For example, among a sample of middle school students, Keyes (2006) reported that a significant number of youth reported low levels of psychological distress but also low psychological well-being. Nonetheless, based on most standardized self-report measures used in schools, which often focus on assessing psychological distress, these students would appear psychologically "healthy" even though their well-being reports would indicate otherwise (see Suldo & Shaffer, 2008, for similar findings). Second, a study of factors that contribute to optimal functioning has intuitive appeal to many stakeholders—most notably to parents. Indeed, the foremost goal of most parents is not to prevent psychopathology but to instill and promote skills and values that contribute to a productive life. To this end, research has shown that numerous psychological, social, and academic benefits are afforded to those individuals who maintain incrementally higher levels of well-being (e.g., Gilman & Huebner, 2006; Haranin, Huebner, & Suldo, 2007). An understanding of the presumed correlates associated with positive psychological constructs would contribute meaningful information toward interventions that enhance optimal functioning among youth having suboptimal levels.

A growing literature base has continued to add to the nomothetic understanding of developmental pathways to optimal functioning in children (see Huebner, Gilman, & Ma, 2011, for a recent review). Positive psychology in youth has been studied in primary prevention (Madden, Green, & Grant, 2011), health disparities (Vera & Shin, 2006), positive youth development (Lerner, Phelps, Forman, & Bowers, 2009), and resilience research (Noble & McGrath, 2012). Other areas have been lacking. Schools, for example, constitute an important and fertile environment in which positive attributes, psychological assets, and character strengths can be developed and maintained. The first edition of this handbook was the first to provide a synthesis of positive psychology theory, application, and research findings within the context of schooling and school-related experiences. Nevertheless, since the publication of the handbook, more than 200 studies have been published that have greatly expanded how positive psychology can be applied to this important setting. The purpose of this revised handbook, undertaken in a relatively short time since its initial release, reflects that speed in which school-based research has rapidly emerged, both in the United States and internationally.

CONCEPTUAL MODEL

It has been noted elsewhere that the positive psychology movement has grown so rapidly that guiding, conceptual frameworks have been elusive (Csikszentmihalyi, 2003). Although some efforts have been made to address this concern within specific positive psychology constructs (e.g., Lent et al., 2005; Seligman, Steen, Park, & Peterson, 2005), concerns regarding a lack of conceptual positive psychology framework that encompasses both individual and contextual factors remain (Schueller, 2009). Such concerns are not reserved to adult samples, however. In our first edition, we introduced a conceptual model within an ecological perspective, reflecting the notion that children live within interlocking systems, all of which are essential to their psychological, social, and educational development. The model itself was based on the work of both Bronfenbrenner's (1979) Ecological Systems Theory and Belsky's (1980) inclusion of ontogenic (i.e., intraindividual) variables. The model also is adapted from Schalock and Alonso's (2002) integrative model of quality of life. These ecological systems are identified in the columns in Figure 1.1. The ontogenic system includes individual differences in aspects such as self-esteem, while the microsystem consists of immediate settings, such as home, peer group, and school, which can influence and be influenced by these ontogenic factors. The mesosystem and its extension, the exosystem, refer to more distal contextual factors, such as the neighborhood, community services, organizations, and interactions between microsystem variables (e.g., parent–school interactions). Finally, the macrosystem refers to the institutional patterns of the culture or subculture (e.g., economic, social, educational, legal, and political systems) that influence the other subsystems.

The positive psychology constructs, which involve individual personal strengths of interest (i.e., physical, cognitive, or social-emotional), are listed along the vertical axis, that is, down the left side of the matrix in Figure 1.1. It is noted that the model itself is

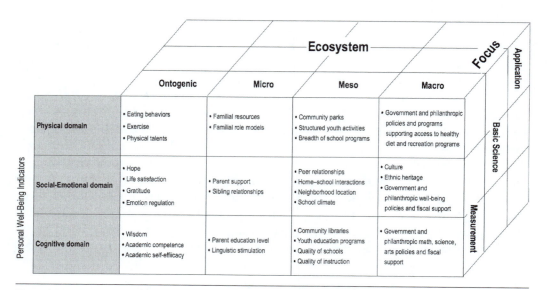

Figure 1.1 Children's positive psychology research summary matrix conceptual framework.

intended to be quite flexible and can accommodate yet unexplored positive psychology constructs. Key correlates of individual differences in the positive psychology variables, some of which have strong, empirical merit—others less so—can be listed within each cell (some examples are provided). In this manner, the extant literature can be summarized, potentially indicating areas that need further investigation. For example, recent studies examining correlates associated with optimal school satisfaction have focused primarily on ontogenic and microsystem levels. There remains a paucity of research at the mesosystem and macrosystem levels (e.g., Gilman & Huebner, 2006; Siddall, Huebner, & Jiang, 2013). Similar listings might be developed for these higher-level systems or for additional positive psychology ontogenic constructs such as hope, optimism, school connectedness, healthy physical activity, and so forth.

The third dimension of the positive psychology matrix reflects three types of research in child-focused positive psychology: measurement, basic science, and applied research. The measurement domain includes research related to the development of psychometrically sound measures of positive psychology constructs for children and youth (e.g., developmentally appropriate measures of life satisfaction, hope, social self-efficacy). The basic research domain includes studies of the development, correlates, and consequences of positive psychological attributes of individuals. Finally, the applied research domain refers to studies of planned and unplanned interventions related to positive psychology constructs (e.g., Suldo, Savage, & Mercer, 2013) or studies of the effects of residential treatment programs on life satisfaction of youth clients (Gilman & Handwerk, 2001). Taken together, this 4 (system) × 3 (social-emotional, cognitive, or physical) × 3 (type of research) matrix provides a conceptual framework that may be useful in organizing, synthesizing, and communicating the results of positive psychology research with children in the context of schools.

Although not reflected in the conceptual scheme in Figure 1.1, we recognize that positive psychology research must consider developmental factors. The specific attributes and processes that define wellness may vary as a function of age group. As a simple example, same-gender peer relationships may be a critical indicator for preadolescents, whereas opposite-gender relationships may assume more prominence for adolescents (Gilligan & Huebner, 2007). Additionally, the nature of determinants and indicators may become more complex as children mature (Gonzales, Casas, & Coenders, 2006). The relative strength of the determinants may fluctuate across time as well. For example, Suldo and Huebner (2004) found that the strength of the relation between parental emotional support and life satisfaction declined across adolescence. Thus, a comprehensive framework of positive psychology research will have to incorporate developmental considerations to capture the changing nature and determinants of well-being in children and adolescents.

In the time since its publication in the first edition of this handbook, this model has been used as a guidepost for positive psychology as applied to youth in school settings. For example, Froh and colleagues (2011) used portions of the model to summarize the relative frequencies of positive psychology topics in four selected school psychology journals during the years from 1963 through 2008. Their content analysis revealed several interesting findings. For example, they were able to identify relatively well-studied positive psychology topics (e.g., competency, self-concept) as well as relatively neglected topics (e.g., optimism, purpose). For another example, they found that 61% of the studies focused on measurement, 22% on intervention, and 5% on basic science. Furthermore, the percentages of articles incorporating positive psychology topics remained relatively consistent (25–33% range) over the approximately 50-year period. Froh and colleagues concluded that positive psychology was alive and well in school psychology, but they also recommended further research attention should be devoted to the (a) basic science foundations underlying applications of positive psychology and (b) relatively new positive psychology constructs (e.g., VIA strengths, purpose, life satisfaction). Future such analyses using the conceptual model may be informative in evaluating the scope and progress of positive psychology research. Given the growing international influence of positive psychology, international comparisons of child-focused (and adult-focused) positive psychology research may be of interest as well.

Two brief notes of caution should be highlighted before concluding. First, the proposed matrix does not provide a dimension that allows for the distinction between determinants and consequences of individual differences in the particular positive psychology attribute. Although some relations may be transactional in nature, some may not. For example, Martin, Huebner, and Valois (2008) found that individual differences in adolescents' life satisfaction significantly predicted subsequent experiences of relational victimization by peers, whereas individual differences in relational victimization did not significantly predict subsequent levels of life satisfaction. These findings suggest that a low level of life satisfaction in adolescents is possibly a causal factor rather than a consequence of relational victimization experiences.

Second, although the matrix provides a possible heuristic tool to organize and synthesize the developing body of positive psychology knowledge for children and youth in school settings, it is not intended to explain the origins and development of individual differences in these constructs. A full picture of wellness in children will need to capture the interactions among the personal and environmental variables, taking into account gender, culture, and developmental considerations. This will not be an easy task, but efforts will likely be needed to model the trajectories of children's development across time and settings. The development of a sophisticated science of "what works" for children and youth within the context of their schooling is underway, but much work remains to be completed.

CONCLUSION

Although remaining in its emergent stage, positive psychology continues to gain traction in children and youth, especially as it pertains to school settings. Nevertheless, as we noted in the first edition, additional areas are in need of attention as these efforts move forward. For example, the development of age-appropriate, psychometrically sound measures of positive psychology constructs for children and youth lags far behind measures that assess psychopathology. America's schools have been criticized for focusing disproportionately on identifying and remediating students' weaknesses while neglecting the identification and nurturing of their strengths (Gordon & Crabtree, 2006), resulting in the failure to maximize student potential. The ongoing development of measures of the key positive psychology strengths that could be included in the proposed matrix could contribute to more comprehensive evaluations of student and school outcomes by assessing the entire spectrum of mental health and social and educational functioning, as suggested by Renshaw and colleagues (2014) in Chapter 2 of this handbook. Such evaluations may contribute important information toward developing educational programs that nurture strengths rather than simply identify problems.

Further, much work remains to be done in terms of basic and applied scientific studies of the development of and interventions designed to heighten positive psychology indicators. Although research has advanced the understanding of the nature and correlates of many positive psychology constructs, the extension of this research to diverse youth populations—including those who reside outside of the United Stated—is scant. One major addition to this new edition is how youth-based positive psychology constructs have been studied and advanced in a number of countries. Nevertheless, the distribution of effort is not uniform; for studies that have illuminated relations with respect to one positive construct, many others have received less attention. Critical questions regarding basic science research in many unexplored areas of positive psychology will likely propel the movement for some time.

Finally, in spite of the advances in defining and exploring relations, empirically validated programs to promote positive psychology constructs are rare. Although there are some noteworthy contributions, many of which are discussed in this new edition of the handbook, school-based programs, more often than not, focus on preventing "pathology" rather than "building health," a point noted more than two decades ago (Cowen, 1991). Additional efforts are necessary not only to promote positive constructs in students but also to examine how such promotion moderates negative outcomes such as distress and poor academic functioning. These efforts are necessary to demonstrate the important, practical applications of positive psychology to address the learning, social, and intrapersonal struggles of many students.

Our hope is that this revised handbook will serve as an important resource for those interested in positive psychology as currently understood. A second and equally important hope is that the book will serve to stimulate additional research on basic science foundations, measurement issues, developmental considerations, and associated interventions across established and emerging areas of positive psychology as applied to youth in school settings. Collectively, such efforts might stimulate alternative and balanced perspectives for legislative bodies, funding sources, and school stakeholders to consider in the shared goal of creating conditions that advance optimal youth and learning development.

REFERENCES

Belsky, J. (1980). Child maltreatment: An ecological integration. *American Psychologist, 35*, 320–335. doi:10.1037/0003-066X.35.4.320

Bronfenbrenner, U. (1979). Toward an experimental ecology of human development. *American Psychologist, 32*, 513–529. doi:10.1037/0003-066X.32.7.513

Cohen, J., McCabe, E. M., Michelli, N. M., & Pickeral, T. (2009). School climate: Research, policy, practice, and teacher education. *Teacher's College Record, 111*, 180–213.

Cowen, E. L. (1991). In pursuit of wellness. *American Psychologist, 46*, 404–408. doi:10.1037/0003-066X.46.4.404

Csikszentmihalyi, M. (2003). Legs or wings? A reply to R. S. Lazarus. *Psychological Inquiry, 14*, 113–115.

Forrest, C. B., Bevans, K. B., Riley, A. W., Crespo, R., & Louis, T. A. (2013). Health and school outcomes during children's transition into adolescence. *Journal of Adolescent Health, 52*, 186–194. doi:10.1016/j.jadohealth.2012.06.019

Fredrickson, B. L., & Losada, M. F. (2005). Positive affect and the complex dynamics of human functioning. *American Psychologist, 60*, 678–686. doi:10.1037/0003-066X.60.7.678

Froh, J. J., Huebner, E. S., Youssef, A., & Conte, V. (2011). Acknowledging and appreciating the full spectrum of the human condition: School psychology's (limited) focus on positive psychological functioning. *Psychology in the Schools, 48*, 110–123. doi:10.1002/pits.20530

Gilligan, T. D., & Huebner, E. S. (2007). Initial development and validation of the Multidimensional Students' Life Satisfaction Scale—Adolescent version. *Applied Research in Quality of Life, 2*, 1–16. doi:10.1007/s11482-007-9026-2

Gilman, R., & Handwerk, M. L. (2001). Changes in life satisfaction as a function of stay in a residential setting. *Residential Treatment for Children and Youth, 18*, 47–65. doi:10.1300/J007v18n04_05

Gilman, R., & Huebner, E. S. (2006). Characteristics of adolescents who report high life satisfaction. *Journal of Youth and Adolescence, 35*, 293–301. doi:10.1007/s10964-006-9036-7

Gilman, R., Huebner, E. S., & Buckman, M. (2008). Positive schooling. In S. J. Lopez (Ed.), *Positive psychology: Exploring the best in people, Vol. 4: Pursuing human flourishing* (pp. 87–98). Westport, CT: Praeger/Greenwood.

Gonzales, M., Casas, F., & Coenders, G. (2006). A complexity approach to psychological well-being in adolescence: Major strengths and methodological issues. *Social Indicators Research, 80*, 267–295. doi:10.1007/s11205-005-5073-y

Gonzalez, R. (2009). Beyond affirmation: How the school context facilitates racial/ethnic identity among Mexican American adolescents. *Hispanic Journal of Behavioral Sciences, 31*, 5–31. doi:10.1177/0739986308328387

Gordon, G., & Crabtree, S. (2006). *Building engaged schools: Getting the most out of America's classrooms.* New York, NY: The Gallup Organization.

Haranin, E. C., Huebner, E. S., & Suldo, S. M. (2007). Predictive and incremental validity of global and domain-based adolescent life satisfaction reports. *Journal of Psychoeducational Assessment, 25*, 127–138. doi:10.1177/0734282906295620

Huebner, E. S., Gilman, R., & Ma, S. (2011). Perceived quality of life among children and youth. In K. Land (Ed.), *Encyclopedia of social indicators and quality of life studies.* New York, NY: Springer.

Ingram, R. E., & Snyder, C. R. (2006). Blending the good with the bad: Integrating positive psychology and cognitive psychotherapy. *Journal of Cognitive Psychotherapy, 20*, 117–122. doi:10.1891/jcop.20.2.117

Jahoda, M. (1958). *Current concepts of positive mental health.* New York, NY: Basic Books.

Keyes, C. L. M. (2005). Mental illness and/or mental health? Investigating axioms of the complete state model of health. *Journal of Consulting and Clinical Psychology, 73*, 539–548. doi:10.1037/0022-006X.73.3.539

Keyes, C. L. M. (2006). Mental health in adolescence: Is America's youth flourishing? *American Journal of Orthopsychiatry, 76*, 395–402. doi:10.1037/0002-9432.76.3.395

Keyes, C. L. M., & Westerhof, G. J. (2012). Chronological and subjective age differences in flourishing mental health and major depressive episode. *Aging & Mental Health, 16*, 67–74. doi:10.1080/13607863.2011.596811

King, L. A. (2011). Are we there yet? What happened on the way to the demise of positive psychology. In K. M. Sheldon, T. B. Kashdan, & M. F. Streger (Eds.), *Designing positive psychology: Taking stock and moving forward* (pp. 439–446). New York, NY: Oxford University Press.

Knoop, H. H. (2011). Education in 2025: How positive psychology can revitalize education. In S. I. Donaldson, M. Csikszentmihalyi, & J. Nakamura (Eds.), *Applied positive psychology: Improving everyday life, health, schools, work, and society* (pp. 97–115). New York, NY: Routledge/Taylor & Francis.

Kristjánsson, K. (2012). Positive psychology and positive education: Old wine in new bottles? *Educational Psychologist, 47*, 86–105. doi:10.1080/00461520.2011.610678

Lapan, R. T., Gysbers, N. C., & Sun, Y. (1997). The impact of more fully implemented guidance programs on the school experiences of high school students: A statewide evaluation study. *Journal of Counseling & Development, 75*, 292–302. doi:10.1002/j.1556-6676.1997.tb02344.x

Lent, R. W., Singley, D., Sheu, H., Gainor, K. A., Brenner, B. R., Treistman, D., & Ades, L. (2005). Social-cognitive predictors of domain and life satisfaction: Exploring the theoretical precursors of subjective well-being. *Journal of Counseling Psychology, 52*, 429–442. doi:10.1037/0022-0167.52.3.429

Lerner, J. V., Phelps, E., Forman, Y., & Bowers, E. P. (2009). Positive youth development. In R. M. Lerner & L. Steinberg (Eds.), *Handbook of adolescent psychology, Vol. 1: Individual bases of adolescent development* (3rd ed., pp. 524–558). Hoboken, NJ: Wiley.

Locke, T. F., & Newcomb, M. D. (2004). Adolescent predictors of young adult and adult alcohol involvement and dysphoria in a prospective community sample of women. *Prevention Science, 5*, 151–168. doi:10.1023/B:PREV.0000037639.78352.3c

Lopez, S. J., Magyar-Moe, J. L., Peterson, S. E., Ryder, J. A., Krieshok, T. S., O'Byrne, K. K., . . . Fry, N. A. (2006). Counseling psychology's focus on positive aspects of human functioning. *The Counseling Psychologist, 34*, 205–227. doi:10.1177/0011000005283393

Madden, W., Green, S., & Grant, A. M. (2011). A pilot study evaluating strengths-based coaching for primary school students: Enhancing engagement and hope. *International Coaching Psychology Review, 6*, 71–83. doi:10.1007/978-94-007-6398-2_13

Martin, K., Huebner, E. S., & Valois, R. F. (2008). Does life satisfaction predict victimization experiences in adolescence? *Psychology in the Schools, 45*, 705–714. doi:10.1002/pits.20336

Myers, D. G. (2000). The funds, friends, and faith of happy people. *American Psychologist, 55*, 56–67. doi:10.1037/0003-066X.55.1.56

Noble, T., & McGrath, H. (2012). Wellbeing and resilience in young people and the role of positive relationships. In S. Roffey (Ed.), *Positive relationships: Evidence based practice across the world* (pp. 17–33). New York, NY: Springer.

Peterson, C. (2006). *A primer in positive psychology.* Oxford, UK: Oxford University Press.

Renshaw, T. L., Furlong, M. J., Dowdy, E., Rebelez, J., Smith, D. C., O'Malley, . . . Strom, I. F. (2014). Covitality: A synergistic conception of adolescents' mental health. In M. J. Furlong, R. Gilman, & E. S. Huebner (Eds.), *Handbook of positive psychology in the schools* (2nd ed., pp. xx–xx). New York, NY: Routledge/Taylor & Francis.

Reynolds, A. J., & Ou, S. R. (2010). Early childhood to young adulthood: An introduction to the special issue. *Children and Youth Services Review, 32*, 1045–1053. doi:10.1016/j.childyouth.2010.03.024

Schalock, R., & Alonso, M. A. V. (2002). *Handbook on quality of life for human service practitioners.* Washington, DC: American Association on Mental Retardation.

Schueller, S. M. (2009). Promoting wellness: Integrating community and positive psychology. *Journal of Community Psychology, 37*, 922–937. doi:10.1002/jcop.20334

Seligman, M. E. P., & Csikszentmihalyi, M. (2000). Special issue on happiness, excellence, and optimal human functioning. *American Psychologist, 55*(1).

Seligman, M. E. P., Steen, T. A., Park, N., & Peterson, C. (2005). Positive psychology progress: Empirical validation of interventions. *American Psychologist, 60*, 410–421. doi:10.1037/0003-066X.60.5.410

Sheldon, K. M., & King. L. (2001). Why positive psychology is necessary. *American Psychologist, 56*, 216–217. doi:10.1037/0003-066X.56.3.216

Siddall, J., Huebner, E. S., & Jiang, X. (2013). A prospective study of differential sources of school-related social support and adolescent global life satisfaction. *American Journal of Orthopsychiatry, 83*, 107–114. doi:10.1111/ajop.12006

Simonton, D. K. (2011). Positive psychology in historical and philosophical perspective: Predicting its future from the past. In K. M. Sheldon, T. B. Kashdan, & M. F. Streger (Eds.), *Designing positive psychology: Taking stock and moving forward* (pp. 447–454). New York, NY: Oxford University Press.

Snyder, C. R., & McCullough, M. E. (2000). A positive psychology field of dreams: "If you build it, they will come . . ." *Journal of Social and Clinical Psychology, 19*, 151–160. doi:10.1521/jscp.2000.19.1.151

Suldo, S. M., & Huebner, E. S. (2004). The role of life satisfaction in the relationship between authoritative parenting dimensions and adolescent problem behavior. *Social Indicators Research, 66*, 165–195. doi:10.1023/B:SOCI.0000007498.62080.1e

Suldo, S. M., Savage, J. A., & Mercer, S. H. (2013). Increasing middle school students' life satisfaction: Efficacy of a positive psychology group intervention. *Journal of Happiness Studies.* First published online February 2013. doi:10.1007/s10902-013-9414-2

Suldo, S. M., & Shaffer, E. J. (2008). Looking beyond psychopathology: The dual-factor model of mental health in youth. *School Psychology Review, 37*, 52–68.

van Grinsven, L., & Tillema, H. (2006). Learning opportunities to support student self-regulation: Comparing different instructional formats. *Educational Research, 48*, 77–91. doi:10.1080/00131880500498495

Vera, E., & Shin, R. Q. (2006). Promoting strengths in a socially toxic world: Supporting resiliency with systemic interventions. *The Counseling Psychologist, 34*, 80–89. doi:10.1177/0011000005282365

Wickrama, T., & Vazsonyi, A. T. (2011). School contextual experiences and longitudinal changes in depressive symptoms from adolescence to young adulthood. *Journal of Community Psychology, 39*, 566–575. doi:10.1002/jcop.20453

World Health Organization. (1948). *Official records of the World Health Organization*, no. 2, p. 100. Geneva, Switzerland: Author.

2

COVITALITY

A Synergistic Conception of Adolescents' Mental Health

Tyler L. Renshaw, Department of Psychology, Louisiana State University, Baton Rouge, Louisiana, USA

Michael J. Furlong, Erin Dowdy, and Jennica Rebelez, Department of Counseling, Clinical, and School Psychology, University of California Santa Barbara, Santa Barbara, California, USA

Douglas C. Smith, Department of Psychology, Southern Oregon University, Ashland, Oregon, USA

Meagan D. O'Malley, WestEd, Los Alamitos, California, USA

Sueng-Yeon Lee, Department of Psychology, Ewha Womans University, Seoul, Korea

Ida Frugård Strøm, Norwegian Centre for Violence and Traumatic Stress Studies Building, Oslo, Norway

DEFINITIONS AND THEORY BASE

Toward Complete Mental Health

Interest in promoting youths' psychological well-being has traditionally taken a *one-dimensional model of mental health*. This perspective considers psychological distress and well-being as being opposite states of human functioning that are represented as opposing poles of a single mental health continuum. Taking from this perspective, reductions in youths' psychological distress (e.g., emotional or behavioral symptoms) are synonymous with enhancements to their well-being (e.g., happiness or prosocial behavior) and vice versa (cf. Keyes, 2007). Although this traditional model is parsimonious and intuitive, whether it is comprehensive enough to adequately describe youth mental health has been questioned in recent years as emerging research has examined multiple-component (e.g., *two-continua* or *dual-factor*) models of mental health. Compared to a one-dimensional model, multicomponent models propose that the elements of psychological distress and well-being are related-yet-distinct aspects of human functioning and they should be represented as separate-yet-associated mental health continua. Several studies have yielded evidence supporting a two-dimensional model of youth mental health by showing that both the presence of distress and the absence of well-being are independently associated with impairments in youths' school performance (Suldo & Shaffer, 2008). Both positive and negative indicators of mental health have been shown to have additive value in predicting students' attendance and academic achievement over time (Suldo, Thalji, & Ferron, 2011). Given these emerging findings, we propose that there is a need to attend to both symptoms of distress and personal strengths and assets when considering youths' complete mental health.

From Positive Traits to Covitality

During the past decade and a half, educational scholars and practitioners have given increasing attention to the influence of strengths and assets on youth development, particularly as framed under the banner of positive psychology (e.g., Chafouleas & Bray, 2004; Huebner & Gilman, 2003; Huebner & Hills, 2011; Seligman, Ernst, Gillham, & Linkins, 2009). The nature and scope of this positive-oriented work has, so far, followed a multiphase trajectory that is similar to previous traditional, negative-oriented mental health work conducted with youth. The first phase of positive psychology's work with youth sought to identify and assess isolated traits (e.g., gratitude, mindfulness, and hope), the majority of which were generalized downward from previous empirical work with adults, and investigated the relations of these individual traits with each other as well as with key quality-of-life outcomes (e.g., positive relationships, physical health, and school achievement). Although this initial measurement phase is still in progress, the validation of several brief instruments for assessing youths' strengths and assets has paved the way for another phase of work, which has been characterized by the development and testing of interventions aiming to cultivate or enhance particular positive traits of youth (e.g., the "counting blessings" exercise for cultivating gratitude and the "mindful breathing" exercise for enhancing mindfulness). Although this targeted intervention phase is still in progress, a third—and more integrative—phase of work has also emerged.

The third phase of positive psychology work with youth, particularly in schools, has been largely shaped by interests in population-based service delivery and is characterized by the development and testing of screening instruments and intervention packages (or curricula) targeting an array of positive-psychological assets in youth (Seligman et al., 2009). The overarching aim of this phase has been to create and validate practices that can be integrated into multitiered systems of student support and function to facilitate "psychologically healthy educational environments for [all] children" (Huebner, Gilman,

Reschly, & Hall, 2009, p. 565). Within the broader positive psychology sphere of interest, for example, Seligman (2011) has offered that it is the combination of positive emotions, engagement, relationships, meaning, and accomplishment (PERMA) that forms the foundation for a flourishing life, with this model being applied in some school settings (e.g., White, 2013). Driven primarily by prevention logic, this phase has drawn inspiration from the childhood risk and resilience scholarship, which has demonstrated that increased numbers of external assets (e.g., supportive family and school relationships) and internal assets (e.g., achievement motivation and coping skills) are predictive of better school achievement and other quality-of-life outcomes for youth (e.g., Scales, 1999).

Although the major thrust of this latest phase has been investigating new multiasset measures (e.g., Positive Experiences at School Scale; Furlong, You, Renshaw, O'Malley, & Rebelez, 2013) and interventions (e.g., Strong Kids; Harlacher & Merrell, 2010), it has also yielded some new conceptual developments, such as the *covitality* construct (e.g., Jones, You, & Furlong, 2013). As the counterpart to comorbidity, covitality has been described as "the synergistic effect of positive mental health resulting from the interplay among multiple positive-psychological building blocks" (Furlong, You, Renshaw, Smith, & O'Malley, 2013). More technically, it is "the latent, second-order positive mental health construct accounting for the presence of several co-occurring, first-order positive mental health indicators" (Furlong et al., 2013). The first study to investigate the applicability of this metaconstruct with youth found that covitality was a better predictor of elementary students' (Grades 4–6) prosocial behavior, caring relationships, school acceptance, and school rejection than were the individual contributions of several school-grounded positive traits (i.e., gratitude, zest, optimism, and persistence). In a parallel study from a cognitive therapy perspective, Keyfitz, Lumley, Hennig, and Dozois (2013) examined the relations among core positive constructs and self-reported aspects of youths' (average age 11 years) problematic and positive development. These authors found that the combination of self-reported self-efficacy, optimism, trust, success, and worthiness was more strongly negatively correlated with scores on scales measuring depression and anxiety and positively correlated with a measure of resilience than were the positive constructs individually. Building on this initial empirical groundwork, we have proposed and investigated an expanded model of covitality for adolescents, which is described and discussed throughout the remainder of this chapter.

A Model of Adolescent Covitality

To investigate the validity and utility of the covitality construct among adolescents, we developed a conceptual model that maps onto a testable measurement model (see Figure 2.1). Our conceptual model of adolescent covitality posits 12 lower-order constructs, which we refer to as *positive-psychological building blocks.* These lower-order traits are ones that have been widely examined by researchers interested in positive psychology (e.g., Toner, Haslam, Robsinson, & Williams, 2012) and positive youth development (e.g., Lynch, Lerner, & Leventhal, 2013). Our proposed model seeks to make a contribution by suggesting that these 12 lower-order traits all contribute to four core constructs, which we call *positive mental health domains.* At its core, the proposed model is cognitively based in that it sees adolescents as actively constructing a

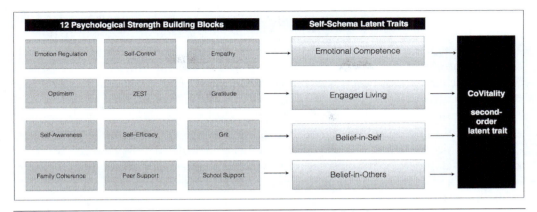

Figure 2.1 Theoretical and measurement model underlying the Social Emotional Health Survey and adolescent covitality.

worldview of who they are and coming to conclusions about their fit within their social contexts. The conceptual grounding for these domains draws on social psychology (e.g., Lips, 1995), self-concept (Chi-Hung, 2005), and cognitive therapy (e.g., Dozois, Eichstedt, Collins, Phoenix, & Harris, 2012; Young, Klosko, & Weishaar, 2003) research, which have suggested that as youth develop and mature, they increasingly develop broad cognitive schemas that are used to efficiently make sense of and organize their life experience.

Markus (1977) suggested that "self-schemata are cognitive generalizations about the self, derived from past experience, that organize and guide the processing of self-related information contained in the individual's social experiences" (p. 64). Subsequently, much of this body of research has focused on the development of maladaptive self-schemas because of legitimate concerns about how they might disrupt positive development, as when they lead to depression (e.g., Carlson, 2001), perceptions of a hostile attribution bias (e.g., Pornari & Wood, 2010), or justification for aggressive behavior (e.g., Calvete & Orue, 2012). However, just as self-schemas can contribute to negative developmental outcomes, it is increasingly recognized that the formation of adaptive self-schemas are associated with resilience (Dozois et al., 2012). In fact, we propose that the vast paradigm-changing resilience research (e.g., Masten & Wright, 2010; Werner, 2013) and the rapidly building positive psychology literature (e.g., Norrish & Vella-Brodrick, 2009; Yates & Masten, 2004) are fundamentally about understanding how positive self-schemas are formed, how they are related to adaptive and thriving developmental outcomes, and how they can be fostered across the lifespan.

Our model proposes four positive core mental health domains or self-schemas. The first, *belief-in-self*, is composed of three constructs investigated in the social-emotional learning (SEL) literature: *self-efficacy* (e.g., "I can work out my problems"), *self-awareness* (e.g., "There is a purpose to my life"), and *persistence* (e.g., "I try to answer all the questions asked in class"). The second domain, *belief-in-others*, consists of three constructs studied primarily in the childhood resilience literature: *school support* (e.g., "At my school there is a teacher or some other adult who believes that I will be a success"), *peer support* (e.g., "I have a friend my age who really cares about me"), and *family support* (e.g., "There is a feeling of togetherness in my family"). Similar to the first domain, the third domain, *emotional competence*, is also composed of three constructs researched primarily in the SEL literature: *emotional regulation* (e.g., "I can deal with being told no"), *empathy* (e.g., "I feel bad when someone gets their feelings hurt"), and *behavioral regulation* (e.g., "I can wait for what I want"). And, the final positive mental health domain, *engaged living*, is composed of three constructs derived from the positive psychology literature: *gratitude* (frequency of feeling thankful), *zest* (frequency of feeling energetic), and *optimism* (e.g., "I usually expect to have a good day"). This model recognizes that these positive domains are correlated; however, as noted previously in this chapter, we extended this reasoning by proposing that these four domains map onto a higher-order construct that we call covitality. Based on a cumulative resilience model, we have proposed that the influences of lower-order positive-psychological building blocks are enhanced when they present in combination (Furlong et al., 2013; Jones et al., 2013)

When transformed into a measurement model, the 12 positive-psychological building blocks are the only constructs from our conceptual model that are measured directly, as both the four positive mental health domains and the overarching covitality construct are inferred as latent constructs. In the next section, we further expand upon our model by providing operational definitions and reviewing relevant research for the 12 positive-psychological building blocks that we situate as the foundation of adolescent covitality, then reviewing research on the development of the Social Emotional Health Survey (SEHS; Furlong et al., 2013) that operationalizes the measurement model. See Furlong and colleagues (2013) for a full description of the SEHS.

REVIEW OF KEY RESEARCH STUDIES

Operational Definitions

Operational definitions for the 12 positive-psychological building blocks underlying our adolescent covitality model are provided in Table 2.1. Although these positive-mental-health constructs are not novel, we recognize that our operationalizations may differ slightly from those used in previous works and that some of our conceptualizations are broader in scope than those employed in several of the studies cited in Table 2.1. For example, while we operationalize our first indicator, *self-awareness*, as "perceiving and attending to the private and public aspects of one's self" (see Table 2.1), the studies we cite in support of this indicator were all investigations of youths' *mindfulness*, which was conceptualized in one study as simply attending to one's present-moment experience (Drake, Duncan, Sutherland, Abernethy, & Henry, 2008) and in other studies as present-moment attention accompanied by a receptive attitude toward one's experiences (Ciarrochi Kashdan, Leeson, Heaven, & Jordan., 2011; Greco, Baer, & Smith, 2011). A comparison of these definitions with our operationalization of self-awareness, as well as a content analysis of the three items making up the self-awareness scale for the SEHS (see Table 2.1), suggests that although our conception of self-awareness encompasses mindfulness, it also extends beyond the boundaries of mindfulness—including awareness of one's "purpose in life" and an intuitive "understanding" of one's behavior, which

Table 2.1 Definitions and Correlates of Covitality Indicators

Covitality Indicator	Construct Definition	Range of r with SWB[1] [95% CI]	References	Range of r with SA[2] [95% CI]	References
BELIEF-IN-SELF					
Self-Awareness	Perceiving and attending to the private and public aspects of one's self (Abrams & Brown, 1989)	.24 – .35 [.17, .43]	Ciarrochi et al., 2011; Drake et al., 2008	~.28 [.23, .33]	Greco et al., 2011
Persistence	Working diligently to accomplish one's goals, including maintaining interest in the face of adversity and failure (Duckworth et al., 2007)	.09 – .34 [–.03, .42]	Garcia, 2011; Garcia et al., 2012	.24 – .32 [.15, .42]	Duckworth & Quinn, 2009; Martin & Marsh, 2006
Self-Efficacy	Sensing one's ability to act effectively to meet environmental demands (Bandura et al., 1996)	.09 – .48 [–.03, .51]	Danielsen et al., 2009; Diseth et al., 2012; Fogle et al., 2002; Lightsey et al., 2011; Vecchio et al., 2007; Vieno et al., 2007	.17 – .44 [.06, .51]	Capara et al., 2011; Zhu et al., 2011; Zuffiano et al., 2013
BELIEF-IN-OTHERS					
Peer Support	Appraising the caring and helpful nature of one's relationships with peers (Farmer & Farmer, 1996)	.23 – .61 [.07, .63]	Danielsen et al., 2009; Flaspohler et al., 2009; Oberle et al., 2011; Schwarz et al., 2012; Vera et al., 2008	.10 – .22 [.01, .33]	Chen, 2005; Danielsen et al., 2009; Ozer & Schotland, 2011; Rosalind, 2010
Teacher Support	Appraising the caring and helpful nature of one's relationships with teachers (Farmer & Farmer, 1996)	.32 –.54 [.29, .61]	Danielsen et al., 2009; Ferguson et al., 2010; Flaspohler et al., 2009; Stewart & Suldo, 2011	.15 – .33 [.05, .43]	Chen, 2005; Danielsen et al., 2009; Rosalind, 2010; Stewart & Suldo, 2011
Family Support	Appraising the caring and helpful nature of one's relationships with family (Farmer & Farmer, 1996)	.32 – .67 [.29, .72]	Danielsen et al., 2009; Ferguson et al., 2010; Oberle et al., 2011; Schwarz et al., 2012; Stewart & Suldo, 2011; Vieno et al., 2007	.23 – .27 [.13, .33]	Chen, 2005; Danielsen et al., 2009; Rosalind, 2010; Stewart & Suldo, 2011
EMOTIONAL COMPETENCE					
Empathy	Perceiving, sharing, and considering the emotional states expressed by others (Garaigordobil, 2004)	~.27 [.08, .44]	Oberle et al., 2010	*No available research*	

(Continued)

Table 2.1 (Continued)

Covitality Indicator	Construct Definition	Range of r with SWB[1] [95% CI]	References	Range of r with SA[2] [95% CI]	References
Emotional Regulation	Effectively expressing one's positive emotions (e.g., happiness) and managing one's negative emotions (e.g., anger; Fry et al., 2012)	.19 – .28 [.10, .38]	Haga et al., 2009; Saxena et al., 2011	.25 – .28 [.19, .45]	Gail & Arsenio, 2002; Vidal Roderio et al., 2012; Vukman & Licardo, 2010
Behavioral Self-Control	Effectively expressing and managing one's behavior within given contexts (Hofer Busch, & Kartner, 2011)	.36 – .48 [.27, .55]	Fry et al., 2012; Hofer, et al., 2011	.25 – .42 [.11, .48]	Bertrams, 2012; Kuhnle et al., 2012; Vidal Roderio et al., 2012
ENGAGED LIVING					
Gratitude	Sensing thankfulness that arises in response to one's benefitting from some kind of transactional means (Emmons, 2007)	.11 – .60 [.06, .66]	Froh et al., 2009, 2011; Proctor et al., 2010	~.28 [.23, .33]	Froh et al., 2011
Zest	Experiencing one's life in the present moment as exciting and energizing (Park & Peterson, 2006b)	.31 – .50 [.24, .59]	Park & Peterson, 2006a, 2006b	*No available research*	
Optimism	Expecting the occurrence of good events and beneficial outcomes in one's future (Utsey et al., 2008).	.24 – .65 [.11, .68]	Chang et al., 2003; Extremera et al., 2007; Froh et al., 2009; Gadermann et al., 2011; Ho et al., 2010; Lai, 2009; Oberle et al., 2011; Piko et al., 2009; Veronese et al., 2012; Wong & Lim, 2009	.13 – .27 [.07, .39]	Creed et al., 2002; Lounsbury et al., 2002; Vidal Roderio et al., 2012

are subphenomena of awareness that have heretofore been uninvestigated in youth. Given this situation, we encourage interested readers to consider the nuances between our definitions of the 12 positive-psychological building blocks and the definitions employed in previous studies.

Quality-of-Life Correlates

In addition to operational definitions, Table 2.1 also provides an overview of the available correlational evidence for the relations among the 12 positive-psychological building blocks and selected quality-of-life (QOL) outcomes—namely, subjective well-being (SWB) and school/student achievement (SA). Given that this overview of the research is purely correlational in nature and focuses on just two key QOL outcomes, we encourage interested readers to explore the additional concurrent validity evidence available for each indicator. For instance, in addition to being positively associated with SWB and SA, youths' *gratitude* has also been shown to be positively associated with perceived social support, provision of emotional support to others, and greater social integration (e.g., Froh et al., 2011), whereas *optimism* has also been demonstrated to be positively associated with successful coping with stress and illness, better college adjustment, more prosocial relationships, better physical health, and greater persistence (e.g., Gillham & Reivich, 2004). Such wider concurrent validity evidence can be found for most of the 12 indicators included in our model. Moreover, further evidence supporting many of these psychological building blocks (including *empathy*, *emotional regulation*, and *behavioral self-control*) is available via findings from treatment studies, such as those demonstrating the effectiveness of school-based universal-level SEL interventions (Durlak, Weissberg, Dymnicki, Taylor, & Schellinger, 2011; Durlak, Weissberg, & Pachan, 2010). Thus, the citations provided in Table 2.1 are best viewed as an introduction to, and not an exhaustive review of, the relevant research literature supporting each indicator.

MEASUREMENT APPROACHES AND ISSUES

Initial Development and Validation of the SEHS

The initial study reporting on the development and validation of the SEHS was conducted with a sample of 4,189 California students in Grades 8, 10, and 12 (Furlong et al., 2013). The overarching purpose of this study was to investigate the SEHS's underlying theoretical and measurement model, which we conceptualized as representing adolescent covitality (see Figure 2.1). This study also aimed to develop a psychometrically sound and socially valid instrument that could be used to assess covitality, its four positive-mental-health domains, and its 12 positive-psychological building blocks. The original version of SEHS consisted of 51 items that were drafted to represent the 12 core positive-psychological building blocks. Following an initial confirmatory factor analysis (CFA) conducted with a split-half of the original sample ($n = 2,056$), the 51-item SEHS was shortened to a 36-item version, which consisted of the three highest-loading items for each subscale. Using the other half of the original sample ($n = 2,133$), a CFA was conducted on the shortened 36-item version of the SEHS, with findings indicating an overall adequate model fit. All items loaded uniquely onto their respective subscales (with no double loadings), the 12 subscales loaded onto their respective hypothesized first-order latent constructs (representing the positive mental health domains), and the four first-order latent constructs further loaded onto one second-order latent construct (representing covitality).

In addition to these factor analyses, results from a latent-variable path analysis indicated that the covitality construct was a significant predictor of adolescents' subjective well-being. Other analyses indicated that the SEHS had full factorial invariance for males and females—supporting its utility as a sound measure of complete mental health for both genders. Moreover, this study yielded further concurrent validity evidence in favor of the covitality construct, demonstrating that higher overall covitality levels were associated with higher self-reported academic achievement and perceptions of school safety. Lower covitality levels were associated with higher self-reported substance use and experiences of depressive symptoms. Taken together, the findings of this study suggested that adolescent covitality, as assessed by the SEHS, was an empirically promising phenomenon warranting further investigation.

Further Validation of the SEHS

A follow-up investigation of the SEHS was conducted with a sample of 2,240 California students in Grades 9 through 12 to further examine the concurrent and predictive utility of the adolescent covitality construct (You et al., 2013). Using a split-half of the original sample (n = 1,120), a CFA was conducted to reconfirm the factor structure of the 12 subscales (see Figure 2.1). Findings from this analysis indicated that, similar to the initial development study, an adequate model fit was obtained—with all items loading onto their 12 hypothesized subscales. Following this analysis, and using the other split-half of the original sample (n = 1,120), another CFA was conducted to confirm the full hypothesized structure of the SEHS. Findings replicated the initial development study with an adequate model fit.

Additional validity analyses using structural equation modeling indicated that covitality was a significant negative predictor of adolescents' social-emotional-behavioral symptoms and that the SEHS had full factorial invariance for younger (ages 13–15 years) and older (ages 16–18 years) adolescents—providing additional support for its utility as an appropriate measure of complete mental health for all adolescents. Further validity evidence in favor of the covitality construct was found in that higher covitality scores predicted higher course grades at the end of the academic term.

In addition to evidence supporting the validity of the SEHS, we found that the total covitality score (summed across all 36 items) has strong reliability (α = .92) and is approximately normally distributed (skewness = –0.54, kurtosis = 0.49). Because the SEHS latent traits are proposed to measure self-schemas, we anticipate that they are consistent over time. To examine this aspect of the SEHS's psychometric properties, 115 adolescents (14–15 years old at Time 1, 55% females) completed the SEHS at two time points, approximately 12 months apart (Furlong et al., 2013). The stability coefficients reflected trait-like stability for all of the SEHS latent constructs: belief-in-self (r_{12} = .56), belief-in-others (r_{12} = .57), emotional competence (r_{12} = .57), engaged living (r_{12} = .45), and covitality (r_{12} = .60). In sum, the SEHS has promising psychometric properties for assessing adolescents' mental health, and the covitality construct is significantly related to and predictive of key school-based and quality-of-life outcomes.

One of the advantages of the SEHS is that because it is normally distributed, it measures a full continuum—both high and low scores of covitality provide meaningful information. As such, it has potential to be used as part of a more general approach to assess complete mental health. We turn now to a discussion of how the SEHS and its covitality construct are being used by educators to assess complete mental health via a schoolwide universal screening process.

EDUCATIONAL APPLICATIONS

Schoolwide Mental Health Screening

Within a schoolwide screening initiative, the SEHS can be used as an instrument for assessing youths' mental health, to identify which students are most likely to need preventive or early intervention services (Doll & Cummings, 2008; Severson, Walker, Hope-Doolittle, Kratochwill, & Gresham, 2007). Although the practice of schoolwide mental health screening is nascent, the majority of available screeners are designed to assess risk factors or clinical symptoms, which are endorsed by no more than 20% of students. Thus, resources are expended to identify a small group of needful or troubled students. One way to remedy this problem and provide information that is relevant to 100% of students is to use a screener that assesses positive aspects of youths' psychological development to complement the traditional risk-and-symptoms–focused screening process. As both high and low scores on the SEHS provide meaningful information, its use in schoolwide screening might be particularly relevant to expand the applicability of schoolwide mental health screening to the entire student body. *All* students, regardless of their level of impairment or risk, have strengths that can be identified and cultivated to facilitate more optimal developmental outcomes. Given this context, school-based student care teams might use SEHS data in conjunction with traditional mental health screening data to gain a better understanding of youths' complete mental health, which could, in turn, help them provide more comprehensive and well-rounded services for improving the academic performance and other QOL outcomes for all students at a given school. To help school-based practitioners and researchers understand how the SEHS could be used for such purposes, we offer, in the next subsection, an example of our use of this measure as a positive mental health screener within a secondary school context.

An Example of Universal Screening With the SEHS

We recently used the SEHS as a part of a complete mental health screening initiative in a large, urban high school in California (Grades 9–12; see Dowdy et al., 2013, for a more detailed description). Prior to beginning the initiative, university-based personnel and school-district personnel met to discuss the aims of the screening project, which included identifying which students were in need of additional supports and gathering an overall profile of the mental health functioning of all the students at the school—so that schoolwide services could be appropriately tailored to fit the school's and the students' needs. Two self-report instruments were chosen to assess students' complete mental health, the SEHS and the Behavior Assessment System for Children-2 (BASC-2) Behavioral and Emotional Screening System (BESS), which is a 30-item behavior rating scale designed to measure risk for behavioral and emotional problems (Kamphaus & Reynolds, 2007).

In the first month of the academic school year, during one hour of the regular school day, members of the school staff and research team canvassed the high school, providing each class with a brief explanation of the screening procedures. All students who consented to participate completed the SEHS and the BESS. Completed surveys were received from approximately 83% of the enrolled student population. An overall T score was provided for each student, which was used to classify each adolescent into one of three risk-level categories: normal, elevated, and extremely elevated, per standard BESS procedures. Based on previous research showing that the sum of the 36 SEHS items was approximately normally distributed (Furlong et al., 2013), the composite scores were used to classify each student into one of four categories: low strengths (< 1 SD), low-average strengths (1 SD to 0 SD), high-average strengths (> 0 SD to 1 SD), or high strengths (> 1 SD). Both schoolwide and student-level results were provided to school personnel. Results describing the school's overall profile of student mental health functioning were presented to school administrators and staff. For example, a graph depicting the percentage of students with low, middle, and high scores for the personal strengths was provided (see Figure 2.2). In response, school personnel discussed strategies to increase peer support and enhance the academic persistence of students.

Additionally, students' responses to both the BESS and the SEHS were combined (see Figure 2.3), resulting in each student being placed into one of the following eight complete mental health functioning categories: *Highest Risk* (extremely elevated BESS score, low or low-average SEHS score), *Moderate Risk* (elevated BESS score, low SEHS score), *Lower Risk* (elevated BESS score, low-average SEHS score), *Languishing* (normal BESS score, low SEHS score), *Getting By* (normal BESS score, low-average SEHS score), *Moderate Thriving* (normal BESS score, high-average SEHS score), *High Thriving* (normal BESS score, high SEHS score), and *Inconsistent* (elevated or extremely elevated BESS score, high-average or high SEHS score). Using these data, individual student reports, organized by risk level, were provided to school personnel, who used the information to determine which students needed additional supports. A triage process was developed to determine the priority of needs, as resources were insufficient to serve all students immediately, and services were provided for students

BESS Risk Groups / SEHS Strength Groups	BESS Normal ($T \leq 60$)	BESS Elevated ($T = 61–70$)	BESS Very Elevated ($T \geq 71$)
Low SEHS Strengths ($z = < -1$ SD)	4. Languishing ($N = 122$)	2. Moderate Risk ($N = 61$)	1. Highest Risk ($N = 25$)
Low Average SEHS Strengths ($z = -1$ SD –0 SD)	5. Getting By ($N = 398$)	3. Lower Risk ($N = 56$)	
High Average SEHS Strengths ($z = 0$ SD –1 SD)	6. Moderate Thriving ($N = 504$)	9. Inconsistent ($N = 31$)	8. Inconsistent ($N = 3$)
High SEHS Strengths ($z = > 1$ SD)	7. High Thriving ($N = 248$)		

Figure 2.2 Example of reporting the results of a complete mental health screening showing the schoolwide covitality building block profile as reported back to the school administrators, teachers, and student care coordination team.

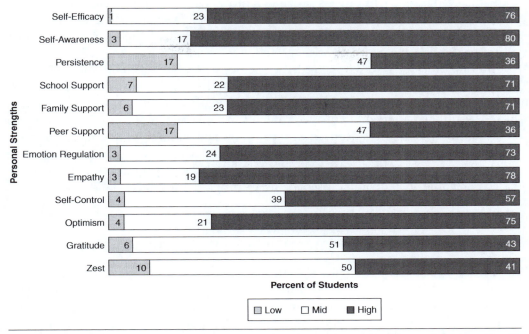

Figure 2.3 Example of reporting the results of a schoolwide universal complete mental health screening process using the Social Emotional Health Survey (SEHS) for psychological strengths and the Behavioral Emotional Screening System (BESS) for psychological distress. School care coordination team engaged in a triage process to provide supports for students in greatest need and to develop schoolwide programs and activities to promote student thriving.

in the Highest Risk group. Overall, using the SEHS as one part of a multicomponent complete mental health assessment resulted in richer information regarding the mental health functioning of each student. Its use facilitated the development of interventions and supports that were grounded in building student strengths, not just remedying symptoms. Most importantly, data provided by the SEHS enabled the school's student care team to consider the complete mental health status of *all* students as opposed to focusing on the negative functioning of only a few students, and thus empowered them to develop support services aiming to benefit the entire student body.

Individual Assessments

The SEHS is likely to be useful as a schoolwide mental health screener, providing schools with the opportunity to assess covitality among all students, in hopes that by identifying strengths to build upon and deficits to remediate, evidence-based support services can be provided. However, the SEHS can also be incorporated into preexisting individualized assessment frameworks, serving as an instrument for measuring and synthesizing strength-based information for use within comprehensive evaluations for determining eligibility for special education. Including strengths-based information within this individualized assessment process provides a broader, more comprehensive perspective on students' functioning, which is likely to facilitate increased satisfaction with assessment and resulting intervention services (Cox, 2006; Epstein, Hertzog, & Reid, 2001; Walrath, Mandell, Holden, & Santiago, 2004).

Although further research is needed to demonstrate the sensitivity of the SEHS to change in response to intervention, the brevity and breadth of the measure suggest that it might also serve as a practical progress-monitoring instrument to evaluate the effects of interventions designed to enhance students' positive mental health. The SEHS may be useful to evaluate the effectiveness of both individual and group-counseling interventions designed to increase student's strengths and assets. Thus, the SEHS might be used at varying points within a comprehensive service-delivery model, from population-based screening to individual assessments to progress monitoring and evaluation of interventions.

DIVERSITY AND DEVELOPMENTAL CONSIDERATIONS

As a unifying construct, covitality potentially offers a framework for understanding the dynamic interplay of a wide range of internal and external assets that work synergistically to enhance overall well-being among youth. A fundamental question remains as to whether and to what extent the covitality framework applies to a broad range of students manifesting individual differences with regard to age, gender, cultural background, and other relevant factors. Although responding to these questions will require considerably more empirical effort, our research group has begun to address the covitality model's applicability to diverse populations by including samples of students across grade levels and from countries outside the United States. In addition to the SEHS described in this chapter, our efforts have included the development of additional covitality scales appropriate for use with students ranging from elementary to university school settings. With each scale, our intention is to determine structural invariance according to age, gender, and nationality, as well as to determine the predictive utility of such scales.

With regard to age and gender differences, the 12 lower-order traits measured by the SEHS have been shown to demonstrate full factorial invariance for males and females in our original California samples, as well as factorial invariance for younger and older secondary level students. There is a need to further examine the SEHS's factorial invariance across more diverse samples of students who may differ not only in terms of age and gender but also with regard to factors such as socioeconomic status, cognitive dimensions including language skills, and broader distinctions related to culture and ethnicity.

In an effort to examine the role of covitality as a predictor of younger students' well-being and engagement in school, Furlong and colleagues (2013) developed the Positive Experiences at School Scale (PEASS) for elementary school children. As a measure of four positive-psychological building blocks, including gratitude, zest, optimism, and persistence, the PEASS was administered to 1,995 students from Grades 4 through 6 from four school districts located in central California. Similar to the findings reported for the SEHS, analyses provided support for covitality as a unifying construct for young students, which demonstrated better concurrent validity in terms of students' positive school development than the four positive-psychological traits considered individually. In addition, the model was found to be sufficiently invariant across males and females in this sample.

In an examination of the covitality model with university students, Jones and colleagues (2013) explored the combination of six first-order positive-psychological constructs, including self-efficacy, hope, life satisfaction, optimism, happiness, and gratitude, with a sample of 528 undergraduate students attending a university in Southern California. Although only five of the six first-order constructs were independently identified on the basis of factor analysis, all of these significantly loaded onto the second-order covitality factor, which itself proved to be a good predictor of positive aspects of mental health as well as negative symptoms of mental distress.

The fact that we were able to identify and replicate the higher-order latent covitality construct as a viable predictor of positive student outcomes with student samples from elementary school through college provides support for an additive, multiple positive-psychological traits model of youth mental health. The high degree of factorial invariance across genders garners additional support for its utility as a sound measure of covitality for students of both sexes.

The evaluation of ethnic and cultural variations with regard to covitality presents numerous measurement challenges for researchers because cross-cultural comparisons can involve cultural differences as well as language differences. At present, we have translated the SEHS into several languages and have collected or are in the process of collecting SEHS data from students in Australia, Japan, Korea, and Peru, with plans to extend this to other Pacific Rim countries. Preliminary analysis of a Japanese translation of the SEHS administered to a sample of approximately 600 public and private school students in and around Tokyo again supported the notion of covitality as a valid, second-order latent construct for predicting a wide range of positive youth outcomes including school engagement and performance (Smith, Ito, Shimoda, You, & Furlong, 2014). Our future plans also include examining data collected from eight California comprehensive high schools that will allow structural comparisons of SEHS data with more diverse ethnic populations, including students from African-American and Asian-American backgrounds.

As this research goes forward, there is a need to explore other iterations of the covitality model, perhaps including additional positive-psychological dispositions or supportive assets with diverse samples of youth. It may well be the case that specific combinations of psychological assets differentially predict a variety of positive outcomes for youth, and these differences may be further influenced by cultural and ethnic factors. In addition, there remains a need to establish structural invariance of existing measurement tools (e.g., PEASS, SEHS) with other populations of students from within the United States as well as internationally.

CONCLUSION

Significant advances have been made toward a more comprehensive understanding of youths' well-being. It has become increasingly clear that there is value in assessing for personal strengths and assets in addition to solely assessing for psychological distress. It is also known that increased numbers of personal strengths and assets are associated with more positive outcomes, and educators are beginning to learn about how those strengths and assets can combine in powerful ways. This chapter introduced covitality as the synergistic effect of positive mental health resulting from the combination of multiple positive-psychological strengths and assets. We provided a conceptual model of adolescent covitality along with development and validity evidence in support of the SEHS, a measure designed to provide an overall measure of covitality. The SEHS represents a potential advancement, as now researchers and practitioners have a psychometrically sound and widely applicable tool to measure and further examine covitality.

We wish to make it clear that we do not present our model as being exhaustive in scope, because it was *not* designed to account for all preexisting, empirically promising indicators of positive youth development. Rather, we put forth our current model as a parsimonious, well-rounded, and conceptually grounded representation of core positive-psychological indicators that have both face validity and empirical promise as predictors and facilitators of students' well-being, school success, and other quality-of-life outcomes. Thus, although we offer a particular conception of covitality, future research will expand on, reduce, and revise our model when such changes are warranted on both theoretical and empirical grounds.

The development of the covitality construct is only in the beginning stages of understanding its complexities and which subcomponents are most related to important educational and QOL outcomes. We continue to be interested to identify (a) profiles of personal strengths that might exist, (b) combinations of assets that are necessary for positive development, and (c) combinations of assets that are sufficient for positive outcomes. Our initial findings suggest that it is the combination of strengths and assets that is the most powerful, rather than any of the unique constructs in isolation. It is also likely that there may be more optimal ways to intervene to enhance covitality rather than developing each skill (e.g., gratitude) in isolation. However, our understanding of the mechanisms involved in the interplay among these constructs is limited, which, in turn, limits our understanding of how to best intervene and help students achieve optimal developmental outcomes. We hope that this current lack of understanding will provide impetus for future conceptual, assessment, and intervention work. In the same way that the study of comorbidity offered new insights into the assessment and treatment of youth with co-occurring problems, we hope that the continued study of covitality will provide further information regarding how to best help students achieve optimal developmental outcomes.

REFERENCES

Abrams, D., & Brown, R. (1989). Self-consciousness and social identity: Self-regulation as a group member. *Social Psychology Quarterly, 52,* 311–318. doi:10.2307/2786994

Bandura, A., Barbaranelli, C., Capara, G.V., & Pastorelli, C. (1996). Multifaceted impact of self-efficacy beliefs on academic functioning. *Child Development, 67,* 1206–1222. doi:10.2307/1131888

Bertrams, A. (2012). How minimal grade goals and self-control capacity interact in predicting test grades. *Learning and Individual Differences, 22,* 833–838. doi:10.1016/j.lindif.2012.07.003

Calvete, E., & Orue, I. (2012). Social information processing as a mediator between cognitive schemas and aggressive behavior in adolescents, *Journal of Abnormal Child Psychology, 40,* 105–117. doi:10.1007/s10802-011-9546-y

Capara, G.V., Vecchione, M., Guido, A., Gerbino, M., & Barbaranelli, C. (2011). The contribution of personality traits and self-efficacy beliefs to academic achievement: A longitudinal study. *British Journal of Educational Psychology, 81,* 78–96. doi:10.1348/2044-8279.002004

Carlson, K. T. (2001). The self—yesterday, today, and tomorrow: Another look at adolescent suicide. *Child & Adolescent Social Work Journal, 18*, 241–252. doi:10.1023/A:1010932916107

Chafouleas, S. M., & Bray, M. A. (2004). Introducing positive psychology: Finding a place within school psychology. *Psychology in the Schools, 41*, 1–5. doi:10.1002/pits.10133

Chang, E. C., Sanna, L. J., & Yang, K. Y. (2003). Optimism, pessimism, affectivity, and psychological adjustment in U.S. and Korea: A test of a mediation model. *Personality and Individual Differences, 34*, 1195–1208. doi:1016/S0191-8869(02)00109-5

Chen, J. J. L. (2005). Relation of academic support from parents, teachers, and peers to Hong Kong adolescents' academic achievement: The mediating role of academic engagement. *Genetic, Social, and General Psychology Monographs, 131*, 77–127. doi:10.3200/MONO.131.2.77-127

Chi-Hung, N. (2005). Academic self-schemas and their self-congruent learning patterns: Findings verified with culturally different samples. *Social Psychology of Education, 8*, 303–328. doi:10.1007/s11218-005-4015-5

Ciarrochi, J., Kashdan, T. B., Leeson, P., Heaven, P., & Jordan, C. (2011). On being aware and accepting: A one-year longitudinal study into adolescent well-being. *Journal of Adolescence, 34*, 695–703. doi:10.1016/j.adolescence.2010.09.003

Cox, K. (2006). Investigating the impact of strength-based assessment on youth with emotional or behavioral disorders. *Journal of Child and Family Studies, 15*, 287–301. doi:10.1007/s10826-006-9021-5

Creed, P. A., Patton, W., & Dee, B. (2002). Multidimensional properties of the LOT-R: Effects of optimism and pessimism on career and well-being related variables in adolescents. *Journal of Career Assessment, 10*, 42–61. doi:10.1177/1069072702010001003

Danielsen, A. G., Samdal, O., Hetland, J., & Wold, B. (2009). School-related social support and students' perceived life satisfaction. *Journal of Educational Research, 102*, 303–320. doi:10.3200/JOER.102.4.303-320

Diseth, A., Danielsen, A. G., & Samdal, O. (2012). A path analysis of basic need support, self-efficacy, achievement goals, life satisfaction and academic achievement level among secondary school students. *Educational Psychology: An International Journal of Experimental Educational Psychology, 32*, 335–354. doi:10.1080/01443410.2012.657159

Doll, B., & Cummings, J. (2008). Best practices in population-based school mental health services. In A. Thomas & J. Grimes (Eds.), *Best practices in school psychology V* (pp. 1333–1347). Bethesda, MD: National Association of School Psychologists.

Dowdy, E., Furlong, M. J., Raines, T. C., Price, M., Murdock, J., & Bovery, B. (2013). *Enhancing school-based mental health services with a preventive and promotive approach to universal screening for complete mental health.* Manuscript submitted for publication.

Dozois, D. J. A., Eichstedt, J. A., Collins, K. A., Phoenix, E., & Harris, K. (2012). Core beliefs, self-perception, and cognitive organization in depressed adolescents. *International Journal of Cognitive Therapy, 5*, 99–112. doi:10.1521/ijct.2012.5.1.99

Drake, L., Duncan, E., Sutherland, F., Abernethy, A., & Henry, C. (2008). Time perspective and correlates of wellbeing. *Time and Society, 17*, 47–61. doi:10.1177/0961463X07086304

Duckworth, A. L., Peterson, C., Matthews, M. D., & Kelly, D. R. (2007). Grit: Perseverance and passion for long-term goals. *Personality Processes and Individual Differences, 92*, 1087–1101. doi:10.1037/0022-3514.92.6.1087

Duckworth, A. L., & Quinn, P. D. (2009). Development and validation of the Short Grit Scale (Grit-S). *Journal of Personality Assessment, 91*, 166–174. doi:10.1080/00223890802634290

Durlak, J. A., Weissberg, R. P., Dymnicki, A. B., Taylor, R. D., & Schellinger, K. B. (2011). The impact of enhancing students' social and emotional learning: A meta-analysis of school-based interventions. *Child Development, 82*, 405–432. doi:10.1111/j.1467-8624.2010.01564.x

Durlak, J. A., Weissberg, R. P., & Pachan, M. (2010). A meta-analysis of after-school programs that seek to promote personal and social skills in children and adolescents. *American Journal of Community Psychology, 45*, 294–309. doi:10.1007/s10464-010-9300-6

Emmons, R. A. (2007). *Thanks!* New York, NY: Houghton Mifflin.

Epstein, M., Hertzog, M., & Reid, R. (2001). The Behavioral and Emotional Rating Scale: Long-term test-retest reliability. *Behavioral Disorders, 26*, 314–320.

Extremera, N., Durán, A., & Rey, L. (2007). Perceived emotional intelligence and dispositional optimism–pessimism: Analyzing their role in predicting psychological adjustment among adolescents. *Personality and Individual Differences, 42*, 1069–1079. doi:10.1016/j.paid.2006.09.014

Farmer, T. W., & Farmer, E. (1996). Social relationships of students with exceptionalities in mainstream classrooms: Social networks and homophily. *Exceptional Children, 62*, 431–450.

Ferguson, Y. L., Kasser, T., & Jahng, S. (2010). Differences in life satisfaction and school satisfaction among adolescents from three nations: The role of perceived autonomy support. *Journal of Research on Adolescence, 21*, 649–661. doi:10.1111/j.1532-7795.2010.00698.x

Flaspohler, P.D., Elfstrom, J.L., Vanderzee, K.L., & Sink, H.E. (2009). Stand by me: The effects of peer and teacher support in mitigating the impact of bullying on quality of life. *Psychology in the Schools, 46,* 636–649. doi:10.1002/pits.20404

Fogle, L.M., Huebner, E.S., & Laughlin, J.E. (2002). The relationship between temperament and life satisfaction in early adolescence: Cognitive and behavioral mediation models. *Journal of Happiness Studies, 3,* 373–392. doi:10.1023/A:1021883830847

Froh, J.J., Fan, J., Emmons, R.A., Bono, G., Huebner, E.S., & Watkins, P. (2011). Measuring gratitude in youth: Assessing the psychometric properties of adult gratitude scales in children and adolescents. *Psychological Assessment, 23,* 311–324. doi:10.1037/a0021590

Froh, J.J., Yurkewicz, C., & Kashdan, T.B. (2009). Gratitude and subjective well-being in early adolescence: Examining gender differences. *Journal of Adolescence, 32,* 633–650. doi:10.1016/j.adolescence.2008.06.006

Fry, M.D., Guivernau, M., Kim, M.S., Newton, M., Gano-Overway, L.A., & Magyar, T.M. (2012). Youth perceptions of a caring climate, emotional regulation, and psychological well-being. *Sport, Exercise, and Performance Psychology, 1,* 44–57. doi:10.1037/a0025454

Furlong, M.J., You, S., Renshaw, T.L., O'Malley, M.D., & Rebelez, J. (2013). Preliminary development of the Positive Experiences at School Scale for elementary school children. *Child Indicators Research.* Advanced online publication. doi:10.1007/s12187-013-9193-7

Furlong, M.J., You, S., Renshaw, T.L., Smith, D.C., & O'Malley, M.D. (2013). Preliminary development and validation of the Social and Emotional Health Survey for secondary students. *Social Indicators Research.* Advanced online publication. doi:10.1007/s11205-013-0373-0

Gadermann, A.M., Schonert-Reichl, K.A., & Zumbo, B.D. (2011). Investigating validity evidence of the Satisfaction With Life Scale adapted for children. *Social Indicators Research, 96,* 229–247. doi:10.1007/s11205-009-9474-1

Gail, G., & Arsenio, W.F. (2002). Emotionality, emotion regulation, and school performance in middle school children. *Journal of School Psychology, 40,* 395–413. doi:10.1016/S0022-4405(02)00108-5

Garaigordobil, M. (2004). Effects of a psychological intervention on factors of emotional development during adolescence. *European Journal of Psychological Assessment, 20,* 66–80. doi:10.1027///1015-5759.20.1.66

Garcia, D. (2011). Two models of personality and well-being among adolescents. *Personality and Individual Differences, 50,* 1208–1212. doi:10.1016/j.paid.2011.02.009

Garcia, D., Kerekes, N., & Archer, T. (2012). A will and a proper way leading to happiness: Self-directedness mediates the effect of persistence on positive affectivity. *Personality and Individual Differences, 53,* 1034–1038. doi:10.1016/j.paid.2012.07.025

Gillham, J., & Reivich, K. (2004). Cultivating optimism in childhood and adolescence. *Annals of the American Academy of Political and Social Science, 591,* 146–163. doi:10.1177/0002716203260095

Greco, L.A., Baer, R.A., & Smith, G.T. (2011). Assessing mindfulness in children and adolescents: Development and validation of the Child and Adolescent Mindfulness Measure (CAMM). *Psychological Assessment, 23,* 606–614. doi:10.1037/a0022819

Haga, S.M., Kraft, P., & Corby, E.K. (2009). Emotion regulation: Antecedents and well-being outcomes of cognitive reappraisal and expressive suppression in cross-cultural samples. *Journal of Happiness Studies, 10,* 271–291. doi:10.1007/s10902-007-9080-3

Harlacher, J.E., & Merrell, K.W. (2010). Social and emotional learning as a universal level of student support: Evaluating the follow-up effect of Strong Kids on social and emotional learning outcomes. *Journal of Applied School Psychology, 26,* 212–229. doi:10.1080/15377903.2010.495903

Ho, M.Y., Cheung, F.M., & Cheung, S.F. (2010). The role of meaning in life and optimism in promoting well-being. *Personality and Individual Differences, 48,* 658–666. doi:10.1016/j.paid.2010.01.008

Hofer, J., Busch, H., & Kartner, J. (2011). Self-regulation and well-being: The influence of identity and motives. *European Journal of Personality, 25,* 211–224. doi:10.1002/per.789

Huebner, E.S., & Gilman, R. (2003). Toward a focus on positive psychology in school psychology. *School Psychology Quarterly, 18,* 99–102. doi:10.1521/scpq.18.2.99.21862

Huebner, E.S., Gilman, R., Reschly, A.L., & Hall, R. (2009). Positive schools. In S.J. Lopez & C.R. Synder (Eds.), *The Oxford handbook of positive psychology* (2nd ed., pp. 561–568). New York, NY: Oxford University Press.

Huebner, E.S., & Hills, K.J. (2011). Does the positive psychology movement have legs for children in schools? *Journal of Positive Psychology, 6,* 88–94. doi:10.1080/17439760.2010.536778

Jones, C.N., You, S., & Furlong, M.J. (2013). A preliminary examination of covitality as integrated well-being in college students. *Social Indicators Research, 111,* 511–526. doi:10.1007/s11205-012-0017-9

Kamphaus, R.W., & Reynolds, C.R. (2007). *BASC-2 Behavioral and Emotional Screening System manual.* Bloomington, MN: Pearson.

Keyes, C. L. M. (2007). Promoting and protecting mental health as flourishing: A complimentary strategy for improving national mental health. *American Psychologist, 62,* 95–108. doi:10.1037/0003-066X.62.2.95

Keyfitz, L., Lumley, M.N., Hennig, K.H., & Dozois, D.J.A. (2013). The role of positive schemas in child psychopathology and resilience. *Cognitive Therapy and Research, 37*(1), 97–108. doi: 10.1007/s10608-012-9455-6

Kuhnle, C., Hofer, M., & Kilian, B. (2012). Self-control as predictor of school grades, life balance, and flow in adolescents. *British Journal of Educational Psychology, 82,* 533–548. doi:10.1111/j.2044-8279.2011.02042.x

Lai, J.C.L. (2009). Dispositional optimism buffers the impact of daily hassles on mental health in Chinese adolescents. *Personality and Individual Differences, 47,* 247–249. doi:10.1016/j.paid.2009.03.007

Lightsey, O.R., Maxwell, D.A., Nash, T.A., Rarey, E.B., & McKinney, V.A. (2011). Self-control and self-efficacy for affect regulation as moderators of the negative affect–life satisfaction relationship. *Journal of Cognitive Psychotherapy: An International Quarterly, 25,* 142–154. doi:10.1891/0889-8391.25.2.142

Lips, H.M. (1995). Through the lens of mathematical/scientific self-schemas: Images of students' current and possible selves. *Journal of Applied Social Psychology, 25,* 1671–1699. Retrieved from http://search.proquest.com/docview/618915232?accountid=14522

Lounsbury, J.W., Sundstrom, E., Loveland, J.L., & Gibson, L.W. (2002). Broad versus narrow personality traits in predicting academic performance of adolescents. *Learning and Individual Differences, 14,* 65–75. doi:10.1016/j.lindif

Lynch, A. D., Lerner, R.M., & Leventhal, T. (2013). Adolescent academic achievement and school engagement: An examination of the role of school-wide peer culture. *Journal of Youth and Adolescence, 42,* 6–19. Retrieved from http://search.proquest.com/docview/1285632683?accountid=14522

Markus, H. (1977). Self-schemata and processing information about the self. *Journal of Personality and Social Psychology, 35,* 63–78.

Martin, A.J., & Marsh, H.W. (2006). Academic resilience and its psychological and educational correlates: A construct validity approach. *Psychology in the Schools, 43,* 267–281. doi:10.1002/pits.20149

Masten, A.S., & Wright, M.O. (2010). *Resilience over the lifespan: Developmental perspectives on resistance, recovery, and transformation* (pp. 213–237). New York, NY: Guilford. Retrieved from http://search.proquest.com/docview/754045132?accountid=14522

Norrish, J.M., & Vella-Brodrick, D. (2009). Positive psychology and adolescents: Where are we now? Where to from here? *Australian Psychologist, 44,* 270–278. doi:10.1080/00050060902914103

Oberle, E., Schonert-Reichl, K.A., & Thomson, K.C. (2010). Understanding the link between social and emotional well-being and peer relations in early adolescence: Gender-specific predictors of peer acceptance. *Journal of Youth and Adolescence, 39,* 1330–1342. doi:10.1007/s10964-009-9486-9

Oberle, E., Schonert-Reichl, K.A., & Zumbo, B.D. (2011). Life satisfaction in early adolescence: Personal, neighborhood, school, family, and peer influences. *Journal of Youth and Adolescence, 40,* 889–901. doi:10.1007/s10964-010-9599-1

Ozer, E.J., & Schotland, M. (2011). Psychological empowerment among urban youth: Measure development and relationship to psychosocial functioning. *Health Education & Behavior, 38,* 348–356. doi:10.1177/1090198110373734

Park, N., & Peterson, C. (2006a). Character strengths and happiness among young children: Content analysis of parental descriptions. *Journal of Happiness Studies, 7,* 323–341. doi:10.1007/s10902-005-3648-6

Park, N., & Peterson, C. (2006b). Moral competence and character strengths among adolescents: The development and validation of the Values in Action Inventory of Strengths for Youth. *Journal of Adolescence, 29,* 891–909. doi:10.1016/j.adolescence.2006.04.011

Piko, B.F., Kovacs, E., & Fitzpatrick, K.M. (2009). What makes a difference? Understanding the role of protective factors in Hungarian adolescents' depressive symptomatology. *European Child and Adolescent Psychiatry, 18,* 617–624. doi:10.1007/s00787-009-0022y

Pornari, C.D., & Wood, J. (2010). Peer and cyber aggression in secondary school students: The role of moral disengagement, hostile attribution bias, and outcome expectancies. *Aggressive Behavior, 36*(2), 81–94. doi:10.1002/ab.20336

Proctor, C., Linley, P.A., & Maltby, J. (2010). Very happy youths: Benefits of very high life satisfaction among adolescents. *Social Indicators Research, 98,* 519–532. doi:10.1007/s11205-009-9562-2

Rosalind, M.H. (2010). Relationship influences on students' academic achievement, psychological health, and well-being at school. *Educational and Child Psychology, 27,* 104–115. doi:10.1111/j.1475-3588.2011.00608.x

Saxena, P., Dubey, A., & Pandey, R. (2011). Role of emotion regulation difficulties in predicting mental health and well-being. *SIS Journal of Projective Psychology & Mental Health, 18,* 147–155.

Scales, P.C. (1999). Reducing risks and building developmental assets: Essential actions for promoting adolescent health. *Journal of School Health, 69,* 113–119. doi:10.1111/j.1746-1561.1999.tb07219.x

Schwarz, B., Mayer, B., Trommsdorff, G., Ben-Arieh, A., Friedlmeier, M., Lubiewska, K., . . . Peltzer, K. (2012). Does the importance of parent and peer relationships for adolescents' life satisfaction vary across cultures? *Journal of Early Adolescence, 32,* 55–80. doi:10.1177/0272431611419508

Seligman, M. E. P. (2011). *Flourish.* New York, NY: Free Press.

Seligman, M. E. P., Ernst, R., Gillham, K., & Linkins, M. (2009). Positive education: Positive psychology and classroom interventions. *Oxford Review of Education, 35,* 293–311. doi:10.1080/03054980902934563

Severson, H. H., Walker, H. M., Hope-Doolittle, J., Kratochwill, T. R., & Gresham, F. M. (2007). Proactive, early screening to detect behaviorally at-risk students: Issues, approaches, emerging innovations, and professional practices. *Journal of School Psychology, 45,* 193–223. doi:10.1016/j.jsp.2006.11.003

Smith, D. C., Ito, A, Shimoda, Y., You, S. & Furlong, M. J. (2014). *Covitality and school performance and engagement among Japanese youth.* Manuscript submitted for publication.

Stewart, T., & Suldo, S. (2011). Relationships between social support sources and early adolescents' mental health: The moderating effect of student achievement level. *Psychology in the Schools, 48,* 1016–1033. doi:10.1002/pits.20607

Suldo, S. M., & Shaffer, E. J. (2008). Looking beyond psychopathology: The dual-factor model of mental health in youth. *School Psychology Review, 37,* 52–68.

Suldo, S. M., Thalji, A., & Ferron, J. (2011). Longitudinal academic outcomes predicted by early adolescents' subjective well-being, psychopathology, and mental health status yielded from a dual-factor model. *Journal of Positive Psychology, 6,* 17–30. doi:10.1080/17439760.2010.536774

Toner, E., Haslam, N., Robinson, J., & Williams, P. (2012). Character strengths and wellbeing in adolescence: Structure and correlates of the Values in Action Inventory of Strengths for Children. *Personality and Individual Differences, 52,* 637–642. doi:10.1016/j.paid.2011.12.014

Utsey, S. O., Hook, J. N., Fischer, N., & Belvet, B. (2008). Cultural orientation, ego resilience, and optimism as predictors of subjective well-being in African Americans. *The Journal of Positive Psychology, 3,* 202–210. doi:10.1080/17439760801999610

Vecchio, G. M., Gerbino, M., Pastorelli, C., Del Bove, G., & Caparara, G. V. (2007). Multi-faceted self-efficacy beliefs as predictors of life satisfaction in late adolescence. *Personality and Individual Differences, 43,* 1807–1818. doi:10.1016/j.paid.2007.05.018

Vera, E., Thakral, C., Gonzales, R., Morgan, M., Conner, W., Caskey, E., . . . Dick, L. (2008). Subjective well-being in urban adolescents of color. *Cultural Diversity and Ethnic Minority Psychology, 14,* 224–233. doi:10.1037/1099-9809.14.3.224

Veronese, G., Castiglioni, M., Tombolani, M., & Said, M. (2012). "My happiness is the refugee camp, my future Palestine": Optimism, life satisfaction and perceived happiness in a group of Palestinian children. *Scandinavian Journal of Caring Sciences, 26,* 467–473. doi:10.1111/j.1471-6712.2011.00951.x

Vidal Roderio, C. L., Emery, J. L., & Bell, J. F. (2012). Emotional intelligence and academic attainment of British secondary school children: A cross-sectional survey. *Educational Studies, 38,* 521–539. doi:10.1080/03055698.2011.643115

Vieno, A., Santinello, M., Pastore, M., & Perkins, D. D. (2007). Social support, sense of community in school, and self-efficacy as resources during early adolescence: An integrative model. *American Journal of Community Psychology, 39,* 177–190. doi:10.1007/s10464-007-9095-2

Vukman, K. B., & Licardo, M. (2010). How cognitive, metacognitive, motivational and emotional self-regulation influence school performance in adolescence and early adulthood. *Educational Studies, 36,* 259–268. doi:10.1080/03055690903180376

Walrath, C. M., Mandell, D., Holden, E. W., & Santiago, R. L. (2004). Assessing the strengths of children referred for community-based mental health services. *Mental Health Services Research, 6*(1), 1–8.

Werner, E. E. (2013). What can we learn about resilience from large-scale longitudinal studies? In S. Goldstein & R. B. Brooks (Eds.), *Handbook of resilience in children* (pp. 87–102). New York, NY: Springer. doi:10.1007/978-1-4614-3661-4_6

White, M. A. (2013). Positive education at Geelong grammar school. In *Proceedings of the Richard and Janet Southby Visiting Fellows Program* (pp. 657–668). New York, NY: Oxford University Press. Available from http://search.proquest.com/docview/1364719225?accountid=14522

Wong, S. S., & Lim, T. (2009). Hope versus optimism in Singaporean adolescents: Contributions to depression and life satisfaction. *Personality and Individual Differences, 46,* 648–652. doi:10.1016/j.paid.2009.01.009

Yates, T. M., & Masten, A. S. (2004). Fostering the future: Resilience theory and the practice of positive psychology. In P. A. Linley & S. Joseph (Eds.), *Positive psychology in practice* (pp. 521–539). Hoboken, NJ: Wiley. Retrieved from http://search.proquest.com/docview/620583191?accountid=14522

You, S., Dowdy, E., Furlong, M. J., Renshaw, T. L., Smith, D. C., & O'Malley, M. D. (2013). *Further validation of the Social and Emotional Health Survey for High School students. Applied Research In Quality of Life. Advanced* online publication. doi:10.1007/s11482-013-9282-2

Young, J. E., Klosko, J. S., & Weishaar, M. E. (2003). *Schema therapy: A practitioner's guide.* New York, NY: Guilford.

Zhu, Y. Q., Chen, L. Y., Chen, H. G., & Chern, C. C. (2011). How does Internet information seeking help academic performance? The moderating and mediating roles of academic self-efficacy. *Computers and Education, 57,* 2476–2484. doi:10.1016/j.compedu.2011.07.006

Zuffiano, A., Alessandri, G., Gerbino, M., Luengo Kanacri, B. P., Di Giunta, L., Milioni, M., & Vittorio Caprara, G. V. (2013). Academic achievement: The unique contribution of self-efficacy beliefs in self-regulated learning beyond intelligence, personality traits, and self-esteem. *Learning and Individual Differences, 23,* 158–162. doi:10.1016/j.lindif.2012.07.010

CHAPTER SUMMARY: COVITALITY

- In contrast to a unidimensional model of mental health, a bidimensional model recognizes that psychological well-being and distress are separate-but-associated states of human functioning and that both positive and negative indicators of mental health deserve consideration.
- Covitality is a positive construct that is a result of the interplay among multiple co-occurring positive social-emotional health dispositions.
- The covitality model presented consists of 12 social-emotional health building blocks that contribute to four core mental health domains or self-schemas (belief-in-self, belief-in-others, emotional competence, and engaged living), which all load on to the higher-order construct called covitality.
- The Social Emotional Health Survey (SEHS) has promising psychometric properties for assessing covitality, its four positive-mental-health domains, and its 12 social-emotional health building blocks and is significantly related to and predictive of important quality-of-life and school-based outcomes.
- The SEHS can be used as part of a complete social-emotional health screening initiative in schools to expand the applicability of results to all students and could be useful as an individual assessment and progress-monitoring tool.
- Most of the current SEHS research involved Californian samples with a preponderance of Latino/a students. The positive psychometric characteristics or structural invariance by gender and age needs to be extended to include other sociocultural groups in the United States and in other countries.
- Continued research on covitality is needed to better understand how to further enhance youths' developmental outcomes.

SUGGESTED READINGS: COVITALITY

Furlong, M. J., You, S., Renshaw, T. L., O'Malley, M. D., & Rebelez, J. (2013). Preliminary development of the Positive Experiences at School Scale for elementary school children. *Child Indicators Research.* Advanced online publication. doi:10.1007/s12187-013-9193-7

This article provides detailed presentation of the development and validation of the 16-item Positive Experiences at School Scale (PEASS). The PEASS includes subscales that measure persistence, gratitude, optimism, and zest with support that they all map on to the higher-order covitality construct.

Furlong, M.J., You, S., Renshaw, T.L., Smith, D.C., & O'Malley, M.D. (2013). Preliminary development and validation of the Social and Emotional Health Survey for secondary students. *Social Indicators Research*. Advanced online publication. doi:10.1007/s11205-013-0373-0

The study presents detailed information about the development and validation of the Social Emotional Health Survey that is described in this chapter. The analyses include multigroup invariance and latent means analyses comparing males and females.

Keyfitz, L., Lumley, M.N., Hennig, K.H., & Dozois, D.J.A. (2013). The role of positive schemas in child psychopathology and resilience. *Cognitive Therapy and Research, 37*(1), 97–108. doi:http://dx.doi.org/10.1007/s10608-012-9455-6

This study uses a small sample to present the preliminary development of the Positive Schema Questionnaire for children ages 9 to 14. Psychometric properties are presented as well as concurrent validity analyses.

Park, N., & Peterson, C. (2006b). Moral competence and character strengths among adolescents: The development and validation of the Values in Action Inventory of Strengths for Youth. *Journal of Adolescence, 29*, 891–909. doi:10.1016/j.adolescence.2006.04.011

The psychometric properties of an adaptation of the Values in Action Survey, based on Seligman and Peterson's Character Strengths framework, is presented.

Suldo, S.M., Thalji, A., & Ferron, J. (2011). Longitudinal academic outcomes predicted by early adolescents' subjective well-being, psychopathology, and mental health status yielded from a dual-factor model. *Journal of Positive Psychology, 6*, 17–30. doi:10.1080/17439760.2010.536774

Suldo is a key contributor to research that examines the use of a dual-factor model of mental health in school contexts. This study further describes the dual-factor model and examines its relations with academic achievement.

Section II
Individual Positive Psychology Assets

3

MEASURING AND PROMOTING HOPE IN SCHOOLCHILDREN

Susana C. Marques, Faculty of Psychology and Educational Sciences, Porto University, Porto, Portugal

Shane J. Lopez, Gallup Organization, Omaha, Nebraska, USA

Sage Rose, Department of Research, Counseling, Special Education, and Rehabilitation, Hofstra University, Hempstead, New York, USA

Cecil Robinson, Department of Educational Studies in Psychology, Research Methodology and Counseling, University of Alabama, Tuscaloosa, Alabama, USA

HOPE THEORY

Snyder and colleagues (Snyder, Harris, et al., 1991) characterized hope as a human strength manifested in capacities to (a) clearly conceptualize goals (goals thinking), (b) develop the specific strategies to reach those goals (pathways thinking), and (c) initiate and sustain the motivation for using those strategies (agency thinking). Goals thinking is ubiquitous in youth but often untamed and unrefined. Pathways and agency thinking are both necessary, but neither by itself is sufficient to sustain successful goal pursuit. As such, pathways and agency thoughts are additive, reciprocal, and positively related, but they are not synonymous.

Whereas other positive psychology constructs (such as goal theory, optimism, self-efficacy, and problem solving) give differentially weighted emphases to the goal itself or to the future-oriented agency or pathways-related processes, hope theory equally emphasizes all of these goal-pursuit components (Snyder, 1994). For detailed comparisons of the similarities and differences between hope theory and other theories (e.g., achievement motivation, flow, mindfulness, optimism, resiliency, self-esteem), see Snyder (1994).

According to hope theory, a goal can be anything that an individual desires to experience, create, get, do, or become. As such, a goal may be a significant, lifelong pursuit (e.g., developing a comprehensive theory of human motivation), or it may be mundane and brief (e.g., getting a ride to school). Goals also may vary in terms of having anywhere from very low to very high perceived probabilities of attainment. On this point, it should be noted that individuals reporting high levels of hope often prefer "stretch goals" that are slightly more difficult than previously attained goals.

High-hope as compared to low-hope individuals are more likely to develop alternative pathways, especially when the goals are important and when obstacles appear (Snyder, Harris et al., 1991). No matter how good the cognitive routing, however, pathways are useless without the associated agency-inducing cognitions (Snyder, Cheavens, & Michael, 1999). These agency thoughts are reflected in the positive self-talk that is exhibited by high-hope individuals (e.g., "I can do this" or "I will not give up"). High-hope people are sustained by their agency thinking when confronted with challenging situations or impediments (Snyder, 1994). Thus, high-hope more than low-hope people exhort themselves to "take the next step" or to take a long-range goal and separate it into steps (i.e., "stepping").

Research demonstrates that hope is built on a foundation of contingency thinking (Snyder, 1994) and that it is socially primed (Snyder, Cheavens, & Sympson, 1997). For example, Marques, Pais-Ribeiro, and Lopez (2007a) identified a moderate relation between children's hope and their parents' in a sample of Portuguese students, which supports previous thinking about how caregivers foster hope development in children. Nevertheless, given the recent efforts in this area, further research is needed to investigate these process mechanisms (see Hoy, Suldo, & Mendez, 2013).

MEASURING HOPE

Hope can exist as a relatively stable personality disposition (i.e., a trait) or as a more temporary frame of mind (i.e., a state). Similarly, hopeful thought can occur at various levels of abstraction. For example, one can be hopeful about achieving goals in general (e.g., a personal trait), goals in a certain life domain (e.g., school), or one goal in particular.

Snyder, Hoza, and colleagues (1997) developed the *Children's Hope Scale* (CHS) as a trait hope measure for children ages 7 through 15 years. The scale is composed of three agency and three pathways items. The CHS has demonstrated satisfactory (a) internal consistencies (overall alphas from .72 to .86), (b) test-retest reliabilities of .71 to .73 over 1 month and (c) convergent and discriminant validities. Furthermore, the scale has been used with (a) physically and psychologically healthy children from public schools, (b) boys diagnosed with attention-deficit/hyperactivity disorder, (c) children with various medical problems, (d) children under treatment for cancer or asthma, (e) child burn victims, (f) adolescents with sickle-cell disease, and (g) early adolescents exposed to violence (Snyder, Hoza, et al., 1997).

To measure the trait aspect of hope in adolescents (and adults) ages 15 and older, Snyder, Harris, and colleagues (1991) developed the *Hope Scale* (HS). This scale consists of four items measuring agency, four items measuring pathways, and four distracter items. Having been used with a wide range of samples, the *Hope Scale* has exhibited acceptable (a) internal consistency (overall alphas from .74 to .88, agency alphas of .70 to .84, and pathways alphas of .63 to .86), (b) test-retest reliabilities ranging from .85 for 3 weeks to .82 for 10 weeks, and (c) concurrent and discriminant validities.

The Gallup Student Poll (GSP; Gallup, 2009) has recently developed an online school-based measure of hope appropriate for student ages 10 to 18 years (for more information, see www.gallupstudentpoll.com). Findings from studies using this scale have demonstrated that half of American students are hopeful, meaning they have many future ideas and goals, cognitive strategies, and motivation to get the things done. The remaining half of students reported that they do not have the hope they need to succeed. These stuck (33%) or discouraged (17%) students may lack the motivation to pursue goals and often give up when facing obstacles because they cannot find alternative pathways or cannot get the support they need to overcome obstacles.

In the remainder of this chapter, we incorporate findings derived from these various measures to differentiate "high-hope" from "low-hope" children (i.e., those who score in the top or bottom third of hope scale distributions, respectively). In an absolute sense, however, it should be noted that the children who score around the mean of these self-report instruments are reporting fairly frequent hopeful thinking.

RESEARCH ON HOPE

Over the last 20 years, researchers have gained a clearer understanding of the relationships between hope and important aspects of students' lives. In this section, we address areas that are most salient to the activities of school professionals.

Views About the Self and the Future

Correlational findings indicate that a child's higher hopeful thinking is positively associated with perceived competence and self-worth (Marques, Pais-Ribeiro, & Lopez, 2009) and negatively associated with symptoms of depression (Snyder, Hoza, et al., 1997). Indeed, researchers have reported that very high-hope students (upper 10% of the distribution) differ from students with average (middle 25%) and very low hope (bottom 10%) on self-esteem, with significant higher self-esteem levels for the very high-hope group (Marques, Lopez, Fontaine, Coimbra, & Mitchell, in press). Also, lower hope predicts more depressive symptoms (Kwon, 2000), and it does so independently of appraisals and other coping strategies (Chang & DeSimone, 2001). Moreover, results from a recent meta-analysis found that hope accounted for 23% of the strength of student assets, making its greatest contributions to self-worth, optimism, and life satisfaction (Lopez, Reichard, Marques, & Dollwet, in press). Additional evidence suggests that high-hope children and adolescents (Snyder, Hoza, et al., 1997) view themselves in a favorable light and have slight positive self-referential allusions.

Regarding views about the future, those with high hope typically are more optimistic, they focus on success when pursuing goals, they develop many life goals, and they perceive themselves as being capable of solving problems that may arise (Snyder, Hoza, et al., 1997). Likewise, higher hope is linked closely to having a greater perceived purpose in life (Feldman & Snyder, 2005).

Satisfaction With Life and Well-Being

Accumulating evidence suggests that hope is related to life satisfaction and well-being. Research suggests that hope scores are correlated negatively with measures of internalizing and externalizing behavior problems, indicators of psychological distress, and school maladjustment (e.g., Gilman, Dooley, & Florell, 2006). Hope in students is strongly correlated (both cross-sectionally and longitudinally 1 and 2 years later) with life satisfaction and mental health (Marques, Pais-Ribeiro, & Lopez, 2007b, 2011a). Moreover, children (Merkas & Brajsa-Zganec, 2011) and adolescents (Gilman et al., 2006; Marques, Lopez, & Mitchell, 2013) with very high hope were more satisfied with their lives and reported better mental health when compared to children with low hope. Finally, hope explained 20% of the magnitude of student liabilities, doing a better job of explaining students' depression than general negative affect (Lopez et al., in press).

Spirituality and Religiosity

There remains a paucity of research examining hope and its relations with spirituality and religiosity. Initial findings with Portuguese adolescents (Marques et al., 2013) indicated that hope is moderately correlated with spirituality but has weak relations with religious practice (as measured by attendance at a place of worship). These associations were stable 6 months and 1 year later. Nevertheless, additional research among children and adolescents from different countries is clearly needed (including different indicators of religiosity).

Physical Health

Research suggests that hope may play a role in student health. Berg, Rapoff, Snyder, and Belmont (2007) investigated the relation between hope and adherence to a daily inhaled steroid regimen among 48 asthma patients ages 8 to 12. A multivariate model with children's hope level entered in the second step predicted adherence. No other demographic or psychosocial variables were significant predictors of adherence. These results support hope as a significant predictor of student adherence to prescribed medication. To explain hope's role in student health perceptions, low-hope individuals may not believe their medication will provide a pathway to their goals of improved health; or it may be that taking the medication is difficult or uncomfortable, thus affecting their agency beliefs (Snyder, 2000). These findings highlight the need to attend to psychosocial predictors of adherence, specifically hope, and might help practitioners target these factors in their efforts to increase adherence among pediatric asthma patients.

Similarly, research on adolescents with diabetes showed that those with higher hope were more likely to adhere to a medical regimen necessary for glycemic control (Lloyd, Cantell, Pacaud, Crawford, & Dewey, 2009). Past research (Lewis & Kliewer, 1996) on children with sickle-cell disease found that those who had the disease but maintained high hope perceptions along with active coping strategies were less likely to experience the negative effects of anxiety. Hope can provide benefits for those struggling with their health, but it can also facilitate healthy behaviors. At the college level, students with high hope were less likely to binge drink and smoke, even when controlling for demographics (Berg, Ritschel, Swan, An, & Ahluwalia, 2011). Further, these high-hope students were more likely to restrict fat in their diet and they engaged in more frequent exercise than low-hope students.

Academic Achievement

Students with low hope experience high anxiety, especially in competitive, test-taking situations. Such anxiety presumably reflects that such students often do not use feedback from failure experiences in an adaptive manner so as to improve their future performances (Onwuegbuzie & Snyder, 2000). That is, rather than using such feedback constructively, low-hope individuals are prone to self-doubt and negative ruminations that interfere with attending to the appropriate cues for both inputting (i.e., studying) and outputting information (i.e., test taking).

High-hope students, on the other hand, do not derogate their abilities when they fail, and they do not let failures affect their self-worth over time. In this regard, the high-hope students make adaptive attributions that the failure feedback merely means that they did not try hard enough in a given instance, or that they did not identify the correct studying or test-taking strategies. The emphases on strategies and effort attributions may explain, in part, why hope is not significantly related to native intelligence (Snyder, McDermott, Cook, & Rapoff, 2002) but instead is related consistently to academic achievement.

Higher levels of hope are related to greater reported scholastic and social competence, as well as to elevated creativity (Onwuegbuzie, 1999). Not surprisingly, high-hope students reported significantly greater academic (and interpersonal) satisfaction than their low-hope counterparts (Chang, 1998), and extremely high-hope students (top 10%) reported greater academic achievement (Marques et al., 2013) and grade point average (Gilman et al., 2006) than average and low-hope students. Given hope's relation with perceived competence and adaptive coping strategies, it follows that high-hope middle school children have better scores on achievement tests (Marques, Pais-Ribeiro, & Lopez, 2011b; Snyder, Hoza et al., 1997), and that high-hope high school (Snyder, Harris et al., 1991) and beginning college students (e.g., Day, Hanson, Maltby, Proctor, & Wood, 2010) have higher overall grade point averages (and dropout less often; see Worrell & Hale, 2001). In these studies, the predictive power of hope remained significant even when controlling for life satisfaction, self-esteem, intelligence, prior grades, personality, and entrance examination scores. Most recently, Lopez and colleagues (in press) found in a meta-analysis that the correlation effect between hope and academic achievement represents a 12% gain in performance.

Identifying how hope differs across domains can help identify weak academic areas. However, some students may experience lower hope in regard to overall academic achievement. For example, Seirup and Rose (2011) investigated the potential benefits of a mandatory intervention course targeting undergraduates placed on academic probation. The authors found that students with higher hope completed the semester with significantly higher GPAs than those with low hope, even when controlling for entering GPAs. The authors speculated that higher-hope students internalized more of the positive strategies offered by the course and effectively applied them to their academic circumstances.

Athletic Achievement

Higher hope has been positively related to superior athletic (and academic) performances among student athletes (Curry, Maniar, Sondag, & Sandstedt, 1999; Curry, Snyder, Cook, Ruby, & Rehm, 1997), even after statistically controlling for variance related to their natural athletic abilities. For example, Curry and colleagues (1997) reported that high-hope student athletes performed significantly better in their track and field events than their low-hope counterparts, with trait and state hope scale scores together accounting for 56% of the variance in subsequent track performances.

Curry and colleagues (1999) examined the efficacy of a semester-long academic class aimed to raise students' levels of hope. After taking this class, students have increased confidence related to their athletic ability, academic achievement, and self-esteem. These gains were retained for at least a year after completion of the athlete class intervention. Also, high- as compared to low-hope children were less likely to consider quitting their sports (Brown, Curry, Hagstrom, & Sandstedt, 1999).

Interpersonal Relationships

When hopeful thinking is stymied, interpersonal struggles may result. For instance, ruminations block adaptive goal-related thinking and cause increased frustration and aggression against others (Collins & Bell, 1997; Snyder, 1994). In addition, the interpersonal problems of others can translate into lowered hope for children. For example, children who have witnessed family members or friends who have been victims of interpersonal violence have shown lower levels of hope than children who have not witnessed such violence (Hinton-Nelson, Roberts, & Snyder, 1996). Conversely, higher hope has been correlated positively with social competence (Barnum, Snyder, Rapoff, Mani, & Thompson, 1998), pleasure in getting to know others, enjoyment in frequent interpersonal interactions (Snyder, Hoza, et al., 1997), and interest in the goal pursuits of others (Snyder et al., 1997). Recent research has found that children with high hope, when compared to children with low hope, reported greater support from others and higher levels of family cohesion (Merkas & Brajsa-Zganec, 2011).

Individual Differences Related to Sex and Race

The findings consistently reveal no differences in hope between girls and boys or young women and men. Further, the differences in the hope scores of children and young adults across ethnic groups have been examined, and it appears that while not statistically significant, Caucasians tend to report fewer obstacles (e.g., oppression, prejudice) in their lives than their ethnic-minority counterparts. However, minority groups have been shown to produce higher average hope scores (see McDermott et al., 1997; Munoz-Dunbar, 1993) and higher average levels of agency thinking (Chang & Banks, 2007) than Caucasians.

To date, few studies have examined the relative levels of hope among gifted students or students with learning disorders or physical disabilities, necessitating additional research among these populations.

ENHANCING HOPE IN STUDENTS

Given the compendium of findings described earlier, we suggest that school-based psychologists consider giving the CHS to younger children and the HS to those who are age 16 and older. Although these scales have been used mostly for research, their consistently high reliabilities and validation support their use with students in actual, applied school settings. In this regard, we suggest that attention be given to the levels of the specific agency and pathways scores. For example, it may be that a student has a full low-hope pattern (i.e., low agency *and* low pathways scores); or, more happily, the student may have the full high-hope pattern (i.e., high agency *and* high pathways), either of which correlates with a variety of academic and health outcomes. Additionally, the student may have a mixed pattern of high agency/low pathways or low agency/high pathways. In these mixed patterns, attention needs to turn to raising the particular hope component that is low.

Students with the lowest levels of hope tend to benefit most from hope interventions (Bouwkamp, 2001); however, our research shows that virtually all students raise their hope levels when taking part in school hope programs (Lopez, Bouwkamp, Edwards, & Teramoto Pedrotti, 2000; Marques, Lopez, & Pais-Ribeiro, 2011). That is to say, mental health and education professionals may want to develop group-based approaches for raising the hopeful thinking of all students, irrespective of their levels of trait or school-related hope. Likewise, for students who are identified as having very low levels of hope, special approaches may be tailored to raise their hopeful thinking. See Table 3.1 for a list of steps to enhance hope in students.

Besides significant increases in hope, there is evidence to suggest that hope-based interventions can produce additional benefits. For example, in comparison to a control group, Marques, Lopez, and colleagues (2011) found that middle school students who participated in a brief hope-based intervention reported significantly higher increases in levels of hope, self-worth, and life satisfaction at both 6 months and 18 months postintervention. Also, Feldman and Dreher (2012) found that college students who participated in a 90-minute intervention to increase their hopeful goal-directed thinking reported significant increases in measures of hope, life purpose, vocational calling, and greater progress on a self-nominated goal relative in comparison to a control group.

In applying hope theory to work in the schools, we aggregate our suggestions into three categories—those involving goals, pathways, and agency. These suggestions, which we discuss next, can be applied in individual or group settings. See Snyder and colleagues (2002) for more detailed information about imparting goal setting, pathways, and agency thinking to students.

Table 3.1 Steps to Enhancing Hope in Students

1. Administration of the Children's or Adult Hope Scale (trait)—The first step in this process is to have the student complete the appropriate measure of hope. The psychologist will then tally the total score and compute subscale scores for both pathway and agency.
2. *Learning about Hope*—Once a baseline hope score is determined, the psychologist can then discuss hope theory with the student and its relevance to the change process and to positive outcomes.
3. *Structuring Hope for the Student*—In this step, the student will create a list of important life components, determine which areas are most important, and discuss the level of satisfaction within those areas.
4. *Creating Positive and Specific Goals*—Using the important life components identified above, the student and psychologist work together to create workable goals that are both positive and specific. These goals should be salient to the student and attainable. Additionally, the student will develop multiple pathways for each goal and identify agency thoughts for each goal.
5. *Practice Makes Perfect*—Once the student and psychologist have agreed upon these goals, the student should visualize and verbalize the steps to reach the goals. With this practice, the student and psychologist can collaborate on the most effective pathways and the agency behind the goals.
6. *Checking In*—Students will incorporate these goals, pathways, and agency into their lives and report back to the psychologist on the process of goal attainment. Again, collaboration can occur to adjust or modify any disparities in actions or thinking that may hinder the successful achievement of their desired goals.
7. *Review and Recycle*—This process is cyclical and requires continual assessment by both the student and the psychologist. Once the student has grasped the concepts of hope theory, however, the student can then assume the bulk of responsibility in the implementation of hope theory to unique life experiences.

Helping Students to Set Goals

The foundation of imparting hope rests on helping students set goals. The goals, of course, must be calibrated to the student's age and specific circumstances.

If the school-based psychologist first gives instruments that measure values, interests, and abilities, then specific goals can be designed for each given student. Likewise, the student can be asked about recent important goals that are quite meaningful and pleasurable. These recent activities then may be used to generate an appropriate future goal. Once the student, with the help of the mental health or education professional, has produced a list of goals, that student then should rank the importance of these goals. In this process, the student learns important skills about how to prioritize goals. Some students, particularly those low in hope, do not prioritize their goals (Snyder et al., 2005); instead, they have the maladaptive practice of impulsively wanting to go after any or all goals that come to their minds.

Assuming students have been helped to establish desired goals, the next step is to teach them how to set clear markers for such goals. These markers enable the students to track progress toward the goals. A common goal, but one in our view that is quite counterproductive, is the vague "getting good grades." This and similar goals are sufficiently lacking in clarity that the student cannot know when they are attained (Pennebaker, 1989) and are more difficult to reach than well-specified goals (Emmons, 1992). Thus, we advocate concrete markers such as "to study an hour each day in preparation for my next biology exam." With this latter goal, students not only can tell when they have reached it, but they also can experience a sense of success.

Another important aspect of helping students is to encourage them to establish approach goals in which they try to move toward getting something accomplished. This is in contrast to avoidance goals, in which students try to prevent something from happening (Snyder, Feldman, Taylor, Schroeder, & Adams III, 2000). We have found that high-hope students are more likely to use approach goals in their lives, whereas low-hope students tend to use avoidance goals. Thus, students should be helped to abandon avoidance goal setting and to embrace the more productive approach goal setting (Snyder et al., 2002).

High-hope people also appear to be interested in other people's goals in addition to their own. Accordingly, we see advantages in instructing students to think in terms of "we" goals and their own "me" goals (Snyder, Cheavens, & Sympson, 1997). For example, encouraging students to help each other on difficult math problems can create a sense of shared accomplishment while deemphasizing competition. This has the benefit of helping students to get along with their peers, and it makes for easier and more fulfilling interpersonal transactions.

Helping Students to Develop Pathways Thinking

Perhaps the most common strategy for enhancing pathways thinking is to help students break down large goals into smaller subgoals. The idea of such "stepping" is to take a long-range goal and separate it into steps that are undertaken in a logical, one-at-a-time sequence. Low-hope students tend to have the greatest difficulty in formulating subgoals (Snyder, Cheavens, & Sympson, 1997). They often hold on to counterproductive and inaccurate beliefs that goals are to be undertaken in an "all at once" manner. Likewise, low-hope students may not have been given much instruction by their caregivers, teachers, or other adult figures in the planning process more generally. Such planning can be learned, however, and with practice in "stepping," students can gain confidence in the fact that they can form subgoals to any of the major goals in their lives.

Perhaps a student's deficiency is not in stepping per se but rather involves difficulty in their identifying several routes to a desired goal. Blockage to desired goals happens frequently in life and, lacking alternative pathways to those goals, a student can become very dejected and give up. This may explain, in part, the previous research findings on low-hope students' high probabilities of dropping out of school (Snyder, Shorey, Cheavens et al., 2002). Thus, we advocate teaching students to have several routes to their desired goals—even before they set out to reach their goals. Likewise, students need to learn that if one pathway does not work, they then have other routes to try.

Additionally, it is crucial for the production of future pathways—as well as for the maintenance of agency—that students learn not to attribute a blockage to a perceived lack of talent. Instead, we believe that a more productive attribution when encountering impediments is to think of that information as identifying the path that does not work—thereby helping one to search productively for another route that may work.

Helping Students to Enhance Their Agency

Although it may seem obvious that students would select goals that are important to them, such goals actually may reflect those imposed by their peers, parents, or teachers.

As such, the student does not obtain an accompanying sense of motivation in pursuing these imposed goals. Related to this point, when students lack personal goals that fill their needs, their intrinsic motivations and performances are undermined (Conti, 2000). Thus, goals that are built on internal, personal standards are more energizing than those based on external standards.

Helping students to set "stretch" goals also is invigorating for them. These "stretch" goals are based on a child or adolescent's previous performances and personally established more complex goals. Stretch goals thus can enhance intrinsic motivation and perseverance when progress is hindered.

Often individuals do not realize the impact their self-talk can have on their goal-attaining abilities. Having students keep a diary of their ongoing self-talk (via a small notebook or audio recorder) can be helpful in determining if their internal dialogues are high or low in agency. We would suggest that the students who have low-hope internal dialogues be taught to dispute their negative, hypercritical self-talk. Emphasize to such students how they can replace the ongoing self-criticism with more realistic, positive, and productive thoughts. This approach requires repeated practice before it begins to work, so it is important to inform students of this fact so as to lessen their needless discouragement.

Hopeful children often draw upon their own memories of positive experiences to keep them buoyant during difficult times. In this way, they tell themselves their own uplifting stories, or they create their own positive personal narratives (Snyder et al., 2002). In contrast, low-hope children may not have a base of positive memories to sustain them. Telling them stories and providing them books that portray how other children have succeeded or overcome adversity can give low-hope children a model on which to begin building their own sense of agency. For suggested children's books, listed by specific hope-related topics (e.g., adoption, alcohol, anger, arguing, attachment, communication, confidence, crying, and death), we refer the reader to the appendices in *The Psychology of Hope: You Can Get There From Here* (Snyder, 1994) and *Hope for the Journey: Helping Children Through the Good Times and Bad* (Snyder et al., 2002) and to Table 3.2, which summarizes daily strategies that can be used to increase hopeful thinking.

Enhancing Hope in Teachers

Just as young children develop hope through learning to trust in the predictability of cause-and-effect interactions with parents and caregivers, so too do schoolchildren build hope through learning to trust in the ordered predictability and consistency of their interactions with their teachers. By being firm, fair, and consistent, teachers engender hope among their students. Along with such order, we believe that the teacher needs to establish an atmosphere in which students are responsible for their actions. This is not to suggest that total obedience to authority is necessary or even desirable but rather that students must be held to reasonably high standards.

With order and responsibility having been established, a teacher then can plant the seeds of trust in the classroom. Whether it is in grade school or junior and senior high school, trust opens the doors to the establishment of growth-inducing stretch goals wherein students build upon previous knowledge and insights.

High-hope teachers are very clear about their objectives, both in the sense of how to master the material in each learning unit and how to attain good grades. Moreover, these teachers take care to convey these objectives to their students (Snyder, Lopez, Shorey,

Table 3.2 Checklist for Enhancing Pathways and Agency in Students

Pathways

DO
- Break a long-range goal into steps or subgoals.
- Begin your pursuit of a distant goal by concentrating on the first subgoal.
- Practice making different routes to your goals and select the best one.
- Mentally rehearse scripts for what you would do should you encounter a blockage.
- If you need a new skill to reach your goal, learn it.
- Cultivate two-way friendships in which you can give and get advice.

DON'T
- Think you can reach your big goals all at once.
- Be too hurried in producing routes to your goals.
- Be rushed to select the best or first route to your goal.
- Overthink with the idea of finding one perfect route to your goal.
- Conclude you are lacking in talent or no good when initial strategy fails.
- Get into friendships in which you are praised for not coming up with solutions to your problems.

Agency

DO
- Tell yourself that you have chosen the goal, so it is your job to go after it.
- Learn to talk to yourself in positive voices (e.g., I can do this!).
- Recall previous successful goal pursuits, particularly when in a jam.
- Be able to laugh at yourself, especially if you encounter some impediment to your goal pursuits.
- Find a substitute goal when the original goal is blocked solidly.
- Enjoy the process of getting to your goals and do not focus only on the final attainment.

DON'T
- Allow yourself to be surprised repeatedly by roadblocks that appear in your life.
- Try to squelch totally any internal put-down thoughts because this may only make them stronger.
- Get impatient if your willful thinking doesn't increase quickly.
- Conclude that things never will change, especially if you are down.
- Engage in self-pity when faced with adversity.
- Stick to a blocked goal when it is truly blocked.
- Constantly ask yourself how are doing to evaluate your progress toward a goal.

Rand, & Feldman, 2003). This may entail having to reinforce any written instructions orally. When goals are made concrete and understandable and are broken down into subgoals, both the teachers and students will be more likely to see growth. Likewise, we would suggest that school psychologists should work with teachers to focus on long-range as opposed to short-term goals.

Beyond setting clear and specific educational goals, hopeful teachers emphasize preparation and planning. Accordingly, learning tasks should be organized in an easily comprehended format. It also is helpful to devise alternate exercises for use if a primary approach does not work. No matter what the exercise, however, teachers should avoid placing an overemphasis on "winning." Instead, attempts should be made to create an atmosphere in which students are more concerned with expending effort and mastering the information than with a sole focus on obtaining good outcomes (e.g., high grades or stellar athletic records; Dweck, 1999). This atmosphere is encouraged through a give-and-take process between teachers and students.

We believe that school-based psychologists are well positioned in school structures to be vigilant for the signs of teacher burnout and the loss of personal hopes that are all too common for teachers and coaches (Snyder et al., 2002). To reach this objective, teachers should be encouraged to remain engaged and invested in pursuing their own important interests and life goals outside of the classroom.

RIPPLES OF HOPE IN TODAY'S SCHOOLS

School-based psychologists can maximize the benefits of the ripple effects of hope in students and teachers through consultation and direct interventions (as discussed previously). Psychologists, in collaboration with the other professionals in the school, also can raise hope in a school building or a school district by facilitating the hope contagions that naturally occur through individual or group achievements. In this section, we share some ideas about maximizing hopeful thinking in school contexts.

The elimination of various forms of "barriers" is essential for spreading hope in each educational community. That is, through assessment and consultation, psychologists can identify the impediments that may be hindering students' academic performance and growth (e.g., learning problems, behavioral problems); moreover, they may generate alternate pathways for circumventing such obstacles. Additionally, psychologists may talk with students, teachers, coaches, and staff members to find any physical or psychological barriers that they may be experiencing. Included in such barriers would be schedule problems, difficulties stemming from the physical layout of the facilities, lack of resources, parental disinterest, stressful societal events, and health-related epidemics.

Facilitating goal setting also is part of a psychologist's acumen. Hope can be promoted by connecting one student's goal (e.g., a child with behavior problems who wants to learn how to play chess) with another student's goal (e.g., a socially awkward student who is good at chess but likes working one on one). We would encourage psychologists to foster interdependence among diverse sets of students, much in the spirit of Aronson's "jigsaw" approach. Within the jigsaw cooperative learning technique, students are divided into diverse groups in which each member of a group receives a portion of material to be learned, which must then be taught to group members. Within each group, all students are dependent on one another and each student is considered an expert on some aspect of the material (Aronson, Bridgeman, & Geffner, 1978; see Internet site of www.jigsaw. org/steps.htm). In this regard, hope appears to be a cooperation-linked concept by its very nature, and efforts repeatedly should be made to facilitate such linkages. Psychologists also can help groups of students or members of an Individual Education Program team set common, attainable goals. The pursuit of shared goals can positively galvanize a group. In this sense, team activities often have inherent hope-inducing repercussions for their participants. Likewise, team activities engendering school pride, when not taken to an extreme, can produce hope.

School-based psychologists who are facile at eliminating barriers and are committed to helping students and teachers pursue meaningful goals become models of healthy goal pursuit. Often, however, the sheer number of institutional obstacles may limit the time that psychologists spend in being hopeful models. Everyone's hopes can grow more easily, however, when there are common goals aimed at lessening the number and magnitude of obstacles in school environments. As key facilitators in this process, we view psychologists as "barrier busters" who help make the attainment of a variety of educational goals more likely in our schools.

CONCLUSION

In this chapter, we presented the fundamentals of hope theory to our school-based psychology colleagues. It probably is accurate to say that engendering hope already is a part of what school-based psychologists do. As such, the present hope theory ideas may help psychologists do an even better job of supporting schools' efforts into arenas in which meaningful goals are set, where the parents, teachers, and students know how to reach those goals, and where everyone involved has the requisite motivations to try hard. *Hopeful thinking can empower and guide a lifetime of learning,* and psychologists help keep this lesson alive.

REFERENCES

Aronson, E., Bridgeman, D. L., & Geffner, R. (1978). Interdependent interactions and prosocial behavior. *Journal of Research and Development in Education, 12,* 16–27.

Barnum, D. D., Snyder, C. R., Rapoff, M. A., Mani, M. M., & Thompson, R. (1998). Hope and social support in the psychological adjustment of pediatric burn survivors and matched controls. *Children's Health Care, 27,* 15–30.

Berg, C. J., Rapoff, M. A., Snyder, C. R., & Belmont, J. M. (2007). The relationship of children's hope to pediatric asthma treatment adherence. *Journal of Positive Psychology, 2,* 176–184. doi:10.1080/17439760701409629

Berg, C. J., Ritschel, L. A., Swan, D. W., An, L. C., & Ahluwalia, J. S. (2011). The role of hope in engaging in healthy behaviors among college students. *American Journal of Health Behavior, 35,* 402–415. doi:10.5993/AJHB.35.4.3

Bouwkamp, J. (2001). *Making hope happen: A program for inner-city adolescents.* Master's thesis: University of Kansas, Lawrence.

Brown, M., Curry, L. A., Hagstrom, H., & Sandstedt, S. (1999, August). *Female teenage athletes, sport participation, self-esteem, and hope.* Paper presented at the Association for the Advancement of Applied Sport Psychology, Banff, Alberta, Canada.

Chang, E. C. (1998). Hope, problem-solving ability, and coping in a college student population: Some implications for theory and practice. *Journal of Clinical Psychology, 54,* 953–962. doi:10.1002/(SICI)1097-4679(199811)54:7<953::AID-JCLP9>3.0.CO;2-F

Chang, E. C. & Banks, K. H. (2007). The color and texture of hope: Some preliminary findings and implications for hope theory and counseling among diverse racial/ethnic groups. *Cultural Diversity & Ethnic Minority Psychology, 13,* 94–103. doi:10.1037/1099-9809.13.2.94

Chang, E. C., & DeSimone, S. L. (2001). The influence of hope on appraisals, coping, and dysphoria: A test of hope theory. *Journal of Social and Clinical Psychology, 20,* 117–129. doi:10.1521/jscp.20.2.117.22262

Collins, K., & Bell, R. (1997). Personality and aggression: The dissipation-rumination scale. *Personality and Individual Differences, 22,* 751–755. doi:10.1016/S0191-8869(96)00248-6

Conti, R. (2000). College goals: Do self-determined and carefully considered goals predict intrinsic motivation, academic performance, and adjustment during the first semester? *Social Psychology of Education, 4,* 189–211. doi:10.1023/A:1009607907509

Curry, L. A., Maniar, S. D., Sondag, K. A., & Sandstedt, S. (1999). *An optimal performance academic course for university students and student-athletes.* Unpublished manuscript, University of Montana, Missoula.

Curry, L. A., Snyder, C. R., Cook, D. L., Ruby, B. C., & Rehm, M. (1997). The role of hope in student-athlete academic and sport achievement. *Journal of Personality and Social Psychology, 73,* 1257–1267.

Day, L., Hanson, K., Maltby, J., Proctor, C., & Wood, A. (2010). Hope uniquely predicts objective academic achievement above intelligence, personality, and previous academic achievement. *Journal of Research in Personality, 44,* 550–553. doi:10.1016/j.jrp.2010.05.009

Dweck, C. S. (1999). Self-theories: Their role in motivation, personality, and development. Philadelphia, PA: Psychology Press.

Emmons, R. A. (1992). Abstract versus concrete goals: Personal striving level, physical illness, and psychological well-being. *Journal of Personality and Social Psychology, 62,* 292–300.

Feldman, D. B., & Dreher, D. E. (2012). Testing the efficacy of a single-session goal-pursuit intervention for college students. *Journal of Happiness Studies, 13,* 745–759. doi:10.1007/s10902-011-9292-4

Feldman, D. B., & Snyder, C. R. (2005). Hope and the meaningful life: Theoretical and empirical associations between goal-directed thinking and life meaning. *Journal of Social & Clinical Psychology, 24,* 401–421. doi:10.1521/jscp.24.3.401.65616

Gallup. (2009). *Hope, engagement, and well-being as predictors of attendance, credits earned, and GPA in high school freshmen.* Unpublished data. Omaha, Nebraska.

Gilman, R., Dooley, J., & Florell, D. (2006). Relative levels of hope and their relationship with academic and psychological indicators among adolescents. *Journal of Social and Clinical Psychology, 25,* 166–178. doi:10.1521/jscp.2006.25.2.166

Hinton-Nelson, M. D., Roberts, M. C., & Snyder, C. R. (1996). Early adolescents exposed to violence: Hope and vulnerability to victimization. *American Journal of Orthopsychiatry, 66,* 346–353. doi:10.1037/a0023867

Hoy, B., Suldo, S., & Mendez, L. (2013). Links between parents' and children's levels of gratitude, life satisfaction, and hope. *Journal of Happiness Studies, 14,* 1343–1361. doi:10.1007/s10902-012-9386-7

Kwon, P. (2000). Hope and dysphoria: The moderating role of defense mechanisms. *Journal of Personality, 68,* 199–223. doi:10.1111/1467-6494.00095

Lewis, H. A., & Kliewer, W. (1996). Hope, coping, and adjustment among children with sickle cell anemia: Tests of mediator and moderator models. *Journal of Pediatric Psychology, 21,* 25–41. doi:10.1007/BF02895780

Lloyd, S. M., Cantell, M., Pacaud, D., Crawford, S., & Dewey, D. (2009). Brief report: Hope, perceived maternal empathy, medical regime adherence, and glycemic control in adolescents with type 1 diabetes. *Journal of Pediatric Psychology, 34,* 1025–1029. doi:10.1093/jpepsy/jsn141

Lopez, S. J., Bouwkamp, J., Edwards, L. E., & Teramoto Pedrotti, J. (2000, October). *Making hope happen via brief interventions.* Presented at the Second Positive Psychology Summit, Washington, DC.

Lopez, S. J., Reichard, R. J., Marques, S. C., & Dollwet, M. (in press). *Relation of hope to academic outcomes: A meta-analysis.* Manuscript submitted for publication.

Marques, S. C., Lopez, S. J., Fontaine, A. M., Coimbra, S., & Mitchell, J. (in press). *How much hope is enough? Levels of hope and students' psychological and school functioning.* Manuscript submitted for publication.

Marques, S. C., Lopez, S. J., & Mitchell, J. (2013). The role of hope, spirituality and religious practice in adolescents' life satisfaction: Longitudinal findings. *Journal of Happiness Studies, 14,* 251–261. doi:10.1007/s10902-012-9329-3

Marques, S. C., Lopez, S. J., & Pais-Ribeiro, J. L. (2011). "Building Hope for the Future"—A program to foster strengths in middle-school students. *Journal of Happiness Studies, 12,* 139–152. doi:10.1007/s10902-009-9180-3

Marques, S. C., Pais-Ribeiro, J. L., & Lopez, S. J. (2007a). *Relationship between children's hope and guardian's hope.* Paper presented at the 10th European Congress of Psychology, Prague, Czech Republic.

Marques, S. C., Pais-Ribeiro, J. P., & Lopez, S. J. (2007b). Validation of a Portuguese version of the Students' Life Satisfaction Scale. *Applied Research in Quality of Life, 2,* 83–94. doi:10.1007/s11482-007-9031-5

Marques, S. C., Pais-Ribeiro, J. L., & Lopez, S. J. (2009). Validation of a Portuguese version of the Children Hope Scale. *School Psychology International, 30,* 538–551. doi:10.1177/0143034309107069

Marques, S. C., Pais-Ribeiro, J. L., & Lopez, S. J. (2011a). Use of the "Mental Health Inventory—5" with middle-school students. *Spanish Journal of Psychology, 14,* 472–479. doi:10.5209/rev_SJOP.2011.v14.nl.43

Marques, S. C., Pais-Ribeiro, J. L., & Lopez, S. J. (2011b). The role of positive psychology constructs in predicting mental health and academic achievement in Portuguese children and adolescents: A 2-year longitudinal study. *Journal of Happiness Studies, 12,* 1049–1062. doi:10.1007/s10902-010-9244-4

McDermott, D., Hastings, S. L., Gariglietti, K. P., Gingerich, K., Callahan, B., & Diamond, K. (1997). A cross-cultural investigation of hope in children and adolescents. *Resources in Education,* CG028078.

Merkas, M., & Brajsa-Zganec, A. (2011). Children with different levels of hope: Are there differences in their self-esteem, life satisfaction, social support, and family cohesion? *Child Indicators Research, 4,* 499–514. doi:10.1007/s12187-011-9105-7

Munoz-Dunbar, R. (1993). *Hope: A cross-cultural assessment of American college students.* Master's thesis. University of Kansas, Lawrence, Kansas.

Onwuegbuzie, A. J. (1999). Relation of hope to self-perception. *Perceptual and Motor Skills, 88,* 535–540. doi:10.2466/pms.1999.88.2.53

Onwuegbuzie, A. J., & Snyder, C. R. (2000). Relations between hope and graduate students' studying and test-taking strategies. *Psychological Reports, 86,* 803–806.

Pennebaker, J. W. (1989). Stream of consciousness and stress: Levels of thinking. In J. S. Uleman & J. A. Bargh (Eds.), *Unintended thought* (pp. 327–349). New York, NY: Guilford.

Seirup, H., & Rose, S. (2011). Exploring the effects of hope on GPA and retention among college undergraduate students on academic probation. *Education Research International, 1,* 1–7. doi:10.1155/2011/381426

Snyder, C. R. (1994). *The psychology of hope: You can get there from here.* New York, NY: Free Press.

Snyder, C. R. (Ed.). (2000). *Handbook of hope: Theory, measures, and applications.* San Diego, CA: Academic Press.

Snyder, C.R., Berg, C., Woodward, J.T., Gum, A., Rand, K.L., Wrobleski, K., ... Hackman, A. (2005). Hope against the cold: Individual differences in trait hope and acute pain tolerance on the cold pressor task. *Journal of Personality, 73,* 287–312. doi:10.1111/j.1467-6494.2005.00318.x

Snyder, C.R., Cheavens, J., & Michael, S.T. (1999). Hoping. In C.R. Snyder (Ed.), *Coping: The psychology of what works* (pp. 205–231). New York, NY: Oxford.

Snyder, C.R., Cheavens, J., & Sympson, S.C. (1997). Hope: An individual motive for social commerce. *Group Dynamics: Theory, Research, and Practice, 1,* 107–118. http://dx.doi.org/10.1037%2F%2F1089-2699.1.2.107

Snyder, C.R., Feldman, D.B., Taylor, J.D., Schroeder, L.L., & Adams III, V. (2000). The roles of hopeful thinking in preventing problems and enhancing strengths. *Applied and Preventive Psychology, 15,* 262–295. http://dx.doi.org/10.1016/S0962-1849(00)80003-7

Snyder, C.R., Harris, C., Anderson, J.R., Holleran, S.A., Irving, L.M., Sigmon, S.T., ... Harney, P. (1991). The will and the ways: Development and validation of an individual-differences measure of hope. *Journal of Personality and Social Psychology, 60,* 570–585. http://dx.doi.org/10.1037%2F%2F0022-3514.60.4.570

Snyder, C.R., Hoza, B., Pelham, W.E., Rapoff, M., Ware, L., Danovsky, M., ... Stahl, K.J. (1997). The development and validation of the Children's Hope Scale. *Journal of Pediatric Psychology, 22,* 399–421. doi:10.1093/jpepsy/22.3.399

Snyder, C.R., Lopez, S., Shorey, H.S., Rand, K.L., & Feldman, D.B. (2003). Hope theory, measurements, and applications to school psychology. *School Psychology Quarterly, 18,* 122–139. doi:10.1521%2Fscpq.18.2.122.21854

Snyder, C.R., McDermott, D., Cook, W., & Rapoff, M. (2002). *Hope for the journey* (revised ed.). Clinton Corners, NY: Percheron.

Snyder, C.R., Shorey, H.S., Cheavens, J., Pulvers, K.M., Adams, V.H., III, & Wiklund, C. (2002). Hope and academic success in college. *Journal of Educational Psychology, 94,* 820–826. doi:10.1037/0022-0663.94.4.820

Worrell, F.C., & Hale, R.L. (2001). The relationship of hope in the future and perceived school climate to school completion. *School Psychology Quarterly, 16,* 370–388. doi:10.1521%2Fscpq.16.4.370.19896

CHAPTER SUMMARY: HOPE

- Hope is conceptualized as a cognitive construct, which reflects people's motivation and capacity to strive toward personally relevant goals.
- Hope in students predicts many important outcomes, from physical and mental health to academic and athletic success.
- Teachers play an important role in children's perceptions about their competences to achieve goals and to cope with obstacles that can arise.
- Students' hope is malleable to change through intentional efforts.
- The school is an ideal place to work hope by integrating hope into curriculum or doing separate and regular hope-enhancing group sessions.

SUGGESTED READINGS: HOPE

Marques, S.C., Lopez, S.J., & Pais-Ribeiro, J.L. (2011). "Building Hope for the Future"—A program to foster strengths in middle-school students. *Journal of Happiness Studies, 12,* 139–152.

This study examined the effectiveness of hope-based intervention in middle school students. Results suggest that a brief hope intervention can increase psychological strengths, and participants continue to benefit up to 1 year and 6 months later.

Snyder, C.R. (Ed.). (2000). *Handbook of hope: Theory, measures, and applications.* San Diego, CA: Academic Press.

This book presents a comprehensive overview of the psychological inquiry into hope, including its measurement, development, how its loss is associated with specific clinical disorders, and therapeutic approaches that can help instill hope in those who have lost theirs. A final section discusses how the use of hope can make one a better coach, teacher, or parent.

Snyder, C.R. (2002). Hope theory: Rainbows in the mind. *Psychological Inquiry, 13,* 249–275.

In this article, hope theory is compared to theories of learned optimism, optimism, self-efficacy, and self-esteem. Higher hope consistently is related to better outcomes in several life arenas. Processes that lessen hope in children and adults are reviewed.

Snyder, C. R., Harris, C., Anderson, J. R., Holleran, S. A., Irving, L. M., Sigmon, S. T., . . . Harney, P. (1991). The will and the ways: Development and validation of an individual-differences measure of hope. *Journal of Personality and Social Psychology, 60,* 570–585.

This article examines the development and the psychometric properties of the Adult Hope Scale.

Snyder, C. R., Hoza, B., Pelham, W. E., Rapoff, M., Ware, L., Danovsky, M., . . . Stahl, K. J. (1997). The development and validation of the Children's Hope Scale. *Journal of Pediatric Psychology, 22,* 399–421.

This article examines the development and the psychometric properties of the Children Hope Scale.

4

OPTIMISM

What It Is and Its Relevance in the School Context

Peter Boman and Amanda Mergler, School of Cultural and Professional Learning, Queensland University of Technology, Brisbane, Queensland, Australia

INTRODUCTION

"For myself, I am an optimist—it does not seem to be much use to be anything else."
Winston Churchill

Optimism has its modern roots in philosophy dating back to the 17th century in the writings of philosophers such as Descartes and Voltaire (Domino & Conway, 2001). Previous to these philosophical writings, the concept of optimism was revealed in the teachings of many of the great spiritual traditions such as Buddhism and Christianity (Miller, Richards, & Keller, 2001). In the 20th century, optimism became defined in juxtaposition to pessimism, sometimes conceptualized as a bipolar unidimensional construct and by others as two related but separate constructs (Garber, 2000).

Contemporary models (Scheier & Carver, 1985; Seligman, 1991) have increasingly focused on distinguishing optimism–pessimism as a general dispositional orientation, as described by expectancy theory, and as an explanatory process, described by explanatory style theory.

OPTIMISM THEORETICAL PERSPECTIVES

Optimism as an expectancy is "a sense of confidence or doubt about the attainability of a goal value" (Carver & Scheier, 1999, p. 183). From the expectancy perspective, optimism and pessimism are forward looking, proactive dispositional tendencies. In explanatory style theory, optimism and pessimism are immediate, reactive tendencies, used to explain the cause of events, which are associated with a general coping response. In these views, expectancy is a generalized belief about goal attainment, and explanatory style describes a predominant process of cognitive mediation.

Optimism and Pessimism as Generalized Expectancy

There are no universally agreed-upon definitions for dispositional optimism and pessimism (Chang, Maydeu-Olivares, & D'Zurilla, 1997). However, researchers have offered related definitions that involve biases in generalized positive or negative expectations for future events (Peterson & Bossio, 1991). Optimism has been defined as (a) the tendency to expect positive outcomes (Kassinove & Sukhodolsky, 1995), (b) the belief that positive events exceed negative ones (Yates, Yates, & Lippett, 1995), or (c) a tendency to look on the bright side of things (Silva, Pais-Ribeiro, & Cardoso, 2004). Conversely, pessimism has been defined as (a) failure expectancy (Kassinove & Sukhodolsky, 1995), (b) anticipating bad outcomes, or (c) a tendency to take a gloomy view of things (Scheier & Carver, 1985).

Both optimism and pessimism have been associated with the coping strategies that individuals use (Chang, 1996; Helton, Dember, Warm, & Matthews, 1999; Scheier, Weintraub, & Carver, 1986). Optimism is linked with adaptive strategies such as problem solving, obtaining social support, and looking for any positive aspects in stressful situations. Pessimism, on the other hand, is related to maladaptive strategies, namely problem avoidance, denial, withdrawal, and the failure to complete goals when a stressor intrudes. In relation to the school environment, Boman and Yates (2001) found that optimistic children were more successful in transitioning from primary school to high school. Overall, optimism and pessimism can be expected to play an important role in generalized outcomes or in situations in which the individual has no previous experience.

Optimism and Pessimism as a Cognitive Explanatory Style

Seligman (1991) advanced another major theory that incorporated constructs of optimism and pessimism. This perspective emphasized the role of cognitive explanatory style and emerged from learned helplessness research that focused on individuals with depression (Seligman, 1975). Learned helplessness refers to expectations that lead depressed persons to conclude there is nothing they can do to help or control future outcomes. This expectation develops from a person's experiences with uncontrollable events in which attempted coping strategies did not help. The belief that one lacks control leads to lowered response initiation and persistence (motivational deficits), an inability to perceive new opportunities for control (cognitive deficits), and lowered self-esteem and increased sadness (emotional deficits; Seligman, 1975).

The theory of learned helplessness, however, was critiqued on several grounds (Nolen-Hoeksema, Girgus, & Seligman, 1986; Seligman, 1991). First, not all vulnerable people became helpless and, of those who did, some never recovered while others responded positively almost immediately. Second, some people only gave up in the immediate situation they faced, whereas others gave up in new situations. Third, some people blamed themselves for their circumstances and others blamed someone or something in the surrounding environment. Seligman and other researchers turned to Weiner's attribution theory to address outcomes that learned helplessness theory did not predict (Seligman, 1991).

Weiner's attribution theory posited that certain causal interpretations of other individuals' behaviors or events largely determine both emotional and behavioral reactions to achievement or failure (Weiner et al., 1971). These include whether the cause is viewed as internal or external to the person, its perception as stable or permanent over time, and the degree to which the other views it as controllable or uncontrollable.

Seligman and others drew from Weiner's theory, but their application differed in several ways (Abramson, Seligman, & Teasdale, 1978; Seligman, 1991). This modified theory stated that individuals have a habitual explanation style, not just a single explanation for each discrete failure experience. To this end, they added the third dimension of pervasiveness to Weiner's permanent and personal dimensions (Seligman et al., 1984; Seligman, Kamen, & Nolen-Hoeksema, 1988). Finally, they shifted the focus from achievement to mental illness and therapy (e.g., Reivich, Gillham, Chaplin, & Seligman, 2005). This became the basis of explanatory style theory as operationalized for children and adolescents (Seligman, Reivich, Jaycox, & Gillham, 1995).

In essence, children and adolescents can differ in their manner of personal attributions—that is, their style of explanation. Those with pessimistic explanatory styles are more inclined to use permanent ("It always happens this way"), personal ("It's my fault"), and pervasive ("It affects everything I do") dimensions of causal attribution when faced with hardship, setbacks, challenges, or stressful circumstances. Those with optimistic explanatory styles are more inclined to perceive setbacks as only temporary, not being their fault, and limited to the immediate incident. When faced with good events, these styles of explanation are reversed. In contrast, those with a pessimistic explanatory style would see a good event as being temporary, not their fault, and only an isolated incident. Conversely, children and adolescents with an optimistic explanatory style see the same event as permanent, being caused by themselves, and as all encompassing. These explanatory styles are influenced by the modeling behavior of parents and other significant adults (Seligman et al., 1995).

Comparing Expectancy and Explanatory Style Perspectives

Scheier and Carver (1992) reported several studies in which explanatory style did not correlate strongly with dispositional optimism and pessimism. Overall, correlations have tended not to be more than .20. In a study with Grade 8 students, Boman and Yates (2001) found a nonsignificant relation between dispositional optimism and explanatory style. Scheier and Carver believe the limited amount of conceptual overlap is due to the different foci of the two theories—that is, causal explanations for specific events opposed to generalized expectations for the future. Garber (2000) suggests that "there is a clear conceptual and empirical difference between attributions and expectancies" (p. 303) but also that attributions may predict expectations. That is, once a person explains the cause of an event, expectations maintain the positive or negative affect associated with that event.

MEASUREMENT OF OPTIMISM

Assessing Optimism and Pessimism as Generalized Expectancy

Despite the generally accepted view that optimism and pessimism play a role in coping and adjustment, there are two opposing views about how they should be measured (Chang et al., 1997; Fischer & Leitenberg, 1986; Myers & Steed, 1999; Olason & Roger, 2001). Some researchers consider optimism and pessimism to be a single bipolar continuum. Therefore, a person is either optimistic or pessimistic but cannot be both. Conversely, the partially dependent view sees both as capable of existing within a person. Scheier and Carver's (1985) unidimensional view of optimism and pessimism has tended to be the dominant view, but not all researchers see an optimist as being totally devoid of pessimism.

Other researchers have suggested optimism and pessimism are partially dependent dimensions (Chang et al., 1997; Fischer & Leitenberg, 1986). All of these studies reveal optimism and pessimism as yielding two separable but correlated factors. However, Lai and Yue (2000) found support for the partially dependent view in the mainland Chinese students only. This may be suggestive of the Western influence in Hong Kong compared to mainland China, where the concepts of optimism and pessimism may not reflect Western culture.

Chang and colleagues (1997) suggest when defining optimism and pessimism as positive or negative outcome expectancies, the partially dependent model appears to be more appropriate. Chang and Bridewell's (1998) study of undergraduate students reported those who endorsed more irrational beliefs (e.g., "I absolutely should not have made obvious mistakes in my life") were found to be significantly more pessimistic. However, they were not found to be less optimistic. This supports the partially dependent view of optimism and pessimism, which states a pessimist is not considered devoid of optimism but has higher numbers of irrational beliefs than an optimist.

Assessing Optimism and Pessimism as Expectancy

The Life Orientation Test (LOT; Scheier & Carver, 1985) and the Revised Life Orientation Test (LOT-R; Scheier, Carver, & Bridges, 1994) are the most widely used assessments of dispositional optimism and pessimism. The LOT and LOT-R were designed to be a unidimensional measure of optimism in that the pessimism scores are reversed and added to the optimism scores. The LOT has 12 items, 4 of which are fillers. Four items are positively worded (e.g., "I always look on the bright side of things") and four are negatively worded ("If something can go wrong for me it will"). The LOT-R has 10 items with 3 positively and 3 negatively worded items plus 4 fillers. It was felt that there was some overlap in the items of the LOT, so some of these were removed (Chang, 2001). Three other scales, the Expanded Life Orientation Test (ELOT; Chang et al., 1997), the Generalized Expectancy for Success Scale (Fibel & Hale, 1978), and the Optimism and Pessimism Scale (Dember, Martin, Hummer, Howe, & Melton, 1989), have been developed but have not been used as extensively in research.

The ELOT has been used in research with adolescents (Boman, Smith, & Curtis, 2003; Boman & Yates, 2001), but more recently, the Youth Life Orientation Test (YLOT) was developed more specifically for use with children and adolescents (Ey et al., 2005; Taylor et al., 2004). The YLOT is a 16-item self-report measure created to better evaluate optimism and pessimism in school-age children. Items from the LOT-R were reworded to be developmentally appropriate for children. Additional items that reflect positive and negative expectations were added to the scale, yielding a total of seven optimism items, seven pessimism items, and two filler items, all on a 4-point Likert scale—children respond using on a scale of 0 to 3 (0 = *not true for me* to 3 = *true for me*). The scale produces three scores: optimism, pessimism, and a total optimism score in response to the long-standing question of whether optimism and pessimism represent two separate constructs or opposite ends of a bipolar continuum. The initial administration of the instrument reported internal consistencies in the acceptable range through Cronbach's alpha coefficients (optimism = .70, pessimism = .78, and total optimism = .83). However, this only applied to Grades 3 through 6 because Cronbach's alphas for the first and second graders were unacceptable. It will need more time and research to determine the validity of the YLOT as a measure of optimism.

Assessing Optimism and Pessimism as an Explanatory Style

In the context of Seligman's theory, explanatory style is a cognitive personality variable that plays a role in adjustment to various life situations (Dykema, Bergbower, Doctora, & Peterson, 1996; Peterson, 2000). Explanatory style is assessed by a person's responses to a specially designed instrument, the Attributional Style Questionnaire (Peterson et al., 1982). The instrument measures personal, permanent, and pervasive dimensions in relation to specific events after initially asking to state a cause for that event. Seligman (1991) suggested the removal of the personal dimension due to the concern over the possible lessening of the sense of personal responsibility through the optimist's use of the blaming of others (externality) for failures. Although originally developed to incorporate positive and negative events, research has revealed that causal explanations about bad events reflect stronger correlates than those for good events (Peterson, 1990). This is not necessarily surprising, as Fincham (2000) explains: Causal explanations are more likely to occur for negative events, as people rarely seek to explain their good fortune.

The Attributional Style Questionnaire (ASQ) is the most commonly used measure associated with evaluating explanatory style (Reivich & Gillham, 2003). Several additional versions of the ASQ have been designed to target specific audiences or settings (Dykema et al., 1996; Furnham, Sadka, & Brewin, 1992; Lieber, 1997; Mayerson, 1991; Norman, 1988; Peterson & Villanova, 1988; Whitley, 1991). This is in line with Peterson's (1990) own development of various forms of the ASQ that use the original format but adjust the stimulus events to be relevant to the target population. The ASQ generally has a series of events to which a person initially responds with a possible cause and then follows with items that measure permanent and pervasive dimensions of explanatory style. For example, Boman and colleagues (2003) developed a version for use with high school students that utilized 12 hypothetical negative events, which reflected situations likely to occur within the school context (e.g., "You fail a test or an examination"). Students were asked to write one main cause for the event and then recorded permanent ("How likely is it that this cause will continue to affect you?") and pervasive ("Is this cause something that just affects failing a test or does it affect other areas of your life?") responses only. The Cronbach's alphas were strong at .90 and .93, respectively.

Children's Attributional Style Questionnaire (CASQ)

The CASQ (Kaslow, Tannenbaum, & Seligman, 1978) is the most widely used measure of explanatory style for children (Reivich & Gillham, 2003). It is a 48-item forced-choice questionnaire designed with the same structure as the ASQ but altered to be developmentally appropriate for children as young as 8 years old. Each item consists of a hypothetical scenario (24 positive negative and 24 negative) followed by two statements explaining why the event happened. Children are asked to choose the statement that best explains why the event took place. For example, with the item "you get an 'A' on a test" the child is asked to choose between because "I am smart" or because "I am good in the subject that the test was in." Items were designed to measure the attributional or explanatory style of the child (internal versus external, global versus specific, and stable versus unstable).

The CASQ yields three scores: positive composite score, negative composite score, and overall composite score. Psychometric examinations of the CASQ show moderate internal consistency for all three scores: .47 to .73 for positive scores, .42 to .67 for negative scores, and .62 for the overall composite scores. In addition, there was moderate stability with test-retest reliability of .71 for positive scores and .66 for negative scores at 6 months and .35 for the overall composite score at 12 months (Thompson, Kaslow, Weiss, & Nolen-Hoeksema, 1998). The CASQ is a widely used instrument that offers valuable information. However, the lengthy nature is not always ideal for limited administration time or when assessing children with short attention spans.

In response to this concern, Kaslow and Nolen-Hoeksema (1991) developed the Children's Attributional Style Questionnaire-Revised (CASQ-R) as a 24-item forced-choice measure adapted from the original CASQ. The measure was designed to be a more user-friendly assessment, catering to children's short attention spans. To create this new revised measure, the original CASQ was administered to 449 elementary school children. The responses were analyzed and the items with the weakest item-total correlations were dropped, leaving 12 positive composite items with a correlation of .14 or greater and 12 negative composite items with a correlation of .08 or greater.

Thompson and colleagues evaluated the psychometric structure of the revised measure to compare reliability and validity to the original CASQ (Thompson et al., 1998). The CASQ-R was then administered to 1,086 (515 boys and 570 girls) students ages 9 to 12 years old. Internal consistency of the CASQ-R using Fisher's r-to-z transformation showed no age or gender differences; however, the CASQ-R was more internally consistent for European-American students than African-American students. No gender, race, or age differences were found in the stability of the CASQ-R over the 6-month period (Thompson et al., 1998). Overall, results comparing the CASQ-R and the CASQ show that the CASQ-R is psychometrically sound and is appropriate when time constraints are an issue. However, if time allows, the CASQ would be the measure of choice.

CAN OPTIMISM BE CHANGED?

Building Optimism in School

In recent years, the important role schools have in developing strengths and positive values in students has been identified (Lovat, Clement, Dally, & Toomey, 2010). The positive psychology movement, with its focus on facilitating individuals to lead flourishing lives centered on well-being (Seligman et al., 1995), has led to the development of programs aimed at enhancing the well-being of all students, not just those facing difficulties (McGrath & Noble, 2010). Many programs take a holistic approach to students and the complexities of their lives, thus exploring a range of areas including individual factors (optimism, personal responsibility, problem solving), social factors (developing friendships, prosocial behavior, bullying), and school-based factors (e.g., student engagement/connection, relationships between teachers and students).

In general, school-based programs to promote optimism, well-being, and mental health have produced mixed results. Seligman and others specifically developed the Penn Prevention Program to help change explanatory style (the way in which we explain the positive and negative events that happen to us) and prevent depressive symptoms developing in at-risk 10- to 13-year-old children in America (Seligman et al., 1995; Shatte, Reivich, Gillham, & Seligman, 1999). The program included training in both developing an optimistic explanatory style (feeling able to positively impact on negative events that affect us and taking appropriate ownership of our role in the positive events we experience) and positive social skills. It was effective in reducing depressive symptoms and improving classroom behavior. A 2-year follow-up study found that the effects of the prevention program were stronger (Gillham, Reivich, Jaycox, & Seligman, 1995). Overall, these children had a positive change in explanatory style and used more optimistic thinking (Shatte et al., 1999). More recently, this program has been called the Penn Resiliency Program (PRP) and subsequent studies have all reported successful results (see Gillham, Hamilton, Freres, Patton, & Gallop, 2006; Reivich, Gillham, Chaplin, & Seligman, 2005). These studies have shown improved explanatory styles and lower levels of depressive tendencies across cultures.

Based on the successful evaluations of PRP in America, a number of similar programs have undergone school-based trials. To date, there have been a limited number of random controlled trials conducted for these programs with varying results, ranging from positive and significant outcomes to inconclusive and insignificant results. It has been suggested, though, that these equivocal findings may be due to the small sample sizes employed in some studies, high attrition rates, and poor design (as per criteria published by the Society for Prevention Research), as opposed to the effectiveness of the programs themselves (Horowitz & Garber, 2006; Spence & Shortt, 2007).

A national initiative occurring in Australia that uses a range of school-based programs to support well-being and mental health is the KidsMatter program. This initiative, funded by the Australian government and developed by the Department of Health and Ageing, beyondblue, the Australian Psychological Society, Early Childhood Australia, Principals Australia, and the Australian Rotary Health Research Fund, supports schools and children from early childhood (including long day care) to primary school

(4 to 12 years of age; Department of Health and Ageing, 2010). The initiative centers on four overarching components: a positive school community, social and emotional learning for students, parenting support and education, and early intervention for students experiencing mental health difficulties. Within each component, a range of school-based programs is available, and schools are encouraged to select programs that they feel would most benefit their school and wider community. While this initiative focuses on and develops many personal characteristics that support students, particular attention is paid to the role of optimism as being a protective factor for an individual child's mental health (Department of Health and Ageing, 2010). The Commonwealth Governments investment in the KidsMatter initiative demonstrates the growing belief that schools play a fundamental role in developing a range of strengths and skills in students, including their social and emotional competence.

One program designed to prevent internalizing problems and enhance optimism in upper primary school students (i.e., Grades 6 to 7), and listed as a resource within the KidsMatter framework, is the Aussie Optimism Program. This program was based directly on the Penn Resiliency Program, although modified to suit the Australian school system timetable and culture (Bishop & Roberts, 2005; Quayle, Dziurawiec, Roberts, Kane, & Ebsworthy, 2001; Roberts, 2006; Roberts, Kane, Bishop, Matthews, & Thomson, 2004; Roberts, Kane, Thomson, Bishop, & Hart, 2003). The program has two components: the Optimistic Thinking Skills Program (Roberts et al., 2002), and the Social Life Skills Program (Roberts, Ballantyne, & van der Klift, 2002). The optimism component explores children's beliefs about themselves, their life circumstances, and their futures and teaches them to identify and challenge those beliefs that are negative. Children are then encouraged to consider explanations for their lives that may be more optimistic and realistic. Importantly, children are taught strategies and techniques to assist them with identifying, labeling, and monitoring their feelings (Roberts, 2006). The social component of the program involves teaching children listening skills, assertiveness, negotiation, social problem-solving skills, decision making, perspective taking, and coping skills (Roberts, 2006).

The Aussie Optimism Program has been used extensively in Western Australia, where it was initially developed, and has been implemented in schools across Australia. Quayle and colleagues (2001) implemented the program with seventh-grade girls (11 and 12 years old) using a random control trials model. Results revealed no significant difference in symptoms of depression, pessimism, or global self-worth between the control and intervention groups at posttest. A significant difference was found between these groups at the 6-month follow-up, however, with girls in the intervention group reporting significantly fewer depressive symptoms than control-group girls. Further evaluation of the program was conducted in a larger random controlled trial for preadolescents with elevated levels of depression (Roberts et al., 2003, 2004). The study found no effect size for depression on any of the follow-up tests. There was a small intervention effect for anxiety at posttest, and at the 6-month and 30-month follow-ups. However, a more recent study by Swannell, Hand, and Martin (2009) showed that Grade 8 students in Queensland who exhibited high levels of depression and emotional/behavioral difficulties before undertaking the program demonstrated significantly lower levels in these areas after completing the intervention.

Another program with varied results is the Problem Solving for Life Program (PSFL) directed at secondary school students (Grades 8 to 10). The program is designed to promote optimistic thinking by teaching better problem-solving skills and was designed as a preventative program for depression in preadolescents. There have been two major random controlled trial studies conducted for the PSFL program, which employed larger sample sizes in comparison to the majority of other program evaluations. The initial results of the first study found a significant decrease in depressive symptoms among the participants in the high-risk-for-depression intervention group compared with the high-risk control group (Spence, Sheffield, & Donovan, 2003). Likewise, the low-risk-for-depression intervention group also showed fewer depressive symptoms than the low-risk control group, although the effect size was smaller. These results were not maintained at the 12-month follow-up. A subsequent study conducted further follow-ups at 2-, 3-, and 4-year points since the initial intervention, which again showed no significant intervention effects at these later stages (Spence, Sheffield, & Donovan, 2005). In the second random controlled trial study, the results were even more disappointing, with interventions showing no effect on any time points (Sheffield et al., 2006).

Overall, while school-based prevention programs for promoting optimism and changing depressive cognitions have yielded some promising and varying results, more research is needed to establish their long-term effectiveness (Merry, McDowell, Hetrick, Bir, & Muller, 2004). Meta-analyses suggest that specific (as opposed to universal) approaches appear to have more consistent results, but the need for routine screening would render these approaches less sustainable over time. Most of the successful outcomes for promoting optimism in particular have been with the preadolescent age group. Limited longitudinal data are available for assessing the long-term effects of increasing optimism and resilience in children in relation to many areas other than protection against some mental health problems.

Despite these limitations, support for school-based programs that promote the development of positive emotions and values, individual strengths, positive character traits, and meaningful connections between students and schools is growing (Noble & McGrath, 2008). Research is beginning to show that school-based programs and whole-school approaches that develop positive values and character traits in students result in positive outcomes for students, teachers, and school communities (Benninga, Berkowitz, Kuehn, & Smith, 2006; DEST, 2008; Lovat et al., 2010). Many teachers choose teaching as their profession as they wish to shape, support, and care for students (O'Sullivan, 2005; Watt & Richardson, 2007). While adopting programs that focus on optimism, life skills, and other supportive factors is one way in which teachers can impact the lives of their students, there are additional everyday classroom practices that can also impact positively on students and their sense of optimism.

BUILDING OPTIMISM IN THE CLASSROOM

Teachers and other significant people, such as coaches, influence children. One could also presume optimistic teachers would be better able to cope with life and school-related stress. A recent study by Tyson, Roberts, and Kane (2009) investigated whether the Aussie Optimism Program provided mental health-related benefits to teachers who teach it. The researchers argued that teachers who were trained to implement the program to support their students might use the strategies learned in their professional lives. Looking specifically at teacher job-related anxiety and depression, the results revealed that teachers who had received training in the program and additional coaching support from school psychologists reported significantly lower levels of job-related anxiety and depression than those teachers in the training-only and control group. It appears from this study that while teaching mental health programs may provide related benefits to teachers, this only occurs when teachers are provided appropriate training and ongoing coaching support. To promote optimism and coping in students, teachers need to have experiences that support the development and maintenance of optimism in their own teaching experiences.

According to Jenson, Olympia, Farley, and Clark (2004), teachers seem to think they are positive and see themselves as using positive techniques to manage behaviors in the classroom. However, these self-reports of positiveness are in contrast to observations of teachers in their classrooms. For example, Boman and Yates (2001) found that although optimism was the single most important predictor of a student's successful transition to high school, the teachers' views of a successful transition were only predicted by gender. That is, although a student may have an optimistic disposition, teachers were not necessarily likely to recognize and develop this asset. In another study that analyzed differences between teachers' beliefs and their behavior, Russo and Boman (2007) found that although teachers reported a very sound knowledge of resilience, they were not as successful in recognizing which children were resilient. That is, teachers may not be as aware of children's strengths or weaknesses as they might suggest. It appears that some teachers may need more professional development in these areas to help them move beyond the theoretical knowledge and develop the necessary practical skills to help children develop their optimism and other positive attributes.

Nevertheless, teachers can generally promote optimism by their attributions in relation to students' successes or failures in the classroom (Dweck, Davidson, Nelson, & Enna, 1978). By attributing success to effort or failure to lack of effort, teachers can help promote a sense of optimism in their students. They can also help students learn to problem solve and look for alternatives in addressing troubling issues (Seligman, 1991; Seligman et al., 1995). The role modeling that teachers do in the classroom is very powerful. Teachers need to demonstrate a positive explanatory style in which they focus on things that are going well and discuss the effort they are committing to a task (Noble & McGrath, 2007). Teachers should model problem solving in the classroom and show students there is always something they can do rather than giving up.

It is integral that teachers make social and emotional learning a normal occurrence in the classroom and that they offer students many opportunities to explicitly learn and practice these skills (Department of Health and Ageing, 2010). Providing group work activities and engaging students in explicit discussions around emotional awareness and prosocial behaviors are meaningful ways in which teachers can help develop optimism and competency in students (Noble & McGrath, 2007). Being realistic in feedback to students is also important in helping to develop optimism. Students know when they have not put their best effort into something. Giving students honest constructive feedback rather than trying to protect their feelings helps them learn that it is their effort or behavior that may be the problem and not them personally.

Sagor (2008) argues that there are two key variables that teachers need to nurture in students in order for students to develop optimism: faith in the future and personal efficacy. Faith in the future requires students to believe that the work they invest energy in today will pay off for them in the future. He argues that while some students can see the benefits of hard work in their environment, other students may not. It is these students who most need teachers who believe in them and offer them insight into the ways in which their effort can be rewarded. Personal efficacy is the deep-seated belief that individuals have in their ability. Students will develop and maintain optimistic thinking when they see that they are capable of achieving what they want to achieve. Teachers can demonstrate to students that effort and hard work will pay off and challenge students to continue with difficult tasks to experience success. Sagor encourages all teachers to ponder whether their students will leave the classroom each day feeling more or less confident that their futures are bright.

CONCLUSION

It is important to understand that optimists' lives are not perfect and they do experience negative events in their lives. It is their ability to recover from these events and use problem-focused coping that is the key. Building children's levels of optimism will not prevent them from encountering problems and trauma in their lives, but it will help ensure that they cope with them positively and adjust psychologically in the best possible way. What more could we ask for our children?

REFERENCES

Abramson, L.Y., Seligman, M.E.P., & Teasdale, J.D. (1978). Learned helplessness in humans: Critique and reformulation. *Journal of Abnormal Psychology, 87,* 49–74. http://psycnet.apa.org/index.cfm?fa=buy.optionTo Buy&id=1979-00305-001

Benninga, J.S., Berkowitz, M.W., Kuehn, P., & Smith, K. (2006). Character and academics: What good schools do. *Phi Delta Kappan, 87,* 448–452.

Bishop, B., & Roberts, C. (2005). The process of embedding and sustaining a mental health promotion program in social contexts. *Community Psychologist, 38,* 14–16.

Boman, P., Smith, D. C., & Curtis, D. (2003). Effects of pessimism and explanatory style on the development of anger in children. *School Psychology International, 24,* 80–94. doi:10.1177/0143034303024001581

Boman, P., & Yates, G.C.R. (2001). Optimism, hostility, and adjustment in the first-year of high school. *British Journal of Educational Psychology, 71,* 401–411. doi:10.1348/000709901158587

Carver, C.S., & Scheier, M.F. (1999). Optimism. In C.R. Snyder (Ed.), *Coping: The psychology of what works* (pp. 182–204). New York, NY: Oxford University Press.

Chang, E. C. (1996). Cultural differences in optimism, pessimism, and coping: Predictors of subsequent adjustment in Asian American and Caucasian American college students. *Journal of Counseling Psychology, 43*(1), 113–123. doi: 10.1037/0022-0167.43.1.113

Chang, E.C. (2001). Introduction: Optimism and pessimism and moving beyond the more fundamental question. In E.C. Chang (Ed.), *Optimism & pessimism: Implications for theory, research, and practice* (pp. 3–12). Washington, DC: American Psychological Association.

Chang, E.C., & Bridewell, W.B. (1998). Irrational beliefs, optimism, pessimism, and psychological distress: A preliminary examination of differential effects in a college population. *Journal of Clinical Psychology, 54,* 137–142. doi:10.1002/(SICI)1097-4679(199802)54:2<137::AID-JCLP2>3.0.CO;2-P

Chang, E.C., Maydeu-Olivares, A., & D'Zurilla, T.J. (1997). Optimism and pessimism as partially independent constructs: Relationships to positive and negative affectivity and psychological well-being. *Personality and Individual Differences, 23,* 433–440. doi:10.1016/S0191-8869(97)80009-8

Dember, W.N., Martin, S., Hummer, M.K., Howe, S., & Melton, R. (1989). The measurement of optimism and pessimism. *Current Psychology: Research and Reviews, 8,* 102–119. ISSN 1936-4733

Department of Health and Ageing. (2010). *KidsMatter: Australian Primary Schools Mental Health Initiative.* Retrieved from http://www.kidsmatter.edu.au/primary/

DEST. (2008). *At the heart of what we do: Values education at the centre of schooling—The final report of the values education good practice schools project—Stage 2 August 2008.* Retrieved from http://www.curriculum.edu.au/verve/_resources/VEGPSP-2_final_3.pdf

Domino, B., & Conway, D.W. (2001). Optimism and pessimism from a historical perspective. In E.C. Chang (Ed.), *Optimism & pessimism: Implications for theory, research, and practice* (pp. 3–12). Washington, DC: American Psychological Association.

Dweck, C.S., Davidson, W., Nelson, S., & Enna, B. (1978). Sex differences in learned helplessness: II. The contingencies of evaluative feedback in the classroom and III. An experimental analysis. *Developmental Psychology, 14,* 268–276. doi:10.1037/0012-1649.14.3.268

Dykema, J., Berbbower, K., Doctora, J.D., & Peterson, C. (1996). An attributional style questionnaire for general use. *Journal of Psychoeducational Assessment, 14,* 100–108. doi:10.1177/073428299601400201

Ey, S., Hadley, W., Allen, D., Palmer, S., Klosky, J., Deptula, D., & Cohen, R. (2005). A new measure of children's optimism and pessimism: The Youth Life Orientation Test. *Journal of Child Psychology and Psychiatry, 46,* 548–558. doi:10.1111/j.1469-7610.2004.00372.x

Fibel, B., & Hale, W.D. (1978). The generalised expectancy for success scale: A new measure. *Journal of Consulting and Clinical Psychology, 46,* 924–931. doi:10.1037/0022-006X.46.5.924

Fincham, F.D., (2000). Optimism and the family. In J.E. Gilham (Ed.), *The Science of optimism and hope: Research essays in honour of Martin E. P. Seligman* (pp. 271–298), West Conshohocken, PA: Templeton Foundation Press.

Fischer, M., & Leitenberg, H. (1986). Optimism and pessimism in elementary school aged children. *Child Development, 57,* 241–248. doi:10.1111/1467-8624.ep7251052

Furnham, A., Sadka, V., & Brewin, C. (1992). The development of an occupational attributional style questionnaire. *Journal of Organizational Behavior, 13,* 27–39. doi:10.1002/job.4030130104

Garber, J. (2000). Optimism: Definitions and origins. In J.E. Gillham (Ed.), *The science of optimism and hope: Research essays in honor of Martin E. P. Seligman* (pp. 299–314). West Conshohocken, PA: Templeton Foundation Press.

Gillham, J. E., Hamilton, J., Freres, D. R., Patton, K., & Gallop, R. (2006). Preventing depression among early adolescents in the primary care setting: A randomized controlled study of the Penn Resiliency Program. *Journal of Abnormal Child Psychology, 34*(2), 195–211. doi: 10.1007/s10802-005-9014-7

Gillham, J.E., Reivich, K.J., Jaycox, L.H., & Seligman, M.E.P. (1995). Prevention of depressive symptoms in school children: Two-year follow up. *Psychological Science, 6,* 343–351. doi:10.1111/j.1467-9280.1995.tb00524.x

Helton, W.S., Dember, W.N., Warm, J.S., & Matthews, G. (1999). Optimism, pessimism, and false failure feedback: Effects on vigilance performance. *Current Psychology, 18,* 311–326. doi:10.1007/s12144-999-1006-2

Horowitz, J., & Garber, J. (2006). The prevention of depressive symptoms in children and adolescents: A meta-analytic review. *Journal of Consulting and Clinical Psychology, 74,* 401–415. doi:10.1037/0022-006X.74.3.401

Jenson, W.R., Olympia, D., Farley, M., & Clark, E. (2004). Positive psychology and externalizing students in a sea of negativity. *Psychology in the Schools, 41,* 67–79. doi:10.1002/pits.10139

Kaslow, N.J., & Nolen-Hoeksema, S. (1991). *Children's Attributional Style Questionnaire-Revised (CASQ-R).* Unpublished manuscript, Emory University, Atlanta, Georgia.

Kaslow, N.J., Tannenbaum, R.L., & Seligman, M.E.P. (1978). *The Kastan: A Children's Attributional Style Questionnaire.* Unpublished manuscript, University of Pennsylvania, Philadelphia.

Kassinove, H., & Sukhodolsky, D.G. (1995). Optimism, pessimism, and worry in Russian and American children and adolescents. *Journal of Social Behaviour and Personality, 10,* 157–168. doi:10.1002/(SICI)1097-4679(199710)53:6<543::AID-JCLP3>3.0.CO;2-L

Lai, J.C.L., & Yue, X. (2000). Measuring optimism in Hong Kong and mainland Chinese with the revised Life Orientation Test. *Personality and Individual Difference, 28,* 781–796. doi:10.1016/S0191-8869(99)00138-5

Lieber, E. (1997). *The Teenage Attributional Style Questionnaire.* Doctoral dissertation, University of Illinois at Urbana-Champaign, 1997. Dissertation Abstracts International, 57(11-B), 7271.

Lovat, T., Clement, N., Dally, K., & Toomey, R. (2010). Values education as holistic development for all sectors: Researching for effective pedagogy. *Oxford Review of Education, 36,* 713–729. doi:10.1080/03054985.2010.501141

Mayerson, D. (1991). *The Parenting Attributional Style Questionnaire.* Dissertation abstracts international. B, The Sciences and Engineering, 51(11-A), 36–76.

McGrath, H., & Noble, T. (2010). Supporting positive pupil relationships: Research to practice. *Educational & Child Psychology, 27,* 79–90. http://hdl.handle.net/10536/DRO/DU:30032674

Merry, S., McDowell, H., Hetrick, S., Bir, J., & Muller, N. (2004). *Psychological and/or educational interventions for the prevention of depression in children and adolescents.* Cochrane Database of Systemic Reviews. No. CD003380. doi:10.1002/14651858.CD003380.pub2

Miller, L., Richards, P.S., & Keller, R.R. (2001). Foreword. In E.C. Chang (Ed.), *Optimism & pessimism: Implications for theory, research, and practice* (pp. xiii–xvii). Washington, DC: American Psychological Association.

Myers, L.B., & Steed, L. (1999). The relationship between dispositional optimism, dispositional pessimism, repressive coping, and trait anxiety. *Personality and Individual Differences, 27,* 1261–1272. doi:10.1016/S0191-8869(99)00071-9

Noble, T., & McGrath, H. (2007). *The Positive Educational Practices Framework: Leadership transforming schools through optimism.* Paper presented at the ACEL/ASCD Conference: New Imagery for Schools and Schooling: Challenging, Creating, and Connecting, Sydney, Australia, October 2007. Retrieved from http://www.acel.org.au/conf07/papers/Noble%20McGrath%20postive%20education.pdf

Noble, T., & McGrath, H. (2008). The positive educational practices framework: A tool for facilitating the work of educational psychologists in promoting pupil wellbeing. *Educational & Child Psychology, 25,* 119–134. Retrieved from http://hdl.handle.net/10536/DRO/DU:30018015

Nolen-Hoeksema, S., Girgus, J. S., & Seligman, M. E. P. (1986). Helplessness in children: A longitudinal study of depression, achievement, and explanatory style. *Journal of Personality and Social Psychology, 51*(2), 435–442. doi:10.1037/0022-3514.51.2.435

Norman, P. (1988). Real Events Attributional Style Questionnaire. *Journal of Social and Clinical Psychology, 7,* 97–100. doi:10.1521/jscp.1988.7.2-3.97

Olason, D.T., & Roger, D. (2001). Optimism, pessimism, and "fighting spirit": A new approach to assessing expectancy and adaptation. *Personality and Individual Differences, 31,* 755–768. doi:10.1016/S0191-8869(00)00176-8

O'Sullivan, S. (2005). The soul of teaching: education teachers of character. *Action in Teacher Education, 26*(4), 3–9. doi:10.1080/01626620.2005.10463338

Peterson, C. (1990). Explanatory style in the classroom and on the playing field. In S. Graham & V. Folkes (Eds.), *Attribution theory: Applications to achievement, mental health, and interpersonal conflict* (pp. 53–75). Hillsdale, NJ: Erlbaum.

Peterson, C. (2000). The future of optimism. *American Psychologist, 55,* 44–55. doi:10.1037/0003-066X.55.1.44

Peterson, C., & Bossio, L.M. (1991). *Health and optimism.* New York, NY: Free Press.

Peterson, C., Semmel, A., von Baeyer, C., Abramson, L.Y., Metalsky, G.I., & Seligman, M. E.P. (1982). The Attributional Style Questionnaire. *Cognitive Therapy and Research, 6,* 287–300. doi:10.1007/BF01173577.

Peterson, C., & Villanova, P. (1988). An Expanded Attributional Style Questionnaire. *Journal of Abnormal Psychology, 97,* 87–89. doi:10.1037/0021–843X.97.1.87

Quayle, D., Dziurawiec, S., Roberts, C., Kane, R., & Ebsworthy, G. (2001). The effect of an optimism and life skills program on depressive symptoms in preadolescence. *Behaviour Change, 18,* 194–203. doi:10.1375/bech.18.4.194

Reivich, K., & Gillham, J. (2003). Learned optimism: The measurement of explanatory style. In S.J. Lopez & C.R. Snyder (Eds.), *Positive psychological assessment: A handbook of models and measures* (pp. 57–74). Washington, DC: American Psychological Association.

Reivich, K., Gillham, J.E., Chaplin, T.M., & Seligman, M.E.P. (2005). From helplessness to optimism: The role of resilience in treating and preventing depression in youth. In S. Goldstein & R.B. Brooks (Eds.), *Handbook of resilience in children* (pp. 223–237). New York, NY: Kluwer Academic/Plenum.

Roberts, C. (2006). Embedding mental health promotion programs in school contexts: The Aussie Optimism Program. *International Society for the Study of Behavior Newsletter, 2*(50), 1–4.

Roberts, C., Ballantyne, F., & van der Klift, P. (2002). *Aussie optimism: Social Life Skills program. Teacher resource.* Perth, Western Australia: Curtin University of Technology.

Roberts, C., Kane, R., Bishop, B., Matthews, H., & Thomson, H. (2004). The prevention of depressive symptoms in rural school children: A follow-up study. *International Journal of Mental Health Promotion, 6,* 4–16. doi:10.1080/14623730.2004.9721934

Roberts, C., Kane, R., Thomson, H., Bishop, B., & Hart, B. (2003). The prevention of depressive symptoms in rural school children: A randomized controlled trial. *Journal of Consulting and Clinical Psychology, 71,* 622–628. doi:10.1037/0022-006X.71.3.622

Roberts, R., Roberts, C., Cosgrove, S., Houston, K., Ludlow, T., Mar, D., . . . vanderKlift, P. (2002). *Aussie Optimism: Optimistic Thinking Skills program. Teacher resource.* Perth, Western Australia: Curtin University of Technology.

Russo, R., & Boman, P. (2007). Primary school teachers' ability to recognise resilience in their students. *The Australian Educational Researcher, 34,* 17–31. http://www.eric.ed.gov/PDFS/EJ766602.pdf

Sagor, R. (2008). Cultivating optimism in the classroom. *Educational Leadership, 65*, 26–31. http://www.ascd.org/publications/educational-leadership/mar08/vol65/num06/Cultivating-Optimism-in-the-Classroom.aspx

Scheier, M.F., & Carver, C.S. (1985). Optimism, coping and health: Assessment and implications of generalized outcome expectancies. *Health Psychology, 4*, 219–247. doi:10.1037/0278-6133.4.3.219

Scheier, M.F., & Carver, C.S. (1992). Effects of optimism on psychological and physical well-being: Theoretical overview and empirical update. *Cognitive Therapy and Research, 16*, 201–228. doi:10.1007/BF01173489

Scheier, M.F., Carver, C.S., & Bridges, M.W. (1994). Distinguishing optimism from neuroticism (and trait anxiety, self-mastery, and self-esteem): A re-evaluation of the Life Orientation Test. *Journal of Personality and Social Psychology, 67*, 1063–1078. doi:10.1037/0022-3514.67.6.1063

Scheier, M. F., Weintraub, J. K., & Carver, C. S. (1986). Coping with stress: Divergent strategies of optimists and pessimists. *Journal of Personality and Social Psychology, 51*(6), 1257–1264. doi:0.1037/0022-3514.51.6.1257

Seligman, M.E.P. (1975). *Helplessness: On depression, development, and death.* San Francisco, CA: Reffman.

Seligman, M.E.P. (1991). *Learned optimism.* New York: Houghton Mifflin.

Seligman, M.E.P., Kamen, L.P., & Nolen-Hoeksema, S. (1988). *Explanatory style across the life-span: Achievement and health.* Hillsdale, NJ: Erlbaum.

Seligman, M.E.P., Peterson, C., Kaslow, N.J., Tanenbaum, R.L., Alloy, L.B., & Abramson, L.Y. (1984). Attributional style and depressive symptoms among children. *Journal of Abnormal Psychology, 93*, 235–238. doi:10.1037/0021-843X.93.2.235

Seligman, M.E.P., Reivich, K., Jaycox, L., & Gillham, J. (1995). *The optimistic child.* New York, NY: Houghton Mifflin.

Shatte, A.J., Reivich, K.J., Gillham, J.E., & Seligman, M.E.P. (1999). Learned optimism in children. In C.R. Snyder (Ed.), *Coping: The psychology of what works* (pp. 165–181). New York, NY: Oxford University Press.

Sheffield, J.K., Spence, S.H., Rapee, R.M., Kowalenko, N., Wignall, A., Davis A., & McLoone, J. (2006). Evaluation of universal, indicated, and combined cognitive-behavioral approaches to the prevention of depression among adolescents. *Journal of Consulting and Clinical Psychology, 74*, 66–79. doi:10.1037/0022-006X.74.1.66

Silva, I., Pais-Ribeiro, J., & Cardoso, H. (2004). Dificuldade em perceber o lado positivo davida? stresse em doentes diabéticos com e sem complicações crónicas da doença / Difficulty in seeing the bright side of life: Stresses in diabetes patients with and without chronic complications from the disease. *Análise Psicológica, 22*, 597–605.

Spence, S., Sheffield, J., & Donovan, C. (2003). Preventing adolescent depression: An evaluation of the Problem Solving for Life program. *Journal of Consulting and Clinical Psychology, 71*, 3–13. doi:10.1037/0022-006X.71.1.3

Spence, S., Sheffield, J., & Donovan, C. (2005). Long-term outcome of a school-based, universal approach to prevention of depression in adolescents. *Journal of Consulting and Clinical Psychology, 73*, 160–167. doi:10.1037/0022-006X.73.1.160

Spence, S., & Shortt, A. (2007). Research review: Can we justify the widespread dissemination of universal, school-based interventions for the prevention of depression among children and adolescents? *Journal of Child Psychology and Psychiatry, 48*, 526–542. doi:10.1111/j.1469-7610.2007.01738.x

Swannell, S., Hand, M. & Martin, G. (2009). The effects of a Universal Mental Health Promotion Programme on depressive symptoms and other difficulties in year eight high school students in Queensland, Australia. *School Mental Health, 1(4)*, 229–239. doi:10.1007/s12310-009-9019-4

Taylor, W.C., Baranowski, T., Klesges, L.M., Ey, S., Pratt, C., Rochon, J., & Zhou, A. (2004). Psychometric properties of optimism and pessimism: Results from the Girls' Health Enrichment Multisite Studies. *Preventative Medicine, 38*, S69–S77. http://dx.doi.org/10.1016/j.ypmed.2003.10.015

Thompson, M., Kaslow, N., Weiss, B., & Nolen-Hoeksema, S. (1998). Children's Attributional Style Questionnaire–Revised: Psychometric examination. *Psychological Assessment, 10*, 166–170. doi:10.1037/1040–3590.10.2.166

Tyson, O., Roberts, C.M., & Kane, R. (2009). Can implementation of a resilience program for primary school children enhance the mental health of teachers? *Australian Journal of Guidance and Counselling, 19*, 116–130. doi:10.1375/ajgc.19.2.116

Watt, H.M.G. & Richardson, P.W. (2007). Motivational factors influencing teaching as a career choice: Development and validation of the 'FIT-Choice' Scale. *Journal of Experimental Education, 75*(3), 167–202. doi:10.3200/JEXE.75.3.167-202

Weiner, B., Frieze, I., Kukla, A., Reed, L., Rest, S., & Rosenbaum, R.M. (1971). *Perceiving the courses of success and failure.* Morristown, NJ: General Learning Press.

Whitley, B. (1991). A short form of the Expanded Attributional Style Questionnaire. *Journal of Personality Assessment, 56*, 365–369. doi:10.1207/s15327752jpa5602_14

Yates, S.M., Yates, G.C.R., & Lippett, R.M. (1995). Explanatory style, ego-orientation, and primary school mathematics achievement. *Educational Psychology, 15*, 23–24. doi:10.1080/0144341950150103

CHAPTER SUMMARY: OPTIMISM

- Optimism has two forms and can be measured as a general dispositional orientation, as described by expectancy theory, and as an explanatory process, described by explanatory style theory.
- Optimism, in expectancy theory, has been defined as (a) the tendency to expect positive outcomes, (b) the belief that positive events exceed negative ones, or a tendency to look on the bright side of things.
- In explanatory style theory, individuals are believed to have a habitual explanation style, not just a single explanation for each discrete failure experience. Children and adolescents with an optimistic explanatory style see the good events as permanent and pervasive. Those with optimistic explanatory styles are more inclined to perceive setbacks as only temporary and limited to the immediate incident.
- The Life Orientation Test and the Revised Life Orientation Test are the most widely used assessments of dispositional optimism and pessimism. The Youth Life Orientation Test (YLOT) has been developed more specifically for use with children and adolescents.
- Explanatory style is assessed by a person's responses to a specially designed instrument, the Attributional Style Questionnaire. The instrument measures the permanent and pervasive dimensions in relation to specific events after initially asking to state a cause for that event. The Children's Attributional Style Questionnaire is the most widely used measure of explanatory style for children.
- In recent years, the important role schools have in developing strengths and positive values in students has been identified. In general, school-based programs to promote optimism, well-being, and mental health have produced mixed results.
- Seligman and others specifically developed the Penn Prevention Program to help change explanatory style (the way in which we explain the positive and negative events that happen to us) and prevent depressive symptoms developing in at-risk 10- to 13-year-old children in America. More recently, this program has been called the Penn Resiliency Program (PRP) and subsequent studies have all reported successful results.
- The Aussie Optimism Program has been used extensively in Western Australia and other Australian states. Although original studies produced inconsistent results, in the most recent study, Grade 8 students in Queensland who exhibited high levels of depression and emotional/behavioral difficulties before undertaking the program demonstrated significantly lower levels in these areas after completing the intervention.

SUGGESTED READINGS: OPTIMISM

Boman, P., Smith, D. C., & Curtis, D. (2003). Effects of pessimism and explanatory style on the development of anger in children. *School Psychology International, 24,* 80–94. doi:10.1177/0143034303024001581

One of the small number of studies that assesses both expectancy and explanatory style in children.

Quayle, D., Dziurawiec, S., Roberts, C., Kane, R., & Ebsworthy, G. (2001). The effect of an optimism and life skills program on depressive symptoms in preadolescence. *Behavior Change, 18,* 194–203. doi:10.1375/bech.18.4.194

Discusses and presents the development of the Aussie Optimism Program.

Sagor, R. (2008). Cultivating optimism in the classroom. *Educational Leadership, 65,* 26–31.

Argues the case that there are two key variables that teachers need to nurture in students in order for students to develop optimism: faith in the future and personal efficacy.

Scheier, M. F., & Carver, C. S. (1985). Optimism, coping and health: Assessment and implications of generalized outcome expectancies. *Health Psychology, 4,* 219–247. doi:10.1037/0278–6133.4.3.219

This study describes the initial development of the Life Orientation Test and gives a sound overview of expectancy theory.

Seligman, M. E. P. (1991). *Learned optimism.* New York: Houghton Mifflin.

This book gives an overview of the development of explanatory style from its roots in learned helplessness and discusses the beginnings of the Penn Prevention Program.

5

GRATITUDE IN SCHOOL
Benefits to Students and Schools

Giacomo Bono, Psychology Department, California State University, Dominguez Hills, Carson, California, USA

Jeffrey J. Froh, Psychology Department, Hofstra University, Hempstead, New York, USA

Rafael Forrett, Psychology Department, California State University, Dominguez Hills, Carson, California, USA

Preparation of this chapter was supported by California State University at Dominguez Hills, Hofstra University, and the John Templeton Foundation.

INTRODUCTION

In the last several years, research has identified a variety of ways that gratitude can benefit youth. Establishing positive social relationships and connections to schools and school programs are critical for youths' development and success in the world. Growing up in today's information society presents many challenges for youths, as they face many choices for what to do, wear, and buy. At the same time, schools are having to learn how to tailor teaching to more diverse populations and provide them with skills in a world challenged by an increasing number of social issues, all while working with increasingly constrained budgets. Meanwhile, families are busier than ever, with more dual-income households. Consider also the alarming rise of commercial forces constantly vying for youths' time, money, and motivations, and it is easy to understand how achieving a positive and purposeful identity has become more challenging than ever. And yet, positive social relationships that help buoy youths' motivations and strengths are necessary if they are to achieve positive selfhood and become healthy, resilient, and successful adults. Gratitude may be key in this respect precisely because it appears to benefit youth both psychologically and socially. Gratitude is unique among the human virtues with its strong link to happiness and malleability; however, despite its promise for transforming youth and institutions, the implementation of school-based programs to enhance gratitude is limited in scope.

There is ample empirical evidence that supportive social networks help buffer individuals from adversity and pathology on one hand and help enhance health and well-being on the other. Social belonging is one of the most essential human needs, and fulfilling it creates protective properties (Patrick, Knee, Canevello, & Lonsbary, 2007). One reason is that supportive relationships make people feel good on a regular basis. Positive emotions initiate cognitive processes that can make people interact in more helpful and socially responsible ways (Fredrickson, 2013); and they foster creative, open-minded thinking that can build lasting resources and make individuals more productive, healthy, and happy (Fredrickson, 2001). Thus, securing caring relationships early on in a child's life can provide bedrock for many positive outcomes in human development. One reliable way to feel good and strengthen supportive social connections is to experience and express gratitude.

Gratitude involves more than just feeling good, as it appears to be linked to positive transformations of selfhood (Bono, Froh, & Emmons, 2012). Gratitude is a common response when one is the beneficiary of a kind act. Opportunities to cooperate and help others abound in school environments and youth programs; and despite ample evidence on the benefits of gratitude and its many potential applications in general (Bono, Emmons, & McCullough, 2004; Bono & McCullough, 2006; Froh, Emmons, Lomas, Mishra, & Bono, in press-b) and for schools in particular (Froh & Bono, 2011), research on gratitude and gratitude applications for youth is still in its early stages (Froh & Bono, 2011). This chapter covers research on gratitude, with particular focus on its relevance to in-school youth and its potential to enhance student achievement, well-being, and social development. After a brief introduction of the concept of gratitude, its measurement in youth, and its relevance to school settings, we turn to the literature on the consequences of gratitude—its links to well-being, supportive relationships, prosocial behavior, and goal striving—and consider how gratitude may be tied to positive youth development. We then cover research on interventions with youth and moderators of gratitude. Finally, we close by touching on potential organizational benefits of gratitude for schools and suggestions for future research.

WHAT IS GRATITUDE?

When people receive a personal gift or benefit that was not earned, deserved, or expected but instead due to the good intentions of another person, a typical emotional response is gratitude (Emmons & McCullough, 2003). As a moral emotion, gratitude is an "other-praising" emotion that is linked to the welfare of other people or society as a whole (Haidt, 2003). People could feel grateful emotions for many reasons—material (e.g., a gift), mundane (e.g., a favor), interpersonal (e.g., support from a friend), or collective (e.g., donations to an organization or cause). People could also experience appreciative states that involve thoughts, beliefs, or attitudes beyond an interpersonal context (e.g., appreciation for God, a beautiful landscape, or a creative work of art). It has been shown that people differ in terms of their disposition to gratitude. Four qualities that distinguish highly grateful people from less grateful people is that they experience gratitude more *intensely* for a positive event, more *frequently* throughout the day, with greater *density* for any given benefit (i.e., grateful to more people), and at any given time they may have a wider *span* of benefits in their lives for which they are grateful (e.g., family, friends, teachers, being included in a special event, having been defended by someone; McCullough, Emmons, & Tsang, 2002).

McCullough, Kilpatrick, Emmons, and Larson (2001) first proposed a conceptualization of gratitude as an emotion that serves three moral functions. First, they hypothesized that gratitude can serve as a *moral barometer* because it indicates change in people's social relationships as a result of recognizing others' roles in augmenting their welfare. Second, gratitude can serve as a *moral reinforcer* because expressing it can increase the chances of benefactors acting kindly again in the future—just as showing ingratitude can instill anger in benefactors and inhibit future benevolent acts. Finally, gratitude can serve as a *moral motive* by motivating a person to reciprocate kindness and inhibit destructive acts toward benefactors or others. McCullough and colleagues (2001) found ample support in the literature for the first two hypotheses and subsequent experiments using behavioral measures of helping provided additional support for the moral motive function (Bartlett & DeSteno, 2006; Tsang, 2006). Experiencing gratitude serves an informational function for the beneficiary, indicating the value relationships with benefactors hold, expressing gratitude serves a motivational function for benefactors to behave prosocially toward the beneficiary again, and experiencing gratitude causes the beneficiary to behave prosocially in response to benefactors as well as toward others.

More recent evidence has indicated that gratitude serves as a moral barometer and a moral motive among youth as well. For instance, social cognitive determinants of gratitude (i.e., the personal value of the benefit, the cost to the benefactor, and the intention of the benefactor) can be trained in children as young as 8 years old, and such an intervention increases gratitude and positive affect over the course of 5 months (Froh et al., in press a). With respect to gratitude as a moral motive among youth, adolescents (ages 11–14) who developed gratitude over a period of 4 years also reported increased prosocial behavior (e.g., "Helped another kid if they fell or hurt themselves") and decreased antisocial behavior (e.g., "Picked on another child in class"), compared to youth who were consistently low in gratitude during this period (Bono, Froh, Emmons, & Card, 2013). Finally, the life satisfaction and prosocial behavior associated with gratitude predicted general motivation to help others and contribute to society 6 months later (Froh, Bono, & Emmons, 2010). In combination, the findings of intervention and correlational research indicate that gratitude is particularly suited to building and strengthening supportive social ties among adults as well as youth. It is worth noting, however, that the development of gratitude or factors that promote or inhibit its emergence remain empirically uncharted.

POTENTIAL BENEFITS OF GRATITUDE IN SCHOOLS

There is increasing awareness that a critical school issue for adolescents is meeting social and academic demands simultaneously and that success in both domains requires effective coordination between tasks and social goals (Wentzel, 2005). Given the centrality of friendships and social acceptance in the lives of adolescents (Hartup & Stevens, 1997), it is important to identify ways to promote both social and academic development. In collaborative learning contexts, positive peer relationships can enable students to engage in learning activities and develop social skills (Wentzel & Watkins, 2002). Indeed, hundreds of studies conducted in the last 30 years covering nearly every subject and grade level show positive links between cooperative learning and achievement (Johnson, Johnson, & Smith, 2007). Therefore, we believe gratitude could be integral to the transformation that is underway—of turning schools into environments that do not just address deficit and pathology but enhance strengths and psychological and social development (Roberts, Brown, Johnson, & Reinke, 2003).

Dual-factor models of mental health suggest that emotional and behavioral problems are independent from well-being and that direct treatment of negative symptomology alone does not necessarily improve youths' well-being (Greenspoon & Saklofske, 2001; Suldo & Shaffer, 2008). Subjective well-being is adaptive for human survival because it motivates exploration and behaviors that build resources for succeeding in life (Diener, 1994). For this reason, school-based interventions that reduce negative symptoms (e.g., depression and anger) and enhance well-being (e.g., self-efficacy and hope) simultaneously are needed. Gratitude interventions have produced improvements in well-being and reductions in negative outcomes (Emmons & McCullough, 2003; Seligman, Steen, Park, & Peterson, 2005). Therefore, school-based interventions that boost positive psychological phenomena like gratitude may effectively promote positive outcomes *and* mitigate negative ones (Froh, Sefick, & Emmons, 2008).

That gratitude seems especially geared for maintaining and producing positive social ties makes it a prime candidate for improving students' satisfaction with life in school and the quality of their peer relationships, which can create lasting resources for well-being and achievement. This may be especially important as adolescents seek greater autonomy and rely increasingly on individuals outside the home during the high school years (Hill & Holmbeck, 1986). School satisfaction, which we found can be increased with a gratitude intervention (Froh et al., 2008), is related to both academic and social success (Verkuyten & Thijs, 2002). Thus, instilling a habit of gratitude early on in a child's life holds promise because it could help adolescents cope successfully with many challenges and broadly facilitate their identity development.

RESEARCH ASSOCIATED WITH GRATITUDE IN YOUTH

Gratitude appears to be universally valued, encouraged by religions and cultures throughout the world (Emmons & Crumpler, 2000) and widely deemed as central to happiness—with more than 90% of American teens and adults indicating that expressing it made them "extremely happy" or "somewhat happy" (Gallup, 1998). Considered an important virtue for "the good life," gratitude is considered a character strength of transcendence because of its potential to provide a sense of meaning and connection to the universe (Emmons, 2004).

Assessment of Gratitude

Froh, Fan, and colleagues (2011) recently assessed the psychometric properties of the GQ-6, the Gratitude Adjective Checklist (GAC; McCullough et al., 2002), and the Gratitude Resentment and Appreciation Test (GRAT-short form; Thomas & Watkins, 2003) using a sample of 1,405 youths ages 10 to 19 years. The aim was to determine which of these adult measures were most appropriate for measuring gratitude in children and adolescents. Results showed that all three gratitude scales were positively correlated among adolescents (ages 14 to 19 years) and that the GRAT-short form displayed low correlations with the other two scales among younger youths (ages 10 to 13 years). These results suggested that the GRAT-short form measures something different when compared to the GQ-6 and the GAC, at least among younger youth. Finally, the GQ-6 was found to perform better with youth only using the first five questions (not the sixth).

Psychological Well-Being and Resilience

Positive emotions can fuel an upward spiral of well-being, optimal functioning, and coping (Fredrickson, 2001; Fredrickson & Joiner, 2002). Because gratitude is strongly linked to well-being, it may engage such healthy processes and promote resilience (Fredrickson, 2004). Indeed, there is evidence that gratitude buffers people from psychiatric disorders like depression and anxiety and from substance abuse (Kendler et al., 2003). It appears to protect people from debilitating emotions and distress as well. For example, Fredrickson, Tugade, Waugh, and Larkin (2003) found that out of 20 emotions, gratitude was the second most commonly experienced after the September 11, 2001, terrorist attacks in the United States (after compassion). Experiencing gratitude actively helped people cope with the disaster. Further, an archival study of newspaper accounts about what children were thankful for before and after the September 11 event found that themes of gratitude for basic human needs (e.g., family, friends, and teachers) increased (Gordon, Musher-Eizenman, Holub, & Dalrymple, 2004). These findings suggested that gratitude, in particular, may foster coping, adjustment, and resiliency in youth.

In a recent longitudinal study (Bono et al., 2012), 436 adolescents (11- to 14-year-olds) were asked to complete self-report questionnaires just before entering high school and then again 4 years later. Measuring gratitude broadly (i.e., as both a trait and affective mood), gratitude at time 1 significantly predicted lower negative emotions and depression (βs = −.14 & −.14) and greater positive emotions, life satisfaction, and happiness (βs = .12, .18, .19, respectively) at time 2 (Bono et al., 2012). When change in gratitude from year 1 to year 4 was examined, even stronger effects were observed—increases in gratitude throughout high school predicted greater increases in positive emotions, life satisfaction, and happiness toward the end of high school (βs = .33, .35, and .39, respectively). Thus, even if the ninth-graders did not have high levels of gratitude when entering high school, if they developed more gratitude during high school then they had more positive outcomes by the time they were seniors. Thus, gratitude seems to improve youths' moods, mental health, and satisfaction with life.

Relational Well-Being

Grateful people tend to be more helpful, supportive, forgiving, and empathic toward others, and they tend to have personalities that are more agreeable, less narcissistic, and less materialistic (McCullough et al., 2002). The experience of gratitude motivates people to reciprocate to benefactors (Bartlett & DeSteno, 2006; Tsang, 2006) and to respond prosocially to other people (Bartlett & DeSteno, 2006). The evidence with adults so strongly supports gratitude's links to relational well-being (Fredrickson, 2004) that gratitude is considered an evolutionary adaptation that sustains reciprocal altruism and ensures positive human relations (McCullough, Kimeldorf, & Cohen, 2008). Evidence supporting these notions among youth is also emerging. For instance, teens reporting higher levels of gratitude also report more relational satisfaction and support (Froh, Yurkewicz, & Kashdan, 2009). Gratitude in teens is also negatively correlated with materialism and envy (Froh, Emmons, Card, Bono, & Wilson, 2010).

In the Bono and colleagues (2012) longitudinal study of high school adolescents, it was also found that increases in gratitude during high school predicted reduced antisocial and delinquency behavior toward the end of high school (βs = −.15 and −.13; Bono et al., 2012). Specifically, teens who reported higher levels of gratitude across a 4-year period also reported lower levels of hitting, teasing, ganging up on, upsetting, threatening, and gossiping about their peers, compared to those who made fewer gains in gratitude. Higher-gratitude youths also reported better conduct at school (e.g., not being sent to the principal's office, not bringing alcohol/drugs to school, not cheating on tests, not skipping school, not getting suspended, and not getting expelled), compared to teens who reported lower gratitude across the 4-year period of the study.

The desire to give back to the neighborhood, community, and the world (i.e., social integration) was observed in another longitudinal study with early adolescents (Froh, Bono, & Emmons, 2010). Results showed that grateful youth were more likely than less grateful youth to report increases in social integration 6 months later, and this effect was partly due to increases in satisfaction with life and engagement in prosocial behaviors at 3 months. Further analyses showed that gratitude and social integration mutually increased each other, partly due to increases in life satisfaction at 3 months, supporting the notion that gratitude may promote upward spirals of emotional and social well-being.

Finally, in an experimental test to further investigate the gratitude–prosocial link, adolescents who kept a gratitude journal were found to be more generous in the amount of money they donated compared to those in the control journal condition. Notably, adolescents who kept a gratitude journal donated 60% more of their earnings compared to those in the control condition (Chaplin, Froh, John, & Rindfleisch, in press). Therefore, promoting gratitude may be an effective way to improve students' social relationships.

Strong social ties may be related to academic achievement more than previously thought, as was found in analyses of the California Healthy Kids Survey and Resilience and Youth Development Module—a comprehensive self-report tool kit for tracking youth risk behaviors and assets linked to student learning and school success (Hanson & Kim, 2007). In diverse samples of California students in Grades 7, 9, and 11, caring community and peer relationships predicted schools' Academic Performance Index (API; the cornerstone of the state's accountability system) as well as or better than many health risks or strengths typically linked to school achievement (Bono, Hanson, Zheng, & Austin, 2007). For instance, caring and supportive relationships with adults in the community, with peers, and with teachers were each related to differences in schools' API quintile scores (effect size Fs across Grades 7, 9 and 11 ranged from .22 to .28, from .20 to .25, and from .15 to .20, respectively) more so than other constructs typically considered by schools for increasing academic achievement (e.g., self-efficacy, problem solving, current alcohol or marijuana use). This is, however, not direct proof that gratitude raises API. But it does suggest that gratitude may play a role in increasing API given its relation to strong social ties (Froh et al., 2009).

The CHKS findings suggest that establishing autonomous, caring social ties with adults in the community, peers, and teachers comprise important student-level determinants of schools' overall achievement. Gratitude, therefore, could help foster relationship resources that are especially important for students and schools. Because gratitude occurs less in relationships in which exchanges are obligatory or habitual (Bar-Tal, Bar-Zohar, Greenberg, & Hermon, 1977), gratitude is especially suited to strengthening social connections of one's own choosing (e.g., peers, mentors, and adults outside the home); and this has implications for individuals' chances of developing optimally and thriving.

CAN GRATITUDE HELP YOUTH FLOURISH?

Cultivating gratitude in youth could spur on other beneficial processes besides helping them with their social and academic development. If gratitude broadens people's habitual thought-action repertoires and helps them build enduring personal resources that increase their likelihood of feeling good and functioning well in the future (Fredrickson, 2004), then it should help youth fulfill their potential and find greater meaning, success, and well-being—that is, to flourish. The existing evidence is consonant with this notion that gratitude promotes positive development in youth as well.

Gratitude appears to fuel intrinsic goal pursuit, other-oriented motivations, and the fulfillment of higher-order needs (e.g., self-expression and purpose), whereas materialism appears to fuel extrinsic goal pursuit, individualistic motivations, and the fulfillment of lower-order needs (e.g., possessions of comfort and safety; Kasser, 2002; Kasser & Ryan, 1996; Polak & McCullough, 2006). Providing support for this notion, one study found gratitude to be negatively related to materialism and positively related to academic, psychological, and social outcomes (Froh et al., 2010). Further, grateful adolescents tended to have higher GPAs, greater absorption in meaningful activities, more life satisfaction, and more social integration and were less envious and depressed than less grateful adolescents. Materialism, on the other hand, was linked to lower GPAs and greater envy. Such findings suggest that gratitude promotes valuing connections to people, purposeful growth, and social capital, so that they are less likely to be materialistic (i.e., primarily focused on status, image, wealth, and acquiring things)—something that poses a rising challenge in society (Chaplin & John, 2007).

The longitudinal findings from Bono and colleagues (2012) suggest that the advantages of gratitude are part of a more general pattern of thriving—gratitude significantly predicted increases in hope and sense of meaning in adolescents 4 years later (βs = .23, .19, respectively). And again, gaining gratitude during the high school years was even more strongly related to increases in hope and meaning by the end of high school (βs = .31, .30, respectively). Therefore, longitudinal evidence indicates that gratitude helps youth thrive during the critical years of identity formation.

WHY GRATITUDE MAY BE A CRITICAL INGREDIENT IN POSITIVE YOUTH DEVELOPMENT (PYD)

PYD theory emphasizes the importance of nurturing young people's potentialities by providing them with environments and opportunities that help build up their strengths (Benson, Scales, Hamilton, & Semsa, 2006). It posits that five strengths are essential if youth are to develop optimally: *competence* (or a positive view of one's actions/skills), *confidence* (or overall self-worth), *connection* (or positive bonds with people, groups, institutions, or communities), *character* (or respect for societal/cultural rules and sense of morality and integrity), and *caring* and compassion (having sympathy and empathy for others; Lerner et al., 2005). PYD theory also emphasizes the importance of youth contributing to their own development, and, in turn, helping to transform the people, groups, institutions or communities that nurture them (Benson et al., 2006).

Gratitude involves empathic processing on the part of the benefactor and beneficiary; hence, it promotes the strength of caring and compassion for both parties involved in beneficial social exchanges. By virtue of its three moral functions (described earlier), gratitude should also feed into the strengths of connection and character; and finally, because it also promotes intrinsic motivation and self-improvement, it should also support the strength of competence. Further, because gratitude appears linked to purposeful life engagement and meaning beyond hedonism, then it should aid youths' adaptive developmental regulation (Brandtstädter, 1998; Lerner, 2004) within their academic and social contexts, help them establish a sense of moral identity (Damon, 1990), and move them closer to the ultimate manifestation of PYD—contribution to society (Lerner et al., 2005). Again, recent longitudinal evidence supports the view that gratitude development is associated broadly with PYD (Bono et al., 2013). For instance, adolescents who approached high school with a moderate amount of gratitude and exhibited steady gains over the subsequent 4 years also reported greater self-awareness, empathy, self-efficacy, goals and plans for the future, and intentional self-regulation and a stronger sense of identification with their community and a motivation to improve society (Bono et al., 2013).

INTERVENTIONS AND MODERATORS: INCREASING GRATITUDE IN CHILDREN AND ADOLESCENTS

Froh and colleagues (2008) conducted an investigation with early adolescents to see if a gratitude intervention (i.e., counting blessings) could influence their well-being. Eleven classrooms were randomly assigned to one of three conditions: gratitude, hassles, or no-treatment control. Measures were completed daily for 2 weeks and then again at a 3-week follow-up. For 2 weeks, students in the gratitude condition were instructed to count up to five things in their lives for which they were grateful. Those in the hassles condition were instructed to focus on irritants. Results indicated that counting blessings was related to more optimism and life satisfaction, fewer physical complaints, and less negative affect. Students who claimed feeling grateful in response to aid reported more positive affect. In fact, feeling grateful for aid demonstrated a linear relation with positive affect throughout the intervention—becoming stronger by the 3-week follow-up. Finally, students who counted blessings reported more school satisfaction both at the immediate posttest and at the 3-week follow-up compared to students in either the hassles or control group.

To further build on the study of gratitude interventions, Froh, Kashdan, Ozimkowski, and Miller (2009) examined whether affect moderated the effects of gratitude interventions on children and adolescents (ages 8 to 19). Students were randomly assigned to do a gratitude visit condition (write a letter to a benefactor who they needed to thank and then reading the letter to the benefactor in person) or to a control condition (wrote about daily events and the way the events made them feel). Compared with youths in the control condition, the youths in the gratitude condition who were also low in positive affect reported more gratitude and positive affect at posttreatment and more positive affect at the 2-month follow-up.

The most recent development in the area of gratitude interventions for youth comes from a gratitude curriculum designed to train the appraisal of helpful exchanges in elementary school students (Froh et al., in press). Using a quasi-experimental design, classrooms (consisting of 8- to 11-year-olds) were randomly assigned to a benefit appraisal curriculum or a control condition. Specifically, experimenters delivered five daily curriculum sessions to 122 students in six different classes in one study and five weekly curriculum sessions to 82 students in four different classrooms in a second study. The benefit appraisal condition trained students to appreciate the personal value of kind actions or gifts, the intention of the benefactor to notice their need and act on it, and the degree to which such actions cost benefactors in terms of time or effort. The control condition had students focus on mundane daily issues in the lives of students that were emotionally neutral and unassociated with beneficial interpersonal exchanges. The lessons included classroom discussions, writing assignments, and role-playing activities that all served to deliver, apply, and learn these three skills of appreciation (in the case of the intervention condition) or not (in the case of the control condition) when reflecting on daily life.

Overall, the authors found evidence that the curriculum intervention helped induce gratitude. In both studies, students receiving the social cognitive appraisal training reported stronger help appraisals and more gratitude than students in the control condition. The daily curriculum produced increases in help appraisals and gratitude immediately (2 days later); and students even wrote 80% more thank-you cards to their Parent Teacher Association (expressing gratitude behaviorally), compared to the control students. The weekly curriculum produced increases in help appraisals, gratitude, and positive affect up to 5 months postintervention. Evidence thus supported the effectiveness of this curriculum intervention, with effect sizes ranging from small to medium. One advantage of this grateful thinking curriculum, as opposed to the other intervention methods, is that it is easier to use with younger participants (i.e., in elementary or middle school), who might not be particularly capable of, or even interested in, keeping a gratitude journal or performing a gratitude visit. Yet another advantage has to do with its practicality and potential for schools; it can easily be infused in any program or activity that involves or has a focus on cooperating, helping, or giving.

When testing the efficacy of gratitude interventions, it is critical to consider moderators, as some subgroups may be more responsive to the intervention than others (Froh et al., 2009). For example, there is evidence that gratitude benefits boys more than it does girls (Froh et al., 2009). Research examining different mechanisms through which gratitude benefits males and females differently will help to produce better interventions. With the use of exercises that are better tailored to the sexes, individuals are more likely to personally "own" and commit to the interventions (Kashdan, Mishra, Breen, & Froh, 2009). The same could be said with other potential moderators, such as positive affect—there is evidence that youth lower in positive affect benefit more from gratitude (Froh et al., 2009)—but cultural factors or attitudinal factors also likely moderate the effects of gratitude on well-being. Recent work by Wood, Brown, and Maltby (2011) suggests that different people will experience different amounts of gratitude for help or gifts they are given, depending on the amount of help or size of gifts they are accustomed to receiving. A better understanding of how gratitude is experienced and expressed in different cultures and in different groups may thus help improve our ability to use gratitude to promote well-being and other related outcomes.

APPLYING GRATITUDE TO SCHOOLS

Simmel (1950) argued that gratitude is the moral glue that bonds people together into a functioning society, and his logic of gratitude as the "moral memory of mankind" (p. 388) can be applied to school communities. School psychologists can help students identify the resources and support provided by school boards (e.g., funding extracurricular activities), school-level administration (e.g., supporting school plays), teachers (e.g., teaching new learning strategies), support staff (e.g., cleaning the facilities), and community volunteers (e.g., committing many hours to organizing or chaperoning enrichment events). Most importantly, recognizing the contributions and investments others make toward their welfare would focus students on concrete ways that they and their progress are valued at the school, and knowing that others believe in and care to bring out the best in them would likely engage students' motivation to better themselves.

Gratitude felt and expressed by students and the improved behaviors that could ensue would likely spread to teachers and staff, encouraging them to work harder on students' behalf and helping to prevent burnout. Though there is no direct evidence for this, there is evidence that a gratitude intervention helped reduce burnout and increase life satisfaction and a sense of personal accomplishment among Chinese schoolteachers (Chan, 2011). Therefore, teaching students to count blessings and develop an attitude of gratitude may foster stronger bonds to schools *and* communities, helping both students and schools to thrive.

Social exchange is necessary for most organizations in society to function properly. A recent experimental study showed that beneficiaries' appreciation of help depends on the degree to which they perceive helpers' actions to facilitate active goals (Converse & Fishbach, 2012), indicating that helpful exchanges help individuals complete tasks and feel good. The positive emotions of leaders (e.g., principals, teachers) predict the performance for their entire group (George, 1995). Indeed, evidence suggests that gratitude promotes social cohesion, relational and job satisfaction, and even enhanced organizational functioning (Emmons, 2003). Thus, gratitude and the valuing of benefits may even be contagious.

CONCLUSION

In this chapter, we reviewed the literature on gratitude in youth so as to bring into focus its relevance to students and schools. Because gratitude leads to many positive outcomes that are of central importance to youth in schools—psychological well-being, satisfaction with school and other domains, prosocial relationships, improved motivation, and a stronger focus on priorities and planning for the future—gratitude applications in schools have much promise for advancing students' learning and engagement with school. For instance, gratitude components could be easily designed into character and civic education programs to help to enhance them and make them more personally relevant and interesting. Moreover, English classes could benefit from the inclusion of gratitude and appreciation exercises; not only would such exercises help develop writing skills in general (given the interpersonal dynamics involved in gratitude experiences), they might help motivate students to focus on their unique life stories and priorities. The prospect that these impacts could even spread to improve the effectiveness of schools as organizations brings even more promise that gratitude could help transform schools into places where youth and their potential are valued above all else and where all people (and communities) involved thrive.

REFERENCES

Bar-Tal, D., Bar-Zohar, Y., Greenberg, M.S., & Hermon, M. (1977). Reciprocity behavior in the relationship between donor and recipient and between harm-doer and victim. *Sociometry, 40,* 293–298. doi:10.1111/j.1467-8721.2008.00590.x

Bartlett, M.Y., & DeSteno, D. (2006). Gratitude and prosocial behavior: Helping when it costs you. *Psychological Science, 17,* 319–325. doi:10.1111/j.1467-9280.2006.01705.x

Benson, P.L., Scales, P.C., Hamilton, S.F., & Semsa, A., Jr. (2006). Positive youth development: Theory, research, and applications. In W. Damon & R.M. Lerner (Chief Eds.), & R.M. Lerner (Ed.), *Handbook of child psychology: Theoretical models of human development* (Vol. 1, 6th ed., pp. 894–941). Hoboken, NJ: Wiley. doi:10.1002/9780470147658.chpsy0116

Bono, G., Emmons, R.A., & McCullough, M.E. (2004). Gratitude in practice and the practice of gratitude. In P.A. Linley & S. Joseph (Eds.), *Positive psychology in practice* (pp. 464–481). New York: Wiley. doi:10.1002/9780470939338.ch29

Bono, G., Froh, J.J., & Emmons, R.A. (2012, August). *Searching for the developmental role of gratitude: A 4-year longitudinal analysis.* Paper presented at the annual meeting of the American Psychological Association, Orlando, Florida.

Bono, G., Froh, J.J., Emmons, R.A., & Card, N.A. (2013, April). *The benefits of gratitude to adolescent development: Longitudinal models of gratitude, well-being and prosocial behavior.* Paper presented at the annual meeting of the Society for Research in Child Development, Seattle, Washington.

Bono, G., Hanson, T., Zheng, C., & Austin, G. (2007). *Analysis of 2004–2006 data from the California Healthy Kids Survey, Resilience and Youth Development Module, and academic performance index.* Unpublished data.

Bono, G., & McCullough, M. E. (2006). Positive responses to benefit and harm: Bringing forgiveness and gratitude into cognitive psychotherapy. *Journal of Cognitive Psychotherapy, 20,* 147–158. doi:10.1891/jcop.20.2.147

Brandtstädter, J. (1998). Action perspectives on human development. In W. Damon & R.M. Lerner (Eds.), *Handbook of child psychology: Theoretical models of human development* (Vol. 1, 5th ed., pp. 807–863). New York, NY: Wiley. doi:10.1002/9780470147658.chpsy0110

Chan, D.W. (2011). Burnout and life satisfaction: Does gratitude intervention make a difference among Chinese school teachers in Hong Kong? *Educational Psychology, 31,* 809–823. doi:10.1080/01443410.2011.608525

Chaplin, L., Froh, J.J., John, D.R., & Rindfleisch, A. (in press). *Reducing materialism in adolescents.* Manuscript submitted for publication.

Chaplin, L.N., & John, D.R. (2007). Growing up in a material world: Age differences in materialism in children and adolescents. *Journal of Consumer Research, 34,* 480–493. doi:10.1086/518546

Converse, B.A., & Fishbach, A. (2012). Instrumentality boosts gratitude: Helpers are more appreciated while they are useful. *Psychological Science, 23,* 560–566. doi:10.1177/0956797611433334

Damon, W. (1990). *The moral child.* New York, NY: Free Press.

Diener, E. (1994). Assessing subjective well-being: Progress and opportunities. *Social Indicators Research, 31,* 103–157. doi:10.1007/978-90-481-2354-4_3

Emmons, R.A. (2003). Acts of gratitude in organizations. In K.S. Cameron, J.E. Dutton, & R.E. Quinn (Eds.), *Positive organizational scholarship* (pp. 81–93). San Francisco, CA: Berrett-Koehler.

Emmons, R.A. (2004). Gratitude. In M.E.P. Seligman & C. Peterson (Eds.), *The VIA taxonomy of human strengths and virtues.* New York, NY: Oxford University Press.

Emmons, R.A., & Crumpler, C.A. (2000). Gratitude as a human strength: Appraising the evidence. *Journal of Social and Clinical Psychology, 19,* 56–69. doi:10.1521/jscp.2000.19.1.56

Emmons, R.A., & McCullough, M.E. (2003). Counting blessings versus burdens: An empirical investigation of gratitude and subjective well-being in daily life. *Journal of Personality and Social Psychology, 84,* 377–389. doi:10.1037/0022-3514.84.2.377

Fredrickson, B.L. (2001). The role of positive emotions in positive psychology: The broaden-and-build theory of positive emotions. *American Psychologist, 56,* 218–226. doi:10.1037//0003-066X.56.3.218

Fredrickson, B.L. (2004). Gratitude, like other positive emotions, broadens and builds. In R.A. Emmons & M.E. McCullough (Eds.), *The psychology of gratitude* (pp. 145–166). New York, NY: Oxford University Press.

Fredrickson, B.L. (2013). Positive emotions broaden and build. *Advances in Experimental Social Psychology, 47,* 1–57. doi:10.1016/B978-0-12-407236-7.00001-2

Fredrickson, B.L., & Joiner, T. (2002). Positive emotions trigger upward spirals toward emotional well-being. *Psychological Science, 13,* 172–175. doi:10.1111/1467-9280.00431

Fredrickson, B.L., Tugade, M.M., Waugh, C.E., & Larkin, G.R. (2003). What good are positive emotions in crises? A prospective study of resilience and emotions following the terrorist attacks on the United States on September 11th, 2001. *Journal of Personality and Social Psychology, 84,* 365–376. doi:10.1037/0022-3514.84.2.365

Froh, J.J., & Bono, G. (2011). Gratitude in youth: A review of gratitude interventions and some ideas for applications. *NASP Communiqué, 39,* 1, 26–28.

Froh, J.J., Bono, G., & Emmons, R.A. (2010). Being grateful is beyond good manners: Gratitude and motivation to contribute to society among early adolescents. *Motivation & Emotion, 34,* 144–157. doi:10.1007/s11031-010-9163-z

Froh, J.J., Bono, G., Fan, J., Emmons, R.A., Henderson, K., Harris, C., Leggio, H., & Wood, A. (in press-a). *Nice thinking! An educational intervention that teaches children how to think gratefully. [Special Issue: Theoretical Frameworks in School Psychology Intervention Research: Interdisciplinary Perspectives and Future Directions].* School Psychology Review.

Froh, J.J., Emmons, R.A., Card, N.A., Bono, G., & Wilson, J. (2011). Gratitude and the reduced costs of materialism in adolescents. *Journal of Happiness Studies, 12,* 289–302. doi:10.1007/s10902-010-9195-9

Froh, J.J., Emmons, R.A., Lomas, T., Mishra, A, & Bono, G. (in press-b). Gratitude interventions: Remaining calm in the excitement. In. A. Parks (Ed.), *Handbook of positive psychological interventions.* Malden, MA: Wiley-Blackwell.

Froh, J.J., Fan, J., Emmons, R.A., Bono, G., Huebner, E.S., & Watkins, P. (2011). Measuring gratitude in youth: Assessing the psychometric properties of adult gratitude scales in children and adolescents. *Psychological Assessment, 23,* 311–324. doi:10.1037/a0021590

Froh, J.J., Kashdan, T.B., Ozimkowski, K.M., & Miller, N. (2009). Who benefits the most from a gratitude intervention in children and adolescents? Examining positive affect as a moderator. *Journal of Positive Psychology, 4,* 408–422. doi:10.1080/17439760902992464

Froh, J.J., Sefick, W.J., & Emmons, R.A. (2008). Counting blessings in early adolescents. An experimental study of gratitude and subjective well-being. *Journal of School Psychology. 46*, 213–233. doi:10.1016/j.jsp.2007.03.005

Froh, J.J., Yurkewicz, C., & Kashdan, T.B. (2009). Gratitude and subjective well-being in early adolescence: Examining gender differences. *Journal of Adolescence, 32*, 633–650. doi:10.1016/j.adolescence.2008.06.006

Gallup, G. (1998). Gallup survey results on "gratitude," adults and teenagers. *Emerging Trends, 20*(4–5), 9.

George, J.M. (1995). Leader positive mood and group performance: The case of customer service. *Journal of Applied Social Psychology, 25*, 778–794. doi:10.1111/j.1559-1816.1995.tb01775.x

Gordon, A.K., Musher-Eizenman, D.R., Holub, S.C., & Dalrymple, J. (2004). What are children thankful for? An archival analysis of gratitude before and after the attacks of September 11. *Applied Developmental Psychology, 25*, 541–553. doi:10.1016/j.appdev.2004.08.004

Greenspoon, P.J., & Saklofske, D.H. (2001). Toward an integration of subjective well-being and psychopathology. *Social Indicators Research, 54*, 81–108. doi:10.1023/A:1007219227883

Haidt, J. (2003). The moral emotions. In R.J. Davidson, K.R. Scherer, & H.H. Goldsmith (Eds.), *Handbook of affective sciences* (pp. 852–870). Oxford, UK: Oxford University Press.

Hanson, T.L., & Kim, J.O. (2007). Measuring resilience and youth development: The psychometric properties of the Healthy Kids Survey. (Issues & Answers Report, REL 2007–No. 034). Washington, DC: U.S. Department of Education, Institute of Education Sciences, National Center for Education Evaluation and Regional Assistance, Regional Educational Laboratory West. Retrieved from http://ies.ed.gov/ncee/edlabs

Hartup, W.W., & Stevens, N. (1997). Friendship and adaptation in the life course. *Psychological Review, 121*, 355–370. doi:10.1037/0033-2909.121.3.355

Hill, J.P., & Holmbeck, G.N. (1986). Attachment and autonomy during adolescence. *Annals of Child Development, 3*, 145–189.

Johnson, D.W., Johnson, R.T., & Smith, K. (2007). The state of cooperative learning in postsecondary and professional settings. *Educational Psychology Review, 19*, 15–29. doi:10.1007/s10648-006-9038-8

Kashdan, T.B., Mishra, A., Breen, W.E., & Froh, J.J. (2009). Gender differences in gratitude: Examining appraisals, narratives, the willingness to express emotions, and changes in psychological needs. *Journal of Personality, 77*, 691–730. doi:10.1111/j.1467-6494.2009.00562.x

Kasser, T. (2002). *The high price of materialism.* Cambridge, MA: MIT Press.

Kasser, T., & Ryan, R.M. (1996). Further examining the American Dream: Differential correlates of intrinsic and extrinsic goals. *Personality and Social Psychology Bulletin, 22*, 281–288. doi:10.1177/0146167296223006

Kendler, K.S., Liu, X., Gardner, C.O., McCullough, M.E., Larson, D., & Prescott, C.A. (2003). Dimensions of religiosity and their relationship to lifetime psychiatric and substance use disorders. *American Journal of Psychiatry, 160*, 496–503. doi:10.1176/appi.ajp.160.3.496

Lerner, R.M. (2004). *Liberty: Thriving and civic engagement among American youth.* Thousand Oaks, CA: Sage.

Lerner, R.M., Lerner, J.V., Almerigi, J.B., Theokas, C., Phelps, E., Gestsdottir, S., . . . Eye, A. (2005). Positive youth development, participation in community youth development programs, and community contributions of fifth-grade adolescents: Findings from the first wave of the 4-H Study of positive youth development. *Journal of Early Adolescence, 25*, 17–71. doi:10.1177/0272431604272461

McCullough, M.E., Emmons, R.A., & Tsang, J. (2002). The grateful disposition: A conceptual and empirical topography. *Journal of Personality and Social Psychology, 82*, 112–127. doi:10.1037/0022-3514.82.1.112

McCullough, M.E., Kilpatrick, S.D., Emmons, R.A., & Larson, D.B. (2001). Is gratitude a moral affect? *Psychological Bulletin, 127*, 249–266. doi:10.1037/0033-2909.127.2.249

McCullough, M.E., Kimeldorf, M.B., & Cohen, A.D. (2008). An adaptation for altruism? The social causes, social effects, and social evolution of gratitude. *Current Directions in Psychological Science, 17*, 281–285.

Patrick, H., Knee, C.R., Canevello, A., & Lonsbary, C. (2007). The role of need fulfillment in relationship functioning and well-being: A self-determination theory perspective. *Journal of Personality and Social Psychology, 92*, 434–457. doi:10.1037/0022-3514.92.3.434

Polak, E., & McCullough, M.E. (2006). Is gratitude an alternative to materialism? *Journal of Happiness Studies, 7*, 343–360.

Roberts, M.C., Brown, K.J., Johnson, R.J., & Reinke, J. (2003). Positive psychology for children: Development, prevention and promotion. In C.R. Synder & S.J. Lopez (Eds.), *Handbook of positive psychology* (pp. 663–675). New York, NY: Oxford University Press.

Seligman, M.E.P., Steen, T.A., Park, N., & Peterson, C. (2005). Positive psychology progress: Empirical validation of interventions. *American Psychologist, 60*, 410–421. doi:10.1037/0003-066X.60.5.410

Simmel, G. (1950). *The sociology of Georg Simmel.* Glencoe, IL: Free Press.

Suldo, S. M., & Shaffer, E. J. (2008). Looking beyond psychopathology: The dual-factor model of mental health in youth. *School Psychology Review, 37*, 52–68.

Thomas, M., & Watkins, P. (2003, April). *Measuring the grateful trait: Development of the revised GRAT.* Poster session presented at the Annual Convention of the Western Psychological Association, Vancouver, BC.

Tsang, J. (2006). Gratitude and prosocial behaviour: An experimental test of gratitude. *Cognition and Emotion, 20*, 138–148. doi:10.1080/02699930500172341

Verkuyten, M., & Thijs, J. (2002). School satisfaction of elementary school children: The role of performance, peer relations, ethnicity, and gender. *Social Indicators Research, 59*, 203–228. doi:10.1023/A:1016279602893

Wentzel, K. R. (2005). Peer relationships, motivation, and academic performance at school. In A. J. Elliot & C. S. Dweck (Eds.), *Handbook of competence and motivation* (pp. 279–296). New York, NY: Guilford.

Wentzel, K. R., & Watkins, D. E. (2002). Peer relationships and collaborative learning as contexts for academic enablers. *School Psychology Review, 31*, 366–367.

Wood, A. M., Brown, G. D. A., & Maltby, J. (2011). Thanks, but I'm used to better: A relative rank model of gratitude. *Emotion, 11*, 175–180. doi:10.1037/a0021553

CHAPTER SUMMARY: GRATITUDE

- Gratitude is a behavior that appears to be linked to positive transformations of selfhood, involving both psychological and social benefits.
- Gratitude acts as a moral barometer (distinguishes more valuable relationships) and has moral motive functions (produces prosocial behavior) among youth, suggesting that it helps build supportive relationships.
- Gratitude could be important for schools to encourage because it promotes positive social relationships and cooperation, supports youths' autonomy and well-being, and improves their satisfaction with school, resilience, and identity development.
- Gratitude is linked to improved psychological functioning (correlations with subjective well-being, mental health, resilience), including 4-year correlations with increased subjective well-being.
- Gratitude is linked to improved relational functioning (more relational satisfaction and support, less materialism and envy), including 4-year correlations with reduced antisocial behavior and delinquency) and 6-month correlations with increased social integration (i.e., motivation to help community and world).
- Measures of a school's caring community and positive peer relationships are more strongly linked to academic performance index scores than many other internal and external assets commonly considered for improving school achievement.
- There is evidence of linking gratitude to thriving, which is relevant for schools' goals of helping social development and curbing vulnerability to health risks.
- Gratitude interventions that can be used in schools include counting blessings, gratitude visits, and benefit appraisal training.
- Gratitude may help boys more, as well as those who are low in positive affect.
- Gratitude promotes outcomes that are important for schools, but it is underutilized.

SUGGESTED READINGS: GRATITUDE

Froh, J. J., Bono, G., & Emmons, R. A. (2010). Being grateful is beyond good manners: Gratitude and motivation to contribute to society among early adolescents. *Motivation & Emotion, 34,* 144–157. doi:10.1007/s11031-010-9163-z

Before this article, research was accumulating showing that gratitude in youth was related with more well-being and less ill-being. This study, however, offers the first longitudinal evidence that not only does gratitude feel good, but it also makes us do good. Here the authors found that gratitude in early adolescents was prospectively related with a passion for wanting to use one's strengths to better one's community 6 months later (i.e., social integration). Further, gratitude sparked an upward positive spiral of helping behavior with gratitude and social integration serially enhancing each other, whereby gratitude lead to more social integration, which lead to more gratitude, and so on.

Froh, J. J., Emmons, R. A., Card, N. A., Bono, G., & Wilson, J. (2011). Gratitude and the reduced costs of materialism in adolescents. *Journal of Happiness Studies, 12,* 289–302. doi:10.1007/s10902-010-9195-9

This is the first known study to demonstrate a negative relationship between gratitude and materialism in late adolescents. Using self-determination theory (SDT) as the conceptual framework, this finding suggests that gratitude and materialism are related to distinct and opposite value systems. Thus, considering the negative effects that materialism can have on youth—poor family and peer relationships, depression, academic hardship, and so forth—this study suggests that teaching youth how to be more grateful may be an effective intervention for making them less materialistic.

Froh, J. J., Sefick, W. J., & Emmons, R. A. (2008). Counting blessings in early adolescents. An experimental study of gratitude and subjective well-being. *Journal of School Psychology. 46,* 213–233. doi:10.1016/j.jsp.2007.03.005

This is the first empirical attempt at investigating the effects of a gratitude intervention with youth. Eleven classes were randomly assigned to one of three conditions: a gratitude condition in which students recorded up to five blessings, a hassles condition in which students recorded up to five irritants, and a control condition in which students just completed measures. Students did this daily for 2 weeks. Results indicated that counting blessings was associated with enhanced self-reported gratitude, optimism, life satisfaction, and decreased negative affect. The most significant finding was the robust relationship between gratitude and satisfaction with school experience at both the immediate posttest and 3-week follow-up.

6

EMPATHY, PROSOCIAL BEHAVIOR, AND POSITIVE DEVELOPMENT IN SCHOOLS

Tracy L. Spinrad and Nancy Eisenberg, Arizona State University, Tempe, Arizona, USA

Writing of this chapter was partially supported by a grant from the National Institute of Mental Health (2 R01 MH60838) and a grant from the National Institute of Child Health and Development (1R01HD068522).

INTRODUCTION

The ability to respond appropriately to others' distress is an important topic in the area of child development. In this chapter, we review findings of studies involving the relations of empathy-related responding (i.e., empathy, sympathy, personal distress) and prosocial behaviors (e.g., helping, sharing) to children's social and academic functioning. In addition, we discuss literature pertaining to the socialization of empathy and prosocial behaviors. Finally, the effectiveness of school programs designed to improve children's social skills (and empathy-related responding) are described.

Prosocial behavior has been defined as voluntary behavior intended to benefit another (Eisenberg & Fabes, 1998). Contemporary researchers have distinguished among several emotional responses thought to contribute to prosocial behavior. These responses include (a) *empathy*, which is defined as an affective response that is identical to or very similar to what another person is feeling or is expected to feel; (b) *sympathy*, which is an affective response that consists of feelings of sorrow or concern for others; and (c) *personal distress,* which is characterized by a proneness to overarousal in the presence of another's distress. Children's empathy and especially sympathy have been positively related to prosocial behavior, such as sharing and helping, especially if they are likely to be altruistic (i.e., motivated by sympathy or perhaps moral values; Batson, 1991; Eisenberg, Fabes, Schaller,

& Miller, 1989; Zahn-Waxler, Robinson, & Emde, 1992), whereas personal distress reactions have been negatively related or unrelated to prosocial actions toward others (Eisenberg et al., 1993; Zahn-Waxler, Cole, Welsh, & Fox, 1995). Although the majority of this chapter focuses on children's empathy and sympathy (rather than personal distress reactions), it is important to differentiate personal distress from other aspects of responding.

DEVELOPMENT OF EMPATHY

Hoffman (1982, 2000) outlined a series of phases in the development of empathy, shifting from self-concern to more empathic, other-oriented concern. Specifically, in infancy, empathic responses are rudimentary reactions, typically marked by reactive or contagious crying in response to the cries of other infants. In the second year of life, toddlers are capable of experiencing concern for another rather than simply seeking comfort for themselves. In this phase, labeled *egocentric empathy*, toddlers demonstrate empathic concern and prosocial behaviors in response to another's distress, although these behaviors likely involve giving the other person what they themselves find comforting (e.g., bringing a favorite teddy bear to a distressed adult). As children cognitively mature and develop more sophisticated perspective-taking skills, they acquire greater awareness of another person's needs. They also understand that these needs differ from their own. For example, older children begin to experience empathy toward people who are not physically present (e.g., if they hear about someone in distress), and by later childhood, the ability to experience empathy for another's life condition or general plight develops (Hoffman, 1982, 2000). Hoffman predicted that this ability could be acquired by 9 or 10 years of age, although there is no direct research on the development of this ability. Nevertheless, empirical research does find that empathy/sympathy and prosocial behavior increase during childhood. For example, Fabes and Eisenberg (1996; Eisenberg & Fabes, 1998) conducted a meta-analysis of developmental trends in prosocial behavior and found that older children exhibited more prosocial behavior than did younger children and were higher in some measures of empathy/sympathy. However, effect sizes for age differences varied as a function of study design (i.e., method, type of prosocial behavior). Thus, although empathy and prosocial behavior sometimes increase as children develop, findings are relatively complex due to varying study characteristics. Indeed, teachers' reports of children's prosocial behavior often decline in childhood (Kokko, Tremblay, Lacourse, Nagin, & Vitaro, 2006; Nantel-Vivier et al., 2009). The development of prosocial behavior in adolescence also is deserving of further research because prosocial behavior has been shown to decline at some points in adolescence and improve at a later age (Carlo, Crocket, Randall, & Roesch, 2007).

THE RELATION OF EMPATHY-RELATED RESPONDING
TO BEHAVIORAL AND ACADEMIC COMPETENCE

Children's appropriate responses to others' distress have important implications for school success. As is noted later in this chapter, empathy and prosocial behavior have been linked with children's social competence and lower problem behaviors, and in much of the work these constructs have been measured in the school context (i.e., reported by teachers). In addition, empathy and prosocial skills have been shown to contribute to academic functioning, although children's social competence and problem behaviors possibly mediate the relation between empathy/prosocial behavior and the level of a child's academic achievement.

Social Competence

Prosocial behavior, and more specifically empathy and sympathy, have consistently been empirically related to children's positive social functioning (see Eisenberg, Fabes, & Spinrad, 2006). Specifically, empathy and sympathy have been correlated with various measures of social competence and socially appropriate behaviors (Eisenberg, Liew, & Pidada, 2001; Sallquist, Eisenberg, Spinrad, Eggum, & Gaertner, 2009; Zhou et al., 2002). In a notable longitudinal study, Eisenberg and colleagues (1996) found that teachers' reports of 6- to 8-year-olds' sympathy were positively related to teacher-rated social skills and socially appropriate behavior concurrently and/or 2 years prior. In a follow-up study when the children were 10 to 12 years old (Murphy, Shepard, Eisenberg, Fabes, & Guthrie, 1999), similar relations were found between sympathy and measures of social competence concurrently and 2, 4, and 6 years earlier. In addition, young adolescents' sympathy was linked with same-sex peers' reports of sociometric status 6 years earlier (Murphy et al., 1999).

Individuals who experience other-oriented emotional reactions and behave prosocially are likely to have positive peer relationships and interactions. Indeed, prosocial children tend to be popular with their peers (Attili, Vermigli, & Roazzi, 2010; Caprara, Barbaranelli, Pastorelli, Bandura, & Zimbardo, 2000; Clark & Ladd, 2000; Denham et al., 2003; Graziano, Keane, & Calkins, 2007; Lansford et al., 2006; Warden & Mackinnon, 2003), are relatively sociable (Robinson, Zahn-Waxler, & Emde, 1994; Young, Fox, & Zahn-Waxler, 1999), engage in less solitary and reticent play (Nelson, Hart, Yang, Wu, & Jin, 2012), and tend to have supportive peer relationships (Clark & Ladd, 2000; Sebanc, 2003). Thus, children who experience concern for others behave sensitively toward others and are viewed positively by adults and peers.

Aggression and Problem Behaviors

The relations of empathy-related responding to children's problem behaviors also have received attention from investigators. This literature is particularly relevant for school personnel because disruptive children are thought to spend less time on task (Arnold et al., 1999; NICHD Early Childcare Research Network, 2004; Ramsey, Patterson, & Walker, 1990), do less homework (Dishion, Loeber, Stouthamer-Loeber, & Patterson, 1984), and may receive less instruction from teachers (Arnold et al., 1999; Coie & Dodge, 1998; Pianta, La Paro, Payne, Cox, & Bradley, 2002). Thus, externalizing problem behaviors in the classroom likely have adverse consequences for children.

Extant research reveals a negative relation between empathy/prosocial behavior and aggression or externalizing problems (Carlo, Mestre, Samper, Tur, & Armenta, 2010; Diener & Kim, 2004; Hastings, Zahn-Waxler, Robinson, Usher, & Bridges, 2000; Strayer & Roberts, 2004), although few studies have examined these constructs longitudinally. In one exception, Zhou and colleagues (2002) assessed elementary school children's facial and self-reported empathic reactions after viewing mildly evocative slides of other people in positive or negative situations. At the first assessment, children who exhibited more facial empathy during the evocative slides were rated by parents and teachers as lower in externalizing problem behaviors (e.g., argues, lies, aggression). Two years later, children's facial empathy and their self-reported empathy (combined in a latent construct) were associated with lower levels of adult-reported externalizing problems. Thus, observed empathy has been found to predict lower levels of externalizing problems in school-aged children across time.

Interestingly, the negative relation between aggressiveness and prosocial behavior may be evident only in the school years (Lovett & Sheffield, 2007). Indeed, aggressive toddlers have been found to display *more* empathic responses than less aggressive toddlers (Gill & Calkins, 2003). It is possible that the lack of social inhibition often associated with aggression allows children to approach and exhibit concern toward an unfamiliar adult. In one study, Spinrad and Stifter (2006) reported that the relation between anger (the emotion thought to underlie aggression; Eisenberg, Cumberland et al., 2001; Rothbart & Bates, 1998) and prosocial behavior in toddlers was moderated by the level of maternal responsiveness. A negative relation between anger and prosocial behavior toward the mother was found when mothers were low in responsiveness. Conversely, when mothers were relatively high in responsiveness, toddlers' anger was positively related to prosocial behavior. Thus, at young ages, the relation between aggression/anger and prosocial behavior is more complex, perhaps because of the measurement of prosocial behavior in young children (toward an unfamiliar person) or because the links are moderated by parental behavior.

Academic Competence

Prosocial behaviors, and more specifically empathy/sympathy, also may play an important role in children's school success. Children who are relatively prosocial or empathic are likely to cooperate in class and exhibit appropriate classroom behavior and/or may be well liked by teachers. In turn, these students may receive more help from teachers and peers and may be more engaged in school activities (Coie & Dodge, 1988; Wentzel, 1993).

Some investigators have obtained positive correlations between empathy or prosocial behavior and measures of intelligence, vocabulary or reading skills, language development, or mental developmental level (Carlo, Hausmann, Christiansen, & Randall, 2003; Cassidy, Werner, Rourke, Zubernis, & Balaraman, 2003; van der Mark, van Ijzendoorn, & Bakermans Kranenburg, 2002). For example, in a longitudinal investigation, Miles and Stipek (2006) found a positive and significant relation between kindergarten or first-grade teachers' ratings of children's prosocial behavior and children's literacy achievement across elementary school (through Grade 5). The authors suggested that perhaps children with strong social skills (i.e., those high in prosocial behavior) develop closer relationships with teachers, and, as a result receive more instruction time from teachers. Similar findings have been noted in other studies. For example, emergent literacy problems in boys were associated with fewer prosocial interactions, suggesting that prosocial boys may receive positive attention from teachers (e.g., increased interactions with teachers) that lead to increased opportunities for learning (Doctoroff, Greer, & Arnold, 2006).

In addition, prosocial behavior and empathy have been found to predict children's grade point average (GPA) and other measures of school-based achievement (e.g., academic self-efficacy, general achievement tests; Bandura, Caprara, Barbaranelli, Pastorelli, & Regalia, 2001; Caprara et al., 2000; Johnson, Beebe, Mortimer, & Snyder, 1998; Wentzel, 2003; Wise & Cramer, 1988). Moreover, these relations have been found over time. For example, Caprara and colleagues (2000) found that early prosocial behavior (in third grade) predicted higher academic achievement in eighth grade, even after accounting for variation in early academic achievement. Thus, prosocial skills may help foster children's academic learning and school success.

It is also important to note that some researchers have found no significant or inconsistent relations between tests of intelligence or academic competence and children's prosocial behavior or sympathy (Jennings, Fitch, & Suwalsky, 1987; Strayer & Roberts, 1989; Turner & Harris, 1984; Wise & Cramer, 1988). It is likely that the relations between empathy or prosocial behavior and academics are mediated by other factors such as more general social competence (i.e., a well-behaved child) and the quality of teacher–child relationships, or that the relations between academics and empathy-related responding are derived from differences in children's attention or regulation abilities. In other words, children who do well in school may have the ability to sit still in class and to focus on the teacher. These same skills (i.e., attention skills, behavioral regulation) may also underlie empathy and prosocial behavior (see Eisenberg et al., 2006). Further research is needed to examine these processes.

SOCIALIZATION OF CHILDREN'S EMPATHY-RELATED RESPONSES TO DISTRESS

Researchers have shown considerable interest in understanding the contribution of the social environment to the development of children's empathy and prosocial behavior (Knafo & Plomin, 2006). Although the majority of work in this area has focused on parental socialization, one might expect similar processes for other socializers, such as peers, teachers, and the school environment. Each socializer will be reviewed in turn.

Parental Socialization

The quality of the parent–child relationship may be an important factor in understanding children's empathy-related responding. A high-quality parent–child relationship (i.e., characterized as secure with low conflict) may facilitate the child's sense of connection or partnership with others (Staub, 1992). Indeed, securely attached children tend to display more concern toward a stranger (van der Mark et al., 2002) and are relatively prosocial (Kestenbaum, Farber, & Sroufe, 1989; Laible, 2006).

Moreover, maternal responsiveness has been positively related to children's empathic responding. Maternal responsiveness (including appropriate, contingent, and sensitive responding to their child's cues) has been linked with higher empathy or prosocial behavior from 18 to 30 months old (Kestenbaum et al., 1989; Kiang, Moreno, &

Robinson, 2004; Kochanska, Forman, & Coy, 1999; Moreno, Klute, & Robinson, 2008; Robinson et al., & Emde, 1994; Zahn-Waxler, Radke-Yarrow, & King, 1979) and in older children (Davidov & Grusec, 2006; Iannotti Cummings, Pierrehumbert, Milano, & Zahn-Waxler, 1992; Janssens & Dekovic, 1997; Robinson et al., 1994). Although most research in this area has used concurrent data, Spinrad and Stifter (2006) found that maternal sensitivity observed in infancy predicted toddlers' higher sympathy responses and prosocial behavior 8 months later. In long-term longitudinal work, Feldman (2007a, 2007b) showed that mother–infant synchrony in the first year of life predicted empathy in adolescence.

In addition, much of the research on the relations of parenting practices to children's empathy/sympathy responses and prosocial behavior has focused on discipline techniques. Specifically, parental induction, which is characterized as attempts to focus on another's emotional reactions or on the consequences of the child's behavior, is considered a practice likely to induce sympathy and prosocial behavior. This supportive practice may promote children's perspective taking and likely contributes to children's internalization of parental values (Hoffman, 1982, 2000). Empirical work supports this notion, as inductions have been linked with children's higher empathy and prosocial behavior (Bar Tal, Nadler, & Blechman, 1980; Krevans & Gibbs, 1996; Laible, Eye & Carlo, 2008; Ramaswarny & Bergin, 2009; Stanhope, Bell, & Parker-Cohen, 1987).

On the other hand, researchers have found that parental punitive responses have been negatively related to prosocial behavior and sympathy (Hastings et al., 2000; Russell, Hart, Robinson, & Olsen, 2003). Punitive and power-assertive discipline practices, such as physical punishment, strict supervision, or deprivation of privileges, may over-arouse children, and the opportunity for children to empathize may be lost. Indeed, such practices have been associated with higher levels of self-focused personal distress reactions in children (Eisenberg, Fabes, Schaller, Carlo, & Miller, 1991). However, the occasional use of power-assertive responses (e.g., physical punishment) in the context of a positive parent–child relationship likely differs from the use of power-assertive techniques as the predominant discipline practice. Indeed, Miller Eisenberg, Fabes, Shell, and Gular (1989) found that physical discipline techniques (including physical punishment) were actually positively associated with children's empathy, but only for children whose mothers also used relatively high levels of inductive discipline.

Learning theories emphasize the importance of modeling and reinforcement, and these aspects of socialization are also associated with children's empathy-related responding. Consistent with this view, parents who model relatively high levels of sympathy are likely to have same-sex children who are willing to help someone in need (Fabes, Eisenberg, & Miller, 1990) or are prone to sympathy (Eisenberg et al., 1991, 1992). Moreover, children model prosocial behavior in adults, such as volunteerism, helping, and altruistic behaviors (Eisenberg et al., 2006; Garner, 2006; McGinley, Lipperman-Kreda, Byrnes & Carlo, 2010). In addition, parental reinforcement for children's empathy-related responding is related to appropriate responses to others' distress (Eisenberg et al., 1992; Hastings, McShane, Parker, & Ladha, 2007), although the use of extrinsic rewards for prosocial behavior may deter future prosocial behavior (see Warneken & Tomasello, 2008).

It is important to note that children's characteristics may interact with the environment when predicting children's empathy and prosocial behavior. For example,

Bakermans-Kranenburg and Van Ijzendoorn (2011) found that 7-year-old children with secure attachment representations were more prosocial (i.e., donated) than their insecure counterparts, but only if they had the DRDR 7-repeat gene. Thus, the relation between parental socialization and children's empathy-related responding is undoubtedly complex.

Nonparental Socialization

Although the majority of research regarding the socialization of prosocial behavior and empathy has focused on mothers' potential influence on children's empathy, peers, teachers, and the school environment also may play a role in this regard. For example, although limited in scope, research finds that peers serve as important socializers of prosocial behavior. Similar to research on parental modeling, investigators have demonstrated that adolescents who volunteer are relatively likely to have friends who are involved in community and volunteer (Zaff, Moore, Papillo, & Williams, 2003) and are less likely to volunteer if they belong to a crowd that places a high value on "having fun" (Youniss, McLellan, & Mazer, 2001; see also Pugh & Hart, 1999). Friends also tend to be similar in their degree of prosocial behavior (Wentzel, Barry, & Caldwell, 2004). Moreover, prosocial peer models have been found to be effective in eliciting prosocial behavior in the laboratory (Owens & Ascione, 1991). Specifically, children were more likely to share if they had observed a peer donating than if they had observed an adult displaying the same activity. In a study of ninth and tenth graders, friends' prosocial behavior predicted adolescents' prosocial behavior through adolescents' prosocial goal pursuit (i.e., trying to accomplish prosocial behaviors; Barry & Wentzel, 2006). Prosocial peer interactions also have been related to increases in positive affect and life satisfaction in middle-school students (Martin & Huebner, 2007).

In addition to modeling, peers may positively reinforce prosocial behavior (Eisenberg, Cameron, Tryon, & Dodez, 1981). For example, Eisenberg and colleagues (1981) reported a positive link between girls' (but not boys') spontaneous prosocial behavior and positive reinforcement for prosocial actions from peers. Fujisawa, Kutsakake, & Hasegawa (2008) showed that children tended to reciprocate prosocial behaviors within dyads; that is, children who received were also likely to give. Thus, peers' responses to children's prosocial behaviors may impact the degree to which children engage in prosocial actions.

Further, the quality of peer relationships may predict children's empathy/sympathy and prosocial behavior. For example, Laible (2007) showed that attachment security with peers in adolescence was related to higher prosocial behavior and sympathy. In addition, mutual positive affect among peers was related to higher social adjustment (a construct that included prosocial behavior with peers; Sallquist, Didonato, Hanish, Martin, & Fabes, 2011).

Teachers are also an important influence on children's empathic responses, with teachers' warmth positively and significantly associated with children's empathy-related responding and prosocial behavior (Kienbaum, Volland, & Ulich, 2001; Luckner & Pianta, 2011). Secure attachments to teachers have been found to predict preschoolers' prosocial behaviors and empathy (Howes, Matheson, & Hamilton, 1994; Mitchell-Copeland,

Denham, & DeMulder, 1997; Palermo, Hanish, Martin, Fabes & Reiser, 2007) and their social competence, a measure that includes their prosocial behavior/empathy (Sette, Spinrad, & Baumgartner, 2013). In a study of first graders, learner-centered practices (i.e., child centered, emphasizing positive social climate) were predictive of a student's greater empathy toward classmates (Donohue, Perry, & Weinstein, 2003). Finally, quality of the childcare or preschool environment, such as high teacher warmth and child-centered care, has been associated with children's empathy and social competence (Brœberg, Hwang, Lamb, & Ketterlinus, 1989; Kienbaum, 2001) and mothers' and caregivers' ratings of children's prosocial behaviors (NICHD Early Child Care Research Network, 2002).

SCHOOL-BASED PROGRAMS TO PROMOTE EMPATHY-RELATED RESPONDING

Capitalizing on the parental socialization literature, school-based programs have been designed to promote empathy and prosocial behavior, and evidence indicates that these programs can be effective. For example, Solomon and colleagues (Solomon, Battistich, Watson, Schaps, & Lewis, 2000; Solomon, Watson, Delucchi, Schaps, & Battistich, 1988) developed a program that promoted positive teacher–child relationships and provided opportunities for children to engage in collaborative interactions. Teachers were trained in child-centered approaches (e.g., students participate in rule setting and decision making, inductive discipline, mutual problem solving), and the program provided children with opportunities to participate in collaborative activities, such as participating in rule setting and engaging in different roles in the classroom. In addition, teachers were trained to promote social understanding (e.g., make use of spontaneous events, such as conflicts among students), highlight prosocial values, and provide helping activities (such as classroom chores, buddies, community service). The program was implemented for 5 consecutive years (kindergarten through Grade 4). Students who participated in the program scored higher on ratings of prosocial behavior compared to children in control classes. Further, these patterns held even when controlling for teachers' general competence and students' participation in cooperative activities (Solomon et al., 1988). The program also was effective in promoting personal, social, and ethical values, attitudes, and motives and reducing substance abuse and other problems when implemented over a 3-year period (Battistich, Schaps, Watson, Solomon, & Lewis, 2000; Solomon et al., 2000).

Interestingly, children enrolled in the program evidenced the highest ratings for prosocial behavior and harmony in kindergarten as opposed to the later years in the program. Thus, it appears that the impact of this program was greatest when first introduced. One explanation for this finding is that the teachers in the program had only 1 year of experience in implementing the program. Had teachers been given additional time to develop their techniques and fully integrate the program into the ongoing routine of the classroom, the program may have had more lasting effects (Battistich, Watson, Solomon, Schaps, & Solomon, 1991).

Other school-based programs designed to promote empathy have demonstrated effectiveness. For example, Feshbach and Feshbach (1982) developed a school-based empathy-training program that involved small-group classroom activities, including role playing and discussions of conflict resolutions. Children in the empathy-training group displayed higher frequencies of helping and cooperative behaviors (Feshbach, 1983; Feshbach & Feshbach, 1982). Moreover, there was a decline in aggressive behavior for children in the empathy-training program (Feshbach, 1983). In another intervention designed to improve girls' social problem solving, social skills training had a positive impact on social behavior. Specifically, for girls with high baseline social problems, participation in the program was linked to increased teacher ratings of prosocial behavior (Cappella & Weinstein, 2006).

A recent study examined the impact of the Roots of Empathy program (ROE; Gordon, 2001) on a sample of fourth- through seventh-grade children. The classroom program involves monthly classroom visits by an infant and his or her parent(s) and bimonthly visits from a program instructor who provides lessons designed to foster empathy, emotional understanding, and sensitivity. The students are also required to engage in lessons that are designed to benefit the infant (e.g., create a recording of nursery rhymes and songs for the infant) with the goal of promoting altruism and prosocial values. Findings showed that children in the ROE group, compared to control children, increased on peer-nominated prosocial behaviors (i.e., sharing, cooperating, helping others) and decreased in teacher-rated aggressive behaviors (Schonert-Reichl, Smith, Zaidman-Zait, & Hertzman, 2012). Finally, Head Start preschool children who participated in an empathy-training program were reported as more tolerant, prosocial, and cooperative than children enrolled in an academic enrichment program that did not involve emotion or empathy training (Chiang, Douglas, Kite, Barber, & Webb, 2007).

Moreover, the use of cooperative educational techniques in classroom activities has been found to promote acceptance of others (Johnson & Johnson, 1987), as well as cooperation and prosocial behavior (Choi, Johnson, & Johnson, 2011; Hertz-Lazarowitz, 1983; Hertz-Lazarowitz, Sharan, & Steinberg, 1980). In addition, Ascione (1992) studied the effects of a humane education program in elementary school children. Humane attitudes and empathy were enhanced for older children (fourth and fifth graders) both immediately and a year later. There were few immediate effects for younger children, although there was an effect on humane attitudes at posttest a year later (Ascione & Weber, 1993).

Other intervention programs using a classroom component and other components, such as parent training, social skills training, and home visiting, have been found to improve social competence and prosocial behavior. For example, the Fast Track Project, targeting children at risk for antisocial behavior, used such an approach. At the end of Grade 1, children in the intervention group engaged in more prosocial activities with peers and showed more improvement in aggressive-disruptive behavior than did children in the control group (Conduct Problems Prevention Research Group, 1999). Children in the Fast Track intervention group also showed improvements in aggressive and prosocial behavior by third grade, and these skills contributed to behavioral outcomes in fourth grade (Conduct Problems Prevention Research Group, 2002). Thus, effective interventions for children are likely to have multiple components including parents and schools.

Thus, a focus on empathy in the school system, including a focus on other people's feelings and on creating a positive atmosphere in the classroom, can enhance children's social functioning. Although there is relatively limited research in this area, it appears that it is a worthwhile investment for teachers to focus not just on academic achievements but also on children's moral emotions and behaviors. In addition, further research on the effectiveness of the programs, including ways to enhance teacher implementation and the generalizability of the findings to later years and other contexts, is needed.

CONCLUSION

Clearly, empathy-related responding is associated with important domains relevant to school functioning. Moreover, socialization by parents, teachers, and others such as peers has been related to and may contribute to individual differences in children's empathy and prosocial behavior. Intervention studies designed to promote children's social skills also can be effective, suggesting that the school environment can be an important context for learning social skills, such as empathy. These findings point to the need for schools to value social skills as part of their curricula.

There is a need to continue to develop programs designed to improve children's prosocial behavior and empathy and to test the complexities involved in supporting children's positive development. For example, the effectiveness in promoting children's empathy-related responding may depend on many factors, such as children's temperament, culture, cognitive development, and gender. In addition, the processes involved (i.e., mediating factors) in the socialization of children's empathy-related responding need to be examined in future research.

REFERENCES

Arnold, D. H., Ortiz, C., Curry, J. C., Stowe, R. M., Goldstein, N. E., Fisher, P., . . . Yershova, K. (1999). Promoting academic success and preventing disruptive behavior disorders through community partnership. *Journal of Community Psychology, 27*, 589–598. doi:10.1002/(SICI)1520-6629(199909)27:5<589::AID-JCOP6>3.0.CO;2-Y

Ascione, F. R. (1992). Enhancing children's attitudes about the humane treatment of animals: Generalization to human-directed empathy. *Anthrozoos, 5*, 176–191. doi:10.2752%2F089279392787011421

Ascione, F. R., & Weber, C. V. (1993, March). *Children's attitudes about the humane treatment of animals and empathy: One-year follow up of a school-based intervention.* Paper presented at the Society for Research in Child Development, New Orleans, LA.

Attili, G., Vermigli, P., & Roazzi, A. (2010). Children's social competence, peer status, and the quality of mother–child and father–child relationships: A multidimensional scaling approach. *European Psychologist, 15*, 23–33. doi:10.1027/1016-9040/a000002

Bakermans-Kranenburg, M. J., & Van Ijzendoorn, M. H. (2011). Differential susceptibility to rearing environment depending on dopamine-related genes: New evidence and a meta-analysis. *Development and Psychopathology, 23*, 39–52. doi:10.1017/S0954579410000635

Bandura, A., Caprara, G. V., Barbaranelli, C., Pastorelli, C., & Regalia, C. (2001). Sociocognitive self-regulatory mechanisms governing transgressive behavior. *Journal of Personality and Social Psychology, 80*, 125–135. doi:10.1037%2F0022-3514.80.1.125

Barry, C. M., & Wentzel, K. R. (2006). Friend influence on prosocial behavior: The role of motivational factors and friendship characteristics. *Developmental Psychology, 42*, 153–163. doi:10.1037%2F0012-1649.42.1.153

Bar Tal, D., Nadler, A., & Blechman, N. (1980). The relationship between Israeli children's helping behavior and their perception of parents' socialization practices. *Journal of Social Psychology, 111*, 159–167.

Batson, C. D. (1991). *The altruism question: Toward a social psychological answer.* Hillsdale, NJ: Erlbaum.

Battistich, V., Schaps, E., Watson, M., Solomon, D., & Lewis, C. (2000). Effects of the Child Development Project on students' drug use and other problem behaviors. *Journal of Primary Prevention, 21*, 75–99.

Battistich, V., Watson, M., Solomon, D., Schaps, E., & Solomon, J. (1991). The Child Development Project: A comprehensive program for the development of prosocial character. In W.M. Kurtines & J.L. Gewirtz (Eds.), *Handbook of moral behavior and development* (Vol. 3, pp. 1–34). New York, NY: Erlbaum.

Broœberg, A., Hwang, C.P., Lamb, M.E., & Ketterlinus, R.D. (1989). Childcare effects on socioemotional and intellectual competence in Swedish preschoolers. In J.S. Lande, S. Scarr, & N. Gunzenhauser (Eds.), *Caring for children: Challenge to America* (pp. 49–76). Hillsdale, NJ: Erlbaum.

Cappella, E., & Weinstein, R. (2006). The prevention of social aggression among girls. *Social Development, 15*, 434–462. doi:10.1111%2Fj.1467-9507.2006.00350.x

Caprara, G.V., Barbaranelli, C., Pastorelli, C., Bandura, A., & Zimbardo, P.G. (2000). Prosocial foundations of children's academic achievement. *Psychological Science, 11*, 302–306. doi:10.1111%2F1467-9280.00260

Carlo, G., Crockett, L.J., Randall, B.A., & Roesch, S.C. (2007). A latent growth curve analysis of prosocial behavior among rural adolescents. *Journal of Research on Adolescence, 17,* 301–324. doi:10.1111%2Fj.1532-7795.2007.00524.x

Carlo, G., Hausmann, A., Christiansen, S., & Randall, B.A. (2003). Sociocognitive and behavioral correlates of a measure of prosocial tendencies for adolescents. *Journal of Early Adolescence, 23*, 107–134.

Carlo, G., Mestre, M.V., Samper, P., Tur, A., & Armenta, B.E. (2010). Feelings or cognitions? Moral cognitions and emotions as longitudinal predictors of prosocial and aggressive behaviors. *Personality and Individual Differences, 48*, 872–877. doi:10.1016%2Fj.paid.2010.02.010

Cassidy, K.W., Werner, R.S., Rourke, M., Zubernis, L.S., & Balaraman, G. (2003). The relationship between psychological understanding and positive social behaviors. *Social Development, 12*, 198–221. doi:10.1111%2F1467-9507.00229

Chiang, T.M., Douglas, S., Kite, K., Barber, C., & Webb, K. (2007). *Emotion coaching of at-risk children's social competence in preschool context.* Paper presented at the Society for Research in Child Development, Boston, MA.

Choi, J., Johnson, D.W., & Johnson, R. (2011). Relationships among cooperative learning experiences, social interdependence, children's aggression, victimization, and prosocial behaviors. *Journal of Applied Social Psychology, 41*, 976–1003. doi:10.1111%2Fj.1559-1816.2011.00744.x

Clark, K.E., & Ladd, G.W. (2000). Connectedness and autonomy support in parent–child relationships: Links to children's socioemotional orientation and peer relationships. *Developmental Psychology, 36*, 485–498. doi:10.1037%2F%2F0012-1649.36.4.485

Coie, J.D., & Dodge, K.A. (1988). Multiple sources of data on social behavior and social status in the school: A cross-age comparison. *Child Development, 59*, 815–829. doi:10.2307%2F1130578

Coie, J.D., & Dodge, K.A. (1998). Aggression and antisocial behavior. In N. Eisenberg (Ed.), *Handbook of child psychology, Vol. 3, social, emotional and personality development* (5th ed., pp. 779–862). New York, NY: Wiley.

Conduct Problems Prevention Research Group. (1999). Initial impact of the Fast Track prevention trial of conduct problems I. The high-risk sample. *Journal of Consulting and Clinical Psychology, 67*, 631–647. doi:10.1037%2F%2F0022-006X.67.5.631

Conduct Problems Prevention Research Group. (2002). Using the Fast Track randomized prevention trial to test the early-starter model of the development of serious conduct problems. *Development and Psychopathology, 14*, 925–943. doi:10.1017/S0954579402004133

Davidov, M., & Grusec, J.E. (2006). Untangling the links of parental responsiveness to distress and warmth to child outcomes. *Child Development, 77*, 44–58. doi:10.1111/j.1467-8624.2006.00855.x

Denham, S.A., Blair, K.A., DeMulder, E., Levitas, J., Sawyer, K., Auerbach-Major, S., & Queenan, P. (2003). Preschool emotional competence: Pathway to social competence. *Child Development, 74*, 238–256. doi:10.1111%2F1467-8624.00533

Diener, M.L., & Kim, D.Y. (2004). Maternal and child predictors of preschool children's social competence. *Journal of Applied Developmental Psychology, 25*, 3–24. doi:10.1016%2Fj.appdev.2003.11.006

Dishion, T.J., Loeber, R., Stouthamer-Loeber, M., & Patterson, G.R. (1984). Skill deficits and male adolescent delinquency. *Journal of Abnormal Child Psychology, 12*, 37–53. doi:10.1007%2FBF00913460

Doctoroff, G.L., Greer, J.A., & Arnold, D.H. (2006). The relationship between social behavior and emergent literacy among preschool boys and girls. *Journal of Applied Developmental Psychology, 27*, 1–13. doi:10.1016%2Fj.appdev.2005.12.003

Donohue, K.M., Perry, K.E., & Weinstein, R.S. (2003). Teachers' classroom practices and children's rejection by their peers. *Journal of Applied Developmental Psychology, 24*, 91–118. doi:10.1016%2FS0193-3973%2803%2900026-1

Eisenberg, N., Cameron, E., Tryon, K., & Dodez, R. (1981). Socialization of prosocial behavior in the preschool classroom. *Developmental Psychology, 17*, 773–782. doi:10.1037%2F%2F0012-1649.17.6.773

Eisenberg, N., Cumberland, A., Spinrad, T.L., Fabes, R.A., Shepard, S.A., Reiser, M., . . . Guthrie, I. K (2001). The relations of regulation and emotionality to children's externalizing and internalizing problem behavior. *Child Development, 72*, 1112–1134. doi:10.1111%2F1467-8624.00337

Eisenberg, N., & Fabes, R.A. (1998). Prosocial development. In W.D. Damon & N. Eisenberg (Eds.), *Handbook of child psychology, Vol. 3. Social, emotional, and personality development* (5th ed., pp. 701–778). New York, NY: Wiley.

Eisenberg, N., Fabes, R.A., Carlo, G., Speer, A.L., Switzer, G., Karbon, M., & Troyer, D. (1993). The relations of empathy-related emotions and maternal practices to children's comforting behavior. *Journal of Experimental Child Psychology, 55*, 131–150. doi:10.1006%2Fjecp.1993.1007

Eisenberg, N., Fabes, R.A., Carlo, G., Troyer, D., Speer, A.L., Karbon, M., & Switzer, G. (1992). The relations of maternal practices and characteristics to children's vicarious emotional responding. *Child Development, 63*, 583–602. doi:10.2307%2F1131348

Eisenberg, N., Fabes, R. A., Murphy, B. C., Karbon, M., Smith, M., & Maszk, P. (1996). The relations of children's dispositional empathy-related responding to their emotionality, regulation, and social functioning. *Developmental Psychology, 32*, 195–209. doi:10.1023/A:1024478415317

Eisenberg, N., Fabes, R.A., Schaller, M., Carlo, B., & Miller, P. (1991). The relations of parental characteristics and practices to children's vicarious emotional responding. *Child Development, 62*, 1393–1408. doi:10.11 11%2Fj.1467-8624.1991.tb01613.x

Eisenberg, N., Fabes, R.A., Schaller, M., & Miller, P.A. (1989). Sympathy and personal distress: Development, gender differences, and interrelations of indexes. In N. Eisenberg (Ed.), *New directions in child development: Vol. 44. Empathy and related emotional responses* (pp. 107–126). San Francisco, CA: Jossey-Bass.

Eisenberg, N., Fabes, R.A., & Spinrad, T.L. (2006). Prosocial development. In W. Damon, R.M. Lerner (Eds.), & N. Eisenberg (Vol. Ed.), *Handbook of child psychology: Vol. 3: Social, emotional and personality development* (6th ed., pp. 646–718). Hoboken, NJ: Wiley.

Eisenberg, N., Liew, J., & Pidada, S.U. (2001). The relations of parental emotional expressivity with quality of Indonesian children's social functioning. *Emotion, 1*, 116–136. doi:10.1037%2F%2F1528-3542.1.2.116

Fabes, R. A., & Eisenberg, N. (1996). *An examination of age and sex differences in prosocial behavior and empathy.* Unpublished manuscript, Arizona State University at Tempe.

Fabes, R.A., Eisenberg, N., & Miller, P.A. (1990). Maternal correlates of children's vicarious emotional responsiveness. *Developmental Psychology, 26*, 639–648. doi:10.1037%2F%2F0012-1649.26.4.639

Feldman, R. (2007a). Mother–infant synchrony and the development of moral orientation in childhood and adolescence: Direct and indirect mechanisms of developmental continuity. *American Journal of Orthopsychiatry, 77*, 582–597. doi:10.1037%2F0002-9432.77.4.582

Feldman, R. (2007b). Parent–infant synchrony and the construction of shared timing; physiological precursors, developmental outcomes, and risk conditions. *Journal of Child Psychology and Psychiatry and Allied Disciplines, 48*, 329–354. doi:10.1111%2Fj.1469-7610.2006.01701.x

Feshbach, N.D. (1983). Learning to care: A positive approach to child training and discipline. *Journal of Clinical Child Psychology, 12*, 266–271. doi:10.1207%2Fs15374424jccp1203_6

Feshbach, N.D., & Feshbach, S. (1982). Empathy training and the regulation of aggression: Potentialities and limitations. *Academic Psychology Bulletin, 4*, 399–413.

Fujisawa, K.K., Kutsukake, N., & Hasegawa, T. (2008). Reciprocity of prosocial behavior in Japanese preschool children. *International Journal of Behavioral Development, 32*, 89–97. doi:10.1177/0165025407084055

Garner, P.W. (2006). Prediction of prosocial and emotional competence from maternal behavior in African American preschoolers. *Cultural Diversity & Ethnic Minority Psychology, 12*, 179–198. doi:10.1037%2F1099-9809.12.2.179

Gill, K.L., & Calkins, S.D. (2003). Do aggressive/destructive toddlers lack concern for others? Behavioral and physiological indicators of empathic responding in 2-year-old children. *Development and Psychopathology, 15*, 55–71. doi:10.1017%2FS095457940300004X

Gordon, M. (2001). *Roots of empathy: Training manual.* Available from www.Rootsofempathy.org

Graziano, W.G., Keane, S.P., & Calkins, S.D. (2007). Cardiac vagal regulation and early peer status. *Child Development, 78*, 264–278. doi:10.1111%2Fj.1467-8624.2007.00996.x

Hastings, P.D., McShane, K.E., Parker, R., & Ladha, F. (2007). Ready to make nice: Parental socialization of young sons' and daughters' prosocial behaviors with peers. *Journal of Genetic Psychology, 168*, 177–200. doi:10.3200% 2FGNTP.168.2.177-200

Hastings, P.D., Zahn-Waxler, C., Robinson, J., Usher, B., & Bridges, D. (2000). The development of concern for others in children with behavior problems. *Developmental Psychology, 36,* 531–546. doi:10.1037%2F%2F0012-1649.36.5.531

Hertz-Lazarowitz, R. (1983). Prosocial behavior in the classroom. *Academic Psychology Bulletin, 5,* 319–338.

Hertz-Lazarowitz, R., Sharan, S., & Steinberg, R. (1980). Classroom learning style and cooperative behavior of elementary school children. *Journal of Educational Psychology, 72,* 99–106. doi:10.1037/0022-0663.72.1.99

Hoffman, M.L. (1982). Development of prosocial motivation: Empathy and guilt. In N. Eisenberg (Ed.), *The development of prosocial behavior* (pp. 218–231). San Diego, CA: Academic Press.

Hoffman, M.L. (2000). *Empathy and moral development: Implications for caring and justice.* New York, NY: Cambridge University Press.

Howes, C., Matheson, C.C., & Hamilton, C.E. (1994). Maternal, teacher, and child care history correlates of children's relationships with peers. *Child Development, 65,* 264–273. doi:10.1111%2Fj.1467-8624.1994.tb00749.x

Iannotti, R.J., Cummings, E.M., Pierrehumbert, M.J., Milano, M.J., & Zahn-Waxler, C. (1992). Parental influences of prosocial behavior and empathy in early childhood. In J.M.A.M. Janssens & J.R.M. Gerris (Eds.), *Child rearing: Influence on prosocial and moral development.* Amsterdam, Netherlands: Swets & Zeitlinger.

Janssens, J.M.A.M., & Dekovic, M. (1997). Child rearing, prosocial moral reasoning, and prosocial behaviour. *International Journal of Behavioral Development, 20,* 509–527. doi:10.1080/016502597385252

Jennings, K.D., Fitch, D., & Suwalsky, J.T. (1987). Social cognition and social interaction in three-year-olds: Is social cognition truly social? *Child Study Journal, 17,* 1–14.

Johnson, D.W., & Johnson, R.T. (1987). *Learning together and alone: Cooperative, competitive, and individualistic learning* (2nd ed.). Upper Saddle River, NJ: Prentice Hall.

Johnson, M.K., Beebe, T., Mortimer, J.T., & Snyder, M. (1998). Volunteerism in adolescence: A process perspective. *Journal of Research on Adolescence, 8,* 309–332. doi:10.1207%2Fs15327795jra0803_2

Kestenbaum, R., Farber, E.A., & Sroufe, L.A. (1989). Individual differences in empathy among preschoolers: Relation to attachment history. *New Directions for Child Development, 44,* 51–64. doi:10.1002%2Fcd.23219894405

Kiang, L., Moreno, A.J., & Robinson, J.L. (2004). Maternal perceptions about parenting predict child temperament, maternal sensitivity, and children's empathy. *Developmental Psychology, 40,* 1081–1092. doi:10.1037/0012-1649.43.2.438

Kienbaum, J. (2001). The socialization of compassionate behavior by childcare teachers. *Early Education and Development, 12,* 139–153. doi:10.1207%2Fs15566935eed1201_8

Kienbaum, J., Volland, C., & Ulich, D. (2001). Sympathy in the context of mother–child and teacher–child relationships. *International Journal of Behavioral Development, 25,* 302–309. doi:10.1080/01650250143000076

Knafo, A., & Plomin, R. (2006). Prosocial behavior from early to middle childhood: Genetic and environmental influences on stability and change. *Developmental Psychology, 42,* 771–786. doi:10.1037%2F0012-1649.42.5.771

Kochanska, G., Forman, D.R., & Coy, K.C. (1999). Implications of the mother-child relationship in infancy for socialization in the second year of life. *Infant Behavior & Development, 22,* 249–265. doi:10.1037/a0028287

Kokko, K., Tremblay, R.E., Lacourse, E., Nagin, D.S., & Vitaro, F. (2006). Trajectories of prosocial behavior and physical aggression in middle childhood: Links to adolescent school dropout and physical violence. *Journal of Research on Adolescence, 16,* 403–428. doi:10.1111/j.1532-7795.2006.00500.x

Krevans, J., & Gibbs, J.C. (1996). Parents' use of inductive discipline: Relations to children's empathy and prosocial behavior. *Child Development, 67,* 3263–3277. doi:10.1111%2Fj.1467-8624.1996.tb01913.x

Laible, D. (2006). Maternal emotional expressiveness and attachment security: Links to representations of relationships and social behavior. *Merrill-Palmer Quarterly, 52,* 645–670. doi:10.1353%2Fmpq.2006.0035

Laible, D. (2007). Attachment with parents and peers in late adolescence: Links with emotional competence and social behavior. *Personality and Individual Differences, 43,* 1185–1197. doi:10.1016%2Fj.paid.2007.03.010

Laible, D., Eye, J., & Carlo, G. (2008). Dimensions of conscience in mid-adolescence: Links with social behavior, parenting, and temperament. *Journal of Youth and Adolescence, 37,* 875–887. doi:10.1007%2Fs10964-008-9277-8

Lansford, J.E., Putallaz, M., Grimes, C.L., Schiro-Osman, K.A., Kupersmidt, J.B., & Coie, J.D. (2006). Perceptions of friendship quality and observed behaviors with friends: How do sociometrically rejected, average, and popular girls differ? *Merrill-Palmer Quarterly, 52,* 694–720. doi:10.1353%2Fmpq.2006.0036

Lovett, B.J., & Sheffield, R.A. (2007). Affective empathy deficits in aggressive children and adolescents: A critical review. *Clinical Psychology Review, 27,* 1–13. doi:10.1016%2Fj.cpr.2006.03.003

Luckner, A.E., & Pianta, R.C. (2011). Teacher–student interactions in fifth grade classrooms: Relations with children's peer behavior. *Journal of Applied Developmental Psychology, 32,* 257–266. doi:10.1016%2Fj.appdev.2011.02.010

Martin, K.M., & Huebner, E.S. (2007). Peer victimization and prosocial experiences and emotional well-being of middle school students. *Psychology in the Schools, 44*, 199–208. doi:10.1002%2Fpits.20216

McGinley, M., Lipperman-Kreda, S., Byrnes, H.F., & Carlo, G. (2010). Parental, social and dispositional pathways to Israeli adolescents' volunteering. *Journal of Applied Developmental Psychology, 31*, 386–394. doi:10.1016%2Fj. appdev.2010.06.001

Miles, S.B., & Stipek, D. (2006). Contemporaneous and longitudinal associations between social behavior and literacy achievement in a sample of low-income elementary school children. *Child Development, 77*, 103–117. doi:10.1111%2Fj.1467-8624.2006.00859.x

Miller, P.A., Eisenberg, N., Fabes, R.A., Shell, R., & Gular, S. (1989). Socialization of empathic and sympathetic responding. In N. Eisenberg (Ed.), *The development of empathy and related vicarious responses: New Directions in child development* (pp. 65–83). San Francisco, CA: Jossey-Bass.

Mitchell-Copeland, J., Denham, S.A., & DeMulder, E.K. (1997). Q-sort assessment of child-teacher attachment relationships and social competence in the preschool. *Early Education and Development, 8*, 27–39. doi:10.1207/s15566935eed0801_3

Moreno, A.J., Klute, M.M., & Robinson, J.L. (2008). Relational and individual resources as predictors of empathy in early childhood. *Social Development, 17*, 613–637. doi:10.1111%2Fj.1467-9507.2007.00441.x

Murphy, B.C., Shepard, S.A., Eisenberg, N., Fabes, R.A., & Guthrie, I.K. (1999). Contemporaneous and longitudinal relations of dispositional sympathy to emotionality, regulation, and social functioning. *Journal of Early Adolescence, 19*, 66–97. doi:10.1177/0272431699019001004

Nantel-Vivier, A., Kokko, K., Caprara, G.V., Pastorelli, C., Gerbino, M.G., Paciello, M., . . . Tremblay, R.E. (2009). Prosocial development from childhood to adolescence: A multi-informant perspective with Canadian and Italian longitudinal studies. *Journal of Child Psychology and Psychiatry, 50*, 590–598. doi:10.1111/j.1469-7610.2008.02039.x

Nelson, L.J., Hart, C.H., Yang, C., Wu, P., & Jin, S. (2012). An examination of the behavioral correlates of subtypes of nonsocial play among Chinese preschoolers. *Merrill-Palmer Quarterly, 58*, 77–109. doi:10.1353%2Fmpq.2012.0006

NICHD Early Child Care Research Network. (2002). The interaction of childcare and family risk in relation to child development at 24 and 36 months. *Applied Developmental Science, 6*, 144–156.

NICHD Early Child Care Research Network. (2004). Trajectories of physical aggression from toddlerhood to middle childhood. *Monographs of the Society for Research in Child Development, 69*, 1–129. doi:10.1111/j.0037-976X.2004.00315.x

Owens, C.R., & Ascione, F.R. (1991). Effects of the model's age, perceived similarity, and familiarity on children's donating. *Journal of Genetic Psychology, 152*, 341–357. doi:10.1080/00221325.1991.9914691

Palermo, F., Hanish, L.D., Martin, C.L., Fabes, R.A., & Reiser, M. (2007). Preschoolers' academic readiness: What role does the teacher–child relationship play? *Early Childhood Research Quarterly, 22*, 407–422. doi:10.1016%2Fj. ecresq.2007.04.002

Pianta, R.C., La Paro, K.M., Payne, C., Cox, M.J., & Bradley, R. (2002). The relation of kindergarten classroom environment to teacher, family, and school characteristics and child outcomes. *Elementary School Journal, 102*, 225–238. doi:10.1086%2F499701

Pugh, M.J., & Hart, D. (1999). Identity development and peer group participation. *New Directions in Child and Adolescent Development, 84*, 55–70. doi:10.1002/cd.23219998406

Ramaswamy, C., & Bergin, C. (2009). Do reinforcement and induction increase prosocial behavior? Results of a teacher-based intervention in preschools. *Journal of Research in Childhood Education, 23*, 527–538. doi:10.1080/02568540909594679

Ramsey, E., Patterson, G.R., & Walker, H.M. (1990). Generalization of the antisocial trait from home to school settings. *Journal of Applied Developmental Psychology, 11*, 209–223. doi:10.1016%2F0193-3973%2890%2990006-6

Robinson, J.L., Zahn-Waxler, C., & Emde, R.N. (1994). Patterns of development in early empathic behavior: Environmental and child constitutional influences. *Social Development, 3*, 125–145. doi:10.1111%2Fj.1467-9507.1994. tb00032.x

Rothbart, M.K., & Bates, J.E. (1998). Temperament. In W. Damon & N. Eisenberg (Eds.), *Handbook of child psychology, vol. 3. Social, emotional, and personality development* (5th ed., pp. 105–176). New York, NY: Wiley.

Russell, A., Hart, C.H., Robinson, C.C., & Olsen, S.F. (2003). Children's sociable and aggressive behavior with peers: A comparison of the US and Australia, and contributions of temperament and parenting styles. *International Journal of Behavioral Development, 27*, 74–86. doi:10.1080%2F01650250244000038

Sallquist, J., Didonato, M.D., Hanish, L.D., Martin, C.L., & Fabes, R.A. (2011). The importance of mutual positive expressivity in social adjustment: Understanding the role of peers and gender. *Emotion, 12,* 304–313. doi:10.1037%2Fa0025238

Sallquist, J., Eisenberg, N., Spinrad, T.L., Eggum, N.D., & Gaertner, B.M. (2009). Assessment of preschoolers' positive empathy: Concurrent and longitudinal relations with positive emotion, social competence, and sympathy. *Journal of Positive Psychology, 4,* 223–233. doi:10.1080%2F17439760902819444

Schonert-Reichl, K., Smith, V., Zaidman-Zait, A., & Hertzman, C. (2012). Promoting children's prosocial behaviors in school: Impact of the "Roots of Empathy" program on the social and emotional competence of school-aged children. *School Mental Health, 4,* 1–21. doi:10.1007/s12310-011-9064-7

Sebanc, A. M. (2003). The friendship features of preschool children: Links with prosocial behavior and aggression. *Social Development, 12,* 249–268. doi:10.1111%2F1467-9507.00232

Sette, S., Spinrad, T. L., & Baumgartner, E. (2013). Links among Italian preschoolers' socioemotional competence, teacher–child relationship quality, and peer acceptance. *Early Education and Development, 24,* 851–864. doi:10.1080/10409289.2013.744684

Solomon, D., Battistich, V., Watson, M., Schaps, E., & Lewis, C. (2000). A six-district study of educational change: Direct and mediated effects of the child development project. *Social Psychology of Education, 4,* 3–51. doi:10.1023/A:1009609606692

Solomon, D., Watson, M.S., Delucchi, K.L., Schaps, E., & Battistich, V. (1988). Enhancing children's prosocial behavior in the classroom. *American Educational Research Journal, 25,* 527–554. doi:10.3102%2F00028312025004527

Spinrad, T.L., & Stifter, C.A. (2006). Toddlers' empathy-related responding to distress: Predictions from negative emotionality and maternal behavior in infancy. *Infancy, 10,* 97–121. doi:10.1207%2Fs15327078in1002_1

Stanhope, L., Bell, R.Q., & Parker-Cohen, N.Y. (1987). Temperament and helping behavior in preschool children. *Developmental Psychology, 23,* 347–353. doi:10.1037%2F%2F0012-1649.23.3.347

Staub, E. (1992). The origins of caring, helping and nonaggression: Parental socialization, the family system, schools, and cultural influence. In P. M. Oliner, S. P. Oliner, L. Baron, & L. Blum (Eds.), *Embracing the other: Philosophical, psychological, and historical perspectives on altruism* (pp. 399–412). New York, NY: New York University Press.

Strayer, J., & Roberts, W. (1989). Children's empathy and role taking: Child and parental factors, and relations to prosocial behavior. *Journal of Applied Developmental Psychology, 10,* 227–239. doi:10.1016%2F0193-3973%2889%2990006-3

Strayer, J., & Roberts, W. (2004). Empathy and observed anger and aggression in five-year-olds. *Social Development, 13,* 1–13. doi:10.1111%2Fj.1467-9507.2004.00254.x

Turner, P.H., & Harris, M.B. (1984). Parental attitudes and preschool children's social competence. *Journal of Genetic Psychology, 144,* 105–113. doi:10.1080%2F00221325.1984.10532455

van der Mark, I.L., van Ijzendoorn, M.H., & Bakermans Kranenburg, M.J. (2002). Development of empathy in girls during the second year of life: Associations with parenting, attachment, and temperament. *Social Development, 11,* 451–468. doi:10.1111/1467-9507.00210

Warden, D., & Mackinnon, S. (2003). Prosocial children, bullies and victims: An investigation of their sociometric status, empathy and social problem-solving strategies. *British Journal of Developmental Psychology, 21,* 367–385. doi:10.1348%2F026151003322277757

Warneken, F., & Tomasello, M. (2008). Extrinsic rewards undermine altruistic tendencies in 20-month-olds. *Developmental Psychology, 44,* 1785–1788. doi:10.1037%2Fa0013860

Wentzel, K.R. (1993). Does being good make the grade? Social behavior and academic competence in middle school. *Journal of Educational Psychology, 85,* 357–364. doi:10.1037%2F%2F0022-0663.85.2.357

Wentzel, K.R. (2003). Sociometric status and adjustment in middle school: A longitudinal study. *Journal of Early Adolescence, 23,* 5–28. doi:10.1177%2F0272431602239128

Wentzel, K.R., Barry, C.M., & Caldwell, K.A. (2004). Friendships in middle school: Influences on motivation and school adjustment. *Journal of Educational Psychology, 96,* 195–203. doi:10.1037%2F0022-0663.96.2.195

Wise, P.S., & Cramer, S.H. (1988). Correlates of empathy and cognitive style in early adolescence. *Psychological Reports, 63,* 179–192. doi:10.2466%2Fpr0.1988.63.1.179

Young, S.K., Fox, N.A., & Zahn-Waxler, C. (1999). The relations between temperament and empathy in 2-year-olds. *Developmental Psychology, 35,* 1189–1197. doi:10.1037%2F%2F0012-1649.35.5.1189

Youniss, J., McLellan, J. A., & Mazer, B. (2001). Voluntary service, peer group orientation, and civic engagement. *Journal of Adolescent Research, 16,* 456–468. doi:10.1177/0743558401165003

Zaff, J. F., Moore, K. A., Papillo, A. R., & Williams, S. (2003). Implications of extracurricular activity participation during adolescence on positive outcomes. *Journal of Adolescent Research, 18,* 599–630. doi:10.1037/0012-1649.44.3.814

Zahn-Waxler, C., Cole, P. M., Welsh, J. D., & Fox, N. A. (1995). Psychophysiological correlates of empathy and pro-social behaviors in preschool children with behavior problems. *Development and Psychopathology, 7,* 27–48. doi:10.1017%2FS0954579400006325

Zahn-Waxler, C., Radke-Yarrow, M., & King, R. A. (1979). Childrearing and children's prosocial initiations toward victims of distress. *Child Development, 50,* 319–330. doi:10.1111/j.1467-8624.1979.tb04112.x

Zahn-Waxler, C., Robinson, J. L., & Emde, R. N. (1992). The development of empathy in twins. *Developmental Psychology, 28,* 1038–1047. doi:10.1037%2F0012-1649.28.6.1038

Zhou, Q., Eisenberg, N., Losoya, S. H., Fabes, R. A., Reiser, M., Guthrie, I. K., . . . Shepard, S. A. (2002). The relations of parental warmth and positive expressiveness to children's empathy-related responding and social function-ing: A longitudinal study. *Child Development, 73,* 893–915. doi:10.1111%2F1467-8624.00446

CHAPTER SUMMARY: EMPATHY

- Children's empathy and prosocial behaviors have received considerable attention in the area of child development. We have found it important to differentiate between empathy and its related responses. In brief, empathy is an affective response that is the same (or very similar) to what another is feeling. Sympathy reflects an other-oriented response involving feelings of concern rather than feeling the same emotion as another. On the other hand, personal distress is a self-focused reaction that involves discomfort or anxiety upon viewing another's distress.

- Empathy and sympathy have been linked to various aspects of social functioning related to school success. For example, sympathy has been shown to predict children's positive social functioning with both peers and adults. In addition, negative relations between empathy and children's aggression and problem behaviors have been demonstrated. Although research examining the relations of academic success and prosocial behavior is limited, investigators have shown positive associations between these variables. It is likely that these relations are mediated by other factors such as social competence and the quality of the teacher–child relationship.

- Importantly, children's empathy and prosocial behaviors are influenced by environmental sources. The majority of work in this area has focused on the role of parents. However, there is also some limited work demonstrating that teachers and peers contribute to the development of these constructs through processes such as developing warm relationships, modeling, and reinforcement.

- Finally, school-based interventions focusing on skills such as social skills training, empathy training, or classroom strategies (i.e., cooperative learning techniques) have been found to be effective in improving children's empathy and prosocial behavior. More work in understanding the specific mechanisms involved in effective interventions is needed.

SUGGESTED READINGS: EMPATHY

Eisenberg, N. (2000). Emotion, regulation, and moral development. In S. T. Fiske, D. L. Schacter, & C. Zahn-Waxler (Eds.), *Annual review of psychology* (Vol. 51, pp. 665–697). Palo Alto, CA: Annual Reviews.

Reviews literature on differences between moral emotions (i.e., shame, embarrassment, guilt) and their relations to moral behavior. In addition, the role of regulation in understanding empathy-related responding is considered. Socialization of moral emotions is also discussed.

Eisenberg, N., Cumberland, A., & Spinrad, T. L. (1998). Parental socialization of emotion. *Psychological Inquiry, 9,* 241–273. doi:10.1207/s15327965pli0904_1

This paper is not directly linked to the study of prosocial behavior. However, the socialization of emotion is relevant to empathy and prosocial development, as individual differences in children's caring behaviors are thought to be promoted by emotion-related parenting practices. This work is recommended in light of the work on parental socialization.

Eisenberg, N., Fabes, R. A., & Spinrad, T. L. (2006). Prosocial development. In W. Damon, R. M. Lerner (Eds.), & N. Eisenberg (Vol. Ed.), *Handbook of child psychology: Vol. 3: Social, emotional and personality development* (6th ed., pp. 646–718). Hoboken, NJ: Wiley.

Extensive review of literature on the major topics in prosocial development. Includes theory as well as the empirical literature related to prosocial responding from infancy through adolescence. This work is known as a reference guide for child psychology research.

Hoffman, M. L. (2000). *Empathy and moral development: Implications for caring and justice*. New York, NY: Cambridge University Press.

This volume focuses on the authors' decades of study of empathy and altruism. Of note, researchers studying the development of empathy and prosocial behaviors have nearly exclusively relied on the theory presented in this book.

Lerner, R. M., Lerner, J. V., Almerigi, J. B., Theokas, C., Phelps, E., Gestdottir, S., . . . von Eye, A. (2005). Positive youth development, participation in community youth development programs, and community contributions of fifth-grade adolescents: Findings from the first wave of the 4-H Study of Positive Youth Development. *Journal of Early Adolescence, 25*, 17–71. doi:10.1177/0272431604272461

The concept of positive youth development (a construct that includes youths' sympathy) is described. Data from the first wave of the 4-H Study of Positive Youth Development are presented, and the findings provide empirical support for the conceptualization of positive youth development.

7

EMOTION REGULATION
Implications for Positive Youth Development

Maureen Buckley and Carolyn Saarni, Counseling Department, Sonoma State University, Rohnert Park, California, USA

INTRODUCTION

The ability to recognize, regulate, and express emotions adeptly plays a crucial role in determining a student's ability to achieve personal or academic goals, as well as cope with life's challenges. Advances in research and theoretical development have bolstered our understanding of children's emotional functioning and its role in positive developmental outcomes (see Saarni, Campos, Camras, & Witherington, 2006). Emotion regulation, an area of focus within emotional development, has been sharpened in its definitions and implications for behavior (e.g., Campos, Frankel, & Camras, 2004; Eisenberg, Spinrad, & Eggum, 2010). We begin this chapter with an overview of emotional regulation, integrating this construct within the larger framework of emotional competence (Saarni, 1999). We then provide a review of recent empirical findings regarding emotional regulation and its impact on developmental outcomes, including social-emotional and academic functioning. The chapter concludes by addressing school-based methods for enhancing emotional competence in general and emotion regulation more specifically.

DEFINITION AND THEORY BASE

Emotional Competence and Emotion Regulation

Saarni's (2000, 2007; Saarni et al., 2006) theoretical model of emotional competence emphasizes emotional skills that bolster self-efficacy, adaptation, and coping. These skills emerge according to a developmental process, through the combined influences of factors such as learning, temperament, cognitive maturity, and developmental history.

Saarni (1999) proposed eight specific but mutually interdependent skills of emotional competence. These skills can be grouped into three broad categories: emotion expression, emotion understanding, and emotion regulation. However, even with this simplification, there is interdependence: Emotion expression includes both verbal and nonverbal emotion communication, yet this requires development in the domain of emotion understanding and emotion regulation. Emotion understanding encompasses the knowledge people have about emotional experiences, both their own and those of others, but this too requires development in the domain of an emotion lexicon. Finally, emotion regulation refers to managing one's emotional reactivity in order to engage with others and cope with challenging circumstances, but students also learn to manage their emotional expressions in order to cope with social demands as well as to modulate their felt sense of arousal (e.g., smiling when feeling anxious).

Effective emotional self-regulation includes both conscious, effortful regulation and unconscious, automatic regulation (Eisenberg & Spinrad, 2004; Eisenberg et al., 2010; Eisenberg & Sulik, 2012; Gross & Thompson, 2007). Effortful control, or the ability to voluntarily inhibit or activate behavior, encompasses attentional control (capacity to focus or shift attention and to persevere on task), as well as abilities related to activating or inhibiting behavior as required for adaptive responding. Effortful control is associated with better adjustment among young people (Eisenberg & Sulik, 2012). In contrast, reactive control refers to a purportedly temperament-linked and thus less voluntary tendency that can range from being overly inhibited to being excessively impulsive. Problems in adjustment may occur due to propensity toward either overcontrolled or undercontrolled behavior.

Definitions of emotion regulation vary to some extent in the developmental psychology and developmental psychopathology literature. The differences tend to pivot around how much emphasis is given to influences that come from *extrinsic* sources, that is, outside the self, such as parents or peers playing a regulatory role in a child's emotional experience, and influences that are *intrinsic* to the self (Eisenberg et al., 2010). Gross and Thompson (2007) conceptualized these intrinsic processes of emotion regulation as strategies involving the individual: (a) selecting situations and/or modifying situations so as to be able to functionally regulate emotion, (b) deploying attention in such a way so as to regulate emotion, (c) altering the cognitive appraisal or meaning of events, and (d) altering the response to an emotion-evocative event. Furthermore, Gross and Thompson contended that emotion regulation should be seen on a continuum, ranging from conscious and effortful regulation at one end to unconscious and effortless (as in automatic or involuntary) regulation at the other end.

The first three strategies of emotion regulation noted above emphasize the modulation of emotional arousal (including its duration, intensity, and latency to emotion evocation). The last emotion regulation strategy, altering one's response to an emotion-evocative event, includes management of emotional expression (the socially effective use of emotionally expressive behavior). Management of emotional expressiveness involves recognition that an inner emotional state need not correspond to outer expression of feelings, both in self and in others. At more mature levels, it reflects the capacity to understand that one's emotional-expressive behavior may affect others and to take this into account in one's self-presentation strategies.

Researchers have also examined how other behaviors become modified or recruited as a function of emotion regulation. For example, if a child has successfully reduced the intensity of her emotional reaction, then she is more likely to access problem-solving strategies as opposed to simply attempting to flee the situation and avoid it in the future. In this example, emotion regulation plays a *mediating* role in how one copes with a particular taxing situation: Modulation of one's emotional arousal allows for a different sort of coping behavior than simple flight or avoidance. However, emotion regulation might in other contexts play a *moderating* role, for example, sustaining the duration of the expressive display of happiness (a genuine smile) influences the likelihood that one's interactant will respond positively in kind. In other words, regulation of emotional-expressive behavior often increases or decreases the sorts of social interaction one desires with another.

Successful young people are equipped with both individual and environmental assets that help them cope with a variety of life events. The skills of emotional competence are one set of resources that students draw upon when faced with challenges. In the specific instance of emotion regulation, children who can manage their feelings and expressive behavior are better equipped to manage impulses, make informed decisions, and persist in pursuing goals. This in turn enhances other characteristics associated with positive developmental outcomes, including feelings of self-efficacy, prosocial behavior, and supportive relationships with others.

REVIEW OF KEY RESEARCH STUDIES

Key Research With Children and Adolescents

Much of the research on emotion regulation in youth is deficit oriented, with evidence suggesting that individuals who are not adept at managing their emotions are at risk for internalizing and externalizing forms of psychopathology (Adrian et al., 2009; Gilbert, 2012; McLaughlin, Hatzenbuehler, & Hilt, 2009). Research implicates emotion dysregulation in a host of problematic youth outcomes, including impulsivity (Schreiber, Grant, & Odlaug, 2012) and mood and anxiety disorders (Carthy, Horesh, Apter, & Gross, 2010; Esbjorn, Bender, Reinholdt-Dunne, Munck, & Ollendick, 2012; Kashdan & Breen, 2008; Rusch, Westermann, & Lincoln, 2012; Tortella-Feliu, Balle, & Sese, 2010; Werner, Goldin, Ball, Heimberg, & Gross, 2011).

Emotion regulation, particularly management of distress, is linked to optimal child functioning, as well as childhood psychopathology (Calkins & Hill, 2007; Eisenberg et al., 2010; Suveg, Southam-Gerow, Goodman, & Kendall, 2007). Navigating social relationships requires continual management of positive and negative emotional arousal. For example, children who cannot contain their joy, to the point of shrieking and running around the classroom, may receive contemptuous stares from peers. Furthermore, it is not surprising to find that children prone to unrestrained episodes of intense negative emotion are socially vulnerable. Young people experiencing emotional dysregulation lack adaptive strategies to modulate their feelings and/or fail to use appropriate goal-assisting strategies when the situation calls for it (Gilbert, 2012).

Emotion regulation is associated with positive social development in both preschool and school-age children (Chang, Shelleby, Cheong, & Shaw, 2012; Denham et al., 2003; Denham, Blair, Schmidt, & DeMulder, 2002; Eisenberg, Fabes, Guthrie, & Reiser, 2000; Hill, Degnan, Calkins, & Keane, 2006; Monopoli & Kingston, 2012). Children's proficiency in controlling their feelings is associated with peer acceptance (Shields, Ryan, & Cicchetti, 2001; Trentacosta & Izard, 2007; Trentacosta & Shaw, 2009). For example, the ability to divert attention from a frustrating situation in early childhood is associated with less peer rejection in middle childhood and, indirectly, with decreased likelihood of antisocial behavior in adolescence (Trentacosta & Shaw, 2009). Likewise, positive emotionality appears to support social competence (Garner & Waajid, 2012). Young people who can accurately appraise emotionally stimulating situations, as well as identify and deploy effective emotion management strategies, enjoy better socioemotional adaption to school (Lopes, Mestre, Guil, Pickard Kremenitzer, & Salovey, 2012). Functional emotion regulation is also associated with closer student–teacher relationships and classroom adjustment (Spritz, Sandberg, Maher, & Zajdel, 2010).

In the following section, we will briefly review some specific instances in which emotional regulation plays a role in developmental outcomes.

The Case of Peer Aggression

Current research suggests that both biological (e.g., temperament) and socialization (e.g., early social interactions) factors contribute to children's psychological difficulties and peer victimization status (Adrian et al., 2009; Rosen, Milich, & Harris, 2009) and that affective control is a key element of the peer victimization cycle (Rosen et al., 2009). Children disposed to negative emotions such as anger are more likely to be victimized by their peers (Champion, 2009; Hanish et al., 2004). Moreover, victimized children demonstrate less ability to appropriately manage the expression of negative emotions (Camodeca & Goossens, 2005; Champion & Clay, 2007; Kochenderfer-Ladd, 2004; Shields & Cicchetti, 2001) and may lack a proper understanding of cultural emotional display rules (Garner & Hinton, 2010). Likewise, children identified as bullies show emotional lability and negativity (Champion, 2009; Garner & Hinton, 2010), and under controlled negative emotion, characteristics associated with externalizing problems such as aggression (Eisenberg et al., 2001).

A child's choice of coping strategy when negative emotions are aroused plays a role in developmental outcomes. Kochenderfer-Ladd (2004) found that students faced with peer aggression showed various emotional reactions, including anger, fear, or embarrassment. Furthermore, the type of emotional response related to the coping strategy used by the child to deal with the aggression. In general, scared or embarrassed children sought advice, whereas angry children sought revenge. The advice-seeking strategy used by children who reacted with fear or embarrassment predicted prosocial attempts at conflict resolution (e.g., telling the perpetrator to stop, taking time to cool down) and was associated with decreased victimization and fewer difficulties with internalizing problems. In contrast, children who reacted to peer aggression with anger were more likely to endorse ineffective coping strategies such as revenge seeking, which were, in turn, related to increased victimization and risk for loneliness, anxiety, and depressive symptoms.

Champion (2009) found that elementary school children low in self-rated anger preferred strategies such as ignoring and distraction when faced with various provocative actions by others. In contrast, anger-reactive children were less likely to endorse these coping responses and less likely to foresee positive outcomes from nonassertive responses such as distraction or walking away. Champion proposes that optimal responses to provocation may differ for children prone to low or high anger reactivity. Nonassertive response may function best for children low in anger, whereas children experiencing greater anger may benefit from learning strategies to help them decrease anger reactivity.

Both bullies and victims are susceptible to intense negative feelings that may overwhelm their ability to implement emotion regulation and conflict-resolution strategies (Champion, 2009; Garner & Hinton, 2010; Rosen, Milich, & Harris, 2007). Rosen and colleagues (2009) propose that some children, through an interaction of victimization experiences and social-cognitive and socioemotional processing, develop a "victim schema." This theory holds that children internalize models of social interaction, which influence scripts, roles, and outcome expectations. A chronically victimized child's victim schema is strengthened through each ill-treatment experience, making it more accessible. Thus, a cycle is created in which children who have a poor ability to regulate their feelings are more likely to have intense emotional experiences. If these same children have also developed a schema in which they expect to be victimized and do not expect to be efficacious in coping with victimization, their level of distress will likely increase. These elevated levels of emotional distress will impede the child's ability to process incoming social cues or engage in appropriate goal-setting and regulation strategies.

Rosen further contends that the type of emotional stimulation may impact goal choice and response production. Thus, children experiencing feelings such as fear or anxiety may try to regulate arousal via submissive or avoidant behaviors, whereas those feeling angry may be reactively aggressive. In either case, these poor emotion management choices lead to higher concurrent and future victimization. Like Champion (2009), Rosen and colleagues (2009) assert that teaching dysregulated children conflict-resolution skills is insufficient, as an activated victim schema and associated emotional reactivity may override prior learning. They argue for interventions that address social-cognitive and emotional processing as well. Once children learn to effectively manage their intense emotions, they can more effectively apply learned social skills. Longitudinal research indicates that chronic stress, such as repeated victimization, taxes the individual's ability to manage negative emotions, exhausting coping resources and diminishing emotion regulation over time (McLaughlin et al., 2009), further supporting the argument for bolstering emotion management prior to teaching conflict-management skills.

The Case of Anxiety and Depression

Emotion regulation also influences a child's ability to cope with worrying circumstances (Werner et al., 2011), and deficits in emotion regulation predict internalizing forms of psychopathology among children and adolescents (McLaughlin et al., 2009; Werner et al., 2011). With mood and anxiety disorders, the implicated factors include maladaptive reappraisal strategies, high levels of negative affect, and poor effortful control (Carthy et al., 2010; Gilbert, 2012; Tortella-Feliu et al., 2010). Individuals with anxiety disorders use more inhibition, suppression, and avoidance of negative emotions, possess fewer adaptive strategies for managing problematic emotions, and report a lower sense of self-efficacy with regard to emotional control (Suveg & Zeman, 2004; Werner et al., 2011).

When faced with negative life events, children with internalizing difficulties (i.e., depression, worry, fearfulness) use less adaptive cognitive coping strategies such as self-blame and catastrophizing (Garnefski, Rieffe, Jellesma, Terwogt, & Kraaij, 2007). In contrast, endorsement of strategies such as positive reappraisal and positive refocusing is associated with decreased depression, worry, and fearfulness (Garnefski et al., 2007). Depressed individuals tend to respond to distress by ruminating, which encourages the continuation of negative affect and diminishes effective problem solving (McLaughlin et al., 2009).

Relations With Educational Outcomes

Research links social and emotional learning and a host of academic attributes (e.g., attitudes, motivation, commitment) and outcomes (e.g., attendance, graduation rates, performance, behavior; CASEL, 2012; Zins, Bloodworth, Weissberg, & Walberg, 2004). According to two recent meta-analyses, students exposed to social and emotional learning show an 11- to 12-percentage-point gain in achievement, as measured by grades and achievement test scores (Durlak, Weissberg, Dymnicki, Taylor, & Schellinger, 2011; Durlak, Weissberg, & Pachan, 2010). More specifically, research supports the important role self-regulation plays in academic achievement (Ursache, Blair, & Raver, 2012). How well a child manages the array of intensive feelings stimulated in the academic environment influences her ability to absorb academic information (Graziano, Reavis, Keane, & Calkins, 2007). Children possessing adaptive emotion regulation skills are better equipped for school (Calkins & Mackler, 2011) and show strong achievement in the early elementary school years (Howse, Calkins, Anastopolous, Keane, & Shelton, 2003; Trentacosta & Izard, 2007).

Research supports the notion that emotion regulation indirectly impacts academic competence in first grade, mediated by teacher rating of behavioral self-regulation (Howse et al., 2003) and attention (Trentacosta & Izard, 2007). Gumora and Arsenio (2002) found a significant relation between emotionality, academic affect, and emotion regulation. Moreover, each of these affect-related variables showed a relation to academic performance. In this study, middle school students reporting higher emotion regulation, framed as effortful control, reported less negative academic affect and their teachers viewed them as having more positive moods. Students prone to negative academic affect achieved lower grades. Graziano and colleagues (2007) found that parent-reported emotion regulation significantly predicts kindergarteners' academic success, parent-reported behavior problems, and the quality of the student–teacher relationships. These studies suggest that students with adaptive emotion regulation skills may more effectively cope with the emotional demands of the learning environment and thus be less vulnerable to emotion-related disruptions in cognitive functioning.

MEASUREMENT APPROACHES AND ISSUES

There are several measures of emotion regulation available for children, and they are best used in a battery of assessments that include evaluation of emotion awareness and understanding to determine a specific child's emotional functioning and well-being. We briefly discuss two of the more recently developed measures of children's emotional regulation. The first is the Emotion Regulation Questionnaire for Children and Adolescents (Gullone & Taffe, 2012). The authors adapted Gross and John's (2003) emotion regulation questionnaire for adults by focusing on two emotion regulation strategies: cognitive reappraisal and expression suppression. The former subscale positively correlated with extraversion and optimism, whereas the latter subscale, expression suppression, positively correlated with depression scores.

The second measure, the Emotion Regulation Index for Children and Adolescents (ERICA; MacDermott, Gullone, Allen, King, & Tonge, 2010) consists of three subscales: Emotional Control (e.g., When things don't go my way I get upset easily—reverse scored), Emotional Self-Awareness (e.g., I handle it well when things change or I have to try something new,), and Situational Responsiveness (e.g., When others are upset, I become sad or concerned for them). This measure showed a somewhat different pattern of convergent validity as compared to the first measure described: The total score and the Emotional Self-Awareness subscale score correlated negatively with depression, and the Situational Responsiveness score correlated positively with empathy and guilt. We await the next study that looks at how both scales correlate with each other.

DIVERSITY ISSUES

Literature on how diversity interacts with emotion regulation suggests that the role of gender is considerable (e.g., Perry-Parrish & Zeman, 2011) but that ethnic differences were difficult to separate from socio-economic status, acculturation stress, and cumulative risk exposure (e.g., Raver, 2004). Disability status and sexual orientation tend to be investigated more within a risk and resilience framework rather than specific to emotion regulation. The aforementioned role of gender was found to be evident in girls having greater leeway in expressing emotions indicating vulnerability (sadness, distress) accompanied by peer and parent acceptance of such emotion expression. For boys, emotional expressive stoicism was the preferred norm (Perry-Parish & Zeman, 2011).

EDUCATIONAL APPLICATIONS

Learning the language of emotion, having the capacity for emotion awareness, and knowing how to regulate one's arousal and expressive behavior are skills developed across multiple settings, and schools figure prominently among these influential contexts. From kindergarten on, school becomes a significant developmental context for children, and teachers may take on the roles of transitional attachment figures and models of emotional competence skills. Teachers are in a unique position to actively educate students about emotion self-regulation (Eisenberg & Sulik, 2012) and are integral players in creating an emotionally safe and responsive learning environment in which students can both fully engage in academic learning and develop the skills of emotional competence.

Gottman, Katz, and Hooven's (1997) work on emotion coaching provides useful information that may be applied to the classroom setting. Although developed with a focus on parenting, we believe this work is relevant for promoting positive emotional development in other key developmental contexts, given that it addresses interventions to bolster the three areas indicated by research as associated with developmental outcomes, emotion regulation, emotion knowledge and attention skills. Emotion coaching includes five key elements: (a) awareness of the child's emotions, (b) understanding of emotion as an opportunity for intimacy and teaching, (c) assistance in helping the child attach verbal labels to emotional experiences, (d) empathy with the child's emotions, and (e) assistance in helping the with child problem solving (Gottman et al., 1997, p. 84). Emotion coaching parents are responsive to the full range of a child's affective experience and strive to maintain warmth and connection even during emotionally charged encounters. They use negatively charged emotional incidents to instruct the child regarding *acceptable behavior*, while conveying that all *feelings* are acceptable.

At first glance, it might seem like a mighty challenge to expect a parent to maintain such a calm, aware, and empathic approach to a child overcome with negative affect and who is discharging this affect in every counterproductive way possible. It might seem absurd to suggest this approach to a teacher who is trying to successfully instruct 25 children. However, Gottman's research indicates that the emotional competence of significant adults plays a key role in the development of emotional competence skills in children.

In the case of both parents and teachers, their own emotional awareness and regulation significantly impacts their ability to achieve optimal levels of emotional attunement and to model skills of emotional competence. Research indicates a relation between emotion regulation and student–teacher relationship; a teacher's ability to modulate his own emotional reactions, especially in the face of difficult students, is essential (Merrell & Gueldner, 2010). Thus, promotion of students' emotional regulation skills may also entail enhancing the emotional regulation of the adults charged with their care.

Mindfulness training is emerging as a fruitful area for both young people and the key adults in their lives. We will address the role of mindfulness for students later in this chapter, but at this juncture we focus on how research in the area of mindful parenting intersects with Gottman's emotion coaching work in its potential to impact school and classroom climate. Mindful parenting approaches focus on increasing emotional awareness on parents' part, which allows them to acknowledge and label a child's affective experiences. Awareness allows parents to avoid automatic responses growing out of emotional reactivity, thus becoming more attuned and attentive to the emotional message conveyed by the child's disruptive behavior.

Duncan, Coatsworth, and Greenberg (2009) outline five goals of mindful parenting, which contain some parallels to emotion coaching. The mindful parent listens to the child with full attention, accepting the child without judgment. The mindful parent remains aware of both his or her own and the child's emotional state while maintaining a compassionate stance for both parties. The parent also attends to self-regulation in the parenting relationship. Relationally oriented mindfulness interventions may positively impact parenting by fostering empathy, social connection, and emotional intelligence in caregivers (Sawyer Cohen & Semple, 2010). Integration of mindful parenting activities may bolster the impact of existing evidence-based parenting programs (Coatsworth, Duncan, Greenburg, & Nix, 2010). For example, as an intervention for children with ADHD, a combination of mindfulness training for both the children and their parents lead to significant reductions in parent-rated ADHD behavior, parent stress, and parent overreactivity (Van der Oord, Bogels, & Peijnenburg, 2012). While there is a dearth of research in the area, mindfulness approaches appear to hold promise for the educational setting, particularly in the area of consultation (Davis, 2012).

We propose that applying the principles of emotion coaching and mindfulness to the school setting optimally entails an exploration of the meta-emotional climate of the individuals making up the system. In other words, how do teachers and other school personnel feel about feelings? An initial assessment would include considering educators', administrators', and support staffs' awareness of and comfort with emotions, both in themselves and in the students. It would also take into account the adults' comfort with emotions and ability to regulate their own emotional states. The proximity or distance from a meta-emotional climate associated with optimal child outcomes could then be assessed, and a plan for altering the school climate to more closely align with emotion coaching and mindfulness principles could be devised. The emotional climate of a school impacts not just the students but also the teachers, administrators, and support personnel. For example, students with poorly regulated affect are a source of stress and emotional exhaustion for teachers, which in turn may impact a teacher's own emotion regulation capacity. The processes associated with emotion coaching and mindfulness would likely benefit all members of the school community.

Mindfulness Training for Students

Mindfulness techniques may also be useful in promoting the emotional competencies of students. While emotion regulation interventions often focus on controlling negative emotions, this approach may be counterproductive. In her writing on self-injury, Gratz (2007) proposes that all emotions serve a function, and thus adaptive emotion regulation should emphasize control of emotion-related behavior but not the emotion itself, although part of this behavioral control may be getting emotional experience down to manageable levels. This notion of acceptance of our emotional experiences is consistent with acceptance-based and mindfulness interventions. These approaches encourage emotional awareness, understanding, and acceptance as a pathway to decreased emotional reactivity. As such, they are consistent with the perspective that emotion awareness and understanding are key aspects of emotion regulation (Saarni, 1999).

Indeed, mindfulness addresses many of the regulation strategies outlined by Gross and Thompson (2007). Mindfulness encourages effortful attention focused on awareness of emotions as they arise, without evaluative appraisals (i.e., attentional deployment). Mindfulness moves the individual away from maladaptive strategies, such as suppression and rumination, as all emotions are acknowledged and accepted. Nonresistance of emotional experiences is in itself a form of cognitive reappraisal. For example, an uncomfortable emotion such as anger, often accompanied by cognitions that it is bad or harmful, loses its potency as it is accepted and acknowledged. Response modulation may ensue, as the emotional experience is allowed and then naturally dissipates. Heightened emotional awareness assists with emotional differentiation relative to both positive and negative emotions (Hill & Updegraff, 2012) and more flexible emotional responses.

As the individual acknowledges and accepts internal and external states, a sense self-efficacy regarding mood regulation is bolstered.

Emerging research suggests that mindfulness-based approaches hold promise with young people, although some developmental modifications may be appropriate (Burke, 2010; Davis, 2012; Thompson & Gauntlett-Gilber, 2008). Positive results have been achieved for management of childhood anxiety, attention-related problems, and impulsivity (Bogels, Hoogstad, van Dun, de Schutter, & Restifo, 2008; Semple, Lee, Rosa, & Miller, 2010; Semple, Reid, & Miller, 2005). There is growing evidence that these interventions are impactful across a range of clinical issues while also holding potential to promote positive outcomes for nonclinical populations (Sawyer Cohen & Semple, 2010), such as helping young people cope with everyday stress (Marks, Sobanski, & Hilne, 2010).

Mindfulness aids in emotion regulation, with self-reported mindfulness coinciding with decreased emotional reactivity and general emotion dysregulation (Hill & Updegraff, 2012). Mindful individuals appear to possess greater emotional intelligence, more positive affect, less negative affect, and more life satisfaction (Schutte & Malouff, 2011). College students with higher levels of dispositional mindfulness show more positive emotions, greater mood regulation expectancies, and greater self-acceptance, thus serving as a possible protective influence against depressive symptoms (Jimenez, Niles, & Park, 2010). For adolescents facing life stressors, rumination may exacerbate depression and anxiety, whereas mindfulness may lessen these types of symptoms (Marks et al., 2010). However, there is a need to explore the specific nature of the relation between mindfulness and emotion regulation (Hill & Updegraff, 2012).

Social-Emotional Learning (SEL)

Any discussion of the promotion of emotion regulation specifically, in our view, must begin with the consideration of social and emotional learning (SEL) in general. SEL subsumes a set of dynamic processes that are broadly described as those avenues "through which children enhance their ability to integrate thinking, feeling and behaving to achieve important life tasks" (Zins et al., 2004, p. 6).

At the forefront of applying SEL research to the school setting is the Collaborative for Academic, Social and Emotional Learning (CASEL). For almost two decades, CASEL has worked to establish effective, evidence-based social and emotional learning as a fundamental element of education from preschool through high school. CASEL's model identifies five core components of comprehensive social and emotional learning (i.e., self-awareness, social awareness, self-management, relationships skills, and responsible decision making; CASEL, 2012, p. 9). The category of self-management is perhaps most closely connected with emotion regulation and encompasses three key areas: (a) impulse control and stress management, (b) self-motivation and discipline, and (c) goal setting and organizational skills (Zins et al., 2004).

CASEL publications demonstrate that social and emotional skills can be developed within the school setting and that the most effective social and emotional learning occurs within the context of developmentally appropriate, comprehensive, and systemically supported interventions (Durlak et al., 2010, 2011; Greenberg et al., 2003;

Zins et al., 2004). The acronym SAFE is used to illustrate core elements of effective programs: sequenced, active, focused, and explicit. Additionally, it is important that SEL programs show evidence that they can fit readily into the existing school day (Merrell & Gueldner, 2010).

For example, Durlak and colleagues (2011) conducted a meta-analysis of 213 school-based, universal social and emotional learning (SEL) programs involving students in kindergarten through high school. The review focused on programs implemented by existing school staff, such as teachers. This comprehensive review found that students participating in school-based SEL programs showed significantly improved social and emotional skills, attitudes, behavior, and academic performance compared to students who did not receive explicit SEL training. A similar meta-analysis for after-school SEL programs showed positive effects in the areas of child self-perception and bonding to school (Durlak et al., 2010).

The *2013 CASEL Guide (CASEL, 2012)* details 23 school-based social and emotional learning programs, with a focus on evidence-based programs that benefit all students and are integrated into the normal school day by existing personnel. The guide offers a systematic framework for evaluating the quality of classroom-based social and emotional learning (SEL) programs and presents best practices for district and school teams on how to select and carry out social and emotional learning programs.

CONCLUSION

As discussed in this chapter, emotional regulation, including the ability to modulate emotional arousal and manage emotional expression, facilitates adaptive coping. Research indicates that emotion regulation skills play a role in developmental outcomes. Children with well-developed emotion regulation skills, particularly in terms of handling strong negative emotions, appear to fare better socially, emotionally, behaviorally, and academically. They are more likely to manage their feelings in a manner that facilitates goal attainment.

Existing research suggests both direct and more complex relations between emotion regulation and developmental outcomes. Of particular note is the increasing evidence that problematic behavioral outcomes are associated with a combination of negative emotionality and the inability to sustain attention. A fruitful area of future research is the exploration of the various pathways through which emotional regulation may exert its influence, such as its relation to academic attitudes and behaviors (e.g., attitudes, motivation, attention) and its connection to social support (e.g., relationships with teachers and peers).

We agree with the researchers at CASEL that attention to the social and emotional lives of children is integral to our educational system's mission. We acknowledge the value of offering and supporting comprehensive, evidence-based social and emotional learning programs and advocate for the specific consideration of emotion regulation as a crucial element of these programs. While the potential utility of interventions such as emotion coaching or mindfulness training for educators is promising, further work is needed to empirically verify their impact on the social-emotional climate of the classroom and students' academic functioning.

REFERENCES

Adrian, J., Zeman, J., Erdley, C., Lisa, L., Homan, K., & Sim, L. (2009). Social contextual links to emotion regulation in an adolescent psychiatric inpatient population: Do gender and symptomatology matter? *Journal of Child Psychology and Psychiatry, 50*, 1428–1436. doi:10.1111/j.1469-7610.2009.02162.x

Bogels, S., Hoogstad, B., van Dun, L., de Schutter, S., & Restifo, K. (2008). Mindfulness training for adolescents with externalizing disorders and their parents. *Behavioural and Cognitive Psychotherapy, 36*, 193–209. doi:10.1017/S1352465808004190

Burke, C. A. (2010). Mindfulness-based approaches with children and adolescents: A preliminary review of current research in an emergent field. *Journal of Child and Family Studies, 19*, 133–144. doi:10.1007/s10826-009-9282-x

Calkin, S. D., & Hill, A. (2007). Caregiver influences on emerging emotion regulations: Biological and environmental transactions in early development. In J. J. Gross (Ed.), *Handbook of emotion regulation* (pp. 229–249). New York, NY: Guilford.

Calkin, S. D., & Mackler, J. S. (2011). Temperament, emotion regulation, and social development. In M. K. Underwood & L. H. Rosen (Eds.), *Social development: Relationships in infancy, childhood, and adolescence* (pp. 44–70). New York, NY: Guilford.

Camodeca, M., & Goossens, F. A. (2005). Aggression, social cognitions, anger and sadness in bullies and victims. *Journal of Child Psychology and Psychiatry, 46*, 186–197. doi:10.1111/j.1467-8624.2004.00681.x

Campos, J., Frankel, C., & Camras, L. (2004). On the nature of emotion regulation. *Child Development, 75*, 377–394. doi:10.1111/j.1467-8624.2004.00681.x

Carthy, T., Horesh, N., Apter, A., & Gross, J. J. (2010). Patterns of emotional reactivity and regulation in children with anxiety disorders. *Journal of Psychopathology and Behavioral Assessment, 32*, 23–26. doi:10.1007/s10862-009-9167-8

CASEL. (2012). *CASEL guide: Effective social and emotional learning programs.* Chicago, IL: Author.

Champion, K. M. (2009). Victimization, anger, and gender: Low anger and passive responses to work. *American Journal of Orthopsychiatry, 79*, 71–82. doi:10.1037/a0015340

Champion, K. M., & Clay, D. L. (2007). Individual differences in response to provocation and frequent victimization by peers. *Child Psychiatry and Human Development, 37*, 205–220. doi:10.1007/s10578-006-0030-9

Chang, H., Shelleby, E. C., Cheong, J., & Shaw, D. S. (2012). Cumulative risk, negative emotionality, and emotion regulation as predictors of social competence in transition to school: A mediated moderation model. *Social Development, 21*, 780–800. doi:10.1111/j.1467-9507.2011.00648.x

Coatsworth, J. D., Duncan, L. G., Greenburg, M. T., & Nix, R. L. (2010). Changing parents' mindfulness, child management skills and relationship quality with their youth: Results from a randomized pilot intervention trial. *Journal of Child and Family Studies, 19*, 203–217. doi:10.1007/s10826-009-9304-8

Davis, T. S. (2012). Mindfulness-based approaches and their potential for educational psychology practice. *Educational Psychology in Practice, 28*, 31–46. doi:10.1080/02667363.2011.639348

Denham, S., Blair, K. A., DeMulder, E., Levitas, J., Sawyer, K., Auerbach-Major, S., & Queenan, P. (2003). Preschool emotional competence: Pathways to social competence? *Child Development, 74*, 238–256. doi:10.1111/1467-8624.00533

Denham, S., Blair, K. A., Schmidt, M., & DeMulder, E. (2002). Compromised emotional competence: Seeds of violence sown early? *American Journal of Orthopsychiatry, 72*, 70–82. doi:10.1037/0002-9432.72.1.70

Duncan, L. G., Coatsworth, J. D., & Greenberg, M. T. (2009). A model of mindful parenting: Implications for parent–child relationships and prevention research. *Clinical Child and Family Psychology Review, 12*, 255–270. doi:10.1007/s10567-009-0046-3

Durlak, J. A., Weissberg, R. P., Dymnicki, A. B., Taylor, R. D., & Schellinger, K. B. (2011). The impact of enhancing students' social and emotional learning: A meta-analysis of school-based universal interventions. *Child Development, 82*, 405–432. doi:10.1111/j.1467-8624.2010.01564.x

Durlak, J. A., Weissberg, R. P., & Pachan, M. (2010). A meta-analysis of after-school programs that seek to promote personal and social skills in children and adolescents. *American Journal of Community Psychology, 45*, 294–309. doi:10.1007/s10464-010-9300-6

Eisenberg, N., Cumberland, A. L., Spinrad, T. L., Fabes, R. A., Shepard, S. A., Reiser, M., . . . Guthrie, I. K. (2001). The relations of regulation and emotionality to children's externalizing and internalizing problem behavior. *Child Development, 64*, 1418–1438. doi:10.1111/1467-8624.00337

Eisenberg, N., Fabes, R., Guthrie, I., & Reiser, M. (2000). Dispositional emotionality and regulation: Their role in predicting quality of social functioning. *Journal of Personality and Social Psychology, 78*, 136–157. doi:10.1037/0022-3514.78.1.136

Eisenberg, N., & Spinrad, T. (2004). Emotion-related regulation: Sharpening the definition. *Child Development, 75*, 334–339. doi:10.1111/j.1467-8624.2004.00674.x

Eisenberg, N., Spinrad, T., & Eggum, N.D. (2010). Emotion-related self-regulation and its relation to children's maladjustment. *Annual Review of Clinical Psychology, 6*, 495–525. doi:10.1146/annurev.clinpsy.121208.131208

Eisenberg, N., & Sulik, M.J. (2012). Emotion-related self-regulation in children. *Teaching and Psychology, 39*, 77–83. doi:10.1177/0098628311430172

Esbjorn, B.H., Bender, P.K., Reinholdt-Dunne, M.L., Munck, L.A., & Ollendick, T.H. (2012). The development of anxiety disorders: Considering the contributions of attachment and emotion regulation. *Clinical Child and Family Psychology Review, 15*, 129–143. doi:10.1007/s10567-011-0105-4

Garnefski, N., Rieffe, C., Jellesma, F., Terwogt, M.M., & Kraaij, V. (2007). Cognitive emotion regulation strategies and emotional problems in 9–11-year-old children: The development of an instrument. *European Child and Adolescent Psychiatry, 16*, 1–9. doi:10.1007/s00787-006-0562-3

Garner, P.W., & Hinton, T.S. (2010). Emotional display rules and emotion self-regulation: Associations with bullying and victimization in community-based after school programs. *Journal of Community and Applied Social Psychology, 20*, 480–496. doi:10.1002/casp.1057

Garner, P.W., & Waajid, B. (2012). Emotion knowledge and self-regulation as predictors of preschoolers' cognitive ability, classroom behavior, and social competence. *Journal of Psychoeducational Assessment, 30*, 330–343. doi:10.1177/0734282912449441

Gilbert, K.E., (2012). The neglected role of positive emotion in adolescent psychopathology. *Clinical Psychology Review, 32*, 467–481. doi:10.1016/j.cpr.2012.05.005

Gottman, J., Katz, L.F., & Hooven, C. (1997). *Meta-emotion*. Hillsdale, NJ: Erlbaum.

Gratz, K.L. (2007). Targeting emotion dysregulation in the treatment of self-injury. *Journal of Clinical Psychology, 63*, 1091–1103. doi:10.1002/jclp.20417

Graziano, P.A., Reavis, R.D., Keane, S.P., & Calkins, S.D. (2007). The role of emotion regulation in children's early academic success. *Journal of School Psychology, 45*, 3–20. doi:10.1016/j.jsp.2006.09.002

Greenberg, M.T., Weissberg, R.P., O'Brien, M.U., Zins, J.E., Fredricks, L., Resnik, H., & Elias, M.J. (2003). Enhancing school-based prevention and youth development through coordinated social, emotional, and academic learning. *American Psychologist, 58*, 466–474. doi:10.1037/0003-066X.58.6-7.466

Gross, J.J., & John, O.P. (2003). Individual differences in two emotion regulation processes: Implications for affect, relationships, and wellbeing. *Journal of Personality and Social Psychology, 85*, 348–362. doi:10.1037/0022-3514.85.2.348

Gross, J.J., & Thomson, R.A. (2007). Emotion regulation: conceptual foundations. In J.J. Gross (Ed.), *Handbook of emotion regulation* (pp. 3–24). New York, NY: Guilford.

Gullone, E., & Taffe, J. (2012). The emotion regulation questionnaire for children and adolescents (ERQ–CA): A psychometric evaluation. *Psychological Assessment, 24*, 409–417. doi:10.1037/a0025777

Gumora, G., & Arsenio, W. (2002). Emotionality, emotion regulation, and school performance in middle school children. *Journal of School Psychology, 40*, 395–413. doi:10.1016/S0022-4405(02)00108-5

Hanish, L., Eisenbeg, N., Fabes, R., Spinrad, T.L., Ryan, P., & Schmidt, S. (2004). The expression and regulation of negative emotions: Risk factors for young children's peer victimization. *Development and Psychopathology, 16*, 335–353. doi:10.1017/S0954579404044542

Hill, A.L., Degnan, K.A., Calkins, S.D., & Keane, S.P. (2006). Profiles in externalizing behavior problems for boys and girls across preschool: The roles of emotion regulation and inattention. *Developmental Psychology, 42*, 913–928. doi:10.1037/0012-1649.42.5.913

Hill, C.L.M., & Updegraff, J.A. (2012). Mindfulness and its relationship to emotional regulation. *Emotion, 12*, 81–90. doi:10.1037/a0026355

Howse, R.B., Calkins, S.D., Anastopoulos, A.D., Keane, S.P., & Shelton, T.L. (2003). Regulatory contributors to children's kindergarten achievement. *Early Education & Development, 14*, 101–119. doi:10.1207/s15566935eed1401_7

Jimenez, S.S., Niles, B.L., & Park, C.L. (2010). A mindfulness model of affect regulation and depressive symptoms: Positive emotions, mood regulation expectancies, and self-acceptance as regulatory mechanisms. *Personality and Individual Differences, 49*, 645–650. doi:10.1016/j.paid.2010.05.041

Kashdan, T.B., & Breen, W.E. (2008) Social anxiety and positive emotions: A prospective examination of a self-regulatory model with tendencies to suppress or express emotions as a moderating variable. *Behavior Therapy, 39*, 1–12. doi:10.1016/j.beth.2007.02.003

Kochenderfer-Ladd, B. (2004). Peer victimization: The role of emotions in adaptive and maladaptive coping. *Social Development, 13*, 329–349. doi:10.1111/j.1467-9507.2004.00271.x

Lopes, P.N., Mestre, J.M., Guil, R., Pickard Kremenitzer, J., & Salovey, P. (2012). The role of knowledge and skills for managing emotions in adaptation to school: Social behavior and misconduct in the classroom. *American Educational Research Journal, 49*, 710–742. doi:10.3102/0002831212443077

MacDermott, S., Gullone, E., Allen, J., King, N., & Tonge, B. (2010). The Emotion Regulation Index for Children and Adolescents (ERICA). *Journal of Psychopathology and Behavioral Assessment, 32*, 301–314. doi:10.1007/s10862-009-9154-0

Marks, A. D.G., Sobanski, D.J., & Hine, D.W. (2010). Do dispositional rumination and/or mindfulness moderate the relationship between life hassles and psychological dysfunction in adolescents? *Australian and New Zealand Journal of Psychiatry, 44*, 831–838. doi:10.1037/t04259-000

McLaughlin, K.A., Hatzenbuehler, M.L., & Hilt, L.M. (2009). Emotion dysregulation as a mechanism linking peer victimization to internalizing symptoms in adolescents. *Journal of Consulting and Clinical Psychology, 77*, 894–904. doi:10.1007/s10802-012-9629-4

Merrell, K.W., & Gueldner, B.A. (2010). *Social and emotional learning in the classroom: Promoting mental health and academic success.* New York, NY: Guilford.

Monopoli, W.J., & Kingston, S. (2012). The relationships among language ability, emotion regulation and social competence in second-grade students. *International Journal of Behavioral Development, 36*, 398–405. doi:10.1177/0165025412446394

Perry-Parrish, C., & Zeman, J. (2011). Relations among sadness regulation, peer acceptance, and social functioning in early adolescence. The role of gender. *Social Development, 20*, 135–153. doi:10.1111/j.1467-9507.2009.00568.x

Raver, C. (2004). Placing emotional self-regulation in sociocultural and socioeconomic contexts. *Child Development, 75*, 346–353. doi:10.1111/j.1467-8624.2004.00676.x

Rosen, P.J., Milich, R., & Harris, M.J. (2007). Victims of their own cognitions: Implicit social cognitions, chronic peer victimization, and the victim schema model. *Journal of Applied Developmental Psychology, 28*, 221–226. doi:10.1016/j.appdev.2007.02.001

Rosen, P.J., Milich, R., & Harris, M.J. (2009). Why's everybody always picking on me? Social cognition, emotion regulation, and chronic peer victimization in children. In M.J. Harris (Ed.), *Bullying, rejection, and peer victimization: A social cognitive perspective* (pp. 79–100). New York, NY: Springer.

Rusch, S., Westermann, S., & Lincoln, T. (2012). Specificity of emotion regulation deficits in social anxiety: An Internet study. *Psychology and Psychotherapy: Theory, Research, and Practice, 85*, 268–277. doi:10.1111/j.2044-8341.2011.02029.x

Saarni, C. (1999). *The development of emotional competence.* New York, NY: Guilford.

Saarni, C. (2000). Emotional competence: A developmental perspective. In R. Bar-On & J.D. Parker (Eds.), *Handbook of emotional intelligence: Theory, development, assessment, and application at home, school, and in the workplace* (pp. 68–91). San Francisco, CA: Jossey-Bass.

Saarni, C. (2007). The development of emotional competence: Pathways for helping children become emotionally intelligent. In R. Bar-On, J. Maree, & M.J. Elias (Eds.), *Educating children and adults to be emotionally intelligent: Guidelines for improving performance* (pp. 15–35). Rondebosch, South Africa: Heinemann Educational.

Saarni, C., Campos, J., Camras, L., & Witherington, D. (2006). Emotional development: Action, communication, and understanding. In N. Eisenberg (Ed.), *Handbook of child psychology: Vol. 3. Social, emotional, and personality development* (6th ed., pp. 226–299). New York, NY: Wiley.

Sawyer Cohen, J.A., & Semple, R.J. (2010). Mindful parenting: A call for research. *Journal of Child and Family Studies, 19*, 145–151. doi:10.1007/s10826-009-9285-7

Schreiber, L.R.N., Grant, J.E., & Odlaug, B.L. (2012). Emotion regulation and impulsivity in young adults. *Journal of Psychiatric Research, 46*, 651–658. doi:10.1016/j.jpsychires.2012.02.005

Schutte, N.S., & Malouff, J.M. (2011). Emotional intelligence mediates the relationship between mindfulness and subjective well-being. *Personality and Individual Differences, 50*, 1116–1119. doi:10.1016/j.paid.2011.01.037

Semple, R.J., Lee, J., Rosa, D., & Miller, L.F. (2010). A randomized trial of mindfulness-based cognitive therapy for children: Promoting mindful attention to enhance social-emotional resiliency in children. *Journal of Child and Family Studies, 19*, 218–229. doi:10.1007/s10826-009-9301-y

Semple, R.J., Reid, E.F.G., & Miller, L. (2005). Treating anxiety with mindfulness: An open trial with mindfulness training for anxious children. *Journal of Cognitive Psychotherapy: An International Quarterly, 19*, 379–392. doi:10.1891/jcop.2005.19.4.379

Shields, A., & Cicchetti, D. (2001). Parental maltreatment and emotion dysregulation as risk factors for bullying and victimization in middle childhood. *Journal of Clinical Child Psychology, 30*, 349–363. doi:10.1207/S15374424JCCP3003_7

Shields, A., Ryan, R. M., & Cicchetti, D. (2001). Narrative representations of caregivers and emotion dysregulation as predictors of maltreated children's rejection by peers. *Developmental Psychology, 37*, 321–337. doi:10.1037/0012-1649.37.3.321

Spritz, B. L., Sandberg, E. H., Maher, E., & Zajdel, R. T. (2010). Models of emotion skill and social competence in the Head Start classroom. *Early Education and Development, 21*, 495–516. doi:10.1080/10409280902895097

Suveg, C., Southam-Gerow, M. A., Goodman, K. L., & Kendall, P. C. (2007). The role of emotion theory and research in child therapy development. *Clinical Psychology: Science and Practice, 14*, 358–371. doi:10.1111/j.1468-2850.2007.00096.x

Suveg, C., & Zeman, J. (2004). Emotion regulation in children with anxiety disorders. *Journal of Clinical Child and Adolescent Psychology, 33*, 750–759. doi:10.1007/978-1-4419-7784-7_12

Thompson, M., & Gauntlett-Gilbert, J. (2008). Mindfulness with children and adolescents: Effective clinical application. *Clinical Child Psychology and Psychiatry, 13*, 395–407. doi:10.1177/1359104508090603

Tortella-Feliu, M., Balle, M., & Sese, A. (2010). Relationship between negative affectivity, emotion regulation, anxiety, and depression symptoms in adolescents as examined through structural equation modeling. *Journal of Anxiety Disorders, 24*, 686–693. doi:10.1016/j.janxdis.2010.04.012

Trentacosta, C. J., & Izard, C. E. (2007). Kindergarten children's emotion competence as a predictor of their academic competence in first grade. *Emotion, 7*, 77–88. doi:10.1037/1528-3542.7.1.77

Trentacosta, C. J., & Shaw, D. S. (2009). Emotional self-regulation, peer rejection, and antisocial behavior: Developmental associations from early childhood to early adolescence. *Journal of Applied Developmental Psychology, 30*, 356–365. doi:10.1016/j.appdev.2008.12.016

Ursache, A., Blair, C., & Raver, C. C. (2012). The promotion of self-regulation as a means of enhancing school readiness and early achievement in children at risk for school failure. *Child Development Perspectives, 6*, 122–128. doi:10.1111/j.1750-8606.2011.00209.x

Van der Oord, S., Bogels, S. M., & Peijnenburg, D. (2012). The effectiveness of mindfulness training for children with ADHD and mindfulness parenting for their parents. *Journal of Child and Family Studies, 21*, 139–147. doi:10.1007/s10826-011-9457-0

Werner, K. H., Goldin, P. R., Ball, T. M., Heimberg, R. G., & Gross, J. J. (2011). Assessing emotion regulation in social anxiety disorder: The Emotion Regulation Interview. *Journal of Psychopathology and Behavioral Assessment, 3*, 346–354. doi:10.1007/s10862-011-9225-x

Zins, J. E., Bloodworth, M. R., Weissberg, R. P., & Walberg, H. J. (2004). The scientific base linking social and emotional learning to school success. In J. Zins, R. Weissberg, M. Wang, & H. J. Walberg (Eds.), *Building academic success on social and emotional learning: What does the research say?* (pp. 3–22). New York, NY: Teachers College.

CHAPTER SUMMARY: EMOTION REGULATION

- Saarni (1999) proposed eight specific but mutually interdependent skills of emotional competence. These skills can be grouped into three broad categories: emotion expression, emotion understanding, and emotion regulation.

- Emotion regulation refers to managing one's emotional reactivity in the service of engaging with others and coping with challenging circumstances.

- Effective emotional self-regulation includes both conscious, effortful regulation and unconscious, automatic regulation.

- Definitions of emotion regulation vary. The differences relate to how much emphasis is given to influences that come from *extrinsic* sources—that is, outside the self, and influences that are *intrinsic* to the self, such as emotion regulation strategies.

- Difficulty with emotion regulation is associated with poor developmental outcomes, including internalizing and externalizing forms of psychopathology, academic difficulties, and problematic social relationships.

- Management of distressing emotions and ability to effectively exert effortful control are key factors related to developmental outcomes.

- Variations in emotional reactivity among students may influence their choice of coping strategy and/or their ability to effectively implement emotional regulation strategies.
- Adaptive emotion regulation capabilities positively influence academic and social-emotional outcomes.
- Interventions to promote emotion regulation may occur at the individual and contextual levels.

RECOMMENDED READING: EMOTION REGULATION

CASEL. (2012). *CASEL guide: Effective social and emotional learning programs.* Chicago, IL: Author.

> The 2013 *CASEL Guide* offers an overview of procedures for evaluating the quality of classroom-based SEL programs. This guide provides comprehensive assessment of SEL programs with demonstrated effectiveness in the school setting. The *Guide* contains a wealth of information of use to educators who are interested in selecting and implementing SEL programs in their districts and schools.

Chen, X. (2012), Culture, peer interaction, and socioemotional development. *Child Development Perspectives, 6,* 27–34. doi:10.1111/j.1750-8606.2011.00187x

> Although not directly addressing emotion regulation, this recent publication offers a contextual-developmental perspective emphasizing the role of peer interaction as a key factor mediating the relation between culture and socioemotional development. The article offers an insightful perspective on the role of cultural norms and values in shaping socioemotional functioning.

Durlak, J. A., Weissberg, R. P., Dymnicki, A. B., Taylor, R. D., & Schellinger, K. B. (2011). The impact of enhancing students' social and emotional learning: A meta-analysis of school-based universal interventions. *Child Development, 82,* 405–432.

> This landmark review provides a timely meta-analysis of 213 school-based, universal social and emotional learning (SEL) programs. This project represents the most ambitious review yet conducted of controlled-outcome research on interventions that promote children's social and emotional development. Focusing on K–12 school, family, and community interventions, the project examined the effect of SEL programs on students' SEL skills, attitudes toward self and others, positive social behavior, conduct problems, emotional distress, and academic performance.

Eisenberg, N., & Sulik, M. J. (2012). Emotion-related self-regulation in children. *Teaching and Psychology, 39,* 77–83.

> This publication provides a review of foundational conceptual issues in research on children's emotion-related self-regulation. A summary of research on developmental changes in self-regulation, as well as issues of measurement, is offered. The article also outlines tactics for teaching students about emotion regulation.

Merrell, K. W., & Gueldner, B. A. (2010). *Social and emotional learning in the classroom: Promoting mental health and academic success.* New York, NY: Guilford.

> This user-friendly book offers practical resources for implementing social and emotional learning (SEL) in K–12 settings. The book includes useful illustrative examples and self-contained chapters. Topics covered include selection of an appropriate SEL program tailored to a school's unique needs and integrating SEL into the classroom curriculum. Strategies related to teaching SEL concepts to students, teachers, and administrators are provided.

8

ACADEMIC SELF-EFFICACY

Dale H. Schunk, School of Education, The University of North Carolina at Greensboro, Greensboro, North Carolina, USA

Maria K. DiBenedetto, Zicklin School of Business, Baruch College, CUNY, New York, New York, USA

INTRODUCTION

Positive psychology is a contemporary movement oriented toward exploring human happiness and thriving (Kristjánsson, 2012). It contrasts with the problems and deficiencies commonly studied by psychologists. Although the movement has no well-defined onset, it received a strong impetus from the publication by Seligman and Csikszentmihalyi (2000). Among its historical precursors are humanistic theories, such as those of Carl Rogers and Abraham Maslow, which emphasize the role of the self in human functioning.

In this chapter we discuss one type of psychological construct that has relevance to the application of positive psychology to education: *self-efficacy,* or one's perceived capabilities for learning or performing actions at designated levels (Bandura, 1997). Self-efficacy is a belief about what one can do. This chapter focuses on self-efficacy theory, research, and applications to academic settings. Our goal is to demonstrate that self-efficacy is a key component of positive psychology and a central influence on individuals' well-being. Researchers have found that self-efficacy influences individuals' learning, motivation, and self-regulation (Bandura, 1997; Pajares, 1996; Schunk & Pajares, 2009).

We initially provide a theoretical overview of self-efficacy to include its grounding in social cognitive theory. We discuss the causes and consequences of self-efficacy and the operation of self-efficacy during academic learning. Key research studies on learning in academic settings are reviewed, along with ways that self-efficacy is assessed. How self-efficacy changes with development is addressed, as well as research on self-efficacy in different cultures. This chapter concludes with suggestions on ways that theoretical principles and research findings can be applied to foster self-efficacy among students and teachers.

THEORETICAL BASE AND DEFINITIONS

Social Cognitive Theory

Self-efficacy is grounded in Bandura's (1986) social cognitive theory, which postulates reciprocal interactions among three sets of influences: personal (e.g., cognitions, beliefs, skills, affects), behavioral, and social/environmental (Schunk, 2012). These reciprocal interactions can be illustrated using self-efficacy, a personal factor. With respect to the interaction of self-efficacy and behavior, research shows that self-efficacy influences achievement behaviors, such as task choice, effort, persistence, and use of effective learning strategies (Schunk & Pajares, 2009). These behaviors also affect self-efficacy. As learners work on tasks and observe their progress, their self-efficacy for continued learning is enhanced.

The link between personal and social/environmental factors can be illustrated with students with learning disabilities, many of whom hold low self-efficacy for learning (Licht & Kistner, 1986). People in their environments may react to them based on common attributes (e.g., low skills) rather than based on their actual capabilities. Social/environmental feedback can affect self-efficacy, as when teachers tell students, "I know you can do this."

The link between behavioral and social/environmental factors is seen in instructional sequences. Social/environmental factors direct behaviors when teachers call students' attention to a display (e.g., "Look at this"), to which students attend without much deliberation. The influence of behavior on the social environment occurs when teachers ask questions and students' answers convey a lack of understanding. Teachers are likely to reteach the material rather than continue with the lesson.

Social cognitive theory reflects a positive psychology view of human agency in which individuals seek to exert a large degree of control over the outcomes of their actions. They hold beliefs that allow them to influence their thoughts, feelings, actions, social interactions, and aspects of their environments. Thus, athletes who want to improve their skills seek out experienced coaches to work with. At the same time, people are influenced by their actions and aspects of their social environments. Athletes are apt to change their behaviors in response to feedback from their coaches.

According to social cognitive theory, strategies for increasing well-being can be aimed at improving emotional, cognitive, or motivational processes, increasing behavioral competencies, or improving aspects of one's environment. Teachers are responsible for promoting learning among their students. Using social cognitive theory as a framework, teachers can seek to improve their students' emotional states and correct their faulty beliefs and habits of thinking (personal factors), raise their academic skills and self-regulation (behaviors), and alter classroom features and social interactions (social/ environmental factors) to ensure student success.

Self-Efficacy: Causes and Consequences

Self-efficacy is hypothesized to influence behaviors and environments and in turn be affected by them (Bandura, 1986, 1997; Schunk, 2012). Students with high self-efficacy for learning are apt to be motivated to learn, engage in self-regulated learning (e.g., set goals, use effective learning strategies, monitor their comprehension, evaluate their goal progress), and create effective environments for learning (e.g., eliminate or minimize distractions, find effective study partners). In turn, self-efficacy can be influenced by the outcomes of behaviors such as goal progress and achievement, as well as by inputs from the environment such as feedback from teachers and social comparisons with peers.

Bandura (1997) postulated that people acquire information to gauge their self-efficacy from their performance accomplishments, vicarious (e.g., modeled) experiences, forms of social persuasion, and physiological indexes. One's performances provide the most reliable information for assessing self-efficacy because they are tangible indicators of one's capabilities. Successful performances raise self-efficacy whereas failures can lower it, although an occasional failure or success after many successes or failures might not have much impact.

Individuals acquire much information about their capabilities through knowledge of how others perform (Bandura, 1997). Similarity to others is a cue for gauging self-efficacy (Schunk, 2012). Observing similar others succeed can raise observers' self-efficacy and motivate them to engage in the task because they may believe that if others can succeed they can as well; however, a vicarious increase in self-efficacy can be negated by subsequent performance failure. Persons who observe similar peers fail may believe they lack the competence to succeed, which may not motivate them to attempt the task.

Individuals also develop self-efficacy from social persuasions they receive from others (Bandura, 1997), such as when a teacher tells a student, "I know you can do this." Social persuasions must be credible to cultivate people's beliefs in their capabilities for successfully attaining outcomes; empty praise is likely to be ineffective. Although positive feedback can raise self-efficacy, the increase will not endure if students subsequently perform poorly (Schunk, 2012). Conversely, negative persuasions can lower self-efficacy.

Individuals acquire self-efficacy information from physiological and emotional states such as anxiety and stress (Bandura, 1997). Strong emotional reactions to a task provide cues about anticipated success or failure. When students experience negative thoughts and fears about their capabilities (e.g., feeling nervous thinking about taking a test), those reactions can lower self-efficacy and trigger additional stress that helps bring about the feared inadequate performance. Learners should be more efficacious when they feel less anxious about academic outcomes.

Although self-efficacy is important, it is not the only influence on behavior. No amount of self-efficacy will produce a competent performance when students lack the necessary skills to succeed (Schunk, 2012). Students' *values* (perceptions of importance and utility of learning) also can affect behavior (Wigfield, Tonks, & Eccles, 2004). Even students who feel highly efficacious in science may not take science courses that they believe are not germane to their goal of becoming a veterinarian. Also important are *outcome expectations*, or beliefs about the anticipated outcomes of actions (Bandura, 1997). Students typically engage in activities that they believe will result in positive outcomes and avoid actions that they believe may lead to negative outcomes, even when they feel efficacious about attaining the latter. Assuming, however, that students possess the requisite skills, as well as positive values and outcome expectations, self-efficacy is a key determinant of individuals' motivation, learning, self-regulation, and achievement (Schunk, 2012).

Self-efficacy can influence the choices people make and the actions they pursue (Schunk & Pajares, 2009). Individuals tend to select tasks and activities in which they feel competent and avoid those in which they do not. Unless people believe that their actions will produce the desired consequences, they have little incentive to engage in those actions.

Self-efficacy also helps determine how much effort students expend, how long they persist when confronting obstacles, and how resilient they are in the face of adversity (Schunk & Pajares, 2009). Students with a strong sense of self-efficacy approach difficult tasks as challenges to be mastered rather than as threats to be avoided. They set challenging goals and maintain strong commitment to them, heighten and sustain their efforts in the face of failure, and quickly recover their sense of self-efficacy after setbacks.

Operation of Self-Efficacy

Researchers have explored the operation of self-efficacy during learning to include determining the effects of instructional and other classroom processes on self-efficacy (Schunk & Pajares, 2009). This body of research shows that when instructional, social, and environmental factors inform students about their learning, they can use this information to assess their self-efficacy for continued learning.

At the outset of a learning activity, students' self-efficacy for learning depends on their prior experiences, personal qualities (e.g., abilities, attitudes), and social supports. The latter include the extent that teachers, parents, and others encourage students to learn, facilitate their access to resources necessary for learning (e.g., materials, facilities), and teach them self-regulatory strategies that enhance skill development.

As students engage in learning activities, they are influenced by personal factors (e.g., goal setting, cognitive information processing) and situational variables (e.g., feedback, social comparisons). These influences provide students with cues about how well they are learning. Their self-efficacy is strengthened when they perceive that they are performing well. Lack of success or slow progress will not necessarily lower self-efficacy if students believe they can perform better, such as by expending greater effort or using more-effective learning strategies (Schunk, 1995). In turn, self-efficacy enhances their motivation and continued learning.

Experimental research supports these hypothesized relations with students in different grade levels (e.g., elementary, middle, high, postsecondary), with diverse abilities (e.g., regular, remedial, gifted), and in different content areas (e.g., reading, writing, mathematics, computer applications; Schunk, 1995, 2012; Schunk & Ertmer, 2000). Some instructional and social processes that raise self-efficacy are having students pursue proximal and specific learning goals, allowing learners to observe models explaining and demonstrating skills, providing students with performance and attributional feedback on their performances, teaching students to use effective learning strategies, having learners verbalize strategies while applying them, linking students' rewards to their learning progress, and teaching students how to monitor and evaluate their learning progress (Schunk & Pajares, 2009). These processes differ in many ways, but they are similar in that they convey information to students about their learning progress, which raises self-efficacy.

RESEARCH EVIDENCE

Researchers have investigated different aspects of academic self-efficacy. This section discusses evidence pertaining to its prediction of educational outcomes, operation during self-regulated learning, and influence on teachers.

Prediction of Educational Outcomes

Researchers have shown that self-efficacy for learning or performing tasks correlates positively and significantly with subsequent achievement on those tasks (Pajares, 1996; Pajares & Urdan, 2006; Schunk & Pajares, 2009). Self-efficacy explains approximately 25% of the variance in academic outcomes beyond that accounted for by instructional variables. Using meta-analytic procedures, Multon, Brown, and Lent (1991) found that self-efficacy related to academic performance ($r_m = .38$) and accounted for 14% of the variance. Stronger effects were obtained with self-efficacy and skill measures that were highly congruent. Self-efficacy also correlates positively with indexes of self-regulation (e.g., goal setting, strategy use, performance monitoring; Schunk & Pajares, 2009).

Researchers have used causal models to test the predictive and mediational power of self-efficacy. Using path analysis, Schunk (1981) found that self-efficacy exerted a direct effect on children's achievement and persistence in mathematics. Pajares and Kranzler (1995) demonstrated that mathematics self-efficacy has as powerful an effect on mathematics performance as does cognitive or mental ability. Zimmerman and Bandura (1994) found that self-efficacy affected achievement directly as well as indirectly through its influence on goals. Schunk and Gunn (1986) found that children's mathematical achievement was directly influenced by use of effective strategies and self-efficacy. Relich, Debus, and Walker (1986) showed that self-efficacy exerted a direct effect on achievement and that instruction had a direct effect on achievement, as well as an indirect effect through self-efficacy.

Self-Efficacy for Self-Regulated Learning

Self-efficacy has been applied extensively to *self-regulated learning*, which refers to learning that results from students' self-generated thoughts, feelings, and behaviors that are systematically oriented toward the attainment of their learning goals (Zimmerman, 2000). Self-regulated learning involves students setting goals and instigating and sustaining goal-directed activities, such as by focusing on task demands, applying effective strategies to learn, establishing productive social and work environments, assessing learning progress, and making strategic adjustments as needed. Developing and maintaining a strong sense of self-efficacy for self-regulated learning motivates students and promotes their learning (Schunk & Usher, 2011).

Zimmerman (2000) developed a model of self-regulated learning that features the role of self-efficacy. This cyclical and recursive model comprises three phases: forethought, performance, and self-reflection. The *forethought* phase involves processes that students engage in prior to learning and includes motivational beliefs and task analysis. Key motivational beliefs are self-efficacy, outcome expectancies, intrinsic interest, and goal orientations (reasons students want to learn). Task analysis includes goal setting (short- and long-term goals) and strategic planning, or deciding what methods to use. While each of these processes is related to achievement, self-efficacy is a strong predictor and affects goal setting and strategic planning (Schunk, 2012; Zimmerman & Bandura, 1994).

The forethought phase initiates the learning activities that occur during the *performance* phase, during which students systematically and actively engage in learning. Key self-regulatory processes are self-control and self-observation. Students exert self-control by using strategies such as imagery, self-instruction, attention focusing, and others targeted at reaching goals (Zimmerman, 2002). Self-observation includes self-monitoring and self-recording learning progress. Students gain progress information from their perceptions and feedback from others (e.g., teachers, peers, parents). Students who are highly self-efficacious about their capability to learn sustain their efforts and adapt their performances better than those with lower self-efficacy (Pajares, 2008).

Based on self-monitoring and feedback from others, students form self-judgments and experience self-reactions in the *self-reflection* phase. Self-judgments include self-evaluations of learning progress and performance attributions (i.e., perceived causes of outcomes; Schunk, 2012). Self-evaluations are based on performance standards that may derive from previous performances, performances by others (e.g., teachers), or absolute criteria (Zimmerman, 2002). Causal attributions may reflect causes that students can control such as strategy use and effort or uncontrollable ones such as luck or ability (Weiner, 1985). Students also react to their performances with self-satisfaction and adaptive/defensive responses. Self-satisfaction refers to the level of contentment students feel about their performance relative to a standard or goal. Adaptive/defensive responses include emotional reactions to performances. Students who react defensively exhibit apathy, helplessness, procrastination, and cognitive disengagement for future learning to preserve their self-worth (Garcia & Pintrich, 1994). Students who respond adaptively adjust their self-regulatory behaviors that might include modifying their motivational beliefs and task analyses.

Self-reflections return learners to the forethought phase, thus forming the recursive loop in the self-regulation cycle. Students who are self-efficacious about their self-regulatory capabilities are likely to persist even when they form negative evaluations (Schunk, 2012). These students may attribute their progress to strategy use and effort and make adjustments in the forethought phase as they plan for subsequent learning.

The development of self-regulatory competence explains how self-efficacy becomes a motivational force behind self-regulated learning. Schunk and Zimmerman's (1997) four-level model includes observation, emulation, self-control, and self-regulation. Initially, social models such as teachers and peers serve as important sources of self-regulatory behaviors and self-efficacy. At the *observation* level, students observe models perform actions and learn many self-regulated learning processes such as strategic planning, self-monitoring, and performance adaptations (Zimmerman, 2000). Students may observe models receive rewards such as praise and good grades. These observations serve as vicarious sources of self-efficacy information.

At the *emulation* level, students practice the behaviors previously demonstrated by the model with assistance from the model as needed (Zimmerman, 2000). Students receive reinforcement from the model and from their sensory and motoric feedback. Students' self-efficacy is strengthened by the model's feedback, along with their perceptions of their increasing capabilities to apply self-regulatory processes needed to complete a task.

In these first two levels, learners derive information about their self-efficacy primarily from external (social) sources (e.g., vicarious experiences, social persuasions). At the third level of *self-control*, students begin to experience self-efficacy from within (Schunk & Zimmerman, 1997). Students have internalized what they previously observed and emulated; however, they are still using the representational patterns of the model to perform behaviors. During this level, students begin to experience self-efficacy as they reflect on their improved capability to match their work against the standards displayed by the model.

At the *self-regulation* level, learners can systematically adapt their performance to different environmental and personal conditions and are motivated by their self-efficacy beliefs (Zimmerman, 2000). They now are capable of initiating the use of strategies, making behavioral adjustments based on situational needs, and evaluating their performances knowing that they can competently make changes as needed. As students engage in the three cyclical phases of self-regulated learning, they strengthen their sense of self-efficacy.

Teacher Self-Efficacy

Teacher (or *instructional*) *self-efficacy* refers to personal beliefs about one's capabilities to help students learn (Tschannen-Moran, Woolfolk Hoy, & Hoy, 1998; Woolfolk Hoy, Hoy, & Davis, 2009). Self-efficacy should influence teachers' activities, effort, and persistence. Teachers with low self-efficacy may avoid planning activities they believe exceed their capabilities, not persist with students having difficulties, expend little effort to find materials, and not reteach content in ways students might better understand (Ashton & Webb, 1986). Teachers with high self-efficacy are more likely to develop challenging activities, help students succeed, and persist with students who have trouble learning. These teachers' behaviors enhance student learning and validate the teachers' sense of self-efficacy for helping students learn.

Ashton and Webb (1986) found that teachers with higher self-efficacy were likely to have a positive classroom environment (e.g., less student anxiety and teacher criticism), support students' ideas, and meet the learning needs of all students. High teacher self-efficacy is positively associated with teachers' use of praise, individual attention, and monitoring students' learning, as well as with higher student achievement.

Collective teacher self-efficacy represents teachers' beliefs that their capabilities as a group can enhance students' learning (Henson, 2002). Teachers develop collective self-efficacy when they work collaboratively to achieve common goals (performance accomplishments), learn from one another and have mentors who serve as role models (vicarious experiences), receive encouragement and support from administrators (forms of social persuasion), and work together to cope with difficulties and alleviate stress (physiological indexes). As collective self-efficacy is strengthened, teachers remain motivated to collaborate to improve students' learning. Collective self-efficacy positively predicts teachers' job satisfaction (Caprara, Barbaranelli, Borgogni, & Steca, 2003).

SELF-EFFICACY ASSESSMENT AND ISSUES

The earliest self-efficacy studies were conducted in clinical settings (Bandura, 1977). Since then, researchers have applied self-efficacy in diverse contexts, which has necessitated changes in forms of assessment. The ways that self-efficacy has been assessed have raised conceptual and methodological issues.

Microanalytic Methodology

Typical of the early studies is the project by Bandura, Adams, and Beyer (1977), who administered a self-efficacy and a behavioral test to adults with snake phobias. The test items consisted of progressively more threatening encounters with a snake (e.g., touch it, allow it to sit in one's lap). For the self-efficacy assessment, participants designated which tasks they felt they could perform and rated how sure they were that they could perform the tasks they felt they could perform. To measure generality, participants rated the same tasks with a type of snake different from the type used on the test. This is a microanalytic research methodology; self-efficacy and skill were assessed at the level of specific tasks. Participants were not asked for a general rating of how well they felt they could cope with snakes. The microanalytic methodology involves obtaining fine-grained measures of students' feelings, thoughts, and actions (DiBenedetto & Zimmerman, 2010). Students are assessed individually, the questions are context specific, and the assessment takes place while students are learning (Cleary, 2012).

Early educational studies used a similar methodology. Schunk (1981) gave children with low mathematical skills self-efficacy and skill tests. For self-efficacy, children were shown pairs of long-division problems; the two problems within each pair were comparable in form and difficulty. For each pair, they judged how certain they were that they could solve problems of that type. For the skill test, children attempted to solve problems that corresponded in form and difficulty to those on the self-efficacy test.

Researchers subsequently have applied the microanalytic methodology in various ways. Cleary and Zimmerman (2001) examined differences between male expert, nonexpert, and novice high school basketball players. Athletes rated their self-efficacy for making two consecutive free throws. Measures of goal setting, strategy choice, and attributions also were obtained. In the forethought phase, experts set more-specific free-throw goals and used more-specific strategies than the participants in the other two groups. Experts had higher self-efficacy for making the free throws than did nonexperts and novices. During self-reflection phase, the experts more often attributed their performances to specific techniques than did the nonexperts and novices.

Kitsantas and Zimmerman (2002) classified college women as expert, nonexpert, or novice volleyball players. The microanalytic assessment obtained measures of several processes related to the overhand serve within the forethought, performance, and self-reflection phases of self-regulated learning. Findings supported the hypothesis that, compared with the other participants, experts engaged in more self-regulated processes, felt more efficacious, were more intrinsically motivated, and had a greater sense of perceived instrumentality or agency regarding overhand serving. These findings support the positive psychology focus on competency and resilience (Clonan, Chafouleas, McDougal, & Rieley-Tillman, 2004).

DiBenedetto and Zimmerman (2010) worked with high school juniors who were high-achieving, average-achieving, or low-achieving science students based on their previous grades. Students were given a passage on tornadoes to read and study. Upon completion of studying, students were tested on the passage. One test question asked students to draw and label the three phases of tornado development. Since there were no images in the text, this question required that students comprehend the text and extrapolate from it.

The microanalytic questions were posed to the participants prior to reading and studying the passage, while reading and studying, and upon completion of the tornado test. Students also were timed on how long they spent studying. During the forethought phase, students were asked questions about their task analysis (goal setting, strategic planning) and their motivational beliefs (self-efficacy, intrinsic interest, outcome expectations). During the performance phase, students were asked questions about their self-control (strategies used for reading and studying) and their self-observations. The self-reflection phase occurred upon completion of the test. Students were asked about their self-judgments (self-evaluations, causal attributions) and their reactions to their performances (satisfaction, adaptive/defensive responses).

The results yielded positive relations between students' level of achievement and their self-regulation, study time, and science performance. High achievers engaged in more strategic planning in the forethought phase, used more strategies and were more meta-cognitively aware during the performance phase, and scored significantly better than the average and low achievers on all processes during the self-reflection phase. High achievers more often attributed their performances to strategy use and effort rather than luck and ability, and they spent significantly more time studying than students in the low achieving group. This study demonstrates how the microanalytic methodology can provide insight into students' beliefs, thinking, behavior, and reflections during academic learning, which can help educators target the areas where students need help and nurture their stronger areas.

Generality of Self-Efficacy

Since Bandura's (1977) initial formulation of self-efficacy, researchers have moved beyond his definition of self-efficacy as a domain-specific variable and assessed self-efficacy at more-general levels with items such as "How well can you get teachers to help you when you get stuck on school work?" and "How well can you study when there are other interesting things to do?" (Schunk & Pajares, 2009). To arrive at these types of judgments, students must integrate their perceptions across different situations (e.g., mathematics, science, social studies).

There is some research evidence for a generalized sense of self-efficacy (Smith, 1989). Certain educational conditions might foster it. School curricula are structured for positive transfer; for example, learning how to divide requires knowing how to estimate, subtract, and multiply. Students who perform well in mathematics might approach division with higher self-efficacy for learning than those who have encountered difficulties.

Even in the absence of specific curricula structure, generalization also might occur when students believe that the new learning will require skills that they previously mastered. For example, writing a research paper requires identifying a topic, conducting a literature review, synthesizing and organizing information, and drawing conclusions. Students likely have used these skills to write papers in English. Students who feel competent in the requisite skills may have higher self-efficacy for writing a research paper than those who question their capabilities.

Evidence for generality does not refute the subject specificity of self-efficacy, but it is important to determine how students weigh and combine efficacy information to arrive at generalized judgments. Developmental factors may be an issue, because we should expect that with development, students should be better able to assess their capabilities in component areas and determine the types of skills needed to succeed.

Calibration

Another assessment issue involves *calibration*, or how well self-efficacy relates to actual performance on the corresponding tasks (Schunk & Usher, 2011). People are well calibrated—and thus their self-efficacy accurately predicts their performances—when they judge that they are capable of performing a task and then perform it or when they judge that they are incapable of performing it and cannot perform it. Conversely, they are poorly calibrated when they judge that they are capable of performing a task but do not perform it or when they judge that they are incapable of performing a task but then perform it.

Calibration is educationally important. When students overestimate their capabilities and then perform poorly, they may lose their sense of hope for learning and not be motivated to learn. Bandura (1997) contended that self-efficacy that slightly exceeds what one can do is desirable because such overestimation can raise effort and persistence, but continual overestimation can lead to many failures with resulting decreases in students' motivation and learning.

Overestimation can result when students do not fully understand the demands of the task. Greater task experience informs students of the skills needed to succeed. In the DiBenedetto and Zimmerman (2010) study, high-achieving students were better calibrated (more accurate) in their beliefs about their capabilities to learn and perform well on the science test than the average and low achievers. This finding suggests that students who overestimate their capabilities might not study sufficiently for an exam because they feel overconfident, whereas high achievers might study for a longer time because of their better estimates of their capabilities.

Calibration also can be affected by instructional and social factors (Schunk & Pajares, 2009). Although instructional practices that provide information about skills required for the task can increase calibration (Schunk, 1981), such practices also can lower it. Students placed in low-ability groups from which they cannot move may feel demoralized and perform poorly, even though they feel efficacious about learning. Teachers who indiscriminately encourage students (e.g., "Come on, I know you can do this") without ensuring that they learn skills might produce highly efficacious students who lack the skills to succeed. The social cultures of schools also may affect calibration (Schunk & Pajares, 2009). Students may perform less than their best—and lower than their self-efficacy would predict—because they do not want to become socially isolated as a result of their peers viewing them as being overly intelligent. Providing students with mastery learning opportunities in which they are evaluated based on their own performances rather than against classroom norms may help them develop higher self-efficacy and satisfaction with their achievements (Zimmerman & DiBenedetto, 2008).

DIVERSITY AND DEVELOPMENTAL CONSIDERATIONS

Self-efficacy does not arise automatically or by chance. The development of self-efficacy begins in infancy. The first influences occur within the family. Like other aspects of human development, self-efficacy is affected by the family's capital. *Capital* includes resources and assets (Bradley & Corwyn, 2002); for example, financial and material resources (e.g., income, assets), human resources (e.g., education levels of parents), and social resources (e.g., those obtained through social networks and connections). Children are motivated to learn when the home is rich in activities and materials that arouse their curiosity and offer challenges. Better-educated parents and those with wide social connections are apt to emphasize education and enroll children in schools and camps that foster their self-efficacy and learning.

Home influences that help children learn to interact effectively with others and their environments build self-efficacy (Schunk & Pajares, 2009). Parents can accelerate their children's academic development by providing a warm, responsive, and supportive home environment, encouraging exploration and curiosity, and providing play and learning materials. Given that mastery experiences are the strongest source of self-efficacy information, parents who facilitate their children experiencing mastery are more apt to develop efficacious youngsters. Family members also are important models. Those who model ways to cope with difficulties, persistence, and effort strengthen their children's self-efficacy. Family members also provide persuasive information. Parents who encourage their children to try different activities and support and encourage their efforts help to develop children who feel more efficacious in meeting challenges.

As children develop, peers become increasingly more important influences on self-efficacy (Schunk & Pajares, 2009). Parents who steer their children toward efficacious peers provide opportunities for vicarious increases in self-efficacy. When children observe similar peers succeed at a task, they are likely to feel efficacious about also succeeding and motivated to try the task.

Additional influence occurs through *peer networks*, or large groups of peers with whom students associate. Students in networks tend to be similar in many ways, and similarity increases the chances of influence by models (Schunk, 2012). Networks affect students' opportunities for social interactions and observations of others, as well as their access to activities.

Peer groups promote socialization. Changes in children's motivation across the school year are predicted well by their peer group membership at the start of the year (Kindermann, McCollam, & Gibson, 1996). Children part of highly motivated groups change positively; those in less motivated groups change negatively. Peer group academic socialization can affect the individual student's and the group's collective self-efficacy (Schunk & Pajares, 2009).

Research also shows that schooling influences the development of self-efficacy. Students' self-efficacy and motivation often decline as they advance in school, which has been attributed to factors such as greater competition, more norm-referenced grading, less teacher attention to individual student progress, and problems associated with school and grade-level transitions (Wigfield & Eccles, 2002). These practices can retard self-efficacy development, especially among students who are poorly prepared to deal effectively with academic challenges.

It is not uncommon for children to report overconfidence about accomplishing difficult tasks (Schunk & Pajares, 2009), even after they are given performance feedback indicating that they performed poorly. Young children may be poorly calibrated because they lack task familiarity and do not fully understand what is required to perform a task successfully. Children may be unduly swayed by task features and decide that they can or cannot perform the task. In subtraction, for example, children may judge longer problems as more difficult than shorter ones, even when the former involve no regrouping. As children's ability to focus on multiple task features develops, they can make more realistic self-efficacy appraisals. Thus, as they gain experience, their self-efficacy actually might decline somewhat but their calibration will improve. As they become more skillful, their self-efficacy rises to high but realistic levels. DiBenedetto and Bembenutty (2012) found that college students' self-efficacy decreased over the course of a semester but became better aligned with final course grades than students' initial self-efficacy beliefs.

Although early self-efficacy research was conducted mostly with students in Western cultures, there has been a proliferation of research across many cultures to the point where today we understand its cross-cultural operation better. Although self-efficacy seems to be an important variable affecting motivation and achievement across cultures, researchers have identified some important differences.

Klassen (2004b) reviewed self-efficacy studies from a cross-cultural perspective and found that self-efficacy tended to be lower for students from non–Western cultures (e.g., Asian and Asian-immigrant students) than for students from Western cultures (e.g., Western Europe, Canada, United States). In some cases, the more modest self-efficacy beliefs of the non–Western students predicted academic outcomes better (i.e., better calibration) than the higher self-efficacy of the Western students. Higher self-efficacy beliefs did not necessarily translate into higher performances.

Cultural dimensions such as individualism and collectivism influence the relation between self-efficacy and academic achievement. According to Kim and Park (2006), the existing psychological and educational theories that emphasize individualistic values (e.g., ability, self-efficacy, intrinsic interest) cannot explain the high achievement of East Asian students. Instead, the Confucian-based socialization practices that promote close parent–child relationships are responsible for high levels of self-regulatory, relational, and social efficacy. Self-regulatory efficacy is a powerful predictor of students' academic performances. In these cultures, relational efficacy (i.e., perceived capabilities for successful familial and social relations) has a powerful influence on students' academic performance. The lower levels of self-efficacy found in some collectivist groups do not always signify lower subsequent performance but instead reflect different conceptualizations of the self. Self-efficacy may be more other-oriented in some non–Western cultures than in Western cultures (Klassen, 2004a).

EDUCATIONAL APPLICATIONS

There are several implications of self-efficacy theory and research for educational practitioners that are consistent with the focus of positive psychology on happiness and thriving. First, we reiterate Pajares's (2009) recommendation, as expressed in the earlier edition of this handbook, that teachers take seriously their responsibility to nurture the academic self-efficacy of their students. Using the four sources of self-efficacy information, teachers can help students identify their strongest qualities and provide struggling students with a sense of hope and optimism that promotes self-efficacy and fosters well-being.

Of the four sources, mastery experiences are the most powerful. The implication is that students need to be taught skills and given opportunities to practice and refine them. As students observe their learning progress, their self-efficacy for continued learning is strengthened. Teachers also can provide vicarious experiences by pointing out how other similar students have mastered skills, as well as persuasive information by encouraging students. Such encouragement must be realistic; telling students "You can do this" when they lack the skills to succeed will prove demoralizing and lower their self-efficacy. Teachers can use physiological indicators, such as when they tell students that they are reacting in a less-stressful way to completing their assignments.

Teachers may be tempted to assist students so that they can be successful. Assistance often is necessary in the early stages of learning. But success gained with much help does not build strong self-efficacy because students are likely to attribute their success to the help they have received. Allowing students to succeed on their own exerts stronger effects on self-efficacy.

Another suggestion is to individualize instruction as much as possible. Students do not learn in the same way or at the same rate. When assignments are not individualized, some students will succeed but others will have difficulty. When those in the latter group socially compare their performances to those of students who have done well, they are apt to doubt their capabilities for learning. Individualizing instruction minimizes opportunities for social comparisons. Teachers can point out to individual students the progress they have made learning (e.g., "See how much better you're doing on these now?"), and the perception of progress by learners helps to build self-efficacy.

We also recommend that students be encouraged to evaluate their learning. Students are not used to assessing their learning; rather, they rely on teachers to provide these assessments. But teachers cannot provide every student progress feedback regularly. Learners can be taught to gauge their own progress. In mathematics, for example, teachers might show students different types of problems and ask them to judge their learning progress on a scale ranging from 1—little progress—to 10—high progress. Students' assessments then can be used to determine where they need further study and which areas they seem to have mastered.

A desirable goal in education is for learners to feel a sense of realistic optimism. Self-efficacy judgments that slightly exceed what they can do can motivate students to expend effort and persist to improve (Bandura, 1997). It is not desirable for learners to have unrealistically high expectations (i.e., no amount of effort and persistence will produce learning) or those that are unrealistically low (i.e., expectations far lower than what students are capable of accomplishing). Teachers need to take into account the potential effects of instructional conditions not only on students' learning but also on their self-efficacy. Helping to produce realistically optimistic learners will improve students' motivation and learning as well as classrooms that are more enjoyable to learn in.

REFERENCES

Ashton, P. T., & Webb, R. B. (1986). *Making a difference: Teachers' sense of efficacy and student achievement.* New York, NY: Longman.

Bandura, A. (1977). Self-efficacy: Toward a unifying theory of behavioral change. *Psychological Review, 84,* 191–215. doi:10.1037/0033-295X.84.2.191

Bandura, A. (1986). *Social foundations of thought and action: A social cognitive theory.* Englewood Cliffs, NJ: Prentice Hall.

Bandura, A. (1997). *Self-efficacy: The exercise of control.* New York, NY: Freeman.

Bandura, A., Adams, N. E., & Beyer, J. (1977). Cognitive processes mediating behavioral change. *Journal of Personality and Social Psychology, 35,* 125–139. doi:10.1037/0022-3514.35.3.125

Bradley, R. H., & Corwyn, R. F. (2002). Socioeconomic status and child development. *Annual Review of Psychology, 53,* 371–399. doi:10.1146/annurev.psych.53.100901.135233

Caprara, G. V., Barbaranelli, C., Borgogni, L., & Steca, P. (2003). Efficacy beliefs as determinants of teachers' job satisfaction. *Journal of Educational Psychology, 95,* 821–832. doi:10.1037/0022-0663.95.4.821

Cleary, T. (2012). Emergence of self-regulated learning microanalysis: Historical overview, essential features, and implications for research and practice. In B. J. Zimmerman & D. H. Schunk (Eds.), *Handbook of self-regulation of learning and performance* (pp. 329–345). New York, NY: Routledge.

Cleary, T., & Zimmerman, B. J. (2001). Self-regulation differences during athletic practice by experts, non-experts, and novices. *Journal of Applied Sport Psychology, 13,* 185–206. doi:10.1080/104132001753149883

Clonan, S. M., Chafouleas, S. M., McDougal, J. L., & Rieley-Tillman, T. C. (2004). Positive psychology goes to school: Are we there yet? *Psychology in the Schools, 41,* 101–110. doi:10.1002/pits.10142

DiBenedetto, M. K., & Bembenutty, H. (2012). Within the pipeline: Self-regulated learning, self-efficacy, and socialization among college students in science courses. *Learning and Individual Differences,* http://dx.doi.org/10.1016/j.lindif.2012.09.015

DiBenedetto, M. K., & Zimmerman, B. J. (2010). Differences in self-regulatory processes among students studying science: A microanalytic investigation. *International Journal of Educational and Psychological Assessment, 5,* 2–24.

Garcia, T., & Pintrich, P. R. (1994). Regulating motivation and cognition in the classroom: The role of self-schemas and self-regulatory strategies. In D. H. Schunk & B. J. Zimmerman (Eds.), *Self-regulation of learning and performance: Issues and educational applications* (pp. 127–153). Hillsdale, NJ: Erlbaum.

Henson, R. K. (2002). From adolescent angst to adulthood: Substantive implications and measurement dilemmas in the development of teacher efficacy research. *Educational Psychologist, 37,* 127–150. doi:10.1207/S15326985EP3703_1

Kim, U., & Park, Y. S. (2006). Factors influencing academic achievement in collectivist societies: The role of self-, relational, and social efficacy. In F. Pajares & T. Urdan (Eds.), *Self-efficacy beliefs of adolescents* (pp. 267–286). Greenwich, CT: Information Age.

Kindermann, T. A., McCollam, T. L., & Gibson, E., Jr. (1996). Peer networks and students' classroom engagement during childhood and adolescence. In J. Juvonen & K. R. Wentzel (Eds.), *Social motivation: Understanding children's school adjustment* (pp. 279–312). Cambridge, UK: Cambridge University Press.

Kitsantas, A., & Zimmerman, B. J. (2002). Comparing self-regulatory processes among novice, non-expert, and expert volleyball players: A microanalytic study. *Journal of Applied Sport Psychology, 14,* 91–105. doi:10.1080/10413200252907761

Klassen, R. M. (2004a). A cross-cultural investigation of the efficacy beliefs of south Asian immigrant and Anglo Canadian nonimmigrant early adolescents. *Journal of Educational Psychology, 96,* 731–742. doi:10.1037/0022-0663.96.4.731

Klassen, R. M. (2004b). Optimism and realism: A review of self-efficacy from a cross-cultural perspective. *International Journal of Psychology, 39,* 205–230. doi:10.1080/00207590344000330

Kristjánsson, K. (2012). Positive psychology and positive education: Old wine in new bottles? *Educational Psychologist, 47,* 86–105. doi:10.1080/00461520.2011.610678

Licht, B. G., & Kistner, J. A. (1986). Motivational problems of learning-disabled children: Individual differences and their implications for treatment. In J. K. Torgesen & B. W. L. Wong (Eds.), *Psychological and educational perspectives on learning disabilities* (pp. 225–255). Orlando, FL: Academic Press.

Multon, K. D., Brown, S. D., & Lent, R. W. (1991). Relation of self-efficacy beliefs to academic outcomes: A meta-analytic investigation. *Journal of Counseling Psychology, 38,* 30–38. doi.apa.org/journals/cou/38/1/30.pdf

Pajares, F. (1996). Self-efficacy beliefs in achievement settings. *Review of Educational Research, 66,* 543–578.

Pajares, F. (2008). Motivational role of self-efficacy beliefs in self-regulated learning. In D. H. Schunk & B. J. Zimmerman (Eds.), *Motivation and self-regulated learning: Theory, research and applications* (pp. 111–139). New York, NY: Taylor & Francis.

Pajares, F. (2009). Toward a positive psychology of academic motivation: The role of self-efficacy beliefs. In R. Gilman, E. S. Huebner, & M. J. Furlong (Eds.), *Handbook of positive psychology in schools* (pp. 149–160). New York, NY: Routledge.

Pajares, F., & Kranzler, J. (1995). Self-efficacy beliefs and general mental ability in mathematical problem-solving. *Contemporary Educational Psychology, 20,* 426–443. http://dx.doi.org/10.1006/ceps.1995.1029

Pajares, F., & Urdan, T. (Eds.). (2006). *Self-efficacy beliefs of adolescents.* Greenwich, CT: Information Age.

Relich, J. D., Debus, R. L., & Walker, R. (1986). The mediating role of attribution and self-efficacy variables for treatment effects on achievement outcomes. *Contemporary Educational Psychology, 11,* 195–216. http://dx.doi.org/10.1016/0361-476X(86)90017-2

Schunk, D. H. (1981). Modeling and attributional effects on children's achievement: A self-efficacy analysis. *Journal of Educational Psychology, 73,* 93–105. doi.apa.org/journals/edu/73/1/93.pdf

Schunk, D. H. (1995). Self-efficacy and education and instruction. In J. E. Maddux (Ed.), *Self-efficacy, adaptation, and adjustment: Theory, research, and application* (pp. 281–303). New York, NY: Plenum.

Schunk, D. H. (2012). Social cognitive theory. In K. R. Harris, S. Graham, & T. Urdan (Eds.), *APA educational psychology handbook: Vol. 1. Theories, constructs, and critical issues* (pp. 101–123). Washington, DC: American Psychological Association.

Schunk, D. H., & Ertmer, P. A. (2000). Self-regulation and academic learning: Self-efficacy enhancing interventions. In M. Boekaerts, P. R. Pintrich, & M. Zeidner (Eds.), *Handbook of self-regulation* (pp. 631–649). San Diego, CA: Academic Press.

Schunk, D. H., & Gunn, T. P. (1986). Self-efficacy and skill development: Influence of task strategies and attributions. *Journal of Educational Research, 79,* 238–244.

Schunk, D. H., & Pajares, F. (2009). Self-efficacy theory. In K. R. Wentzel & A. Wigfield (Eds.), *Handbook of motivation at school* (pp. 35–53). New York, NY: Routledge.

Schunk, D. H., & Usher, E. L. (2011). Assessing self-efficacy for self-regulated learning. In B. J. Zimmerman & D. H. Schunk (Eds.), *Handbook of self-regulation of learning and performance* (pp. 282–297). New York, NY: Routledge.

Schunk, D. H., & Zimmerman, B. J. (1997). Social origins of self-regulatory competence. *Educational Psychologist, 32,* 195–208. doi:10.1207/s15326985ep3204_1

Seligman, M. E. P., & Csikszentmihalyi, M. (2000). Positive psychology: An introduction. *American Psychologist, 55,* 5–14. doi:10.1037/0003-066X.55.1.5

Smith, R. E. (1989). Effects of coping skills training on generalized self-efficacy and locus of control. *Journal of Personality and Social Psychology, 56,* 228–233. doi:10.1037/0022-3514.56.2.228

Tschannen-Moran, M., Woolfolk Hoy, A., & Hoy, W. K. (1998). Teacher efficacy: Its meaning and measure. *Review of Educational Research, 68,* 202–248.

Weiner, B. (1985). An attributional theory of achievement motivation and emotion. *Psychological Review, 12,* 1–14.

Wigfield, A., & Eccles, J.S. (2002). The development of competence beliefs, expectancies for success, and achievement values from childhood through adolescence. In A. Wigfield & J.S. Eccles (Eds.), *Development of achievement motivation* (pp. 91–120). San Diego, CA: Academic Press.

Wigfield, A., Tonks, S., & Eccles, J.S. (2004). Expectancy value theory in cross-cultural perspective. In D.M. McInerney & S. Van Etten (Eds.), *Big theories revisited* (pp. 165–198). Greenwich, CT: Information Age.

Woolfolk Hoy, A., Hoy, W.K., & Davis, H.A. (2009). Teachers' self-efficacy beliefs. In K.R. Wentzel & A. Wigfield (Eds.), *Handbook of motivation at school* (pp. 627–653). New York, NY: Routledge.

Zimmerman, B.J. (2000). Attaining self-regulation: A social cognitive perspective. In M. Boekaerts, P.R. Pintrich, & M. Zeidner (Eds.), *Handbook of self-regulation* (pp.13–39). San Diego, CA: Academic Press.

Zimmerman, B.J. (2002). Becoming a self-regulated learner: An overview. *Theory Into Practice, 41,* 64–70.

Zimmerman, B.J., & Bandura, A. (1994). Impact of self-regulatory influences on writing course achievement. *American Educational Research Journal, 31,* 845–862.

Zimmerman, B.J., & DiBenedetto, M.K. (2008). Mastery learning and assessment: Implications for students and teachers in an era of high-stakes testing. *Psychology in the Schools, 45,* 206–216.

CHAPTER SUMMARY: SELF-EFFICACY

- The construct of self-efficacy reflects positive psychology's focus on well-being.
- Theory and research support the idea that self-efficacy influences learning, motivation, and self-regulation.
- From instructional and social/environmental sources, students acquire information that affects their self-efficacy, and in turn, self-efficacy influences various achievement behaviors.
- Teachers should determine how various facets of instruction may affect learning, motivation, and self-efficacy.
- By helping to produce learners with a sense of realistic optimism, teachers can help ensure that students will be successful, find learning enjoyable, and be motivated to continue learning outside of school.

SUGGESTED READINGS: SELF-EFFICACY

Bandura, A. (1977). Self-efficacy: Toward a unifying theory of behavioral change. *Psychological Review, 84,* 191–215.

The initial publication on self-efficacy theory, which also describes early clinical research.

DiBenedetto, M.K., & Zimmerman, B.J. (2010). Differences in self-regulatory processes among students studying science: A microanalytic investigation. *International Journal of Educational and Psychological Assessment, 5,* 2–24.

Provides an excellent example of the microanalytic methodology.

Klassen, R.M. (2004). Optimism and realism: A review of self-efficacy from a cross-cultural perspective. *International Journal of Psychology, 39,* 205–230.

Gives a thorough overview of self-efficacy research conducted in international settings.

Pajares, F. (2009). Toward a positive psychology of academic motivation: The role of self-efficacy beliefs. In R. Gilman, E.S. Huebner, & M.J. Furlong (Eds.), *Handbook of positive psychology in schools* (pp. 149–160). New York, NY: Routledge.

The chapter in the previous edition on which the current chapter is based.

Schunk, D.H. (2012). Social cognitive theory. In K.R. Harris, S. Graham, & T. Urdan (Eds.), *APA educational psychology handbook: Vol. 1. Theories, constructs, and critical issues* (pp. 101–123). Washington, DC: American Psychological Association.

Provides a comprehensive overview of social cognitive theory.

9

PROMOTING POSITIVE MOTIVATIONAL GOALS FOR STUDENTS

Lynley H. Anderman and Stephanie Levitt, Department of Educational Studies, College of Education and Human Ecology, The Ohio State University, Columbus, Ohio, USA

THEORY BASE AND DEFINITIONS

Public conversation and formal educational policy reveal clear conflicts in beliefs about the goals of education and schooling. The prevalence of high-stakes testing programs, demands for teacher accountability, and ongoing concern about students' college readiness send a strong message to many students that the main purpose of education is performing well on examinations (Nichols & Berliner, 2006). The idea that the purpose of schooling is developing knowledge and promoting learning often gets lost behind the strong emphasis on assessment. This focus on differing purposes and goals for education lies at the heart of goal orientation theory.

Goal orientation theory (also referred to as goal theory or achievement goal theory) is a social-cognitive theory of academic motivation that focuses on individuals' perceptions of the meanings and purposes of achievement. Note that this theoretical approach is distinct from other, more behavioral approaches that use the term "goals" to refer to learning or behavioral objectives (e.g., Locke & Latham, 1990). In goal orientation theory, "goals" refer to a broad understanding of the reasons for striving and achieving, the overall purposes of achievement behavior, and the ways in which success is defined. In goal orientation theory, the emphasis is not on *what* a student is trying to achieve but *why* the student is trying to achieve (Ames & Archer, 1988; Anderman & Wolters, 2006). That is, the focus is not on differences in the amount of students' motivation (this student is more motivated than that one) but on qualitative differences in the nature of their motivation (Ames, 1987, 1992; Dweck, 1986; Nicholls, 1989).

Although debate continues in the field, most research on goal orientations has focused on two major categories of beliefs, each of which has been further subdivided into subtypes. A major distinction is between focusing on learning, improvement, and mastering content contrasted with focusing on demonstrating competence in relation to an externally defined standard or in relation to the performance of others. These orientations are referred to as a *mastery goal orientation* (also sometimes known as a learning goal or a task goal) and a *performance goal orientation* (also sometimes known as an ego goal or an ability goal), respectively. Each of these general orientations can manifest itself in terms of either an *approach* tendency (moving toward success) or an *avoidance* tendency (moving away from failure). Thus, a *mastery approach orientation* refers to students who view tasks as an opportunity to learn, progress, and master content—to **improve** their competence. A *mastery avoidance orientation* refers to students who focus on avoiding a lack of progress or understanding (Cury, Elliot, Da Fonseca, & Mollar, 2006; Elliot, 1999; Hulleman, Schrager, Bodmann, & Harackiewicz, 2010; Pintrich, 2000). In contrast, a *performance approach orientation* refers to students who view tasks as an opportunity to demonstrate their knowledge and skills—to **prove** their competence, as evidenced by external markers such as grades, awards, or position relative to their peers. Finally, a *performance avoidance orientation* refers to students who focus on avoiding the appearance of lack of ability, low grades, or poor relative performance (Elliot & Harackiewicz, 1996; Middleton & Midgley, 1997). These distinctions are summarized in Table 9.1.

A final distinction in goal orientation theory is that between individuals' beliefs about their own reasons for striving and achieving (as just described) and the goal orientations that are emphasized and communicated in various achievement-related social contexts. That is, classrooms and schools also can be oriented toward mastery and performance; at the contextual level, these orientations are referred to as *goal structures* (e.g., Meece, Anderman, & Anderman, 2006; Midgley, 2002; Urdan, 2004b). Thus, we can think about classes as emphasizing some combination of mastery approach, mastery avoidance, performance approach, and performance avoidance orientations. A central and important assumption of goal orientation theory is that the goal structures emphasized in a particular setting influence individual students' adoption of similar goal orientations for themselves (Kaplan, Middleton, Urdan, & Midgley, 2002). That is, students are more likely to become personally oriented toward mastery in contexts they perceive as emphasizing a mastery orientation. This assumption has been supported in a number of

Table 9.1 Major Categories of Achievement Goal Orientations

	Mastery Goal Orientation	Performance Goal Orientation
Approach Tendency	• Focus on learning, improvement, and gaining mastery • Success is defined in terms of progress and knowledge gain	• Focus on demonstrating competence and skill, appearance of ability • Success is defined in terms of grades, awards, and relative standing
Avoidance Tendency	• Focus on avoiding misunderstanding and declining competence • Success is defined in terms of maintaining skill and not being confused	• Focus is on avoiding the appearance of incompetence or lack of ability • Success is defined in terms of not failing on external measures, not being worse than others

empirical studies (e.g., Anderman & Midgley, 1997; Bong, 2008; Kim, Schallert, & Kim, 2010; Roeser, Midgley & Urdan, 1996; Urdan, 2004a; Wolters, 2004).

REVIEW OF KEY RESEARCH STUDIES

A great deal of empirical research has been conducted on students' goal orientations and classroom goal structures over more than 20 years. Much of that work has been conducted with school-aged populations and in regular school settings. There is some evidence that personal goal orientations may relate to educationally relevant outcomes differently at different levels of schooling; that is, patterns of findings with college-aged samples seem to differ from those with elementary and middle school samples (e.g., Harackiewicz, Barron, & Elliot, 1998; Midgley, Middleton, & Kaplan, 2001). In the discussion of major research findings that follows, we highlight those areas in which differences have been reported.

In comparison to developmental differences, relatively little research has reported differential patterns of findings based on either students' race and ethnicity or gender. Studies that have explicitly explored potential ethnic group differences have found considerable consistency with the general research body with samples of both African American (e.g., Kaplan & Maehr, 1999) and Hispanic students (Stevens, Hamman, & Olivarez, 2007).

Relations With Educational Outcomes

Academic Achievement, Motivation, and School-Related Affect

The most consistent findings related to goal orientations reveal positive associations between a mastery approach orientation and a range of desirable learning-related outcomes. When students adopt a mastery orientation, they are more likely to choose moderately challenging tasks (as opposed to those that are too easy or too difficult); use deeper cognitive processing strategies during learning tasks and self-regulate better (e.g., thinking about how newly learned material relates to prior knowledge); put forth effort and persist in the face of difficulty; and attribute any failures to lack of effort rather than lack of ability (for reviews, see E. Anderman & Maehr, 1994; Meece et al., 2006; Urdan, 1997).

One of the most intriguing findings in the goal orientation literature, however, is that mastery goals are seldom directly predictive of students' grades. Although a number of studies have examined the relations between mastery goals and grades (e.g., Shim, Ryan, & Anderson, 2008), many find no evidence of this relation (for reviews, see Anderman & Wolters, 2006; Meece et al., 2006). Given the established associations between mastery goals and improved perseverance and strategy use, this pattern is surprising. One possible explanation is that the assessment strategies regularly used to measure achievement in most educational settings do not match deep learning and engagement with the content. That is, being oriented toward mastery may improve learning in ways that current assessments do not detect (Grant & Dweck, 2003; Meece et al., 2006). An alternative explanation may be that mastery goals do not and should not be expected to have a direct effect on achievement but, instead, may influence grades indirectly. For example, in a longitudinal study examining the relation between mastery goals and learning about current events during adolescence, E. Anderman and Johnston (1998) found that students with a mastery orientation were more likely to seek their news outside of the school environment, which, in turn, predicted current events knowledge. Thus, being mastery oriented predicted a behavior (attending to news outside of the classroom) that subsequently contributed to acquired knowledge. This relation held up even when controlling for prior knowledge.

In terms of learning strategies, Lau and Lee (2008) found a strong relation between perceived classroom mastery goal structure and strategy use (i.e., making a plan to study before taking a test). Coutinho and Neuman (2008) also found that students who have a mastery-approach goal orientation tended to use deep processing (i.e., critical thinking) and also surface-processing (i.e., rote memorization) strategies, demonstrating that they may be able to select and make decisions about best ways to learn material. In contrast, Phan (2009) only found a link between mastery goal orientation and deep processing. Taken together, these studies suggest that students with a mastery goal orientation may be more likely to think critically about material or perhaps better able to determine how to learn material.

The adoption of mastery goals is also related to many other long-term beneficial educational outcomes. For example, in physical education classes, Halvari, Skjesol, and Bagøien (2011) found that a more positive mastery climate predicted positive outcomes such as competence, attendance, and positive attitude in adolescent students. The adoption of mastery goals is also related to future enrollment in courses, when coursework becomes optional. For example, Harackiewicz and her colleagues found that the adoption of mastery goals in introductory psychology courses was related to taking more psychology courses during the remainder of college and to choosing to major in psychology (Harackiewicz, Barron, Tauer, Carter, & Elliot, 2000).

Other research has linked mastery goal orientation to intrinsic motivation. Spinath and Steinmayr (2012) followed 48 11th-grade German students over a year and found that perceiving a mastery goal structure predicted positive change in students' intrinsic motivation. Similarly, Jagacinksi, Kumar, Boe, Lam, and Miller (2010) found a positive relation between mastery goals early in a semester and final interest in an introductory psychology college course. Sungur and Senler (2010) demonstrated a positive association between both kinds of approach goals (mastery and performance) and intrinsic motivation in elementary students (Grades 4–8). Additionally, Gehlbach (2006) examined student motivation in a social studies course for ninth- and tenth-grade students over an academic year, finding that when students had higher mastery goals, they also had higher levels of interest, among other positive outcomes (such as course satisfaction and knowledge of content). Finally, Roeser and colleagues (1996) reported an indirect effect of personal mastery goals on grades through an increase in academic self-efficacy, and Coutinho and Neuman (2008) found that mastery-approach goals predicted self-efficacy for college students. Therefore, students' perceptions of a mastery goal structure in their classes may prove to be a very important predictor in self-efficacy and intrinsic motivation, which may, by extension, impact achievement.

Finally, holding a mastery goal orientation has been linked to positive affect in the classroom. Huang (2011) completed a meta-analysis of 78 articles examining the associations between students' goal orientations and their emotions. He found that mastery goals were associated with strong, positive emotions and suggested that mastery goals can have a positive impact on psychological well-being for students. Several studies by Kaplan and colleagues also demonstrate relations between goal orientation and affect. Kaplan and Maehr (1999) found that holding a mastery goal orientation was positively associated with students' sense of well-being, whereas holding a performance goal orientation had a negative relation with feelings about school and sense of well-being. In a further study, Kaplan and Midgley (1999) demonstrated that such relations between goal orientations and school-related affect were mediated by students' coping strategies, with a mastery orientation being associated with more adaptive coping than a performance orientation. More research is needed examining associations between goal orientations and goal structures on one hand and students' affective outcomes on the other. The results to date, however, are consistent in finding that mastery goal emphases are associated with greater well-being among school-aged students than are performance goals.

In-School Behavior

Endorsing a mastery goal orientation has been linked to positive outcomes for all students but may be particularly helpful for students who are at risk of participating in maladaptive behaviors. For example, Agbuga, Xiang, and McBride (2010) examined disruptive behaviors in a program that took place after school. Using a sample of 158 students in Grades 3 through 6, these researchers found that students who had a mastery goal orientation were less likely to participate in disruptive behaviors than were their peers. Building on previous work that linked goal orientation to disruptive behavior (Kaplan & Maehr, 1999), Kaplan and colleagues (2002) found that students' endorsement of a personal mastery goal orientation was associated with lower levels of self-reported disruptive behavior in class; in contrast, both performance-approach and performance-avoidance goal orientations were associated with higher levels of disruptive behavior. Furthermore, these researchers found differences in levels of disruptive behavior between different classes. Students' perceptions of a mastery goal structure in class, when averaged at the classroom level, were associated with lower levels of disruptive behavior, whereas the averaged perception of a classroom climate that emphasized a performance approach structure was associated with higher levels of disruptive behavior. One possible explanation for this pattern of findings is provided by Kaplan and Midgley (1999), discussed earlier, who found that early adolescent students' perceptions of classroom goal structures were associated longitudinally with differential patterns of academic coping strategies and school-related affect. Perceptions of a mastery goal structure were predictive of adaptive coping strategies and positive affect, whereas perceptions of a performance goal structure were associated with maladaptive coping and negative affect. Such patterns of student affect may then manifest in disruptive behaviors.

A mastery goal orientation is also associated with students' persistence with classroom tasks. Sideridis and Kaplan (2011) demonstrated that, when confronted with experiences of failure, college students who had a mastery orientation persisted longer compared to students with a performance-approach or -avoid orientation. Additionally, Lau and Nie (2008) found that both personal mastery orientation and perceptions of a classroom mastery structure had negative relationships with students' avoidance coping and effort withdrawal—that is, with being less likely to avoid doing work and less likely to give up when the work presented was perceived as either boring or difficult. Therefore, a mastery goal structure in classes may be important not only to prevent maladaptive behaviors but also to encourage persistence in the face of failure or challenge.

Self-Handicapping

The study of academic self-handicapping explores student behaviors that, at least superficially, are difficult to explain. In the face of important academic tasks or assessment situations, some students engage in apparently self-defeating behaviors, such as socializing instead of completing an important project or failing to get sufficient sleep the night before an important test. Self-handicapping is defined as a proactive strategy that occurs before an achievement event, which provides the basis for a face-saving explanation for later poor performance (Urdan & Midgley, 2001). That is, if students are concerned about their ability to perform well, self-handicapping creates a plausible explanation for their poor outcome without implying that they lack academic ability. Unfortunately, the very behaviors that are designed to protect students' sense of self-worth in the short term will have detrimental effects on their long-term learning and achievement.

Researchers exploring the reasons for students' self-handicapping behaviors have found consistently that endorsing performance-avoidance goals is significantly associated with the use of self-handicapping (e.g., Elliot & Church, 2003; Midgley & Urdan, 1995; Urdan, 2004a; Urdan, Midgley, & Anderman, 1998). That is, when students are focused on avoiding failure or avoiding negative judgments of their ability ("looking dumb"), they are more likely to engage in these self-defeating strategies. The focus on how their performance is going to be judged can lead them to engage in behaviors that will actually hurt that performance. In contrast, endorsing mastery goals and perceiving a mastery goal structure in classes is associated with lower levels of self-handicapping (Midgley & Urdan, 2001; Pintrich, 2000b). When students are focused on learning and progress, they are less likely to engage in behaviors that will ultimately detract from that outcome.

Cheating and Academic Dishonesty

Academic cheating and plagiarism represent another set of undesirable classroom behaviors that have been found to be associated with students' goal orientations. As with self-handicapping, students who are mastery goal oriented have few reasons to engage in cheating behaviors. The focus on mastering tasks and understanding content makes dishonest behaviors self-defeating (Anderman, Griesinger, & Westerfield, 1998). In contrast, students may view cheating as a viable alternative strategy to studying when they focus on demonstrating their ability or, particularly, avoiding the appearance of lack of ability. These patterns of findings have been supported in empirical research. Students with a mastery goal orientation are less likely than their peers to cheat, even after other known predictors of cheating are taken into account. This is true for cheating on academic assignments and examinations, as well as for plagiarism in written assignments (Stephens & Gehlbach, 2007). Similarly, Anderman and Midgley (2004) found that self-reported cheating increased across the transition from middle school to high school if students moved from a classroom that emphasized mastery goals to one with less emphasis on mastery goals. Anderman, Cupp, and Lane (2010) also found that for students who reported extensive involvement in cheating, the perception of a classroom mastery goal structure led to less cheating.

Despite these mostly consistent patterns of findings, it is important to note that some studies that have included both mastery and performance goal orientations have found no effect for mastery goals once performance goals are taken into consideration. That is, when both sets of goal orientations are included in analyses, performance goals often emerge as the stronger predictor variable—predicting increased likelihood of cheating—whereas mastery goals are unrelated (e.g., Anderman et al., 1998; Murdock, Hale, & Weber, 2001). In other words, the emphasis on demonstrating ability (or avoiding demonstrating the lack of ability) may be a more important variable in understanding academic dishonesty than the emphasis on mastery per se. Given the role of academic assessments in determining the judgment of students' ability, this pattern is not surprising.

In terms of undesirable classroom behaviors, therefore, the findings related to different patterns of goal orientation are somewhat mixed. Performance goals are associated with classroom behaviors in complex ways, varying considerably depending on the age of students, the context of learning, and the specific outcome behaviors in question. In contrast, however, mastery goals are consistently associated with a matrix of positive beliefs and behaviors and, at least, are unrelated to undesirable outcomes. Therefore, although the advisability of promoting or trying to decrease a performance goal orientation is still being debated, the evidence for promoting a mastery goal orientation is clear.

MEASUREMENT APPROACHES AND ISSUES

Both students' personal goal orientations and their perceptions of the goal structures in educational settings are conceptualized as subjective cognitions and, thus, most appropriately measured through self-report. A number of group-administered survey measures have been developed to assess goal orientation constructs with students at different age and grade levels. Typically, however, these measures are not recommended for administration to students below third grade, when students' responses to questionnaire items are of questionable validity.

The best-known survey instrument for use with school-aged populations is the Patterns of Adaptive Learning Survey (PALS; Midgley et al., 2000). The PALS was initially developed for use with elementary and middle school samples and has been revised several times to reflect theoretical developments over time. It should be noted, however, that the PALS does not include a measure of mastery-avoidance orientations, which emerged theoretically after the publication of these scales. Scales from the PALS have also been used with older student populations, including at the high school (e.g., E. Anderman & Midgley, 2004; Gutman, 2006) and college undergraduate (e.g., Hsieh, Sullivan, & Guerra, 2007; Shim & Ryan, 2005) levels. The PALS has been administered to students representing both ethnic and socioeconomic diversity and, to a smaller degree, to students identified as having learning disabilities (e.g., E. Anderman & Young, 1994; Barron,

Evans, Baranik, Serpell, & Buvinger, 2006). Evidence of the psychometric properties of the original set of measures is reported in Midgley and colleagues (1998). In addition, information regarding the internal consistency and factor structure of the updated measures is provided in the survey manual (www.umich.edu/~pals/manuals.html). Information regarding the PALS, including all survey items, manuals for administration, and a bibliography of related publications, is freely available (www.umich.edu/~pals/).

Alternative survey measures of students' personal goals include the Motivated Strategies for Learning Questionnaire (MSLQ; Pintrich, Smith, Garcia, & McKeachie, 1993) and the Achievement Goals Scale (Elliot & Church, 1997). Both of these surveys have been used extensively and have demonstrated strong psychometric properties, although typically with a focus on older students than is the case for the PALS. The MSLQ has been administered to students from junior high school age (e.g., Pintrich & de Groot, 1990) through college undergraduates. Elliot and Church's measures are most commonly used with college students (Church, Elliot, & Gable, 2001).

Finally, although classroom goal structures are conceptualized as student perceptions, researchers have attempted to assess observable teacher behaviors that are theoretically linked to those perceptions. Patrick, Anderman, Ryan, Edelin, & Midgley (2001) developed a classroom observation instrument, Observing Patterns of Adaptive Learning (OPAL; Patrick et al., 1997), that explicitly focuses on those dimensions of instructional practice. Compared to the survey instruments available, much less information is available regarding the robustness of the OPAL. The manual for this instrument is available (www.umich.edu/~pals/manuals.html).

EDUCATIONAL IMPLICATIONS

Since classroom goal structures are particularly important for students' own goal orientations (Bong, 2008; Kim et al., 2010), the messages teachers send about the purposes of academic work and achievement can impact students' personal motivational beliefs. While the research mostly focuses on late elementary and middle school students, holding a mastery goal orientation has been shown to have positive outcomes for high school and college students as well (Coutinho & Neuman, 2008; Jagacinksi et al., 2010; Sideridis & Kaplan, 2011; Spinath & Steinmayr, 2012). Given the clear patterns of associations between mastery goal structures and positive outcomes, we propose that teachers should focus on communicating a clear mastery structure in their classrooms. Messages that encourage a mastery orientation, then, should start early and be consistent throughout a student's educational career.

For teachers interested in promoting a mastery goal structure in the classroom, a useful tool is the TARGET framework (Tasks, Authority, Recognition, Grouping, Evaluation, Time; Ames, 1992). This framework describes specific dimensions of classroom practice that can communicate a mastery goal focus in the classroom. For example, teachers can consider the ways that their approaches to grouping students, providing recognition, or allocating instructional time send a message of individual progress and learning as compared to an emphasis on demonstrating prowess or speed with tasks. Recently, some authors have suggested that a seventh dimension, Social Support, should be added to this model, creating the TARGETS framework (i.e., Patrick & Ryan, 2008).

Specific characteristics of classroom practices related to each of these dimensions are shown in Table 9.2.

Examples of the ways these dimensions of classroom practice play out and sometimes interact with one another are provided by a limited number of qualitative and multiple-methods studies. Patrick and colleagues (2001) describe their observations of fifth-grade teachers who were perceived by their students as promoting differing goal structures. For example, they show how, in terms of *Authority*, a mastery-oriented teacher might focus on having students participate in creating the rules of the classroom. Similarly, mastery-oriented teachers provided students with opportunities to have autonomy or focus on improvement as opposed to achievement when providing *Recognition*. Other

Table 9.2 Characteristics of Classroom Practices That Promote a Mastery Goal Structure

	Emphasize	De-emphasize
Tasks	• Appropriately challenging • Reasons for learning the material • Provide variety and choice • Emphasize complexity, problem solving, higher-order thinking	• Overuse of routine, low-level tasks • Having all students work on the same tasks at the same time • Teaching "to the test"
Authority	• Appropriate student participation in decision making • Controlled choices and opportunities for self-regulation • Accepting alternative views, opinions, and ways of answering questions	• Sole reliance on "top-down" decision making • Communicating that there is only one "right way" to solve problems
Recognition	• Progress, effort, and intellectual risk taking • Consider providing recognition and feedback in private	• Public displays of "best work" or other signs of relative performance • Excessive praise for relatively simple tasks • Comparing students' accomplishments
Grouping	• Flexible grouping that is heterogeneous when appropriate • Sometimes forming groups based on student interest or choice • Group collaboration	• Long-term placement in ability groups • Competition within and between groups
Evaluation	• Use formal assessments diagnostically to design instruction • Include students' self-evaluation • Base evaluations on multiple sources of evidence • Include student progress and effort	• Over-reliance on a single test score or form of assessment • Comparisons among students
Time	• Use time flexibly to allow students to explore content in depth • Provide for self-pacing	• Time-pressured tasks • Expecting all students to complete tasks in the same time frame
Social Support	• Consistent personal warmth and support • Communicate intellectual support through commitment and confidence in students' learning • Encourage peer collaboration and mutual support	• Focusing attention and participation only on certain students • Communicating fixed expectations for students' success • Focusing exclusively on individual work

Note. See L. Anderman, Patrick, Hruda, & Linnenbrink (2002), L. Anderman, Andrzejewski, & Allen (2011), Midgley & Urdan (1992), and Patrick (2004).

recent qualitative studies have provided rich detail as to specific kinds of behaviors and communication that are perceived as supporting a mastery orientation (Anderman et al., 2011; Turner & Meyer, 2004). These studies shed light on mastery-oriented teachers presenting both challenge and caring, together, in the classroom, as well as the importance of instructional pacing, encouraging help seeking, and using methods to promote positive affect in the classroom. Finally, Patrick and Ryan (2008) explored students' perceptions when evaluating their teachers on their mastery goal orientation. Students discussed the importance of teachers providing students with enough time to understand their work, allowing mistakes and giving students opportunities to redo work, recognizing effort, and caring relationships with teachers. These studies provide detailed examples of teacher behavior and communication that promote a mastery structure in the classroom, demonstrating what mastery-oriented instruction can look like in practice.

Finally, the importance of developing and promoting a mastery goal structure does not stop in the classroom. Many schoolwide policies have the potential to undermine efforts made in individual classrooms (Maehr & Midgley, 1991). This conflict might be seen, for example, if a classroom focuses on reading high-quality, individually appropriate books, while the school as a whole has a goal of reading a certain number of books or only rewards "top readers." Maehr and Midgley (1991) suggest practices in line with the TARGET framework that would apply to the school level as well as to the classroom. For example, in terms of *Task,* Maehr and Midgley (1991) raise questions about the nature of academic tasks, such as "Are they meaningful, challenging, interesting, and important?" (p. 412). Schools as a whole should consider these questions when making decisions about curriculum materials or specific instructional programs. This may mean involving teachers in curriculum decisions and perhaps getting feedback from students and teachers about their experiences with different programs. Similarly, in terms of *Evaluation*, statewide assessments and high-stakes testing have become even more critical since the era of No Child Left Behind. These kinds of assessments have a strong potential to promote a performance goal–oriented community in our schools in which students, teachers, and districts spend a great deal of time preparing for these exams and focusing on achieving specific scores. Decisions at the school and district levels can help to buffer these messages to students to try to maintain an emphasis on learning and personal improvement. For example, Anderman, Anderman, Yough, and Gimbert (2010) suggested that value-added assessments (in which the focus is on a longitudinal assessment of an individual) could help to reduce the most negative effects of high-stakes assessments on students' motivation. Again, each of the elements of the TARGET framework can be used as a way to consider a mastery orientation not just in individual classrooms but also at the schoolwide level.

In conclusion, the development of goal orientation theory has led to a rich body of empirical research on students' motivation over several decades. Despite ongoing debate about some aspects of the theory, particularly in relation to the nature and implications of a performance goal orientation, the benefits of a mastery approach goal orientation are widely accepted (e.g., Anderman & Maehr, 1994; Anderman & Wolters, 2006; Meece et al., 1996; Urdan, 1997). Perhaps more importantly, however, goal orientation theory provides specific recommendations for analyzing, evaluating, and guiding educational practice at the classroom, school, and more general policy levels. The empirical evidence continues to grow that educators at all levels can and do influence the personal goal orientations that students adopt. When educators communicate an emphasis on deep understanding, improvement, and self-referenced evaluation, they stand to improve a range of academic, motivational, and affective outcomes for those students.

REFERENCES

Agbuga, B., Xiang, P., & McBride, R. (2010). Achievement goals and their relations to children's disruptive behaviors in an after-school physical activity program. *Journal of Teaching in Physical Education, 29,* 278–294.

Ames, C. (1987). The enhancement of student motivation. In M. L. Maehr & D. Kleiber (Eds.), *Advances in motivation and achievement, Vol. 5: Enhancing motivation* (pp. 123–148). Greenwich, CT: JAI Press.

Ames, C. (1992). Classrooms: Goals, structures, and student motivation. *Journal of Educational Psychology, 84,* 261–271.

Ames, C., & Archer, J. (1988). Achievement goals in the classroom: Students' learning strategies and motivation processes. *Journal of Educational Psychology, 80,* 260–267.

Anderman, E. M., Anderman, L. H., Yough, M. S., & Gimbert, B. G. (2010). Value-added models of assessment: Implications for motivation and accountability. *Educational Psychologist, 45,* 123–137.

Anderman, E. M., Cupp, P. K., & Lane, D. (2010). Impulsivity and academic cheating. *Journal of Experimental Education, 78,* 135–150.

Anderman, E. M., Griesinger, T., & Westerfield, G. (1998). Motivation and cheating during early adolescence. *Journal of Educational Psychology, 90,* 84–93.

Anderman, E. M., & Johnston, J. (1998). Television news in the classroom: What are adolescents learning? *Journal of Adolescent Research, 13,* 73–100. doi:10.1177/0743554898131005

Anderman, E. M., & Maehr, M. L. (1994). Motivation and schooling in the middle grades. *Review of Educational Research, 64,* 287–309. doi:10.3102/00346543064002287

Anderman, E. M., & Midgley, C. (1997). Changes in personal achievement goals and the perceived goal structures across the transition to middle schools. *Contemporary Educational Psychology, 22,* 269–298.

Anderman, E. M., & Midgley, C. (2004). Changes in self-reported academic cheating across the transition from middle school to high school. *Contemporary Educational Psychology, 29,* 499–517. doi:10.1016/j.cedpsych.2004.02.002

Anderman, E. M., & Wolters, C. (2006). Goals, values and affect. In P. Alexander & P. Winne (Eds.), *Handbook of educational psychology* (2nd ed., pp. 369–390). Mahwah, NJ: Erlbaum.

Anderman, E. M., & Young, A. J. (1994). Motivation and strategy use in science: Individual differences and classroom effects. *Journal of Research in Science Teaching, 31,* 811–831. doi:10.1002/tea.3660310805

Anderman, L. H., Andrzejewski, C. E., & Allen, J. (2011). How do teachers support students' motivation and learning in their classrooms? *Teachers College Record, 113,* 969–1003.

Anderman, L. H., Patrick, H., Hruda, L. Z., & Linnenbrink, L. (2002). Observing classroom goal structures to clarify and expand goal theory. In C. Midgley (Ed.), *Goals, goal structures, and patterns of adaptive learning* (pp. 243–278). Hillsdale, NJ: Lawrence Erlbaum.

Barron, K. E., Evans, S. W., Baranick, L. E., Serpell, N. Z., & Buvinger, E. (2006). Achievement goals of students with ADHD. *Learning Disability Quarterly, 29,* 137–158. http://www.jstor.org/stable/30035504

Bong, M. (2008). Effect of parent-child relationship and classroom goal structures on motivation, help-seeking avoidance, and cheating. *Journal of Experimental Education, 76,* 191–217.

Church, M. A., Elliot, A. J., & Gable, S. L. (2001). Perceptions of classroom environment, achievement goals, and achievement outcomes. *Journal of Educational Psychology, 93,* 43–54. doi:10.1037//0022-0663.93.1.43

Coutinho, S. A., & Neuman, G. (2008). A model of metacognition, achievement goal orientation, learning style and self-efficacy. *Learning Environment Research, 11,* 131–151. doi:10.1007/s10984-008-9042-7

Cury, F., Elliot, A. J., Da Fonseca, D., & Moller, A. C. (2006). The social-cognitive model of achievement motivation and the 2 X 2 achievement goal framework. *Journal of Personality and Social Psychology, 90,* 666–679. doi:10.1037/0022-3514.90.4.666

Dweck, C. S. (1986). Motivational processes affecting learning. *Journal of Personality and Social Psychology, 31,* 474–482.

Elliot, A. J. (1999). Approach and avoidance motivation. *Educational Psychologist, 34,* 169–189. doi:10.1207/s15326985ep3403_3

Elliot, A.J., & Church, M.A. (1997). A hierarchical model of approach and avoidance achievement motivation. *Journal of Personality and Social Psychology, 72,* 218–222.

Elliot, A.J., & Church, M.A. (2003). A motivational analysis of defensive pessimism and self-handicapping. *Journal of Personality, 71,* 369–396.

Elliot, A.J., & Harackiewicz, J.M. (1996). Approach and avoidance achievement goals and intrinsic motivation: A mediational analysis. *Journal of Personality and Social Psychology, 70,* 461–475.

Gehlbach, H. (2006). How changes in students' goal orientations relate to outcomes in social studies. *Journal of Educational Research, 99,* 358–370. doi:10.3200/JOER.99.6.358–370

Grant, H., & Dweck, C. (2003). Clarifying achievement goals and their impact. *Journal of Personality and Social Psychology, 85,* 541–553. doi:10.1037/0022-3514.85.3.541

Gutman, L.M. (2006). How student and parent goal orientations and classroom goal structures influence the math achievement of African Americans during the high school transition. *Contemporary Educational Psychology, 31,* 44–63. doi.org/10.1016/j.cedpsych.2005.01.004

Halvari, H., Skjesol, K., & Bagøien, T.E. (2011). Motivational climates, achievement goals, and physical education outcomes: A longitudinal test of achievement goal theory. *Scandinavian Journal of Educational Research. 55,* 79–104. doi:10.1080/00313831.2011.539855

Harackiewicz, J.M., Barron, K., & Elliot, A. (1998). Rethinking achievement goals: When are they adaptive for college students and why? *Educational Psychologist, 33,* 1–21.

Harackiewicz, J.M., Barron, K.E., Tauer, J.M., Carter, S.M., & Elliot, A.J. (2000). Short-term and long-term consequences of achievement goals: Predicting interest and performance over time. *Journal of Educational Psychology, 92,* 316–330. doi:10.1037/0022-0663.94.3.638

Hsieh, P., Sullivan, J.R., & Guerra, N.S. (2007). A closer look at college students: Self-efficacy and goal orientations. *Journal of Advanced Academics, 18,* 454–476. doi:10.4219/jaa-2007-500

Huang, C. (2011). Achievement goals and achievement emotions: A meta-analysis. *Educational Psychology Review, 23,* 359–388. doi:10.1007/s10648-011-9155-x

Hullman, C.S., Schrager, S.M., Bodmann, S.M., & Harackiewicz, J.M. (2010). A meta-analytic review of achievement goal measures: Different labels for the same constructs or different constructs with similar labels? *Psychological Bulletin, 136,* 422–449. doi:10.1037/a0018947

Jagacinski, C.M., Kumar, S., Boe, J.L., Lam, H., & Miller, S.A. (2010). Changes in achievement goals and competence perceptions across the college semester. *Motivation and Emotion, 34,* 191–204. doi:10.1007/s11031-010-9165-x

Kaplan, A., Gheen, M., & Midgley, C. (2002). Classroom goal structure and student disruptive behavior. *British Journal of Educational Psychology, 72,* 191–211. doi:10.1348/000709902158847

Kaplan, A., & Maehr, M.L. (1999). Achievement goals and student wellbeing. *Contemporary Educational Psychology, 24,* 330–358. doi:10.1006/ceps.1999.0993

Kaplan, A., Middleton, M.J., Urdan, T.C., & Midgley, C. (2002). Achievement goals and goal structures. In C. Midgley (Ed.), *Goals, goal structures, and patterns of adaptive learning* (pp. 55–84). Mahwah, NJ: Erlbaum.

Kaplan, A., & Midgley, C. (1999). The relationship between perceptions of the classroom goal structure and early adolescents' affect in school: The mediating role of coping strategies. *Learning and Individual Differences, 11,* 187–212. doi:10.1016/S1041-6080(00)80005-9

Kim, J., Schallert, D.L., & Kim, M. (2010). An integrative cultural view of achievement motivation: Parental and classroom predictors of children's goal orientations when learning mathematics in Korea. *Journal of Educational Psychology, 102,* 418–437. doi:10.1037/a0018676

Lau, K., & Lee, J. (2008). Examining Hong Kong students' achievement goals and their relations with students' perceived classroom environment and strategy use. *Educational Psychology, 28,* 357–372. doi:10.1080/01443410701612008

Lau, S., & Nie, Y. (2008). Interplay between personal goals and classroom goal structures in predicting student outcomes: A multilevel analysis of person–context. *Journal of Educational Psychology, 100,* 15–29. doi:10.1037/0022-0663.100.1.15

Locke, E.A., & Latham, G.P. (1990). *A theory of goal setting and task performance.* Englewood Cliffs, NJ: Prentice Hall.

Maehr, M.L., & Midgley, C. (1991). *Transforming school cultures.* Boulder, CO: Westview.

Meece, J.L., Anderman, E.M., & Anderman, L.H. (2006). Structures and goals of educational settings: Classroom goal structure, students' motivation, and academic achievement. In S.T. Fiske, A.E. Kazdin, & D.L. Schacter (Eds.), *Annual review of psychology* (Vol. 57, pp. 487–504). Stanford, CA: Annual Reviews. doi:10.1146/annurev.psych.56.091103.070258

Middleton, M.J., & Midgley, C. (1997). Avoiding the demonstration of lack of ability: An underexplored aspect of goal theory. *Journal of Educational Psychology, 89,* 710–718. doi:10.1037//0022-0663.89.4.710

Midgley, C. (Ed.). (2002). *Goals, goal structures, and patterns of adaptive learning.* Mahwah, NJ: Erlbaum.

Midgley, C., Kaplan, A., Middleton, M., Maehr, M. L., Urdan, T., Anderman, L., . . . Roeser, R. (1998). The development and validation of scales assessing students' achievement goal orientations. *Contemporary Educational Psychology, 23,* 113–131. doi:10.1006/ceps.1998.0965

Midgley, C., Maehr, M. L., Hruda, L. Z., Anderman, E., Anderman, L., Freeman, K. E., . . . Urdan, T. (2000). *Manual for the Patterns of Adaptive Learning Scales (PALS).* Ann Arbor, MI: University of Michigan.

Midgley, C., Middleton, M., & Kaplan, A. (2001). Performance-approach goals: Good for what, for whom, under what circumstances, and at what cost? *Journal of Educational Psychology, 93,* 77–86. doi:10.1037/0022-0663.93.1.77

Midgley, C., & Urdan, T. (1992). The transition to middle level schools: Making it a good experience for all students. *Middle School Journal, 24*(2), 5–14.

Midgley, C., & Urdan, T. (1995). Predictors of middle school students' use of self-handicapping strategies. *Journal of Early Adolescence, 15,* 389–411. doi:10.1177/0272431695015004001

Midgley, C., & Urdan, T. (2001). Academic self-handicapping and achievement goals: A further examination. *Contemporary Educational Psychology, 26,* 61–75. doi:10.1006/ceps.2000.1041

Murdock, T. B., Hale, N. M., & Weber, M. J. (2001). Predictors of cheating among early adolescents: Academic and social motivations. *Contemporary Educational Psychology, 26,* 96–115. doi:10.1006/ceps.2000.1046

Nicholls, J. (1989). *The competitive ethos and democratic education.* Cambridge, MA: Harvard University Press.

Nichols, S. L., & Berliner, D. C. (2006). The pressure to cheat in a high stakes testing environment. In E. M. Anderman & T. B. Murdock (Eds.), *Psychological perspectives on academic cheating* (pp. 289–301). San Diego, CA: Elsevier.

Patrick, H. (2004). Re-examining classroom mastery goal structure. In P. R. Pintrich & M. L. Maehr (Eds.), *Advances in motivation and achievement, Vol. 13, Motivating students, improving schools: The legacy of Carol Midgley* (pp. 233–263). New York, NY: Elsevier.

Patrick, H., Anderman, L. H., Ryan, A. M., Edelin, K. C., & Midgley, C. (2001). Teachers' communication of goal orientations in four fifth-grade classrooms. *Elementary School Journal, 102,* 35–58.

Patrick, H., & Ryan, A. M. (2008). What do students think about when evaluating their classroom's mastery goal structure? An examination of young adolescents' explanations. *Journal of Experimental Education, 77,* 99–124.

Patrick, H., Ryan, A. M., Anderman, L. H., Middleton, M. J., Linnenbrink, L., Hruda, L. Z., . . . Midgley, C. (1997). *Observing Patterns of Adaptive Learning (OPAL): A protocol for classroom observation.* Ann Arbor: University of Michigan. Retrieved from http://www.umich.edu/-pals/finalopal.pdf

Phan, H. P. (2009). Relations between goals, self-efficacy, critical thinking and deep processing strategies: A path analysis. *Educational Psychology, 29,* 777–799. doi:10.1080/01443410903289423

Pintrich, P. R. (2000). Multiple goals, multiple pathways: The role of goal orientation in learning and achievement. *Journal of Educational Psychology, 92,* 544–555. doi:10.1037/0022-0663.92.3.544

Pintrich, P. R., & de Groot, E. (1990). Motivational and self-regulated learning components of classroom academic performance. *Journal of Educational Psychology, 82,* 33–40. doi:10.1037/0022-0663.82.1.33

Pintrich, P. R., Smith, D. A. G., Garcia, T., & McKeachie, W. J. (1993). Reliability and predictive validity of the Motivated Strategies for Learning Questionnaire (MSLQ). *Educational and Psychological Measurement, 53,* 801–813. doi:10.1177/0013164493053003024

Roeser, R. W., Midgley, C., & Urdan, T. (1996). Perceptions of the school psychological environment and early adolescents' psychological and behavioral functioning in school. *Journal of Educational Psychology, 88,* 408–422. doi:10.1037//0022–0663.88.3.408

Shim, S., & Ryan, A. (2005). Changes in self-efficacy, challenge avoidance, and intrinsic value in response to grades: The role of achievement goals. *Journal of Experimental Education, 73,* 333–349. doi:10.3200/JEXE.73.4.333-349

Shim, R., Ryan, A. M., & Anderson, C. J. (2008). Achievement goals and achievement during early adolescence: Examining time-varying predictor and outcome variables in growth-curve analysis. *Journal of Educational Psychology, 100,* 655–671. doi:10.1037/0022-0663.100.3.655

Sideridis, G. D., & Kaplan, A. (2011). Achievement goals and persistence across tasks: The roles of failure and success. *Journal of Experimental Education, 79,* 429–451. doi:10.1080/00220973.2010.539634

Spinath, B., & Steinmayr, R. (2012). The roles of competence beliefs and goal orientations for change in intrinsic motivation. *Journal of Educational Psychology, 104,* 1135–1148. doi:10.1037/a0028115

Stephens, J. M., & Gehlbach, J. (2007). Under pressure or under-engaged: Motivational profiles and academic cheating in high school. In E. M. Anderman & T. B. Murdock (Eds.), *Psychological perspectives on academic cheating* (pp. 107–139.) San Diego, CA: Elsevier.

Stevens, T., Hamman, D., & Olivarez, A., Jr. (2007). Hispanic students' perception of White teachers' mastery goal orientation influences sense of school belonging. *Journal of Latinos and Education, 6,* 55–60. doi:10.1080/15348430709336677

Sungur, S., & Senler, B. (2010). Students' achievement goals in relation to academic motivation, competence expectancy, and classroom environment perceptions. *Educational Research and Evaluation, 16,* 303–324. doi:10.1080/13803611.2010.523291

Turner, J.C., & Meyer, D.K. (2004). Are challenge and caring compatible in middle school mathematics classrooms? In P.R. Pintrich & M.L. Maehr (Eds.), *Advances in motivation and achievement, Volume 13, Motivating students, improving schools: The legacy of Carol Midgley* (pp. 331–360). Oxford, UK: Elsevier.

Urdan, T.C. (1997). Achievement goal theory: Past results, future directions. In M.L. Maehr & P.T. Pintrich (Eds.), *Advances in motivation and achievement* (Vol. 10, pp. 99–141). Greenwich, CT: JAI.

Urdan, T.C. (2004a). Predictors of academic self-handicapping: Examining achievement goals, classroom goal structures, and culture. *Journal of Educational Psychology, 96,* 251–264. doi:10.1037/0022-0663.96.2.251

Urdan, T.C. (2004b). Using multiple methods to assess students' perceptions of classroom goal structures. *European Psychologist, 9,* 222–231. doi:10.1027/1016-9040.9.4.222

Urdan, T.C., & Midgley, C. (2001). Academic self-handicapping: What we know, what more there is to learn. *Educational Psychology Review, 13,* 115–138. doi:10.1023/A:1009061303214

Urdan, T.C., Midgley, C., & Anderman, E.M. (1998). The role of classroom goal structure in students' use of self-handicapping strategies. *American Educational Research Journal, 35,* 101–122. doi:10.3102/00028312035001101

Wolters, C.A. (2004). Advancing achievement goal theory: Using goal structures and goal orientations to predict students' motivation, cognition, and achievement. *Journal of Educational Psychology, 96,* 236–250. doi:10.1037/0022-0663.96.2.236

CHAPTER SUMMARY: MOTIVATION

- Students approach academic tasks with differing *achievement goals*; or *goal orientations*—that is, different understanding of the reasons for striving and achieving, the overall purposes of achievement behavior, and the ways in which success is defined.
- *Mastery goals* refer to an emphasis on learning and improving one's ability; *performance goals* refer to an emphasis on demonstrating and proving one's ability.
- Mastery and performance goals are not the opposite ends of a continuum. A student can hold any combination of mastery and/or performance goals, and goals can vary across subjects, contexts, and time.
- Mastery goals are consistently associated with a wide range of positive academic, behavioral, and affective outcomes in students at all grade levels. Findings for performance goals are much more mixed and vary depending on students' age, the instructional setting, and whether students are focused more on success or on avoiding failure.
- Classrooms, schools, and other achievement-related contexts can also be thought of as emphasizing mastery and/or performance goals. At the contextual level, the term *goal structure* is used.
- Educational policies and instructional practices communicate goal emphases to students and shape their individual beliefs. This communication is not necessarily verbal but embedded in decisions related to the design, delivery, and assessment of instruction.

SUGGESTED READINGS: MOTIVATION

Anderman, E.M., & Anderman, L.H. (2013). *Classroom motivation* (2nd ed.). Columbus, OH: Merrill/Pearson.

This readable textbook, designed for educators, is organized around dimensions of instructional practice rather than around theories of motivation. Several current theories, including goal theory, are discussed in relation to specific policies and practices.

Anderman, E. M., & Wolters, C. A. (2006). Goals, values and affect. In P. Alexander & P. Winne (Eds.), *Handbook of educational psychology* (2nd ed., pp. 369–390). Mahwah, NJ: Erlbaum.

This chapter provides a comprehensive review of the research evidence related to students' achievement goals, as well as other motivational variables.

Maehr, M. L., & Midgley, C. (1991). *Transforming school cultures*. Boulder, CO: Westview Press.

This book describes a school reform effort based in goal theory. A team of researchers worked with one elementary and one middle school to try to bring about theory-based reform to support and improve students' academic motivation.

Midgley, C. (Ed.). (2002). *Goals, goal structures, and patterns of adaptive learning*. Mahwah, NJ: Erlbaum.

This book summarizes the development and findings of a longitudinal study of students' motivation from a goal theory perspective as they transition from elementary school into the middle school years and beyond.

Patrick, H., Anderman, L. H., Ryan, A. M., Edelin, K., & Midgley, C. (2001). Teachers' communication of goal orientations in four fifth-grade classrooms. *Elementary School Journal, 102*, 35–58.

This article provides detailed descriptions of four teachers' practices framed within a goal theory framework. It provides specific examples of different ways some teachers created a mastery goal structure in their fifth-grade classrooms.

10

ACHIEVEMENT EMOTIONS

Reinhard Pekrun, Department of Psychology,
University of Munich, Munich, Germany

INTRODUCTION

Achievement emotions are essential for human learning, development, and performance. This is especially true for positive achievement emotions such as enjoyment of learning activities, hope for success, or pride in one's accomplishments. Positive emotions help envision goals and challenges, open the mind to creative problem solving, lay the groundwork for students' self-regulation, and protect health by fostering self-esteem and resiliency. Even negative achievement emotions such as anger, anxiety, or shame can sometimes be beneficial. Until recently, these emotions did not receive much attention by researchers except studies on test anxiety (Zeidner, 1998). During the past dozen years, however, there has been growing recognition that emotions are central to students' academic agency. In this nascent research, emotions are recognized as being of critical importance for students' learning and achievement (Efklides & Volet, 2005; Pekrun & Linnenbrink-Garcia, 2013; Schutz & Pekrun, 2007).

In this chapter, I first discuss the concepts of emotion and achievement emotion. Next, I provide summaries of key theories and empirical evidence on achievement emotion. In the subsequent section, issues of diversity, universality, and development are addressed. In conclusion, I discuss approaches to the measurement of achievement emotions and implications for educational practice.

DEFINITION OF EMOTION AND ACHIEVEMENT EMOTION

There seems to be consensus that *emotions* are multifaceted phenomena involving sets of coordinated psychological processes, including affective, cognitive, physiological, motivational, and expressive components (Shuman & Scherer, in press). For example, a student's anxiety before an exam can be comprised of nervous, uneasy feelings (affective); worries about failing the exam (cognitive); increased cardiovascular activation (physiological); impulses to escape the situation (motivation); and anxious facial expression (expressive). As compared to intense emotions, *moods* are of lower intensity and lack a specific referent.

Achievement emotions are seen as emotions that relate to achievement activities (e.g., studying) or achievement outcomes (success and failure; Pekrun, 2006; see Table 10.1). Most emotions pertaining to attending class, doing homework assignments, or taking tests and exams are considered achievement emotions because they relate to activities and outcomes that are judged according to competence-based standards of quality. However, not all of the emotions experienced in academic settings are achievement emotions. Social emotions are frequently experienced in these same settings, such as empathy for a classmate. Achievement and social emotions can overlap, as in emotions directed toward the achievement of others (e.g., contempt, envy, empathy, or admiration; Weiner, 2007). Furthermore, topic emotions and epistemic emotions also are important for learning. Topic emotions relate to the contents of learning material, such as students' frustration when Pluto was redefined as a dwarf planet (Broughton, Sinatra, & Nussbaum, 2013). Epistemic emotions pertain to the cognitive process of knowledge generation that is inherent to constructive learning and problem solving, such as surprise, curiosity, or confusion triggered by cognitive incongruity (D'Mello, Lehman, Pekrun, & Graesser, 2014).

Past research on achievement emotions focused on emotions induced by achievement outcomes, such as hope and pride related to success or anxiety and shame related to failure (Weiner, 1985; Zeidner, 1998, in press). However, emotions directly pertaining to learning activities are also to be considered achievement emotions and are of equal relevance for students' achievement strivings. The excitement arising from the commencement of a new class, boredom experienced when performing monotonous assignments, or anger felt when the demands of an exam seem unreasonable are examples of activity-related emotions.

Achievement emotions can be organized in a three-dimensional taxonomy (Pekrun, Goetz, Titz, & Perry, 2002; Table 10.1). In this taxonomy, the differentiation of activity versus outcome emotions pertains to the *object focus* of these emotions. In addition, as emotions more generally, achievement emotions can be grouped according to their

Table 10.1 A Three-Dimensional Taxonomy of Achievement Emotions

Object Focus	Positive[a]		Negative[b]	
	Activating	Deactivating	Activating	Deactivating
Activity	Enjoyment	Relaxation	Anger	Boredom Frustration
Outcome/ Prospective	Hope Joy[c]	Relief[c]	Anxiety	Hopelessness
Outcome/ Retrospective	Joy Pride	Contentment Relief Gratitude	Shame Anger	Sadness Disappointment

[a] Positive = pleasant emotion. [b] Negative = unpleasant emotion. [c] Anticipatory joy/relief.

valence and to the degree of *activation* implied. In terms of valence, positive emotions can be distinguished from negative emotions, such as pleasant enjoyment versus unpleasant anxiety. In terms of activation, physiologically activating emotions can be distinguished from deactivating emotions, such as activating excitement versus deactivating relaxation. By using the dimensions valence and activation, the taxonomy is consistent with circumplex models that arrange affective states in a two-dimensional (valence × activation) space (Feldman Barrett & Russell, 1998).

THEORIES OF ACHIEVEMENT EMOTIONS

Theoretical work on achievement emotions has focused on the origins of these emotions. Generally, emotions are influenced by numerous factors including cognitive appraisals, situational perceptions, genetic dispositions, neurohormonal processes, and sensory feedback from facial and postural expression (Davidson, Scherer, & Goldsmith, 2003). Among these factors, cognitive appraisals are likely to play a major role in the arousal of achievement emotions. As such, most theories of achievement emotions focus on the emotional relevance of self-related and task-related appraisals. In the following sections, I outline basic propositions of these appraisal theories. In addition, I will consider theoretical work on the functions of emotions for learning and on reciprocal causation and emotion regulation.

Appraisal Theories

Transactional Model of Test Anxiety

Test anxiety is a prospective emotion related to threat of failure on an upcoming or ongoing evaluation (i.e., test or exam). Therefore, many authors have regarded threat-related appraisals as the main proximal determinants of test anxiety (Zeidner, 1998, in press). More specifically, from the perspective of R.S. Lazarus's transactional model of stress and negative emotions (Lazarus & Folkman, 1984), test anxiety is based on two kinds of appraisals. The *primary appraisal* pertains to the likelihood and subjective importance of failure. In the *secondary appraisal*, possibilities to cope with the situation are explored cognitively. Depending on the combined result of the two appraisals, different emotions can be aroused. It is assumed that anxiety is instigated in the case of threat and insufficient perceived control over threatening failure.

It is thought that situational appraisals are based on objective characteristics of the setting, such as the relative difficulty of exam material, but they are also influenced by individual achievement beliefs. These beliefs can take "irrational" forms (Ellis, 1962), for example, when failure is appraised as likely despite high individual ability, or when failure on an unimportant exam is perceived as undermining self-worth. Irrational beliefs can make students highly vulnerable to anxiety and related negative achievement emotions, like shame and hopelessness ("I am not allowed to fail. If I fail, I am a worthless person").

Attributional Theory

Extending the perspective beyond anxiety, B. Weiner proposed an attributional approach to the origins of achievement emotions following success and failure (Weiner, 1985).

In his theory, causal attributions of success and failure are considered primary deter-minants of these emotions. More specifically, it is assumed that achievement outcomes are first subjectively evaluated as success or failure. This outcome appraisal immediately leads to cognitively less elaborated, attribution-independent emotions, namely happi-ness following success and frustration and sadness following failure. Subsequent to these immediate emotional reactions, causal ascriptions are sought that lead to differentiated, attribution-dependent emotions.

Three dimensions of causal attributions are assumed to play key roles in determin-ing attribution-dependent emotions: (a) the perceived *locus of causality* differentiating internal versus external causes of achievement (e.g., effort vs. environmental circum-stances); (b) their perceived *controllability* (e.g., effort vs. uncontrollable ability), and (c) their perceived *stability* (e.g., stable ability vs. unstable chance). Weiner (1985) posits that pride should be experienced when success is attributed to internal causes (e.g., ability); that shame should be experienced when failure is attributed to uncontrollable, internal causes (e.g., lack of ability); and that gratitude and anger should be experienced when success or failure, respectively, are attributed to external, other-controlled causes. Hope-fulness and hopelessness are expected to be experienced when past success and failure, respectively, are attributed to stable causes (e.g., stable ability). Weiner (2007) recently extended his theory by also speculating about the causal attributional antecedents of "moral" emotions like envy, scorn, sympathy, admiration, regret, and "Schadenfreude."

Control-Value Theory

In R. Pekrun's (2006; Pekrun et al., 2002) control-value theory of achievement emotions, propositions of the transactional stress model and attributional theory are revised to explain a broader variety of emotions, including both outcome emotions and activity emotions. The theory posits that achievement emotions are induced when the individ-ual feels in control of or out of control of activities and outcomes that are subjectively important—implying that appraisals of control and value are the proximal determi-nants of these emotions. Control appraisals pertain to the perceived controllability of achievement-related actions and outcomes, as implied by causal expectations (e.g., self-efficacy expectations), causal attributions of achievement, and competence appraisals (e.g., self-concepts of ability). Value appraisals relate to the subjective importance of these activities and outcomes.

Different kinds of control and value appraisals are assumed to instigate different kinds of achievement emotions (Table 10.1). It is expected that prospective joy and hopeless-ness are triggered when there is high perceived control (joy) or a complete lack of per-ceived control (hopelessness). For example, a student who believes she has the abilities to excel on an exam may feel joyous about the prospect of receiving her exam grade. Prospective hope and anxiety are instigated when there is uncertainty about control, the attentional focus being on anticipated success in the case of hope and on anticipated failure in the case of anxiety. For example, a student who is unsure about being able to master an important exam may hope for success, fear failure, or both. Pride, shame, gratitude, and anger are expected to be induced by perceptions of the controllability of success and failure, as implied by causal attributions of these achievement outcomes.

In addition, all of these outcome-related emotions are thought to depend on the subjective importance of success and failure, implying that they are a joint function of perceived control and value. For instance, a student should feel worried if he judges himself incapable of preparing for an exam (low controllability) that is important (high value). In contrast, if he feels that he is able to prepare (high controllability) or is indifferent about the exam (low value), his anxiety should be low.

Regarding activity emotions, enjoyment of learning is proposed to depend on positive competence appraisals and positive appraisals of the intrinsic value of learning. For example, a student is expected to enjoy learning if she feels competent to meet the demands of the learning task and values the learning material. If she feels incompetent or is disinterested in the material, studying is not enjoyable. Anger and frustration are aroused when the value of the activity is negative (e.g., when working on a difficult project is perceived as taking too much effort, which is experienced as aversive). Finally, boredom is experienced when the activity lacks any incentive value (Pekrun, Goetz, Daniels, Stupnisky, & Perry, 2010).

Theories on the Functions of Achievement Emotions

Theoretical work on the functions of emotions has addressed various mechanisms that impact students' learning and achievement, including cognitive resources available for task performance, motivational processes, memory processes, and styles of cognitive problem solving, among others. Different models address different subsets of these mechanisms; as such, theories on the functions of emotion for learning are in a fragmented state to date.

Theories on *cognitive resources* have posited that emotions produce task-irrelevant thinking, thereby depleting working memory resources that may be needed for task performance. For example, a student who worries about possibly failing an upcoming exam may experience difficulties in focusing attention on the learning material. By implication, emotions are thought to impair learning and performance on tasks that demand cognitive resources, such as cognitive problem-solving tasks. This proposition was part of early interference and attentional deficit models of test anxiety. These models assume that anxiety produces task-irrelevant thinking that reduces on-task attention and, therefore, interferes with performance on tasks requiring working memory capacity (e.g., Wine, 1971). Resource-oriented theories were later generalized for negative mood (Ellis & Ashbrook, 1988) as well as positive affective states (Meinhardt & Pekrun, 2003).

Resource allocation theories posit detrimental effects for both negative and positive emotion. In contrast, theories on *styles of information processing* propose that emotions can facilitate performance, with positive versus negative emotions promoting different modes of cognitive problem solving. Specifically, in mood-as-information approaches (see Clore & Huntsinger, 2007), it is assumed that positive moods signal that "all is well," whereas negative moods signal that the situation is problematic. "All is well" conditions imply safety and the discretion to creatively explore the environment, broaden one's cognitive horizon, and build new actions, as addressed by Fredrickson's (2001) broaden-and-build model of positive emotion. In contrast, if there are problems threatening well-being and agency, it may be wise to focus on these problems in cognitively cautious ways. Accordingly, positive affective states are thought to promote holistic, creative, and flexible ways of thinking, whereas negative states are expected to facilitate analytical and detail-oriented processing of information.

These theories focus on distinguishing between the effects of positive versus negative emotions. However, different emotions within these two categories may serve different functions. In the *cognitive/motivational model of emotion effects* that is part of Pekrun's (2006) control-value theory, an attempt is made to provide a more nuanced theoretical account by taking both the valence and activation dimensions of emotion into account. Doing so renders four broad categories of emotion: positive activating, positive deactivating, negative activating, and negative deactivating (Table 10.1). Emotions from these four categories are posited to influence both cognitive and motivational mechanisms of learning.

Positive activating emotions such as enjoyment of learning are thought to generally preserve cognitive resources and focus attention on learning tasks; promote interest and intrinsic motivation; facilitate the use of flexible, creative learning strategies such as organization and elaboration of learning material; and have positive effects on students' self-regulation of learning. The opposite pattern of effects is expected for negative deactivating emotions such as boredom and hopelessness: depletion of cognitive resources (e.g., due to daydreaming when feeling bored); undermining effects on any kind of motivation to learn; shallow information processing; and under-use of any effortful learning strategies. As a consequence, positive activating emotions are expected to promote academic performance in most students and under most task conditions, whereas deactivating negative emotions are expected to be generally detrimental.

In contrast, the effects of positive deactivating emotions (e.g., relief, relaxation) and negative activating emotions (e.g., anger, anxiety, or shame) are expected to be more complex. For example, anxiety can distract attention and undermine interest and intrinsic motivation. On the other hand, anxiety can induce strong motivation to invest effort in order to avoid failure, and can promote detail-oriented ways of learning (e.g., rigid rehearsal) that can be beneficial for academic performance. Therefore, the overall effects of these emotions on students' achievement are thought to be more variable.

Reciprocal Causation and Emotion Regulation

In Lazarus's transaction model (Lazarus & Folkman, 1984) as well as Pekrun's (2006) control-value theory, emotions, their antecedents, and their effects are thought to be linked by reciprocal causation. Emotions influence learning and performance, but performance outcomes are expected to reciprocally influence antecedent appraisals and environmental factors (Figure 10.1). Positive feedback loops likely are commonplace (e.g., teachers' and students' frustration reciprocally reinforcing each other), but negative feedback loops can also be important (e.g., when a student's failure on an exam induces anxiety, and anxiety motivates the student to avoid failing the next exam).

Reciprocal causation has implications for the regulation and treatment of achievement emotions. Since emotions, their antecedents, and their effects can be reciprocally linked over time, addressing any of the elements involved in these cyclic feedback processes can change emotions. Regulation and treatment can target (a) the emotion

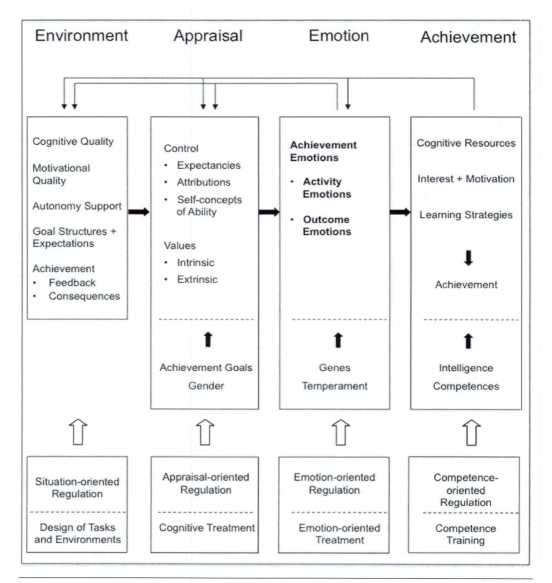

Figure 10.1 Reciprocal linkages between achievement emotions, their antecedents, and their effects (adapted from Pekrun, 2006).

itself (*emotion-oriented* regulation and treatment, such as using relaxation techniques to cope with anxiety or interest-enhancing strategies to reduce boredom; Sansone, Weir, Harpster, & Morgan, 1992); (b) the control and value appraisals underlying emotions (*appraisal-oriented* regulation and treatment, e.g., attributional retraining, Ruthig, Perry, Hall, & Hladkyj, 2004); (c) the competences determining students' academic agency (*competence-oriented* regulation and treatment, e.g., training of learning skills); and (d) the learning environment (*situation-oriented regulation*, e.g., designing tasks and environments to enhance students' enjoyment of learning).

REVIEW OF KEY RESEARCH FINDINGS

Due to the focus of researchers' attention on test anxiety, there is cumulative evidence on the origins and functions of students' anxiety. Evidence on achievement emotions other than anxiety is still scarce. In the following sections, key findings on the origins, functions, and development of both test anxiety and other achievement emotions are summarized.

Individual and Social Origins

Appraisals and Achievement Goals

The available empirical evidence is in line with the propositions of appraisal theories. Test anxiety research has shown that test anxiety correlates negatively with variables of perceived control, such as self-concepts of ability and self-efficacy expectations, and positively with students' expectations of failure (Hembree, 1988; Pekrun, Goetz, Frenzel, Barchfeld, & Perry, 2011; Zeidner, 1998). In attributional studies, retrospective achievement emotions such as pride and shame have been linked to causal attributions of success and failure (Weiner, 1985). Most of these studies used a scenario approach asking students how they might react to success and failure, implying that they asked for participants' subjective theories about links between attributions and emotions. However, there also are experimental and field studies corroborating the validity of attributional assumptions (Heckhausen, 1991).

Studies testing the control-value theory (Pekrun, 2006) have found that both perceived control and perceived value are predictive for outcome emotions such as hope and anxiety, and for activity emotions such as enjoyment and boredom (e.g., Pekrun et al., 2010). Focusing on positive achievement emotions, Goetz, Frenzel, Stoeger, and Hall (2010) have shown that perceived control and value interact in predicting these emotions. For example, enjoyment of achievement activities was high when both control and value related to these activities were high, and low when control, or value, or both were low, in line with the propositions of the theory. Overall, the available evidence corroborates that achievement emotions are closely linked to students' achievement-related appraisals.

Students' appraisals are likely to be influenced by their achievement goals. For example, mastery goals can focus attention on the controllability and positive value of achievement activities (Pekrun, Elliot, & Maier, 2006). Performance-approach goals can facilitate positive appraisals of success, while performance-avoidance goals can sustain appraisals of the uncontrollability and negative value of failure. In line with these considerations, empirical findings show that students' mastery goals relate positively to their enjoyment of learning, performance-approach goals to their hope and pride, and performance-avoidance goals to their anxiety (Linnenbrink & Pintrich, 2002; Pekrun et al., 2006).

Classroom Instruction and Test Taking

Lack of structure and clarity in classroom instruction as well as excessive task demands relate positively to students' test anxiety (Zeidner, 1998, in press). The effects of these factors are likely mediated by students' appraisals of lack of control and failure expectancies

(Pekrun, 1992). Lack of structure and transparency regarding exams has also been shown to contribute to students' anxiety. Furthermore, the format of items has been found to be relevant, with open-ended formats inducing more anxiety than multiple-choice formats. Open-ended formats require more working memory capacity, which may be less available in states of anxiety due to the consumption of cognitive resources by worrying, thus inducing more threat and debilitating performance in anxious students.

A few studies have investigated relations between classroom instruction and students' positive emotions. Teacher-centered instruction emphasizing rigid drill and exercise relates negatively to students' positive emotional attitudes toward school (Valeski & Stipek, 2001). In contrast, the cognitive quality of instruction oriented toward creative mental modeling rather than algorithmic routine procedures has been found to correlate positively with students' enjoyment of learning (Pekrun et al., 2007). In addition, support for students' autonomy at learning also correlated positively with students' enjoyment in Pekrun et al.'s (2007) study. Finally, teachers' own enjoyment and enthusiasm during teaching has been found to relate positively to students' enjoyment, suggesting transmission of positive emotions from teachers to students (Frenzel, Goetz, Lüdtke, Pekrun, & Sutton, 2009).

Social Environments

High achievement expectancies from parents and teachers, negative feedback after achievement, negative consequences of failure, and competition in the classroom were found to correlate positively with students' test anxiety (Zeidner, 1998, in press), likely because these factors reduce perceived control and increase the importance of avoiding failure. In contrast, social support by parents and teachers and a cooperative classroom climate often fail to correlate with students' anxiety scores (Hembree, 1988). This surprising lack of correlation may be due to coercive components of efforts to support students, which can counteract beneficial effects of support per se. A second explanation would be negative feedback loops between support and anxiety, implying that social support alleviates anxiety (negative effect of support on anxiety), but that anxiety provokes support in the first place (positive effect of anxiety on demanding support), thus yielding an overall zero correlation.

Functions for Learning and Performance
Positive Emotions

Traditionally, it was often assumed that positive emotions are maladaptive by inducing unrealistic appraisals, fostering superficial information processing, and reducing motivation to pursuit challenging goals. As summarized by Aspinwall (1998), traditional approaches to positive emotions imply that "our primary goal is to feel good, and feeling good makes us lazy thinkers who are oblivious to potentially useful negative information and unresponsive to meaningful variations in information and situation" (p. 7). However, experimental mood research has shown that positive mood can enhance divergent thinking and flexible problem solving, thus contradicting views that positive emotions are uniformly detrimental for motivation and performance (Clore & Huntsinger, 2007).

Direct evidence on the effects of students' positive emotions is scarce but supports the view that activating positive emotions can enhance motivation and performance. Specifically, enjoyment of learning, hope, and pride have been found to correlate positively with students' interest, effort, elaboration of learning material, self-regulation of learning, and academic achievement, thus corroborating that these emotions can be beneficial for students' academic agency (Pekrun et al., 2002, 2011). However, in some studies, measures of positive affective states did not correlate with performance indicators (Linnenbrink, 2007; Pekrun, Elliot, & Maier, 2009). One possible explanation is that the measures used did not clearly differentiate between activating and deactivating variants of positive affect. As such, null correlations may be due to having measured relaxation and task-irrelevant positive affect rather than task-related enjoyment.

Negative Activating Emotions

The effects of test anxiety have been analyzed in several hundreds of studies (Hembree, 1988; Zeidner, 1998, in press). Experimental studies have shown that test anxiety impairs performance on complex or difficult tasks that demand cognitive resources (e.g., difficult intelligence test items). Performance on easy and less complex tasks need not suffer or is even enhanced. In line with this evidence, field studies have shown that test anxiety correlates moderately negatively with students' academic performance (Hembree, 1988; Zeidner, 1998). However, sometimes zero and positive correlations with performance have been found, in line with the complexity of anxiety-achievement relationships noted earlier. Anxiety likely has deleterious effects in many students, but it may induce motivation to study harder and thus facilitate overall performance in those who are more resilient.

A few studies have addressed the effects of students' anger and shame. The findings suggest that students' anger at school correlates positively with task-irrelevant thinking and negatively with academic self-efficacy, interest, self-regulation of learning, and performance (Boekaerts, 1993; Pekrun et al., 2011). Similarly, students' achievement-related shame shows negative overall correlations with their effort and academic performance (Pekrun et al., 2011). However, as with anxiety, the underlying pattern of functional mechanisms may be complex and imply more than just negative effects. For example, Turner and Schallert (2001) showed that students experiencing shame following negative exam feedback increased their motivation when continuing to be committed to academic goals and holding positive expectancies to reach these goals.

Negative Deactivating Emotions

Reduced levels of physiological and cognitive activation characterize negative deactivating emotions (e.g., boredom and hopelessness). In spite of the frequency of boredom experienced by students, this emotion has received scant attention, as has the less frequent but devastating emotion of achievement-related hopelessness. Boredom at work was researched early as being induced by monotonous assembly-line work (e.g., Wyatt, 1930) and was discussed as being experienced by gifted students in recent years. In empirical research, boredom was found to correlate negatively with students' attention, motivation to learn, and use of learning strategies and to be a negative predictor of academic achievement (Ahmed, van der Werf, Kuyper, & Minnaert, 2013; Pekrun et al., 2010). Similarly, students' achievement-related hopelessness correlates negatively with measures of motivation, study behavior, and achievement (Pekrun et al., 2011).

In sum, the available evidence suggests that emotions exert profound effects on students' motivation, learning, and achievement. Typically, these effects are positive for positive emotions and negative for negative deactivating emotions. The effects of negative activating emotions such as anxiety, anger, and shame are more complex. From an educator's perspective, however, any benefits of these emotions in resilient, highly motivated students are certainly outweighed by their negative effects in the vast majority of students. Also, beyond effects on academic learning, achievement-related anxiety and shame can have severe consequences for students' long-term psychological well-being, social adaptation, and physical health (Zeidner, 1998).

DIVERSITY, UNIVERSALITY, AND DEVELOPMENT

Diversity and Universality of Achievement Emotions

The general functional mechanisms of achievement emotions may be bound to universal, species-specific characteristics of our mind. In contrast, the specific contents and reference objects of these emotions, the frequency of their occurrence, as well as process parameters, such as intensity and duration, can vary widely among different individuals, genders, achievement settings, and socio-cultural contexts. Accordingly, the basic structures and causal mechanisms of achievement emotions are expected to follow nomothetic principles, whereas occurrence and phenomenology follow principles of variation and diversity (Pekrun, 2009).

For example, we found that the relations between girls' and boys' appraisals and their achievement emotions in mathematics were structurally equivalent across the two genders (Frenzel, Pekrun, & Goetz, 2007; Goetz, Bieg, Lüdtke, Pekrun, & Hall, in press). However, perceived control in this domain was substantially lower for girls. As a consequence, girls reported less enjoyment in mathematics, as well as more anxiety and shame. Concerning achievement settings, we found that students' emotions experienced in mathematics, science, and languages differed in mean levels across subject domains, but showed equivalent internal structures and linkages with academic achievement across domains (Goetz, Frenzel, Pekrun, Hall, & Lüdtke, 2007). Similarly, in a cross-cultural comparison of Chinese and German students' achievement emotions, we found that mean levels of emotions differed between cultures, with Chinese students reporting more achievement-related enjoyment, pride, anxiety, and shame, and less anger. Nevertheless, the functional linkages of these emotions with perceived control, important others' expectations, and academic achievement were equivalent across cultures (Frenzel, Thrash, Pekrun, & Goetz, 2007).

Development Across the School Years

Achievement emotions also differ as a function of age. However, basic capabilities to experience these emotions develop early in childhood. At the age of 2 to 3 years, children are able to express pride and shame when successfully solving tasks or failing to do so, suggesting that they are able to differentiate internal versus external causation of success and failure. During the early elementary school years, they additionally acquire capabilities to distinguish between different internal and external causes, such as ability and effort, to develop related causal expectancies, and to cognitively combine expectancies and value-related information (Heckhausen, 1991). By implication, students have developed the cognitive competencies to experience all major types of achievement emotions early in their academic careers.

Empirical evidence on the development of these emotions at school is scarce. Again, research on test anxiety is an exception. This research has shown that average scores for test anxiety are low at the beginning of elementary school but increase substantially during the elementary school years (Hembree, 1988). This development is congruent to the decline of self-concepts of ability during this period and is likely due to increasing realism in academic self-perceptions and to the cumulative failure feedback many students receive. After elementary school, average anxiety scores stabilize and remain at high levels throughout middle school, high school, and college. However, stability at the group level notwithstanding, anxiety can change in individual students. One important source for individual dynamics is the change of reference groups implied by transitions between schools and classrooms (Zeidner, 1998). The likelihood of low achievement relative to peers is higher in high-ability classrooms and lower in low-ability classrooms. Therefore, changing from a low-ability to a high-ability classroom can increase anxiety, whereas the reverse can happen when entering a low-ability classroom.

Congruent to the increase of average levels of anxiety, positive emotions such as enjoyment of learning seem to decrease across the elementary school years (Helmke, 1993). The decrease of enjoyment can continue through the middle school years (Pekrun et al., 2007), which is consistent with the decline of average scores for subject-matter interest and general attitudes toward school (e.g., Fredricks & Eccles, 2002). Important factors responsible for this development may be an increase of teacher-centered instruction and academic demands in middle school, the competition between academic and nonacademic interests in adolescence, and the stronger selectivity of subject-matter interest that is part of adolescent identity formation.

Approaches to Measurement

Due to the multicomponent nature of emotion, there are various ways to assess achievement emotions. Self-report is used most often and has the clear advantage of providing a differentiated account of these emotions. Alternative methods include assessment of physiological processes and observation of facial and postural expression.

Self-Report Measures

Most of the available self-report instruments focus on measuring test anxiety. Self-report scales can be employed to assess students' momentary emotional reactions to tests and exams (*state* test anxiety), as well as their habitual tendency to react, typically, by experiencing anxiety when being confronted with tests or exams (*trait* test anxiety). In the early stages of test anxiety research, measurement instruments conceived the construct as being one-dimensional (e.g., the Test Anxiety Questionnaire, TAQ; Mandler & Sarason, 1952).

Following the proposal by Liebert and Morris (1967) to distinguish affective and physiological components (*emotionality*) from cognitive components (*worry*) of test anxiety, more recent measures take the multifaceted nature of this emotion into account (e.g., the Test Anxiety Inventory, TAI; Spielberger, 1980). Today, most of the available test anxiety scales possess good psychometric properties. Coefficients of internal reliability often are above alpha = .85, structural validity is ensured by use of confirmatory factor analysis, and external construct validity by correlations with measures of academic learning and performance (Zeidner, 1998).

Measures for achievement emotions other than anxiety are still largely lacking. An exception is the Achievement Emotions Questionnaire (AEQ; Pekrun et al., 2011). The AEQ is a multidimensional instrument measuring a variety of major achievement emotions for each of the three main categories of academic achievement situations: attending class, studying, and writing tests and exams. In its current version, the AEQ assesses nine different achievement emotions within each of these categories (enjoyment, hope, pride, relief, anger, anxiety, shame, hopelessness, and boredom). The original version of the instrument measures emotions as experienced by university students. We also constructed domain-specific variants of the AEQ assessing elementary, middle, and high school students' emotions relating to specific school subjects (Lichtenfeld, Pekrun, Stupnisky, Reiss, & Murayama, 2012; Pekrun et al., 2011). Reliability coefficients confirm the psychometric quality of the AEQ scales (alpha range = .75 to .93). The structural validity of the AEQ scales has been corroborated by confirmatory factor analysis and external validity by correlations with students' appraisals, motivation, study behavior, academic achievement, and school dropout, as well as classroom climate and health (Pekrun et al., 2011).

Alternative Types of Assessment

Self-report methods for assessing emotions share a number of limitations. Self-report may be subject to biases (e.g., responding according to social desirability), cannot cover subconscious processes, and is not well suited to analyze the dynamics of emotional processes with sufficient temporal resolution. Alternative methods compensate for some of these disadvantages. Neuroimaging techniques (e.g., fMRI, EEG) assess physiological brain processes, thus making it possible to examine brain systems underlying affective processes and their links with cognitive achievement (Immordino-Yang & Christodoulou, in press). Measurement of peripheral physiological processes allows examining processes of physiological activation and deactivation that are part of achievement emotion arousal (e.g., Spangler, Pekrun, Kramer, & Hofmann, 2002). Finally, observation of nonverbal behavior such as facial expression, postural expression, and prosodic features of verbal speech make it possible to evaluate various discrete emotions in academic settings (Reisenzein, Junge, & Huber, in press).

Systems for coding expressive behavior, such as the Facial Action Coding System (FACS; Ekman & Rosenberg, 1997), are currently used to develop automatic affect-decoding systems as well as intelligent tutors based on such systems ("affective computing"; Calvo & D'Mello, 2012). These new technological developments are promising in terms of potentially superior measurement quality and saving the time needed for coding by human observers. However, one obvious limitation for use in academic settings is that emotions may be only partially displayed by students, making it necessary to complement behavioral observation by self-report or physiological assessment (Reisenzein et al., in press).

IMPLICATIONS FOR EDUCATIONAL PRACTICE

The evidence summarized in this chapter implies that achievement emotions can profoundly influence students' learning and academic performance. Accordingly, educators are well advised to consider these emotions. However, given the scarcity of knowledge about the influence of education on these emotions, it would be premature to derive firm conclusions for educational practice, with the possible exception of recommendations related to test anxiety. Judging from appraisal theories (see Pekrun, 2006) and test anxiety studies (Zeidner, 1998, in press), the following factors should be considered by educators in helping students to develop positive achievement emotions, reduce negative emotions, and productively use the energy provided by negative emotions if they cannot be prevented (Figure 10.1).

Cognitive Quality of Instruction

Well-structured instruction and clear explanations likely contribute to adaptive student emotions by raising students' competencies and feelings of control. By implication, adaptive student emotions likely can be fostered and maladaptive emotions reduced by raising the cognitive quality of instruction.

Motivational Quality of Instruction

Teachers deliver direct messages conveying academic values as well as more indirect messages implied by their behavior. Two ways of inducing values and related emotions may be most important. First, if learning environments meet the needs of students, positive activity-related emotions likely are fostered. For example, learning environments that support cooperative learning should help students to fulfill needs for social relatedness, thus making learning enjoyable. Second, the enjoyment and enthusiasm experienced by teachers themselves can facilitate students' adoption of positive emotions by way of observational learning and emotional contagion (Frenzel et al., 2009).

Support of Autonomy and Self-Regulated Learning

Learning environments supporting students' self-regulated learning can be assumed to increase their sense of control and related positive emotions. In addition, such environments can foster positive emotions by meeting students' need for autonomy. However, these beneficial effects likely depend on the match between students' competence and need for academic autonomy, on the one hand, and the affordances of these environments, on the other. In case of a mismatch, loss of control and negative emotions can result. By implication, teachers should attend to matching demands for autonomy to students' competencies and needs.

Goal Structures and Achievement Expectations

Academic achievement can be defined by standards of individual mastery, by normative standards based on competitive social comparison, or by standards pertaining to cooperative group performance. These different standards imply individualistic (mastery), competitive (normative performance), and cooperative goal structures in the classroom (Johnson & Johnson, 1974). Goal structures and grading practices determine students' opportunities for experiencing success and perceiving control, thus influencing their emotions. Specifically, competitive goal structures imply, by definition, that some students experience success, whereas others have to experience failure, thus increasing levels of anxiety and hopelessness. Similarly, the demands implied by excessively high achievement expectancies of teachers and parents can lead to lowered control perceptions and related negative emotions. Accordingly, as seen from an emotion perspective, educators should adapt expectancies to students' competencies and should refrain from using goal structures inducing individual competition between students.

Test Taking, Feedback, and Consequences of Achievement

Educators can reduce students' test anxiety by increasing structure and transparency of tests and exams (e.g., by providing clear information on demands, materials, and grading practices). In addition, use of structured item formats and giving second chances in terms of retaking tests and exams can help reducing test anxiety (Zeidner, 1998). Furthermore, cumulative success and failure feedback likely is a major factor underlying students' achievement emotions (Pekrun, 1992). Success experiences can strengthen perceived control and related positive emotions, whereas repeated failure can undermine subjective control and, therefore, instigate negative emotions. In addition, the perceived consequences of success and failure are important. Positive future-related student emotions can be increased if academic success is seen to produce beneficial long-term outcomes (such as future career opportunities). Negative outcomes of academic failure, on the other hand, can increase students' anxiety and hopelessness. By implication, providing success experiences, defining mistakes as opportunities to learn rather than as personal failure, linking attainment to beneficial outcomes, and avoiding high-stakes testing involving negative consequences also are important for helping students to develop adaptive emotions.

CONCLUSION

Achievement emotions are among the most frequently experienced and functionally most important kinds of emotions at school. However, except for studies examining test anxiety, a popular construct since the 1950s (Zeidner, 1998), research on achievement emotions is clearly in a nascent stage. Psychological researchers are just beginning to acknowledge the importance of these emotions. The fragmented research efforts in this field need more integration, and need to pay attention to the functions of achievement emotions not only for performance, but also for well-being and health. Of specific importance, little is known to date about regulation, treatment, and design of academic settings targeting achievement emotions other than anxiety. The few attempts to design learning environments that foster students' positive achievement emotions have met with partial success at best (Glaeser-Zikuda, Fuss, Laukenmann, Metz, & Randler, 2005). However, the success story of test anxiety treatment (Zeidner, 1998) suggests that future research can be successful in developing ways to shape academic settings so that adaptive achievement emotions are promoted and maladaptive emotions reduced.

REFERENCES

Ahmed, W., van der Werf, G., Kuyper, H., & Minnaert, A. (2013). Emotions, self-regulated learning, and achievement in mathematics: A growth curve analysis. *Journal of Educational Psychology, 105,* 150–161. doi:10.1037/a0030160

Aspinwall, L. (1998). Rethinking the role of positive affect in self-regulation. *Motivation and Emotion, 22,* 1–32. doi:10.1023/A:1023080224401

Boekaerts, M. (1993). Anger in relation to school learning. *Learning and Instruction, 3,* 269–280.

Broughton, S.H., Sinatra, G.M., & Nussbaum, E.M. (2013). "Pluto has been a planet my whole life!" Emotions, attitudes, and conceptual change in elementary students' learning about Pluto's reclassification. *Research in Science Education, 43,* 529–550. doi:10.1007/s11165-011-9274-x

Calvo, R.A., & D'Mello, S.K. (Eds.). (2012). *New perspectives on affect and learning technologies.* New York, NY: Springer.

Clore, G.L., & Huntsinger, J.R. (2007). How emotions inform judgment and regulate thought. *Trends in Cognitive Sciences, 11,* 393–399. doi:10.1016/j.tics.2007.08.005

Davidson, R.J., Scherer, K.R., & Goldsmith, H.H. (Eds.). (2003). *Handbook of affective sciences.* Oxford, UK: Oxford University Press.

D'Mello, S., Lehman, B., Pekrun, R., & Graesser, A. (2014). Confusion can be beneficial for learning. *Learning and Instruction. 29,* 153–170. doi:10.1016/j.learninstruc.2012.05.003

Efklides, A., & Volet, S. (Eds.). (2005). Feelings and emotions in the learning process [special issue]. *Learning and Instruction, 15,* 377–515. doi:10.1016/j.learninstruc.2005.07.006

Ekman, P., & Rosenberg, E.L. (Eds.). (1997). *What the face reveals: Basic and applied studies of spontaneous expression using the Facial Action Coding System (FACS).* New York, NY: Oxford University Press.

Ellis, A. (1962). *Reason and emotion in psychotherapy.* New York, NY: Lyle Stuart.

Ellis, H.C., & Ashbrook, P.W. (1988). Resource allocation model of the effect of depressed mood states on memory. In K. Fiedler & J. Forgas (Eds.), *Affect, cognition, and social behavior* (pp. 25–43). Toronto, Canada: Hogrefe International.

Feldman Barrett, L., & Russell, J.A. (1998). Independence and bipolarity in the structure of current affect. *Journal of Personality and Social Psychology, 74,* 967–984. doi:10.1037/0022–3514.74.4.967

Fredricks, J.A., & Eccles, J. (2002). Children's competence and value beliefs from childhood through adolescence: Growth trajectories in two male-sex-typed domains. *Developmental Psychology, 38,* 519–533. doi:10.1037//0012-1649.38.4.519

Fredrickson, B.L. (2001). The role of positive emotions in positive psychology: The broaden-and-build theory of positive emotions. *American Psychologist, 56,* 218–226. doi:10.1037/0003-066X.56.3.218

Frenzel, A.C., Goetz, T., Lüdtke, O., Pekrun, R., & Sutton, R. (2009). Emotional transmission in the classroom: Exploring the relationship between teacher and student enjoyment. *Journal of Educational Psychology, 101,* 705–716. doi:10.1037/a0014695

Frenzel, A.C., Pekrun, R., & Goetz, T. (2007). Girls and mathematics—a "hopeless" issue? A control-value approach to gender differences in emotions towards mathematics. *European Journal of Psychology of Education, 22,* 497–514.

Frenzel, A.C., Thrash, T.M., Pekrun, R., & Goetz, T. (2007). Achievement emotions in Germany and China: A cross-cultural validation of the Academic Emotions Questionnaire-Mathematics (AEQ-M). *Journal of Cross-Cultural Psychology, 38,* 302–309. doi:10.1177/0022022107300276

Glaeser-Zikuda, M., Fuss, S., Laukenmann, M., Metz, K., & Randler, C. (2005). Promoting students' emotions and achievement—Instructional design and evaluation of the ECOLE-approach. *Learning and Instruction, 15,* 481–495. doi:10.1016/j.learninstruc.2005.07.013

Goetz, T., Bieg, M., Lüdtke, O., Pekrun, R., & Hall, N.C. (in press). Do girls really experience more anxiety in mathematics? *Psychological Science.*

Goetz, T., Frenzel, A.C., Pekrun, R., Hall, N.C., & Lüdtke, O. (2007). Between- and within-domain relations of students' academic emotions. *Journal of Educational Psychology, 99,* 715–733. doi:10.1037/0022-0663.99.4.715

Goetz, T., Frenzel, A.C., Stoeger, H., & Hall, N.C. (2010). Antecedents of everyday positive emotions: An experience sampling analysis. *Motivation and Emotion, 34,* 49–62. doi:10.1007/s11031-009-9152-2

Heckhausen, H. (1991). *Motivation and action.* New York, NY: Springer.

Helmke, A. (1993). Die Entwicklung der Lernfreude vom Kindergarten bis zur 5. Klassenstufe [Development of enjoyment of learning from kindergarten to grade 5]. *Zeitschrift für Pädagogische Psychologie, 7,* 77–86.

Hembree, R. (1988). Correlates, causes, effects, and treatment of test anxiety. *Review of Educational Research, 58,* 47–77. doi:10.3102/00346543058001047

Immordino-Yang, M.H., & Christodoulou, J.A. (in press). Neuroscientific contributions to understanding and measuring emotions in educational contexts. In R. Pekrun & L. Linnenbrink-Garcia (Eds.), *Handbook of emotions in education.* New York, NY: Taylor & Francis.

Johnson, D.W., & Johnson, R.T. (1974). Instructional goal structure: Cooperative, competitive or individualistic. *Review of Educational Research, 4,* 213–240. doi:10.3102/00346543044002213

Lazarus, R.S., & Folkman, S. (1984). *Stress, appraisal, and coping.* New York, NY: Springer.

Lichtenfeld, S., Pekrun, R., Stupnisky, R.H., Reiss, K., & Murayama, K. (2012). Measuring students' emotions in the early years: The Achievement Emotions Questionnaire–Elementary School (AEQ-ES). *Learning and Individual Differences, 22,* 190–201. doi:10.1016/j.lindif.2011.04.009

Liebert, R.M., & Morris, L.W. (1967). Cognitive and emotional components of test anxiety: A distinction and some initial data. *Psychological Reports, 20,* 975–978.

Linnenbrink, E.A. (2007). The role of affect in student learning: A multi-dimensional approach to considering the interaction of affect, motivation, and engagement. In P.A. Schutz & R. Pekrun (Eds.), *Emotion in education* (pp. 107–124). San Diego, CA: Academic Press.

Linnenbrink, E.A., & Pintrich, P.R. (2002). Achievement goal theory and affect: An asymmetrical bidirectional model. *Educational Psychologist, 37,* 69–78.

Mandler, G., & Sarason, S.B. (1952). A study of anxiety and learning. *Journal of Abnormal and Social Psychology, 47,* 166–173.

Meinhardt, J., & Pekrun, R. (2003). Attentional resource allocation to emotional events: An ERP study. *Cognition and Emotion, 17,* 477–500. doi:10.1080/02699930244000039

Pekrun, R. (1992). Expectancy-value theory of anxiety: Overview and implications. In D.G. Forgays, T. Sosnowski, & K. Wrzesniewski (Eds.), *Anxiety: Recent developments in self-appraisal, psychophysiological and health research* (pp. 23–41). Washington, DC: Hemisphere.

Pekrun, R. (2006). The control-value theory of achievement emotions: Assumptions, corollaries, and implications for educational research and practice. *Educational Psychology Review, 18,* 315–341. doi:10.1007/s10648-006-9029-9

Pekrun, R. (2009). Global and local perspectives on human affect: Implications of the control-value theory of achievement emotions. In M. Wosnitza, S.A. Karabenick, A. Efklides, & P. Nenniger (Eds.), *Contemporary motivation research: From global to local perspectives* (pp. 97–115). Cambridge, MA: Hogrefe.

Pekrun, R., Elliot, A.J., & Maier, M.A. (2006). Achievement goals and discrete achievement emotions: A theoretical model and prospective test. *Journal of Educational Psychology, 98,* 583–597. doi:10.1037/0022-0663.98.3.583

Pekrun, R., Elliot, A.J., & Maier, M.A. (2009). Achievement goals and achievement emotions: Testing a model of their joint relations with academic performance. *Journal of Educational Psychology, 101,* 115–135. doi:10.1037/a0013383

Pekrun, R., Goetz, T., Daniels, L.M., Stupnisky, R.H., & Perry, R.P. (2010). Boredom in achievement settings: Control-value antecedents and performance outcomes of a neglected emotion. *Journal of Educational Psychology, 102,* 531–549. doi:10.1037/a0019243

Pekrun, R., Goetz, T., Frenzel, A.C., Barchfeld, P., & Perry, R.P. (2011). Measuring emotions in students' learning and performance: The Achievement Emotions Questionnaire (AEQ). *Contemporary Educational Psychology, 36,* 36–48.

Pekrun, R., Goetz, T., Titz, W., & Perry, R.P. (2002). Academic emotions in students' self-regulated learning and achievement: A program of quantitative and qualitative research. *Educational Psychologist, 37,* 91–106.

Pekrun, R., & Linnenbrink-Garcia, L. (Eds.). (in press). *Handbook of emotions in education.* New York, NY: Taylor & Francis.

Pekrun, R., vom Hofe, R., Blum, W., Frenzel, A.C., Goetz, T., & Wartha, S. (2007). Development of mathematical competencies in adolescence: The PALMA longitudinal study. In M. Prenzel (Ed.), *Studies on the educational quality of schools* (pp. 17–37). Münster, Germany: Waxmann.

Reisenzein, R., Junge, M., & Huber, O. (in press). Observational approaches to the measurement of emotions. In R. Pekrun & L. Linnenbrink-Garcia (Eds.), *Handbook of emotions in education.* New York, NY: Taylor & Francis.

Ruthig, J.C., Perry, R.P., Hall, N.C., & Hladkyj, S. (2004). Optimism and attributional retraining: Longitudinal effects on academic achievement, test anxiety, and voluntary course withdrawal in college students. *Journal of Applied Social Psychology, 34,* 709–730. doi:10.1111/j.1559–1816.2004.tb02566.x

Sansone, C., Weir, C., Harpster, L., & Morgan, C. (1992). Once a boring task always a boring task? Interest as a self-regulatory mechanism. *Journal of Personality and Social Psychology, 63,* 379–390.

Schutz, P.A., & Pekrun, R. (Eds.). (2007). *Emotion in education.* San Diego, CA: Academic Press.

Shuman, V., & Scherer, K.R. (in press). Concepts and structure of emotions. In R. Pekrun & L. Linnenbrink-Garcia (Eds.), *Handbook of emotions in education.* New York, NY: Taylor & Francis.

Spangler, G., Pekrun, R., Kramer, K., & Hofmann, H. (2002). Students' emotions, physiological reactions, and coping in academic exams. *Anxiety, Stress and Coping, 15,* 413–432.

Spielberger, C.D. (1980). *Test Anxiety Inventory: Preliminary professional manual.* Palo Alto, CA: Consulting Psychologist Press.

Turner, J.E., & Schallert, D.L. (2001). Expectancy-value relationships of shame reactions and shame resiliency. *Journal of Educational Psychology, 93,* 320–329. doi:10.1037/0022–0663.93.2.320

Valeski, T.N., & Stipek, D.J. (2001). Young children's feelings about school. *Child Development, 72,* 1198–1213.

Weiner, B. (1985). An attributional theory of achievement motivation and emotion. *Psychological Review, 92,* 548–573.

Weiner, B. (2007). Examining emotional diversity on the classroom: An attribution theorist considers the moral emotions. In P.A. Schutz & R. Pekrun (Eds.), *Emotion in education* (pp. 73–88). San Diego, CA: Academic Press.

Wine, J.D. (1971). Test anxiety and the direction of attention. *Psychological Bulletin, 76,* 92–104.

Wyatt, S. (1930). The problem of monotony and boredom in industrial work. *Industrielle Psychotechnik, 7,* 114–123.

Zeidner, M. (1998). *Test anxiety: The state of the art.* New York, NY: Plenum.

Zeidner, M. (in press). Anxiety in education. In R. Pekrun & L. Linnenbrink-Garcia (Eds.), *Handbook of emotions in education.* New York, NY: Taylor & Francis.

CHAPTER SUMMARY: ACHIEVEMENT EMOTIONS

- **Definition.** Achievement emotions are emotions that relate to achievement activities (e.g., enjoyment of learning, boredom) or achievement outcomes (success and failure; e.g., hope, anxiety, pride, shame).

- **Appraisal determinants.** Perceived control over achievement is a predictor of positive achievement emotions, and perceived lack of control is a predictor of negative achievement emotions. The perceived value of achievement is positively related with both positive and negative achievement emotions (i.e., more intense emotions with higher importance).

- **Development.** On an average, achievement anxiety increases over the elementary school years and stays at relatively high levels thereafter, whereas positive achievement emotions decline over the school years.

- **Effects of positive emotions.** Positive activating emotions such as enjoyment of learning facilitate students' attention, interest, motivation to learn, use of flexible learning strategies, self-regulation of learning, and academic achievement.

- **Effects of negative emotions.** Negative activating emotions such as anxiety, anger, and shame undermine attention and intrinsic motivation but can induce motivation to avoid failure and can facilitate the use of rigid learning strategies. Negative deactivating emotions such as boredom and hopelessness have uniformly negative effects on attention, motivation, and strategy use. Both types of negative emotions relate negatively to academic achievement.

- **Reciprocal causation.** Achievement emotions, their individual and social antecedents, and their effects are likely to be linked by reciprocal causation over time.
- **Emotion regulation.** Achievement emotions can be changed by directly targeting components of the emotion and by changing appraisals, competencies, or learning environments (emotion-oriented, appraisal-oriented, competence-oriented, and situation-oriented regulation, respectively).
- **Diversity and universality.** Achievement emotions vary widely between individuals, genders, academic settings, and sociocultural context; however, their links with appraisal antecedents and performance outcomes are likely to follow universal principles.
- **Measurement.** Ways to measure achievement emotions include self-report, neuroimaging, assessment of peripheral physiological processes, and observation of expressive behavior.
- **Implications for education.** Educators can help students develop adaptive achievement emotions and reduce maladaptive emotions by increasing the cognitive and motivational quality of instruction, providing sufficient autonomy support, using mastery-oriented goal structures and achievement standards, providing positive feedback about achievement, and avoiding high-stakes testing.

SUGGESTED READINGS: ACHIEVEMENT EMOTIONS

Pekrun, R. (2006). The control-value theory of achievement emotions: Assumptions, corollaries, and implications for educational research and practice. *Educational Psychology Review, 18,* 315–341. doi:10.1007/s10648-006-9029-9

Provides an overview of Pekrun's control-value theory. The theory addresses origins, functions, situational specificity, individual differences, and regulation of achievement emotions.

Pekrun, R., & Linnenbrink-Garcia, R. (Eds.). (in press). *Handbook of emotions in education.* New York, NY: Taylor & Francis.

First handbook on emotions in education. Includes chapters on structures of emotion, major theories of emotion and emotion regulation, emotions in different academic domains and settings, and approaches to measurement and methodology.

Schutz, P.A., & Pekrun, R. (Eds.). (2007). *Emotion in education.* San Diego, CA: Academic Press.

Includes overviews of theories and research on achievement emotions.

Weiner, B. (1985). An attributional theory of achievement motivation and emotion. *Psychological Review, 92,* 548–573.

Provides an overview of Weiner's attributional theory. The theory addresses causal attributions as antecedents of achievement emotions.

Zeidner, M. (1998). *Test anxiety: The state of the art.* New York, NY: Plenum.

Comprehensive review of research on test anxiety. Includes summaries of evidence on origins, development, individual differences, effects on achievement, and therapy.

11

CREATIVITY IN THE SCHOOLS
Renewed Interest and Promising New Directions

James C. Kaufman, Department of Educational Psychology, University of Connecticut, Storrs, Connecticut, USA

Ronald A. Beghetto, College of Education, University of Oregon, Eugene, Oregon, USA

The authors acknowledge Heather Roessler for assistance in preparing the manuscript.

INTRODUCTION

Educators and psychologists have long viewed creativity as an important yet often neglected educational goal (Aljughaiman & Mowrer-Reynolds, 2005; Beghetto & Plucker, 2006; Guilford, 1950; Vygotsky 1967/2004). Interest in making creativity a more central goal in schools has grown steadily in recent years. Indeed, in the years that have transpired since our first version of this chapter, creativity in education has received headline attention in popular media outlets (e.g., *Newsweek, Wall Street Journal*), become the focus of widely popular talks given by public intellectuals (e.g., TED talks), and is frequently highlighted in both popular sources of information (e.g., blog posts) and various scholarly outlets (e.g., edited books, scholarly and practitioner-based journals). One reason for this increased interest is that creativity is viewed as a basic competency for being able to navigate the increasingly complex and unpredictable nature of life in a digital age (Craft, 2011). Not surprisingly, then, creativity has been featured as a central skill in the national curricula of various countries around the world (Beghetto, 2010; Craft, 2007). With respect to the United States, interest in the role that creativity can and should play in the K–12 curriculum has also grown steadily (Beghetto & Kaufman,

2013), as evidenced in recent national curricular guidelines that view creativity as a key component to development in students. For instance, the *Partnership for 21st Century Skills* (www.P21.org) includes creativity as one of its core learning skills.

Coupled with renewed interest in creativity are new concerns about the potentially stifling effects of schools and classrooms on the development of students' creative potential—leading to the report of "a creativity crisis" in U.S. schools (Bronson & Merryman, 2010; Kim, 2011). Teachers are caught somewhere in the middle. Although most teachers recognize the value of creativity, mandated accountability standards often place pressure on teachers to increase standardized test scores. Thus, concerns are expressed that nurturing creativity will come at the cost of covering the curriculum and even lead the class off topic—drifting toward curricular chaos (see essays in Beghetto & Kaufman, 2010). Unless teachers and researchers have a clear understanding of the nature of creativity and how it can coexist in a context of academic accountability, it is unlikely that renewed interest in creativity will lead to substantive changes in classroom practice.

In this chapter, we begin by discussing standard definitions and concepts of creativity, and we elaborate on our Four C Model of Creativity, which we believe is a more encompassing approach to creativity. We then discuss the conditions necessary for nurturing students' development of creativity, including types of educational environments conducive to nurturing creative development and the importance of teaching students when (and when not) to be creative. We close with a summary of key points from the chapter and highlight a few key resources for anyone interested in learning more about creativity in the schools.

WHAT IS CREATIVITY?

Until the 1950s, creativity research was minimal, if barely existent. Less than 0.2% of all entries of *Psychological Abstracts* concentrated on creativity (Guilford, 1950). In his seminal address at the 1950 convention of the American Psychological Association, Guilford persuasively argued for the practical application and scientific merits of creativity research (Kaufman, 2009). Since that influential address, creativity has grown to be a key topic of research studied by numerous scholars representing varied disciplines (e.g., psychology, sociology, philosophy, the arts, and education) throughout the world.

One way of conceptualizing how creativity is researched across the world is to focus on *whose* creativity is being studied. By way of example, the focus of study in creativity depends on whether one is studying internationally famous movie director Steven Spielberg, his plumber (who may creatively fix troublesome leaks), his computer-scientist father and musician mother (both accomplished in their own right), his daughter Mikaela, or her fifth-grade teacher. Thus, the best way to measure creativity may shift according to the creator. Regardless of focus, most definitions of creativity now comprise two components. First, creative ideas need to represent something different, new, or innovative. Second, creative ideas must also be appropriate to the task. Thus, a creative response is original and appropriate as defined in a particular context (Kaufman & Sternberg, 2007; Plucker, Beghetto, & Dow, 2004).

THE FOUR C MODEL

Big-C Approaches

Most investigations of creativity tend to take one of two directions. The first direction focuses on works from eminent individuals, particularly those that are time honored. These types of studies and theories are typically referred to as studying "Big-C" creativity. Examples of studies include those that examine the creative contributions of eminent classical and opera composers whose works have lasted centuries (e.g., Simonton, 1977, 1997) or legendary scientists (Simonton, 2009). Much of the Big-C research uses the historiometric method, which analyzes data taken from biographies or reference sources, thus allowing researchers to examine cross-group patterns in a way that would be impossible to do by interviewing each individually. Many creativity theories have focused on Big-C concepts. For example, the Propulsion Theory of Creative Contributions (Sternberg & Kaufman, 2012; Sternberg, Kaufman, & Pretz, 2002) focuses on how an individual's creative act potentially changes an entire field. The authors outline eight different types of creative contributions, with each representing a different way that a creator can impact a field. The first four contributions all stay within the framework of an existing paradigm. The most basic type of contribution is *replication*, which simply reproduces the past work of others. In comparison, *redefinition* tries to present a different perspective to an established concept, comparable to how a director might re-envision a classic play. The third contribution is *forward incrementation*, which pushes forward a field of study just a little. Maybe the creator makes a slight change in what already exists, such as a slight twist on a genre novel. These additions usually are not groundbreaking—it takes the field of study in the same direction it was heading. The final contribution is the *advance forward incrementation*. This contribution pushes the field of study far ahead—and the creator often suffers for being too far ahead of the times. The remaining four creative types discussed in propulsion theory represent attempts to reject and replace the current paradigm. *Redirection* represents an attempt to take a field of study in a new direction. If most of these contribution types represent forward momentum, *reconstruction/redirection* is an attempt to move the field back to where it once was (a reconstruction of the past) so that it may move forward from this point—but in a different direction. Perhaps the most radical of all of the creative contributions is *reinitiation*. In *reinitiation*, the creator tries to move the field to a new (as-yet-unreached) starting point, then progress from there (e.g., Marcel DuChamp entering a urinal in an art exhibit and declaring it art). Finally, the last contribution is *integration*, in which two diverse domains are merged to create a new idea (e.g., the iPhone, which combines a handheld computer and cell phone).

Little-c Approaches

The other predominant approach to creativity focuses on creative activities conducted every day by laypersons or individuals who would not necessarily be considered experts or luminaries (e.g., Richards, 2007). The theories and studies along this line of thinking are usually said to focus on "little-c." Areas of research that focus on little-c creativity may be aimed at developing and warranting the assertion that everyone has creative potential (for reviews, see Kaufman & Baer, 2005; Plucker et al., 2004). Some examples of little-c research include investigations of layperson perceptions of creativity (i.e., how a layperson's concept of creativity may differ from how a researcher might define the construct) and cross-cultural comparisons of beliefs about creativity (Lim & Plucker, 2001; Paletz & Peng, 2008).

There are several creativity theories that seem grounded in little-c, such as the Investment Theory of Creativity (Sternberg & Lubart, 1995), which argues that the key to being creative is to identify ideas or areas of research that have received only minimal attention, research these ideas, and convince others of how important they might be—and then, when other people have begun to study this topic, move on to another "unpopular" area of research. Sternberg and Lubart (1995) list six variables as being essential to creativity: intelligence, knowledge, personality, environment, motivation, and thinking styles. There are, indeed, patterns in these six variables that would describe a creative person. For example, people who are born into environments that value and nurture creativity tend to grow up to be more creative than people who grow up in environments that do not value (and may even punish) creativity. Another theory is Amabile's (1996) Componential Model of Creativity, which contends that three variables are needed for creativity to occur: *domain-relevant skills* (knowledge of a particular field of study; having technical skills or talent within that domain); *creativity-relevant skills* (personal characteristics such as tolerance for ambiguity, ability to consider divergent perspectives, having creative metacognition, being self-disciplined, willingness to take risks); and *task motivation* (e.g., intrinsic or deep interest in the task).

Beyond Big-C and little-c

Although the distinction between Big-C and little-c creativity has been useful for helping to clarify different levels of creative magnitude, important ambiguities remain. There are people who are extremely creative and accomplished, but not at the Big-C level—should they be lumped in with little-c creators? If so, then little-c becomes a very broad category. Further, how are these models applied to K–12 and college-level learning?

The creative interpretations made by students as they learn a new concept or make a new metaphor are given short shrift in most conceptions of creativity. Consider, for example, the earlier-noted and standard definitions of creativity, which emphasize the combination of novelty and usefulness as defined within a particular sociocultural context (e.g., Plucker et al., 2004). Such definitions highlight the important role that the sociocultural context (e.g., eighth-grade poetry club vs. the *Norton Anthology of Poetry*) plays in determining what will be considered novel and useful. These core components of creativity (i.e., novelty, usefulness, social context) seem most salient to the little-c model. For instance, if an amateur poet shared some poems with a friend, he or she would not expect that friend to begin a critique by comparing the poems to Robert Frost or T.S. Eliot. Indeed, to reach the level of publishable work usually takes approximately 10 years (Hayes, 1989). The friend would likely evaluate the poems by determining whether there was something new and original about them and making sure that the poems followed some basic conventions of poetry. At the Big-C level, on the other hand, the twin components of novelty and usefulness are automatically assumed to be present. An analyst who studies the poetry of Emily Dickenson or W.B. Yeats does not need to begin by asserting that the poems are new or useful. Rather, the larger question rests on how these poets impacted the field and influenced generations of young writers.

Where does this leave the creative insights had by students who are still learning how to write poetry? A student's initial efforts at poetry will not likely be judged to be novel or useful. As such, standard (little-c) definitions of creativity are not applicable (because the standard definition relies on external judgments of novelty and usefulness). Importantly, however, the student's early poems can still represent work that is personally new and meaningful to *him or her*. Even though the poem likely will not represent anything new to the field, the very process of learning a field (like writing poetry) presents many opportunities for students to experience creative insights and interpretation.

Big-C and little-c conceptions of creativity are not enough to capture the complex nature of creativity. Kaufman and Beghetto (2009, 2013; Beghetto & Kaufman, 2007), therefore, proposed a Four C Model of Creativity that included two additional categories over what has been proposed in existing models: "Pro-c" and "mini-c." Pro-c creativity is expert-level creativity that has not yet attained legendary status: If Jascha Heifitz is a Big-C violinist, then a Pro-c violinist might be the first chair of the Los Angeles Philharmonic. Mini-c creativity constitutes the lowest level of the hierarchy—self-discovering or gleaning personally meaningful insights and interpretations inherent in the learning process (Beghetto & Kaufman, 2007). As one example that distinguishes the little-c from the mini-c, someone who plays violin for a community orchestra would be at the little-c category, while a sixth-grade starting violin lessons would be at the mini-c category.

Given that mini-c is most applicable to school-aged youth, we focus on that concept here. Mini-c creativity broadens traditional conceptions of creativity to include creative insights and interpretations. Occasionally, such insights and interpretations may develop into little-c (or perhaps even Big-C) contributions (Beghetto & Kaufman, 2007). In this way, mini-c creativity can also serve as natural progression to more mature and impactful forms of creativity (little-c and Big-C). For example, the invention of Velcro (Big-C creativity) started with George de Mestral's mini-c insight he had after examining the burs that latched onto his clothing while hiking in the Swiss Alps. Of course, the ability to move from such a mini-c insight into the manufacturing of a Big-C product (like Velcro) requires expert knowledge, persistence, resources, and some degree of luck (see Simonton, 2009). Still, it is important to note that the unambiguous, creative end product (in this case, Velcro) can overshadow the recognition that the process started with a mini-c (intrapersonal) insight. Although not everyone's insights will lead to innovative and high-impact products, the genesis of such products (i.e., mini-c insights) occurs nearly every day and is available to most anyone (be they world-renowned inventors or grade school children).

The Promise of mini-c Creativity for Schools and Classrooms

We see the concept of mini-c creativity as holding great promise for helping educators make room for creativity in schools and classrooms. Traditional conceptions of creativity, which focus on eminent levels of creative breakthrough and high levels of productivity, make it difficult for educators to justify spending time on activities with such a low probability of manifesting "creativity" in their students (i.e., revolutionary breakthroughs and high levels of productivity in some domain). It is, therefore, not surprising that while teachers generally value creativity, they fail to see its relevance or importance in their own classroom (Beghetto, 2007; Beghetto & Plucker, 2006).

The marginalization of creativity in schools and classrooms is also underwritten by a host of negative stereotypes and perceptions about creative students. These negative beliefs and perceptions are found across cultures and have long histories. For example, some teachers in Western cultures seem to value creative students less than they value bright students, in part because they associate creativity with nonconformity, impulsivity, and disruptive behavior (e.g., Dawson, 1997; Scott, 1999). Other studies find that teachers feel favorably about creative students (e.g., Runco, Johnson, & Baer, 1993), although they may not be fully clear on what creativity means (Aljughaiman & Mowrer-Reynolds, 2005). For example, in one study, teachers reported liking creative students but then defined creativity with adjectives such as "well-behaved" or "conforming." These perceptions changed for the negative when the same teachers were given descriptors that were more typically used to describe creative people, such as "impulsive" or "tries to do what others call impossible" (Westby & Dawson, 1995).

Several other investigations have found that teachers' understanding of creativity is often poor. Diakidoy and Phtiaka (2002), for example, discovered that teachers associated creativity primarily with the arts and did not associate "knowledge" as a meaningful component of creativity (see also Seo, Lee, & Kim, 2005). Further, de Souza Fleith (2000) found that although teachers articulated how their attitudes might impact student creativity, they did not consider concepts such as self-evaluation, rewards, or intrinsic motivation as being related to creativity. These negative or misinformed perceptions of creativity can transcend cultures. For example, Tan (2003) reported that student teachers in Singapore favored students who had pleasant dispositions (e.g., kind, friendly) over students who were more creative and risk taking. Chan and Chan (1999) found that Chinese teachers associated socially undesirable traits with student creativity, arguing that in Chinese cultures, nonconforming or expressive behavior can be interpreted as arrogant or rebellious. Similar findings have been found in Turkish teachers (Güncer & Oral, 1993).

Mini-c creativity offers teachers another way of thinking about student creativity. Indeed, mini-c creativity highlights the creative processes inherent in the development of creative potential. The concept of mini-c helps teachers recognize that creativity most likely manifested in their classroom will be of a different caliber and require more nurturance than what traditional conceptions of creativity would allow. Importantly, mini-c creativity reframes creativity in a more positive light for teachers. Rather than creativity being viewed as something extraordinary (and therefore extracurricular), mini-c stresses that creative insights and interpretations are present in students' everyday learning of core curricular topics. When teachers recognize this, it is hoped that they will be in a better position to provide supportive feedback aimed at helping students develop their creative potential.

Supportive teacher feedback is an important issue when it comes to students' creativity development. For instance, Beghetto (2006) found that middle and secondary students' reports of teachers providing positive feedback on their creativity were the strongest predictors of beliefs in their own creativity. As such, teachers have good reason to actively seek out (and develop) strategies for providing supportive feedback that helps students develop their confidence in their own creativity. Doing so may help students move from mini-c interpretations to real-world innovations.

How might this feedback look in the classroom? Beghetto (2007) discussed how teachers can encourage movement from mini-c interpretations to little-c expressions by: (a) taking the time to hear and attempt to understand how students are interpreting what they are learning; (b) helping students recognize when their contributions are not making sense given the domain constraints, conventions, and standards of a particular activity or task; and (c) providing multiple opportunities for students to practice developing the skills of a particular domain or task. These suggestions, as well as other practical recommendations (see Beghetto, 2005), provide tangible illustrations of how teachers can recognize the value of students' mini-c creativity.

ENVIRONMENTS SUPPORTIVE OF CREATIVE EXPRESSION

The policies, practices, and procedures of schools and classrooms are laden with goal-related messages that influence the motivational beliefs and subsequent achievement behavior of students (Pintrich & Schunk 2002). Everything from grading practices to honor rolls to displaying student work in hallways and classrooms communicates what is valued in the school/classroom and provides an underlying rationale for engaging in (or avoiding) achievement-directed behaviors. For instance, if displays of student writing in classrooms are finalized products (as opposed to drafts leading to finalized products), then the importance of outperforming others or avoiding the appearance of incompetence may be (unintentionally) stressed.

Motivation researchers have categorized the messages emphasized by learning environments into two major types: *mastery goal structures* and *performance goal structures* (see Anderman and Anderman, this book). Mastery goal structures have been linked to intrinsic motivation, whereas performance goal structures can trigger extrinsic motivation (Pintrich & Schunk 2002). Many research studies (Amabile, 1996; Amabile, Hennessey, & Grossman, 1986; Amabile, Hill, Hennessey, & Tighe, 1994) report that creativity is typically increased when students have intrinsic motivation about a task. However, the relation between motivation, goal structure, and creativity is not necessarily completely straightforward. Although limited empirical work has directly examined the influence of classroom goal structures on student creativity, the conceptual links between creativity, classroom goal structures, and students' motivational beliefs likely are complex, nuanced, and extend beyond the good/bad dichotomy in which mastery and performance goals are often portrayed. For example, Beghetto (2006) found a positive association between middle and secondary students' creative self-efficacy beliefs (i.e., self-assessments of creativity) and mastery goal orientations (i.e., focus on improvement). Interestingly, a positive relation was also found between students' creativity self-efficacy beliefs and their performance approach beliefs. This finding suggests that there may be an optimal "additive pattern" (Barron & Harackiewicz, 2001) of mastery and performance approach beliefs and creative self-efficacy beliefs. In other words, it may be the case that the combination of mastery *and* performance goals actually bolsters and protects creativity self-beliefs.

At this point, such assertions require further study and, importantly, should not underplay the potentially negative impact that external rewards may have on creativity (particularly in the absence of mastery goals that may counterbalance their negative effects). Indeed, the very presence of rewards for creative work can impact creativity and the desire to be creative in multiple ways. In one study, even with tasks presented in a context that emphasized intrinsic motivation, extrinsic rewards had a negative impact on performance (Cooper, Clasen, Silva-Jalonen, & Butler, 1999). Others argue that rewards can be beneficial if given wisely. For example, neither an individual's intrinsic motivation nor creativity were negatively affected—and could actually be enhanced—if the reward (particularly a verbal reward) was delivered after the creative activity (Eisenberger & Selbst, 1994). Eisenberger and Shanock (2003), in reviewing the many studies on the harm or benefits of reward, concluded that much of the debate involves methodological issues. Specifically, they argued that rewarding creative performance increases both intrinsic motivation and creativity (traditionally measured at the mini-c or little-c level), whereas rewarding conventional performance decreases both intrinsic motivation and creativity.

Given the strong connection among the school environment, motivation, and creativity, educators have a responsibility to actively consider how the motivational messages sent by school and classroom policies, practices, and procedures may influence students' willingness to develop and express their creativity. Beghetto (2005) provides several general recommendations for supporting student creativity in educational settings. Those recommendations include: (a) setting challenging but realistic goals for students and focusing on the features of a task that are interesting and personally meaningful (rather than attempting to motivate students to complete tasks simply because they are assigned and will be graded); (b) supporting creative expression by encouraging the generation of novel ideas and helping students then select the most promising and appropriate ideas for a given task; (c) minimizing the pressures of assessment; (d) helping students recognize that the primary reason for engaging in a task is self-improvement rather than just showing others that they can successfully complete a task; (e) helping students learn from mistakes and recognize that making mistakes is a natural part of learning; and (f) helping students consider what their assigned grade meant rather than focusing solely on letter grades and test scores (i.e., what they did well and how they might improve in the future).

TEACHING STUDENTS WHEN (AND WHEN NOT) TO BE CREATIVE

Given the recent attention paid to creativity and the interest on the part of policy makers and business leaders to make creativity a more prominent educational goal in the United States and abroad (Craft, 2007; www.P21.org), the message that may be sent to teachers and students is that they should somehow strive to be creative at all times and in all places. We worry that this is the wrong message.

Part of developing a creative skillset includes learning when (and when not) to be creative. This knowledge, called creative metacognition (Kaufman & Beghetto, 2013), refers to a combination of creative self-knowledge (knowing one's own creative strengths and limitations, both within a domain and as a general trait) and contextual knowledge (knowing when, where, how, and why to be creative). Prior research has provided evidence that creative people have higher creative metacognition (CMC). For example, Silvia (2008) asked people to pick their best responses to a divergent-thinking task and found that more creative people were more likely to choose accurately. Similarly, Runco and his colleagues (Runco & Dow, 2004; Runco & Smith, 1992) found that people who tend to produce more original responses are also better at rating their most original responses to a divergent thinking task. Such insight could also be used to determine times when creativity might be best reined in. For example, a student may have a very creative idea about butterflies during a multiplication test, but the best course of action is probably to finish the test first.

A key area of future research is thus to explore how teachers might best encourage students to be creative and, at the same time, teach students how to "read a situation" and determine whether and how to express one's creative ideas, insights, and behaviors. One place to start would be in how teachers provide students with informative feedback—highlighting students' creative strengths (what they can already do well) and limitations (where they need to continue to learn and improve). For example, researchers might explore how use of the Goldilocks Principle of feedback (Beghetto & Kaufman, 2007) supports the development of CMC. Specifically, this principle highlights the importance of providing feedback that is not too harsh (stifling students' motivation) yet not too gentle (little attention to real-world standards).

REFERENCES

Aljughaiman, A., & Mowrer-Reynolds, E. (2005). Teachers' conceptions of creativity and creative students. *Journal of Creative Behavior, 39,* 17–34. doi:10.1002/j.2162-6057.2005.tb01247.x

Amabile, T. M. (1996). *Creativity in context: Update to the social psychology of creativity.* Boulder, CO: Westview.

Amabile, T. M., Hennessey, B. A., & Grossman, B. S. (1986). Social influences on creativity: The effects of contracted-for reward. *Journal of Personality and Social Psychology, 50,* 14–23. doi:10.1037/0022-3514.50.1.14

Amabile, T. M., Hill, K. G., Hennessey, B. A., & Tighe, E. M. (1994). The work preference inventory: Assessing intrinsic and extrinsic motivational orientations. *Journal of Personality and Social Psychology, 66,* 950–967. doi:10.1037/0022-3514.66.5.950

Barron, K. E., & Harackiewicz, J. M. (2001). Achievement goals and optimal motivation: Testing multiple goal models. *Journal of Personality and Social Psychology, 80,* 706–722. doi:10.1037/0022-3514.80.5.706

Beghetto, R. A. (2005). Does assessment kill student creativity? *Educational Forum, 69,* 254–263. doi:10.1080/00131720508984694

Beghetto, R. A. (2006). Creative self-efficacy: Correlates in middle and secondary students. *Creativity Research Journal, 18,* 447–457. doi:10.1207/s15326934crj1804_4

Beghetto, R. A. (2007). Ideational code-switching: Walking the talk about supporting student creativity in the classroom. *Roeper Review, 29,* 265–270. doi:10.1080/02783190709554421

Beghetto, R. A. (2010). Creativity in the classroom. In J. C. Kaufman & R. J. Sternberg (Eds.), *Handbook of creativity* (pp. 447–466). New York, NY: Cambridge University Press.

Beghetto, R. A., & Kaufman, J. C. (2007). Toward a broader conception of creativity: A case for "mini-c" creativity. *Psychology of Aesthetics, Creativity, and the Arts, 1,* 13–79. doi:10.1037/1931-3896.1.2.73

Beghetto, R. A., & Kaufman, J. C. (Eds.). (2010). *Nurturing creativity in the classroom.* New York, NY: Cambridge University Press.

Beghetto, R. A., & Kaufman, J. C. (2013). Fundamentals of creativity. *Educational Leadership, 70,* 10–15.

Beghetto, R. A., & Plucker, J. A. (2006). The relationship among schooling, learning, and creativity: "All roads lead to creativity" or "You can't get there from here?" In J. C. Kaufman & J. Baer (Eds.), *Creativity and reason in cognitive development* (pp. 316–332). Cambridge, UK: Cambridge University Press. doi:10.1017/CBO9780511606915.019

Bronson, P.O., & Merryman, A. (2010, July 19). The creativity crisis. *Newsweek*, 44–50.

Chan, D.W., & Chan, L.K. (1999). Implicit theories of creativity: Teachers' perception of student characteristics in Hong Kong. *Creativity Research Journal, 12,* 185–195. doi:10.1207/s15326934crj1203_3

Cooper, B.L., Clasen, P., Silva-Jalonen, D.E., & Butler, M.C. (1999). Creative performance on an in-basket exercise: Effects of inoculation against extrinsic reward. *Journal of Managerial Psychology, 14,* 39–56. doi:10.1108/02683949910254747

Craft, A. (2007). Possibility thinking in the early years and primary classroom. In A.G. Tan (Ed.), *Creativity: A handbook for teachers* (pp. 231–249.) Singapore: World Scientific.

Craft, A. (2011). *Creativity and education futures: Learning in a digital age.* Staffordshire, UK: Trentham Books.

Dawson, V.L. (1997). In search of the wild bohemian: Challenges in the identification of the creatively gifted. *Roeper Review, 19,* 148–152. doi:10.1080/02783199709553811

de Souza Fleith, D. (2000). Teacher and student perceptions of creativity in the classroom environment. *Roeper Review, 22,* 148–153. doi:10.1080/02783190009554022

Diakidoy, I.N., & Phtiaka, H. (2002). Teachers' beliefs about creativity. In S.P. Shohov (Ed.), *Advances in psychology research* (Vol. 15, pp. 173–188). Hauppauge, NY: Nova Science.

Eisenberger, R., & Selbst, M. (1994). Does reward increase or decrease creativity? *Journal of Personality and Social Psychology, 66,* 1116–1127. doi:10.1037/0022-3514.66.6.1116

Eisenberger, R., & Shanock, L. (2003). Rewards, intrinsic motivation, and creativity: A case study of conceptual and methodological isolation. *Creativity Research Journal, 15,* 121–130. doi:10.1207/S15326934CRJ152&3_02

Guilford, J.P. (1950). Creativity. *American Psychologist, 5,* 444–454. doi:10.1037/h0063487

Güncer, B., & Oral, G. (1993). Relationship between creativity and nonconformity to school discipline as perceived by teachers of Turkish elementary school children, by controlling for their grade and sex. *Journal of Instructional Psychology, 20,* 208–214.

Hayes, J.R. (1989). *The complete problem solver* (2nd ed.). Mahwah, NJ: Erlbaum.

Kaufman, J.C. (2009). *Creativity 101.* New York, NY: Springer.

Kaufman, J.C., & Baer, J. (Eds.). (2005). *Creativity across domains: Faces of the muse.* Mahwah, NJ: Erlbaum.

Kaufman, J.C., & Beghetto, R.A. (2009). Beyond big and little: The Four C Model of Creativity. *Review of General Psychology, 13,* 1–12. doi:10.1037/a0013688

Kaufman, J.C., & Beghetto, R.A. (2013). In praise of Clark Kent: Creative metacognition and the importance of teaching kids when (not) to be creative. *Roeper Review, 35,* 155–165.

Kaufman, J.C., & Sternberg, R.J. (2007). Resource review: Creativity. *Change, 39,* 55–58.

Kim, K.H. (2011). The creativity crisis: The decrease in creative thinking scores on the Torrance Tests of Creative Thinking. *Creativity Research Journal, 23,* 285–295. doi:10.1080/10400419.2011.627805

Lim, W., & Plucker, J. (2001). Creativity through a lens of social responsibility: Implicit theories of creativity with Korean samples. *Journal of Creative Behavior, 35,* 115–130. doi:10.1002/j.2162-6057.2001.tb01225.x

Paletz, S., & Peng, K. (2008). Implicit theories of creativity across cultures: Novelty and appropriateness in two product domains. *Journal of Cross-Cultural Psychology, 39,* 286–302. doi:10.1177/0022022108315112

Pintrich, P.R., & Schunk, D.H. (2002). *Motivation in education: Theory, research, and applications* (2nd ed.). Upper Saddle River, NJ: Merrill/Prentice Hall.

Plucker, J.A., Beghetto, R.A., & Dow, G.T. (2004). Why isn't creativity more important to educational psychologists? *Educational Psychologist, 39,* 83–96. doi:10.1207/s15326985ep3902_1

Richards, R. (Ed.). (2007). *Everyday creativity and new views of human nature: Psychological, social, and spiritual perspectives.* Washington, DC: American Psychological Association Press. doi:10.1037/11595-000

Runco, M.A., & Dow, G.T. (2004). Assessing the accuracy of judgments of originality on three divergent thinking tests. *Korean Journal of Thinking & Problem Solving, 14,* 5–14.

Runco, M.A., Johnson, D.J., & Bear, P.K. (1993). Parents' and teachers' implicit theories of children's creativity. *Child Study Journal, 23,* 91–113.

Runco, M.A., & Smith, W.R. (1992). Interpersonal and intrapersonal evaluations of creative ideas. *Personality and Individual Differences, 13,* 295–302.

Scott, C.L. (1999). Teachers' biases toward creative children. *Creativity Research Journal, 12,* 321–337. doi:10.1207/s15326934crj1204_10

Seo, H., Lee, E., & Kim, K. (2005). Korean science teachers' understanding of creativity in gifted education. *Journal of Advanced Academics, 16,* 98–105.

Silvia, P.J. (2008). Discernment and creativity: How well can people identify their most creative ideas? *Psychology of Aesthetics, Creativity, and the Arts, 2,* 139–146. doi:10.1037/1931-3896.2.3.139

Simonton, D.K. (1977). Creative productivity, age, and stress: A biographical time-series analysis of 10 classical composers. *Journal of Personality and Social Psychology, 35*, 791–804. doi:10.1037/0022-3514.35.11.791

Simonton, D.K. (1997). Creative productivity: A predictive and explanatory model of career trajectories and landmarks. *Psychological Review, 104*, 66–89. doi:10.1037/0033-295X.104.1.66

Simonton, D. K. (2009). *Genius 101*. New York, NY: Springer.

Sternberg, R.J., & Kaufman, J.C. (2012). When your race is almost run, but you feel you're not yet done: Application of the Propulsion Theory of Creative Contributions to late-career challenges. *Journal of Creative Behavior, 46*, 66–76. doi:10.1002/jocb.005

Sternberg, R.J., Kaufman, J.C., & Pretz, J.E. (2002). *The creativity conundrum*. Philadelphia. PA: Psychology Press.

Sternberg, R.J., & Lubart, T.I. (1995). *Defying the crowd: Cultivating creativity in a culture of conformity*. New York, NY: Free Press.

Tan, A.G. (2003). Student teachers' perceptions of teacher behaviors for fostering creativity: A perspective on the academically low achievers. *Korean Journal of Thinking and Problem Solving, 13*, 59–71.

Vygotsky, L.S. (2004). Imagination and creativity in childhood. (M.E. Sharpe, Inc., Trans.) *Journal of Russian and East European Psychology, 42*, 7–97. (Original work published 1967)

Westby, E.L., & Dawson, V.L. (1995). Creativity: Asset or burden in the classroom? *Creativity Research Journal, 8*, 1–10. doi:10.1207/s15326934crj0801_1

CHAPTER SUMMARY: CREATIVITY

- Creativity is originality plus task appropriateness.
- There are different types of creative impact.
- There are different levels of creativity.
- Features of the classroom can support creative expression.
- Features of the classroom can suppress creative expression.
- There is a time and place for creativity.

SUGGESTED READINGS: CREATIVITY

Beghetto, R.A. (2010). Creativity in the classroom. In J.C. Kaufman & R.J. Sternberg (Eds.), *The Cambridge handbook of creativity* (pp. 447–466). Cambridge, UK: Cambridge University Press.

This chapter, in the *Cambridge Handbook of Creativity*, goes into depth about creativity in the classroom.

Beghetto, R.A., & Kaufman, J.C. (2007). Toward a broader conception of creativity: A case for mini-c creativity. *Psychology of Aesthetics, Creativity, and the Arts, 1*, 73–79. doi:10.1037/1931-3896.1.2.73

In this paper, the authors first propose the construct of mini-c.

Kaufman, J.C. (2009). *Creativity 101*. New York, NY: Springer.

This brief book is an overview of the field of creativity studies.

Kaufman, J.C., & Beghetto, R.A. (2009). Beyond big and little: The Four C Model of Creativity. *Review of General Psychology, 13*, 1–12. doi:10.1037/a0013688

In this paper, the authors present the full Four C Model.

12

STUDENT ENGAGEMENT

Jill D. Sharkey, Matthew Quirk, and Ashley M. Mayworm, Department of Counseling, Clinical, and School Psychology, University of California Santa Barbara, Santa Barbara, California, USA

DEFINITIONS AND THEORY BASE

Scholars and school professionals have identified student engagement as critical to student success in school. Although student attendance can be mandated, student participation or engagement in learning involves a complex interaction between children and their learning environments (Appleton, Christenson, & Furlong, 2008) and is an essential protective factor that promotes students' positive educational and social outcomes (O'Farrell & Morrison, 2003). As research focused on student engagement has progressed, scholars have developed an increasingly sophisticated and specific understanding of student engagement that distinguishes between a myriad of related concepts (Appleton et al., 2008; Unrau & Quirk, in press). Research has focused on measuring and examining facilitators, indicators, and outcomes of student engagement. Scholars have recognized that there are individual student factors as well as school system factors related to student engagement (Sharkey, You, & Schnoebelen, 2008). This chapter provides an orientation to student engagement including definitions, theories, facilitators, indicators, and outcomes. Future directions and practical implications conclude the discussion.

Although variability exists in the definition and measurement of student engagement and related concepts (O'Farrell & Morrison, 2003), researchers concur that the term represents a multidimensional construct encompassing a student's feelings, beliefs, thoughts, and behaviors related to the school context (Appleton et al., 2008). Although many different frameworks have been proposed to conceptualize student engagement, the two most commonly applied in current research include three (Fredricks, Blumenfeld, & Paris, 2004) or four (Appleton et al., 2008) dimensions.

In their seminal synthesis of the engagement literature, Fredricks and colleagues (2004) presented a tripartite conceptualization that included affective, behavioral, and cognitive dimensions. From this perspective, *affective engagement* refers to a student's emotional reactions at school including interest, boredom, happiness, sadness, and anxiety. *Behavioral engagement* includes positive conduct defined as following rules of the school and adhering to norms, as well as the absence of disruptive behaviors, the student's participation in learning and academic tasks, and participation in school-related activities. Finally, *cognitive engagement* is students' investment in learning, self-regulation, and use of strategies to gain knowledge and skills.

More recently, Appleton and colleagues (2008) proposed a framework that included four components of student engagement: academic, behavioral, cognitive, and psychological. These four components were based on a comprehensive review of literature related to student engagement and particularly the work of Finn (1989), Connell and Wellborn (1991), and McPartland (1994). Although similar to the ideas of Fredricks and colleagues (2004), this four-component model included academic engagement, which refers to a subset of academic behaviors traditionally included within the behavioral dimension such as credits earned, homework completion, and time on task. In addition, this framework proposed a psychological dimension of student engagement. While similar to previous conceptualizations of affective engagement, this psychological dimension specified students' relationships with teachers and peers, as well as feelings of belonging.

The student engagement literature has its origins in delinquency research with the work of Hirschi (1969), who proposed a social bonding theory to explain antisocial behavior. He conceptualized *school bonding* as including four components of social bonds: attachment, commitment, involvement, and beliefs. He suggested that people follow rules and norms of society because of their bonds to people or institutions and, conversely, people commit crimes if they are not bonded socially. Gottfredson and Hirschi (1990) later revised this social control theory to suggest that self-control mediated the relation between social bonding and delinquency. That is, students with low self-control—defined as impulsivity, insensitivity, high sensation seeking, and poor decision-making ability—do not effectively socially bond with others, which can contribute to delinquent behavior. Gottfredson and Hirschi (1990) suggested that attachments to adults promote self-control through monitoring, reinforcement, and punishment.

Early conceptualizations of social bonding in the study of delinquency have expanded to integrate developmental, ecological, and transactional influences to enhance understanding of the underlying processes that influence student engagement. A social development model emphasizes that each developmental period provides various opportunities for social involvement in different contexts or "socializing forces" (Maddox & Prinz, 2003). A social ecology model provides further understanding by incorporating additional influences in family, school, and individual domains such as family relationships and school climate (Maddox & Prinz, 2003). An ecological-developmental perspective (Fraser, 1996) adds sophistication by noting the transactional nature of individual and contextual factors including opportunities for involvement—the student is engaged within and by the social context. Therefore, student engagement fluctuates and is informed by a student's history of experiences within various social contexts. Moreover, student engagement is alterable and can be influenced, for better or for worse, by intervention in these social contexts (Reschly & Christenson, 2006).

KEY RESEARCH WITH CHILDREN AND ADOLESCENTS

Given a comprehensive conceptual foundation for student engagement, numerous personal factors and environmental contexts may influence student engagement including individual factors, peer relationships, home influences, teacher interactions, and the schoolwide context. For example, using multilevel growth curve analyses, You and Sharkey (2009) found that student-level factors (i.e., student self-esteem, locus of control, peer academic value, parental expectations, and friend dropout history) and school-level factors (i.e., school safety, teacher support, and teacher rules about homework) were significantly related to both the initial status and growth rate of student engagement. The complex interplay among factors in different areas of youths' lives on engagement is illustrated in a study conducted by Garcia-Reid (2007), which showed that teacher support, friend support, and parent support directly and positively affected school engagement and that the absence of perceived neighborhood danger was associated with greater engagement. Results of these studies point to the importance of understanding how factors in multiple aspects of students' lives facilitate or hinder their engagement in school.

Individual Characteristics

Several individual characteristics are related to student engagement. For example, student engagement is positively correlated with higher levels of career planning and expectations (Kenny, Blustein, Haase, Jackson, & Perry, 2006) and academic self-concept (Seaton & Taylor, 2003) and is negatively correlated with low expectations for success and low self-esteem (Jessor, Turbin, & Costa, 1998). Generalized self-efficacy and goal orientation (Caraway, Tucker, Reinke, & Hall, 2003), as well as self-efficacy in school, self-esteem, and perceived quality of relationships with others are positively associated with student engagement (Connell, Halpern-Felsher, Clifford, Crichlow, & Usinger, 1995). In addition, researchers have found middle school students' life satisfaction at the beginning of the school year to predict cognitive engagement five months later (Lewis, Huebner, Malone, & Valois, 2011). Taken together, these studies demonstrate that students' internal traits have an impact on their level of engagement in school. However, many of these internal traits are likely impacted by external factors.

Peer Relationships

Students' peer relationships have been found to play an important role in student engagement, with this influence varying developmentally. As students progress from early middle school to high school, student school compliance, extracurricular involvement, and valuing of learning tend to decrease (Wang & Eccles, 2012). Social networks have an increasingly important influence on students' attitudes toward schooling and on their academic motivation and success as students enter middle school (Furlong et al., 2003). Children's feelings of belonging with peers (Furrer & Skinner, 2003) and their peer friendship quality (Perdue, Manzeske, & Estell, 2009) are predictive of later school engagement. In a longitudinal study of middle schoolers, Li, Lynch, Kalvin, Liu, and Lerner (2011) found that peer support predicts both behavioral and emotional school engagement, whereas having friends who engage in problem behaviors and/or bullying is negatively associated with school engagement.

Family Factors

Factors related to the family and home have also been found to impact student engagement. Both elementary and secondary students who report a supportive relationship with their parents are more likely to be engaged at school (Wentzel, 1998). In a sample of predominately Latino/a students and families, the quality of the parent–child relationship accounted for a significant amount of variance in student self-reported engagement, grades, and achievement (Murray, 2009). Family involvement in education and educational expectations for their children is related to students' engagement in elementary and high school, even when controlling for prior achievement (Gutman & Midgley, 2000). Parental involvement in school may be particularly important for disadvantaged youths; Cooper and Crosnoe (2007) found that when economically disadvantaged children have parents with high involvement, they are more academically oriented than advantaged youths with either involved or uninvolved parents. Parenting practices have both a direct and an indirect impact on student engagement; Simons-Morton and Chen (2009) found that authoritative parenting not only directly impacts student engagement but also promotes student engagement by discouraging relationships with problem-behaving friends and assisting in adjustment to school.

School-Based Factors

Research has found that school-based factors can impact student engagement beyond the influence of family factors (Sharkey et al., 2008) and the quality of parent and peer relationships (Elmore & Huebner, 2010). Students whose teachers communicate clear expectations, provide consistent feedback, show positive interest in the children, provide both formal and informal evaluations of their work, and show respect for students by considering their opinions when making decisions are more likely to have higher levels of engagement (Skinner, Wellborn, & Connell, 1990; Wentzel, 1998). Classroom environments that allow students to feel comfortable expressing opinions, sharing ideas, and taking risks are more likely to be positive environments in which students feel they belong. In their research, Patrick, Ryan, and Kaplan (2007) found that when students felt supported emotionally by their teacher, able to discuss their work, and academically supported by their peers, they were more likely to use self-regulatory strategies and engage in task-related interactions. The classroom emotional climate is predictive of student grades, and this relation is mediated by student engagement (Reyes, Brackett, Rivers, White, & Salovey, 2012). Thus, classrooms in which positive emotion-related interactions take place are more likely to foster student engagement and, in turn, improve student academic achievement.

In addition to the classroom, the schoolwide context plays an important role in influencing the development and maintenance of students' engagement. Nasir, Jones, and

McLaughlin (2011) found that, for African-American students in low-income urban high schools, students who felt both interpersonally and institutionally connected to school had higher grades and graduation rates; students with only interpersonal connection or no connection to school fared the worst. School climate is affected by the structural and regulatory mechanisms that schools employ. Students at schools with strong disciplinary climates and high expectations for student success tend to be more engaged in school (Willms, 2003). In contrast, strict and arbitrary discipline procedures (e.g., zero tolerance) disrupt the learning environment and have a negative impact on student engagement (Gonsoulin, Zablocki, & Leone, 2012). Harsh discipline policies may send the message to students that they are not truly welcome at school and do little to help the distressed student develop positive coping strategies (Morrison, Anthony, Storino, & Dillon, 2001). Ultimately, student engagement is influenced by numerous factors in the individual, peer, family, classroom, and school contexts; therefore, approaches to improving student engagement should consider these various aspects of youths' lives.

RELATIONS WITH EDUCATIONAL OUTCOMES

Existing literature describes student engagement as a construct that aids in the promotion of positive outcomes and the protection against negative outcomes. Recent research has advanced from cross-sectional investigation to clarify the longitudinal impacts of student engagement on academic and behavioral outcomes for diverse students around the world. Moreover, scholars have started to examine the bidirectionality of these associations and to distinguish outcomes resulting from subtypes of student versus social engagement.

Academic Achievement

Many studies have provided evidence suggesting a positive association between various aspects of engagement and students' academic achievement (Skinner et al., 1990) across diverse student populations (Irvin, 2012; Li & Lerner, 2011; Seelman, Walls, Hazel, & Wisneski, 2011) and developmental stages (Ladd & Dinella, 2009). Although the majority of studies have examined links between behavioral engagement and achievement (Fredricks et al., 2004), an increasing number of studies have focused attention on emotional and cognitive indicators of engagement and their respective influences on children's academic performance (e.g., Sciarra & Seirup, 2008).

Research has also been devoted to developing process models that explain the relations between various personal and contextual factors, student engagement, and academic achievement. For example, Reyes and colleagues (2012) found evidence that the positive relation between classroom emotional climate and students' grades was mediated by engagement, controlling for other potentially influential factors such as teacher and institutional characteristics. Other recent studies have found that associations between peer relationships (Liem & Martin, 2011), peer victimization, effortful control (Iyer, Kochenderfer-Ladd, Eisenberg, & Thompson, 2010), classroom context (Dotterer & Lowe, 2011), and teacher–student relationships (Hughes, Luo, Kwok, & Loyd, 2008) and students' academic achievement are mediated by various aspects of engagement. This growing body of evidence emphasizes the critical role that engagement plays within the various interconnected systems of factors that influence children's academic achievement.

Traditionally, studies examining relations between student engagement and academic achievement have taken a variable-oriented approach, with little attention on subtypes of engagement and how various engagement profiles are related to academic outcomes (Janosz, 2012). A few recent studies have examined these issues using person-oriented approaches. For example, Li and Lerner (2011) identified four distinct developmental engagement trajectories among a sample of 1,977 students by tracking engagement and achievement variables across Grades 5 through 8. Results demonstrated that engagement trajectory group membership predicted academic as well as behavioral/emotional outcomes and that developmental group membership was associated with multiple student demographic characteristics (e.g., sex, race/ethnicity, and family socioeconomic status). Additional research is needed to better understand various profiles or subtypes of engagement (across behavioral, emotional, and cognitive dimensions) that commonly occur in different student populations and how these engagement profiles are related to longitudinal outcomes or achievement trajectories.

In-School Behavior

The majority of past research on student engagement has focused on its importance as a buffer against life challenges that may deter negative developmental outcomes (Maddox & Prinz, 2003). Student engagement is associated with the reduced risk of long-term negative behavioral outcomes such as substance abuse (Guo, Hawkins, Hill, & Abbott, 2001), depression (Mylant, Ide, Cuevas, & Meehan, 2002), school dropout (Archambault, Janosz, Fallu, & Pagani, 2009), teen pregnancy (Manlove, 1998), and antisocial delinquent behavior (Morrison, Robertson, Laurie, & Kelly, 2002).

The link between student engagement and delinquency is well established and continues to be replicated in more sophisticated research. For example, Li, Zhang, Liu, Arbeit, and Schwartz (2011) conducted discrete-time survival analysis with data spanning 7 years and found that student engagement predicted less initiation of delinquency and drug use. To uncover important distinctions between types or aspects of student engagement and delinquency, as well as the bidirectionality of these impacts, Hirschfield and Gasper (2011) examined longitudinal survey data collected twice annually with primarily African-American and Latino/a students in urban Chicago. They measured emotional, behavioral, and cognitive engagement, controlling for common causes of delinquency (parent attachment and peer delinquency). As predicted, emotional and behavioral engagement predicted decreases in delinquency. Surprisingly, cognitive engagement predicted *increases* in delinquency while delinquency predicted decreased cognitive engagement but not decreased emotional or behavioral engagement. These results further reveal the complexity of student engagement and that further study is needed to explain these phenomena.

Recent studies have provided further insight into the complex interactions among students, their social and educational context, and school dropout, which has been identified as the process of student disengagement from school (Rumberger & Rotermund, 2012). Conducting structural equation modeling with data from the National Education

Longitudinal Study of 1988, Ream and Rumberger (2008) found that students who are behaviorally engaged meet and befriend similarly engaged peers who promote educational attainment, whereas students who are not engaged meet and befriend other disengaged peers. Janosz, Archambault, Morizot, and Pagani (2008) conducted growth mixture modeling with 13,300 French-speaking Canadians living in Quebec who were participating in a longitudinal study to identify school engagement trajectories in adolescence. They found that students with unstable engagement trajectories were most likely to drop out of school. Even youth in the moderate yet stable group were much less likely (0%) to drop out of school than students in the transitory increasing (42%) or increasing (10%) trajectories. Janosz and colleagues (2008) argued that engagement stability might reflect other aspects of stability in youths' lives that protect them from negative outcomes.

Student engagement is also related to diverse students' reports of experiencing all types of victimization (O'Brennan & Furlong, 2010), a finding that appears to be true across race and nationality. In a study of student engagement of African-American youth in poor, rural areas in the southern United States, self-reported behavioral engagement in middle school predicted lower peer-assessed aggression in ninth-grade boys, whereas self-reported psychological engagement in middle school had a main effect on peer-assessed aggression for girls in ninth grade (Irvin, 2012). In a convenience sample of 1,452 students Grades 7 through 10 in Bangladesh, participants were more likely to report they would intervene in school bullying if they also reported feeling emotionally connected to school on scenario-based self-report measures (Ahmed, 2008).

Less often studied is the link between student engagement and positive outcomes. Carter, McGee, Taylor, and Williams (2007) examined the associations between connectedness to family and peers and student engagement, as well as specified health-promoting and health-compromising behaviors with 652 adolescents in New Zealand. Logistic regression examined how family, peer, and school variables were related to health behaviors; student engagement showed the most pervasive associations with health behaviors and high levels of health-promoting behaviors. Additional studies are needed to further elucidate the role of student engagement in promoting positive health behaviors.

MEASUREMENT APPROACHES AND ISSUES

The initial and one of the most critical steps in measuring any psychological construct is to develop a clearly conceptualized operational definition (Dawis, 1987). Theoretical ambiguity regarding how student engagement is defined has contributed to variation in how the construct is measured, which presents challenges when attempting to synthesize results across studies (Fredricks & McColskey, 2012). Beyond how engagement is defined or conceptualized, engagement scholars have also employed many different methodologies in measuring the construct. Fredricks and colleagues (2011) provided a comprehensive review of engagement measures that have been used in published studies since 1979. Of the 21 measures reviewed, the vast majority utilized student self-report (67%), followed by observational measures (19%) and teacher report measures (14%). In addition, researchers examining "flow" have utilized a method called experience sampling (ESM; Hektner, Schmidt, & Csikszentmihalyi, 2007) in which individuals carry electronic devices that alert them to fill out self-report questionnaires at various time points to capture context-specific indications of behavioral, affective, and cognitive responses. Finally, a relatively small number of studies have used interviews to access more detailed accounts of why some students are engaged and others remain disengaged in various school experiences (Conchas, 2001). Each method presents a combination of both strengths and weaknesses. For example, self-report measures are efficient and can be administered to large samples at relatively low cost; however, they are also susceptible to socially desirable response bias and can lack sensitivity in terms of fluctuations to engagement across time and specific contexts.

In addition to summarizing the methodological approaches used in measuring engagement, Fredricks and colleagues (2011, 2012) also provide summaries of the psychometric evidence available for specific instruments. Across each of the self-report engagement measures for which information on reliability was available, all exhibited upper-bound reliability coefficients that exceeded a widely applied benchmark of acceptability (Cronbach's alpha of .70 or higher; Leary, 2004). However, only 30% of the measures had lower-bound reliability estimates that exceeded the same benchmark, indicating that the reliability of engagement measures should be carefully considered. Similarly, research has provided evidence to support criterion-related validity for the majority of engagement measures, usually in the form of correlations with related outcomes such as student achievement (Pintrich & DeGroot, 1990) and participation (Fredricks et al., 2011). Fewer measures have construct validity evidence, such as factor analytic results (Betts, Appleton, Reschly, & Christenson, 2010) to empirically support the dimensionality of engagement scales.

There are many measures available to practitioners and scholars interested in gathering information on students' engagement in schools; however, additional research is needed to build on the foundation of information and measures currently available. Scholarship is needed to improve conceptual clarity, including additional research that examines how measures can better distinguish factors that facilitate engagement (e.g., motivation and contextual elements) from actual indicators of engagement (Unrau & Quirk, in press). In terms of methodology, most current measures do not allow raters to identify the degree to which the student is engaged; thus, absolute levels of engagement remain unknown. Also, engagement is commonly conceptualized as both a state variable and a developmental process; however, most existing measures focus solely on the student's engagement at a particular point in time. In order to better understand the process of student engagement, future measures should be taken over time and consider developmental trajectories. Finally, ongoing scholarship is needed to more deeply examine the psychometrics of various measures, with particular attention to factor analyses and tests of invariance (Betts et al., 2010) across various cultural, linguistic, and ethnic groups.

EDUCATIONAL APPLICATIONS

As is clear from the research literature, student engagement is related to numerous positive outcomes in youths. Research findings suggest that schools play a significant role in facilitating student engagement and inhibiting student disengagement by altering school-based factors (Sharkey et al., 2008). By employing school practices and interventions that promote student engagement, educators can promote student identification as members of the school community, with the ultimate goal of enhancing positive youth development.

Furlong and colleagues (2003) conceptualized student engagement as a set of behaviors along a continuum from high to low levels of school involvement, which is supported by recent empirical research that identified different developmental pathways of engagement including high stable, decreasing, and low (Li & Lerner, 2011). Thus, it makes sense that strategies to encourage student engagement should also occur at multiple levels. Furlong, Pavelski, and Saxton (2002) suggest five domains of prevention effort within the school environment.

First, schools can establish school- and classroomwide activities that *reaffirm* relationships with the majority of students. A variety of classroom variables, including positive student–teacher relationships, use of a cooperative learning instructional strategy, and promoting mutual respect within the classroom, have been found to increase a student's sense of belonging to a positive learning community and may lead to an increase in student engagement (Furlong et al., 2003). Increasing students' autonomy, competence, and relatedness has been found to increase student engagement and academic achievement (Connell & Wellborn, 1991). For example, schools that emphasize relational learning (e.g., group decision making, credit rather than grades) may lead to greater student engagement, interest, and enjoyment during school than traditional high school classroom strategies (Johnson, 2008).

Interventions that address schoolwide student engagement using multiple methods show promising results. Researchers examined the effects of a social development intervention on school bonding trajectories. Using hierarchical linear modeling, results indicated that 13- to 18-year-old students who received the full intervention were significantly more bonded to school than the control group (Hawkins, Guo, Hill, Battin-Pearson, & Abbott, 2001). Other schoolwide programs that show promise for increasing student engagement include CareerStart (Orthner et al., 2010) and Rights Respecting Schools (Covell, 2010).

Second, schools can reach out to and *reconnect* with students who are marginally involved with school and may not respond to universal strategies. For example, schools might implement positive behavioral support strategies or involve at-risk youth in afterschool programs. An example of such a program is Check & Connect (C&C), a targeted intervention used to facilitate student engagement and school completion (Anderson, Christenson, Sinclair, & Lehr, 2004). The C&C model includes the core elements of relationship building, routine monitoring of alterable risk factors, individualized intervention, continuous monitoring of targeted students, teaching problem-solving skills, building affiliation with school, and a persistent reinforcement of academic behaviors. Within this program, data are systematically used to guide intervention plans and improve the program at each school site (Stout & Christenson, 2009). There is also evidence that using cross-age peer mentors (Karcher, 2009) and adult mentoring (Holt, Bry, & Johnson, 2008) with students at risk of disengaging in school can yield improvements in student engagement.

Third, schools may need to *reconstruct* relationships with students who show more serious emotional and behavioral difficulties through intensive interventions. Research has consistently shown that students with more serious school-related difficulties, including delinquency and antisocial behavior, benefit from multimodal interventions that link the individual, peer, school, and family domains. For example, the Fast Track Project (Conduct Problems Prevention Research Group, 2011) is a multifaceted prevention and intervention program for youths with serious conduct problems. The program includes parent training, academic tutoring, child social skills training, parent–child interaction sessions, and peer pairing and tutoring, as well as universal school-based intervention (PATHS) at various stages throughout Grades 1 through 10. Other interventions that may be effective in reducing serious school-related concerns and lead to enhanced student engagement include the Family Check-Up (Dishion & Stormshak, 2007), social skills groups, behavior management programs, and group and individual counseling.

Fourth, for a small group of students who have been victims of serious or chronic violence at school, schools will need to *repair* the students' relationship with the school through interventions that renew a sense of school safety and membership. For marginalized students, opportunities to repair bonds across social contexts may be of particular importance. If a student is significantly disengaged from school and possibly other environments (home and community), it may be necessary to use multiple agencies to intervene and create opportunities for attachment and the development of self-efficacy.

Finally, schools need to be vigilant in order to *protect* relationships with youth who are vulnerable to negative influences in other contexts, such as the home or community. Part of this protection of relationships includes protecting and supporting the relationship between students and their teachers. Hughes and Kwok (2007) investigated the influence of student–teacher and parent–teacher relationships on student engagement and achievement. They found that the quality of teachers' relationships with students and their parents explained the relation between students' background and classroom engagement. Classroom engagement, in turn, mediated the relations between student–teacher and parent–teacher relatedness and student achievement the following year. Results indicated that schools should not only work on parental involvement in school but also develop relationships between parents and teachers, particularly with families experiencing low income or whose children are from minority ethnic backgrounds. Teachers may also need training in how to build successful relationships with parents and how to create supportive classroom environments.

When engagement is addressed at all of these levels, schools help increase engagement for all students, prevent future disengagement, and increase engagement in students who are currently disengaged. Ultimately, identifying as a member of the school community has been associated with positive youth development (Voelkl, 2012). Schools should strive to create communities in which students experience continual and rewarding engagement in school, which will likely lead to a sense of being a valued and contributing member of the school. By developing school practices and interventions that address student engagement at the universal, targeted, and intensive levels, schools can help students to flourish as learners and individuals.

DIVERSITY AND DEVELOPMENTAL CONSIDERATIONS

Improving engagement for all students is crucial, as our review of international research has demonstrated the consistent benefit of student engagement across diverse socio-cultural populations. Unfortunately, marginalized students have shown less favorable patterns of student engagement than their more privileged peers. For example, among early elementary students, Latino/a English language learners were less engaged than English-proficient students (Morrison, Cosden, O'Farrell, & Campos, 2003). Students with disabilities may also be at risk for lower levels of student engagement. Reschly and Christenson (2006) found that students with learning disabilities or emotional behavioral disorders reported lower engagement than their typically achieving peers. Student engagement variables were significant predictors of school dropout and completion for students with and without disabilities, indicating that students with disabilities are at higher risk of negative outcomes due to lower levels of engagement. Students with developmental or social pressures may need additional intervention to support their engagement with school than students who are more privileged.

Other research comparing groups has found that unique factors may contribute to student engagement based on group membership. For example, Liljeberg, Eklund, Fritz, and af Klinteberg (2011) examined gender differences with 788 adolescents and found that school attachment, school commitment, and teacher attachment predicted delinquency for males, but only teacher attachment predicted delinquency for girls. Examining bidirectional effects, delinquency was predictive of poor school commitment for both sexes and school attachment for girls only. Recent studies have also focused on the school engagement of sexual minority students, finding that the presence of an adult ally at school and student engagement were related to decreased fear-based truancy (Seelman et al., 2011). These results suggest that the impact of promoting student engagement might not be equivalent across diverse groups and thus, additional research is needed to further explore what works for whom and under what circumstances.

REFERENCES

Ahmed, E. (2008). "Stop it, that's enough": Bystander intervention and its relationship to school connectedness and shame management. *Vulnerable Children and Youth Studies: An International Interdisciplinary Journal for Research, Policy and Care, 3*, 203–213.

Anderson, A.R., Christenson, S.L., Sinclair, M.F., & Lehr, C.A. (2004). Check & Connect: The importance of relationships for promoting engagement with school. *Journal of School Psychology, 42*, 95–113. doi:10.1016/j.jsp.2004.01.002

Appleton, A.R., Christenson, S.L., & Furlong, M.J. (2008). Student engagement with school: Critical conceptual and methodological issues of the construct. *Psychology in the Schools, 45*, 369–386. doi:10.1002/pits.20303

Archambault, I., Janosz, M., Fallu, J.-S., & Pagani, L.S. (2009). Student engagement and its relationship with early high school dropout. *Journal of Adolescence, 32*, 651–670. doi:10.1016/j.adolescence.2008.06.007

Betts, J.E., Appleton, J.J., Reschly, A.L., & Christenson, S.L. (2010). A study of the factorial invariance of the Student Engagement Instrument (SEI): Results from middle and high school students. *School Psychology Quarterly, 25*, 84–93. doi:10.1037/a0020259

Caraway, K., Tucker, C.M., Reinke, W.M., & Hall, C. (2003). Self-efficacy, goal orientation, and fear of failure as predictors of school engagement in high school students. *Psychology in the Schools, 40*, 417–427. doi:10.1002/pits.10092

Carter, M., McGee, R., Taylor, B., & Williams, S. (2007). Health outcomes in adolescence: Associations with family, friends, and student engagement. *Journal of Adolescence, 30*, 51–62. doi:10.1016/j.adolescence.2005.04.002

Conchas, G.Q. (2001). Structuring failure and success: Understanding the variability in Latino school engagement. *Harvard Educational Review, 71*, 475–504. Retrieved from http://search.proquest.com/docview/619598568?accountid=14522

Conduct Problems Prevention Research Group. (2011). The effects of the Fast Track preventive intervention on the development of conduct disorder across childhood. *Child Development, 82*, 331–345. doi:10.1111/j.1467-8624.2010.01558.x

Connell, J.P., Halpern-Felsher, B.L., Clifford, E., Crichlow, W., & Usinger, P. (1995). Hanging in there: Behavioral, psychological, and contextual factors affecting whether African American adolescents stay in high school. *Journal of Adolescent Research, 10*, 41–63. doi:10.1177/0743554895101004

Connell, J.P., & Wellborn, J.G. (1991). Competence, autonomy, and relatedness: A motivational analysis of self-system processes. In M.R. Gunnar & L.A. Sroufe (Eds.), *Self-processes and development* (Vol. 23). Hillsdale, NJ: Erlbaum. doi:10.1177/0743554895101004

Cooper, C.E., & Crosnoe, R. (2007). The engagement in schooling of economically disadvantaged parents and children. *Youth & Society, 38*, 372–392. doi:10.1177/0044118X06289999

Covell, K. (2010). School engagement and rights-respecting schools. *Cambridge Journal of Education, 40*, 39–51. doi:10.1080/03057640903567021

Dawis, R.V. (1987). Scale construction. *Journal of Counseling Psychology, 34*, 481–489. doi:10.1037/0022-0167.34.4.481

Dishion, T.J., & Stormshak, E.A. (2007). The ecological family intervention and therapy model. In T.J. Dishion & E.A. Stormshak (Eds.), *Intervening in children's lives: An ecological, family-centered approach to mental health care* (pp. 49–67). Washington, DC: American Psychological Association. doi:10.1037/11485-004

Dotterer, A.M., & Lowe, K. (2011). Classroom context, school engagement, and academic achievement in early adolescence. *Journal of Youth and Adolescence, 40*, 1649–1660. doi:10.1007/s10964-011-9647-5

Elmore, G.M., & Huebner, E.S. (2010). Adolescents' satisfaction with school experiences: Relationships with demographics, attachment relationships, and school engagement behavior. *Psychology in the Schools, 47*, 525–537. doi:10.1002/pits.20488

Finn, J.D. (1989). Withdrawing from school. *Review of Educational Research, 59*, 117–142. doi:10.3102/00346543059002117

Fraser, M.W. (1996). Aggressive behavior in childhood and early adolescence: An ecological-developmental perspective on youth violence. *Social Work, 41*, 347–357.

Fredricks, J.A., Blumenfeld, P.C., & Paris, A.H. (2004). School engagement: Potential of the concept, state of the evidence. *Review of Educational Research, 74*, 59–109. doi:10.3102/00346543074001059

Fredricks, J., & McColskey, W. (2012). The measurement of student engagement: A comparative analysis of various methods and student self-report instruments. In S.L. Christenson, A.L. Reschley, & C. Wylie (Eds.), *Handbook of research on student engagement* (pp. 763–782). New York, NY: Springer. doi:10.1007/978-1-4614-2018-7_37

Fredricks, J., & McColskey, W., with Meli, J., Mordica, J., Montrosse, B., & Mooney, K. (2011). *Measuring student engagement in upper elementary through high school: A description of 21 instruments* (Issues & Answers Report, REL 2011–No. 098). Washington, DC: U.S. Department of Education, Institute of Education Sciences, National Center for Education Evaluation and Regional Assistance, Regional Educational Laboratory Southeast. Retrieved from http://ies.ed.gov/ncee/edlabs

Furlong, M.J., Pavelski, R., & Saxton, J. (2002). The prevention of school violence. In S. Brock, P. Lazarus, & S. Jimerson (Eds.), *Best practices in school crisis management* (pp. 131–150). Washington, DC: National Association of School Psychologists.

Furlong, M.J., Whipple, A.D., St. Jean, G., Simental, J., Soliz, A., & Punthuna, S. (2003). Multiple contexts of school engagement: Moving toward a unifying framework for educational research and practice. *The California School Psychologist, 8*, 99–114.

Furrer, C., & Skinner, E. (2003). Sense of relatedness as a factor in children's academic engagement and performance. *Journal of Educational Psychology, 95*, 148–162. doi:10.1037/0022-0663.95.1.148

Garcia-Reid, P. (2007). Examining social capital as a mechanism for improving school engagement among low-income Hispanic girls. *Youth & Society, 39*, 165–182. doi:10.1177/0044118X07303263

Gonsoulin, S., Zablocki, M., & Leone, P.E. (2012). Safe schools, staff development, and the school-to-prison pipeline. *Teacher Education and Special Education, 35*, 309–319. doi:10.1177/0888406412453470

Gottfredson, M., & Hirschi, T. (1990). *A general theory of crime*. Stanford, CA: Stanford University Press.

Guo, J., Hawkins, J.D., Hill, K.G., & Abbott, R.D. (2001). Childhood and adolescent predictors of alcohol abuse and dependence in young adulthood. *Journal of Studies on Alcohol, 62*, 754–762. NIHMS18670

Gutman, L.M., & Midgley C. (2000). The role of protective factors in supporting academic achievement of poor African American students during the middle school transition. *Journal of Youth and Adolescence, 29*, 223–248. doi:10.1023/A:1005108700243

Hawkins, J.D., Guo, J., Hill, K.G., Battin-Pearson, S., & Abbott, R.D. (2001). Long-term effects of the Seattle Social Development Intervention on school bonding trajectories. *Applied Developmental Science, 5*, 225–236. doi:10.1207/S1532480XADS0504_04

Hektner, J.M., Schmidt, J.A., & Csikzentmihalyi, M. (2007). *Experience sampling method: Measuring the quality of everyday life*. Thousand Oaks, CA: Sage.

Hirschfield, P.J., & Gasper, J. (2011). The relationship between school engagement and delinquency in late child-hood and early adolescence. *Journal of Youth and Adolescence, 40*, 3–22. doi:10.1007/s10964-010-9579-5

Hirschi, T. (1969). *Causes of delinquency.* Berkeley, CA: University of California Press.

Holt, L.J., Bry, B.H., & Johnson, V.L. (2008). Enhancing school engagement in at-risk, urban minority adolescents through a school-based, adult mentoring intervention. *Child & Family Behavior Therapy, 30*, 297–318. doi:10.1080/07317100802482969

Hughes, J., & Kwok, O. (2007). Influence of student–teacher and parent–teacher relationships on lower achieving readers' engagement and achievement in the primary grades. *Journal of Educational Psychology, 99*, 39–51. doi:10.1037/0022-0663.99.1.39

Hughes, J.N., Luo, W., Kwok, O., & Loyd, L.K. (2008). Teacher–student support, effortful engagement, and achievement: A 3-year longitudinal study. *Journal of Educational Psychology, 100*, 1–14. doi:10.1037/0022-0663.100.1.1

Irvin, M.J. (2012). Role of student engagement in the resilience of African American adolescents from low-income rural communities. *Psychology in the Schools, 49*, 176–193. doi:10.1002/pits.20626

Iyer, R.V., Kochenderfer-Ladd, B., Eisenberg, N., & Thompson, M. (2010). Peer victimization and effortful control: Relations to school engagement and academic achievement. *Merrill-Palmer Quarterly, 56*, 361–387. doi:10.1353/mpq.0.0058

Janosz, M. (2012). Outcomes of engagement and engagement as an outcome: Some consensus, divergences, and unanswered questions. In S.L. Christenson, A.L. Reschley, & C. Wylie (Eds.), *Handbook of research on student engagement* (pp. 695–703). New York: Springer. doi:10.1007/978-1-4614-2018-7_33

Janosz, M., Archambault, I., Morizot, J., & Pagani, L.S. (2008). School engagement trajectories and their differential predictive relations to dropout. *Journal of Social Issues, 64*, 21–40. doi:10.1111/j.1540-4560.2008.00546.x

Jessor, R., Turbin, M.S., & Costa, F.M. (1998). Risk and protection in successful outcomes among disadvantaged adolescents. *Applied Developmental Science, 2,* 194–208. doi:10.1207/s1532480xads0204_3

Johnson, L.S. (2008). Relationship of instructional methods to student engagement in two public high schools. *American Secondary Education, 36*, 69–87.

Karcher, M. (2009). Increases in academic connectedness and self-esteem among high school students who serve as cross-age peer mentors. *Professional School Counseling, 12*, 292–299. doi:10.5330/PSC.n.2010-12.292

Kenny, M.E., Blustein, D.L., Haase, R.F., Jackson, J., & Perry, J.C. (2006). Setting the stage: Career development and the student engagement process. *Journal of Counseling Psychology, 53*, 272–279. doi:10.1037/0022-0167.53.2.272

Ladd, G.W., & Dinella, L.M. (2009). Continuity and change in early school engagement: Predictive of children's achievement trajectories from first to eighth grade? *Journal of Educational Psychology, 101*, 190–206. doi:10.1037/a0013153

Leary, M.R. (2004). *Introduction to behavioral research methods* (4th ed.). Boston, MA: Pearson Education.

Lewis, A.D., Huebner, E.S., Malone, P.S., & Valois, R.F. (2011). Life satisfaction and student engagement in adolescents. *Journal of Youth Adolescence, 40*, 249–262. doi:10.1007/s10964-010-9517-6

Li, Y., & Lerner, R.M. (2011). Trajectories of school engagement during adolescence: Implications for grades, depression, delinquency, and substance use. *Developmental Psychology, 47*, 233–247. doi:10.1037/a0021307

Li, Y., Lynch, A.D., Kalvin, C., Liu, J., & Lerner, R.M. (2011). Peer relationships as a context for the development of school engagement during early adolescence. *International Journal of Behavioral Development, 35*, 329–342. doi:10.1177/0165025411402578

Li, Y., Zhang, W., Liu, J., Arbeit, M.R., & Schwartz, S.J. (2011). The role of school engagement in preventing adolescent delinquency and substance use: A survival analysis. *Journal of Adolescence, 34*, 1181–1192. doi:10.1016/j.adolescence.2011.07.003

Liem, G., & Martin, A.J. (2011). Peer relationships and adolescents' academic and non-academic outcomes: Same-sex and opposite-sex peer effects and the mediating role of school engagement. *British Journal of Educational Psychology, 81*, 183–206. doi:10.1111/j.2044-8279.2010.02013.x

Liljeberg, J.F., Eklund, J.M., Fritz, M.V., & af Klinteberg, B. (2011). Poor school bonding and delinquency over time: Bidirectional effects and sex differences. *Journal of Adolescence, 34*, 1–9. doi:10.1016/j.adolescence.2010.03.008

Maddox, S.J., & Prinz, R.J. (2003). School bonding in children and adolescents: Conceptualization, assessment, and associated variables. *Clinical Child and Family Psychology Review, 6*, 31–49. doi:10.1023/A:1022214022478

Manlove, J. (1998). The influence of high school dropout and school disengagement on the risk of school-age pregnancy. *Journal of Research on Adolescence 8*, 187–220. doi:10.1207/s15327795jra0802_2

McPartland, J.M. (1994). Dropout prevention in theory and practice. In R.J. Rossi (Ed.), *Schools and students at risk: Context and framework for positive change* (pp. 255–276). New York, NY: Teachers College.

Morrison, G. M., Anthony, S. A., Storino, M., & Dillon, C. (2001). An examination of the disciplinary histories of the individual and educational characteristics of students who participate in an in-school suspension program. *Education and Treatment of Children, 24*, 276–293.

Morrison, G. M., Cosden, M. A., O'Farrell, S. L., & Campos, E. (2003). Changes in Latino students' perceptions of school belonging over time: Impact of language proficiency, self-perceptions, and teacher evaluations. *California School Psychologist, 8*, 87–98.

Morrison, G. M., Robertson, L., Laurie, B., & Kelly, J. (2002). Protective factors related to antisocial behavior trajectories. *Journal of Clinical Psychology* (Special Issue: A second generation of resilience research), *58*, 277–290.

Murray, C. (2009). Parent and teacher relationships as predictors of school engagement and functioning among low-income urban youth. *Journal of Early Adolescence, 29*, 376–405. doi:10.1177/0272431608322940

Mylant, M., Ide, B., Cuevas, E., & Meehan, M. (2002). Adolescent children of alcoholics: Vulnerable or resilient? *Journal of American Psychiatric Nurses Association, 8*, 57–64. doi:10.1067/mpn.2002.125037

Nasir, N. S., Jones, A., & McLaughlin, M. (2011). School connectedness for students in low-income urban high schools. *Teachers College Record, 113*, 1755–1805.

O'Brennan, L. M., & Furlong, M. J. (2010). Relations between students' perceptions of school connectedness and peer victimization. *Journal of School Violence, 9*, 375–391. doi:10.1080/15388220.2010.509009

O'Farrell, S. L., & Morrison, G. M. (2003). A factor analysis exploring school bonding and related constructs among upper elementary students. *The California School Psychologist, 8*, 53–72.

Orthner, D. K., Akos, P., Rose, R., Jones-Sanpei, H., Mercado, M., & Woolley, M. E. (2010). CareerStart: A middle school student engagement and academic achievement program. *Children & Schools, 32*, 223–234. doi:10.1093/cs/32.4.223

Patrick, H., Ryan, A. M., & Kaplan, A. (2007). Early adolescents' perceptions of the classroom social environment, motivational beliefs, and engagement. *Journal of Educational Psychology, 99*, 83–98. doi:10.1037/0022-0663.99.1.83

Perdue, N. H., Manzeske, D. P., & Estell, D. B. (2009). Early predictors of school engagement: Exploring the role of peer relationships. *Psychology in the Schools, 46*, 1084–1097. doi:10.1002/pits.20446

Pintrich, P. R., & DeGroot, E. (1990). Motivational and self-regulated learning components of classroom academic performance. *Journal of Educational Psychology, 82*, 33–40. doi:10.1037/0022-0663.82.1.33

Ream, R. K., & Rumberger, R. W. (2008). Student engagement, peer social capital, and school dropout among Mexican American and non–Latino White students. *Sociology of Education, 81*, 109–139. doi:10.1177/003804070808100201

Reschly, A., & Christenson, S. L. (2006). Research leading to a predictive model of dropout and completion among students with mild disabilities and the role of student engagement. *Remedial and Special Education, 27*, 276–292. doi:10.1177/07419325060270050301

Reyes, M. R., Brackett, M. A., Rivers, S. E., White, M., & Salovey, P. (2012). Classroom emotional climate, student engagement, and academic achievement. *Journal of Educational Psychology, 104*, 700–712. doi:10.1037/a0027268

Rumberger, R. W., & Rotermund, S. (2012). The relationship between engagement and high school dropout. In S. L. Christenson, A. L. Reschly, & C. Wylie (Eds.), *Handbook of research on student engagement* (pp. 491–513). New York, NY: Springer.

Sciarra, D. T., & Seirup, H. J. (2008). The multidimensionality of school engagement and math achievement among racial groups. *Professional School Counseling, 11*, 218–228. doi:10.5330/PSC.n.2010-11.218

Seaton E. K., & Taylor, R. D. (2003). Exploring familial processes in urban, low-income African American families. *Journal of Family Issues, 24*, 627–644. doi:10.1177/0192513X03024005003

Seelman, K. L., Walls, E. N., Hazel, C., & Wisneski, H. (2011). Student school engagement among sexual minority students: Understanding the contributors to predicting academic outcomes. *Journal of Social Service Research, 38*, 3–17. doi:10.1080/01488376.2011.583829

Sharkey, J. D., You, S., & Schnoebelen, K. (2008). Relations among school assets, individual resilience, and student engagement for youth grouped by level of family functioning. *Psychology in the Schools, 45*, 402–418. doi:10.1002/pits.20305

Simons-Morton, B., & Chen, R. (2009). Peer and parent influences on school engagement among early adolescents. *Youth & Society, 41*, 3–26. doi:10.1177/0044118X09334861

Skinner, E. A., Wellborn, J. G., & Connell, J. P. (1990). What it takes to do well in school and whether I've got it: A process model of perceived control and children's engagement and achievement in school. *Journal of Educational Psychology, 82*, 22–32. doi:10.1037/0022-0663.82.1.22

Stout, K. E., & Christenson, S. L. (2009). Staying on track for high school graduation: Promoting student engagement. *The Prevention Researcher, 16*, 17–20.

Unrau, N., & Quirk, M. (in press). Reading motivation and reading engagement: Clarifying commingled conceptions. *Reading Psychology.*

Voelkl, K.E. (2012). School identification. In K.E. Voelkl (Ed.), *Handbook of research on student engagement* (pp. 193–218). New York, NY: Springer. doi:http://dx.doi.org/10.1007/978-1-4614-2018-7_9

Wang, M., & Eccles, J. S. (2012). Social support matters: Longitudinal effects of social support on three dimensions of school engagement from middle to high school. *Child Development, 83,* 877–895. doi:10.1111/j.1467-8624.2012.01745.x

Wentzel, K.R. (1998). Social relationships and motivation in middle school: The role of parents, teachers, and peers. *Journal of Educational Psychology, 90,* 202–209. doi:10.1037/0022-0663.90.2.202

Willms, J.D. (2003). *Student engagement at school: A sense of belonging and participation.* Paris, France: OECD: Programme for International Student Assessment.

You, S., & Sharkey, J.D. (2009). Testing a developmental-ecological model of student engagement: A multilevel latent growth curve analysis. *Educational Psychology, 29,* 659–684. doi:10.1080/01443410903206815

CHAPTER SUMMARY: STUDENT ENGAGEMENT

- Student engagement is a multidimensional construct that involves academic, behavioral, cognitive, and psychological engagement with school.
- Student engagement plays an important role in promoting youth success and in preventing youth problems for diverse sociocultural groups.
- Student engagement is impacted by transactions within and across multiple contexts, including the individual youth, peer groups, family, classrooms, and schools. Interventions in any of these contexts may improve student engagement.
- Historically, research on student context is particularly focused on students at risk for adverse outcomes. Scholarship is still needed to understand student engagement as a resilience-enhancing process that improves developmental outcomes across the lifespan. Future research may also investigate student engagement and its relation to other positive psychology constructs such as optimism and hope.
- Measurement strategies need to be improved to adequately assess student engagement.
- Additional scholarship needs to focus on understanding the development of student engagement, including various types of student engagement trajectories and the bidirectional impact of student engagement.
- Research needs to continue to expand the study of student engagement across diverse groups including gender, sexuality, disability, race, SES, and nationality to determine what works for whom under what circumstances.

SUGGESTED READINGS: STUDENT ENGAGEMENT

Appleton, A.R., Christenson, S.L., & Furlong, M.J. (2008). Student engagement with school: Critical conceptual and methodological issues of the construct. *Psychology in the Schools, 45,* 369–386. doi:10.1002/pits.20303

Examines the engagement construct as used in extant research and proposes how to integrate perspectives to advance future scholarship.

Fredricks, J., & McColskey, W., with Meli, J., Mordica, J., Montrosse, B., & Mooney, K. (2011). *Measuring student engagement in upper elementary through high school: A description of 21 instruments* (Issues & Answers Report, REL 2011–No. 098). Washington, DC: U.S. Department of Education, Institute of Education Sciences, National Center for Education Evaluation and Regional Assistance, Regional Educational Laboratory Southeast. Retrieved from http://ies.ed.gov/ncee/edlabs

A report that reviews and summarizes the properties of 21 measures of student engagement.

Furlong, M.J., Whipple, A. D., St. Jean, G., Simental, J., Soliz, A., & Punthuna, S. (2003). Multiple contexts of school engagement: Moving toward a unifying framework for educational research and practice. *The California School Psychologist, 8*, 99–114.

Presents a conceptual framework for student engagement that organizes current research and practice and accounts for multiple contextual influences.

Li, Y., & Lerner, R.M. (2011). Trajectories of school engagement during adolescence: Implications for grades, depression, delinquency, and substance use. *Developmental Psychology, 47*, 233–247. doi:10.1037/a0021307

A longitudinal study of student engagement trajectories, which differed by sex, SES, and race/ethnicity. Trajectories were associated with negative outcomes.

Sharkey, J.D., You, S., & Schnoebelen, K. (2008). Relations among school assets, individual resilience, and student engagement for youth grouped by level of family functioning. *Psychology in the Schools, 45*, 402–418. doi:10.1002/pits.20305

A cross-sectional study with a large diverse sample that demonstrates school assets have an impact on student engagement above and beyond the impact of internal assets, regardless of family functioning.

13

LIFE SATISFACTION AND SCHOOLING

E. Scott Huebner, Kimberly J. Hills, James Siddall, Department of Psychology, University of South Carolina, Columbia, South Carolina, USA

Rich Gilman, Cincinnati Children's Hospital Medical Center, University of Cincinnati Medical School, Cincinnati, Ohio, USA

INTRODUCTION

In the chapter on life satisfaction (LS) in the first edition of this handbook, Suldo, Huebner, Friedrich, and Gilman (2009) quoted Noddings's (2003) contention that student happiness should be a central aim of education because "happiness and education are properly, intimated related" (p. 1). However, Noddings provided little empirical evidence to support her claim. In the previous edition, the authors summarized the scant literature available at the time. Since then, the research base has increased substantially (Proctor, Linley, & Maltby, 2009a). Based on current research, we critically evaluate the support for her notion that happiness, in the form of LS, is related to important educational processes and outcomes in school children. In doing so, we tentatively conclude that the relation is significant but complex, with happiness related more strongly to school behavior and academic self-perception variables than academic performance variables. Furthermore, based on the research, we provide recommendations for the promotion of positive LS in schoolchildren.

DEFINITION AND THEORY BASE

The study of LS in psychological and social indicators research has been largely influenced by Diener (Diener, 1984) and his work on positive subjective well-being (SWB).

Although definitions of SWB have been controversial, it is widely accepted that global LS is a major component along with the experience of frequent positive emotions and infrequent negative emotions (Diener, 1984). A commonly used definition in the literature provided by Shin and Johnson (1978) states that it is "a global assessment of a person's quality of life according to his (sic) own chosen criteria" (p. 478). Thus, global or overall LS can be thought of as a cognitive judgment made by individuals about the quality of their lives as a whole. Because individuals differ in the degree to which specific domains of their life affect their global LS (e.g., the importance of family relationships, economic resources, and physical health), these cognitive judgments are often measured using domain-free items (e.g., "I have a good life") rather than using items addressing specific domains. Nevertheless, assessment of satisfaction within specific domains can and has been assessed, with these judgments closely tied to concrete experiences (e.g., "I have a good family life"). Research has shown that LS judgments extend beyond momentary experiences, yielding more stable measures of SWB (Kim-Prieto, Diener, Tamir, Scollon, & Diener, 2005). Global LS judgments are also distinguishable from measures of positive affect, negative affect, and related constructs (e.g., self-esteem) in students as early as third grade (Huebner, 1991a).

MEASUREMENT APPROACHES AND ISSUES

Given that the study of LS among children and adolescents is a fairly new area of research, there are few appropriate measures developed for research or clinical purposes. Nevertheless, the volume of research in this area has continued to grow (Proctor, Linley, & Maltby, 2009a). A central component of the definition of LS is that it represents the subjective experiences of individuals, and thus the scales designed to measure this construct are typically self-reports. Youth LS measures can be categorized as either unidimensional or multidimensional. Unidimensional measures assess LS globally by asking only domain-free questions (e.g., *Students' Life Satisfaction Scale*; Huebner, 1991b) or by summing responses to items covering a variety of specific domains to derive a total LS score (e.g., *Perceived Life Satisfaction Scale*; Adelman, Taylor, & Nelson, 1989). Multidimensional measures, such as the *Comprehensive Quality of Life Scale—Student Version* (Cummins, 1997) and *Multidimensional Students' Life Satisfaction Scale* (Huebner, 1994) derive scores separately for youths' satisfaction for various domains (e.g., school, family, peers).

Several LS measures display acceptable internal consistency, meaningful stability, and evidence of construct validity, including predictive validity (Huebner & Hills, 2013; Proctor, Linley, & Maltby, 2009b). Factor analytic studies have revealed comparability for some measures across youth from various countries (e.g., Gilman et al., 2008). Studies have also shown that despite the relatively stable nature of LS, youth LS reports fluctuate in meaningful ways relative to planned interventions as well as unplanned life changes (e.g., Farrell, Valois, Meyer, & Tidwell, 2003; Froh, Sefick, & Emmons, 2008). For instance, a longitudinal study of students in a residential program revealed that their global and domain-specific LS reports decreased from baseline as they experienced more stress in their lives but increased from baseline as their circumstances improved (Gilman & Handwerk, 2001).

Concerns regarding self-report methods with youth include social desirability responding as well as contextual influences, such as mood or situational factors. However, research has shown little empirical support for these concerns (Proctor et al., 2009b).

In summary, the existing research suggests that several youth LS instruments show acceptable reliability and validity for research and some applied purposes. Given the increasing interest in students' LS, it is likely that more refined measures will become available. Innovative approaches will be needed to overcome the unique challenges of assessing LS in very young children, including preschool children and early elementary school children. To date, there is a lack of suitable measures for children under the age of 8. For an exception, see the Personal Wellbeing Index—Preschool Version (PWI-PS: Cummins & Lau, 2005).

KEY RESEARCH WITH CHILDREN AND ADOLESCENTS

Levels and Correlates of LS

Studies of children in multiple nations suggest that most children and adolescents are satisfied with their lives overall (Proctor et al., 2009a). Nevertheless, individual differences are apparent, with significant numbers of youth reporting dissatisfaction with their lives. Furthermore, using multidimensional measures of LS, some studies suggest variability among mean levels of satisfaction. For example, two studies of U.S. secondary school students demonstrated that students are more satisfied with their lives overall than within some specific life domains, such as schooling (Huebner, Drane, & Valois, 2000; Huebner, Valois, Paxton, & Drane, 2005). Although 11% of the students in the Huebner et al. (2000) study reported low levels of *global* LS (i.e., scores below the neutral point), nearly 23% of the students reported low school satisfaction, with almost 10% describing their school experiences as "terrible."

Researchers have investigated the antecedents and consequences of individual differences in global and context-specific LS. Although early work focused on the origins of LS differences, researchers have recently begun paying greater attention to the consequences of LS and related variables (e.g., positive affect). Indeed, a meta-analysis of correlational, longitudinal, and experimental studies yielded the conclusion that LS may not only be a correlate but may also be a cause of desirable life outcomes in adulthood, including comfortable incomes, high-quality interpersonal relationships, superior mental health, and longer lives (Lyubormirsky, King, & Diener, 2005). With respect to school outcomes, lower LS in college students predicts subsequent interpersonal rejection (Furr & Funder, 1998) and school dropout (Frisch et al., 2005).

Research on LS among children is sparse compared to that of adults. Nevertheless, studies have already revealed a wide array of LS correlates, including possible consequences of LS differences. For example, cross-sectional studies have shown robust relations between LS and positive cognitions (e.g., hope, gratitude, and adaptive attribution styles), coping behavior (e.g., approach coping behavior), frequent positive emotions, good interpersonal relationships, and mental and physical health (see Proctor et al., 2009a). A few recent short-term longitudinal studies provide some support for the notion that high LS may also operate as a protective factor among adolescents. For instance, longitudinal analyses have found low global LS to be a significant predictor of peer relational victimization and neglect (Martin, Huebner, & Valois, 2008), withdrawal of parent emotional support (Saha, Huebner, Suldo, & Valois, 2010), and disengagement from schooling (Lewis, Huebner, Malone, & Valois, 2011). Suldo and Huebner (2004) also found that adolescents with high global LS were less likely to exhibit externalizing behaviors after experiencing significant life stressors. Such findings underscore the critical contribution of LS to positive youth development. Thus, studies of the origins of individual differences appear warranted to identify key risk and protective factors in the development of positive LS in children and adolescents. The following sections review the literature on intrapersonal, interpersonal, as well as school-related factors associated with LS.

Demographic and Intrapersonal Factors

Similar to adults, the relationship between school-age students' global LS and socioeconomic status appears to be modest, especially when basic needs have been met (Proctor et al., 2009a). Similarly, relations with other demographic variables (e.g., gender, parental marital status) appear modest. However, personality/temperament variables have demonstrated moderate relations with global LS. For example, LS has been found to be moderately negatively associated with neuroticism (Fogle, Huebner, & Laughlin, 2002) and moderately positively associated with extraversion (Heaven, 1989). Studies of cognitive variables have yielded even stronger relations. For one example, youth who believe they have more personal control over the events in their lives report higher LS than those who perceive less control (Gilman & Huebner, 2006; Nevin, Carr, Shevlin, Dooley, & Breaden, 2005). For other examples, adolescents who report adaptive causal attributions, high personal standards and self-confidence, and hopeful thinking indicate higher LS (Extremera, Durán, & Rey, 2007; Gilman & Ashby, 2003; Rigby & Huebner, 2005; Valle, Huebner & Suldo, 2006).

Research has also been conducted on how having a disability affects global LS, but findings have been equivocal. For instance, while students diagnosed with severe hearing loss have reported lower levels of LS (Gilman, Easterbrooks, & Frey, 2004), students with cognitive impairments have reported comparable levels of LS compared to nondisabled peers (Brantley, Huebner, & Nagle, 2002; Shogren, Lopez, Wehmeyer, Little, & Pressgrove, 2006). Youth LS also appears unrelated to IQ scores (Huebner & Alderman, 1993).

Environmental Factors

Although research indicates that environmental factors contribute to LS, little is known about the specific environmental features that make a difference. Research has focused mainly on the relation between LS and the *overall* perceived quality of adolescents' family, neighborhood, school, and peer relationships. Each of these contexts appears to exert a significant influence on children's LS. For instance, youth who report very high levels of global LS (i.e., in the top 20% of students surveyed) also report greater social support from teachers, family, and peers (Gilman & Huebner, 2006; Suldo & Huebner, 2006). Multiple studies have confirmed the importance of each of these groups; research has demonstrated that from the ages of 8 to 18, positive parent–child relationships are a stronger correlate than peer relationships (Huebner, 1991b; Man, 1991). Among high school students, perceived positive parent–child relationships were also a stronger correlate of global LS than perceptions of physical appearance and academic self-concept (Dew & Huebner, 1994). More specifically, a qualitative study identified the following key features of positive family/home environments: a safe and comfortable home, a loving atmosphere, open and trusting communication, consistent parental monitoring and involvement in adolescents' activities, a communicated sense of importance within the family, and family support for children's relationships with people outside the family (Joronen & Åstedt-Kurki, 2005).

Although research has shown parent–child relationships to be the stronger predictor of adolescent LS, positive peer relationships are also strong predictors of adolescents' LS, especially among older adolescents and females. Youth who report higher LS also report higher levels of peer attachment (i.e., relationships characterized as having high loyalty, mutual caring, and commitment; Nickerson & Nagle, 2004). Further studies have characterized peer relationships that promote higher levels of LS as displaying frequent positive and reciprocal supportive interactions (Martin, Huebner, & Valois, 2008).

Relations between children's global LS and chronic (i.e., daily) and acute life events have received some research attention. McCullough, Huebner, and Laughlin (2000) found that life events contributed significant variance to the prediction of LS, over and above that of global self-concept, with chronic experiences (e.g., ongoing family conflict) contributing unique variance over and above that of acute, major life events (e.g., parental separation). Furthermore, they found that while only negative daily events were uniquely related to adolescents' reports of positive and negative affect, only positive daily events were uniquely related to their LS. This finding suggested that positive everyday experiences have a larger impact than negative daily events on students' LS. However, Ash and Huebner (2001) found chronic life experiences and acute life events, both positive and negative, to be significantly related to global LS in adolescents. Additionally, both positive long-term resources and chronic stressors added significant variance over and above acute positive and negative events. Although much more research is needed, these studies highlight the importance of everyday experiences and suggest that positive, daily experiences (e.g., experiencing frequent, positive teacher–student interactions) may enhance adolescents' LS more than brief positive experiences (e.g., winning an award).

School-Related Factors

In Noddings's (2003) aforementioned book titled *Happiness and Education,* she concluded that "happy people are rarely mean, violent, or cruel" and "children learn best when they are happy" (p. 2). She also noted that in many nations, including the United States, education as a discipline does not strive to monitor, understand, or promote students' happiness. Despite this alleged lack of attention to happiness, considerable research has illuminated the importance of school-related factors to children's LS. Numerous studies have shown that children's satisfaction with school is a significant, but moderate correlate (around $r = .30$) of global LS relative to the stronger relations observed between global LS and satisfaction with family, friends, self, and living environment. The relation between school satisfaction and global LS also seems to vary as a function of culture or between subgroups in the same culture. For instance, Park and Huebner (2005) found that school satisfaction had a much stronger relation with LS for South Korean students than U.S. students. In addition, Ash and Huebner (1998) found that school satisfaction was a stronger predictor of LS among gifted students than nongifted peers. Finally, a link between the overall school context and global LS has been demonstrated by the study of Oberle, Schonert-Reichl, and Zumbo (2011), which revealed significant differences in students' mean levels of global LS across different schools. Although particular features of the schools were not investigated, the demonstration of significant school–student LS linkages supports the notion that the effects of school experiences extend beyond the schools' doors, influencing children's pervasive sense of LS.

Recent variable- and person-centered approaches have highlighted the importance of including *positive* indicators in comprehensive assessments of students. As an example of variable-centered research, Lewis, Huebner, Reschly, and Valois (2009) found that incorporating measures of positive emotions yielded incremental validity relative to negative emotions in predicting students' school engagement levels and social coping behaviors. Using person-centered analyses, Gilman and Huebner (2006) also found that students with "very high" LS demonstrated superior levels of hope, social stress, and attitudes toward teachers compared to students with "average" LS. Furthermore, Anta-ramian, Huebner, Hills, and Valois (2010) found that four distinct groups of adolescents could be identified using assessments that included positive indicators of LS along with measures of internalizing and externalizing behavior problems. Among the four groups, one group was composed of significant number of students (around 10%) who showed both low levels of LS and low levels of psychopathological symptoms. These children (referred to as "vulnerable" students) would typically not be identified using traditional, pathology-based measures of mental health. However, these vulnerable students showed significantly lower behavioral, cognitive, and affective school engagement along with lower grade point averages when compared to peers who also had low psychopathologi-cal symptoms but *high* global LS. Furthermore, these vulnerable students were similar to the group of "troubled" students who exhibited both low LS and high psychopathologi-cal symptoms (see also Suldo & Shaffer, 2008). At a 5-month follow-up, 54% of these vulnerable students remained at risk or developed clinically significant levels of psycho-logical symptoms (Kelly, Hills, Huebner, & McQuillin, 2012).

The following sections cover some of the most important school-related variables connected with LS.

School-Related Social Support

Students' perceptions regarding their school social climate and school experiences sig-nificantly relate not only to their academic performance and behavior at school but also to their LS (Flanagan & Stout, 2010; Suldo, Shaffer, & Riley, 2008; Wang, 2009). In par-ticular, students who do not feel safe at school (e.g., they fear being threatened or injured or having property stolen or damaged) report lower LS than students who feel safe at school (Valois, Zullig, Huebner, & Drane, 2001). Unsurprisingly, lower levels of LS can be found among students who report physical or relational peer victimization (Flouri &

Buchanan, 2002). For example, Flaspohler, Elfstrom, Vanderzee, Sink, and Birchmeier (2009) demonstrated that students who bully or are bully victims experience reduced LS, but support from peers and teachers mitigates the effect of bullying. Furthermore, Martin and colleagues (2008) found that students who received few prosocial acts from peers were also more likely to experience low LS, suggesting that LS may be influenced by benign neglect as much as by active peer victimization. Finally, research with minority youth has shown that life events involving perceived discrimination by other youth has detrimental effects on LS (Seaton, Caldwell, Sellers, & Jackson, 2010).

Although peer relations appear very important to students' LS, studies examining the magnitude of the relationships between school social climate variables and LS have reported mixed findings regarding the relative importance of peer, parental, and teacher support. Suldo et al. (2008) found that among six different school-climate dimensions (including student relationships, teacher–student relationships, and parental involvement), only teacher–student relationships and parental involvement were unique predictors of students' LS. However, subsequent work by Suldo, Thalji-Raitano, Hasemeyer, Gelley, and Hoy (20113) found all three types of social support (student relationships, teacher–student relationships, and parental involvement) were statistically significant and independently related to LS of middle school students.

Danielsen, Samdal, Hetland, and Wold (2009) found that only parental support and peer support showed significant unique, direct effects on the LS of early adolescents. Suldo, McMahan, Chappel, and Loker (2012) also observed this finding in U.S. high school students and found gender differences in the relation between social support and LS, with a stronger positive relation for girls. Although these studies demonstrated strong connections between school-related social support and LS, a major limitation is that they were all cross-sectional, limiting causal inferences. To address this gap, Siddall, Jiang, and Huebner (2013) examined the prospective impact of teacher–student relationships and peer and parent support for learning on changes in U.S. middle schoolers' LS across a 5-month period. They found that only parental involvement in schooling at Time 1 was uniquely related to students' global LS at Time 2, when controlling for students' LS at Time 1. This finding suggests the importance of more distal variables (e.g., parent involvement in schooling) as well as proximal variables (e.g., student–teacher interactions) on early adolescents' LS.

Academics

A few studies have investigated the link between global LS and academic success, with most studies reporting a modest to moderate relation. For instance, Gilman and Huebner (2006) found that students with very low LS (lowest 20% of the sample) reported significantly lower GPAs ($M = 3.01$) than students with average and high levels of LS ($M = 3.42$ and 3.49, respectively). The correlation between LS and self-reported GPA was .32 for their entire sample. However, the correlations reported for the relation between global LS and *actual* GPAs have been more modest, with correlations ranging from approximately .14 (Huebner, 1991b) to .29 (Cheng & Furnham, 2002). When evaluated within the previously mentioned dual-factor model of mental health, an effect size (Cohen's d) of .52 was obtained for the difference in report card grades between the vulnerable students (low LS coupled with low levels of psychological symptoms) and the positive-mental-health students (high LS coupled with low psychological symptoms; Antaramian et al. 2010).

Interestingly, Quinn and Duckworth (2007) reported a reciprocal relation between U.S. fifth graders' LS and their academic performance. Specifically, students with higher LS earned higher grades on their subsequent report card (controlling for prior grades), while higher grades also predicted higher LS (controlling for prior LS).

Although the connections between academic performance (as measured by GPA) and global LS may be moderate, one robust finding is that youth who report higher LS also report higher academic self-efficacy (Suldo & Huebner, 2006). Among adolescents in Hong Kong, a correlation of .52 was observed between LS and perceived academic competence (Leung & Bond, 2004). Thus, student expectations and demonstrated performance in school may both be related to their LS. However, LS appears more strongly related to *perceived* competence than demonstrated competence, at least when the latter is indexed by school grades.

Student Behavior and Participation

Relations between global LS and student behavior problems have been investigated more frequently (for a review see Proctor et al., 2009a), with several monomethod studies demonstrating relatively strong linkages between self-reported lower LS and self-reported internalizing and externalizing behaviors (e.g., Haranin, Huebner, & Suldo, 2007). Beyond such monomethod studies, Huebner and Alderman (1993) found a .35 correlation between a composite score for *teacher*-reported internalizing and externalizing behaviors and student-reported LS. Studies have also found a significant link between LS and specific risk behaviors such as physical fighting, carrying a weapon to school (Valois et al., 2001), and suicidal ideation and behavior (Valois, Zullig, Huebner, & Drane, 2004a). Increased classroom behavior problems have also been linked to greater dissatisfaction with school (Elmore & Huebner, 2010).

Participation in school-related, extracurricular activities seems to have a significant positive relationship with students' LS. For instance, Gilman (2001) found that participating in structured extracurricular activities appears to be a protective factor related to higher LS. Vilhjalmsson and Thorlindsson (1992) also found a positive relation between LS and participation in clubs and social groups. In particular, playing on sports teams may have a significant positive impact on students for both social and physical health reasons. LS has been found to be positively related to engaging in strenuous activities (Vilhjalmsson & Thorlindsson, 1992) and negatively related to not exercising at least 20 minutes per week (Valois, Zullig, Huebner, & Drane, 2004b), which may explain why Valois and colleagues found that not playing on a sports team was inversely associated with LS.

School Engagement and Dropout

Student engagement in schooling relates significantly to high global LS. For example, Lewis and colleagues (2011) demonstrated significant cross-sectional correlations between LS and behavioral, cognitive, and affective engagement. Furthermore, longitudinal analyses revealed significant bidirectional relations between students' cognitive engagement and LS. Several studies have additionally linked low levels of school engagement with eventual student dropout (Appleton, Christenson, & Furlong, 2008). The links among students' global LS, school engagement, and dropout perhaps explain why Frisch and colleagues (2005) found that low LS significantly predicted school dropout in undergraduate students. Taken together, this research suggests that school engagement and LS are significantly interrelated, again supporting the role of schooling in children's overall development.

Summary of School-Related Variables

Overall, although more research is needed, it seems safe to draw two tentative, major conclusions from the extant research on children's LS and school-related factors. First, Noddings's (2003) contention that happiness and education are interrelated appears to be supported by the wide range of school-related variables associated with the *global* LS of school-age children. These findings are not inconsistent with the social-cognitive model of LS proposed by Suldo, Shaffer, and Riley (2008) in which cognitive factors (e.g., academic self-efficacy) mediate the relations between contextual factors (e.g., school-related social support) and school satisfaction, as well as global LS. Second, Noddings's contention that happy students learn and behave best also appears to be somewhat supported, although the evidence for the influence of LS on behavior in the classroom is perhaps stronger than the evidence for its influence on academic performance, particularly when measured by GPA. However, much work remains in order to understand fully the complex relations among student individual difference variables, environmental influences, and students' LS and school functioning. Clearly, some of the relations in the social-cognitive model may be bidirectional, and additional factors may moderate the various relations (e.g., personality, cultural, and developmental factors). Longer-term prospective studies are especially needed as the effects of high (or low) LS may differ across time. For example, a student with higher LS might not only show better classroom behavior and academic success in one school year, but such behavior may lead to an upward spiral (Fredrickson, 2008), in which the student has an increased probability of acquiring greater academic resources in the future (e.g., subsequent teacher support, admission to more challenging classes, increasing peer acceptance). Finally, measures of specific domains (e.g., family satisfaction) may be more sensitive to the influence of some conditions (e.g., parental divorce) than global satisfaction measures.

EDUCATIONAL APPLICATIONS AND RESEARCH IMPLICATIONS

Empirical work expanding psychology's focus to include factors related to illness *and* well-being has demonstrated consistently that the absence of illness is not sufficient for youth to flourish. The development of measures to assess negative *and* positive aspects of mental health and educational functioning has facilitated the beginnings of a science of well-being, which should inform school professionals in their efforts to promote youth well-being in a more comprehensive way. Given that youth spend a significant amount of time in school, a context that is intricately related to other contexts (e.g., peers, community), schools provide an important opportunity to address their overall LS.

Interventions to Increase LS

Current research suggests that school-age students' LS is influenced by a number of personal and contextual variables. Although some personal and contextual variables (e.g., stressful life events) show significant relations to global LS, alterable social, cognitive, and behavioral characteristics show even stronger relations. Two generic approaches have been considered with respect to promoting youth LS. One approach involves identifying specific, empirically validated conditions associated with children's LS (e.g., poor teacher–student relationships) and making efforts to infuse the conditions throughout the child's school experiences. For example, a teacher might change her behavioral responses across the school day in the hopes of improving the teacher–student relationship, in turn increasing student LS (Noddings, 2003). Such strategies are discussed in various chapters throughout this handbook and will not be discussed here.

An alternative approach involves the development and implementation of time-limited, packaged (e.g., manualized) interventions designed to enhance LS and other possible outcomes. Such standardized approaches are typically installed through delivering a curriculum at a specific time in the school day. Since the publication of the last edition, several packaged programs have demonstrated promising results with respect to sustainable LS gains. Noteworthy programs include Building Hope for the Future (Marques, Lopez, & Pais-Ribeiro, 2011), Responding in Peaceful and Positive Ways (Farrell et al. 2003), and gratitude interventions (Froh et al., 2008).

Studies using such intervention programs vary in the breadth of intervention strategies. Whereas some studies employed a single intervention strategy, others comprise a variety of strategies. These activities vary across studies and include but are not limited to writing about one's "best possible self," practicing gratitude, learning conflict-management skills, using character strengths, and practicing optimistic thinking. For example, recent studies have demonstrated that the practice of grateful thinking by "counting one's blessings" enhances LS (Froh et al., 2008). For another example, Proctor and colleagues (2011) demonstrated that the use of character strengths exercises within a school curriculum (i.e., Strengths Gym) is a promising strategy to increase LS.

Research using multicomponent interventions is still in a nascent stage. Although a meta-analysis of 51 intervention studies revealed that positive psychology interventions significantly increase SWB (mean $r = .29$), all but two of the studies targeted adults, limiting inferences to children and adolescents (Sin & Lyubormirsky, 2009). The two studies that targeted children and adolescents yielded minimal ($r = .04$) to negative effect sizes ($r = -.15$). Such findings are consistent with recent dissertation and research studies implementing positive psychology interventions with youth. For example, Long and Davis (2011) evaluated the effects of an expressive writing intervention (e.g., writing for 15 minutes for 5 consecutive days about future life goals, things they were grateful for) on 25 male juvenile offenders' SWB. Their results indicated improvements in optimism and mood, but not in LS. In an unpublished doctoral dissertation, Savage (2011) investigated the variance in SWB of 54 early adolescents exposed to a positive psychology intervention aimed at increasing positive affect (PA) and LS as well as decreasing negative affect through intentional activities (e.g., gratitude journals, acts of kindness, use of character strengths). Although the data showed a trend that approached significance, the effects were not statistically significant.

The effects of interventions may be contingent on participant factors as well as the length, fidelity, and dosage levels associated with the interventions. For example, a portion of the work supporting the efficacy of gratitude interventions has involved comparing a gratitude intervention to a control condition inducing negative affect (e.g., recording daily hassles). When using more neutral control conditions, gratitude interventions have shown more limited benefits. Froh, Kashdan, Ozimkowski, and Miller (2009) addressed such issues by conducting a study hypothesizing that people high in trait PA would be less susceptible to experiencing gains in SWB, whereas people lower in PA may have "more room for improvement." Specifically, they examined whether individual differences in PA moderated the effects of a gratitude intervention on SWB using a sample of 89 youth who were randomly assigned to the gratitude intervention (i.e., writing and delivering a letter to someone to whom they were grateful) or a control condition (i.e., writing about daily events). The results confirmed their hypothesis. Compared to youth who were high in PA, the youth who were low in PA reported higher gratitude and more positive emotions at immediate posttreatment and more positive emotions at the 2-month follow-up. These results are similar to findings of Sin and Lyubomirsky's (2009) meta-analysis, which demonstrated that depression status moderated the effectiveness of positive interventions on SWB, such that clinically depressed individuals experienced enhanced well-being compared to their nondepressed counterparts. Of course, personal preferences and self-selection may also influence the usage and utility of positive psychology interventions (Lyubomirsky, Dickerhoof, Boehm, & Sheldon, 2011).

Research conducted since the first edition of this text continues to delineate more precisely the specific conditions that influence the effectiveness of positive psychology interventions, including interventions designed to increase LS. Research with adults demonstrates that using optimal timing and variation of positive activities/intervention may be essential to foster and maintain increases in LS (Boehm, Lyubormirsky, & Sheldon, 2011). That is, higher levels of LS may be most sustainable when individuals practice multiple strategies *across time* (Sin & Lyubomirsky, 2009). The benefits of such strategies may not begin immediately but rather may show delayed (but long-term) effects (Seligman, Steen, Park, & Peterson, 2005). Nonetheless, most of this research is based on adult populations and further work is essential in understanding the effectiveness of various methods with youth, whose psychosocial, cognitive, and physical characteristics are markedly different from those of adults.

The research reviewed within this chapter indicates a growing interest in student SWB, including LS, in schools. Research published since the last edition of this text provides considerable additional, *empirical* support for Noddings's (2003) argument that children's school experiences and LS are interrelated. Thus, in order to be most effective in preparing students for the future as well as facilitating a current, positive quality of school life, school professionals need to attend to students' academic *and* social-emotional (e.g., LS) needs. Because LS and school behavior and success are interrelated, efforts to enhance one area must address the other area as well to maximize effectiveness.

For some schools, this means expanding their major goals for children beyond success in traditional academic areas. To accomplish such well-being goals, attention to individual and systemic factors, like school climate, will likely be necessary to promote the LS of *all* students. As the literature suggests, promoting positive, everyday school experiences (e.g., frequent positive interactions with school staff, small-group instructional activities) may be as (or more) influential in maintaining high student LS as implementing major, one-time, or infrequent classroom or system-wide events (e.g., sponsoring an annual "student of the year" award dinner, distributing quarterly report cards) or possibly even empirically validated packaged strategies that are initiated and implemented for a specified time but are not employed in an ongoing fashion with students.

Given the limited availability of comprehensive, empirically validated, packaged strategies to increase LS in youth, it may be most realistic for schools to consider selecting the evidence-based strategies relevant to their context. This plan should involve three major components. First, school personnel should develop and implement a comprehensive schoolwide assessment system to monitor student well-being (including LS) and key associated factors (e.g., school climate), along with their schoolwide academic measures. Consistent with a dual-factor model, this screening effort should not be limited to "negative" health indicators (e.g., psychological symptoms, risk behavior) but should also include "positive" indicators to comprehensively assess nuances in levels and changes in student well-being. Second, based on these results, school professionals should design multitier intervention strategies, including schoolwide efforts to promote the LS of all children, along with individualized efforts for individuals or groups of students who need more intensive intervention strategies. Third, school professionals should continually evaluate the success of their programs, making changes accordingly to ensure success. Given space limitations, see Huebner and Hills (2013) for a more detailed description of such an approach.

REFERENCES

Adelman, H. S., Taylor, L., & Nelson, P. (1989). Minors' dissatisfaction with their life circumstances. *Child Psychiatry & Human Development, 20*, 135–147. doi:10.1007/BF00711660

Antaramian, S. P., Huebner, E. S., Hills, K. J., & Valois, R. F. (2010). A dual-factor model of mental health: Toward a more comprehensive understanding of youth functioning. *American Journal of Orthopsychiatry, 80*, 462–472. doi:10.1111/j.1939-0025.2010.01049.x.

Appleton, J. J., Christenson, S. L., & Furlong, M. J. (2008). Student engagement with school: Critical conceptual and methodological issues of the construct. *Psychology in the Schools, 45*, 369–386. doi:10.1002/pits.20303

Ash, C., & Huebner, E. S. (1998). Life satisfaction reports of gifted middle-school children. *School Psychology Quarterly, 13*, 310–321. doi:10.1037/h0088987

Ash, C., & Huebner, E. S. (2001). Environmental events and life satisfaction reports of adolescents: A test of cognitive mediation. *School Psychology International, 22*, 320–336. doi:10.1177/0143034301223008

Boehm, J. K., Lyubormirsky, S., & Sheldon, K. M. (2011). A longitudinal experimental study of comparing the effectiveness of happiness-enhancing strategies in Anglo Americans and Asian Americans. *Cognition and Emotion, 25*, 1152–1167. doi:10.1080/02699931.2010.541227

Brantley, A., Huebner, E. S., & Nagle, R. J. (2002). Multidimensional life satisfaction reports of adolescents with mild mental disabilities. *Mental Retardation, 40*, 321–329. doi:10.1352/0047-6765(2002)040<0321:MLSROA>2.0.CO;2

Cheng, H., & Furnham, A. (2002). Personality, peer relations, and self-confidence as predictors of happiness and loneliness. *Journal of Adolescence, 25*, 327–339. doi:10.1006/jado.2002.0475

Cummins, R. A. (1997). *Manual for the Comprehensive Quality of Life Scale-student (Grades 7–12): ComQol-S5.* Melbourne, Australia: Deakin University School of Psychology.

Cummins, R. A., & Lau, A. L. (2005). *Personal Wellbeing Index-Pre-School* (PWI-PS: 3rd ed.). Available from http://www.deakin.edu.au/research/acqol/instruments/wellbeing-index/pwi-ps-english.pdf-567.71KB-06-10-2010

Danielsen, A. G., Samdal, O., Hetland, J., & Wold, B. (2009). School-related social support and students' perceived life satisfaction. *Journal of Educational Research, 102*, 303–320. doi:10.3200/JOER.102.4.303-320

Dew, T., & Huebner, E. S. (1994). Adolescents' perceived quality of life: An exploratory investigation. *Journal of School Psychology, 33*, 185–199. doi:10.1016/0022-4405(94)90010-8

Diener, E. (1984). Subjective well-being. *Psychological Bulletin, 95*, 542–575. doi:10.1037/0033-2909.95.3.542

Elmore, G. M., & Huebner, E. S. (2010). Adolescents' satisfaction with school experiences: Relationships with demographics, attachment relationships, and school engagement behavior. *Psychology in the Schools, 47*, 525–537. doi:10.1002/pits.20488

Extremera, N., Durán, A., & Rey, L. (2007). Perceived emotional intelligence and dispositional optimism–pessimism: Analyzing their role in predicting psychological adjustment among adolescents. *Personality and Individual Differences, 42*, 1069–1079. doi:10.1016/j.paid.2006.09.014

Farrell, A. D., Valois, R. F., Meyer, A. L., & Tidwell, R. P. (2003). Impact of the RIPP violence prevention program on rural middle school students. *Journal of Primary Prevention, 24*, 143–167. doi:10.1023/A:1025992328395

Flanagan, C., & Stout, M. (2010). Developmental patterns of social trust between early and late adolescence: Age and school climate effects. *Journal of Research on Adolescence, 20*, 748–773. doi:10.1111/j.1532-7795.2010.00658.x

Flaspohler, P. D., Elfstrom, J. L., Vanderzee, K. L., Sink, H. E., & Birchmeier, Z. (2009). Stand by me: The effects of peer and teacher support in mitigating the impact of bullying on quality of life. *Psychology in the Schools, 46*, 636–649. doi:10.1002/pits.20404

Flouri, E., & Buchanan, A. (2002). Life satisfaction in teenage boys: The moderating role of father involvement and bullying. *Aggressive Behavior, 28*, 126–133. doi:10.1002/ab.90014

Fogle, L. M., Huebner, E. S., & Laughlin, J. E. (2002). The relationship between temperament and life satisfaction in early adolescence: Cognitive and behavioral mediation models. *Journal of Happiness Studies, 3*, 373–392. doi:10.1023/A:1021883830847

Fredrickson, B. L. (2008). Promoting positive affect. In M. Eid & R. J. Larsen (Eds.), *The science of subjective well-being* (pp. 449–468). New York, NY: Guilford.

Frisch, M. B., Clark, M. P., Rouse, S. V., Rudd, M. D., Paweleck, J. L., Greenston, A., & Kopplin, D. A. (2005). Predictive and treatment validity of life satisfaction and the Quality of Life Inventory. *Assessment, 12*, 66–78. doi:10.1177/1073191104268006

Froh, J. J., Kashdan, T. B., Ozimkowski, K. M., & Miller, N. (2009). Who benefits the most from a gratitude intervention in children and adolescents? Examining positive affect as a moderator. *Journal of Positive Psychology, 4*, 408–422.

Froh, J. J., Sefick, W. J., & Emmons, R. A., (2008) Counting blessings in early adolescents: An experimental study of gratitude and subjective well-being. *Journal of School Psychology, 46*, 213–233. doi:10.1080/17439760902992464

Furr, R. M., & Funder, D. C. (1998). A multimodal analysis of personal negativity. *Journal of Personality and Social Psychology, 74*, 1580–1591. doi:10.1037/0022-3514.74.6.1580

Gilman, R. (2001). The relationship between life satisfaction, social interest, and frequency of extracurricular activities in adolescent students. *Journal of Youth and Adolescence, 30*, 749–767.

Gilman, R., & Ashby, J. S. (2003). A first study of perfectionism and multidimensional life satisfaction among adolescents. *Journal of Early Adolescence, 23*, 218–235. doi:10.1177/0272431603023002005

Gilman, R., Easterbrooks, S. R., & Frey, M. (2004). A preliminary study of multidimensional life satisfaction among deaf/hard of hearing youth across environmental settings. *Social Indicators Research, 66*, 143–164. doi:10.1023/B:SOCI.0000007495.40790.85

Gilman, R., & Handwerk, M. (2001). Changes in life satisfaction as a function of stay in a residential setting. *Residential Treatment for Children and Youth, 21*, 19–41. doi:10.1300/J007v18n04_05

Gilman, R., & Huebner, E. S. (2006). Characteristics of adolescents who report very high life satisfaction. *Journal of Youth and Adolescence, 35*, 311–319. doi:10.1007/s10964-006-9036-7

Gilman, R., Huebner, E. S., Tian, L., Park, N., O'Byrne, J., Schiff, M., . . . Langknecht, H. (2008). Cross-national adolescent multidimensional life satisfaction reports: Analyses of mean scores and response style differences. *Journal of Youth and Adolescence, 37*, 142–154. doi:10.1007/s10964-007-9172-8

Haranin, E. C., Huebner, E. S., & Suldo, S. M. (2007). Predictive and incremental validity of global and domain-based adolescent life satisfaction reports. *Journal of Psychoeducational Assessment, 25*, 127–138. doi:10.1177/0734282906295620

Heaven, P. (1989). Extraversion, neuroticism, and satisfaction with life among adolescents. *Personality and Individual Differences, 10*, 489–492. doi:10.1016/0191-8869(89)90029-9

Huebner, E.S. (1991a). Further validation of the Students' Life Satisfaction Scale: The independence of satisfaction and affect ratings. *Journal of Psychoeducational Assessment, 2*, 363–368. doi:10.1177/073428299100900408

Huebner, E.S. (1991b). Correlates of life satisfaction in children. *School Psychology Quarterly, 6*, 103–111. doi:10.1037/h0088805

Huebner, E.S. (1994). Preliminary development and validation of a multidimensional life satisfaction scale for children. *Psychological Assessment, 6*, 149–158. doi:10.1037/10403590.6.2.149

Huebner, E., S., & Alderman, G.L. (1993). Convergent and discriminant validation of a children's life satisfaction scale: Its relationship to self- and teacher–reported psychological problems and school functioning. *Social Indicators Research, 30*, 71–82. doi:10.1007/BF01080333

Huebner, E.S., Drane, J.W., & Valois, R.F. (2000). Levels and demographic correlates of adolescent life satisfaction reports. *School Psychology International, 21*, 281–292. doi:10.1177/0143034300213005

Huebner, E.S., & Hills, K.J. (2013). Assessment of life satisfaction in children and youth. In D. Saklofske, V. Schwean, & C.R. Reynolds (Eds.), *Oxford handbook of psychological assessment of children and adolescents* (pp. 773–787). New York, NY: Oxford University Press.

Huebner, E.S., Valois, R.F., Paxton, R.J., & Drane, J.W. (2005). Middle school students' perceptions of quality of life. *Journal of Happiness Studies, 6*, 15–24. doi:10.1007/s10902-004-1170-x

Joronen, K., & Åstedt-Kurki, P. (2005). Familial contribution to adolescent subjective well-being. *International Journal of Nursing Practice, 11*, 125–133. doi:10.1111/j.1440-172X.2005.00509.x

Kelly, R.M., Hills, K.J., Huebner, E.S., & McQuillin, S.D. (2012). The longitudinal stability and dynamics of group membership in the dual-factor model of mental health: Psychosocial predictors of mental health. *Canadian Journal of School Psychology, 27*, 337–355. doi:10.1177/0829573512458505

Kim-Prieto, C., Diener, E., Tamir, M., Scollon, C., & Diener, M. (2005). Integrating the diverse definitions of happiness: A time-sequential framework of subjective well-being. *Journal of Happiness Studies, 6*, 261–300. doi:10.1007/s10902-005-7226-8

Leung, K., & Bond, M.H. (2004). Social axioms: A model of social beliefs in multicultural perspective. In M.P. Zanna (Ed.), *Advances in experimental social psychology* (pp. 119–197). San Diego, CA: Elsevier.

Lewis, A.D., Huebner, E.S., Malone, P.S., Valois, R.F. (2011). Life satisfaction and student engagement in adolescents. *Journal of Youth and Adolescence, 40*, 249–262. doi:10.1007/s10964-010-9517-6

Lewis, A.D., Huebner, E.S., Reschly, A., & Valois, R.F. (2009). Incremental validity of positive emotions in predicting school satisfaction, engagement, and academic success. *Journal of Psychoeducational Assessment, 27*, 397–408. doi:10.1177/0734282908330571

Long, J.J., & Davis, J.O. (2011). Pen and paper: A prescription for adolescents' emotional and psychological well-being? *Journal of Correctional Education, 62*, 7–25.

Lyubomirsky, S., Dickerhoof, R., Boehm, J.K., & Sheldon, K.M. (2011). Becoming happier takes both a will and a proper way: An experimental longitudinal intervention to boost well-being. *Emotion, 11*, 391–401. doi:10.1037/a0022575

Lyubomirsky, S., King, L., & Diener, E. (2005). The benefits of frequent positive affect: Does happiness lead to success? *Psychological Bulletin, 131*, 803–855. doi:10.1037/0033-2909.131.6.803

Man, P. (1991). The influence of peers and parents on youth life satisfaction in Hong Kong. *Social Indicators Research, 24*, 347–365. doi:10.1007/BF00383734

Marques, S.C., Lopez, S.J., & Pais-Ribeiro, J.L. (2011). Building hope for the future: A program to foster strengths in middle school students. *Journal of Happiness Studies, 12*, 129–152. doi:10.1007/s10902-009-9180-3

Martin, K., Huebner, E.S., & Valois, R.F. (2008). Does life satisfaction predict victimization experiences in adolescence? *Psychology in the Schools, 45*, 705–714. doi:10.1002/pits.20336

McCullough, G., Huebner, E.S., & Laughlin, J.E. (2000). Life events, self-concept, and adolescents' positive subjective well-being. *Psychology in the Schools, 37*, 281–290. doi:10.1002/(SICI)1520-6807(200005)37:3<281::AID-PITS8>3.0.CO;2-2

Nevin, S., Carr, A., Shevlin, M., Dooley, B., & Breaden, C. (2005). Factors related to well-being in Irish adolescents. *Irish Journal of Psychology, 26*(3–4), 123–136. doi:10.1080/03033910.2005.10446215

Nickerson, A.B., & Nagle, R.J. (2004). The influence of parent and peer attachments on life satisfaction in middle childhood and early adolescence. *Social Indicators Research, 66*, 35–60. doi:10.1023/B:SOCI.0000007496.42095.2c

Noddings, N. (2003). *Happiness and education.* Cambridge, UK: Cambridge University Press.

Oberle, E., Schonert-Reichl, K.S., & Zumbo, B.D. (2011). Life satisfaction in early adolescence: Personal, neighborhood, school, family, and peer influences. *Journal of Youth and Adolescence, 40*, 889–901. doi:10.1007/s10964-010-9599-1

Park, N., & Huebner, E.T. (2005). A cross-cultural study of the levels and correlates of life satisfaction among adolescents. *Journal of Cross-Cultural Psychology, 36*, 444–456. doi:10.1177/0022022105275961

Proctor, C.L., Linley, P.A., & Maltby, J. (2009a). Youth life satisfaction: A review of the literature. *Journal of Happiness Studies*, *10*, 583–630. doi:10.1007/s10902-008-9110-9

Proctor, C., Linley, P.A., & Maltby, J. (2009b). Youth life satisfaction measures: A review. *Journal of Positive Psychology*, *4*, 128–144. doi:10.1080/17439760802650816

Proctor, C., Tsukayama, E., Wood, A. M., Maltby, J., Eades, J.F., & Linley, P.A. (2011). Strengths Gym: The impact of a character strengths-based intervention on the life satisfaction and well-being of adolescents. *Journal of Positive Psychology*, *6*, 377–388. doi:10.1080/17439760.2011.594079

Quinn, P.D., & Duckworth, A.L. (2007, May). *Happiness and academic achievement: Evidence for reciprocal causality*. Poster session presented at the annual meeting of the American Psychological Society, Washington, DC.

Rigby, B.T., & Huebner, E.S. (2005). Do causal attributions mediate the relationship between personality characteristics and life satisfaction in adolescence? *Psychology in the Schools*, *42*, 91–99. doi:10.1002/pits.20026

Saha, R., Huebner, E.S., Suldo, S.M., & Valois, R.F. (2010). A longitudinal study of adolescent life satisfaction and parenting. *Child Indicators Research*, *3*, 149–165. doi:10.1007/s12187-009-9050-x

Savage, J.A. (2011*). Increasing adolescents' subjective well-being: Effects of a positive psychology intervention in comparison to the effects of therapeutic alliance, youth factors, and expectancy for change*. Unpublished Doctoral Dissertation, University of South Florida. ProQuest LLC.

Seaton, E.K., Caldwell, C.H., Sellers, R.M., & Jackson, J.S. (2010). An intersectional approach for understanding perceived discrimination and psychological well-being among African American and Caribbean Black youth. *Developmental Psychology*, *46*, 1372–1379. doi:10.1037/a0019869

Seligman, M.E.P., Steen, T.A., Park, N., & Peterson, C. (2005). Positive psychology progress: Empirical validation of interventions. *American Psychologist*, *60*, 410–421. doi:10.1037/0003-066X.60.5.410

Shin, D. C., & Johnson, D.M. (1978). Avowed happiness as an overall assessment of the quality of life. *Social Indicators Research*, *5*, 475–492. doi:10.2307/27521880

Shogren, K.A., Lopez, S.J., Wehmeyer, M.L., Little, T.D., & Pressgrove, C.L. (2006). The role of positive psychology constructs in predicting life satisfaction in adolescents with and without cognitive disabilities: An exploratory study. *Journal of Positive Psychology*, *1*, 37–52. doi:10.1080/17439760500373174

Siddall, J., Jiang, X., & Huebner, E.S. (2013). A prospective study of differential sources of school-related social support and adolescents' global life satisfaction. *American Journal of Orthopsychiatry*, *83*, 107–114. doi:10.1111/ajop.12006

Sin, N.L., & Lyubomirsky, S. (2009). Enhancing well-being and alleviating depressive symptoms with positive psychology interventions: A practice-friendly meta-analysis. *Journal of Clinical Psychology*, *65*, 467–487. doi:10.1002/jclp.20593

Suldo, S.M., & Huebner, E.S. (2004). Does life satisfaction moderate the effects of stressful life events on psychopathological behavior during adolescence? *School Psychology Quarterly*, *19*, 93–105. doi:10.1521/scpq.19.2.93.33313

Suldo, S.M., & Huebner, E.S. (2006). Is extremely high life satisfaction during adolescence advantageous? *Social Indicators Research*, *78*, 179–203. doi:10.1007/s 11205-005-8208-2

Suldo, S.M., Huebner, E.S., Friedrich, A.A., & Gilman, R. (2009). Life satisfaction. In R. Gilman, E.S., Huebner, & M.J. Furlong (Eds.), *Handbook of positive psychology in the schools* (pp. 27–35). New York, NY: Routledge.

Suldo, S.M., McMahan, M.M., Chappel, A. M., & Loker, T. (2012). Relationships between perceived school climate and adolescent mental health across genders. *School Mental Health*, *4*, 69–80. doi:10.1007/s12310-012-9073-1

Suldo, S.M., & Shaffer, E.J. (2008). Looking beyond psychopathology: The dual-factor model of mental health in youth. *School Psychology Review*, *37*, 52–68.

Suldo, S.M., Shaffer, E.J., & Riley, K.N. (2008). A social-cognitive-behavioral model of academic predictors of adolescents' life satisfaction. *School Psychology Quarterly*, *23*, 56–66. doi:10.1037/1045-3830.23.1.56

Suldo, S.M., Thalji-Raitano, A., Hasemeyer, M., Gelley, C.D., & Hoy, B. (2013). Understanding middle school students' life satisfaction: Does school climate matter? *Applied Research in Quality of Life*, *8*, 169–182. doi:10.1007/s11482-012-9185-7

Valle, M.F., Huebner, E.S., & Suldo, S.M. (2006). An analysis of hope as a psychological strength. *Journal of School Psychology*, *44*, 393–406. doi:10.1016/j.jsp.2006.03.005

Valois, R.F., Zullig, K.J., Huebner, E.S., & Drane, J.W. (2001). Relationship between life satisfaction and violent behaviors among adolescents. *American Journal of Health Behavior*, *25*, 353–366. doi:10.5993/AJHB.25.4.1

Valois, R.F., Zullig, K.J., Huebner, E.S., & Drane, J. W. (2004a). Relationship between life satisfaction and suicide ideation and behavior. *Social Indicators Research*, *66*, 81–105. doi:10.1023/B:SOCI.0000007499.19430.2f

Valois, R.F., Zullig, K.J., Huebner, E.S., & Drane, J.W. (2004b). Physical activity behaviors and perceived life satisfaction among public high school adolescents. *Journal of School Health*, *74*, 59–65. doi:10.1111/j.1746-1561.2004.tb04201.x

Vilhjalmsson, R., & Thorlindsson, T. (1992). The integrative and physiological effects of sport participation: A study of adolescents. *Sociological Quarterly, 33*, 637–647. doi:10.1111/j.1533-8525.1992.tb00148.x

Wang, M. (2009). School climate support for behavioral and psychological adjustment: Testing the mediating effect of social competence. *School Psychology Quarterly, 24*, 240–251. doi:10.1037/a0017999

CHAPTER SUMMARY: LIFE SATISFACTION

- Life satisfaction shows a meaningful network of relations with important personal and contextual variables.
- Empirically supported, developmentally appropriate measures of global and domain-specific life satisfaction are now available for some research and applied purposes with children and adolescents. A case example can be found in Huebner and Hills (2013).
- Most school-age children and adolescents report satisfaction with their lives.
- Students with higher life satisfaction report better psychosocial, health, and school outcomes, although life satisfaction may be more strongly related to student classroom behavior than academic success.
- A group of students report low life satisfaction and low levels of psychological symptoms. These "vulnerable" students show school engagement levels and grades that are significantly lower than "positive mental health" students who report high life satisfaction and low levels of psychological symptoms. Such differences underscore the importance of comprehensive assessments that incorporate negative *and* positive measures of well-being.
- School-related experiences play a major role in life satisfaction. Ongoing, everyday experiences appear to be more strongly related to life satisfaction than various acute life events. Some empirically validated interventions have been reported.

RECOMMENDED READINGS: LIFE SATISFACTION

Antaramian, S. P., Huebner, E. S., Hills, K. J., & Valois, R. F. (2010). A dual-factor model of mental health: Toward a more comprehensive understanding of youth functioning. *American Journal of Orthopsychiatry, 80*, 462–472.

Important person-centered study on the importance of subjective well-being to student engagement and student academic success.

Diener, E. (2009). *The science of well-being: The collected works of Ed Diener. Social Indicators Research Series*, Vol. 37. Dordrecht, Netherlands: Springer.

Collection of key articles on the basic science of subjective well-being by the leading researcher.

Huebner, E. S., & Hills, K. J. (2013). Assessment of subjective well-being in children and adolescents. In D. Saklofske, V. Schwean, & C. R. Reynolds (Eds.), *Oxford handbook of psychological assessment of children and adolescents* (pp. 773–787). Oxford, UK: Oxford University Press.

Literature review on assessment of subjective well-being, including life satisfaction, in youth, which contains implications for practice and a case study.

Noddings, N. (2003). *Happiness and education.* New York, NY: Cambridge University Press.

Philosophical treatise on happiness as both a means and end of education.

Suldo, S. M., Shaffer, E. J., & Riley, K. N. (2008). A social-cognitive-behavioral model of academic predictors of adolescents' life satisfaction. *School Psychology Quarterly, 23*, 56–66.

Important, empirical study of cognitive mediators of the relation between school climate and students' global life satisfaction.

Section III

Contextual Educational Factors and Resources

14

FLOW IN SCHOOLS REVISITED

Cultivating Engaged Learners and Optimal Learning Environments

David J. Shernoff, Beheshteh Abdi, and Brett Anderson, Department of Leadership, Educational Psychology, and Foundations at Northern Illinois University, DeKalb, Illinois, USA

Mihaly Csikszentmihalyi, Distinguished Professor of Psychology, Claremont Graduate University, Claremont, California, USA

INTRODUCTION

Public schools are continually characterized by pervasive boredom (Goodlad, 1984; Steinberg, Brown, & Dornbusch, 1996). For example, the 2009 High School Survey of Student Engagement found that two thirds (66%) of students reported being bored at least every day in high school, and approximately one in six students (17%) was bored in every class (Yazzie-Mintz, 2010). Of concern to teachers for decades (Pickens, 2007; Singh, Granville, & Dika, 2002; Theobald, 2006), boredom and apathy in class are primary reasons that many students do not become engaged in school (Pekrun, Goetz, Daniels, Stupnisky, & Perry, 2010). Studies have reported that disengagement is strongly related to poor attendance and dropout, substance abuse, and criminal offending (Conner & Pope, 2014; Henry, Knight & Thornberry, 2011). Pervasive student disengagement is both a national and an international problem, with 20 to 25% of students in 28 OECD countries (i.e., those belonging to the Organisation for Economic Co-operation) classified as having low participation and/or a low sense of belonging (Willms, 2003).

Schools have historically struggled to provide meaningful and engaging experiences for many youth. Many students in public schools see themselves as passive participants in a mass, anonymous educational system (Larson & Richards, 1991). Accordingly, fostering engagement and enjoyment in learning has become a dominant concern for educators, researchers, policy makers, and other stakeholders of the U.S. public school system. Yet many students remain apathetic toward school.

Can positive psychology foster healthier schools with its focus on optimal health and human functioning rather than illness? The concept of optimal experience, or flow, has served as a theoretical cornerstone of positive psychology (Seligman & Csikszentmihalyi, 2000). In this chapter, we focus on how optimal learning experiences as theoretically rooted in the concept of flow have direct and meaningful application to student engagement in schools. Our review, guided by multiple studies bearing on this topic in the last 20 years, specifically focuses on the perceptual and environmental factors that can influence student engagement and their resultant outcomes. We also highlight several promising contexts for fostering optimal experiences and engaged learning before closing with some new directions in this line of research.

FLOW IN LEARNING

By interviewing individuals from diverse backgrounds about their peak experiences, Csikszentmihalyi (1990) and colleagues identified the phenomenological characteristics of the most meaningful and satisfying moments in people's lives. From rock climbers and chess players to accomplished scientists and artists, optimal experiences in diverse activities were often described in similar terms: intense concentration and absorption in an activity with no psychic energy left over for distractions, a merging of awareness with action, a feeling of control, loss of self-consciousness, and a contraction of the normal sense of time (i.e., time seems to fly). Csikszentmihalyi subsequently coined the term "flow" to describe experiences when skillful and successful action seems effortless, even when a great deal of physical or mental energy is exerted. Subsequent research on flow finds that the experience is enhanced by certain properties of the task. Specifically, in most flow activities, goals are clear, and feedback with respect to meeting those goals is immediate and forthcoming. The activities also are often *autotelic*, or a goal in and of itself performed for the sheer experience of it—sometimes even in the face of personal risk or danger. Perhaps the most central condition for flow experiences to occur is that the challenge of the activity is well matched to the individual's skills. Typically, the challenge and skill are high and in balance—individuals stretch their skills to their limits in pursuit of a challenging goal. The various combinations of high or low challenges and skills predict distinct psychological states: (a) apathy, resulting from low challenge and low skill; (b) relaxation, resulting from high skill but low challenge; (c) anxiety, resulting from high challenge but low skill; and (d) flow, resulting from high challenge combined with high skill. This model later evolved into one with eight flow channels including four intermediary or transitional states between these four quadrants (see Strati, Shernoff, & Kacker, 2012); however, we discuss only the four quadrants here for simplicity.

As concrete examples of these states, an intermediate-level female skier may find herself in apathy waiting in line at the ski lift before any challenge is present. Once on the mountain, if the first slope is a bunny trail, she finds she has more skills than required and feels only relaxation as she takes in the scenery. Later in the day, when confronted with a slope that is too steep, bumpy, or icy for her ability, anxiety sets in until she safely navigates her way down. Only on her favorite slopes that are quite challenging for her ability, but not excessively so, does she feel herself enter into an enjoyable, rhythmic peak experience in which time seems to stand still. The exhilaration of these flow experiences is typically the main reason skiers invest the time, money, and energy to hit the slopes in the first place (Csikszentmihalyi, 1990).

Flow experiences can involve mental tasks as much as physical ones. Anyone who has been "sucked into" a good novel that could not be set down implicitly understands the phenomenon. Recent experiments in neuroscience have demonstrated that when a reader is fully engrossed in a novel, the human brain is activated not only in areas responsible for attention; it also dramatically "lights up" in areas controlling affect and emotion (Thomson & Vedansom, 2012). Still, an experienced reader is unlikely to enter flow reading a children's book. A more sophisticated novel not only appeals to one's reading ability but also stimulates a full array of skills: to understand the geographical and historical context, infer the motivations of the characters, or solve the central mystery. The relation between flow and the balance of challenge and skills has been empirically supported in numerous settings (e.g., Csikszentmihalyi & Csikszentmihalyi, 1988).

The theory of flow, then, is inherently related to learning. When learning a new skill, the challenge of even a basic task may exceed a student's beginning level of ability, and hence one may feel overwhelmed. Even "Twinkle, Twinkle Little Star" may be too difficult for a beginner pianist. To reach flow, the level of skill must increase to match the challenge. Much like Vygotsky's (1978) *zone of proximal development,* the level at which most learning occurs is just one step beyond the skills one has already mastered. In this case, sufficient practice may be needed until the song is mastered. Once the song is played comfortably with relative ease (causing a state of "relaxation"), only one thing can restart a cycle of fresh learning: a new song at a higher level of challenge, causing one's skill to increase yet again. Thus, the pianist may progress through increasingly difficult songs at ever-higher levels of skill. Flow is expected to peak at the highest level of challenge and skill, as when a master pianist is playing a Mozart concerto with great poise and skill. Fullagar, Knight, and Sovern (2013) found that the balance between the challenge of a passage of music and the skills utilized to play the passage is significantly and consistently correlated with optimal experience. This balance of challenge and skills increases motivation, enhances competence, fosters growth, and extends the student's capacities (Csikszentmihalyi, Abuhamdeh, & Nakamura, 2005; Fullagar et al., 2013).

Also applicable to learning is the finding that flow activities tend to be selected and replicated over time because they are so gratifying. This process of *psychological selection* plays a crucial role in the development of specific interests, goals, and talents over the course of one's life (Delle Fave & Massimini, 2003).

MEASURING FLOW AND ENGAGEMENT IN LEARNING

In the last 25 years, the study of flow has been pursued mainly through the use of the Experience Sampling Method (or ESM; Hektner, Schmidt, & Csikszentmihalyi, 2007). Respondents carry a paging device (traditionally a programmable wristwatch, but more recently smartphones and pagers), which signals them at random moments throughout the day. Each time a respondent is signaled, he or she completes a brief questionnaire containing open-ended and scaled questions about the day and time of the signal, the current activity, and the cognitive, affective, and motivational qualities of her or his experience pertaining to the activity. Example items include: "As you were beeped, did you *enjoy* what you were doing?" "How well were you *concentrating*?" "Was this activity *interesting*?" In addition, ratings are given for the challenge of the activity and the respondent's skill in the activity. The ESM thus solicits repeated "snapshots" of subjective experience, improving upon the problem of recall and estimation errors inherent to one-time surveys and interviews. For reliability and validity information regarding the ESM, the reader is referred to Hektner and colleagues (2007).

Based on flow theory, *student engagement* has been conceptualized as the simultaneous occurrence of high *concentration, interest,* and *enjoyment* (Shernoff, 2010b). *Concentration* or *absorption*, which is central to flow (Csikszentmihalyi, 1990), is related to meaningful learning (Montessori, 1967), including depth of cognitive processing and academic performance (Corno & Mandinach, 1983). *Interest* directs attention, reflects intrinsic motivation, stimulates the desire to continue engagement in an activity, and is related to school achievement (Hidi, 1990; Schiefele, Krapp, & Winteler, 1992). *Enjoyment* is a positive feeling related to the demonstration of competencies, creative accomplishment, and school performance (Csikszentmihalyi, Rathunde, & Whalen, 1993; Nakamura, 1988). In this conceptualization, student engagement is highest when all three components are simultaneously stimulated. As flow theory would predict, student engagement was maximized in classroom experiences in which perceived challenge and skill were above average compared to those marked by apathy (i.e., low challenge, low skill), anxiety (i.e., high challenge, low skill), or relaxation (i.e., low challenge, high skill; Shernoff, Csikszentmihalyi, Schneider, & Shernoff, 2003).

WHAT FLOW THEORY AND THE ESM HAVE TAUGHT US ABOUT STUDENT ENGAGEMENT IN PUBLIC SCHOOLS

Initial ESM research in U.S. public schools has highlighted the rarity with which students experience flow while in school (Csikszentmihalyi & Larson, 1984). On average, high school students are less engaged while in classrooms than anywhere else. Their concentration is higher than in activities outside of classrooms, but their level of interest in classroom activities is lower, and their enjoyment is especially low. Students are also found to be thinking about topics entirely unrelated to academics a full 40% of the time while in classrooms (Shernoff, 2010b). Overall, studies suggest that alternative approaches are needed in order to provide what is most lacking: greater enjoyment, motivation, and opportunities for action in the learning process (Bassi & Delle Fave, 2004; Shernoff et al., 2003).

PERCEPTUAL AND CONTEXTUAL FACTORS INFLUENCING STUDENT ENGAGEMENT

Perceptual Factors Influencing Engagement

Concentration, attention, and engagement, all hallmarks of flow, have been shown to be significantly higher when instruction is perceived as challenging and relevant. Several studies have shown that students experience greater enjoyment, motivation, self-esteem, and engagement when they perceive themselves to be active, in control, and skilled in the activity or subject at hand (Shernoff, 2010b; Shernoff et al., 2003). Consistent with flow theory, these findings suggest that students are more likely to become engaged when academic work intellectually involves them in active processes of meaningful inquiry (Newmann, Wehlage, & Lamborn, 1992). Furthermore, such findings suggest that the perception of competence and autonomy contributes to students' engagement, likely by increasing self-efficacy and perceptions of self-worth as suggested in much of the motivational literature (e.g., Schunk, Pintrich, & Meece, 2008).

Flow and Learning Goals

Learning goal orientation refers to students' purposes for engaging in their learning activities. *Mastery goal orientation* is defined as a focus on mastering a task according to self-set standards or for improvement. Alternatively, a *performance goal orientation* represents a focus on demonstrating ability or competence according to how one will be judged by others (Ames, 1992; Elliott & Dweck, 1988). Students' goal orientation is recognized to be crucial to academic engagement (Martin, Marsh, Debus, & Malmberg, 2008).

Sharifah, Habibah, Samsilah, and Sidek (2011) investigated the potential of learning goals to influence flow among high school students in Malaysia. Results of the study demonstrated that mastery goals made a significant contribution to explaining flow, whereas performance goals were not a significant predictor of flow. While recognizing that performance goals can have a beneficial role in learning, the researchers emphasized promoting mastery goals as the main ingredient for students to become highly engaged in their learning tasks.

The Influence of Classroom Context and the Learning Environment

Student engagement appears to be significantly influenced by contextual and classroom factors, such as instructional format and learning environment. For example, students have more engagement when doing group and individual work than while listening to a lecture or watching TV or a video. Overall, students reported being more engaged during instructional methods that present opportunities for action and to demonstrate their skills (Shernoff, Knauth, & Makris, 2000).

More recent studies further qualify the importance of instructional format. For example, in a study of seven academic classes in two schools in which interactions in high school classrooms across a variety of academic subjects were videotaped and matched to ESM data, some of the highest levels of engagement were reported during lecture formats, provided that they involved Socratic questioning, while some of the lowest levels of engagement were reported during large-group discussions that featured a high level of discourse (Shernoff, Tonks, Anderson, & Dortch, 2011; Shernoff, Tonks, & Anderson, 2014). Results support the proposition that more specific, qualifying instructional features, such as rules, goals of the activity, and quality of the learning environment were more operative in influencing student engagement than the main instructional format. As one concrete example, "interactive presentations" in which the instructor frequently asked questions were generally more engaging than "lectures" in which students were not actively questioned. In line with these findings, another recent study found that messages teachers send to students specifically about the learning *goal* (i.e., performance or mastery goal) of a given instructional format have a greater impact on student engagement than the format itself (Zaleski, 2012).

Constructivist classroom principles such as reciprocal instruction, cooperative learning, and a supportive classroom climate are believed to shape students' experiences (Zhang, Scardamalia, Reeve, & Messina, 2009). Thus, the extent to which the learning environment, characterized as a whole, predicted fluctuations in engagement was also examined by Shernoff and colleagues (2011, 2013). Motivational characteristics of the learning environment in high school classrooms were coded from an observational instrument and matched to ESM data. The primary characteristic of optimal learning environments, in which engagement was high, was the *environmental complexity*, or the simultaneous combination of environmental challenge and environmental support. Environmental challenge was characterized by the importance of the instructional activity and the clarity of its goals. Environmental support was characterized by support for motivational drives (for example, support of the learner's sense of autonomy or perceived competency), the availability of performance feedback, and positive relationships with teachers and peers. Therefore, when students believed that what they were doing was both important and had clear goals, they were more likely to interact within the classroom environment with interest and absorb what is available in the environment. When they additionally were supported to reach those goals, both emotionally and with timely performance feedback, they adopted an attitude of excitement, fun, and interest in learning.

Engagement and Educational Outcomes

Some studies on adolescents shed light on how the quality of experience in learning activities affects short-term and long-term educational outcomes. With respect to short-term outcomes, recent research has shown a significant positive relation between student engagement and reported grades in the same academic year after controlling for background characteristics (Shernoff & Schmidt, 2008). Several other studies have found that high-achieving, adolescent-aged students who develop their talents in specific domains are more likely to be in flow when working in their area of talent development than lower-achieving students (Csikszentmihalyi et al., 1993; Nakamura, 1988).

In order to examine longer-term outcomes associated with engagement in high school, researchers interviewed a sample of college students several years after participating in an ESM study in high school (Shernoff & Hoogstra, 2001). After accounting for student background characteristics including academic performance, engagement was a significant predictor of continuing motivation in science. Enjoyment and interest "in the moment" during high school science class were significant predictors of choosing a science-related major in college. In addition, student engagement in high school math and science classes was the strongest predictor of reported grades in college compared to a variety of individual background characteristics—for example, stronger than grades in high school. These findings suggest that spontaneous engagement with school learning may operate in subtle ways that have important, long-term effects on students' intellectual and professional development.

Conceptual Model of Student Engagement and
Optimal Learning Environments

Based on previous ESM studies (Shernoff, 2010b; Shernoff et al., 2003), the two sep-arate processes that describe the formation of meaningful student engagement are (a) *academic intensity,* which refers to heightened concentration and effort in skill-building activities (e.g., taking a test or a quiz, or completing tasks in math class in which stu-dents are usually very challenged and concentrate hard) and (b) *positive emotional response,* which refers to spontaneous enjoyment undergirding intrinsic interest and continued motivation (e.g., watching a video, attending an art class, or other activity that students find enjoyable). Consistent with the notion of flow as combining both work-like and play-like aspects of engagement, researchers have found that both pro-cesses are integral parts of optimal engagement in the learning process, but they sel-dom operate together during school instruction (Csikszentmihalyi & Schneider, 2000; Rathunde, 1993).

Activities or environments that can combine both aspects of engagement, as is not uncommon during individual work in computer science class or a group lab activity in science class, are of utmost importance, however, because they provide opportunities for *meaningful engagement* (Shernoff et al., 2011). Optimal learning environments thus (a) include activities that are challenging and relevant and yet also allow students to feel confident and in control; (b) exact concentration but also provide enjoyment; (c) are intrinsically satisfying in the short term as well as build a foundation of skills and inter-est for the future; (d) involve both intellect and feeling; and (e) are both work-like and play-like—which is to say that they *meaningfully engage* (Shernoff, 2010b).

EDUCATIONAL CONTEXTS PROMOTING ENGAGEMENT

To summarize our research so far: There is not a great deal of flow or engagement in traditional U.S. public schools as a whole, but there are exceptions to this trend. Over the past decade, researchers have gained insights into ways to promote optimal learning environments in which experiencing flow and high engagement are the norm rather than the exception. We will now review recent research in several educational contexts that hold promise for understanding optimal learning environments: Montessori middle schools, organized after-school programs, and educational video games.

Montessori Middle Schools

Rathunde and Csikszentmihalyi (2005a, 2005b) conducted a large-scale study measuring the quality of experience of students ($n = 290$) from several Montessori middle schools and that of a comparison group of demographically matched public middle school students from the Sloan Study of Youth and Social Development (SSYSD; see Csikszentmihalyi & Schneider, 2000). Because we have already described engagement in the traditional public schools from the SSYSD study, we will focus here on describing the Montessori middle schools.

To set up optimal environments for student engagement through challenge and emotional support, the Montessori philosophy emphasizes the creation of a "prepared environment" that integrates both freedom and high demands in order to increase the likelihood of spontaneous concentration in learning activities (Rathunde & Csikszentmihalyi, 2005a). The researchers found that Montessori students reported higher combinations of high intrinsic motivation and importance, indicative of *meaningful engagement*, compared to public school students (Rathunde & Csikszentmihalyi, 2005a). In contrast, public school students reported greater salience and importance, but low intrinsic motivation, a combination suggestive of a performance-goals orientation.

In a more recent ESM study, Rathunde (2013) assessed whether the Montessori practice of 30-minute morning nature walks would have a positive effect on students' attention and concentration during subsequent academic work when in class. Short-term effects of the walk were captured by a questionnaire completed immediately after the walks; and the ESM captured the lingering effects of the walk when students were later in class (approximately 2,500 signals across 4 days). The study found that students who felt fascinated while taking the walks were less distractible and mentally fatigued immediately after the nature walks; and the same students showed improved concentration lasting approximately 4 hours into the school day after the walk.

Organized After-School Programs

In contrast to formal classrooms, extracurricular activities that include academically enriching activities, athletics, and the arts have been associated with heightened levels of challenge, enjoyment, intrinsic motivation, initiative, and academic performance among adolescents (Mahoney, Larson, & Eccles, 2005). Few studies, however, have explicitly examined whether engagement and related experiential factors in after-school programs help account for these outcomes. A recent study, therefore, examined if middle school students' experiences and perceptions in after-school programs mediate the relation between after-school program participation and socioemotional and academic outcomes (Shernoff, 2010a). Specifically, the research tested whether engagement and flow played a mediating role in the development of social competency (i.e., student reports of goal setting and planning, conflict resolution, nonconformity, teamwork, and perspective taking) and achievement (i.e., math and English grades) over 1 year of middle school students' participation in school-based after-school programs.

Results showed that engagement and flow during program experiences accounted for a significant portion of the positive association between program participation and social competence. In addition, students who were more engaged in an after-school program, feeling that their after-school experiences were more challenging and important to them compared to their experiences in other out-of-school settings, went on to earn higher end-of-year grades in math and English. The amount of time students spent in these programs did not have a significant effect on students' engagement or on positive outcomes; thus, overall the results suggested that relative *quality* of experience in programs may be a stronger predictor of positive outcomes like academic performance than the *quantity* of experience in programs.

NEW DIRECTIONS IN STUDENT ENGAGEMENT RESEARCH

Computer and Video Games and Flow

Research on student engagement in educational video games has grown a great deal in the last two decades as their popularity has grown, and they have been used to increase one's desire to learn (Abrantes & Gouveia, 2012; Roberts, Foehr, & Rideout, 2005; Scoresby & Shelton, 2007). Flow theory has been the theoretical base for exploring learning through immersion or "being enveloped" by a virtual learning environment since the emotional composition of these experiences resembles flow. This sense of "presence," "being there," or "flow" while immersed in virtual-reality interfaces has been shown to facilitate efficient or deep learning of the content and skills that are integral to successful game play (e.g., Abrantes & Gouveia, 2012; Johnson, Vilhjalmsson, & Marsella, 2005; Liu, Chen & Huang, 2011; Procci, Singer, Levy, & Bowers, 2012; Van Eck, 2006).

Coller, Shernoff, and Strati (2011) examined the impact of applying a video game approach in teaching an undergraduate mechanical engineering course on engagement and learning. The video game developed by Coller, *EduTorcs,* is similar to commercial car racing games, except that student drivers write computer programs drawing on principles from mechanical engineering to race the car. The researchers found that students using the video game approach experienced significantly more engagement, intrinsic motivation, and positive affect—again as measured by the ESM—during their homework and labs, compared to a control group using traditional methods (i.e., solving problem sets from a textbook). A subsequent study showed that students using the video game approach made considerably greater learning gains as demonstrated by their course test performance, scoring almost one standard deviation higher on the tests than the control group (Shernoff & Coller, 2013). These learning gains were, in turn, linked to students' enhanced experience while doing their homework and labs with the game as measured by ESM items assessing if the learning activity seemed more like work, more like play, neither, or both. Reported levels of engagement, skill use, and the perception of the gaming experience as both "like play" and "like work" (indicative of flow experiences and *meaningful engagement*) predicted learning gains.

What About the Teacher's Role in Fostering Engagement?

An obvious influence on students' engagement and flow experience is the teacher. Although teaching and learning have traditionally been studied as separate processes (Kunter et al., 2008; Shuell, 1993), in reality, teachers and students cocreate the pattern of classroom interactions together, which, in turn, impacts both teacher and student motivation (Turner & Warzon, 2009). According to Pianta, Hamre, and Allen (2012), the nature and quality of interactions between teachers and students are fundamental to understanding student engagement.

Shernoff and colleagues (2011) found that how teachers set up the learning environment—especially in creating an environment supporting positive relationships and student motivation—was just as salient in fostering student engagement as direct classroom-management skills. Specific instructional behaviors found to be associated with high engagement included interactivity, teacher's sense of humor, and use of hands-on activities; those associated with low engagement included basing class activities on reading assignments (typically because some students may not have completed the reading) and allowing for homework completion during class time. However, further research is needed to determine the generalizability these results.

Turner and Meyer (e.g., Turner & Meyer, 2004; Turner et al., 1998) provided a rich, contextualized picture of how skilled teachers go about achieving optimal levels of challenge and support to create high student engagement. For example, optimally engaging teachers might administer fewer problems to students, but they make these problems sufficiently challenging. Such teachers also provide support for students to solve them independently. They also ask questions for higher-order conceptual understanding, combined with providing feedback and emotionally supportive encouragement (i.e., conveying enthusiasm, demonstrating a sense of humor).

Şentürk (2011) investigated teachers' and students' perceptions about the existence of flow experiences in English courses in Turkey. Findings revealed that teachers could facilitate a flow experience for students by developing tasks that provide optimal challenge and support in areas of need. For example, setting up challenging tasks and supporting students who had poor vocabulary and grammar knowledge to express themselves effectively led directly to more flow experiences.

TEACHER'S FLOW

Although most engagement research has focused on student engagement, it is also critical to study teacher engagement. One obvious reason is to reduce teacher attrition. The attrition rate for U.S. public school teachers is estimated at 25% (Kaufman & Ring, 2011), with some estimates as high as 50% for new teachers with less than 5 years of service (Hughes, 2012). Teachers frequently cite job dissatisfaction as the primary reason for leaving (Hughes, 2012). Therefore, it is important to understand the conditions leading to teacher engagement. Another reason for its importance is that teachers who regularly experience flow are those who continually improve their skills to meet the needs of their students (Smith, 2009).

Under what conditions, then, do teachers experience flow? Basom and Frase (2004) reported that teachers frequently claim that their sense of flow was derived from students' engagement, just as students claim that their flow was caused by the teachers' engagement and enthusiasm. In one study, Smith (2009) demonstrated that teachers who applied differentiated instruction (a kind of instruction that requires close and individualized interaction between teacher and student) were more likely to experience higher levels of flow. In particular, when teachers assessed students' differences based on their interests and abilities and then accounted for these differences in their instructional approach, serving each individual student became like a puzzle to be solved, instilling flow and a spirit of artistry. Smith (2009) found that of nine domains of flow studied (i.e., challenge-skill balance, merging of actions and awareness, clear goals, unambiguous feedback, total concentration, sense of control, loss of self-consciousness, transformation of time, and autotelic experience), all of them were positively correlated with differentiating instruction. Smith concluded that the more teachers take into account the students that they are teaching and how those students will best learn, the more engaged they become in their teaching.

When in flow, teachers reported feeling connected to their class; they maintained good eye contact and could sense the attentiveness of the class. One study of 178 music teachers and 605 students in 16 different music schools tested the hypothesis that flow experiences can "cross over" from teachers to their students (Bakker, 2005). The study found students' and teachers' flow were indeed positively related: The more flow the teachers experienced, the more the students experienced. When this occurs, the classroom dynamic may be experienced as "group flow" (Custodero, 2005; Shernoff & Csikszentmihalyi, 2009). Overall, student and teacher engagement appears to be highly interactive.

IMPLICATIONS FOR PROMOTING STUDENT ENGAGEMENT

Several implications for practice may be derived from our analysis of flow as it relates to student engagement and learning in schools. Flow is a useful model with which to conceptualize student engagement in classrooms. Although there has not been a great deal of engagement or flow found in U.S. public schools, factors such as student perceptions and goal orientation, instructional formats, the learning environment, and teacher behaviors all influence student engagement. Most available research tends to converge on the observation that optimal learning environments combine both environmental challenge and environmental support in order for learning to become both playful and challenging, both spontaneous and important (e.g., Rathunde & Csikszentmihalyi, 2005a; Shernoff, 2013; Turner & Meyer, 2004). Optimal learning environments can be achieved when teachers support students' autonomy and initiative, as well provide the opportunity for students to interact with peers and adults to obtain a sense of belongingness. In such environments, teachers provide activities that are challenging and relevant and also allow students to feel confident and in control—those that exact concentration but also induce enjoyment. However, the opportunity for action and to build skills seems to be the key.

Some innovative school models are living examples that supporting students' natural desire to learn, especially through relationship support, is an important key to fostering optimal learning environments (in addition to Montessori schools, see Shernoff, 2012, for other empirically supported models). Organized after-school programs for students in traditional public schools can be extremely effective at both engaging students and cultivating their development (Mahoney et al., 2005; Shernoff, 2010a). Budding research suggests that new technologies that have the ability to "envelop" the learner in a virtual learning environment can be extremely flow-inducing and increase learning (Pearce, 2005; Scoresby & Shelton, 2007). Finally, teachers may experience more flow if they work to understand and account for individual students' interests, abilities, and skills. The teacher's flow can also be contagious, having the potential to cross over and stimulate students' flow (Bakker, 2005; Basom & Frase, 2004).

Using the flow model, researchers have discovered that creating engaged learners and optimal learning environments requires attention to a variety of contextual, instructional, developmental, and interpersonal factors beyond the preoccupation with educational "outcomes" narrowly defined. In addition, research is demonstrating that optimal learning environments must be *intentionally designed* to support these factors (Shernoff, 2013).

REFERENCES

Abrantes, S., & Gouveia, L. (2012). Using games for primary school: Assessing its use with flow experience. In M.M. Cruz-Cunha (Ed.), *Handbook of research on serious games as educational, business and research tools* (pp. 769–781). Hershey, PA: Information Science Reference.

Ames, C. (1992). Classrooms: Goals, structures, and student motivation. *Journal of Educational Psychology, 84,* 261–271. doi:10.1037/0022-0663.84.3.261

Bakker, A. B. (2005). Flow among music teachers and their students: The crossover of peak experiences. *Journal of Vocational Behavior, 66,* 26–44. doi.org/10.1016/j.jvb.2003.11.001

Basom, M. R., & Frase, L. (2004). Creating optimal work environments: Exploring teacher flow experiences. *Mentoring and Tutoring, 12,* 241–258. doi:10.1080/1361126042000239965

Bassi, M., & Delle Fave, A. (2004). Adolescence and the changing context of optimal experience in time: Italy 1986–2000. *Journal of Happiness Studies, 5,* 155–179. doi:10.1023/B:JOHS.0000035914.66037.b5

Coller, B. D., Shernoff, D. J., & Strati, A. D. (2011). Measuring engagement as students learn dynamic systems & control with a video game. *Advances in Engineering Education, 2*(3), 1–32.

Conner, J., & Pope, D. (2014). Student engagement in high-performing schools: Relationships to mental and physical health. In D. Shernoff & J. Bempechat (Eds.), *Engaging youth in schools: Evidence-based models to guide future innovations.* New York, NY: NSSE Yearbook by Teachers College Record.

Corno, L., & Mandinach, E. B. (1983). The role of cognitive engagement in classroom learning and motivation. *Educational Psychologist, 18,* 88–108. doi:10.1080/00461528309529266

Csikszentmihalyi, M. (1990). *Flow: The psychology of optimal experience.* New York, NY: Harper Perennial.

Csikszentmihalyi, M., Abuhamdeh, S., & Nakamura, J. (2005). Flow. In A. J. Elliott & C. S. Dweck (Eds.), *Handbook of competence and motivation* (pp. 598–608). New York, NY: Guilford.

Csikszentmihalyi, M., & Csikszentmihalyi, I. S. (Eds.). (1988). *Optimal experience: Psychological studies of flow in consciousness.* New York, NY: Cambridge University Press.

Csikszentmihalyi, M., & Larson, R. (1984). *Being adolescent: Conflict and growth in the teenage years.* New York, NY: Basic Books.

Csikszentmihalyi, M., Rathunde, K., & Whalen, S. (1993). *Talented teenagers: The roots of success and failure.* New York, NY: Cambridge University Press.

Csikszentmihalyi, M., & Schneider, B. (2000). *Becoming adult: How teenagers prepare for the world of work.* New York, NY: Basic Books.

Custodero, L. A. (2005). Observable indicators of flow experience: A developmental perspective on musical engagement in young children from infancy to school age. *Music Education Research, 7,* 185–209. doi:10.1080/14613800500169431

Delle Fave, A., & Massimini, F. (2003). Optimal experience in work and leisure among teachers and physicians: Individual and bio-cultural implications. *Leisure Studies, 22,* 323–342. doi:10.1080/02614360310001594122

Elliott, E. S., & Dweck, C. S. (1988). Goals: An approach to motivation and achievement. *Journal of Personality & Social Psychology, 54,* 5–12.

Fullagar, C. J., Knight, P. A., & Sovern, H. S. (2013). Challenge/skill balance, flow, and performance anxiety. *Applied Psychology: An International Review, 62,* 236–259. doi:10.1111/j.146-0597.2012.00494

Goodlad, J. I. (1984). *A place called school: Prospects for the future.* New York, NY: McGraw-Hill.

Hektner, J. M., Schmidt, J. A., & Csikszentmihalyi, M. (2007). *Experience sampling method: Measuring the quality of everyday life.* Thousand Oaks, CA: Sage.

Henry, K. L., Knight, K. E., & Thornberry, T. P. (2011). School disengagement as a predictor of dropout, delinquency, and problem substance use during adolescence and early adulthood. *Journal of Youth and Adolescence, 41,* 156–166. doi:10.1007/s10964-011-9665-3

Hidi, S. (1990). Interest and its contribution as a mental resource for learning. *Review of Educational Research, 60,* 549–571. doi:10.3102/00346543060004549

Hughes, G. D. (2012). Teacher retention: Teacher characteristics, school characteristics, organizational characteristics, and teacher efficacy. *Journal of Educational Research, 105,* 245–255. http://dx.doi.org/10.1080/00220671.2011.584922

Johnson, W. L., Vilhjalmsson, H., & Marsella, S. (2005). Serious games for language learning: How much game, how much AI? In C. Looi & G. McCalla (Eds.), *Proceeding of the 2005 conference on artificial intelligence in education: Supporting learning through intelligent and socially informed technology* (pp. 306–313). Amsterdam, Netherlands: IOS Press Amsterdam.

Kaufman, R.C., & Ring, M. (2011). Pathways to leadership and professional development. *Teaching Exceptional Children, 43*, 52–60.

Kunter, M., Tsai, Y.-M., Klusmann, U., Brunner, M., Krauss, S., & Baumert, J. (2008). Students' and mathematics teachers' perceptions of teacher enthusiasm and instruction. *Learning and Instruction, 18*, 468–482. doi:10.1016/j.learninstruc.2008.06.008

Larson, R.W., & Richards, M.H. (1991). Boredom in the middle school years: Blaming schools versus blaming students. *American Journal of Education, 99*, 418–443.

Liu, C.C., Chen, Y.B., & Huang, C.W. (2011). The effect of simulation games on the learning of computational problem solving. *Computer and Education, 57*, 1907–1918. doi:10.1016/j.compedu.2011.04.002

Mahoney, J.L., Larson, R.W., & Eccles, J.S. (Eds.). (2005). *Organized activities as contexts of development: Extracurricular activities, after-school and community programs.* Mahwah, NJ: Erlbaum.

Martin, A.J., Marsh, H.W., Debus, R.L., & Malmberg L.E. (2008). Performance and mastery orientation of high school and university/college students—a Rasch perspective. *Educational and Psychological Measurement, 68*, 464–487. doi:10.1177/0013164407308478

Montessori, M. (1967). *The absorbent mind* (1st ed.). New York, NY: Holt, Rinehart, and Winston.

Nakamura, J. (1988). Optimal experience and the uses of talent. In M. Csikszentmihalyi & I.S. Csikszentmihalyi (Eds.), *Optimal experience: Psychological studies of flow in consciousness* (pp. 319–326). New York, NY: Cambridge University Press.

Newmann, F.M., Wehlage, G.G., & Lamborn, S.D. (1992). The significance and sources of student engagement. In F.M. Newmann (Ed.), *Student engagement and achievement in American secondary schools* (pp. 11–39). New York, NY: Teachers College Press.

Pearce, J.M. (2005). *Engaging the learner: How can the flow experience support e-learning?* Paper presented at the E-Learn 2005 Conference, Vancouver, British Columbia, Canada.

Pekrun, R., Goetz, T., Daniels, L.M., Stupnisky, R.H., & Perry, R.P. (2010). Boredom in achievement settings: Exploring control-value antecedents and performance outcomes of a neglected emotion. *Journal of Educational Psychology, 102*, 531–549. doi:10.1037/a0019243

Pianta, R.C., Hamre, B.K., & Allen, J.P. (2012). Teacher–student relationships and engagement: Conceptualizing, measuring, and improving the capacity of classroom interactions. In S. L Christenson, A.L. Reschly, & C. Wylie (Eds.), *Handbook of research on student engagement* (pp. 365–386). New York, NY: Springer Science.

Pickens, M.T. (2007). *Teacher and students perspectives on motivation within the high school science classroom.* Unpublished doctoral dissertation, Auburn University, Auburn, Alabama.

Procci, K., Singer, A.R., Levy, K.R., & Bowers, C. (2012). Measuring the flow experience of gamers: An evaluation of the DFS-2. *Computers in Human Behavior, 28*, 2306–2312. doi:10.1016/j.chb.2012.06.039

Rathunde, K. (1993). Undivided interest and the growth of talent: A longitudinal study of adolescents. *Journal of Youth and Adolescence, 22*, 385–405. doi:10.1007/BF01537720

Rathunde, K. (2013). Understanding the context for optimal school experience: Contributions from Montessori education. In D. Shernoff & J. Bempechat (Eds.), *Engaging youth in schools: Evidence-based models to guide future innovations.* New York, NY: NSSE Yearbook by Teachers College Record.

Rathunde, K., & Csikszentmihalyi, M. (2005a). Middle school students, motivation and quality of experience: A comparison of Montessori and traditional school environments. *American Journal of Education, 111*, 341–371. doi:10.1086/428885

Rathunde, K., & Csikszentmihalyi, M. (2005b). The social context of middle school: Teachers, friends, and activities in Montessori and traditional school environments. *Elementary School Journal, 106*, 59–79. doi:10.1086/496907

Roberts, D.F., Foehr, U.G., & Rideout, V. (2005). *Generation M: Media in the lives of 8–18-year-olds.* Menlo Park, CA: Kaiser Family Foundation.

Schiefele, U., Krapp, A., & Winteler, A. (1992). Interest as a predictor of academic achievement: A meta-analysis of research. In K.A. Renninger, S. Hidi, & A. Krapp (Eds.), *The role of interest in learning and development* (pp. 183–212). Hillsdale, NJ: Erlbaum.

Schunk, D.H., Pintrich, P.R., & Meece, J.L. (Eds.). (2008). *Motivation in education: Theory, research, and applications* (3rd ed.). Upper Saddle River, NJ: Merrill Prentice Hall.

Scoresby, J., & Shelton, B.E. (2007). *Visual perspectives within educational computer games: Effects on presence and flow within virtual learning environments.* Paper presented at the annual meeting of the American Educational Research Association, Chicago, IL.

Seligman, M.E.P., & Csikszentmihalyi, M. (2000). Positive psychology: An introduction. *American Psychologist, 55*, 5–14. doi:10.1037/0003-066X.55.1.5

Şentürk, B. A. (2012). Teachers' and students' perception of flow in speaking activities. *Journal of Managerial Economics and Business, 8*(16), 284–306.

Sharifah, M. S. M., Habibah, E., Samsilah, R., & Sidek, M. N. (2011). Can mastery and performance goals predict learning flow among secondary school students? *International Journal of Humanities and Social Science, 1*(11), 93–98.

Shernoff, D. J. (2010a). Engagement in after-school programs as a predictor of social competence and academic performance. *American Journal of Community Psychology, 45,* 325–337. doi:10.1007/s10464-010-9314-0

Shernoff, D. J. (2010b). *The experience of student engagement in high school classrooms: Influences and effects on long-term outcomes.* Saarbruken, Germany: Lambert Academic Publishing.

Shernoff, D. J. (2012). Engagement and positive youth development: Creating optimal learning environments. In K. R. Harris, S. Graham, & T. Urdan (Eds.), *The APA educational psychology handbook.* (Vol. 3, pp. 195–220). Washington, DC: American Psychological Association.

Shernoff, D. J. (2013). *Optimal learning environments to promote student engagement.* New York, NY: Springer.

Shernoff, D. J., & Coller, B. D. (2013, April). *A quasi-experimental comparison of learning and performance in engineering education via video game versus traditional methods.* Paper presented at the annual meeting of the American Educational Research Association, San Francisco, CA.

Shernoff, D. J., & Csikszentmihalyi, M. (2009). Flow in schools: Cultivating engaged learners and optimal learning environments. In R. Gilman, E. S. Heubner, & M. J. Furlong (Eds.), *Handbook of positive psychology in schools* (pp. 131–145). New York, NY: Routledge.

Shernoff, D. J., Csikszentmihalyi, M., Schneider, B., & Shernoff, E. S. (2003). Student engagement in high school classrooms from the perspective of flow theory. *School Psychology Quarterly, 18,* 158–176. doi:10.1521/scpq.18.2.158.21860

Shernoff, D. J., & Hoogstra, L. (2001). Continuing motivation beyond the high school classroom. *New Directions for Child and Adolescent Development, 93,* 73–87. doi:10.1002/cd.26

Shernoff, D. J., Knauth, S., & Makris, E. (2000). The quality of classroom experiences. In M. Csikszentmihalyi & B. Schneider (Eds.), *Becoming adult: How teenagers prepare for the world of work* (pp. 141–164). New York, NY: Basic Books.

Shernoff, D. J., & Schmidt, J. A. (2008). Further evidence of an engagement–achievement paradox among U.S. high school students. *Journal of Youth and Adolescence, 37,* 564–580. doi:10.1007/s10964-007-9241-z

Shernoff, D. J., Tonks, S., & Anderson, B. G. (2014). The impact of the learning environment on student engagement in high school classrooms. In D. J. Shernoff & J. Bempechat (Eds.), *Engaging youth in schools: Evidence-based models to guide future innovations.* New York, NY: NSSE Yearbook by Teachers College Record.

Shernoff, D. J., Tonks, S., Anderson, B., & Dortch, C. (2011). *Linking instructional practices with student engagement from moment to moment in high school classrooms.* Paper presented at the Annual Meeting of the American Educational Research Association, New Orleans, LA.

Shuell, T. J. (1993). Toward an integrated theory of teaching and learning. *Educational Psychologist, 28,* 291–311. doi:10.1207/s15326985ep2804_1

Singh, K., Granville, M., & Dika, S. (2002). Mathematics and science achievement: Effects of motivation, interest, and academic engagement. *Journal of Educational Research, 95,* 323–333. doi:10.1080/00220670209596607

Smith, M. P. (2009). *Differentiated instruction and teacher flow.* Unpublished doctoral dissertation, Saint Mary's University of Minnesota.

Steinberg, L., Brown, B. B., & Dornbusch, S. M. (1996). *Beyond the classroom: Why school reform has failed and what parents need to do.* New York, NY: Simon & Schuster.

Strati, A. D., Shernoff, D. J., & Kackar, H. Z. (2012). Flow. In R. Levesque (Ed.), *Encyclopedia of adolescence* (pp. 1050–1059). New York, NY: Springer.

Theobald, M. (2006). *Increasing student motivation: Strategies for middle and high school teachers.* Thousand Oaks, CA: Corwin.

Thompson, H., & Vedantam, S. (2012). A lively mind: Your brain on Jane Austen. *NPR: National Public Radio Website.* Retrieved from http://www.npr.org/blogs/health/2012/10/09/162401053/a-lively-mind-your-brain-on-jane-austen

Turner, J. C., & Meyer, D. K. (2004). A classroom perspective on the principle of moderate challenge in mathematics. *Journal of Educational Research, 97,* 311–318. doi:10.3200/JOER.97.6.311-318.

Turner, J. C., Meyer, D. K., Cox, K. E., Logan, C., DiCintio, M., & Thomas, C. T. (1998). Creating contexts for involvement in mathematics. *Journal of Educational Psychology, 90,* 730–745. doi:10.1037/0022-0663.90.4.730

Turner, J. C., & Warzon, K. B. (2009). *Pathways to teacher motivation: The outcomes of teacher–student interaction.* Paper presented at the annual meeting of the American Educational Research Association, San Diego, CA.

Van Eck, R. (2006). Digital game-based learning: It's not just the digital natives who are restless. *Educase Review, 41*, 16–30.

Vygotsky, L. S. (1978). *Mind in society: The development of higher mental processes.* Cambridge, MA: Harvard University Press.

Willms, J. D. (2003). *Student engagement at school: A sense of belonging and participation. Results from PISA 2000.* Paris, France: OECD.

Yazzie-Mintz, E. (2010). *Charting the path from engagement to achievement: A report of the 2009 High School Survey of Student Engagement.* Bloomington, IN: Center for Evaluation & Education Policy.

Zaleski, D. J. (2012). *The influence of momentary classroom goal structures on student engagement and achievement in high school science.* Unpublished doctoral dissertation. Northern Illinois University, DeKalb, IL.

Zhang, J., Scardamalia, M., Reeve, R., & Messina, R. (2009). Designs for collective cognitive responsibility in knowledge-building communities. *Journal of the Learning Sciences, 18*, 7–44. doi:10.1080/10508400802581676.

CHAPTER SUMMARY: FLOW

- The concept of optimal experience, or flow, can be used to characterize student engagement in learning, especially since its central phenomenological components of *concentration*, *enjoyment*, and *interest* are the foundations of meaningful learning. As flow theory would predict, student engagement in the high school classroom is greatly enhanced when the challenge of the activity is perceived to be high and students assess their skills to be equally high.

- Student engagement in public high school is rare; however, certain conditions make it more likely, such as perceptual factors (e.g., high challenges and skills, relevance, and control), mastery learning goals, instructional factors (e.g., activity type and characteristics of the teacher's implementation), and the academic ability or achievement of the student.

- The chief characteristic of optimal learning environments, in which research shows that engagement is high, is *environmental complexity*, or the simultaneous combination of environmental challenge and environmental support. Environmental challenge is characterized by working on tasks of sufficient complexity for the learner's skill level (usually with a domain-specific tool), clear goals, perceived importance of the task, the building of conceptual understanding and/or language skills, and the opportunity to demonstrate one's performance through assessment. Environmental support is characterized by positive relationships with teachers and peers, support for motivational drives (e.g., support for competence and autonomy), constructive performance feedback, and opportunities to be both active and interactive.

- Recent research has shown that optimal learning environments and environmental complexity are illustrated by Montessori schools, high-quality after-school programs, and educational video games that immerse players in complex learning tasks. High engagement in such environments has been related to numerous positive developmental and academic outcomes such as increased learning and academic performance, stronger interpersonal relationships, and social competency.

- Research shows that the teachers' flow and students' flow are frequently related and interactive.

- Creating optimal learning environments requires attention to a variety of contextual, instructional, developmental, and interpersonal factors. Research is demonstrating that optimal learning environments must be *intentionally designed* to support these factors.

SUGGESTED READINGS: FLOW

Csikszentmihalyi, M., Abuhamdeh, S., & Nakamura, J. (2005). Flow. In A. J. Eliot & C. S. Dweck (Eds.), *Handbook of competence and motivation* (pp. 598–608). New York, NY: Guilford.

This chapter provides a conceptual overview of flow as related to motivation and the development of competence, plus a summary of related research.

Hektner, J. M., Schmidt, J. A., & Csikszentmihalyi, M. (2007). *Experience Sampling Method: Measuring the quality of everyday life.* Thousand Oaks, CA: Sage.

This valuable book describes the theoretical foundations, reliability and validity information, and practical applications of the Experience Sampling Method. It also provides logistical information for carrying out the method, from conceiving of a research question to analyzing the data; and it includes a chapter on ESM research in education.

Shernoff, D. J. (2012). Engagement and positive youth development: Creating optimal learning environments. In K. R. Harris, S. Graham, & T. Urdan (Eds.), *The APA educational psychology handbook.* (Vol. 3, pp. 195–220). Washington, DC: American Psychological Association.

This chapter overviews research on engagement and highlights influences on engagement as conceptually based in flow theory. Evidence-based, alternative models to improve engagement are highlighted, and implications for educational philosophy, practice, and policy are also discussed.

Shernoff, D. J. (2013). *Optimal learning environments to promote student engagement.* New York, NY: Springer.

This book conceptualizes and analyzes optimal learning environments to promote student engagement from multiple perspectives, framing it as critical to learning and development. Drawing on positive psychology and flow studies, the book conceptualizes engagement as a learning experience, explaining how schools can maximize it among adolescents.

Shernoff, D. J., & Bempechat, J. (Eds.). (2014). *Engaging youth in schools: Evidence-based models to guide future innovations.* New York, NY: NSSE Yearbook by Teachers College Record.

This volume intentionally selects and emphasizes a variety of optimally engaging learning environments for youth, not only to provide research evidence of their power to engage but also, more importantly, to describe in rich detail how these proven environments work in order to be of maximum usefulness to educators and policy makers.

15

MEANINGFUL ACTIVITY PARTICIPATION AND POSITIVE YOUTH DEVELOPMENT

Bonnie L. Barber, Bree D. Abbott, Corey J. Blomfield Neira, School of Psychology and Exercise Science, Murdoch University, Perth, Australia

Jacquelynne S. Eccles, Psychology Department, University of Michigan, Ann Arbor, Michigan, USA

Work on this chapter was supported by a grant from the Australian Research Council to Barber and Eccles. We thank Margaret Stone for her contributions over the years to our views about the role of activity participation in the lives of youth.

INTRODUCTION

When adolescents decide how to use their leisure time, most choose at least one organized structured activity—a sport, performing art, academic club, service activity, or church youth group. Sports are the most commonly reported activities, followed by performing arts (Eccles, & Barber, 1999; Feldman & Matjasko, 2007; Zill, Nord, & Loomis, 1995). Voluntary community service is also reported by between a third and a half of all youth (Youniss et al., 2002). Girls tend to participate in more types of activities, whereas boys are most likely to play sports (Eccles & Barber, 1999; Feldman & Matjasko, 2007; Mahoney & Cairns, 1997). Given the prevalence of extracurricular activities in the daily lives of youth, it is important to understand their role in successful development and healthy adjustment.

Meaningful activity participation is important for successful development, with mounting evidence that school- and community-based activity participation facilitates healthy outcomes, including achievement, self-esteem, ability to overcome adversity, willingness to help others, leadership qualities, physical health, educational and occupational attainment, and civic involvement (e.g., Eccles & Barber, 1999; Eccles & Gootman, 2002; Holland & Andre, 1987; Larson, 2000; Mahoney & Vest, 2012; Marsh & Kleitman, 2002; Youniss & Yates, 1997). Although activities may help reduce risks for students, Pittman reminds us that being problem free is not the same as being fully prepared (Pittman, Irby, Tolman, Yohalem, & Ferber, 2002). As noted by Lerner (2001), positive development is more than simply avoiding delinquency and substance use. Students need opportunities to meet challenges as well as help resolve issues of identity, develop increasing autonomy, and acquire educational and other experiences needed for adult work roles. This chapter focuses on the role of adolescent activity participation in the accomplishment of a range of developmental tasks. First, an overview of the conceptual approaches to operationalizing meaningful activities is presented. Second, the role of structured organized activities in the psychological, academic, and psychosocial development of youth is examined. The strengths and limitations of existing research in these areas are briefly considered, and the chapter concludes with suggestions for further research.

HOW HAVE MEANINGFUL ACTIVITIES BEEN DEFINED AND STUDIED?

Most of the North American research on the role of participation in meaningful activities has focused on organized, adult-supervised activities. It is to be noted that "meaningfulness" has primarily been defined in terms of the structure of the activity itself—not in terms of its psychological meaningfulness to the participants. In keeping with this focus, this chapter draws on research on extracurricular activity participation in the following contexts: (a) school (e.g., academic clubs, service clubs, student government, drama and music, and school spirit–associated activities); (b) organized sports programs both in and out of school; (c) service and faith-based activities in the community; (d) organized community-based activities at such places as the YMCA, Boys and Girls Club, Girls Inc., 4-H centers, and other such organizations; and (e) community-based music, drama, and art activities.

Initially, benefits of leisure activities were compared between those who participated and those who did not. However, the assessment of activity participation has moved beyond these dichotomous comparisons. Activity participation is multifaceted and as such, several dimensions are needed to capture the complex nature of participation (Bonhert, Fredricks, & Randell, 2010). As evidence has grown for the benefits of activities, research has begun to focus on questions of dosage and content, seeking to explain when and why participation yields positive results. Dosage of activity participation has been operationalized in terms of the number or breadth, duration, and perceived intensity of the activities. Developmental benefits afforded to adolescents can depend on the range of chosen activities, the frequency and consistency of engagement, and the number of years the young person participates (Feldman Farb & Matjasko, 2012). In terms of content or process, there has been some research focused on the nature and quality of experiences in these types of activities and participants' engagement, to probe the causal mechanisms underlying the influence of participation on development. We briefly summarize the general nature of the findings related to dosage below before turning to how the content of some activities may influence specific developmental outcomes.

Breadth of Activities

An approach that combines both metric and activity content measures is a *breadth index*, which indicates the degree of eclectic participation. By participating in a wide variety of activities, youth have the opportunity to experience a broad range of different activity contexts, potentially exposing them to a greater variety of developmental experiences (Hansen, Larson, & Dworkin, 2003) and diverse peer groups (Eccles & Barber, 1999; Fredricks & Eccles, 2005). Breadth may be explored using the total number of activities or activity contexts, or it may be examined using dispersion methods or cluster analyses to create participation profiles.

We have found that the extent of participation across a broader range of activity domains such as music, art, sports, leadership, and community service predicted greater school attachment, higher GPA, greater likelihood of college attendance, and more years of education completed, even after controlling for math and verbal aptitude (Barber & Eccles, 1997; Barber, Stone, & Eccles, 2005, 2010; Fredricks & Eccles, 2006a, 2006b). Greater activity breadth during early and mid-adolescence has also been associated with greater civic development and academic orientation in late adolescence (Denault & Poulin, 2009). Overall, youth who participate in a wide range of leisure activities have more positive social and academic outcomes (Bonhert et al., 2010).

There has been a recent call for researchers to take a person-centered approach by considering the *patterns* or *profiles* of participation when examining breadth, that is, ways that students combine multiple activities (Bonhert et al., 2010; Feldman & Matjasko, 2007; Feldman Farb & Matjasko, 2012). For example, some students play on a sport team or two, while others spend their time in academic clubs, and still others participate in a combination of different activities. Using the nationally representative Add Health data set, Feldman and Matjasko (2007) found that multiple activity portfolios were the most common profiles of participation, with 43% of students engaged in more than one type of activity, with one or more sports activities being the most common. Adolescents involved in activity profiles that consist of both a sport and a nonsport report having a greater social self-concept and a sense of general self-worth than adolescents in profiles consisting of a single activity type and those who did not participate in any activities (Blomfield & Barber, 2009).

Dosage of Activities

Generally, there is a positive relation between *the frequency of activity participation* and a wide range of developmental outcomes for adolescents (Feldman & Matjasko, 2005). Furthermore, the absolute number of different activities predicts better developmental outcomes, even when prior levels of the specific developmental outcomes are controlled (Barber & Eccles, 1997). Studies on the stability or *duration* of involvement provide evidence that greater continuity of participation across several years predicts more positive development. Benefits include lower levels of loneliness (Randall & Bohnert, 2009), better grades, psychological resilience, and school belonging (Darling, 2005; Eccles, Barber, Stone, & Hunt, 2003; and for duration of school club participation, but not sports—Fredricks & Eccles, 2006a), and higher educational attainment in young adulthood (e.g., Mahoney, Cairns, & Farmer, 2003).

In spite of these consistent and positive findings, some scholars and child advocates have raised concerns that too much participation in organized activities robs adolescents of the time they need to be creative and increases parental pressure to perform (for a detailed response to these concerns, see Mahoney, Harris, & Eccles, 2006). In fact, research investigating the *intensity* of involvement—or total amount of time spent participating—has found that students reporting greater intensity in activities also report more positive outcomes (Bonhert et al., 2010) including higher achievement, stronger school connections, and better school adjustment (Cooper, Valentine, Nye, & Lindsay 1999; Mahoney et al., 2006). A few studies have found diminishing benefits at the highest levels of participation (Cooper et al., 1999; Fredricks, 2012; Zill et al., 1995); but even so, there remains a developmental advantage to the highest-level participants compared to those students who did not participate at all. Overall, greater time spent in organized activities is related to positive developmental outcomes for adolescents from various demographic and economic backgrounds (Bonhert et al., 2010; Mahoney & Vest, 2012).

Student Engagement

Studying attendance or participation alone may not be sufficient to understand the link between activities and positive outcomes. These quantifying approaches do not consider student engagement. Engagement can vary substantially across different activity settings, with high engagement associated with high attention, enjoyment, effort toward skill mastery, and interest, and low engagement characterized by boredom, passivity, apathy, and inattentiveness (Larson, 2000). Engagement is a multidimensional construct and can be measured cognitively, behaviorally, and emotionally using a variety of methods such as the experience sampling method (ESM), observational methods, self-report questionnaires, and teacher/leader reports (Bonhert et al., 2010).

ACTIVITIES AS DEVELOPMENTAL ASSETS FOR INDIVIDUAL PSYCHOLOGICAL DEVELOPMENT

If adolescents are often bored and unmotivated (Larson, 2000), then they need something in which to become engaged. Meaningful activities provide a forum in which to explore and express one's identity, talents, and passion and to gain a sense that one "matters" (Csikszentmihalyi & Kleiber, 1991; Eccles & Gootman, 2002; Kleiber, 1999). Adolescents likely choose activities that reflect core aspects of their self-beliefs, and that participation can, in turn, both reinforce and channel both the way that youth think about themselves and how they behave. In the process, positive development in a range of domains can be facilitated, including identity, body image, initiative, life satisfaction, and conduct. We examine each of these areas below.

Self-System

The opportunity to both express and refine one's identity is a key aspect of socioemotional development during adolescence, and activity participation offers a meaningful and constructive domain for such work. This context is unique, as other areas of an adolescent's life, such as school, work, and church, are more rigidly structured and may provide less freedom to explore and express identity options than discretionary activities. Therefore, voluntary participation in extracurricular activities provides an opportunity for adolescents to be personally expressive and to communicate to both themselves and others that "this is who I am" (Barber, Stone, Hunt, & Eccles, 2005; Coatsworth et al., 2005). Eccles and her colleagues (1983) refer to this quality of activities as attainment value, or the value of an activity to demonstrate that one is the kind of person one most hopes to be. In support of this idea, Coatsworth and his colleagues (2005) reported that youth consider a broad range of activities to be "self-defining," including organized activities such as sports, performing arts, and religious and altruistic activities. Within those activities, it appears that greater personal expressiveness of activities predicts lower delinquency (Palen & Coatsworth, 2007) and helps to explain the link between activity participation and adolescent wellness (Coatsworth, Palen, Sharpe, & Ferrer-Wreder, 2006). Thus, the more congruent an activity is with an adolescent's self-perspective, the greater the potential benefits.

In addition to reinforcing one's personal identity, activity participation offers an opportunity to explore a range of social identities, such as where one fits in the leisure context, peer culture, and the community. Adolescents develop a social sense of self in addition to an individual sense of self as they participate in activities (Stone & Brown, 1998; Youniss & Smollar, 1985). Participating in a particular activity type provides the opportunity for adolescents to associate themselves with an activity-based peer culture, with their self-identity influenced by the meaning attached to that activity (Eccles et al., 2003). We have explored these connections and have found clear links between high school social identities and specific activities and that consistency between one's identity and one's activities predicts better psychological and academic functioning (et al., 2005; Eccles & Barber, 1999). Meaningful civic activities such as volunteering and service learning provide a platform to explore community-based social identities and to integrate experiences addressing social problems into their self-concepts of ability to contribute to the community (Youniss & Yates, 1997) and adopt and maintain prosocial values (Horn, 2012).

The exploration of different identities that is afforded by activity participation provides youth with the opportunity to develop and refine their self-concept. Self-concept refers to an individual's perceptions or knowledge structure of the self across several domains (academic, social, physical, and behavioral conduct) and is formed through experience (Harter, 1999). Participation in activities is consistently associated with a more positive self-concept in adolescence (Blomfield & Barber, 2009; Eccles & Barber 1999; Fredricks & Eccles 2006b; Marsh, 1992), with youth who participate in a combination of both sport and nonsport activities appearing to benefit the most (Blomfield & Barber, 2009). In our research, we have found the opportunity to explore and reflect on one's identity, in conjunction with the more concrete developmental experiences that activities provide, such as skills in perseverance and goal setting, to be some of the underlying mechanisms by which activity participation is linked to a more positive self-concept (Blomfield & Barber, 2011).

Body Image

Body image also is positively influenced by meaningful activity participation. Some aspects of activity participation may help to counteract the tendency for Western societies to objectify and sexualize the female body (Fredrickson & Roberts, 1997), perhaps reducing the extent to which females are socialized to view their bodies as objects to be viewed and evaluated by others for their aesthetic appeal rather than for their function. The more value and investment that is placed on the functional aspects of the body, the more satisfied both male and female adolescents are with their bodies' function and form (Abbott & Barber, 2010). Extracurricular activities that focus on function over form have a positive impact on the development of a healthy body image among adolescents—particularly among adolescent girls. We have found that girls involved in sport have greater value of, investment in, and satisfaction toward their functional bodies than non-participants (Abbott & Barber, 2011). Furthermore, the type of sport made a difference, with girls participating in nonaesthetic sports reporting greater investment in and satisfaction with the functional dimension of the body than girls who participated in aesthetic sports (such as dance or gymnastics). Brady (2005) suggested that sports programs have the potential to deliver healthy messages to females and encourage an identity and body image that are based upon physical skill and potential rather than looks and sexuality.

Sports also reinforce the masculine cultural stereotype and muscular body ideal for male participants. Males are socialized to focus on the functional aspects of their bodies, and participation in sports and physical activity may therefore reinforce this process. Adolescent males who participate in sports or physical activity report higher body satisfaction than those who do not (Frost & McKelvie, 2005), particularly in the areas of muscle power in the shoulders and chest and the upper body in general (Aşçi, Gőkmen, Tiryaki, & Aşçi, 1997).

Initiative

Larson (2000) proposed that participation in certain types of organized activities is vital to the development of *initiative*. Initiative is defined as the capacity to achieve specific goals through the use of skills such as planning, time management, problem solving, and contingency thinking over a period of time (Larson, Hansen, & Walker, 2005). However, adolescents are rarely given the opportunity to engage in activities that require them to use these skills. Organized meaningful activities provide an alternative context in which adolescents can become intrinsically motivated and voluntarily establish self-directed attention, control, self-discipline, and decision-making skills (Crean, 2012; Kleiber, 1999; Larson, 2000). For example, when asked about why basketball was his favorite activity, one boy noted, "it requires more skill, more focused teamwork and concentration" (Abbott & Barber, 2007). The aspects of activities that facilitate the development of initiative, such as challenge and skill enhancement, also make them enjoyable pursuits.

Structured extracurricular activities provide youth with more experiences that promote the development of initiative than do activities such as school classes or hanging out with friends (Abbott & Barber, 2007; Hansen et al., 2003; Larson, Hansen, & Moneta, 2006). According to Larson and colleagues, adolescents reported that arts and sports activities, in particular, allowed them to exercise more initiative than involvement in other organized activities, but all organized activities examined offered more opportunities for taking initiative than core school classes alone.

Risk Taking and Problem Behavior

Activity participation is associated with lower levels of illegal and problem behavior in adolescence (Davis & Menard, 2013; Mahoney, Larson, Eccles, & Lord, 2005). Feldman and Matjasko's (2005) comprehensive review evaluated the evidence for the protective role of participation and highlighted a number of studies linking participation to less delinquency. Mahoney (2000) reported a significant link between extended participation in extracurricular activities during high school and reduced rates of criminal offending, particularly for high-risk youth.

The evidence for extracurricular participation to protect against substance use is more equivocal than that for delinquency. Participation in community-service activities predicts lower rates of drinking and drug use in adolescence (Eccles & Barber, 1999; Youniss, McLellan, Su, & Yates, 1999) and young adulthood (Barber, Eccles, & Stone, 2001). Further, participation generally predicts less marijuana and other drug use, as well as less smoking and drinking (Darling, 2005; Mahoney et al., 2006; Rawana & Ames, 2012; Zill et al., 1995). There is some evidence, however, that not all types of activities provide equal protection. For example, some studies have found that sports participation predicts greater substance use (Barber et al., 2001; Fauth, Roth, & Brooks-Gunn, 2007). This connection between sports and alcohol can be attributed, at least in part, to the peer associations formed with other athletes, who themselves are also likely to drink (Blomfield & Barber, 2008; Eccles & Barber, 1999).

ACTIVITIES AS DEVELOPMENTAL ASSETS
FOR ACADEMIC DEVELOPMENT

School-sponsored activities such as sports and performing arts are important contexts that can support or undermine academic developmental goals (Barber et al., 2001). Research suggests that school activities link students to the larger society of the school (Entwisle, 1990) and that these experiences are positively related to adolescents' feelings of personal competence, efficacy, and academic achievement (Holland & Andre, 1987; Marsh & Kleitman, 2002). Research consistently reports a positive relation between activity participation and higher academic focus (Broh, 2002; Darling, Cadwell, & Smith, 2005; Guest & Schneider, 2003; Marsh, 1992; Videon, 2002) and a reduced likelihood of dropping out of school (Mahoney, 2000; Mahoney & Cairns, 1997; Zill et al., 1995). School-based activities also offer opportunities that regular classroom activities might not, including the exercise of initiative, identity work, and engagement (Dworkin, Larson, & Hansen, 2003; Larson, 2000; Larson et al., 2006), increasing the likelihood that students will feel connected to their school (Feldman & Matjasko, 2005; Knifsend & Graham, 2012). It should not be surprising, therefore, that participation predicts academic achievement and educational attainment.

School Connection and Involvement

We have argued that although a sense of belonging at school can result from a number of personal and social contextual factors, extracurricular activities are an especially likely path to school attachment, particularly for youth who do not excel academically (Eccles et al., 2003). Participation in extracurricular activities can facilitate connections in the school context that satisfy adolescents' developmental need for social relatedness, competence, and autonomy. Highly involved adolescents report greater school satisfaction and belonging than their peers who have little to no activity participation (Darling et al., 2005; Gilman, 2001). Blomfield and Barber (2010) found that 88% of activity participants responded affirmatively when asked if their activity made school more enjoyable, with comments such as, "It stops you stressing out about tests, school in general, so when you are at school you have a calmer mind," "I am not constantly focused on my study. I can have a break" and "Because it makes me feel accepted." Activities also contribute to one's identity as a valued member of the school community. In turn, a strong attachment to one's school can facilitate the internalization of other aspects of the school's agenda, such as those related to academics. In support of this idea, research has documented the connections between activity participation and higher achievement and aspirations (e.g., Barber et al., 2001; Cooper et al., 1999; Darling et al., 2005; Knifsend & Graham, 2012, Mahoney & Cairns, 1997; Mahoney et al., 2003; Marsh & Kleitman, 2002).

Academic Achievement

Participation in organized activities has been shown to be positively related to academic performance, with students who participate in activities such as sports, performing arts, service learning, and academic clubs receiving better grades than their nonparticipating peers (Broh, 2002; Eccles et al., 2003; Fredricks & Eccles, 2006b; Guest & Schneider, 2003; Marsh & Kleitman, 2003; Metsäpelto & Pulkkinen, 2012). These relations generally hold up even when key variables are controlled, including family background, prior achievement, and scores on standardized aptitude tests. Several researchers have documented an especially pronounced benefit from sports involvement in the United States. (e.g., Barber et al., 2001; Mahoney & Cairns, 1997; Marsh & Kleitman, 2002). For example, in National Educational Longitudinal Survey (NELS) data, sport participation was related to numerous positive academic indicators (Marsh & Kleitman, 2002, 2003), and the number of sports teams on which a student played also predicted increased likelihood of college attendance and a higher GPA, with higher levels of athletic participation associated with greater benefits. In addition, higher breadth and intensity of activity participation have been positively associated with math test scores, higher grade point average (GPA), and educational expectations in high school students (Fredricks, 2012).

Educational and Occupational Attainment

A long research tradition in sociology has focused on the beneficial link between adolescents' extracurricular activities and their future educational attainment, occupation, and income (Hanks & Eckland, 1976; Holland & Andre, 1987; Otto, 1975; Otto & Alwin, 1977). We have found in our research that participation in sports, school-based leadership and spirit activities, and academic clubs predicted an increased likelihood of being enrolled full time in college at age 21 (Eccles et al., 2003). Beal and Crockett (2010) demonstrated that the link between educational and occupational aspirations in high school and adult educational attainment was partially mediated by extracurricular activity participation. Participation in extracurricular and service learning activities has also been linked to better job quality, more active participation in the political process and other types of volunteer activities, and better mental health during young adulthood (Barber et al., 2001; Marsh, 1992; Youniss et al., 1999).

ACTIVITIES AS FACILITATORS OF SOCIAL DEVELOPMENT

As noted, there is increasing and convincing evidence to indicate that activities are important assets for intrapersonal and academic development. Less is known about the importance of activities for the development of interpersonal relationships and social connections. Evidence is accruing that activity participation is significantly related to more positive relationships with adults and friendships with more prosocial peers. These two social networks are briefly reviewed.

The Role of Adult Leaders

Structured extracurricular activities provide adolescents with access to caring non-familial adults, who are often teachers or counselors acting as coaches and leaders. Coaches, club advisors, and other involved adults often invest a great deal of time and attention to participants, acting as teachers, mentors, and problem solvers (e.g., Youniss & Yates, 1997). This investment provides adolescents with a range of social developmental opportunities, establishes supportive networks of adults and adolescents, integrates adolescents into adult-sponsored culture, and allows them to achieve positive recognition (e.g., Eccles et al., 2003). Links to competent supportive adults in after-school activities can also contribute to psychological well-being (Mahoney, Schweder, & Stattin, 2002).

A key characteristic of structured activities is the guidance and monitoring provided by an adult during the activity. However, the amount of guidance provided by adult leaders should be tailored to the skills and competence of the participants. Adolescents may require initial direction from a more competent adult or peer, but assistance should gradually decrease as the competence of the adolescents increases (Vygotsky, 1978).

Larson, Walker, and Pearce (2005) compared the benefits and limitations of both adult-driven and youth-driven activities. The adult-driven approach to activities appears to be more beneficial for activities that require adolescents to master a specific skill or knowledge base (for example, performing arts or sports). However, if adult leaders are insensitive to the competencies of their participants or provide either too much or too little guidance, the participant may lose interest in the activity or drop out altogether (Dworkin & Larson, 2006).

Youth-driven activities (such as student council committees, protest rallies) are those that encourage youth to become involved in higher levels of decision making and planning (Larson et al., 2005). Although an adult facilitator might supervise these activities, youth take responsibility for their own progress and learning and as a result experience a sense of empowerment and ownership. However, adolescents may

lack the skills required to maintain focus and keep track of long-term goals. Therefore, for both youth-driven and adult-driven activities to be beneficial and facilitative,
any adult involvement needs to be adaptive, monitored, and guiding, keeping youth on
track while at the same time allowing youth to maintain their own self-direction and
explore their own capabilities and limits (Larson et al., 2005; Larson et al., 2005).

Friendship Networks and Peer Groups

Participation in organized activities facilitates achievement of a primary developmental task of adolescence—namely, meaningful connections to peers. In many
organized activities, that connection is made to a group of peers likely to encourage
academic success and avoid risk behavior (e.g., Barber et al., 2005). Involvement in
a sport, club, performing art, or service activity provides shared opportunities and
challenges with such prosocial peers and can reinforce friendships. To the extent that
one spends a lot of time in these activity settings with the other participants, it is
likely that one's friends will be drawn from among the other participants. It is also
likely that the collective behaviors of such peer groups will influence the behaviors of
each member. Thus, some of the behavioral differences associated with activity participation appear to be a consequence of the behavioral expectations and influence
of the peer groups (Barber et al., 2010; Eccles et al., 2003; Fredricks & Eccles, 2005;
Mahoney, 2000).

We have found significant relations between friendship network characteristics and activity participation (Barber et al., 2005; Blomfield & Barber, 2008; Fredricks & Eccles, 2005). Adolescents engaged in extracurricular activities generally have
more academically oriented friends and fewer friends who skip school and use drugs
than do adolescents who do not participate in activities (Eccles & Barber, 1999).
In turn, having more studious and fewer risky friends predicts other positive outcomes
for adolescents (Fredricks & Eccles, 2005).

Conversely, being part of a peer network that includes a high proportion of youth
who engage in and encourage risky behaviors predicts increased involvement in such
conduct and a decreased likelihood of completing high school and going to college. Patterson and colleagues (Patterson, Dishion, & Yoerger, 2000) have documented a pattern
wherein early involvement with deviant peers is associated with more "mature" forms
of deviance, such as risky sexual behavior, substance abuse, and crime. Such a dynamic
makes it imperative to understand how some activities facilitate membership in positive
peer networks while others facilitate membership in more problematic peer networks
(Blomfield & Barber, 2008; Denault & Poulin, 2012).

Disadvantaged Youth

Despite the numerous benefits consistently associated with activity participation, for
many youth, access to such activities and programs continues to be beyond reach. Adolescents from disadvantaged backgrounds (low socioeconomic status, ethnic minority) are
much less likely to participate in extracurricular activities in comparison to their peers
from more advantaged backgrounds (Blomfield & Barber, 2011; Bouffard et al., 2006;

Dearing et al., 2009). Numerous constraints exist for these youth, which make participation more difficult, with the financial cost of activities often a primary reason for nonparticipation. In a national survey, only 39% of ethnic minority parents reported being able to afford extracurricular activities, compared with 62% of white parents (Duffett & Johnson, 2004). Often youth from disadvantaged backgrounds have considerable familial responsibilities, which take priority over their own individual desire to participate in activities (Perkins et al., 2007). The ability to access activities has been highlighted as a major barrier to participation for youth from disadvantaged backgrounds (Eccles & Gootman, 2002), and schools with a poorer student population are found to offer fewer extracurricular activities than schools in more affluent communities (Stearns & Glennie, 2010).

The disproportionately low participation of youth from disadvantaged backgrounds is of further concern as it is these youth who may gain the most from involvement. Though the majority of research on meaningful activity participation is based on middle-class youth, studies incorporating disadvantaged populations have found that associations between activity participation and positive indicators are strongest for youth from such backgrounds (Blomfield & Barber, 2011; Mahoney & Cairns, 2007; Marsh, 1992, Marsh & Kleitman, 2002). We have examined the links between developmental experiences, self-concept, and school SES (Blomfield & Barber, 2011). Youth from disadvantaged schools reported higher rates of nonparticipation than those from more advantaged schools. The developmental experiences afforded to youth in activities were found to positively predict self-worth, social self-concept, and academic self-concept among all youth; however, these links were much stronger for youth from disadvantaged schools. It is possible that the developmentally rich environment that extracurricular activities can provide is of particular importance to youth with limited access to such experiences elsewhere, and therefore it is of utmost importance to determine ways in which to reduce and remove barriers to participation for disadvantaged youth.

METHODOLOGICAL ISSUES

The research summarized to this point documents statistical relations between activity participation and positive youth development. However, the causal inferences we can draw from these data are quite limited. The growing evidence for the benefits of participation in organized activities has been encouraging, with a major caveat—we often do not know to what extent the "effects" are attributable to the characteristics of the youth who nominate for and stay in the programs. One of the major challenges to those studying extracurricular activities is, thus, the issue of "selection effects" (for a detailed discussion of the characteristics of youth, their families, and their communities that predict initial and continued participation in various types of organized activities, see Barber et al., 2010). Scholars interested in the effects of activities (as well as those who study other potentially beneficial experiences) have pointed out that activity participation may not be a cause of positive adaptation but rather a result or marker of pre-existing positive characteristics and developmental assets (Mahoney, 2000). It is clear that more motivated, competent, and socially advantaged youth are more likely to select opportunities to participate in activities and to choose to continue their participation. To what, then, should we attribute good outcomes for extracurricular activity participants?

Activities: "Markers" or Promoters of Well-Being?

The importance of the issue of selection effects is related to both practical concerns and basic theoretical and methodological challenges. When interpreting apparent effects in research, it is important not to overestimate the effects of activities. Numerous sources of differences among participants are evident in the literature on extracurricular activity participation. Youth characteristics such as gender, ethnicity, socioeconomic background, and earlier participation history have been shown to have an impact on participation in school-based activities (Videon, 2002). More "psychological" individual attributes (e.g., motivation, self-concept, aptitude, personality, and more positive feelings about one's family context) have also been shown to predict which leisure activities adolescents choose and whether they persist (e.g., Persson, Kerr, & Stattin, 2004). Youth with substantial pre-existing assets are likely to experience positive outcomes with or without activities. Therefore, we should not credit positive development of asset-rich youths who participate as resulting from their participation. Furthermore, some of the same factors that predict activity participation also predict positive outcomes (e.g., parental support and involvement).

This theoretical and practical challenge is made more complicated by the tendency for resources and risk factors to occur in correlated "packages" of "developmental constraints" (Cairns, 1996). This phenomenon can be illustrated by the example of a student from an advantaged background whose intelligence and supportive family are coupled with private tutoring, relationships with peers who encourage academic engagement, constructive experiences in the school math club, and a positive identity based on her achievements. Because such developmental assets are not independent, numerous researchers and theorists have suggested that development must be viewed "organismically," such that any one asset can only be seen to have an effect in the context of its relation and its bidirectional transactions with other asset and risk systems (Barber et al., 2005, 2010; Bronfenbrenner, 1979; Cairns, 1996; Mahoney, 2000).

One way to address these methodological issues and probe the causal links between activity participation and youth outcomes is to conduct longitudinal studies that examine whether change in activity involvement predicts change in youth outcomes. Such an approach does not eliminate selection issues, however. The use of propensity score matching, a statistical technique incorporating multiple covariates, has recently been used in this field by treating activity participation as a "treatment" condition and thus matching participants with nonparticipants on a range of relevant indicators in an attempt to reduce the issue of selection effects (O'Connor & Jose, 2012). An even more compelling method is to try to experimentally change activity involvement and test whether those changes result in enhanced youth development (Bronfenbrenner, 1979). Such experiments have not been conducted for the majority of organized activities (such as sports, band, and student council) that we have described in this chapter—such activities have long been part of most school extra-curricula and do not therefore lend themselves to manipulation or random assignment. However, some opportunities for participation, particularly in the area of community service and cross-age tutoring, have been the focus of evaluation research, with encouraging results (e.g., Cohen, Kulik, & Kulik, 1982; Philliber & Allen, 1992).

CONCLUSION

The evidence base on the salutary effects of meaningful activities continues to grow. A great deal has been learned about the key attributes to consider in determining the quality of experiences adolescents gain from activities. Larson (2000) stressed the importance of activities being voluntary and requiring concerted engagement over time so that participants can learn the skills associated with taking initiative. Eccles and Gootman (2002), in their report on community-based activities for youth, sponsored by the National Research Council, reiterated these criteria and added the following characteristics:

1. opportunities to do things that really matter to the organization and the community in which the adolescents live (e.g., service activities and leadership activities)
2. opportunities to learn quite specific cognitive, social, and cultural skills
3. opportunities to form close social relationships with nonfamilial adults
4. clear and consistently reinforced positive social norms and rules
5. practices that both respect the adolescents' growing maturity and expertise and foster strong bonding of the adolescents with prosocial community institutions

Hansen and Larson (2007) articulate amplifiers of developmental experiences in activities: amount of time spent in the activity, involvement in a leadership role, and ratio of adults to youth. Future research needs to consider more of these attributes in attempting to explain the benefits of some activities and the ineffectiveness of others. We are hopeful that more comprehensive investigations of these aspects of participation will further improve our understanding of the importance of activities in successful adolescent pathways.

REFERENCES

Abbott, B.D., & Barber, B.L. (2007). Not just idle time: Adolescents' developmental experiences provided by structured and unstructured leisure activities. *The Australian Educational and Developmental Psychologist, 24*, 59–81.

Abbott, B.D. & Barber, B.L. (2010). Embodied image: Gender differences in functional and aesthetic body image among Australian adolescents. *Body Image, 7*, 22–31. doi:10.1016/j.bodyim.2009.10.004

Abbott, B.D. & Barber, B.L. (2011). Differences in functional and aesthetic body image between sedentary girls and girls involved in sports and physical activity: Does sport type make a difference? *Psychology of Sport & Exercise, 12*, 333–342. doi:10.1016/j.psychsport.2010.10.005

Aşçi, F.H., Gőkmen, H., Tiryaki, G., & Aşçi, A. (1997). Self-concept and body image of Turkish high school male athletes and nonathletes. *Adolescence, 32*(128), 959–968.

Barber, B.L., & Eccles, J.S. (1997, April). *Student council, volunteering, basketball, or marching band: What kind of extracurricular involvement matters?* Paper presented at the biennial meeting of the Society for Research on Child Development, Washington, DC.

Barber, B.L., Eccles, J.S., & Stone, M.R. (2001). Whatever happened to the Jock, the Brain, and the Princess? Young adult pathways linked to adolescent activity involvement and social identity. *Journal of Adolescent Research, 16*, 429–455. doi:10.1177/0743558401165002

Barber, B.L., Stone, M.R., & Eccles, J.S. (2005). Adolescent participation in organized activities. In K. Moore & L.H. Lippman (Eds.), *Conceptualizing and measuring indicators of positive development: What do children need to flourish?* (pp. 133–146). New York, NY: Springer. doi:10.1007/0–387–23823–9_9

Barber, B.L., Stone, M.R., & Eccles, J.S. (2010). Protect, prepare, support, and engage: The roles of school-based extracurricular activities in students' development. In J. Meece & J. Eccles (Eds.), *Handbook of research on schools, schooling, and human development* (pp. 366–378). New York, NY: Routledge.

Barber, B. L., Stone, M. R., Hunt, J., & Eccles, J. S. (2005). Benefits of activity participation: The roles of identity affirmation and peer group norm sharing. In J. L. Mahoney, R. W. Larson, & J. S. Eccles (Eds.), *Organized activities as contexts of development: Extracurricular activities, after-school and community programs* (pp. 185–210). Mahwah, NJ: Erlbaum.

Beal, S. J., & Crockett, L. J. (2010). Adolescents' occupational and educational aspirations and expectations: Links to high school activities and adult educational attainment. *Developmental Psychology, 46,* 258–265. doi:10.1037/a0017416

Blomfield, C. J., & Barber, B. L. (2008, March). *Risks linked to Australian adolescents' extracurricular activity participation: Is the relationship mediated by peer attributes?* Paper presented at the biennial meeting of the Society for Research on Adolescence, Chicago, IL.

Blomfield, C. J., & Barber, B. L. (2009). Performing on the stage, the field, or both? Extracurricular activity participation and Australian adolescent self-concept. *Journal of Adolescence, 32,* 733–739. doi:10.1016/j.adolescence.2009.01.003

Blomfield, C. J., & Barber, B. L. (2010). Australian adolescents' extracurricular activity participation and positive development: Is the relationship mediated by peer attributes? *Australian Journal of Educational & Developmental Psychology, 10,* 114–128.

Blomfield, C. J., & Barber, B. L. (2011). Developmental experiences during extracurricular activities and Australian adolescents' self-concept: Particularly important for youth from disadvantaged schools. *Journal of Youth & Adolescence, 40,* 582–594. doi:10.1007/s10964-010-9563-0

Bonhert, A., Fredricks, J., & Randell, E. (2010). Capturing unique dimensions of youth organised activity involvement: Theoretical and methodological considerations. *Review of Educational Research, 80,* 576–610. doi:10.3102/0034654310364533

Bouffard, S. M., Wimer, C., Caronongan, P., Little, P. M. D., Dearing, E., & Simpkins, S. D. (2006). Demographic differences in patterns of youth out-of-school time activity participation. *Journal of Youth Development, 1*(1), 24–39.

Brady, M. (2005). *Letting girls play: Using sport to create safe spaces and build social assets.* New York, NY: Population Council.

Broh, B. A. (2002). Linking extracurricular programming to academic achievement: Who benefits and why? *Sociology of Education, 75,* 69–91. doi:10.2307/3090254

Bronfenbrenner, U. (1979). *The ecology of human development: Experiments by nature and design.* Cambridge, MA: Harvard University Press.

Cairns, R. B. (1996). Socialization and sociogenesis. In D. Magnusson (Ed.), *The lifespan development of individuals: Behavioral, neurobiological, and psychosocial perspectives: A synthesis* (pp. 277–295). New York, NY: Cambridge University Press.

Coatsworth, J. D., Palen, L. A., Sharpe, E. H., & Ferrer-Wreder, L. (2006). Self-defining activities, expressive identity, and adolescent wellness. *Applied Developmental Science, 10,* 157–170. doi:10.1207/s1532480xads1003_5

Coatsworth, J. D., Sharp, E. H., Palen, L. A., Darling, N., Cumsille, P., & Marta, E. (2005). Exploring adolescent self-defining leisure activities and identity experiences across three countries. *International Journal of Behavioral Development, 29,* 361–370. doi:10.1080/01650250500166972

Cohen, P. A., Kulik, J. A., & Kulik, C.-L. C. (1982). Education outcomes of tutoring: A meta-analysis of findings. *American Educational Research Journal, 19,* 237–248. doi:10.3102/00028312019002237

Cooper, H., Valentine, J. C., Nye, B., & Lindsay, J. J. (1999). Relationship between five after-school activities and academic achievement. *Journal of Education Psychology, 91,* 369–378. doi:10.1037//0022-0663.91.2.369

Crean, H. F. (2012). Youth activity involvement, neighborhood adult support, individual decision making skills, and early adolescent delinquent behaviors: Testing a conceptual model. *Journal of Applied Developmental Psychology, 33,* 175–188. doi:10.1016/j.appdev.2012.04.003

Csikszentmihalyi, M., & Kleiber, D. A. (1991). Leisure and self-actualization. In B. L. Driver, P. J. Brown, & G. L. Peterson (Eds.), *Benefits of leisure* (pp. 91–102). State College, PA: Venture.

Darling, N. (2005). Participation in extracurricular activities and adolescent adjustment: Cross-sectional and longitudinal findings. *Journal of Youth and Adolescence, 34,* 493–505. doi:10.1007/s10964-005-7266-8

Darling, N., Cadwell, L. L., & Smith, R. (2005). Participation in school-based extracurricular activities and adolescent adjustment. *Journal of Leisure Research, 37,* 51–76.

Davis, B. S., & Menard, S. (2013). Long-term impact of youth sports participation on illegal behavior. *Social Science Journal, 50,* 34–44. doi:10.1016/j.soscij.2012.09.010

Dearing, E., Wimer, C., Simpkins, S. D., Lund, T., Bouffard, S., & Caronongan, P. (2009). Do neighborhood and home contexts help explain why low-income children miss opportunities to participate in activities outside of school? *Developmental Psychology, 45,* 1545–1562. doi:10.1037/a0017359

Denault, A.-S., & Poulin, F. (2009). Intensity and breadth of participation in organised activities during the adolescent years: Multiple associations with youth outcomes. *Journal of Youth & Adolescence, 38,* 1199–1213. doi:10.1007/s10964-009-9437-5

Denault, A.-S., & Poulin, F. (2012). Peer group deviancy in organized activities and youths' problem behaviours. *Canadian Journal of Behavioral Science, 44,* 83–92. doi:10.1037/a0025705

Duffett, A., & Johnson, J. (2004). *All work and no play?* Washington, DC: Public Agenda.

Dworkin, J.B., & Larson, R. (2006). Adolescents' negative experiences in organized youth activities. *Journal of Youth Development, 1*(3), 1–19.

Dworkin, J.B., Larson, R., & Hansen, D. (2003). Adolescents' accounts of growth experiences in youth activities. *Journal of Youth and Adolescence, 32,* 17–26.

Eccles (Parsons), J., Adler, T.F., Futterman, R., Goff, S.B., Kaczala, C.M., Meece, J.L., & Midgley, C. (1983). Expectations, values and academic behaviors. In J.T. Spence (Ed.), *Perspective on achievement and achievement motivation* (pp. 75–146). San Francisco, CA: W.H. Freeman.

Eccles, J.S., & Barber, B.L. (1999). Student council, volunteering, basketball, or marching band: What kind of extracurricular involvement matters? *Journal of Adolescent Research, 14,* 10–43. doi:10.1177/0743558499141003

Eccles, J.S., Barber, B.L., Stone, M., & Hunt, J. (2003). Extracurricular activities and adolescent development. *Journal of Social Issues, 59,* 865–890. doi:10.1046/j.0022-4537.2003.00095.x

Eccles, J.S., & Gootman, J.A. (2002). *Community programs to promote youth development.* Washington, DC: National Academy Press.

Entwisle, D.R. (1990). Schools and the adolescent. In S. Feldman & G. Elliot (Eds.), *At the threshold: The developing adolescent* (pp. 197–224). Cambridge, MA: Harvard University Press.

Fauth, R.C., Roth, J.L., & Brooks-Gunn, J. (2007). Does the neighborhood context alter the link between youth's after-school time activities and developmental outcomes? A multilevel analysis. *Developmental Psychology, 43,* 760–777. doi:10.1037/0012-1649.43.3.760

Feldman, A.M., & Matjasko, J.L. (2005). The role of school-based extracurricular activities in adolescent development: A comprehensive review and future directions. *Review of Educational Research, 75,* 159–210. doi:10.3102/00346543075002159

Feldman, A.M., & Matjasko, J.L. (2007). Profiles and portfolios of adolescent school-based extracurricular activity participation. *Journal of Adolescence, 30,* 313–322. doi:10.1016/j.adolescence.2006.03.004

Feldman Farb, A.M., & Matjasko, J.L., (2012). Recent advances in research on school-based extracurricular activities and adolescent development. *Developmental Review, 32,* 1–48. doi:10.1016/j.dr.2011.10.001

Fredricks, (2012). Extracurricular participation and academic outcomes: Testing the over-scheduling hypothesis. *Journal of Youth & Adolescence, 41,* 295–306. doi:10.1007/s10964-011-9704-0

Fredricks, J.A., & Eccles, J.S. (2005). Developmental benefits of extracurricular involvement: Do peer characteristics mediate the link between activities and youth outcomes? *Journal of Youth and Adolescence, 34,* 507–520. doi:10.1007/s10964-005-8933-5

Fredricks, J.A., & Eccles, J.S. (2006a). Extracurricular involvement and adolescent adjustment: Impact of duration, number of activities, and breadth of participation. *Applied Developmental Science, 10,* 132–146. doi:10.1207/s1532480xads1003_3

Fredricks, J.A., & Eccles, J.S. (2006b). Is extracurricular activity participation associated with beneficial outcomes? Concurrent and longitudinal relations. *Developmental Psychology, 42,* 698–713.

Fredrickson, B.L., & Roberts, T. (1997). Objectification theory: Toward understanding women's lived experiences and mental health risks. *Psychology of Women Quarterly, 21,* 173–206. doi:10.1111/j.1471-6402.1997.tb00108.x

Frost, J., & McKelvie, S.J. (2005). The relationship of self-esteem and body satisfaction to exercise activity for male and female elementary school, high school, and university students. *Athletic Insight: The Online Journal of Sport Psychology, 7*(4). Available from http://www.athleticinsight.com/Vol7Iss4/Selfesteem.htm

Gilman, R. (2001). The relationship between life satisfaction, social interest and frequency of extracurricular activities among adolescent students. *Journal of Youth and Adolescence, 30,* 749–767.

Guest, A., & Schneider, B. (2003). Adolescents' extracurricular participation in context: The mediating effects of schools, communities, & identity. *Sociology of Education, 76,* 89–109. doi:10.2307/3090271

Hanks, M.P., & Eckland, B.K. (1976). Athletics and social participation in the educational attainment process. *Sociology of Education, 49,* 271–294. doi:10.2307/2112314

Hansen, D.M., & Larson, R.W. (2007). Amplifiers of developmental and negative experiences in organized activities: Dosage, motivation, lead roles, and adult-youth ratios. *Journal of Applied Developmental Psychology, 28,* 360–374. doi:10.1016/j.appdev.2007.04.006

Hansen, D. M., Larson, R. W., & Dworkin, J. B. (2003). What adolescents learn in organized activities: A survey of self-reported developmental experiences. *Journal of Research on Adolescence, 13,* 25–55. doi:10.1111/1532-7795.1301006

Harter, S. (1999). *The construction of the self. A developmental perspective.* New York, NY: Guilford.

Holland, A., & Andre, T. (1987). Participation in extracurricular activities in secondary school: What is known, what needs to be known? *Review of Educational Research, 57,* 437–466. doi:10.3102/00346543057004437

Horn, A. S. (2012). A cultivation of prosocial value orientation through community service: An examination of organizational context, social facilitation and duration. *Journal of Youth & Adolescence, 41,* 948–968. doi:10.1007/s10964-011-9714-y

Kleiber, D. (1999). *Leisure experience and human development: A dialectical interpretation.* New York, NY: Basic Books.

Knifsend, C. A., & Graham, S. (2012). Too much of a good thing? How breadth of extracurricular participation relates to school-related affect and academic outcomes during adolescence. *Journal of Youth and Adolescence, 41,* 379–389. doi:10.1007/s10964-011-9737-4

Larson, R., Walker, K., & Pearce, N. (2005). A comparison of youth-driven and adult-driven youth programs: Balancing inputs from youth and adults. *Journal of Community Psychology, 33,* 57–74. doi:10.1002/jcop.20035

Larson, R. W. (2000). Toward a psychology of positive youth development. *American Psychologist, 55,* 170–183. doi:10.1037/0003-066X.55.1.170

Larson, R. W., Hansen, D. M., & Moneta, G. (2006). Differing profiles of developmental experiences across types of organized youth activities. *Developmental Psychology, 42,* 849–863. doi:10.1037/0012-1649.42.5.849

Larson, R. W., Hansen, D., & Walker, K. (2005). Everybody's gotta give: Development of initiative and teamwork within a youth program. In J. L. Mahoney, R. W. Larson, & J. S. Eccles (Ed.), *Organized activities as contexts of development: Extracurricular activities, after-school and community programs* (pp. 159–183). Mahwah, NJ: Erlbaum.

Lerner, R. (2001). Promoting promotion in the development of prevention science. *Applied Developmental Science, 5,* 254–257. doi:10.1207/S1532480XADS0504_06

Mahoney, J. L. (2000). School extracurricular activity participation as a moderator in the development of antisocial patterns. *Child Development, 71,* 502–516. doi:10.1111/1467-8624.00160

Mahoney, J. L., Cairns, B. D., & Farmer, T. W. (2003). Promoting interpersonal competence and educational success through extracurricular activity participation. *Journal of Educational Psychology, 95,* 409–418. doi:10.1037/0022-0663.95.2.409

Mahoney, J. L., & Cairns, R. B. (1997). Do extracurricular activities protect against early school dropout? *Developmental Psychology, 33,* 241–253. doi:10.1037//0012-1649.33.2.241

Mahoney, J. L., Harris, A. L., & Eccles, J. S. (2006). Organized activity participation, positive youth development, and the over-scheduling hypothesis. *Social Policy Report, 20,* 3–31.

Mahoney, J. L., Larson, R. W., Eccles, J. S., & Lord, H. L. (2005). Organized activities as developmental contexts for children and adolescents. In J. L. Mahoney, R. W. Larson, & J. S. Eccles (Eds.), *Organized activities as contexts of development: Extracurricular activities, after-school and community programs* (pp. 3–22). Mahwah, NJ: Erlbaum.

Mahoney, J. L., Schweder, A. E., & Stattin, H. (2002). Structured after-school activities as a moderator of depressed mood for adolescents with detached relations to their parents. *Journal of Community Psychology, 30,* 69–86. doi:10.1002/jcop.1051

Mahoney, J. L., & Vest, A. E. (2012). The over-scheduling hypothesis revisited: Intensity of organized activity participation during adolescence and young adult outcomes. *Journal of Research on Adolescence, 22,* 409–418. doi:10.1111/j.1532-7795.2012.00808.x

Marsh, H. (1992). Extracurricular activities: Beneficial extension of the traditional curriculum or subversion of academic goals? *Journal of Educational Psychology, 84,* 553–562. doi:10.1037//0022-0663.84.4.553

Marsh, H., & Kleitman, S. (2002). Extracurricular school activities: The good, the bad, and the non-linear. *Harvard Educational Review, 72,* 464–514.

Marsh, H. W., & Kleitman, S. (2003). School athletic participation: Mostly gain with little pain. *Journal of Sport and Exercise Psychology, 25,* 205–228.

Metsäpelto, R.-L. & Pulkkinen, L. (2012). Socioemotional behaviour and school achievement in relation to extracurricular activity participation in middle childhood. *Scandinavian Journal of Educational Research, 56,* 167–182. doi:10.1080/00313831.2011.581681

O'Connor, S., & Jose, P.E. (2012). A propensity score matching study of participation in community activities: A path to positive outcomes for youth in New Zealand? *Developmental Psychology, 48*, 1563–1569. doi:10.1037/a0027597

Otto, L.B. (1975). Extracurricular activities in the educational attainment process. *Rural Sociology, 40*, 162–176.

Otto, L.B., & Alwin, D. (1977). Athletics, aspirations and attainments. *Sociology of Education, 50*, 102–113. doi:10.2307/2112373

Palen, L.A., & Coatsworth, J.D. (2007). Activity-based identity experiences and their relations to problem behavior and psychological well-being in adolescence. *Journal of Adolescence, 30*, 721–737. doi:10.1016/j.adolescence.2006.11.003

Patterson, G., Dishion, T., & Yoerger, K. (2000). Adolescent growth in new forms of problem behavior: Macro- and micro-peer dynamics. *Prevention Science, 1*, 3–13.

Perkins, D.F., Borden, L.M., Villarruel, F.A., Carlton-Hig, A., Stone, M.R., & Keith, J.G. (2007). Participation in youth programs. Why ethnic minority urban youth choose to participate—or not to participate. *Youth & Society, 38*, 420–442. doi:10.1177/0044118X06295051

Persson, A., Kerr, M., & Stattin, H. (2004). Why a leisure context is linked to normbreaking for some girls and not others: Personality characteristics and parent–child relations as explanations. *Journal of Adolescence, 27*, 583–598. doi:10.1016/j.adolescence.2004.06.008

Philliber, S., & Allen, J.P. (1992). Life options and community service: Teen Outreach program. In *Preventing adolescent pregnancy: Model programs and evaluations* (Vol. 140, pp. 139–155). Thousand Oaks, CA: Sage.

Pittman, K., Irby, M., Tolman, J., Yohalem, N., & Ferber, T. (2002). *Preventing problems, promoting development, encouraging engagement: Competing priorities or inseparable goals?* Washington, DC: The Forum of Youth Investment.

Randall, E.T., & Bonhert, A.M. (2009). Organized activity involvement, depressive symptoms, and social adjustment in adolescents: Ethnicity and socioeconomic status as moderators. *Journal of Youth & Adolescence, 38*, 1187–1198. doi:10.1007/s10964-009-9417-9

Rawana, J.S., & Ames, M.E. (2012). Projective predictors of alcohol use trajectories among Canadian aboriginal youth. *Journal of Youth & Adolescence, 41*, 229–243. doi:10.1007/s10964-011-9716-9

Stearns, E., & Glennie, E.J. (2010). Opportunities to participate: Extracurricular activities' distribution across academic correlates in high schools. *Social Science Research, 39*, 296–309. doi:10.1016/j.ssresearch.2009.08.001

Stone, M.R., & Brown, B.B. (1998). In the eye of the beholder: Adolescents' perceptions of peer crowd stereotypes. In R. Muuss (Ed.), *Adolescent behavior and society: A book of readings* (5th ed., pp. 158–169). Boston, MA: McGraw-Hill College.

Videon, T.M. (2002). Who plays and who benefits: Gender, interscholastic athletics, and academic outcomes. *Sociological Perspectives, 45*, 415–444. doi:10.1525/sop.2002.45.4.415

Vygotsky, L.S. (1978). *Mind in society: The development of higher psychological processes.* Cambridge, MA: Harvard University Press.

Youniss, J., Bales, S., Christmas-Best, V., Diversi, M., McLaughlin, M., & Silbereisen, R. (2002). Youth civic engagement in the twenty-first century. *Journal of Research on Adolescence, 12*, 121–148. doi:10.1111/1532-7795.00027

Youniss, J., McLellan, J.A., Su, Y., & Yates, M. (1999). The role of community service in identity development: Normative, unconventional, and deviant orientations. *Journal of Adolescent Research 14*, 248–261. doi:10.1177/0743558499142006

Youniss, J., & Smollar, J. (1985). *Adolescent relations with mothers, fathers, and friends.* Chicago. IL: University of Chicago Press.

Youniss, J., & Yates, M. (1997). *Community service and social responsibility in youth.* Chicago, IL: University of Chicago Press.

Zill, N., Nord, C.W., & Loomis, I.S. (1995). *Adolescent time use, risky behavior, and outcomes: An analysis of national data.* Rockville, MD: Westat.

CHAPTER SUMMARY: MEANINGFUL ACTIVITY

- Meaningful activity participation is very common during adolescence and is linked to a broad range of positive outcomes for students. This is generally true in whichever way participation is studied—how many activities, how much time is spent in them, or how long participation has been ongoing.

- Activities offer rich opportunities for students to explore and express who they are, find opportunities to make a difference, and practice skills such as time management, planning, problem solving, and contingency thinking.
- Many school-based activities are linked with greater academic achievement, higher academic goals, greater connection and engagement with school, and a lower likelihood of school dropout.
- Participation in activities creates a social community of invested adult leaders and committed peers who can have strong positive influences on adolescents.
- The personal developmental benefits of activities are particularly salient for adolescents from disadvantaged backgrounds, who are generally afforded limited opportunities for positive development.
- Because of selection issues, caution is needed in attributing positive developmental indicators to activity participation. However, with the growing methodological sophistication of the research, we can have some confidence that the positive experiences found in meaningful activities are beneficial.

SUGGESTED READINGS: MEANINGFUL ACTIVITY

Bonhert, A., Fredricks, J., & Randell, E. (2010). Capturing unique dimensions of youth organised activity involvement: Theoretical and methodological considerations. *Review of Educational Research, 80,* 576–610. doi:10.3102/0034654310364533

This article explores theoretical background and measurement issues for four dimensions of extracurricular activity participation: breadth, intensity, duration, and engagement with activities. Developmental benefits of each dimension are examined and conceptual considerations for strengthening future research across the various dimensions are discussed.

Eccles, J.S., Barber, B.L., Stone, M., & Hunt, J. (2003). Extracurricular activities and adolescent development. *Journal of Social Issues, 59,* 865–890. doi:10.1046/j.0022-4537.2003.00095.x

This article explores the relationships between youth involvement in extracurricular activities, educational outcomes, and risky behavior. Generally, prosocial activities, performing arts, team sports, school spirit and support activities, and academic clubs were protective against risky behavior and promoted positive educational outcomes. Participants' peer associations, relationships with nonfamilial adults, and identity exploration are discussed as possible mediators in this relationship.

Feldman Farb, A. M., & Matjasko, J. L. (2012). Recent advances in research on school-based extracurricular activities and adolescent development. *Developmental Review, 32,* 1–48. doi:10.1016/j.dr.2011.10.001

This article reviews the most recent literature on adolescent extracurricular activity participation and links to developmental outcomes. Focusing specifically on academic achievement, substance use, sexual activity, psychological adjustment, and delinquency, this review explores extracurricular activity participation as a potential moderator or mediator for positive youth outcomes.

16

CULTIVATING MINDFULNESS IN STUDENTS

Tyler L. Renshaw, Department of Psychology, Louisiana State University, Baton Rouge, Louisiana, USA

Meagan D. O'Malley, Health & Human Development Program, WestEd, Los Alamitos, California, USA

DEFINITIONS AND THEORY BASE

Origins of Mindfulness

Mindfulness is an ancient psychological construct that primarily originated with the teachings of the Buddha and the Eastern religious traditions that evolved from them. It was not until the 1970s that mindfulness moved out of the realm of religion and became a modern, applied psychological construct. This secularizing shift was spurred by the work of Jon Kabat-Zinn (1990) and his colleagues, who redefined mindfulness and repackaged it as the core construct in a stress-reduction intervention designed for inpatients experiencing severe pain—claiming that mindfulness "can be learned or practiced . . . without appealing to Oriental culture or Buddhist authority to enrich it or authenticate it" (p. 12). Since that time, Kabat-Zinn (1994) has redefined mindfulness several times, yet his most popular definition is a state of consciousness wherein one "pay[s] attention in a particular way: on purpose, in the present moment, and nonjudgmentally" (p. 4). Smalley and Winston (2010) have offered a similar definition of mindfulness as a state of conscious wherein one "observ[es] [one's] physical, emotional, and mental experiences with deliberate, open, and curious attention" (p. 11). Moreover, Brown, Ryan, and Creswell (2007) have redefined it as having "receptive attention to and awareness of present events and experience" (p. 212). In an effort to consolidate and interpret the essence of these similar definitions, Renshaw (2012) has offered a unifying, common-core-components model of mindfulness, wherein the construct is conceptualized as a state of consciousness that is composed of three distinct subphenomena: attentive awareness, a receptive attitude, and intentionality.

Components of Mindfulness

Attentive Awareness

The first core component of mindfulness, *attentive awareness*, refers to the quality and duration of one's contact with whatever stimuli present themselves to one's mind in the here and now. Stimuli, in this sense, are broadly construed as any information consciously registered via the five basic senses (i.e., tactile, visual, auditory, gustatory, and olfactory), the three bodily senses (i.e., emotional, vestibular, and kinesthetic), as well as the thought-based activities of the mind (e.g., judgments and conceptualizations; Brown et al., 2007). The key feature of this component is not just that awareness is achieved but that it is captivated and focused for a sustained period of time instead of wandering to and fro as usual. The mechanism of change posited to underlie attentive awareness is a growing familiarity with the true nature of the stimuli and the contingencies involved in the larger stimuli-person-environment situation, which empowers one to respond more willfully (instead of reacting automatically) in the face of deep-rooted habits (Brown & Ryan, 2003). For example, by repeatedly being attentively aware to her pretest anxiety, a student may learn the ins and outs of her symptoms as well as come to an understanding of the larger train of events of which they are part. Such knowledge could then empower her to make positive, proactive choices in the situation that will enhance her well-being (e.g., practicing relaxation techniques) instead of defaulting to automatic, reactive habits that are likely to exacerbate her symptoms (e.g., engaging in excessive eating or negative self-talk).

Receptive Attitude

The second core component of mindfulness, *receptive attitude*, refers to one's outlook toward and reaction to the particular stimuli that arise in awareness and are attended to in the present moment. Although the details of this outlook have been described differently by various mindfulness scholars, most agree that it is characterized by some combination of the following qualities: curiosity, openness, acceptance, and self-compassion (Siegel, 2007). It is this positive, constructive attitudinal orientation that distinguishes a mindful approach to awareness from common unhelpful approaches to awareness (e.g., habitual avoidance of negative emotion) as well as a mindful form of sustained attention from common unhealthy forms of sustained attention (e.g., rumination on negative self-talk). The mechanism of change posited to underlie a receptive attitude is a loving tolerance of one's experiences, especially those that are aversive in nature, which enables individuals to experience their symptoms from more of a third-person point of view and, as a result, disrupt problematic habits that have formed in conjunction with their symptoms (Brown & Ryan, 2003). For example, by bringing a receptive attitude toward his impulses to speak out in class or interrupt the teacher, a student could learn to be aware and compassionately accepting of his unwanted impulses. In turn, such awareness and self-acceptance could empower him to consciously disrupt the behavioral habits that typically get him in trouble, as his impulses no longer automatically compel him to action.

Intentionality

Given that attentive awareness and a receptive attitude can both manifest by happenstance, and that, because of interindividual differences, they are more likely to be more frequently achieved by some youth than by others, the third and final core component of mindfulness is *intentionality*. In short, intentionality refers to one's deliberate cultivation of an attentive awareness that is characterized by a receptive attitude, as opposed to simply recognizing or taking advantage of such features of one's mind whenever they chance to occur (Brown et al., 2007). Thus true mindfulness is characterized by significant individual effort and grit, both beginning and persisting with purpose. That said, although intentionality is not theoretically connected with a psychological mechanism of change, we conceptualize it as having a commensurable contribution to that of attentive awareness and a receptive attitude in comprising the overall mindfulness construct. To represent this relation visually, we offer the "Mindfulness Molecule" (Figure 16.1), in which each core component is coequal in creating the overall structure

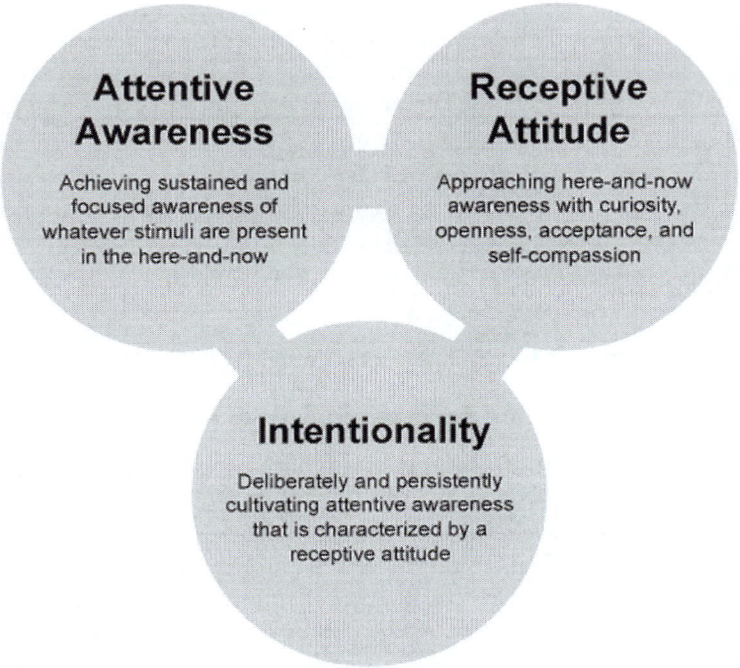

Attentive Awareness

Achieving sustained and focused awareness of whatever stimuli are present in the here-and-now

Receptive Attitude

Approaching here-and-now awareness with curiosity, openness, acceptance, and self-compassion

Intentionality

Deliberately and persistently cultivating attentive awareness that is characterized by a receptive attitude

Figure 16.1 The mindfulness molecule core construct components.

of the mindfulness construct. In this view, if one component is absent, mindfulness fails to manifest; if all components are present but then one fails, mindfulness ceases. Given the delicate relations among these core components, achieving and sustaining mindfulness by sheer willpower is often a difficult and short-lived experience, especially for youth. For this reason, various practices and therapies have been developed to help make experiences of mindfulness more habitual.

Mindfulness Therapies

Beginning with Kabat-Zinn's (1990) use of mindfulness-based stress reduction (MBSR) in inpatient settings, mindfulness-based interventions (MBIs) have become increasing prevalent over the past few decades, being adopted by various applied mental health professionals (psychiatrists, psychologists, social workers, and counselors) as either an adjunct or primary approach to treatment (Siegel, 2007). Besides MBSR, other common, contemporary MBIs for youth have included mindfulness-based cognitive therapy (MBCT), dialectical behavior therapy (DBT), and acceptance and commitment therapy (ACT), as well as various nonsystematized treatment packages (Greco & Hayes, 2008). Interestingly, despite the existence of formalized MBIs such as MBSR, MBCT, DBT, and ACT, our review of the empirical research literature suggests that the majority of MBIs conducted with youth (and subsequently published in professional journals) have used idiosyncratic, nonstandardized protocols (e.g., Huppert & Johnson, 2010). That said, a more careful look at the makeup of these nonstandardized MBIs reveals that they employ similar kinds of key practices for cultivating youths' mindfulness, including formal meditations (i.e., breathing, walking/movement, and body-scan exercises), psychoeducation about the core components of mindfulness (similar to information provided earlier), as well as metaphorically grounded experiential exercises (e.g., "Taking Your Mind for a Walk" or "Thoughts in Flight"; see Twohig, Hayes, & Berlin, 2008, for details and other examples). To date, the relative effectiveness of each genre of practice (e.g., formal meditation vs. experientially grounded exercises) and the particular practices that make up each genre (e.g., breathing meditation vs. body-scan meditation) is unknown. What is known, however, and what can be concluded from the empirical research is that mindfulness correlates positively with and that MBIs have positive effects on various aspects of youths' well-being.

REVIEW OF KEY RESEARCH STUDIES

Core Research Involving Youth

The benefits and effects of mindfulness in youth have been investigated through two distinct forms of research: measurement studies and clinical/educational intervention studies. Measurement studies have tended to conceptualize mindfulness within the classical state–trait paradigm, investigating the relations among measures of trait mindfulness and various positive and negative psychological traits and other life outcomes. Clinical/educational intervention studies, on the other hand, have tended to conceptualize mindfulness as a "skill that can be learned like any other skill" (Smalley & Winston, 2010, p. 6), investigating the effects of mindfulness training on various positive and negative indicators of personal, relational, and educational functioning. Interestingly, these two areas of research have been conducted largely in isolation from each other, rarely crossing paths, as the majority of intervention studies have failed to assess the effects of MBIs on the development of youths' trait mindfulness (e.g., Haydicky, Wiener, Badali, Milligan, & Ducharnme, 2012), although there are some exceptions (e.g., Brown, West, Loverich, & Biegel, 2011). The simplest explanation for this state of affairs seems to be that interest in the applied science of mindfulness is, to date, greater than interest in the basic science of mindfulness. This discrepancy between the amount of research devoted to construct validation and intervention will be seen more clearly later in this chapter, where we review findings from each body of literature. In the remainder of this section, we provide a highlight-driven overview of the research regarding MBIs with youth. Yet in the following section on measurement issues, we provide a more comprehensive review of relevant construct validation studies.

MBIs for Children and Adolescents

In 2010, Burke published the first—and, so far, only—comprehensive review of mindfulness-based interventions conducted with youth samples. Of the published studies she reviewed ($N = 14$), six were conducted with primary school-aged children and eight with secondary school-aged adolescents. Moreover, four studies were conducted in school settings, while all others were conducted in a variety of outpatient or community settings. Nine studies were conducted with clinical samples and five with nonclinical samples. Six studies used pre–post between-group designs, four reported wait-list or intent-to-treat controls, and two reported other nontreatment activities. As described earlier, although all studies were considered MBIs, each employed different treatment packages aimed at enhancing mindfulness, consisting of some combination of formal meditations (included in all treatment packages), psychoeducation (included in many treatment packages), and metaphorically grounded experiential exercises (included in some treatment packages). Burke's review provided evidence indicating that MBIs are feasible and acceptable treatments for youth. Her review also provided preliminary evidence indicating that, beyond social validity, MBIs have promising clinical and educational treatment utility—showing positive effects on various aspects of youths' social (e.g., Napoli, Krech, & Holley, 2005), emotional (e.g., Lee, Semple, Rosa, & Miller, 2008), physiological (e.g., Bootzin & Stevens, 2005), cognitive (e.g., Bögels, Hoogstad, van Dun, De Shutter, & Restifo, 2008), behavioral (e.g., Singh et al., 2007), and academic functioning (e.g., Beauchemin, Hutchins, & Patterson, 2008).

Since the publication of Burke's (2010) initial review, several more studies of MBIs, utilizing similar treatment packages yet more rigorous evaluation methods, have been carried out with youths in medical, community, and educational settings. These studies offer more evidence in support of MBIs having both high social validity and wide-ranging clinical utility. For example, a recent randomized-controlled study investigating the effects of a 20-week mindfulness training program on a group of adolescents ($N = 21$) diagnosed with a learning disability, or comorbid learning disability with attention-deficit/hyperactivity disorder and/or an anxiety disorder, showed that the intervention yielded positive improvements in youths' parent-rated social, externalizing, and internalizing symptoms (Haydicky et al., 2012). Another recent randomized-controlled study, investigating the effects of a 12-week MBI on urban children in fourth and fifth grades ($N = 50$), indicated that intervention-group students demonstrated marked declines in negative coping experiences, including rumination, intrusive cognitions, and emotional arousal (Mendelson et al., 2010). Furthermore, beyond these gold-standard studies, other recent and more naturalistic (i.e., quasi-experimental) investigations have also indicated that MBIs can positively affect youth in schools, enhancing their behavioral regulation, attention, metacognition, emotional competence, subjective well-being, and school performance (e.g., Flook et al., 2010; Schonert-Reichl & Lawlor, 2010).

MBIs for Parents and Teachers

In addition to research focused particularly on youth outcomes, a recent wave of MBIs has investigated the effects of mindfulness training on the quality of caregiving and well-being of parents and educators of children with and without disabilities. Findings from a few small, randomized-controlled studies within this line of research have shown that MBIs can positively enhance caregivers' competence, effectiveness, and relationships with the youths they care for (Coatsworth, Duncan, Greenberg, & Nix, 2010), significantly reduce perceived stress and negative emotional symptoms while boosting mindfulness, self-compassion, personal growth (Benn, Akiva, Arel, & Roeser, 2012), and substantially improve general health conditions (Ferraioli & Harris, 2012). Considered in light of the findings from student-focused studies (reviewed earlier), findings from these caregiver-focused studies suggest that mindfulness training is a promising intervention for school-based treatment and prevention, as it seems capable of reducing various forms of psychological distress and enhancing several aspects of psychological well-being for students and their caregivers. Nevertheless, given the still-preliminary status of MBI research, we reiterate the call of Greenberg and Harris (2012) for future intervention scholarship that (a) is designed to provide high-quality evidence, (b) assumes a strong developmental perspective, (c) further develops mindfulness theory, (d) provides clearer descriptions of intervention components, and (e) examines the role of dosage-response effects. In fact, such rigorous research is necessary to determine if MBIs will ever warrant the "best practice" label in schools.

MEASUREMENT APPROACHES AND ISSUES

Surveying Trait Mindfulness

To date, all measures of youths' mindfulness have been conceptualized as tools for assessing trait (or dispositional) mindfulness. Given the common-core-components model of mindfulness—a state of consciousness characterized by attentive awareness, a receptive attitude, and intentionality (Renshaw, 2012; see Figure 16.1)—youths' trait mindfulness might be best understood as the regularity with which they experiences mindful states of consciousness. In this way, not only may persons be considered to be more or less mindful in a particular moment in time (i.e., state mindfulness), but they might also be described as more or less mindful individuals in general (i.e., trait mindfulness). Similar to other survey instruments measuring state-trait distinctions, mindfulness measures were originally developed with university students and adult-aged samples. In recent years, however, surveys of trait mindfulness have been successfully tested with youth, while surveys of state mindfulness have been ignored and left unexplored. So far, only two survey instruments have been developed for assessing youths' trait mindfulness: the adolescent version of the Mindfulness Attention Awareness Scale (Brown et al., 2011) and the Child and Adolescent Mindfulness Measure (Greco, Baer, & Smith, 2011).

Mindful Attention Awareness Scale

The Mindful Attention Awareness Scale (MAAS) was originally designed to assess differences in trait mindfulness within and between adults across time (Brown & Ryan, 2003). In the original psychometric study of the MAAS, samples of predominantly Caucasian, university-aged students (ages 17 to 32) and adults (ages 18 to 77) in the northeastern region of the United States were used to test the instrument's reliability and structural validity. The authors determined that a single-factor model demonstrated a satisfactory fit for both samples, suggesting that overall MAAS scores represented a unidimensional mindfulness trait. In this same initial study, Brown and Ryan also reported sufficient evidence for discriminant validity, suggesting that trait mindfulness (as represented by MAAS scores), although significantly positively correlated with other measures of well-being (e.g., self-esteem, positive and negative affect, autonomy, relatedness), was sufficiently different to warrant examination as a distinct psychological construct. Lastly, in this initial development study, Brown and Ryan (2003) also reported that the MAAS had strong internal consistency (Cronbach's α = .80 to .87) and good test-retest reliability (intraclass correlation = .81).

To adapt the MAAS to adolescents, Brown and colleagues (2011) reduced the MAAS by one item, reasoning that it lacked sufficient face validity for all adolescents (i.e., "I drive places on 'automatic pilot' and then wonder why I went there"), and then labeled the remaining 14-item scale the MAAS-Adolescent (MAAS-A). They tested the MAAS-A with samples of predominantly Caucasian students (89.1%) from the midwestern region of United States (M_{age} = 16.7 years), confirming the single-factor structure for the MAAS-A and showing it to have high internal consistency (Cronbach's α = .85 to .88) and acceptable test-retest reliability (intraclass correlation = .79). Findings from this study also provided evidence regarding divergent and convergent validity, indicating that overall MAAS-A scores were significantly negatively correlated with perceived stress, neuroticism, negative affect, substance use, and psychiatric symptoms, as well as significantly positively correlated with agreeableness, conscientiousness, positive affect, life satisfaction, wellness, happiness, and healthy self-regulation.

Following in the footsteps of Brown and colleagues (2011), Black, Sussman, Johnson, and Milam (2012) recently extended the psychometric evidence for the MAAS to international adolescent samples, testing it with a large group of adolescent students (M_{age} = 16.2 years) in Chengdu, China. In addition to replicating the unidimensional factor structure advanced by Brown and Ryan (2003) and Brown and colleagues (2011), the authors showed the MAAS to be configurally invariant across gender. Black and colleagues (2012) also reported the MAAS's strong internal consistency and discriminant validity when measured against similar traits in youth (e.g., self control, social self-efficacy), and they demonstrated the validity of a brief, six-item MAAS for adolescents, confirming a single-factor structure and showing the scale to be fully invariant across gender with strong reliability. Results from this study also indicated evidence regarding divergent and convergent validity, with brief-MAAS scores showing significant negative correlations with depression, perceived stress, aggression, impulsive behavior, and psychiatric symptoms, as well as a significant positive correlation with self-control.

Finally, Hansen, Lundh, Homman, and Wångby-Lundh (2009) tested the MAAS in a sample of Swedish adolescents (M_{age} = 16.2 years). Although their analysis was less sophisticated than that of Black and colleagues (2012), results suggest that the MAAS was similarly reliable in this sample (Cronbach's α = .85). Furthermore, evidence regarding divergent and convergent validity indicated that overall MAAS scores were significantly negatively correlated with self-harming behaviors and significantly positively correlated with self-esteem.

Child and Adolescent Mindfulness Measure

Unlike the MAAS, the Child and Adolescent Mindfulness Measure (CAMM), developed by Greco and colleagues (2011), was not adapted or generalized from an adult survey. Rather, Greco and colleagues (2011) argued that because existing instruments for measuring mindfulness in youth were limited in quantity and contained language that was either too complex or not relevant to youth, an entirely new youth-centered measure was warranted. Also unlike the MAAS, which intentionally developed items to measure as a unidimensional trait, the CAMM was designed with items intended to tap into four mindfulness-related phenomena: observing one's here-and-now experience, acting with awareness in the present moment, acting without judgment, and describing details of the here and now. After submitting an original set of 25 items to an expert review panel, the authors tested the CAMM in a sample of public school students from the southern region of the United States (M_{age} = 12.6). Following a series of item reduction decisions, the authors confirmed a modest statistical fit of 10 items to a unidimensional mindfulness model, which disconfirmed their initial four-factor hypothesis and provides additional support for the unidimensional model of mindfulness assessed via the MAAS. Unfortunately, no reliability estimates were reported in this initial study; however, discriminant validity evidence was provided, suggesting that trait mindfulness (as measured by CAMM scores) was unique from similar constructs in youth (i.e., social skills). Moreover, divergent and convergent validity evidence were also provided, indicating that overall CAMM scores were significantly negatively correlated with self-reported somatic complaints, internalizing symptoms, externalizing symptoms, thought suppression, psychological inflexibility, and teacher-reported problem behaviors, as well as significantly positively correlated with self-reported quality of life and teacher-reported academic competency.

Although the psychometric evidence for the CAMM and MAAS are promising, further testing in a variety of domestic and international samples is warranted to further validate their utility as measures of youths' trait mindfulness. Moreover, given that the CAMM and the MAAS both intend to measure trait mindfulness in youth but both were developed with different theoretical frameworks in mind (i.e., a multidimensional versus a unidimensional model of mindfulness), further research is also needed to investigate the convergent validity of these measures with each other. Taken together, however, findings from studies related to both measures suggest that mindfulness might be conceptualized as a legitimate positive psychological construct for youth, as empirical evidence supports both its divergent relations with traditional indicators of unhealthy psychological functioning (e.g., internalizing and externalizing symptoms) as well as its convergent relations with contemporary indicators of psychological well-being (e.g., life satisfaction and happiness). Furthermore, these findings suggest that, similar to how some negative psychological characteristics (e.g., anxiety and depression) are commonly "comorbid" with other psychological difficulties in youth (e.g., attention deficit/hyperactivity disorder), mindfulness might be a key indicator of psychological functioning that is commonly "covital" with other indicators of youths' well-being (cf. Jones, You, & Furlong, 2012).

Individual Variation in Trait Mindfulness

To successfully validate measures of trait mindfulness for youth, as well as the construct of trait mindfulness in general, the next step in the construct validation process is to investigate the variation of dispositional mindfulness within and between individuals over time. In order to demonstrate that trait mindfulness is a meaningful psychological construct worth measuring, researchers must show that it varies predictably across individuals and groups and that it predicts important psychosocial and/or physical outcomes. In other words, researchers must answer the question, "Do some individuals or groups of individuals have more trait mindfulness than others and does having more or less trait mindfulness matter?" One method for demonstrating that trait mindfulness varies across individuals is to describe the trait within groups of individuals that share some identifying characteristic. Using this approach, Brown and Ryan (2003) asked a small sample of individuals currently practicing meditation in the United States to report on their current meditation practice, duration of practice history, and time spent in daily practice. Results from this investigation showed that MAAS scores were significantly positively related to meditation practitioners' number of years in practice and the intensity of their belief that their meditation practice was generalized throughout the day. To date, this approach has not been tested with youths; however, given that select groups of youths (e.g., young Buddhists and yoga practitioners) are known to regularly engage in mindfulness-based practices, it certainly could be.

Also commonly studied within this paradigm are samples of individuals sharing the same stressor, such as those under medical care for similar physical or mental health-related disorders. For example, Jedel and colleagues (2012) studied trait mindfulness in individuals with inflammatory bowel disease (IBD), finding that mindfulness varied between individuals and that those with high levels of the trait had significantly lower scores on measures of anxiety, depression, and perceived stress as well as significantly higher life satisfaction scores. Similar to the previously described approach, this technique has yet to be used with children and adolescents, but there is no reason why it could not be. Moreover, another route for examining variation in trait mindfulness is to demonstrate how it changes between groups that participate in MBIs. These studies lend particularly strong evidence if selection for participation in the MBI is random and if there is a control sample for comparison. An example of this approach is the intervention study by Brown and colleagues (2011), described previously, in which a test–retest analysis using the MAAS-A was conducted in conjunction with a randomized controlled study of psychiatric outpatient adolescents receiving an MBI. Findings from this study indicated that youth who were assigned to the active treatment group showed significant increases in their MAAS-A scores after the 8-week intervention, compared to no change for the participants assigned to the control group. Considering this study in light of other adolescent mindfulness measurement research, more work is needed to investigate individual variation in trait mindfulness. That said, preliminary evidence suggests that adolescent trait mindfulness is an empirically promising construct that appears to have applicability within educational settings.

POSSIBLE EDUCATIONAL APPLICATIONS

To effectively integrate the construct of mindfulness within schools, it can be conceptualized as a positive-psychological trait that is amenable to change via skill training—similar to how empathy is currently defined and handled with youth (e.g., Şahin, 2012). Viewing it in this way allows both educators and school-based mental health professionals to strive to cultivate mindfulness in students similarly to how they might cultivate any other positive psychological trait (e.g., gratitude or hope), using empirically grounded assessments and interventions. Considering the research conducted to date, mindfulness appears warranted to play a minor, complementary role in supporting the well-being of students and their caregivers in the schools, serving as both an outcome of interest (e.g., as one of the many indicators assessed through schoolwide mental health screening) and/or an approach to intervention (e.g., as an adjunct unit to a traditional social skills training curriculum).

Multitiered Framework of Student Support

If used to serve students at the schoolwide level, mindfulness and MBIs could be feasibly integrated within a multitiered framework of student support (cf. Renshaw, 2012). Although most empirical studies have investigated MBIs as stand-alone practices at the universal or targeted levels, there is currently no compelling empirical support for any particular MBI protocol—suggesting that, in real-life practice, MBIs should be used in conjunction with other proven treatment and prevention methods (e.g., social skills training). An example of this hybrid intervention approach would be adapting a schoolwide social-emotional learning (SEL; Merrell, Gueldner, & Tranh, 2008) curriculum to include a unit on mindfulness. Furthermore, although there is promising evidence indicating that mindfulness is "covital" with other indicators of children's and adolescents' psychological well-being, there is no evidence showing that it is a better or more comprehensive indicator than other aspects of positive-psychological functioning—suggesting that, when used in schools, trait mindfulness should be assessed alongside other indicators of youths' mental health. Examples of such integrated assessment could be progress-monitoring a group SEL intervention with a mindfulness measure combined with other measures of social-emotional functioning or including a brief mindfulness scale within a schoolwide screener assessing student well-being. Finally, although there is some evidence suggesting that MBIs may be useful for more intensive, individualized therapy with adolescents diagnosed with particular developmental disorders and presenting with specific emotional and behavioral symptoms (e.g., Singh et al., 2007), the research in this area is still scant and developing—suggesting that practitioners should generalize individualized MBIs into school-based practice with caution and not use them as the sole or primary therapeutic technique.

Caregiver Prevention and Intervention

Beyond its possible educational applications for students, current empirical evidence also suggests that the mindfulness construct and MBIs have potential utility in supporting the competency, effectiveness, and well-being of students' caregivers. Although this area of research is rather new and still developing, preliminary findings indicate that MBIs provided to youths' parents and teachers have been shown to have positive effects on both adults and youth (e.g., Benn et al., 2012; Coatsworth et al., 2010). Gutkin and Conoley (1990) have called this kind of indirect service delivery approach, in which educators and mental health professionals must "concentrate their attention and professional expertise on adults" in order to best serve students, the "paradox of school psychology" (p. 212). Although we do not go as far as they do in suggesting that service providers should "first and foremost" focus on adults at the expense of children, we concur that the most effective approaches to cultivating the well-being of youth will also include efforts to cultivate the well-being of their caregivers. Relative to the use of mindfulness in schools, then, possible caregiver prevention and intervention efforts could include MBIs in the form of parent–child after-school workshops or as part of staff development trainings. But given that only a few studies, so far, have investigated MBIs as caregiver interventions, practitioners would do well to use them as an adjunct to other indirect techniques that target parents and teachers for the purpose of improving youths' school functioning (e.g., behavioral consultation; Erchul & Schulte, 2009).

DIVERSITY AND DEVELOPMENTAL CONSIDERATIONS

Traditionally, the majority of mindfulness training methods have been targeted to and developed with adult populations (e.g., Stahl & Goldstein, 2010); however, in recent years, more and more mindfulness training methods have been targeted to and developed with young children (e.g., Greenland, 2010) and adolescents (e.g., Biegel, 2009). To make mindfulness training socially valid for youth, both Biegel (2009) and Greenland (2010) have developed methods that are couched in developmentally appropriate language (e.g., using simple, memorable acronyms and phrasings), supported by multimodal instruction (e.g., experiential activities paired with journaling and direct instruction), varied according to time and content (e.g., adaptable to group implementations or individual counseling sessions), and grounded in real-life, youth-friendly examples (e.g., common school-day experiences). Moreover, to further improve the social validity and effectiveness of MBIs for youth, others have recommended that:

1. frequent analogy and metaphor be employed (e.g., Twohig et al., 2008)
2. the applicability of mindfulness to one's life be emphasized beyond the session, school day, and target concerns (e.g., mindful texting or mindful Internet surfing; Thompson & Gauntlett-Gilbert 2008)
3. group training formats be used to enhance social support and provide external motivation for maintaining practice (e.g., Semple, Lee, & Miller, 2006)
4. parental participation be recruited to help model mindful behaviors and reinforce mindfulness practice (e.g., Wagner, Rathus, & Miller, 2006)
5. clinicians develop a personal mindfulness practice, which will enable them to relay techniques and empathize with barriers encountered during youth's practice in a more fluent and authentic manner (Thompson & Gauntlett-Gilbert, 2008)

Adaptations for Special Populations

Beyond general developmental considerations, mindfulness applications may sometimes necessitate adaptations for special populations of youth, such as those from particular cultural backgrounds or those presenting with specific disabling conditions. For example, given that mindfulness has its origins in ancient Eastern Buddhist traditions, youth or their caregivers from various cultural backgrounds (e.g., students attending or teachers working at a private Christian school) might be wary of or express discomfort with mindfulness training and its possible religious implications. To handle such situations sensitively, mindfulness training methods can be adapted to include an educational component that informs stakeholders about the historical development of mindfulness from an ancient religious concept to a contemporary, secularized, applied psychological construct that has proven clinical utility for adults and promising educational utility for children. Furthermore, some populations of youths might present with a variety of disabling conditions that hamper their participation in mindfulness training or their acquisition of mindfulness skills. For instance, students with preexisting attention-regulation or emotion-regulation difficulties might find mindfulness practice more challenging and frustrating than students without such difficulties. Given that the nature and extent of such disabling conditions vary widely among youth, practitioners utilizing mindfulness and MBIs in schools could seek to resolve therapeutic impasses of any sort by seeking direct feedback from students and their caregivers and then focusing on cultivating the core ingredients of effective behavior change: simple procedural steps, a supportive environment, personal motivation, and repetition (cf. Strayhorn, 2002). Finally, MBIs can also be adapted to special-needs populations by having them intentionally cultivate attentive awareness and a receptive attitude toward whatever difficulties hamper their cultivation of mindfulness in the first place (e.g., behavioral impulsivity or emotional distress).

CONCLUSION

This chapter provided a modern overview of the ancient psychological construct of mindfulness, discussing its theoretical and empirical bases, related intervention techniques, contemporary measurement issues, possible educational applications, and some special considerations for school-based practice. Given all of this, we conclude by reiterating a few key sentiments expressed throughout the preceding sections, which are especially important to impress upon the minds of researchers and practitioners interested in progressing the use of mindfulness in the schools. Foremost, the theoretical and empirical evidence suggests that mindfulness can be conceptualized as a contemporary positive-psychological trait that is "covital" with various other indicators of thriving and well-being in youth. Second, mindfulness-based interventions appear capable of enhancing various aspects of well-being for both youth and their caregivers. Next, MBIs could be feasibly integrated into multitiered systems of student support, as either complementary or supplementary elements. And finally, synthesizing the three previous conclusions, mindfulness is a positive-psychological trait that can be actively cultivated in students for the purposes of enhancing their well-being.

REFERENCES

Black, D. S., Sussman, S., Johnson, C. A., & Milam, J. (2012). Trait mindfulness helps shield decision-making from translating into health-risk behavior. *Journal of Adolescent Health, 51,* 588–592. doi:10.1016/j.jadohealth.2012.03.011

Beauchemin, J., Hutchins, T. L., & Patterson, F. (2008). Mindfulness meditation may lessen anxiety, promote social skills, and improve academic performance among adolescents with learning difficulties. *Complementary Health Practice Review, 13,* 34–45. doi:10.1177/1533210107311624

Benn, R., Akiva, T., Arel, S., & Roeser, R. W. (2012). Mindfulness training effects for parents and educators of children with special needs. *Developmental Psychology, 48,* 1476–1487. doi:10.1037/a0027537

Biegel, G. M. (2009). *The stress reduction workbook for teens.* Oakland, CA: New Harbinger.

Bögels, S., Hoogstad, B., van Dun, L., De Shutter, S., & Restifo, K. (2008). Mindfulness training for adolescents with externalising disorders and their parents. *Behavioural and Cognitive Psychotherapy, 36,* 193–209. doi:10.1017/S1352465808004190

Bootzin, R. R., & Stevens, S. J. (2005). Adolescents, substance abuse, and the treatment of insomnia and daytime sleepiness. *Clinical Psychology Review, 25,* 629–644. doi:10.1016/j.cpr.2005.04.007

Brown, K. W., & Ryan, R. M. (2003). The benefits of being present: Mindfulness and its role in psychological well-being. *Journal of Personality and Social Psychology, 84,* 822–848. doi:10.1037/0022-3514.84.4.822

Brown, K. W., Ryan, R. M., & Creswell, J. D. (2007). Mindfulness: Theoretical foundations and evidence for its salutary effects. *Psychological Inquiry, 18,* 211–237. doi:10.1080/10478400701598298

Brown, K. W., West, A. M., Loverich, T. M., & Biegel, G. M. (2011). Assessing adolescent mindfulness: Validation of an adapted Mindful Attention Awareness Scale in adolescent normative and psychiatric populations. *Psychological Assessment, 23,* 1023–1033. doi:10.1037/a0021338

Burke, C. A. (2010). Mindfulness-based approaches with children and adolescents. *Journal of Child and Family Studies, 19,* 133–144. doi:10.1007/s10826-009-9282-x

Coatsworth, J. D., Duncan, L. G., Greenberg, M. T., & Nix, R. L. (2010). Changing parents' mindfulness, child management skills and relationships quality with their youth: Results from a randomized pilot intervention. *Journal of Child and Family Studies, 19,* 203–217. doi:10.1007/s10826-00909304-8

Erchul, W. P., & Schulte, A. C. (2009). Behavioral consultation. In A. Akin-Little, S. G. Little, M. A. Bray, & T. J. Kehle (Eds.), *Behavioral interventions in schools: Evidence-based positive strategies* (pp. 13–26). Washington, DC: American Psychological Association.

Ferraioli, S. J., & Harris, S. L. (2012). Comparative effects of mindfulness and skills-based parent training programs for parents of children with autism: Feasibility and preliminary outcome data. *Mindfulness.* Advanced online publication. doi:10.1007/s12671-012-0099-0

Flook, L., Smalley, S. L., Kitil, M. J., Galla, B. M., Greenland, K. S., Locke, J., . . . Kasari, C. (2010). Effects of mindful awareness practices on executive functions in elementary school children. *Journal of Applied School Psychology, 26,* 70–95. doi:10.1080/15377900903379125

Greco, L. A., Baer, R. A., & Smith, G. T. (2011). Assessing mindfulness in children and adolescents: Development and validation of the Child and Adolescent Mindfulness Measure (CAMM). *Psychology Assessment, 23,* 606–614. doi:10.1037/a0022819

Greco, L. A., & Hayes, S. C. (Eds.). (2008). *Acceptance and mindfulness treatments for children and adolescents.* Oakland, CA: New Harbinger.

Greenberg, M. T., & Harris, A. R. (2012). Nurturing mindfulness in children and youth: Current state of research. *Child Development Perspectives, 6,* 161–166.

Greenland, S. K. (2010). *The mindful child.* New York, NY: Free Press.

Gutkin, T. B., & Conoley, J. C. (1990). Reconceptualizing school psychology from a service delivery perspective: Implications for practice, training, and research. *Journal of School Psychology, 28,* 203–223.

Hansen, E., Lundh, L., Homman, A., & Wångby-Lundh, M. (2009). Measuring mindfulness: Pilot studies with the Swedish versions of the Mindful Attention Awareness Scale and the Kentucky Inventory of Mindfulness Skills. *Cognitive Behaviour Therapy, 38,* 2–15. doi:10.1080/16506070802383230

Haydicky, J., Wiener, J., Badali, P., Milligan, K., & Ducharme, J. M. (2012). Evaluation of a mindfulness-based intervention for adolescents with learning disabilities and co-occurring ADHD and anxiety. *Mindfulness, 3,* 151–164. doi:10.1007/s12671-012-0089-2

Huppert, F. A., & Johnson, D. M. (2010). A controlled trial of mindfulness training in schools: The importance of practice for an impact on well-being. *Journal of Positive Psychology, 5,* 264–274. doi:10.1080/1743976100379418

Jedel, S., Merriman, P., Hoffman, A., Swanson, B., Fogg, L., & Keshavarzian, A. (2012). Relationship of mindfulness, quality of life, and psychiatric symptoms among patients with ulcerative colitis. *Mindfulness*. Advanced online publication. doi:10.1007/s12671-012-0128-z

Jones, C. N., You, S., & Furlong, M. J. (2012). A preliminary examination of covitality as integrated well-being in college students. *Social Indicators Research*, 9, 1–16. doi:10.1007/s11205-012-0017-9

Kabat-Zinn, J. (1990). *Full catastrophe living.* New York, NY: Bantam.

Kabat-Zinn, J. (1994). *Wherever you go, there you are.* New York, NY: Hyperion.

Lee, L., Semple, R. J., Rosa, D., & Miller, L. (2008). Mindfulness-based cognitive therapy for children: Results of a pilot study. *Journal of Cognitive Psychotherapy*, 22, 15–28. doi:10.1891/0889.8391.22.1.15

Mendelson, T., Greenberg, M. T., Dariotis, J. K., Gould, L. F., Rhoades, B. L., & Leaf, P. J. (2010). Feasibility and preliminary outcomes of a school-based mindfulness intervention for urban youth. *Journal of Abnormal Child Psychology*, 38, 985–994. doi:10.1007/s10802-010-9418-x

Merrell, K. W., Gueldner, B. A., & Tran, O. K. (2008). Social and emotional learning: A school-wide approach to intervention for socialization, friendship problems, and more. In B. Doll & J. A. Cummings (Eds.), *Transforming school mental-health services* (pp. 165–185). Thousand Oaks, CA: Corwin.

Napoli, M., Krech, P. R., & Holley, L. C. (2005). Mindfulness training for elementary school students: The Attention Academy. *Journal of Applied School Psychology*, 21, 99–109. doi:10.1300/J008v21n01_05

Renshaw, T. L. (2012). Mindfulness-based practices for crisis prevention and intervention. In S. E. Brock & S. R. Jimerson (Eds.), *Handbook of school crisis prevention and intervention* (2nd ed., pp. 401–422). Bethesda, MA: National Association of School Psychologists.

Şahin, M. (2012). An investigation into the efficiency of empathy training program on preventing bullying in primary schools. *Children and Youth Services Review*, 34, 1325–1330. doi:10.1016/j.childyouth.2012.03.013

Schonert-Reichl, K. A., & Lawlor, M. S. (2010). The effects of a mindfulness-based education program on pre- and early adolescents' well-being and social and emotional competence. *Mindfulness*, 1, 137–151. doi:10.1007/s12671-010-0011-8

Semple, R. J., Lee, J., & Miller, L. F. (2006). Mindfulness-based cognitive therapy for children. In R. A. Baer (Ed.), *Mindfulness-based treatment approaches* (pp. 143–166). Oxford, UK: Elsevier.

Siegel, D. J. (2007). *The mindful brain.* New York, NY: Norton.

Singh, N. N., Lancioni, G. E., Singh Joy, S. D., Winton, A. S. W., Sabaawi, M., Wahler, R. G., & Singh, J. (2007). Adolescents with conduct disorder can be mindful of their aggressive behavior. *Journal of Emotional and Behavioral Disorders*, 15, 56–63. doi:10.1177/10634266070150010601

Smalley, S. L., & Winston, D. (2010). *Fully present.* Philadelphia, PA: De Capo.

Stahl, B., & Goldstein, E. (2010). *A mindfulness-based stress reduction workbook.* Oakland, CA: New Harbinger.

Strayhorn, J. M. (2002). Self-control: Toward systematic training programs. *Journal of American Academy of Child and Adolescent Psychiatry*, 41, 17–27.

Thompson, M., & Gauntlett-Gilbert, J. (2008). Mindfulness with children and adolescents: Effective clinical application. *Clinical Child Psychology and Psychiatry*, 13, 395–407. doi:10.1177/1359104508090603

Twohig, M. P., Hayes, S. C., & Berlin, K. S. (2008). Acceptance and commitment therapy for childhood externalizing disorders. In L. A. Greco & S. C. Hayes (Eds.), *Acceptance and mindfulness treatments for children and adolescents* (pp. 163–186). Oakland, CA: New Harbinger.

Wagner, E. E., Rathus, J. H., & Miller, A. L. (2006). Mindfulness in dialectical behavior therapy (DBT) for adolescents. In R. A. Baer (Ed.), *Mindfulness-based treatment approaches* (pp. 143–166). Oxford, UK: Elsevier.

CHAPTER SUMMARY: MINDFULNESS

- Mindfulness is composed of three coequal core components: attentive awareness, receptive attitude, and intentionality.
- Familiarity with one's present-moment experiences as well as loving tolerance in relation to such experiences are the two main mechanisms of change underlying mindfulness.
- Mindfulness-based interventions (MBIs) are treatment packages consisting of some combination of formal meditations (i.e., breathing, body scan, and walking/movement), psychoeducation about mindfulness, and metaphorically grounded experiential exercises.

- Intervention research shows that MBIs have positive effects on various aspects of youths' social, emotional, cognitive, physiological, behavioral, and academic well-being, as well as upon the competency, effectiveness, psychological well-being, and health of parents and teachers.
- Mindfulness in adults has been measured as both a state and a trait construct, yet current research with youth has focused solely on assessing trait mindfulness in adolescents—showing that it is commonly "covital" with other indicators of psychological well-being. Future measurement research should focus on assessing variations in youths' trait mindfulness across populations and subgroups.
- Possible educational applications of mindfulness could include integrating mindfulness measures and MBIs into multitiered systems of students support as well as into caregiver prevention and intervention efforts.
- Special considerations for practitioners using mindfulness in the schools include adapting MBIs designed for adults to be socially valid and developmentally appropriate for youth, accounting for possible cultural resistance to mindfulness, as well as supporting any disabling conditions that may hamper students' engagement with MBIs.
- Mindfulness is a positive-psychological trait in youth that can be cultivated in students to help enhance their well-being.

SUGGESTED READINGS: MINDFULNESS

Biegel, G. M. (2009). *The stress reduction workbook for teens.* Oakland, CA: New Harbinger.

A collection of 37 lessons/activities for introducing adolescents to the notion of mindfulness, linking mindfulness with their mental health, and teaching them mindfulness-based stress reduction skills.

Greenland, S. K. (2010). *The mindful child.* New York, NY: Free Press.

An anecdotal account of one practitioner's experiences adapting and implementing mindfulness-based interventions with preschoolers, young elementary school students, and parent–child dyads.

Schoeberlein, D. (2009). *Mindful teaching and teaching mindfulness.* Somerville, MA: Wisdom Publications.

An introduction to potential applications of mindfulness within K–12 education settings, including a collection of teacher-friendly mindfulness-based exercises that could be feasibly implemented within classroom contexts.

Siegel, D. J. (2007). *The mindful brain.* New York, NY: Norton.

A review of contemporary mindfulness research and theory, focusing especially on the role neuroscience plays in understanding the mechanisms of action underlying mindfulness-based interventions.

Smalley, S. L., & Winston, D. (2010). *Fully present.* Philadelphia, PA: De Capo.

An overview of the current state of the art regarding mindfulness and mindfulness-based interventions from childhood to adulthood, including practical examples and scripts for guided mindfulness meditations.

17

PEER RELATIONSHIPS AND POSITIVE ADJUSTMENT AT SCHOOL

Kathryn Wentzel, Shannon Russell, and Sandra Baker, Department of Human Development, University of Maryland, College Park, Maryland, USA

INTRODUCTION

Relationships with peers are of central importance to children throughout childhood and adolescence. They provide companionship and entertainment, help in solving problems, personal validation and emotional support, and especially during adolescence, a foundation for identity development. In addition, positive peer interactions tend to promote the development of perspective-taking and empathic skills that serve as bases for cooperative, prosocial, and nonaggressive types of behavior; positive relationships with peers also have been related consistently to a range of positive academically related accomplishments (Wentzel, 2005).

In light of this evidence that links children's adaptive functioning across social and academic domains, a central question that will be addressed in this chapter is how students' peer-related activities serve to promote these positive social and academic competencies. Toward this end, we first review the literature relating peer relationships and activities to positive outcomes at school, including students' pursuit of socially valued goals, behavioral competence, and academic performance. Next we discuss the underlying reasons and mechanisms for why these relations might exist, providing general criteria for defining social competence that can be used to understand the contribution of students' peer relationships to the achievement of educational objectives.

To guide our discussion, an ecological approach is proposed in which school-related competence is viewed as a highly context-specific outcome reflecting the degree to which students are able to meet the demands of the classroom environment as well as achieve their own personal goals. Research on ways in which peers can support students' achievement of these dual sets of goals is then reviewed. We end with a discussion of ways in which classroom and school contexts can support the development of positive peer relationships and conclude with suggestions for future work in this area.

PEER ACTIVITIES AND SCHOOL-RELATED COMPETENCE

Researchers typically have studied children's involvement with peers at school in two ways: within the context of relationships (e.g., degree of peer acceptance by the larger peer group, membership in specific peer groups, and dyadic friendships; see Juvonen, Espinoza, & Knifsend, 2012; Ladd, Herald-Brown, & Kochel, 2009; Ryan & Ladd, 2012; Wentzel, 2009) and within structured interactions related to instruction (e.g., cooperative and collaborative learning; see Wentzel & Watkins, 2011). Each of these aspects of peer relationships and their correlates will be described in the following sections.

Peer Acceptance and Sociometric Status

An extensive body of work supports the notion that peer acceptance and peer sociometric status are related to children's motivational and academic functioning at school. Peer acceptance and sociometric status variables typically are based on unilateral assessments of a child's relative standing or reputation within the peer group. Scores reflect either a continuum of social preference ranging from well accepted to rejected (e.g., How much do you like this person?) or assignment to a sociometric status group (i.e., popular, rejected, neglected, controversial, and average status; see Asher & Dodge, 1986).

Research indicates that sociometrically popular children (those who are well liked and not disliked by peers) are academically proficient, whereas sociometrically rejected children (those who are not well liked and highly disliked) experience academic difficulties; studies based on social preference scores yield highly similar findings (see Cillessen & van den Berg, 2012; Wentzel, 2005). Results are most consistent with respect to classroom grades, although peer acceptance has been related positively to standardized test scores as well as to IQ. These findings are robust for elementary-aged children as well as adolescents, and longitudinal studies document the stability of relations between peer acceptance and academic accomplishments over time. Sociometric status and peer acceptance also have been related to positive aspects of academic motivation, including pursuit of goals to learn, interest in school, and perceived academic competence.

An extensive body of work also has documented associations between peer acceptance and social behavioral outcomes. In general, when compared to their average-status peers, popular students tend to be more prosocial and sociable and less aggressive, and rejected students less compliant, less self-assured, less sociable, and more aggressive and withdrawn (Asher & McDonald, 2009; Card & Little, 2006). Peer status also has been related to pursuit of goals to be prosocial (defined as helping, sharing, cooperating) and to be socially responsible (following rules, keeping commitments) during middle school (Wentzel, 2005).

Peer Crowds and Groups

Students' membership in specific peer crowds and groups has been studied most frequently in adolescent samples (see Brown, 1989; Brown & Dietz, 2009). Typical adolescent crowds include "Populars," students who engage in positive forms of academic as well as social behavior but also in some delinquent activities; "Jocks," students characterized by athletic accomplishments but also relatively frequent alcohol use; more alienated groups (e.g., "Druggies") characterized by poor academic performance and engagement in delinquent and other illicit activities; and "Normals," who tend to be fairly average students who do not engage in delinquent activities. Research on peer group membership has been mostly descriptive, identifying the central norms and values that uniquely characterize adolescent crowds. In contrast to sociometrically popular students who are typically characterized in positive terms, members of "Popular" crowds are often described in negative terms such as being dominant and exclusionary (Brown, 2011).

The influence of peer crowds on adolescent functioning is illuminated in ethnographic studies that describe how peer crowds facilitate the formation of students' identity and self-concept and structure their ongoing social interactions (Brown & Dietz, 2009). Crowds provide prototypical examples of various identities for those who wish to "try out" different lifestyles and, in doing so, can affirm an adolescent's sense of self. The power of crowd influence also is reflected in relations between crowd membership and adolescents' attitudes toward academic achievement. Adolescent peer groups differ in the degree to which they pressure members to become involved in academic activities, with "Jocks" and "Popular" groups providing significantly more pressure for academic involvement than other groups.

Researchers who identify friendship-based peer groups using statistical procedures also have found relations between group membership and academic motivation and performance (Kindermann & Gest, 2009; Kindermann & Skinner, 2012). For example, elementary-aged students tend to self-select into groups of peers that have motivational orientations to school similar to their own. Over the course of the school year, these orientations became stronger and more similar within groups. Friendship-based groups in middle school also have been related to changes in academic performance over the course of the school year (see Wentzel, 2009).

Friendships

Peer relationships also are studied with respect to dyadic friendships. In this case, students are asked to nominate their best friends at school; nominations are then matched to determine reciprocity, or best friendships. The central distinction between having friends and involvement with larger peer groups is that friendships reflect relatively private, egalitarian relationships often formed on the basis of idiosyncratic criteria. In contrast, peer groups are defined by publicly acknowledged and therefore easily identified and predictable characteristics that are valued by the group. In addition, whereas friendships are enduring aspects of children's peer relationships at all ages, peer groups and crowds emerge primarily during middle school, peak at the beginning of high school, and then diminish in prevalence as well as influence by the end of high school (Brown, 1989).

Simply having a friend at school appears to be related to a range of positive outcomes. Children with friends tend to be more sociable, cooperative, and self-confident when compared to their peers without friends; children with reciprocated friendships also tend to be more independent, emotionally supportive, altruistic and prosocial, and less aggressive than those who do not have such friendships (Newcomb & Bagwell, 1995). In addition, the behavioral characteristics of friends have been related to students' prosocial behavior (Barry & Wentzel, 2006; Wentzel, Barry, & Caldwell, 2004).

Having friends also has been related positively to grades and test scores (Jones, Audley-Piotrowski, & Kiefer, 2012; Wentzel & Caldwell, 1997; Wentzel et al., 2004), and to positive aspects of motivation and engagement in school-related activities (see Kindermann & Skinner, 2012; Wentzel, 2005). In this regard, children entering kindergarten with existing friends and those who make new friends quickly appear to make better social and academic adjustments to school than those who do not (e.g., Ladd, 1990). Similar findings have been reported for students making the transition to middle school (Molloy, Gest, & Rulison, 2011; Wentzel et al., 2004). During adolescence, friends are likely to support academic engagement in the form of studying and making plans for college (e.g., Alvarado, Elias, & Turley, 2012; Epstein, 1983).

Cooperative and Collaborative Interactions

Research on peer interactions within cooperative and collaborative learning structures has been widespread. Experimental studies have documented that active discussion, problem solving, and elaborative feedback among peers are associated with advances in a range of cognitive competencies (e.g., problem solving and conceptual understanding) in samples ranging from preschool to high school (see Gauvain & Perez, 2007). Of particular interest is that collaborating with friends rather than acquaintances tends to yield more predictable cognitive advances, presumably because friends have well-established interaction patterns, are sensitive to each other's interests and needs, and interact with each other in relatively positive ways (e.g., Fonzi, Schneider, Tani, & Tomada, 1997; Swenson & Strough, 2008). However, results of classroom intervention studies have been less conclusive. Reviews of these studies indicate that dyadic peer interactions contribute most (albeit modestly) to learning outcomes for minority, urban-dwelling, and young children, and when dyads are homogeneous with respect to gender (e.g., Rohrbeck, Ginsburg-Block, Fantuzzo, & Miller 2003).

The effects of cooperative learning (i.e., peers working in larger groups) on social and academic outcomes are generally positive (Slavin, 2011; Slavin, Hurley, & Chamberlain, 2003). Results of quasi-experimental and experimental studies suggest that the most successful cooperative learning activities are those that require positive interdependence among group members, individual accountability, face-to-face interactions among students, and learning social skills necessary to work cooperatively. Effects on academic achievement and cognitive outcomes are consistently positive when students work toward group goals while individual group members are simultaneously held accountable for progress (i.e., individual testing). Increases in intrinsic motivation, positive attitudes toward school, persistence, self-efficacy, and self-esteem also have been documented. Finally, positive group relations across ability levels and ethnic groups, and displays of prosocial behavior have been associated consistently with cooperative learning strategies. As with collaborative interactions, however, group learning also tends to be largely unsuccessful in producing cognitive gains when group members differ as a function of ability, race, ethnicity, and SES (Cohen, 1986).

Summary of Peer Activities

The literature on peer relationships and interactions provides strong and convincing evidence that peer-related activities predict a wide range of social and academic competencies at school, including frequent displays of prosocial behavior (e.g., helping, sharing, caring), relatively infrequent displays of antisocial and disruptive behavior, and some modicum of academic success. Many of these characteristics also are endorsed by adolescent peer groups, although less predictably. Collaborative and cooperative interactions also appear to be related to these same social and academic outcomes.

For the most part, this evidence is based on correlational studies lacking strong bases for drawing causal inferences. Similarly, experimental work often has not included important controls. Therefore, it is not clear whether positive social and academic outcomes are the result of intellectual gains or social skill development emanating directly from positive interactions with peers, or from the motivational, social, and behavioral benefits of having positive peer relationships. In fact, direct pathways from collaborative and cooperative forms of learning to cognitive gains rarely have been established when accounting for the complex social and motivational aspects of peer interactions in groups. In either case, however, it is reasonable to assume that for many children, peers have the power to influence the development of social and academic competencies in positive ways. The following section will discuss multiple perspectives on why and how such influence might take place.

THEORETICAL PERSPECTIVES

How and why might students' relationships with peers be related to positive school-related accomplishments? Traditionally, theoretical explanations have focused on the broad notion that positive interactions with peers contribute directly to intellectual and social functioning. For example, Piaget (e.g., 1965) proposed that mutual discussion, perspective taking, and conflict resolution with peers can motivate the accommodation of new and more sophisticated cognitive approaches to problem solving, including problems in the social domain. For Piaget, development was contingent on the relatively symmetrical nature of same-aged peer interactions that allowed conflict resolution within the context of mutual reciprocity. Conversely, Vygotsky (1978) suggested that peers can contribute directly to the development of academic and social skills when competent students teach specific strategies and standards for performance to peers who are less skilled. In this case, asymmetrical interactions were believed to contribute to competent development, primarily by way of cooperative and collaborative exchange.

A more recent approach to answering these questions has been to consider the nature of social competence and how students' relationships with each other can provide access to critical supports that facilitate healthy adaptation to school. To describe this perspective more fully, we first present a definition of social competence derived from theoretical perspectives on person–environment fit and personal goal setting. This definition is then applied to the realm of schooling and students' relationships with peers. Ways in which peers provide school-based supports for competence development are then described.

Social Competence as Person–Environment Fit

In the social developmental literature, social competence has been described from a variety of perspectives, ranging from the development of individual skills to a more general adaptation within a particular setting. In these discussions, social competence frequently is associated with outcomes such as effective behavioral repertoires, social problem-solving skills, positive beliefs about the self, achievement of social goals, and positive interpersonal relationships (see Rose-Krasnor, 1997). In addition, central to many definitions of social competence is the notion that contextual affordances and constraints contribute to and mold the development of these individual outcomes in ways that enable them to contribute to the social good (Bronfenbrenner, 1989). In this manner, social contexts are believed to play an integral role in providing opportunities for healthy social development as well as in defining the appropriate parameters of children's social accomplishments (Bronfenbrenner, 1989; Bronfenbrenner & Morris, 2006).

Ford (1992) expanded on this notion by specifying dimensions of contextual support such that competence is achieved when (a) information is provided concerning what is expected and valued in the classroom; (b) attempts to achieve these valued outcomes are met with help and instruction; (c) attempts to achieve outcomes can be made in a safe, nonthreatening environment; and (d) individuals are made to feel like a valued member of the group.

Social Competence at School

The application of this perspective to the realm of schooling results in a multifaceted description of children who are socially competent and well adjusted. Socially competent students achieve goals that are personally valued as well as those that are sanctioned by others; they pursue goals that result in social integration (e.g., cooperative behavior, social approval and acceptance) as well as in positive developmental outcomes (e.g., perceived competence, feelings of self-determination, feelings of emotional well-being). From this description it follows that social competence is achieved to the extent that students accomplish goals that have personal as well as social value in a manner that supports continued psychological and emotional well-being.

In addition, the application of Ford's dimensions of supportive contexts specifically to peer-related activities in classroom and school settings implies that students will engage in the pursuit of adaptive goals, in part, when their peers communicate expectations and standards for achieving multiple goals; provide direct assistance and help in achieving them; and create a climate of emotional support that facilitates positive engagement in socially valued classroom activities, including protection from physical threats and harm. A consideration of peer relationships as contextual affordances reflects the notion that at the core of positive peer relationships are the benefits they provide in the form of these social supports. Findings relevant to these dimensions of peer support are described next.

Communicating Goals and Expectations for Performance

Research on the school-related goals that students value has not been frequent. However, pursuit of goals to be prosocial and socially responsible has been related consistently and positively to displays of prosocial and responsible behavior and to peer acceptance (see Wentzel, 2005, 2009). A limited number of studies also document that students report trying to achieve positive social and academic outcomes, including social goals to have fun and to be dependable and responsible, and task-related goals to learn new things and to get good grades (Allen, 1986; Ryan, Jamison, Shin, & Thompson, 2012; Wentzel, 1989).

Although not well documented, it is reasonable to assume that students communicate to each other specific academic values and expectations for performance (see Wentzel, Baker, & Russell, 2012; Wentzel, Battle, Russell, & Looney, 2010). In addition, peers also provide proximal input concerning reasons for engaging in academic tasks (e.g., because it is important or fun; Wentzel, 2004; Wentzel, Filisetti, & Looney, 2007). Therefore, students who see that their peers value and enjoy engaging in specific academic tasks and in positive social interactions are likely to form similar positive opinions and attitudes about those same tasks (Bandura, 1986).

Finally, peers also can contribute to students' goals and expectations for performance by influencing perceptions of ability, which are powerful predictors of academic performance (Schunk & Pajares, 2009). Experimental work has shown that peers serve as powerful models that influence the development of academic self-efficacy (Schunk & Pajares, 2009), especially when children observe similar peers who demonstrate successful ways to cope with failure. These modeling effects are most likely to occur when students are friends (Crockett, Losoff, & Petersen, 1984; Ricciardelli & Mellor, 2012).

Providing Help and Assistance

Help giving is perhaps the most explicit and obvious way in which peers can have a direct influence on students' academic and social competence. Indeed, students who enjoy positive relationships with their peers will also have greater access to resources and information that can help them accomplish academic and social tasks than those who do not. At least during adolescence, students report that their peers are as or more important sources of instrumental aid than their teachers (Lempers & Clark-Lempers, 1992). One reason for this growing dependence on peers is that when adolescents enter high school, the relative uncertainty and ambiguity of having multiple teachers and different sets of classmates for each class, new instructional styles, and more complex class schedules necessitates that they turn to each other for social support, ways to cope, and academic help.

Providing Emotional Support

Feelings of emotional security and being socially connected are believed to facilitate both the adoption of goals and interests valued by others and desires to contribute in positive ways to the overall functioning of the social group (Connell & Wellborn, 1991). Support for this notion stems from an extensive literature relating positive academic outcomes to perceived emotional support from peers. Students who perceive that their peers support and care about them tend to be interested and engaged in academic pursuits, whereas students who do not perceive their relationships with peers as positive and supportive tend to be at risk for motivational and academic problems (Wentzel, Donlan, & Morrison, 2012; Wentzel et al., 2010). Similarly, perceived social support also has been related to prosocial outcomes in the classroom, such as helping, sharing, and cooperating, and related negatively to antisocial forms of behavior (e.g., Wentzel, 1994).

One reason for these findings is that children without friends or who are socially rejected often report feeling lonely, emotionally distressed and depressed (e.g., Buhs & Ladd, 2001; Wentzel et al., 2004; Wentzel & Caldwell, 1997). In turn, negative affect is likely to result in negative attitudes toward school, poor academic performance, school avoidance, and low levels of classroom participation (Buhs & Ladd, 2001; Wentzel, Weinberger, Ford, & Feldman, 1990).

Providing a Safe Environment

Of final interest is that students who enjoy positive peer relationships are more likely to enjoy a relatively safe school environment and less likely to be the targets of peer-directed violence and harassment than their peers who do not have friends (e.g., Schwartz, Dodge, Pettit, Bates, & The Conduct Problems Prevention Research Group, 2000). In addition, young children who have friends who display prosocial behavior are less likely to respond in a hostile or impulsive manner in response to peer provocation or bullying behaviors than are children without highly prosocial friends (Lamarche et al., 2006). Further, having highly prosocial friends has been found to protect against the negative relation between peer victimization and academic competence during the middle school years (e.g., Schwartz, Gorman, Dodge, Pettit, & Bates, 2008). Presumably, this is because prosocial friends are able to provide instrumental help as well as model effective ways to decrease and defuse threats from peers.

The general effects of peer harassment on student motivation and academic competence have not been studied frequently. However, peer abuse and exclusion are likely to be associated with academic achievement by way of emotional distress (Flook, Repetti, & Ullman, 2005; Rueger, Malacki, & Demaray, 2011). Therefore, having supportive peers in negatively charged peer situations can have positive direct and indirect effects on a wide range of social, motivational, and academic outcomes.

Processes of Influence

How and why might these peer supports be related to positive engagement and school-related accomplishments? Several theoretical perspectives provide insights into possible mechanisms of influence. At the simplest level, social cognitive theory (Bandura, 1986) suggests that direct communication and instruction provide students with valuable information about what is expected and how to accomplish various tasks. Therefore, peers who convey expectations that academic engagement and positive social interactions are important and enjoyable are likely to lead others to form similar positive attitudes (Bandura, 1986). Although this type of support is probably provided most frequently within dyadic or small-group interactions, the larger peer group also can be a source of behavioral standards, with group pressures providing a mechanism whereby adherence to group standards and expectations is monitored and enforced (see Brown, Bakken, Ameringer, & Mahon, 2008). However, peer monitoring of behavior will contribute to positive motivational orientations only insofar as peers have adopted adult standards for achievement and norms for conduct.

Modeling is a second social cognitive mechanism by which peers can influence students' adoption of goals and standards for behavior and academic performance (Bandura, 1986). Indeed, students might develop specific behavioral styles or interests because they are desirable characteristics modeled by their peers (see Barry & Wentzel, 2006; Wentzel et al., 2004). A final mechanism involves the critical impact that peers can have on adolescents' emotional functioning. Few would argue that the need to belong and to experience a sense of relatedness with others is a powerful motivator of behavior (see Baumeister & Leary, 1995). Theoretical perspectives suggest that strong affective bonds and perceived support from others serve as buffers from stress and anxiety and contribute to a positive sense of emotional well-being (Sarason, Sarason, & Pierce, 1990). In turn, feelings of emotional security and being socially connected are believed to facilitate the adoption of goals and interests valued by others, including goals to contribute in positive ways to the overall functioning of the social group (e.g., Ryan & Deci, 2000).

Summary of Peer Relations and Social Competence

We have defined social competence as the achievement of context-specific goals that result in positive outcomes for the self but also for others. Our definition holds that contextual supports are crucial for the achievement of these multiple goals. In this regard, we have argued that peers can provide essential supports in the form of expectations and values, instrumental help, emotional support, and safety from physical threats and harm. In turn, these supports can facilitate the development of positive social and academic outcomes.

Of additional interest, however, is that teachers and administrators are the primary architects of classroom and school contexts. In the following section, we describe the potential impact that teachers and the broader school context can have on students' ability to support each other's accomplishments at school.

THE ROLE OF TEACHERS AND THE SCHOOL CONTEXT

In recent years, research has begun to focus on the impact that contextual factors might have on children's peer-related experiences. There is evidence that teachers' beliefs and behaviors, classroom organization, and schoolwide structure, composition, and climate affect students' interactions and relationships with peers. In the following sections, research on teachers and classroom contexts and then on school-level influences will be described.

Teachers and Classrooms

Teacher characteristics and instructional practices have been related to a number of peer-related outcomes. Teachers' expectations concerning students' aptitude and performance have been related to levels of peer acceptance and rejection, regardless of whether these expectations are reported by students (e.g., Donohue, Perry, & Weinstein, 2003), or teachers themselves (Farmer, Irvin, Sgammato, Dadisman, & Thompson, 2009; Mikami, Griggs, Reuland, & Gregory, 2012). Teachers' verbal and nonverbal behavior toward certain children, especially when critical, also has been related to how these children are treated by their peers (Harper & McCluskey, 2003).

The instructional approach that a teacher adopts also appears to have an impact on students' relationships with peers (Epstein, 1983; Farmer et al., 2009). For example, students enjoy more positive relationships with classmates when teachers use learner-centered practices (e.g., involving students in decision making) as opposed to teacher-centered practices (e.g., focusing on rote learning, norm-referenced evaluation; Donohue et al., 2003) and competitive practices (Mikami et al., 2012). The way in which teachers group students also has been associated with the quality of peer relations (Gest & Rod-kin, 2011) and interactions (Luckner & Pianta, 2011). Finally, middle and high school students in classrooms in which students are encouraged to talk to each other about class assignments, to work in small groups, and to move about while working on activities also are less likely to be socially isolated or rejected by their classmates, enjoy greater numbers of friends, and experience more diversity and stability in their friendships (e.g., Epstein, 1983; Gest & Rodkin, 2011).

Variations in the social, academic, ethnic, and gender composition of classrooms also are known to influence friendship dynamics. Classrooms that are homogenous with respect to low levels of student ability and problem behavior can be deleterious to the formation and maintenance of positive, high-quality peer relationships over time (Barth, Dunlop, Dane, Lochman, & Wells, 2004). The gender composition of a classroom also can influence the relationships students form with each other in that elementary-aged boys who transition to same-sex classrooms tend to develop more friendships than do girls (Barton & Cohen, 2004), and classrooms with more females tend to have students that are more connected to one another (Cappella & Neal, 2012). Finally, the degree to which classrooms and schools are ethnically diverse also is related to more positive outcomes for some students (Jackson, Barth, Powell, & Lochman, 2006; Urberg, Degirmen-cioglu, Tolson, & Halliday-Scher, 1995; cf., Ryabov, 2011).

Finally, the quality of students' relationships with teachers also is relevant for this discussion. For example, research indicates that preschool children who enjoy emotionally secure relationships with their teachers are more likely to demonstrate prosocial, gregarious, and complex play with peers and less likely to show hostile aggression and withdrawn behavior toward their peers (e.g., Howes & Hamilton, 1993). Moreover, the affective quality of individual teacher–student relationships predicts peer-related competencies up to 8 years later (Hamre & Pianta, 2001), as well as the relation between students externalizing behavior and peer social preference across the school year (Mikami et al., & Gregory, 2012).

SCHOOL-LEVEL INFLUENCES

Evidence of school-level influence on peer interactions and relationships has been less forthcoming. However, school-level norms can have a negative impact on ways in which students interact with each other when they reflect competitive academic standards and norm-referenced criteria for evaluating achievements that heighten social comparison among students. High levels of social comparison tend to result in students adopting orientations toward learning that focus on performance rather than mastery of subject matter and in lowered levels of academic efficacy and aspirations for achievement, especially among low-ability students (Butler, 2005).

On a positive note, schoolwide policies and programs that accentuate the importance of students' prosocial development can facilitate the development of positive peer relationships (Durlak, Weissberg, Dymnicki, Taylor, & Schellinger, 2011; Gresham, Van, & Cook, 2006). Social skills training programs can increase the prevalence of prosocial behaviors (e.g., sharing, cooperating) displayed by students in the classroom by teaching them how to recognize emotions more effectively, negotiate conflict resolutions, and control impulsive behaviors (Gresham et al., 2006). These programs also facilitate a reduction in the use of maladaptive social skills, thus enabling the formation of more functional relationships with peers (Wilson & Lipsey, 2007).

Other systematic efforts to enhance prosocial behavior and positive peer interactions are exemplified by the Caring School Community program (CSC, formerly known as the Child Development Project, Developmental Studies Center). The CSC curriculum provides cooperative learning and class activities designed to reinforce positive behavioral and social norms of the classroom, foster cognitive and social problem solving, and build classroom unity and a sense of community (e.g., Battistich, Solomon, Kim, Watson, & Schaps, 1995; Schaps, 2005). The effectiveness of the program on student behavior has also been acknowledged by the What Works Clearinghouse (2007).

Similarly, the Fast Track Program (see Bierman et al., 1999), a school-based intervention designed in part to promote friendship-building skills and social problem-solving strategies, has documented improvements in the quality of elementary-aged students' peer relationships and social interactions (Lavallee, Bierman, & Nix, 2005), as well as prosocial and aggressive behavior (Conduct Problems Prevention Research Group, 2010).

Finally, teachers and school administrators can play critical roles in creating schools that are free of peer harassment and in alleviating the negative effects of harassment once it has occurred. For example, the Olweus Bullying Prevention Program that focuses on improving peer relationships by creating and fostering a safe and positive school environment has been consistently associated with declines in bullying and increases in teachers' actions to prevent bullying (Olweus & Limber, 2009).

Summary of Teacher, Classroom, and School Effects

The literature offers a range of practices that can facilitate the formation and maintenance of positive peer relationships at school. Heterogeneous classrooms and learner-centered instruction can facilitate positive peer interactions and friendship formation. Efforts to deter negative peer interactions such as bullying and harassment should include clear messages from administrators and teachers that such behavior is not condoned, consistent enforcement of rules when antisocial behavior occurs, and ongoing discussions that focus on the negative consequences of these interactions and how to combat them. Similarly, schools can implement strategies to promote the development of positive peer interactions, such as frequent communication of prosocial values, use of inductive discipline to promote empathy and interpersonal understanding, use of collaborative and cooperative activities for instruction, and encouragement of students to help each other (Battistich et al., 1995). Finally, students can be taught a range of friendship-making strategies and other specific peer interaction skills (see Gresham et al., 2006).

REMAINING ISSUES AND FUTURE DIRECTIONS

The underlying premise of this chapter is that having friends and establishing positive interactions with the larger peer group have the potential to support and facilitate the development of other positive social and academic competencies at school (Wentzel, 2005). Therefore, finding ways to facilitate the development of children's positive peer relationships remains a central and important challenge for educators. However, there are many unanswered questions concerning when and how peers exert their influence. For example, an important question is whether there are critical periods during which peer relationships have more powerful effects.

Some researchers have suggested that the cumulative experience of having friendships is more important to development than any one particular friendship at one point in time (Hartup & Stevens, 1997). From a developmental perspective, the role of peers in motivating academic and social accomplishments is likely to be especially critical during the middle and high school years. During this time, children exhibit increased interest in their peers, spend more time with them, and exhibit a growing psychological and emotional dependence on them for support and guidance as they make the transition into adolescence (Youniss & Smollar, 1989). Moreover, peer groups and crowds emerge primarily in the middle school years, peak at the beginning of high school, and then diminish in prevalence as well as influence by the end of high school (Brown, 1989). Therefore, efforts to understand the positive influence of peer relationships on school-related outcomes must be sensitive to the qualities and types of relationships that students form with each other at different points in their educational careers.

Additional questions concern the causal nature of peer relationships. For instance, do children have high-quality friendships because they already possess the necessary skills to make friends, or do they develop positive social skills within the context of their friendships? Empirical findings provide support for observational learning explanations of influence, whereby a friend or peer models behavior or motivational orientations that are subsequently adopted by a child (e.g., Wentzel et al., 2004). Evidence also supports theoretical propositions that positive interactions with peers contribute directly to intellectual development and functioning that, in turn, can influence social as well as academic problem solving (e.g., Piaget, 1965; Vygotsky, 1978). However, research that addresses this question is limited; longitudinal studies that assess the characteristics of both friends at multiple points in time are necessary to determine the nature and timing of change over the course of a friendship.

In conclusion, a full appreciation of how and why students thrive at school requires an understanding of a student's social interactions and personal relationships with peers. These social aspects of students' lives have the potential to have a significant and positive impact on students' personal interests and goals, including motivation to achieve academically, positive behavioral styles, and academic accomplishments. However, to fully realize the powerful and positive roles of peers at school, the "developmentally instigating" properties (Bronfenbrenner, 1989) of the classroom that support and promote the development of positive interactions and relationships with peers must also be in place. Understanding ways in which teachers, classroom climates, and school-level policies contribute to these positive outcomes remains an important objective for future studies in this area. Peer relationship skills also might be especially important for adjustment in schools in which peer cultures are particularly strong or in which collaborative and cooperative learning is emphasized. Achieving a better understanding of such interactions deserves our full attention.

REFERENCES

Allen, J. D. (1986). Classroom management: Students' perspectives, goals, and strategies. *American Educational Research Journal, 23*, 437–459. http://www.jstor.org/stable/1163059

Alvarado, S., Elias, L., & Turley, R. (2012). College-bound friends and college application choices: Heterogeneous effects for Latino and White students. *Social Science Research, 41*, 1451–1468. doi:10.1016/j.ssresearch.2012.05.017

Asher, S. R., & Dodge, K. A. (1986). Identifying children who are rejected by their peers. *Developmental Psychology, 22*, 444–449. doi:10.1037/0012-1649.22.4.444

Asher, S. R., & McDonald, K. L. (2009). The behavioral basis of acceptance, rejection, and perceived popularity. In K. Rubin, W. Bukowski, & B. Laursen (Eds.), *Handbook on peer relationships* (pp. 232–248). New York, NY: Guilford.

Bandura, A. (1986). *Social foundations of thought and action: A social cognitive theory*. Englewood Cliffs, NJ: Prentice-Hall.

Barry, C., & Wentzel, K. R. (2006). The influence of middle school friendships on prosocial behavior: A longitudinal study. *Developmental Psychology, 42*, 153–163. doi:10.1037/0022-0663.96.2.195

Barth, J., Dunlap, S., Dane, H., Lochman, J., & Wells, K. (2004). Classroom environment influences on aggression, peer relations, and academic focus. *Journal of School Psychology, 42*, 115–133. doi:10.1016/j.jsp.2003.11.004

Barton, B., & Cohen, R. (2004). Classroom gender composition and children's peer relations. *Child Study Journal, 34*, 29–45.

Battistich, V., Solomon, D., Kim, D., Watson, M., & Schaps, E. (1995). Schools as communities, poverty levels of student populations, and students' attitudes, motives, and performance: A multilevel analysis. *American Educational Research Journal, 32*, 627–658. http://www.jstor.org/stable/1163326

Baumeister, R. F., & Leary, M. R. (1995). The need to belong—Desire for interpersonal attachments as a fundamental human motivation. *Psychological Bulletin, 117*, 497–529. doi:10.1037/0033-2909.117.3.497

Bierman, K., Coie, J., Dodge, K., Greenberg, M., Lochman, J., McMahon, R., & Pinderhughes, E. (1999). Initial impact of the Fast Track Prevention Trial for conduct problems: II. Classroom effect. *Journal of Consulting and Clinical Psychology, 67*, 648–657. http://psycnet.apa.org/doi/10.1037/0022-006X.67.5.631

Bronfenbrenner, U. (1989). Ecological systems theory. In R. Vasta (Ed.), *Annals of child development* (Vol. 6, pp. 187–250). Greenwich, CT: JAI.

Bronfenbrenner, U., & Morris, P. A. (2006). The bioecological model of human development. In W. Damon (Series Ed.) & R. Lerner (Vol. Ed.), *Handbook of child psychology: Vol. 1. Theoretical models of human development* (6th ed., pp. 793–828). Hoboken, NJ: Wiley.

Brown, B. B. (1989). The role of peer groups in adolescents' adjustment to secondary school. In T. J. Berndt & G. W. Ladd (Eds.), *Peer relationships in child development* (pp. 188–215). New York, NY: Wiley.

Brown, B. B. (2011). Popularity in peer group perspective: The role of status in adolescent peer systems. In A. Cillessen, D. Schwartz, & L. Mayeux (Eds.), *Popularity in the peer system* (pp. 165–192). New York, NY: Guilford.

Brown, B. B., Bakken, J. P., Ameringer, S. W., & Mahon, S. D. (2008). A comprehensive conceptualization of the peer influence process in adolescence. In M. Prinstein & K. Dodge (Eds.), *Understanding peer influence in children and adolescents* (pp. 17–44). New York, NY: Guilford.

Brown, B. B., & Dietz, E. L. (2009). Informal peer groups in middle childhood and adolescence. In K. Rubin, W. Bukowski, & B. Laursen (Eds.), *Handbook on peer relationships* (pp. 361–376). New York, NY: Guilford.

Buhs, E. S., & Ladd, G. W. (2001). Peer rejection as an antecedent of young children's school adjustment: An examination of mediating processes. *Developmental Psychology, 37*, 550–560.

Butler, R. (2005). Competence assessment, competence, and motivation between early and middle childhood. In A. Elliot & C. Dweck (Eds.), *Handbook of competence and motivation* (pp. 202–221). New York, NY: Guilford.

Cappella, E., & Neal, J. (2012). A classmate at your side: Teacher practices, peer victimization, and network connections in urban schools. *School Mental Health, 4*(2), 81–94. doi:10.1007/s12310-012-9072-2

Card, N. A., & Little, R. D. (2006). Proactive and reactive aggression in childhood and adolescence: A meta-analysis of differential relations with psychosocial adjustment. *International Journal of Behavioral Development, 30*, 466–480.

Cillessen, A., & van den Berg, Y. (2012). Popularity and school adjustment. In A. Ryan & G. Ladd (Eds.), *Peer relationships and adjustment at school* (pp. 135–164). Charlotte, NC: IAP Information Age.

Cohen, E. G. (1986). *Designing group work: Strategies for the heterogeneous classroom*. New York, NY: Teachers College Press.

Conduct Problems Prevention Research Group. (2010). The effects of a multiyear universal social–emotional learning program: The role of student and school characteristics. *Journal of Consulting and Clinical Psychology 78*, 156–168. http://psycnet.apa.org/doi/10.1037/a0018607

Connell, J., & Wellborn, J. (1991). Competence, autonomy, and relatedness: A motivational analysis of self-system processes. In M. Gunnar & L. A. Sroufe (Eds.), *Self processes and development* (pp. 43–77). Hillsdale, NJ: Erlbaum.

Crockett, L., Losoff, M., & Petersen, A. C. (1984). Perceptions of the peer group and friendship in early adolescence. *Journal of Early Adolescence, 4*, 155–181. doi:10.1177/0272431684042004

Donohue, K., Perry, K., & Weinstein, R. (2003). Teachers' classroom practices and children's rejection by their peers. *Journal of Applied Developmental Psychology, 24*, 91–118. doi:10.1016/S0193-3973(03)00026-1

Durlak, J. A., Weissberg, R. P., Dymnicki, A. B., Taylor, R. D., & Schellinger, K. B. (2011). The impact of enhancing students' social and emotional learning: A meta-analysis of school-based universal interventions. *Child Development, 82*, 405–432. doi:10.1111/j.1467-8624.2010.01564.x

Epstein, J. L. (1983). The influence of friends on achievement and affective outcomes. In J. L. Epstein & N. Karweit (Eds.), *Friends in school* (pp. 177–200). New York, NY: Academic Press.

Farmer, T. W., Irvin, M. J., Sgammato, A. N., Dadisman, K., & Thompson, J. H. (2009). Interpersonal competence configurations in rural Appalachian fifth graders: Academic achievement and associated adjustment factors. *Elementary School Journal, 109*, 301–321. http://dx.doi.org/10.1086%2f592309

Flook, L., Repetti, R. L., & Ullman, J. B. (2005). Classroom social experiences as predictors of academic performance. *Developmental Psychology, 41*, 319–327. doi:10.1037/0012-1649.41.2.319

Fonzi, A., Schneider, B. H., Tani, F., & Tomada, G. (1997). Predicting children's friendship status from their dyadic interaction in structured situations of potential conflict. *Child Development, 68*, 496–506. doi:10.1111/j.1467-8624.1997.tb01954.x

Ford, M. E. (1992). *Motivating humans: Goals, emotions, and personal agency beliefs*. Newbury Park, CA: Sage.

Gauvain, M., & Perez, S. M. (2007). The socialization of cognition. In J. E. Grusec & P. Hastings (Eds.), *Handbook of socialization: Theory and research* (pp. 588–613). New York, NY: Guilford.

Gest, S. D., & Rodkin, P. C. (2011). Teaching practices and elementary classroom peer ecologies. *Journal of Applied Developmental Psychology, 32*, 288–296. http://dx.doi.org/10.1016/j.appdev.2011.02.004

Gresham, F., Van, M., & Cook, C. (2006). Social-skills training for teaching replacement behaviors: Remediating acquisition in at-risk students. *Behavioral Disorders, 31*, 363–377.

Hamre, B. K., & Pianta, R. C. (2001). Early teacher–child relationships and the trajectory of children's school outcomes through eighth grade. *Child Development, 72*, 625–638. doi:10.1111/1467-8624.00301

Harper, L. V., & McCluskey, K. S. (2003). Teacher–child and child–child interactions in inclusive preschool settings: Do adults inhibit peer interactions? *Early Childhood Research Quarterly, 18*, 163–184. http://psycnet.apa.org/doi/10.1016/S0885-2006(03)00025-5

Hartup, W. W., & Stevens, N. (1997). Friendships and adaptation in the life course. *Psychological Bulletin, 121*, 355–370. http://psycnet.apa.org/doi/10.1037/0033-2909.121.3.355

Howes, C., & Hamilton, C. (1993). The changing experience of child care: Changes in teachers and in teacher–child relationships and children's social competence with peers. *Early Childhood Research Quarterly, 8*, 15–32.

Jackson, M., Barth, J., Powell, N., & Lochman, J. (2006). Classroom contextual effects of race on children's peer nominations. *Child Development, 77*, 1325–1337. doi:10.1111/j.1467-8624.2006.00937.x

Jones, M. H., Audley-Piotrowski, S., & Kiefer, S. M. (2012). Relationships among adolescents' perceptions of friends' behaviors, academic self-concept, and math performance. *Journal of Educational Psychology, 104*, 19–31. http://psycnet.apa.org/doi/10.1037/a0025596

Juvonen, J., & Espinoza, E., & Knifsend, C. (2012). The role of peer relationships in student academic and extracurricular engagement. In S. L. Christenson, A. L. Reschly, & C. Wylie (Eds.), *Handbook on student engagement* (pp. 387–401). New York, NY: Springer.

Kindermann, T. A., & Gest, S. D. (2009). Assessment of the peer group: Identifying naturally occurring social networks and capturing their effects. In K. Rubin, W. Bukowski, & B. Laursen (Eds.), *Handbook on peer relationships* (pp. 100–120). New York, NY: Guilford.

Kindermann, T. A., & Skinner, E. A. (2012). Will the real peer group please stand up? A "tensegrity" approach to examining the synergistic influences of peer groups and friendship networks on academic development. In A. Ryan & G. Ladd (Eds.), *Peer relationships and adjustment at school* (pp. 51–77). Charlotte, NC: IAP Information Age.

Ladd, G.W. (1990). Having friends, keeping friends, making friends, and being liked by peers in the classroom: Predictors of children's early school adjustment. *Child Development, 61*, 1081–1100.

Ladd, G.W., Herald-Brown, S.L., & Kochel, K.P. (2009). Peers and motivation. In K.R. Wentzel & A. Wigfield (Eds.), *Handbook of motivation at school* (pp. 531–547). New York, NY: Taylor Francis.

Lamarche, V., Brendgen, M., Boivin, M., Vitaro, F., Perusse, D., & Dionne, G. (2006). Do friendships and sibling relationships provide protection against peer victimization in a similar way? *Social Development, 15*, 373–393.

Lavallee, K.L., Bierman, K.L., & Nix, R.L. (2005). The impact of first-grade "friendship group" experiences on child social outcomes in the Fast Track Program. *Journal of Abnormal Child Psychology, 33*, 307–324. doi:10.1007/s10802-005-3567-3

Lempers, J.D., & Clark-Lempers, D.S. (1992). Young, middle, and late adolescents' comparisons of the functional importance of five significant relationships. *Journal of Youth and Adolescence, 21*, 53–96. doi:10.1007/BF01536983

Luckner, A.E., & Pianta, R.C. (2011). Teacher–student interactions in fifth-grade classrooms: Relations with children's peer behavior. *Journal of Applied Developmental Psychology, 32*, 257–266. http://dx.doi.org/10.1016/j.appdev.2011.02.010

Molloy, L.E., Gest, S.S., & Rulison, K. (2011). Peer influences on academic motivation: Exploring multiple methods of assessing youths' most "influential" peer relationships. *Journal of Early Adolescence, 31*, 13–40. doi:10.1177/0272431610384487

Mikami, A.Y., Griggs, M.S., Reuland, M.M., & Gregory, A. (2012). Teacher practices as predictors of children's classroom social preference. *Journal of School Psychology, 50*, 95–111. http://dx.doi.org/10.1016/j.jsp.2011.08.002

Newcomb, A.F., & Bagwell, C.L. (1995). Children's friendship relations: A meta-analytic review. *Psychological Bulletin, 117*, 306–347.

Olweus, D., & Limber, S.P. (2009). The Olweus Bullying Prevention Program: Implementation and evaluation over two decades. In S.R. Jimerson, S.M. Swearer, & D.L. Espelage (Eds.), *Handbook of bullying in schools: An international perspective* (pp. 377–402). New York, NY: Routledge.

Piaget, J. (1965). *The moral judgment of the child*. New York, NY: The Free Press (Originally published 1932)

Ricciardelli, L.A., & Mellor, D. (2012). Influence of peers. In N. Rumsey & D. Harcourt (Eds.), *The Oxford handbook of the psychology of appearance* (pp. 253–272). New York, NY: Oxford University Press.

Rohrbeck, C.A., Ginsburg-Block, M.D., Fantuzzo, J.W., & Miller, T.R. (2003). Peer-assisted learning interventions with elementary school students: A meta-analytic review. *Journal of Educational Psychology, 95*, 240–257. doi:10.1037/0022-0663.95.2.240

Rose-Krasnor, L. (1997). The nature of social competence: A theoretical review. *Social Development, 6*, 111–135. doi:10.1111/j.1467-9507.1997.tb00097.x

Rueger, S., Malecki, C., & Demaray, M (2011). Stability of peer victimization in early adolescence: Effects of timing and duration. *Journal of School Psychology, 49*, 443–464. doi:10.1016/j.jsp.2011.04.005

Ryabov, I. (2011). Adolescent academic outcomes in school context: Network effects reexamined. *Journal of Adolescence, 34*, 915–927. doi:10.1016/j.adolescence.2010.12.004

Ryan, A., & Ladd, G. (2012). *Peer relationships and adjustment at school*. Charlotte, NC: IAP Information Age.

Ryan, A. M., Jamison, R.S., Shin, H., & Thompson, G. (2012). Social achievement goals and adjustment at school during early adolescence. In A. Ryan & G. Ladd (Eds.), *Peer relationships and adjustment at school* (pp. 165–186). Charlotte, NC: IAP Information Age.

Ryan, R.M., & Deci, E.L. (2000). Self-determination theory and the facilitation of intrinsic motivation, social development, and well-being. *American Psychologist, 55*, 68–78. http://psycnet.apa.org/doi/10.1037/0003-066X.55.1.68

Sarason, B.R., Sarason, I.G., & Pierce, G.R. (1990). Traditional views of social support and their impact on assessment. In B.R. Sarason, I.G. Sarason, & G.R. Sarason (Eds.), *Social support: An interactional view* (pp. 9–25). New York, NY: Wiley.

Schaps, E. (2005). *The role of supportive school environments in promoting academic success* (pp. 39–56). Retrieved from http://www.devstu.org

Schunk, D.H., & Pajares, F. (2009). Self-efficacy theory. In K. Wentzel & A. Wigfield (Eds.), *Handbook of motivation at school* (pp. 35–54). Mahwah, NJ: Erlbaum.

Schwartz, D., Dodge, K.A., Pettit, G.S., Bates, J.E., & The Conduct Problems Prevention Research Group. (2000). Friendship as a moderating factor in the pathway between early harsh home environment and later victimization in the peer group. *Developmental Psychology, 36*, 646–662. doi:10.1037//0012-1649.36.5.646

Schwartz, D., Gorman, A., Dodge, K.A., Pettit, G.S., & Bates, J.E. (2008). Friendships with peers who are low or high in aggression as moderators of the link between peer victimization and declines in academic functioning. *Journal of Abnormal Child Psychology, 36*, 719–730. http://dx.doi.org/10.1007%2Fs10802-007-9200-x

Slavin, R.E. (2011). Instruction based on cooperative learning. In R. Mayer & P. Alexander (Eds.), *Handbook of research on learning and instruction* (pp. 344–360). New York, NY: Routledge.

Slavin, R.E., Hurley, E.A., & Chamberlain, A. (2003). Cooperative learning and achievement: Theory and research. In W. Reynolds & G. Miller (Eds.), *Handbook of psychology, Vol. 7: Educational psychology* (pp. 177–198). New York, NY: Wiley.

Swenson, L.M., & Strough, J. (2008). Adolescents' collaboration in the classroom: Do peer relationships or gender matter? *Psychology in the Schools, 45*, 715–728. doi:10.1002/pits.20337

Urberg, K., Degirmencioglu, S., Tolson, J., & Halliday-Scher, K. (1995). The structure of adolescent peer networks. *Developmental Psychology, 31*, 540–547. doi:10.1037/0012-1649.31.4.540

Vygotsky, L.S. (1978). *Mind in society: The development of higher psychological processes.* Cambridge, MA: Harvard University Press.

Wentzel, K.R. (1989). Adolescent classroom goals, standards for performance, and academic achievement: An interactionist perspective. *Journal of Educational Psychology, 81*, 131–142. doi:10.1037/0022-0663.81.2.131

Wentzel, K.R. (1994). Relations of social goal pursuit to social acceptance, classroom behavior, and perceived social support. *Journal of Educational Psychology, 86*, 173–182. http://psycnet.apa.org/doi/10.1037/0022-0663.86.2.173

Wentzel, K.R. (2004). Understanding classroom competence: The role of social-motivational and self-processes. In R. Kail (Ed.), *Advances in child development and behavior* (Vol. 32, pp. 213–241). New York, NY: Elsevier.

Wentzel, K.R. (2005). Peer relationships, motivation, and academic performance at school. In A. Elliot & C. Dweck (Eds.), *Handbook of competence and motivation* (pp. 279–296). New York, NY: Guilford.

Wentzel, K.R. (2009). Peer relationships and motivation at school. In K. Rubin, W. Bukowski, & B. Laursen (Eds.), *Handbook on peer relationships* (pp. 531–547). New York, NY: Guilford.

Wentzel, K.R., Baker, S.A., & Russell, S.L. (2012). Young adolescents' perceptions of teachers' and peers' goals as predictors of social and academic goal pursuit. *Applied Psychology: An International Review, 61*, 605–633. doi:10.1111/j.1464-0597.2012.00508.x

Wentzel, K.R., Barry, C., & Caldwell, K. (2004). Friendships in middle school: Influences on motivation and school adjustment. *Journal of Educational Psychology, 96*, 195–203. http://psycnet.apa.org/doi/10.1037/0022-0663.96.2.195

Wentzel, K.R., Battle, A., Russell, S.L., & Looney, L.B. (2010). Social supports from teachers and peers as predictors of academic and social motivation. *Contemporary Educational Psychology, 35*, 193–202. http://dx.doi.org/10.1016/j.cedpsych.2010.03.002

Wentzel, K.R., & Caldwell, K. (1997). Friendships, peer acceptance, and group membership: Relations to academic achievement in middle school. *Child Development, 68*, 1198–1209. doi:10.1111/j.1467-8624.1997.tb01994.x

Wentzel, K.R., Donlan, A., & Morrison, D. (2012). Peer relationships and motivation at school. In A. Ryan & G. Ladd (Eds.), *Peer relationships and adjustment at school* (pp. 79–108). Charlotte, NC: IAP Information Age.

Wentzel, K.R., Filisetti, L., & Looney, L. (2007). Adolescent prosocial behavior: The role of self-processes and contextual cues. *Child Development, 78*, 895–910. http://dx.doi.org/10.1111/j.1467-8624.2007.01039.x

Wentzel, K.R., & Watkins, D.E. (2011). Peer relationships and learning: Implications for instruction. In R. Mayer & P. Alexander (Eds.), *Handbook of research on learning and instruction* (pp. 322–343). New York, NY: Routledge.

Wentzel, K.R., Weinberger, D.A., Ford, M.E., & Feldman, S.S. (1990). Academic achievement in preadolescence: The role of motivational, affective, and self-regulatory processes. *Journal of Applied Developmental Psychology, 11*, 179–193. http://dx.doi.org/10.1016/0193-3973(90)90004-4

What Works Clearinghouse. (2007). *Caring school community.* Retrieved from http://www.ies.ed.gov/ncee/wwc/

Wilson, S., & Lipsey, M.W. (2007). School-based interventions for aggressive and disruptive behavior: Update of a meta-analysis. *American Journal of Preventive Medicine, 33*(2, Suppl), S130–S143. http://dx.doi.org/10.1016%2Fj.amepre.2007.04.011

Youniss, J., & Smollar, J. (1989). Adolescents' interpersonal relationships in social context. In T.J. Berndt & G. Ladd (Eds.), *Peer relationships in child development* (pp. 300–316). New York, NY: Wiley.

CHAPTER SUMMARY: PEER RELATIONSHIPS

- Peer-related activities predict a wide range of social and academic competencies at school.
- Collaborative and cooperative interactions also appear to be related to these same social and academic outcomes.

- Socially competent students achieve goals that are personally valued as well as those that are sanctioned by others; they pursue goals that result in social integration (e.g., cooperative behavior, social approval and acceptance) as well as in positive developmental outcomes (e.g., perceived competence, feelings of self-determination, feelings of emotional well-being).
- Students will engage in the pursuit of adaptive goals, in part, when their peers communicate expectations and standards for achieving multiple goals; provide direct assistance and help in achieving them; and create a climate of emotional support that facilitates positive engagement in socially valued classroom activities, including protection from physical threats and harm.
- Heterogeneous classrooms and learner-centered instruction can facilitate positive peer interactions and friendship formation.
- Efforts to deter negative peer interactions such as bullying and harassment should include clear messages from administrators and teachers that such behavior is not condoned, consistent enforcement of rules when antisocial behavior occurs, and ongoing discussions that focus on the negative consequences of these interactions and how to combat them.
- Schools can implement strategies to promote the development of positive peer interactions, such as frequent communication of prosocial values, use of inductive discipline to promote empathy and interpersonal understanding, use of collaborative and cooperative activities for instruction, and encouragement of students to help each other.
- Educators can facilitate positive peer relationships by teaching students a range of friendship-making strategies and other specific peer interaction skills.

SUGGESTED READINGS: PEER RELATIONSHIPS

Brown, B.B., Bakken, J.P., Ameringer, S.W., & Mahon, S.D. (2008). A comprehensive conceptualization of the peer influence process in adolescence. In M. Prinstein & K. Dodge (Eds.), *Understanding peer influence in children and adolescents* (pp. 17–44). New York, NY: Guilford.

The authors review work on adolescent peer influence and then present a comprehensive model of ways in which peers can influence a range of social and academic outcomes. The authors acknowledge that peers have the potential to influence each other in positive as well as negative ways.

Juvonen, J., & Espinoza, E., & Knifsend, C. (2012). The role of peer relationships in student academic and extracurricular engagement. In S. L. Christenson, A. L. Reschly, & C. Wylie (Eds.), *Handbook on student engagement* (pp. 387–401). New York, NY: Springer.

The authors describe how peers can motivate students to engage in school work as well as in extracurricular activities. The chapter covers the effects of peer support and belongingness, ways in which selection of friends, quality of friendships, and type of friendship support can influence engagement in learning and in activities inside and outside of school. Implications for school policy are discussed.

Ladd, G.W., Herald-Brown, S.L., & Kochel, K.P. (2009). Peers and motivation. In K.R. Wentzel & A. Wigfield (Eds.), *Handbook of motivation at school* (pp. 531–547). New York, NY: Taylor & Francis.

The authors discuss the role of peers in motivating positive emotional, behavioral, and cognitive outcomes related to school. The authors examine recent theory and evidence pertaining to the influence of classmates in school-related outcomes, and they critically appraise what has been learned thus far about specific mechanisms of influence.

Ryan, A., & Ladd, G. (2012). *Peer relationships and adjustment at school*. Charlotte, NC: IAP Information Age.

This book covers a broad range of topics that address peers' influence on adolescents' beliefs and behaviors in the school context. The chapters cover the influence of various types of peer relationships, multiple mechanisms and processes of influence, issues related to development and grade level, and ways in which teachers and practitioners can facilitate positive peer relationships at school.

Wentzel, K. R., & Watkins, D. E. (2011). Peer relationships and learning: Implications for instruction. In R. Mayer & P. Alexander (Eds.), *Handbook of research on learning and instruction* (pp. 322–343). New York, NY: Routledge.

The authors address the question of how students' involvement with peers might be related to academic motivation and accomplishments. Evidence that links involvement with peers at school to learning and intellectual outcomes is reviewed, and theoretical and conceptual models that might explain these links are presented. Ways in which evidence and theory can be applied to classroom instruction and school-based practices also are discussed.

18

CLASSMAPS CONSULTATION
Integrating Evaluation Into Classrooms to Promote Positive Environments

Beth Doll, Robert A. Spies, Anne E. Thomas, Jonathon D. Sikorski, Mindy R. Chadwell, Brooke A. Chapla, and Erika R. Franta, University of Nebraska–Lincoln, Lincoln, Nebraska, USA

INTRODUCTION

Classroom learning environments are critical to the academic and personal success of students and represent a particularly significant context for student development. During their formative years, students spend more than 15,000 hours in schools (Rutter & Maugham, 2002). These hours represent students' opportunity to interact and achieve independent of their parents' careful oversight. Consequently, a primary goal of schools should be to enhance natural supports for psychological wellness in the school environments in which students reside. Strong school environments enhance the social and emotional well-being of students and maximize students' academic success by fostering increased attendance, engagement, work completion, and work accuracy.

This chapter proposes ClassMaps Consultation as a comprehensive framework designed to create optimal classrooms for learning and development. Integral to this overall program is the use of the ClassMaps Survey as a practical and reliable measure of the complex classroom environment. Information from the survey is then used in a problem-solving process that identifies intervention strategies designed to establish or reinstate essential contextual supports in classrooms and to verify the effectiveness of those supports once they are implemented. The chapter closes with a discussion of the implications of ClassMaps Consultation for classroom and school strategies that promote positive psychology.

A CONCEPTUAL FRAMEWORK OF EFFECTIVE CLASSROOMS

Our framework for effective classroom environments has its foundation in developmental research on childhood resilience in the face of adversity. Between 1955 and the present, numerous prospective, longitudinal studies have examined the developmental competence of students exposed to multiple risk factors including poverty, limited parental education, family conflict, ineffective parenting, child maltreatment, poor physical health of the child or parents, and parental mental illness (Werner, 2013). Although initially focused on identifying variables that increased students' maladjustment, the researchers' attention subsequently turned to an even more interesting question: What made it possible for students to unexpectedly succeed in the face of adversity? Examples of these studies include:

- the Kauai Longitudinal study (Werner & Smith, 2001) that began in 1955 and sought to identify the origins of developmental disabilities in young children
- the Newcastle Thousand Family study (Kolvin, Miller, & Fleeting, 1988), which investigated deprivation and its effects on criminality over 15 years
- the Isle of Wight study (Rutter, Cox, Tupling, Berger, & Yule, 1975; Rutter & Maughan, 2002), which investigated factors that increased the risk of psychiatric disorders for students
- the Rochester Longitudinal study (Sameroff, Seifer, Baldwin, & Baldwin, 1993), which followed children of mothers with mental illness from early childhood through Grade 12

Comprehensive reviews of these and other studies can be found in Werner (2013).

Developmental research has repeatedly demonstrated that resilience is interdependent with risk and both are systemic and dynamic mechanisms (Masten & Powell, 2003). Figure 18.1 describes this interdependence in graphic terms. This system is characterized by both *multifinality* (the same risk or protective factors in childhood can result in different adult outcomes) and *equifinality* (the same adult outcomes can be reached by a variety of different risk or protective factors in childhood). The likelihood of positive adult outcomes increases geometrically with each additional protective factor, while the likelihood of poor outcomes increases geometrically with each additional risk factor. Furthermore, both risk and protective factors occur within intercorrelated clusters. For example, the risk factors of poverty, premature birth, parental mental illness, and maltreatment often co-occur, as do the protective factors of educational opportunity, financial stability, and access to competent adult role models. As another example, the unique circumstances of minority students who encounter pervasive racism, classism, or cultural hegemony may interact to magnify the impact of risk factors, while extended family networks may act in ways to protect minority students from these hardships (García Cöll et al., 1996). As students develop, it becomes more difficult to disentangle the unique effect of any single risk or protective factor (Masten & Powell, 2003).

Three systems of resilience have been identified that form a human adaptational system: individual attributes, family qualities, and supportive systems outside the family.

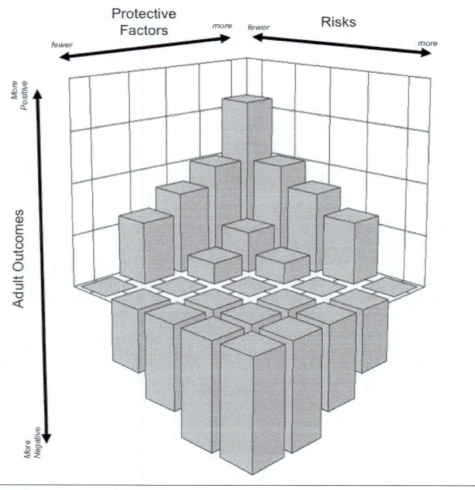

Figure 18.1 The dynamic risk and protective system.

For example, parental competence is a significant family factor in childhood resilience, as an early history of positive and supportive care allows children and adolescents to successfully adapt in adulthood (Werner, 2013). The absence of parental competence can lead to poor adult coping, as expressed in such problems as financial dependence, substance abuse, or dysfunctional relationships. Students with average or above-average intelligence, low emotionality, and an internal locus of control are less vulnerable to family adversities than students without these individual characteristics of resilience. Moreover, students who are denied effective caretaking from their parents can sometimes receive compensatory support from other people in their communities. Students who successfully cope despite serious adversities almost always have strong and caring relationships with siblings, extended family members, caregivers, teachers, or peers. In fact, in a follow-up to the classic Kauai longitudinal study (Werner & Johnson, 2004), children of alcoholics who showed resilience and developed successful adult coping skills were the same children who relied heavily on social supports from their neighbors, peers, religious communities, or schools. Thus, interventions that strengthen protective systems outside the family have the potential to enhance students' opportunities for success. Interventions that appropriately address the culturally specific experiences of students and their families will be even more effective (Varjas, Nastasi, Bernstein-Moore, & Jayasena, 2005).

Schools are a significant and malleable protective presence in students' lives and represent one of the most important community support systems contributing to childhood resilience (Wentzel, 2009; Werner, 2013). Importantly, almost half of students who grew into competent adults despite early hardships cited a supportive teacher as a positive role model in their youth (Werner & Johnson, 2004). It is reassuring to realize that childhood resilience emerges out of such ordinary adaptive phenomena as a warm relationship with a teacher, close friendships with peers, or the mastery of self-regulatory skills and that strengthening these can greatly increase the likelihood that even disadvantaged students can be successful (Masten, 2001). Strengthening supportive school environments benefits all students and especially benefits those at risk (Downer, Rimm-Kauffman, & Pianta, 2007; Pianta et al., 2005).

Developmental research on risk and resilience identifies several characteristics of communities and schools that promote resilience and foster success in children and adolescents (Masten, 2001; Werner, 2013). We selected six of these factors for our description of positive classroom environments because they were alterable and could be framed as features of classroom contexts. These include classroom practices that (a) foster caring and authentic relationships between adults and students (Teacher–Student Relationships); (b) maximize opportunities for ongoing and rewarding friendships with peers (Peer Relationships); (c) strengthen home–school collaboration (Home–School Relationships); (d) foster students' self-identities as competent and effective learners (Academic Efficacy); (e) support opportunities for students to set and work toward ambitious, self-set goals (Academic Self-Determination); and (f) promote student self-control of their behavior so that their conduct is appropriate and adaptive (Behavioral Self-Control). The following descriptions briefly explain why each of the six factors was retained in the definition of resilient classrooms by describing the factor's relation to the developmental competence and academic success of children who learn there.

Relational Features of Resilient Classrooms

Teacher–Student Relationships

Of all the relationships that students have at school, teacher–student relationships are the most influential for school success (Doll, LeClair, & Kurien, 2009). Teachers' relationships with their students have been described as an attachment bond that is similar to the parent–child bond (Ahnert, Harwardt-Heinecke, Kappler, Eckstein-Madry, & Milatz 2012). Like parents, teachers can provide support and encouragement, influencing students' academic and social development. Students feel stronger connections to teachers who are warm and authoritative in their interactions. These emotionally supportive teachers are helpful, even tempered, demonstrate respect for students, engage students in frequent and enjoyable conversations, and encourage their students to develop personal autonomy (Hamre & Pianta,

2005; Merritt, Wanless,Rimm-Kaufman, Cameron, & Peugh, 2012). Emotionally support-ive teacher–child interactions have been associated with lower levels of child aggression and higher levels of behavioral self-control (Merritt et al., 2012). Strong teacher–student bonds are particularly important for students at risk of school failure because they serve as pro-tective factors that moderate or even reverse the detrimental effects of other hardships (Hamre &Pianta, 2005).

An important difference between teacher–student and parent–child relationships is that students' relationships with their teachers are embedded within the social context of a classroom (Pianta, 1999). This phenomenon is particularly important because negative interactions may develop between teachers and certain students that damage teachers' relationships with all other students who observe or are affected by these interactions. Damaging conflict or discord between teachers and their students is more destructive to student learning than the absence of positive interactions (Murray & Murray, 2004). Thus, reducing negative interactions between teachers and their students appears to be more important than increasing positive interactions for promoting students' academic success (Ang, 2005).

Peer Relationships

Like teacher–student relationships, rewarding peer relationships strengthen the social climate of the classroom and the social competence of students while also encouraging students' active participation, interest, and success in learning (Wentzel, 2009; Wentzel, Barry, & Caldwell, 2007). Classmates make learning enjoyable, and they give and receive assistance to each other as needed (Wentzel & Watkins, 2002). Within the classroom, strong peer relationships are demonstrated by high rates of mutual friendships and by classmates' capacity to successfully resolve conflicts without upsetting their friendships (Doll & Brehm, 2010). Thus, the development of any single student's peer relationships is influenced by the student's personal social competence, by the collective climate of acceptance in the classrooms, and by the number and strength of opportunities for stu-dents to have fun together. For most students, classmates make school an inviting place to be, and the large majority of students have three or more friends among their class-mates (Doll, Brehm, & Zucker, 2014).

Interpersonal conflict is also important to classrooms' social climate, and its destruc-tive aspects can be lessened or eliminated with routines and practices that promote positive conflict management (Doll & Brehm, 2010). Students experience teasing and arguments as a normal part of friendships, and this only becomes troublesome when it is hurtful or persists to a point that it interrupts friendships. When this occurs, most students will compromise, share, take turns, apologize, and forgive each other when nec-essary to protect a valued friendship. As a result, most conflicts with friends are quickly resolved. This conflict with friends is distinct in important ways from peer bullying in that a bully is someone who is not a friend and who repeatedly and deliberately harms and intimidates the child (Pellegrini & Bartini, 2001). Within classrooms, students are most worried about and afraid of bullying when they feel unable to defend themselves. Thus, classwide routines to diminish victimization and intimidation are valuable attributes of resilient classrooms. These routines are closely related to the routines that encourage peer friendships. One powerful defense against victimization is friendships with class-mates who are willing to protect students from peer aggression (Song & Stoiber, 2008).

Home–School Relationships

Students' success in school is strongest when their home and schools are compatible partners in childrearing (Christenson, 2004). Early research on home–school partner-ships focused on teacher perceptions of parental involvement such as parental atten-dance at school functions, assemblies, and parent–teacher conferences (Anderson & Minke, 2007). However, recent studies have broadened the definition of successful home–school partnerships to include the many different actions parents take to support their children's school success, such as monitoring television, reinforcing school disci-pline, checking homework, and providing students a quiet work environment (Epstein et al., 2002). Classrooms with strong home–school relationships are approachable and welcoming and provide parents with the sense that they can contribute in important ways to the work of their children at school and at home (Fan, 2001; Hong & Ho, 2005). When parents feel disengaged or left out of the educational experience of their children, students have lower attendance in school and higher dropout rates and are more often found to be delinquent or adjudicated youth (Doll, Spies, & Champion, 2012; Fan, 2001).

Students with involved parents are more successful at school as demonstrated by their higher homework completion rates (Epstein & Van Voorhis, 2001) and higher test scores and overall grades (Fan, 2001; Hill et al., 2004). Parent involvement is correlated with better student attendance, lower suspension rates, and higher rates of school completion (Anguiano, 2004; Epstein & Sheldon, 2002; Fan, 2001; Hill et al., 2004). Finally, students with involved parents have higher educational and career aspirations (Hill et al., 2004). Both teachers and parents benefit from positive home–school relationships: teachers report higher job satisfaction and parents report increased satisfaction with their child's school and teacher (Fan, 2001; Hong & Ho, 2005; Ingram, Wolfe, & Lieberman, 2007).

Self-Regulatory Features of Resilient Classrooms

Academic Efficacy

Academic efficacy refers to students' beliefs that they can be successful in the classroom (Bandura, 1997). It describes a cycle of self-fulfilling prophesy—students who believe that they can succeed are more likely to develop skills and behave in ways that promote success, which strengthens their efficacy or expectations of success. Schools provide some of the first opportunities for students to complete tasks, receive feedback, and experience successes and failures, which lead to the development of efficacious beliefs (Pastorelli et al., 2001). These opportunities promote high academic efficacy when students experi-ence success in their daily classwork, vicariously observe their classmates' success, and receive comments and praise from classmates and teachers that celebrate their achieve-ments (Bandura, Caprara, Barbaranelli, Gerbino, & Pastorelli, 2003).

Academic efficacy prompts students to engage in challenging and difficult tasks (Schraw, Kauffman, & Lehman, 2002). Indeed, compared to students with higher aca-demic efficacy, students with lower academic efficacy tend to avoid learning tasks that they expect to fail and are more likely to engage in risky behaviors than their peers (Pajares, 2006). Students with higher academic efficacy undertake more rigorous course material, ask for help more often, and are more persistent (Doll et al., 2014; Schunk & Pajares, 2005). Given higher self-efficacy, students develop strong self-regulatory skills such as goal setting, using appropriate academic strategies, self-monitoring, and self-evaluation (Brophy, 2010). As a result, they are less anxious and more confident in their schoolwork, and they perceive failures to be temporary setbacks (Pajares & Schunk, 2002). In contrast, students with lower academic efficacy often believe that tasks are too difficult for them, become anxious and stressed, identify fewer alternative solutions for challenging problems, and attribute failure to their own lack of ability. This pattern can escalate as students move from elementary to the secondary grades. Over time, they may repeatedly miss out on key activities that enrich their educational experience, develop a sense of shame, and even become socially isolated (Christensen & Thurlow, 2004). Thus, a key feature of resilient classrooms is that they interrupt the cycle of diminishing efficacy and reinstate students' expectations for success.

Academic Self-Determination

As most students grow and develop, their natural inclination toward autonomy, competence, and relatedness will prompt them to form intrinsically motivated goals and regulate their own behavior to meet those goals (Deci & Ryan, 2012). In school, students demonstrate autonomy when they willingly and purposefully articulate their aspirations for learning and then take concrete steps to reach these goals (Niemiec & Ryan, 2009). This is because students who recognize the importance of learning to their own purposes will systematically plan how they will reach their goals, and when challenges or difficulties stand in their way, they will flexibly use problem-solving strategies for working around these (Deci & Ryan, 2008). Their emerging autonomy is also closely related to the six features of resilient classrooms. These self-determined behaviors are magnified when students feel a sense of relatedness within the classroom and when they believe teachers like, respect, and value them (Niemiec & Ryan, 2009).

Once students recognize the relevance of the classroom's work to their personal goals, the task of teaching becomes much easier. Meaningful learning allows the teacher's role to shift to that of a guide and mentor rather than an enforcer of extrinsic goals. Classroom practices can facilitate students' realizations by assigning work that is interesting to students and matters for their personal lives (Reeve & Halusik, 2009). Self-determined students then work to "master" material (i.e., a mastery goal) rather than working to outperform classmates (i.e., a competitive goal; Pajares & Schunk, 2002). Classrooms further strengthen students' academic self-determination with direct instruction in goal-setting and by teaching students to self-monitor their own learning progress (Doll et al., 2014).

Behavioral Self-Control

Behavioral self-control is the degree to which students' behavior is self-regulated and appropriate (Doll et al., 2014). Learning to behave in socially acceptable ways lays the groundwork for students to develop and maintain strong social relationships (Rudasill & Rimm-Kaufman, 2009). Moreover, students who are attentive, regulated, and persistent in their work receive higher grades, while those who lack behavioral self-control often underachieve academically (Wanless, McClelland, Acock et al., 2011). Limited behavioral self-control challenges academic achievement in the elementary years, and early difficulties with self-control are likely to persist into later grades (Wanless, McClelland, Tominey, & Acock, 2011). By the secondary grades, academic difficulties contribute to increases in rule-breaking behaviors both in school and the surrounding community (Hawkins et al., 2003; Wills, Pokhrel, Morehouse, & Fenster, 2011). Fortunately, prevention programs that increase school success have shown potential to reduce future behavior problems.

Students' behavioral self-control emerges from internal characteristics of students (such as their desire to please and expectations of success) and ecological classroom routines and practices. Early in the year, students help teachers develop behavioral expectations for the class, and they learn routines that script positive behavioral actions for challenging times in the day such as transitioning between subjects or coming in from recess (Doll et al., 2014). Subsequently, instructional practices can enhance behavioral self-control by actively engaging students in learning with instruction that is quick paced and interesting and gives students frequent opportunities to respond (Linan-Thompson & Vaugn, 2010). Peers can also prompt classmates to behave appropriately. Peer behavior coaches have demonstrated effectiveness in improving behavioral self-control and academic engagement in both elementary (Menesses & Gresham, 2009) and middle school students (Mitchem, Young, West, & Benyo, 2001).

Summary

Six characteristics provide a coherent description of classroom environments that promote self-regulatory elements of developmental competence (academic efficacy, academic self-determination, and behavioral self-control) and relational aspects of psychological wellness (peer relationships, teacher–student relationships, and home–classroom relationships). Classrooms possessing these characteristics foster students' psychological wellness, academic success, and successful outcomes in adulthood. Within traditional perspectives, each has been considered to be an important characteristic of the individual child. However, our analysis also considers them to be attributes of the school environments within which students grow, develop, and learn.

FOSTERING RESILIENCE IN CLASSROOMS

Schools continually strive to create optimal classroom learning environments for their students. However, when those environments show signs of disturbance or disruption, data-based problem-solving strategies can be used to promote more effective classroom routines. ClassMaps Consultation is a familiar four-step problem-solving strategy that emphasizes systematic data-based decision making to strengthen the six characteristics of optimal classroom learning environments. In Step One, a needs assessment is conducted of the classroom learning environment using the ClassMaps Survey (CMS). CMS items examine all six features of resilient classrooms, implicitly prompting teachers and their colleagues to consider both relational and self-regulatory supports in the classroom. In Step Two, data gathered from the needs assessment are carefully analyzed in partnership with colleagues and the students who learn in the classroom. The classroom works to identify those aspects of the classroom that need to be strengthened. During Step Three, changes are identified that have the potential to foster stronger relationships and more proficient self-regulation in the classroom, and these changes are crafted into a classroom plan for intervention. One key component of every classroom plan is a strategy for monitoring whether improvements in classroom characteristics occur in response to the planned changes. Subsequently in Step Four, data describing the impact of the classroom changes are examined and, if necessary, the classroom plan is revised. Clearly, this is a cyclical process because teachers and their students can decide to revisit Step One and begin anew with another goal once the initial goal is met. Many of the changed classroom routines that are planned in Step Two and implemented in Step Three do not qualify as evidence based because these may not have been demonstrated to be effective in multiple well-controlled empirical studies. However, in a specific classroom in which ClassMaps Consultation is occurring, the changes are monitored through ongoing data collected within the classroom, and the classroom's plan for change will be systematically modified in response to that data until the goal for the improved learning environment has been met. When followed as a cycle, ClassMaps Consultation prompts teachers and students to work purposefully together to create the classroom environments that support student success.

The framework of ClassMaps Consultation is deceptively simple, but applying it in practice can be challenging. Classrooms can differ in important ways, and the intervention plans that are effective in one classroom may be much less effective in another. Moreover, the skills underlying data-based problem solving are frequently unfamiliar to classroom teachers (Doll et al., 2005). Consequently, teachers require a certain professional confidence to actively lead a classroom change effort even though they are uncertain of the underlying principles. Most classrooms benefit from a consultative team approach in which the classroom teacher collaborates and problem solves with colleagues, a school mental health professional, or a parent. Working within a team expands the number of ideas for intervention, provides alternative perspectives on the classroom, and contributes new knowledge and professional support to the teacher. Students, too, should be fully involved, because through their participation, they share responsibility for solving problems identified in the classroom and thereby contribute to the sustainability of classroom change over time.

A more detailed description of each step of ClassMaps Consultation is provided in the following sections. A comprehensive description of the data-based problem-solving process is found in Doll and colleagues (2014).

Step One: Classroom Needs Assessment

A necessary first step in ClassMaps Consultation is conducting a reliable needs assessment that describes the classroom context for learning. The ClassMaps Survey (CMS) was developed for this purpose. Administering the CMS to all students measures, counts, and quantifies the six classroom characteristics so that they become visible to the team and available for modification (Doll et al., 2014). To strengthen its utility as a measure of classroom learning environment, the CMS was designed to be brief to administer, easy to code and analyze, easily converted to graphic display so that teachers and students could plan from the information, and to have face validity so that teachers and students are more likely to respect the results.

The CMS uses an aggregated rating strategy in which all students in a class rate items describing what it is like to be in their classroom. Individual ratings are then aggregated across students to represent a classroom measure. This strategy was used to create eight subscales assessing the six classroom characteristics. Three subscales assess the collective self-regulation of students in the class: academic efficacy (Believing in Me; BIM), academic self-determination (Taking Charge; TC), and behavioral self-control (Following Class Rules; FCR). Five subscales assess the classroom relationships: teacher–student relationships (My Teacher; MT), home–school relationships (Talking with My Parents; TWP), peer friendships (My Classmates; MC), peer conflict (Kids in this Class; KITC), and concerns about bullying (I Worry That; IWT). Each of the eight subscales is composed of 5 to 8 items, and the full survey is 55 items in length. Students select their response from a four-point scale (never, sometimes, often, or almost always). The survey is completed by the entire class in about 15 to 25 minutes. A practical feature of the CMS is that it can be readministered periodically to assess the impact of planned interventions; it may be most appropriate to readminister only those subtests that are most relevant to the goal.

Individual students' responses to the CMS are anonymous to elicit more accurate and frank responses. Aggregated responses are then graphed, designed to provide quick visual feedback that is easy for teachers and students to understand. Figure 18.2 shows how the survey results are displayed using bar graphs that describe the frequency of each

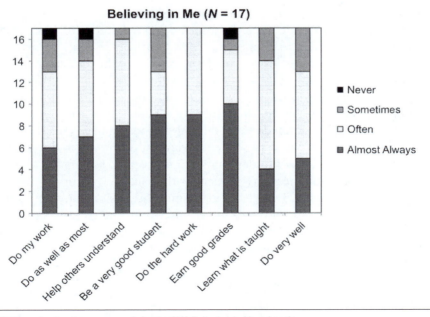

Figure 18.2 Example of a classroom graph for the CMS Believing in Me subscale.

response to each item. In previous applications, these graphs have been easily understood by students as young as second or third graders. The most current version of the CMS is computer administered, allowing students to complete the surveys electronically and teachers to download a classroom graph as soon as the last student has completed the survey.

The CMS was designed to be internally consistent, related to other indices of academic success in the classroom, capable of repeated administrations without practice effects, and sensitive to changes in the elements that might occur in response to interventions. These technical properties have been comprehensively reviewed by Doll and colleagues (2009), Doll, Spies, Champion, and colleagues (2010), and Doll, Spies, LeClair, and colleagues (2010). Despite the CMS subscales' brevity, individual subscales have shown strong internal consistency, with subscale coefficient alphas ranging from .82 to .91 with middle school students (Doll, Spies, Champion et al., 2010) and ranging from .79 to .93 with elementary school students (Doll, Spies, LeClair et al., 2010). Subsequently, two exploratory factor analyses (Doll & Spies, 2007; Doll et al., 2010) and one confirmatory analysis (Doll, Spies, Champion et al., 2010) have supported the factor structure of the CMS subscales. Other studies have described the CMS's correlation with equivalent measures of school learning environments (Doll, Spies, Champion et al., 2010; Paul, 2005).

Step Two: Making Meaning of the Classroom Data

Once the needs assessment has been conducted, the classroom's teacher and students examine the data graph, discuss the results, and articulate the strengths and weakness of the classroom. In a classroom meeting, data graphs are shown to the students, who then comment on the accuracy of the data, explain why they think that the weaknesses exist, and suggest strategies and changes that might strengthen the classroom environment. Students and the teacher decide upon the most important change to make in the classroom and discuss what the classroom would look like if the changes occurred. Student involvement is essential for the developmental sensitivity of the plan for change because students have the unique capacity to understand the classroom from the perspective of participants. Many of the student suggestions are unusually innovative and insightful. For example, in one fourth-grade classroom, students explained that much of their teasing and arguing was prompted by the difficulty choosing teams for the daily soccer game. Once this problem was understood, an obvious next step was to design an efficient team-forming routine that every student in the class accepted as fair.

Teachers also discuss the needs assessment with colleagues or other adults in their classroom consultation team. Even brief 20-minute discussions are sufficient for the team to isolate the weaknesses. In addition to discussing the conditions under which weaknesses occur, the team will make hypotheses as to why weaknesses have emerged. These hypotheses may point to ways to fix the weaknesses.

Step Three: Planning and Carrying Out Classroom Changes

A plan for classroom change is developed in Step Three. Two types of change strategies form the bases for the plan: micro changes and manualized classroom interventions.

As the name implies, micro changes are small modifications that can be made in daily routines and practices and that strengthen conditions for learning. For example, in one second-grade classroom, students completing the CMS described ambivalent relationships with their teacher. In response, the teacher made a point of smiling more often, injected more humor and learning games into the school day, and attended more closely to the students' descriptions of daily triumphs and hassles. Several months later, the students' CMS reports showed stronger teacher–student relationships. In a separate instance, eighth-grade students described substantial conflicts during lunch and teachers concurred, noting that they were worried about high rates of suspensions due to fights. In a meeting with their teachers, students suggested that the problems were primarily due to the barren and boring playground environment where they gathered. Once more games were added to the lunchtime recess, the number of suspensions decreased two or three suspensions each month to one single suspension for the last 3 months of the school year. Ideas for micro changes might emerge out of teachers' prior experiences, the suggestions of colleagues, suggestions made by the students themselves, or case examples in professional journals or newsletters. In some cases, the relevance of a micro change is immediately obvious once teachers understand the classroom events.

The second type of change strategies is manualized classroom interventions; these may be necessary when classroom problems are severe or intractable. Consistent with accepted standards for evidence-based interventions, manualized interventions are those that have been examined in multiple well-designed studies with results demonstrating meaningful positive outcomes for students (U.S. Department of Health and Human Services, 1999). The principle underlying this selection is simple: Comprehensive manualized interventions will only be worth the extraordinary effort if there is some evidence that these have worked to advance similar goals in other classrooms and schools. Doll and Brehm (2010) describe manualized interventions designed to discourage aggression, strengthen peer relationships, and increase prosocial behaviors on playgrounds. Doll and colleagues (2014) describe evidence-based interventions for all six classroom characteristics.

The written plan for intervention includes a description of each activity, when and how often it will occur, and the person responsible for carrying out the activity. Copies of the written plan serve as a checklist on which each activity can be checked off as it occurs, and activities that are inadvertently omitted can be circled. The checklists serve as a record of the degree to which the classroom changes were carried out as planned. The fidelity with which a plan was implemented is described in terms of its accuracy and its duration. Interventions with good fidelity are those for which at least 90% of the planned activities occurred, and the changes were in place for at least 2 weeks—long enough for the changes to have become predictable for the classroom's students. Intervention plans also include a component for monitoring the classroom's progress toward its goal. Monitoring plans may be as simple as collecting student answers to a daily question about recess problems, collating existing class records on seatwork completion or accuracy, using a stopwatch to track the time needed for classroom transitions, or counting disciplinary incidents. In one case, the ClassMaps My Classmates subscale was completed weekly in fourth-grade classrooms to monitor changes in their classroom friendships (Murphy, 2002).

In some cases, it becomes immediately apparent that a planned classroom change is impractical or simply too awkward to implement with fidelity. For example, a middle school teacher had planned to eat lunch with a few select students each week to reward them for their improved work completion. However, students quickly declined the invitation, preferring to eat with their friends. A high school classroom for students with behavior disorders was implementing an evidence-based intervention to teach students alternatives to aggression. However, when colleagues observed the intervention sessions, they noted that the students were not paying attention, did not participate in the activities and, on several occasions, were sent out of the group because of their disruptive behavior. In other cases, it becomes clear that the students or the teacher find a change to be too distasteful to make. For example, in addition to an ambitious refinement of soccer routines and rules, a fourth-grade classroom had developed a "teasing form" that was supposed to be completed whenever one student teased another. Teasing decreased from an average daily rating of 5 on the classroom's teasing thermometer ("90% teasing and 10% not") to an average rating of 2 ("10% teasing and 90% not; mostly not"); however, there was not a single instance in which a teasing form was completed.

Ongoing review of the activity checklists will make it obvious if planned classroom changes are not being implemented with fidelity. When fewer than 90% of the activities are carried out, teachers and their teams have three options: (a) to make a more concerted effort to follow the plan meticulously, (b) to revise the plan in small ways that fix the impractical components, or (c) to develop a new plan that is more likely to address the classroom's goal. Both activity checklists describing the implementation fidelity and classroom data monitoring progress toward the goal will help teams make this decision. In the teasing form example, the activity checklists showed that all of the new soccer routines were implemented immediately and 100% of the time. The teasing form, while available, was never used but student ratings showed that teasing had decreased regardless. In this case, the teacher proceeded with the original plan minus the component of the teasing form. Although the original plan was flawed, the activity checklists provided good information about the changes that had been made with fidelity in the classroom. The middle school students who declined lunch invitations from the teacher were responding to a more problematic classroom plan. After 8 class days, the activity checklists showed only one student had agreed to eat with the teacher, and the teacher's record book showed no changes in work completion rates. This teacher decided to ask the students what they wanted as rewards for improving their work and then changed the plan to include a menu of rewards that the students had suggested. The school high classroom had a more challenging task in fixing the evidence-based alternatives-to-aggression intervention. Because the curriculum had proven effective in well-controlled studies, the teachers were committed to its continued use. However, they also consulted with the intervention's authors to identify strategies that could heighten the activities' appeal for students and reinforce student participation.

Step Four: Evaluating the Impact of the Classroom Changes

In Step Four, the team examines the progress of the plan and evaluates whether it is actually working. Monitoring data are used to determine whether the class is on target for reaching its goals. For example, in the fourth-grade classroom discussed earlier, the class decided to choose soccer teams for the week on each Monday. Students then collected daily "teasing thermometer ratings" from every student describing how much teasing and arguing had occurred. These daily ratings showed a decline in teasing and arguing, and so the Monday team-choosing routine was used consistently. Like this fourth grade group, whenever a classroom's plan is successful, the effective changes can usually be integrated into its ongoing routines and practices.

Sometimes a plan is partially successful. For example, a needs assessment in one second-grade class showed serious problems with students' participation and work completion during the science period. The students helped the teacher plan a stoplight system in which a yellow light warned the students that they were not paying good attention and a red light warned them that additional violations would result in lost recess minutes. The system improved work completion rates from 58% to 75%, but the teacher expected rates of 95% or higher. The class then added a second component to their plan—they graphed daily work completion rates on a bulletin board located at the front of the room and spent a few moments each day talking about their progress. Work completion rates quickly rose above the targeted goal of 95%. Other strategies for adjusting classroom plans might include increasing the amount or dosage of a classroom change or changing to a new intervention.

Some unsuccessful classroom plans indicate a need for an entirely new plan or a more ambitious intervention. Classrooms may decide to return to Step One and collect additional needs assessment data or return to Step Two and reconsider the existing data in a new classroom meeting. Even classrooms that have met with good success in their plans sometimes decide to return to the beginning of the cycle and address the next most important goal.

IMPLICATIONS FOR RESEARCH AND EDUCATIONAL PRACTICE

This chapter demonstrates how it is possible to combine a data-based problem-solving process with an operational definition of effective classroom learning environments to promote the well-being of students. Aggregated student responses to the CMS represent a first step toward data-based decision making about classwide interventions. The CMS's operational definition interjects an emphasis on positive, developmentally protective classroom environments into the ClassMaps Consultation procedures. Once these resilient environments have been described in concrete terms, it becomes easier to systematically intervene to create these supports in individual classrooms. Within the framework of developmental risk and resilience, stronger classrooms have enhanced potential to counteract adversities facing students in other aspects of their daily lives.

Another important benefit of using student surveys is that students' voices are acknowledged during classroom planning and intervention. Student perceptions are crucial because students are integral to the system of the classroom and their endorsement can contribute to the success of classroom changes because their insights may provide teachers with new explanations for classroom problems and unanticipated suggestions for solutions. Engaging students can distribute the work of classroom change efforts so that the strategies are more practical for very busy classroom teachers.

While other intervention strategies promote healthy relationships and self-regulation in school-age children, ClassMaps Consultation seeks to foster these attributes in the naturally occurring groups of the classroom. An obvious benefit of intervening with groups of students in public schools is that the programs are delivered to more students in a more efficient and cost-effective way. A second benefit is that CMS consultation targets the behavior of the full group. This is particularly important in fostering peer relationships, in which group social behavior is at least as important as that of individual students. However, another notable benefit is that the ClassMaps Consultation strengthens the system of the classroom. These systemic changes have the potential to persist over time, and changes that benefit one aspect of the child-in-classroom system might be expected to prompt additional benefits at other points in the system.

Obvious beneficiaries of ClassMaps Consultation are the classroom teachers whose data-based decision-making skills are strengthened. It can be paradigm shifting for teachers to use classroom data to fuel modifications that strengthen their classroom environments. This framework provides teachers with a common language that stretches across theoretical perspectives, enhancing their communication with colleagues about their classroom environments. It makes good use of teacher expertise and leadership and provides them with convincing case examples that they can share with parents and administrators to highlight the good work of the classroom.

CONCLUSION

ClassMaps Consultation research is still in its early stages. Several years were spent developing the CMS to be a practical and technically sound measure of positive classroom environments. An early challenge was the relative difficulty of operationally defining *positive*, wellness-promoting characteristics of classrooms relative to the historical ease with which classroom *problems* had been assessed and refined. More recent research is streamlining the ClassMaps Consultation procedures so that teachers believe that these are worth the effort required to use them. Will teachers be willing to integrate these classroom-based problem-solving procedures into their routine practices? Do the changes translate into greater student engagement in learning and stronger student success in the classroom? Are these worth the time that teachers invest? Because the ClassMaps change strategies are inextricably entwined with teachers' instructional decisions, teachers need to be fully prepared to direct the process. Consequently, current research is examining the most efficient ways to prepare teachers to collect data about their classrooms, collate and graph it, make sense of the results, and use the data to problem solve promising classroom changes and interventions. All of this is complicated by the variability in classrooms—early ClassMaps research has shown that the important needs of one classroom may not be very prominent in a second classroom, and the classroom changes that are very effective in one classroom may be less effective in another classroom with the same goals for change. It is a very complicated task to examine the impact of ClassMaps Consultation using well-controlled research designs while also respecting this variability in classroom needs, monitoring data, and intervention plans. Ultimately, this will be the important challenge of the ClassMaps research: capturing the complexity of classroom interventions that take place in actual school settings while gathering reliable and valid data describing the outcomes of data-based classroom change.

REFERENCES

Ahnert, L., Harwardt-Heinecke, E., Kappler, G., Eckstein-Madry, T., & Milatz, A. (2012). Student–teacher relationships and classroom climate in first grade: How do they relate to students' stress regulation? *Attachment & Human Development, 14*, 249–263. doi:10.1080/14616734.2012.673277

Anderson, K. J., & Minke, K. M. (2007). Parent involvement in education: Toward an understanding of parents' decision making. *Journal of Educational Research, 100*, 311–323. doi:10.3200/JOER.100.5.311-323

Ang, R. (2005). Development and validation of the Teacher–Student Relationship Inventory using exploratory and confirmatory factor analysis. *Journal of Experimental Education, 74*, 55–73. doi:10.3200/JEXE.74.1.55-74

Anguiano, R. P. V. (2004). Families and schools: The effect of parental involvement on high school completion. *Journal of Family Issues, 25*, 61–85. doi:10.1177/0192513X03256805

Bandura, A. (1997). *Self-efficacy: The exercise of control*. New York, NY: W. H. Freeman.

Bandura, A., Caprara, G. V., Barbaranelli, C., Gerbino, M., & Pastorelli, C. (2003). Role of affective self-regulatory efficacy in diverse spheres of psychosocial functioning. *Child Development, 74*, 769–782. doi:10.1111/1467-8624.00567

Brophy, J. E. (2010). *Motivating students to learn* (3rd ed.). New York, NY: Routledge.

Christenson, S. L. (2004). The family–school partnership: An opportunity to promote the learning competence of all students. *School Psychology Review, 33*, 83–104. doi:10.1521/scpq.18.4.454.26995

Christenson, S. L., & Thurlow, M. L. (2004). Keeping kids in school: Efficacy of Check & Connect for dropout prevention. *NASP Communiqué, 32*, 37–40.

Deci, E. L., & Ryan, R. M. (2008). Facilitating optimal motivation and psychological well-being across life's domains. *Canadian Psychology, 49*, 14–23. doi:10.1037/0708-5591.49.1.14

Deci, E. L., & Ryan, R. M. (2012). Motivation, personality, and development within embedded social contexts: An overview of self-determination theory. In R. M. Ryan (Ed.), *Oxford handbook of human motivation* (pp. 85–107). Oxford, UK: Oxford University Press. doi:10.1093/oxfordhb/9780195399820.001.0001

Doll, B., with Brehm, K. (2010). *Resilient playgrounds*. New York, NY: Routledge.

Doll, B., Brehm K., & Zucker, S. (2014). *Resilient classrooms* (2nd ed.). New York, NY: Guilford.

Doll, B., Haack, M. K., Kosse, S., Osterloh, M., Siemers, E., & Pray, B. (2005). The dilemma of pragmatics: Why schools don't use quality team consultation practices. *Journal of Educational and Psychological Consultation, 16*, 127–155. doi:10.1207/s1532768xjepc1603_1

Doll, B., Kurien, S., LeClair, C., Spies, R., Champion, A., & Osborn, A. (2009). The ClassMaps Survey: A framework for promoting positive classroom environments. In R. Gilman, E. S. Huebner, & M. J. Furlong (Eds.), *Handbook of positive psychology in the schools* (pp. 213–227). New York, NY: Routledge.

Doll, B., LeClair, C., & Kurien, S. (2009). Effective classrooms: Classroom learning environments that foster school success. In T. Gutkin & C. Reynolds (Eds.), *The handbook of school psychology* (pp. 791–807). Hoboken, NJ: Wiley.

Doll, B., & Spies, R. A. (2007, March). *The CMS*. A paper presented at the Annual Convention of the National Association of School Psychologists, New York.

Doll, B., Spies, R., & Champion, A. (2012). Contributions of ecological school mental health services to students' academic success. *Journal of Educational and Psychological Consultation, 22*, 44–61. doi:10.1080/10474412.2011.649642

Doll, B., Spies, R., Champion, A., Guerrero, C., Dooley, K., & Turner, A. (2010). The ClassMaps Survey: A measure of middle school science students' perceptions of classroom characteristics. *Journal of Psychoeducational Assessment, 28*, 338–348. doi:10.1177/0734282910366839

Doll, B., Spies, R., LeClair, C., Kurien, S., & Foley, B. (2010). Student perceptions of classroom learning environments: Development of the ClassMaps survey. *School Psychology Review, 39*, 203–218. doi:10.1177/0734282910366839

Downer, J., Rimm-Kaufman, S., & Pianta, R. (2007). How do classroom conditions and children's risk for school problems contribute to children's behavioral engagement in learning? *School Psychology Review, 36*, 413–432.

Epstein, J. L., Sanders, M. G., Simon, B. S., Salinas, K. C., Jansorn, N. R., & Van Voorhis, F. L. (2002). *School, community, and community partnerships: Your handbook for action* (2nd ed.). Thousand Oaks, CA: Corwin.

Epstein, J. L., & Sheldon, S. B. (2002). Present and accounted for: Improving student attendance through family and community involvement. *Journal of Educational Research, 95*, 308–318. doi:10.1080/00220670209596604

Epstein, J. L., & Van Voorhis, F. L. (2001). More than minutes: Teachers' roles in designing homework. *Educational Psychologist, 36*, 181–193. doi:10.1207/S15326985EP3603_4

Fan, X. (2001). Parental involvement and students' academic achievement: A growth modeling analysis. *Journal of Experimental Education, 70*, 27–61. doi:10.1080/00220970109599497

García Cöll, C., Lamberty, G., Jenkins, R., MCadoo, H. P., Crnic, K., Waskik, B. H., & Vasquez Garcia, H. (1996). An integrative model for the study of developmental competencies in minority children. *Child Development, 67*, 1891–1914. doi:10.2307/1131600

Hamre, B., & Pianta, R. (2005). Can instructional and emotional support in the first-grade classroom make a difference for children at risk for school failure? *Child Development, 76*, 949–967. doi:10.1111/j.1467-8624.2005.00889.x

Hawkins, J. D., Smith, B. H., Hill, K. G., Kosterman, R. F. C., Catalano, F. C., & Abbott, R. D. (2003). Understanding and preventing crime and violence: Findings from the Seattle Social Development Project. In T. P. Thornberry & M. D. Krohn (Eds.), *Taking stock of delinquency: An overview of findings from contemporary longitudinal studies* (pp. 255–312). New York, NY: Kluwer Academic/Plenum Press. doi:10.1007/0-306-47945-1_8

Hill, N. E., Castellino, D. R., Lansford, J. E., Nowlin, P., Dodge, K. A., Bates, J. E., & Pettit, G. S. (2004). Parent academic involvement as related to school behavior, achievement, and aspirations: Demographic variations across adolescence. *Child Development, 75*, 1491–1509. doi:10.1111/j.1467-8624.2004.00753.x

Hong, S., & Ho, H. (2005). Direct and indirect longitudinal effects of parental involvement on student achievement: Second-order latent growth modeling across ethnic groups. *Journal of Educational Psychology, 97*, 32–42. doi:10.1037/0022-0663.97.1.32

Ingram, M., Wolfe, R. B., & Lieberman, J. M. (2007). The role of parents in high-achieving schools serving low-income, at-risk populations. *Education and Urban Society, 39*, 479–497. doi:10.1177/0013124507302120

Kolvin, I., Miller, F. J., & Fleeting, M. (1988). Social and parenting factors affecting criminal-offence rates: Findings from the Newcastle Thousand Family Study (1947–1980). *British Journal of Psychiatry, 152*, 80–90. doi:10.1192/bjp.152.1.80

Linan-Thompson, S., & Vaughn, S. (2010). Evidence-based reading instruction: Developing and implementing reading programs at the core, supplemental, and intervention levels. In G. Peacock, R. Ervin, E. Daly, & K. Merrell (Eds.), *Practical handbook of school psychology. Effective practices for the 21st century* (pp. 274–287). New York, NY: Guilford.

Masten, A. S. (2001). Ordinary magic: Resilience processes in development. *American Psychologist, 56*, 227–238. doi:10.1037/0003-066X.56.3.227

Masten, A. S., & Powell, J. L. (2003). A resilience framework for research, policy, and practice. In S. S. Luthar (Ed.), *Resilience and vulnerability: Adaptation in the context of childhood adversities* (pp. 1–25). New York, NY: Cambridge University Press. doi:10.1017/CBO9780511615788.003

Menesses, K. F., & Gresham, F. M. (2009). Relative efficacy of reciprocal and nonreciprocal peer tutoring for students at risk for academic failure. *School Psychology Quarterly, 24*, 266–275. doi:10.1037/a0018174

Merritt, E. G., Wanless, S. B., Rimm-Kaufman, S. E., Cameron, C., & Peugh, J. L. (2012). The contributions of teachers' emotional support to children's social behaviors and self-regulatory skills in first grade. *School Psychology Review, 41*, 141–159.

Mitchem, K. J., Young, K. R., West, R. P., & Benyo, J. (2001). CWPASM: A Classwide Peer-Assisted Self-Management Program for general education classrooms. *Education and Treatment of Children, 24*, 111–141. doi:10.1177/074193250102200202

Murphy, P. S. (2002). *The effect of classroom meetings on the reduction of recess problems: A single case design.* Unpublished doctoral dissertation, University of Denver, Denver, CO.

Murray, C., & Murray, K. (2004). Child level correlates of teacher–student relationships: An examination of demographic characteristics, academic orientations, and behavioral orientations. *Psychology in the Schools, 41*, 751–762. doi:10.1002/pits.20015

Niemiec, C. P., & Ryan, R. M. (2009). Autonomy, competence, and relatedness in the classroom: Applying self-determination theory to educational practice. *Theory and Research in Education, 7*, 133–144. doi:10.1177/1477878509104318

Pajares, F. (2006). Self-efficacy during childhood and adolescence. In F. Pajares & T. C. Urdan (Eds.), *Self-efficacy beliefs of adolescents* (pp. 339–367). Greenwich, CT: Information Age.

Pajares, F., & Schunk, D. H. (2002). Self and self-belief in psychology and education: A historical perspective. In J. Aronson (Ed.), *Improving academic achievement: Impact of psychological factors on education* (pp. 3–21). San Diego, CA: Academic Press. doi:10.1016/B978-012064455-1/50004-X

Pastorelli, C., Caprara, G.V., Barbaranelli, C., Rola, J., Rozsa, S., & Bandura, A. (2001). The structure of children's perceived self-efficacy: A cross-national study. *European Journal of Psychological Assessment, 17*, 87–97. doi:10.1027//1015-5759.17.2.87

Paul, K. (2005). *SchoolMaps: A reliability and validity study for a secondary education school climate instrument* (Unpublished doctoral dissertation). University of Nebraska-Lincoln, Lincoln, NE.

Pellegrini, A. D., & Bartini, M. (2001). Dominance in early adolescent boys: Affiliative and aggressive dimensions and possible functions. *Merrill-Palmer Quarterly, 47*, 142–163. doi:10.1353/mpq.2001.0004

Pianta, R.C. (1999). *Enhancing relationships between children and teachers.* Washington, DC: American Psychological Association. doi:10.1037/10314-005

Pianta, R., Howes, C., Burchinal, M., Bryant, D., Clifford, R., Early, D., & Barbarin, O. (2005). Features of pre-kindergarten programs, classrooms, and teachers: Do they predict observed classroom quality and child–teacher interactions? *Journal of Applied Developmental Science, 9*, 144–159. doi:10.1207/s1532480xads0903_2

Reeve, J., & Halusic, M. (2009). How K–12 teachers can put self-determination theory principles into practice. *Theory and Research in Education, 7*, 145–154. doi:10.1177/14778785091-04319

Rudasill, K.M., & Rimm-Kaufman, S.E. (2009). Teacher–child relationship quality: The roles of child temperament and teacher–child interactions. *Early Childhood Research Quarterly, 24*, 107–120. doi:10.1016/j.ecresq.2008.12.003

Rutter, M., Cox, A., Tupling, C., Berger, M., & Yule, W. (1975). Attainment and adjustment in two geographic areas: I. The prevalence of psychiatric disorder. *British Journal of Psychiatry, 126*, 493–509. doi:10.1192/bjp.126.6.493

Rutter, M., & Maughan, B. (2002). School effectiveness findings, 1979–2002. *Journal of School Psychology, 40*, 451–475. doi:10.1016/S0022-4405(02)00124-3

Sameroff, A.J., Seifer, R., Baldwin, A., & Baldwin, C. (1993). Stability of intelligence from preschool to adolescence: The influence of social and family risk factors. *Child Development, 64*, 80–97. doi:10.1111/j.1467-8624.1993.tb02896.x

Schraw, G., Kauffman, D.R., & Lehman, S. (2002). Self-regulated learning theory. In L. Nadel (Ed.), *The encyclopedia of cognitive science* (pp. 1063–1073). London, UK: Nature Publishing Group.

Schunk, D.H., & Pajares, F. (2005). Competence perceptions and academic functioning. In A.J. Elliot & C.S. Dweck (Eds.), *Handbook of competence and motivation* (pp. 85–104). New York, NY: Guilford.

Song, S.Y., & Stoiber, K. (2008). Children exposed to violence at school: An evidence-based intervention agenda for the "real" bullying problem. *Special Issue on Children Exposed to Violence, Journal of Emotional Abuse, 8*, 235–253. doi:10.1080/10926790801986205

U.S. Department of Health and Human Services. (1999). *Mental health: A report of the Surgeon General.* Rockville, MD: U.S. Department of Health and Human Services, Substance Abuse and Mental Health Services Administration, Center for Mental Health Services, National Institutes of Health, National Institute of Mental Health.

Varjas, K., Nastasi, B.K., Bernstein Moore, R., & Jayasena, A. (2005). Using ethnographic methods for development of culture-specific interventions. *Journal of School Psychology, 43*, 241–258. doi:10.1016/j.jsp.2005.04.006

Wanless, S.B., McClelland, M.M., Acock, A.C., Ponitz, C.C., Son, S.H., Lan, X., . . . & Li, S. (2011). Measuring behavioral regulation in four societies. *Psychological Assessment, 23*, 364–378. doi:10.1037/a0021768

Wanless, S.B., McClelland, M.M., Tominey, S.L., & Acock, A.C. (2011). The influence of demographic risk factors on children's behavioral regulation in prekindergarten and kindergarten. *Early Education & Development, 22*, 461–488. doi:10.1080/10409289.2011.536132

Wentzel, K.R. (2009). Students' relationships with teachers as motivational contexts. In K.R. Wentzel & A. Wigfield (Eds.), *Handbook of motivation at school* (pp. 301–322). New York, NY: Routledge.

Wentzel, K.R., Barry, C.M., & Caldwell, K.A. (2007). Friendships in middle school: Influences on motivation and school adjustment. *Journal of Educational Psychology, 96*, 195–203. doi:10.1037/0022-0663.96.2.195

Wentzel, K.R., & Watkins, D.E. (2002). Peer relationships and collaborative learning as contexts for academic enablers. *School Psychology Review, 31*, 366–377.

Werner, E.E. (2013). What can we learn about resilience from large-scale longitudinal studies? In S. Goldstein & R.B. Brooks (Eds.), *Handbook of resilience in children* (pp. 87–103). New York, NY: Springer. doi:10.1007/978-1-4614-3661-4_6

Werner, E.E., & Johnson, J.L. (2004). The role of caring adults in the lives of children of alcoholics. *Substance Use and Abuse & Misuse, 39*, 699–720. doi:10.1081/JA-120034012

Werner, E.E., & Smith, R.S. (2001). *Journeys from childhood to midlife: Risk, resilience, and recovery.* Ithaca, NY: Cornell University Press.

Wills, T.A., Pokhrel, P., Morehouse, E., & Fenster, B. (2011). Behavioral and emotional regulation and adolescent substance use problems: A test of moderation effects in a dual-process model. *Psychology of Addictive Behaviors*, 25, 279–292. doi:10.1037/a0022870

CHAPTER SUMMARY: CLASSMAPS

- Schools and classrooms are significant malleable presences in students' lives, and effective classrooms can contribute to students' resilience.
- Resilience-promoting classrooms are those in which strong and caring relationships exist between teachers and students, students and their peers, and the classroom and students' families.
- Also, resilience-promoting classrooms support students' self-regulatory competence including their self-efficacy, academic self-determination, and behavioral self-control.
- Teachers and school mental health professionals can use familiar data-based problem-solving procedures to strengthen the relational and self-regulatory characteristics of classrooms.
- The ClassMaps Survey is a brief and practical measure that uses student ratings aggregated across all students in a classroom to assess the adequacy of a classroom's relational and self-regulatory characteristics. A copy of the ClassMaps Survey is available from the first author upon request.
- Students' perceptions of their classroom data, including their discussions of the data's accuracy and meaning, can contribute to a meaningful understanding of the classroom assessment results.
- Classroom changes that are planned in response to a classroom assessment might include micro changes, or simple changes in classroom routines and practices, or evidence-based interventions that have been manualized and have been shown to be effective in well-controlled studies.
- Classroom plans for change have been implemented with fidelity when 90% of the planned activities have actually occurred and when the plan was implemented for 8 or more classroom days.
- Simple classroom data are used to monitor progress toward the classroom goals for change.
- Current ClassMaps research is streamlining the consultation procedures to make these more practical for use in schools and examining strategies to best prepare teachers to gather and use classroom data to strengthen the resilience-promoting characteristics of their classrooms.

SUGGESTED READINGS: CLASSMAPS

Brophy, J.E. (2010). *Motivating students to learn* (3rd ed.). New York, NY: Routledge.

Brophy's text summarizes three decades of research in classroom motivation in easily understood language and draws out its practical implications for teaching and classroom routines. All of the ClassMaps relational and self-regulatory classroom characteristics are discussed at some point in this very comprehensive book.

Cummings, J., Doll, B., & Chapla, B. (in press). Best practices in population-based mental health services. In A. Thomas & P. Harrison (Eds.), *Best practices in school psychology* (6th ed.). Bethesda, MD: National Association of School Psychologists.

ClassMaps Consultation is an example of a population-based mental health service because it promotes the resilience of all students who are enrolled in a classroom. In this chapter, Cummings and his colleagues provide the rationale for the use of population-based services and explain how population-based services interface with traditional school mental health services.

Doll, B., Brehm, K., & Zucker, S. (2014). *Resilient classrooms: Creating healthy environments for learning* (2nd ed.). New York, NY: Guilford.

This second edition of the *Resilient Classrooms* book provides a detailed 10-chapter description of the Class-Maps Consultation data-based problem-solving procedure. A copy of the ClassMaps Survey and worksheets that guide teachers through the four problem-solving steps are included in an appendix.

Odom, S. L., Hanson, M., Lieber, J., Diamond, K., Palmer, S., Butera, G., & Horn, E. (2010). Prevention, early childhood intervention, and implementation science. In B. Doll, W. Pfohl, & J. Yoon (Eds.), *Handbook of youth prevention science* (pp. 413–432). New York, NY: Routledge.

Manualized interventions that have been shown to be effective well-controlled clinical trials are not always adopted for use in actual practice settings. This chapter by Odom and his colleagues describes the emerging prominence of implementation science for examinations of this research-to-practice gap and of strategies for addressing.

Werner, E. E. (2013). What can we learn about resilience from large-scale longitudinal studies? In S. Goldstein & R. B. Brooks (Eds.), *Handbook of resilience in children* (pp. 87–103). New York, NY: Springer.

Werner reviews six decades of developmental resilience research and then discusses its implications for current practices in community supports for the psychological wellness of children and adolescents.

19

BUILDING RESILIENCE IN SCHOOLS THROUGH SOCIAL AND EMOTIONAL LEARNING

Oanh K. Tran, Department of Educational Psychology, California State University, East Bay, Hayward, California, USA

Barbara A. Gueldner, Steamboat Springs, Colorado, USA

Douglas Smith, Department of Psychology, Southern Oregon University, Ashland, Oregon, USA

INTRODUCTION

In a time in which children and youth are pressured toward academic standards and high-stakes testing while being exposed to a variety of risk factors (e.g., poverty, harsh parenting, single-parent homes), the risk for mental distress increases. Research suggests that an estimated 20% of students display mental health problems (Myers & Holland, 2000); that is, 4 million children in the United States suffer from a diagnosable mental disorder (National Alliance on Mental Illness, 2010). Sadly, 75 to 80% do not receive appropriate services (Greenberg et al., 2003). If mental health needs are left untreated, symptoms and needs intensify, thus requiring more intensive resources—which schools are already lacking. Unfortunately, schools are often unprepared to respond effectively to the increasing mental health needs of students. Without adequate supports, students are vulnerable for other comorbid disorders. Additionally, these youths often engage in multiple high-risk behaviors that impede their ability and potential for school and life success. Although the challenges for today's children and youth may be daunting, schools can play a critical role in building resilient behaviors and skills to enhance healthy coping skills, social and emotional development, school achievement, and long-term health and productivity.

In this chapter, we discuss the concept of resilience, how social and emotional learning can promote resilient behaviors in schools, and research supporting social and emotional learning outcomes and apply *Strong Kids* as an example of a resilience-building program in schools. The chapter emphasizes an ecological perspective in building resilient behaviors through school-based programming for school and life success.

THEORIES AND DEFINITIONS

The Importance of Resilience

Although the concept of resilience has transformed over the years as research reveals its complex nature, resilience is widely accepted to represent humans' capacity to adapt in a positive manner despite exposure to adversity (Masten & Obradovic, 2006). Increasingly in popular culture, individuals are recognized for their resilient qualities, which are perceived not only to help them triumph over difficult circumstances but also to result in a level of accomplishment never before imagined. While such biographies are admittedly inspirational, it is the ordinary and daily expression of resilience that is perhaps more applicable and meaningful for most. Educators are particularly interested in ways in which resilience can be taught to students to maximize the chance that inevitable life stressors and adversities will be navigated and deleterious outcomes minimized.

Research and Development of Resilience

Early experimental and epidemiological research paved the way for what is now thought to be a complex dance among many mechanisms to produce resilience. Singular variables were studied in the mid-20th century, such as environmental deprivation and its negative impact on human and primate development (Bowlby, 1954; Harlow & Woolsey, 1958; Spitz & Wolf, 1946), and risk factors were identified through controlled study. Later, longitudinal studies illuminated that despite chronic and severe exposure to multiple stressors and adversities, many children defied the odds and displayed healthy adjustment and competence in adulthood (Garmezy, Masten, & Tellegen, 1984; Rutter, 1985, 1987; Werner, 1993; Werner & Smith, 1977).

Subsequent research led to identifying within-individual and contextual risk and protective correlates to adjustment as a means of fine-tuning predictions of outcomes and to intervene when known risk factors were present (see Doll & Lyon, 1998). Individual correlates to resilience have included intelligence, social and emotional competence, and self-esteem, while environmental variables such as socioeconomic resources, parenting style, family functioning, and relationships with caregivers, adults, and peers represent common contextual factors (Doll & Lyon, 1998; Masten & Coatsworth, 1998). Most recently, epigenetic research provides another window into this elaborate labyrinth of childhood development and promises fascinating discoveries regarding gene expression and transmission (Hermann et al., 2011). Reducing risk and enhancing protection means taking into account the *transactional* processes among ecological systems (i.e., micro- through macrosystems) that result in a variety of outcomes across the lifespan, which are difficult to predict (Sameroff, 1995). Pianta and Walsh (1998) summarized a (now) 21st-century perspective on the development of resilience when they stated, "Risk and resilience are not a characteristic of a child or a family or a school but are characteristic of a process involving the interactions of systems" (p. 411).

In more recent years, schools have increasingly been considered as naturally occurring systems that can actively mitigate risk factors and enhance protective factors (Doll, Jones, Osborn, Dooley, & Turner, 2011; Doll & Lyon 1998; Zimmerman & Arunkumar, 1994). The prevention science research movement launched preventive intervention initiatives in schools to promote overall health and development (Catalano et al., 2012). Programming can range from altering classroom variables (Doll, Zucker, & Brehm, 2004) to targeting a specific risk factor or problem via specialized curricula (Weissberg, Caplan, & Sivo, 1989) to creating unified partnerships that include schools, families, and communities (Catalano et al., 2012). There is a growing body of evidence supporting an active prevention agenda in schools that aims to affect social, emotional, and academic competence (Catalano et al., 2012; Durlak, Weissberg, Dymnicki, Taylor, & Schellinger, 2011). The field has increasingly moved toward a universal approach, whereby all students have exposure to preventive interventions (Merrell & Gueldner, 2010).

SOCIAL AND EMOTIONAL LEARNING APPROACHES

What Is Social and Emotional Learning (SEL)?

The concept of social and emotional learning (SEL) gained momentum in the mid-1990s when researchers collaborated to promote prevention mental health initiatives for children (Greenberg et al., 2003). SEL includes a broad range of tools and systematic techniques used to promote mental health, teach social, emotional, and life skills, and prevent negative life outcomes through effective curricular programming as an integral part of the school's mission (Ragozzino, Resnik, O'Brien, & Weissberg, 2003; Zins, Bloodworth, Weissberg, Walberg, 2004). Specifically, social and emotional learning principles entail students learning and applying "skills necessary to understand and manage emotions, set and achieve positive goals, feel and show empathy for others, establish and maintain positive relationships, and make responsible decisions" (Collaborative for Academic, Social, and Emotional Learning [CASEL], 2012, p. 6). The concept of wellness is important to mental health promotion, as Lorion (2000) noted that "[it] refers to the psychological capacity to cope with the demands arising across time, circumstance, and setting" (p. 15). . . "and [is] a positive state in and of itself rather than merely serving as an index that dysfunction has been avoided" (p. 17). In other words, there is more to mental health and wellness than preventing negative outcomes. The assumption, as illustrated in the SEL Logic Model (CASEL, 2003), is that when students learn how to be resilient and prosocial, they become more engaged and positively active in their environments—students have healthy coping mechanisms with desirable outcomes and productivity beyond schooling (see Figure 19.1). Rather than simply being able to cope with adversity, students are thus equipped to thrive both within and outside the school environment (Benson & Scales, 2009).

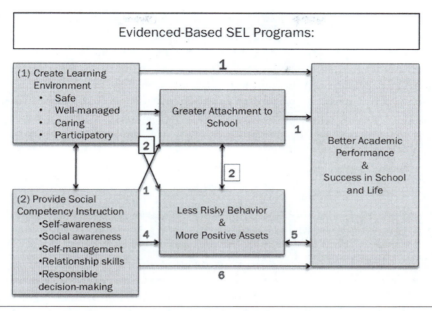

Figure 19.1 Social and emotional learning (SEL) logic model (used with permission of the authors. Evidence-Based SEL Programs. Chicago: Collaborative for Academic, Social, and Emotional Learning [CASEL], 2003).

Promoting SEL and Resilience in Schools

Much like public health initiatives used to promote physical health and development, schools are focusing on building social and emotional competence, as research repeatedly demonstrates the interrelationship among these areas and enhanced academic performance (National Association for the Education of Young Children, 2009; Pellegrino & Hilton, 2012). The goal is to provide students with evidence-based, developmentally and culturally appropriate programming, which utilizes quality instructional techniques so that students may learn, practice, and activate strategies known to mitigate risk and promote healthy development over time (Greenberg et al., 2003). It is highly preferred that SEL efforts be coordinated over time (e.g., prekindergarten through Grade 12) and place (e.g., school, home, and community; Greenberg et al., 2003). This task is undeniably daunting and a work in progress. However, SEL is now viewed as so essential that some state governments (e.g., Illinois and New York) are pressing forward with legislation and policies to ensure that mental health promotion is infused into educational standards (see Merrell & Gueldner, 2010; www.casel.org for more information). The SEL movement has also helped transform education internationally, most notably in parts of Europe, Singapore, Australia, and Israel.

For SEL to be most advantageous, schools must consider a proactive and preventive approach to service delivery (Tran & Merrell, 2010; Weissberg, Caplan, & Harwood, 1991). That is, social and emotional learning should be introduced within a continuum of services using a prevention science model for mental illness (Tran & Merrell, 2010). Such a prevention model suggests school-based services to be implemented at three levels of support. At the universal (primary) level, all students receive resilience training and 80 to 85% of students respond to learning at this level. At the targeted (secondary) level, students receive more intensive or small-group, pullout instruction and 10 to 15% of students respond to learning at this level. And finally at the indicated (tertiary) level, intensive, individualized support is offered and 1 to 5% of students respond at this level. Within a mental health prevention model, the root cause of the problem, the onset or protection from particular disorders, and negative stressors are identified to better understand the student's mental health needs (Tran & Merrell, 2010). Ultimately, educators are better prepared to teach and promote resilient behaviors for positive and healthy outcomes.

Key Studies

Research shows SEL to be an effective approach in school-based prevention and intervention programming to enhance students' academic, social, and emotional development (Durlak et al., 2011; Elias et al., 1997; Weissberg, Walberg, O'Brien, & Kuster, 2003; Zins & Elias, 2006). These studies document the utility of SEL for promoting many of the positive attributes needed for students to deal with life's adversities and expected stressors, resulting in better outcomes with regard to academic performance, antisocial and aggressive behaviors, depressive symptoms, drug use, mental health, problem behaviors, and positive youth development.

The largest meta-analysis study to date examined 213 school-based social and emotional learning programs involving more than 270,000 students in grades kindergarten through high school (Durlak et al., 2011) on multiple outcome factors, unlike previous studies. Study results indicated significantly improved social and emotional skills, attitudes, behaviors, and academic performance. Notably, an 11-percentile increase in academic achievement was universally documented. SEL programming was found to be effective in both school and after-school settings for students with and without social, emotional, or behavioral problems. SEL was applicable to students from racially or ethnically diverse groups, as well as urban, rural, and suburban settings. The findings from this meta-analysis support the benefits of SEL for school-aged children in building resilient behaviors. These results are especially relevant as schools consider and prioritize universal, evidence-based prevention and intervention programming to be a customary part of children's educational experiences.

EDUCATIONAL APPLICATIONS

Examples of SEL Programs

The types of SEL programming that are available range from direct instruction on social and emotional learning skills (e.g., emotion identification and management, empathy for others, problem solving) to a broader focus on such issues as character development, violence prevention, and substance use and abuse. Often it is quite challenging for school districts to choose a program that seems "right" for them. Additionally, there is an increasing expectation to use evidence-based practices in naturalistic settings. In light of these demands and improved research technology whereby programming is more rigorously and systematically evaluated (CASEL, 2012), it is now more likely that the selection of high-quality SEL programs, implemented with a high degree of fidelity, will lead to successful outcomes for students.

There are *many* programs on the commercial market designed to promote mental health and resilience. Examples of programs specifically focused on SEL promotion and instruction in schools include and are not limited to *Caring School Community*, *I Can Problem Solve*, *Promoting Alternative Thinking Strategies*, *Second Step*, *Social Decision Making/Social Problem Solving*, and the *Strong Kids* curriculum. These programs highlight an emphasis on core principles of SEL: understanding self and others, making responsible decisions, setting goals, and building relationships. The Collaborative for Academic, Social, and Emotional Learning (CASEL, 2012) recently published its revised guide to selecting SEL programs called *Effective Social and Emotional Learning Programs: Preschool and Elementary School Edition*, which is useful for schools working through the selection, implementation, and sustainability process. Although CASEL admittedly was quite selective in the programs chosen as having met rigorous standards and inclusion, their guide also lists areas to consider when reviewing potential SEL programs: grade levels covered, number of sessions per year, classroom instructional methods used to deliver program content, how skills can be practiced in other settings, ways in which progress is monitored, and the research conducted that provided evidence of effectiveness.

SEL Challenges, Obstacles, and Considerations

Implementing SEL is not limited to selecting an evidence-based program. Attention must be paid to the groundwork essential prior to adopting a program, fostering supportive relationships between teachers and students, implementation fidelity, providing support and resources, utilizing effective disciplinary practices, capitalizing upon ample opportunities to practice skills and receive feedback, and coordinating instruction through school-to-family/community partnerships (for this discussion, see CASEL, 2012). The 2012 CASEL Guide provides a framework that can help school districts strategically plan for, implement, and sustain SEL to maximize their ability to be successful and to maximize benefits for students.

Specifically, when considering the ecological infrastructure within a school system, it should be noted that a high turnover rate of staff or administrators could impede systems to develop the knowledge base necessary for implementation and sustainability. Those who remain in schools may be disengaged or unmotivated (Elias, Zins, Graczyk, & Weissberg, 2003). In addition, school-based programs are often replaced with new programs without considering current programming or discounting the successful aspects of the current system. Oftentimes, schools may overlook their readiness for change and planning. It is advisable that schools account for these changes and have personnel trained to provide leadership and consultative roles (Elias et al., 2003). Key elements of an ecological model for school implementation of SEL programming include (a) engaging stakeholders in planning and implementing SEL, (b) assessing the need for SEL and available resources, (c) creating a vision and plan, (d) developing standards and measurement options to monitor progress, (e) providing professional development, (f) insuring all adults develop individual competence in SEL that they can use and model, and (g) having a shared vision. For program effectiveness and sustainability, schools must consider these challenges and issues (Elias et al., 2003; Stoiber, 2011). To do otherwise risks perpetual frustration, ineffectiveness, and wasted time and resources.

The Strong Kids Curriculum

To provide a more detailed account of a specific SEL program, we use the *Strong Kids* curriculum as an example. *Strong Kids* was developed under the direction of the late Kenneth W. Merrell and with his colleagues through the Oregon Resiliency Project at the University of Oregon. The curriculum was designed to promote resilience through social and emotional skills for students deemed to be at risk and as a universal mental health promotion program within an SEL framework. That is, *Strong Kids* can be used within a continuum of support services (primary, secondary, and tertiary) in mental health prevention (Tran & Merrell, 2010). In the development of *Strong Kids*, Merrell and his team were keenly aware that while there were effective SEL programs available, they wanted a program that had considerable reach, could be adopted relatively easily, and could be implemented with a high degree of fidelity without the need for the substantial federal funding often required of very effective programming (for a detailed description of program theory and development, see Merrell, 2010; Merrell & Buchanan, 2006). Content was shaped not only by the five principles of SEL but also by the work of Cowen (1994) and his proposed five "pathways to wellness," which highlight the importance of acquiring early attachments, age-appropriate competencies, exposure to settings (such as schools) that can promote wellness outcomes, an internal locus of control, and strategies to cope effectively with stress.

Strong Start contains 10 lessons and *Strong Kids* and *Strong Teens* contain 12 lessons, all focused on delivering content via explicit and instructional design properties known to be highly effective in classrooms (e.g., brisk pacing, immediate feedback, structured review, and high student engagement; Coyne, Kame'enui, & Carnine, 2006). Given the evidence for providing SEL instruction over multiple years, the curriculum includes five grade-specific versions: *Strong Start for Pre–K* (Merrell, Whitcomb, & Parisi, 2009), *Strong Start for Grades K–2* (Merrell, Parisi, & Whitcomb, 2007), *Strong Kids for Grades 3–5*, *Strong Kids for Grades 6–8*, and *Strong Teens for Grades 9–12* (Merrell, Carrizales, Feuerborn, Gueldner, & Tran, 2007a, 2007b, 2007c, respectively). The series was designed to be brief, easy to use, able to be naturally embedded into the course of everyday academic courses, and target skills known to build competence against internalizing problems in particular, such as symptoms and behaviors associated with depression and anxiety. Lessons highlight concepts in emotion identification and management, behavioral activation, managing stress and relaxation strategies, identifying cognitive errors and reframing techniques, social problem solving, and goal setting. Students are active participants in role playing and engagement in regular discussions and real-world applications. A list of lessons is provided in Table 19.1.

A typical lesson starts with a review of the previous lesson's main ideas and introducing new content. Professionals implementing the lesson (typically a teacher or school-based mental health professional) have the option of reading from a sample script to deliver the content. Classroom activities and facilitator-led discussions allow for opportunities to illustrate the content in ways that are relevant to students and to

Table 19.1 Lessons in the Strong Kids Curriculum by Specific Manual

	Strong Start Pre–K Strong Start K–2	Strong Kids Grades 3–5 Strong Kids Grades 6–8 Strong Teens Grades 9–12
Lesson 1	The Feelings Exercise Group	About Strong Kids: Emotional Strength Training
Lesson 2	Understanding Your Feelings 1	Understanding Your Feelings 1
Lesson 3	Understanding Your Feelings 2	Understanding Your Feelings 2
Lesson 4	When You're Angry	Dealing With Anger
Lesson 5	When You're Happy	Understanding Other People's Feelings
Lesson 6	When You're Worried	Clear Thinking 1
Lesson 7	Understanding Other People's Feelings	Clear Thinking 2
Lesson 8	Being a Good Friend	The Power of Positive Thinking
Lesson 9	Solving People Problems	Solving People Problems
Lesson 10	Finishing Up!	Letting Go of Stress
Lesson 11		Behavior Change: Setting Goals and Staying Active
Lesson 12		Finishing Up!

practice new skills with peers. For example, in Lesson Six: Clear Thinking 1, after the lesson content is presented, students participate in an activity in which they identify emotions using an "intensity thermometer" to rate their emotions and discuss how emotions and thoughts can exist simultaneously. Students then learn about six common thinking errors and practice, with sample scenarios, the thinking error that might be in play and contribute to the student's subsequent distress. The lesson concludes with a general review of content, with ideas for classrooms to infuse these concepts over time and contexts. Booster sessions are available to refresh the concepts taught throughout the curriculum.

Assessing changes that may be due to students having participated in the curriculum is important to monitoring progress. A variety of measures have been used over the years to assess constructs such as strengths and assets, social and emotional knowledge, depression and anxiety symptoms, and global social functioning. In addition, measuring fidelity of implementation, or the extent to which the program was delivered in the manner it was designed and intended, is valuable in determining whether student changes could be attributed to the program. If program delivery strays from the original design, it is much more difficult to assign student progress or regression to the curriculum.

Application of Strong Kids *in Classrooms and Schools*

The *Strong Kids* curriculum series has been widely adopted and used in general education classrooms, special education classrooms, and residential facilities with students ranging from kindergarten age through adolescence. It has been used with normally functioning students as well as those exhibiting a range of behavioral and emotional challenges. The evidence to support its effectiveness, feasibility, and acceptability is quite promising. Merrell (2010) provides the most comprehensive discussion of findings.

The strongest and most striking evidence of effectiveness is shown by students' increased knowledge of social and emotional learning concepts when students' knowledge was measured before participating in the curriculum and comparing this to a measurement taken afterward, as well as comparing these posttest results with a control comparison group that did not receive the curriculum. Effect sizes most often were measured near or just above 1.0, demonstrating large and meaningful change (Castro-Olivo & Merrell, 2012; Feuerborn, 2004; Gueldner & Merrell, 2011; Harlacher & Merrell, 2010; Isava, 2006; Marchant, Brown, Caldarella, & Young, 2010a; Merrell, Juskelis, Tran, & Buchanan, 2008; Nakayama, 2008; Tran, 2007). In terms of problem symptom reduction, several studies reported statistically significant reductions in internalizing symptoms (Caldarella, Christensen, Kramer, & Kronmiller, 2009; Faust, 2006; Feuerborn, 2004; Isava, 2006; Marchant, Brown, Caldarella, & Young; 2010b; Merrell et al., 2008; Tran, 2007), while other studies did not measure a reduction in symptoms (Gueldner & Merrell, 2011; Nakayama, 2008). Measurement issues might have contributed to these differences, as some studies included at-risk students, while others took place in general education classrooms where it might be presumed that most students did not manifest internalizing problems, thereby making the goal of symptom reduction less likely. Subsequent research has aimed to assess program effectiveness not only by examining problematic symptom reduction but also by assessing increases in social-emotional competence (Caldarella et al., 2009; Harlacher & Merrell, 2010; Kramer, Caldarella, Christensen, & Shatzer, 2010; Nakayama, 2008). Treatment fidelity is also essential to realizing successful outcomes from an evidence-based program, and multiple studies indicated high levels can be attained with little support from outside resources and funding (Caldarella et al., 2009; Feuerborn, 2004; Gueldner & Merrell, 2011; Harlacher & Merrell, 2010; Isava, 2006; Kramer et al., 2010; Levitt, 2009; Marchant et al., 2010a; Nakayama, 2008; Tran, 2007; Whitcomb & Merrell, 2012). These same studies also demonstrated acceptance or social validity among users, with anecdotal comments considered in revising and improving upon the series. Cultural adaptations of the curriculum for Latino/a immigrant adolescents are also promising, including a useful extension of the *Strong Teens* version of the curriculum (Castro-Olivo & Merrell, 2012).

In sum, research to date is encouraging that the *Strong Kids* curriculum series might be an effective programming option for users who wish to implement SEL using a structured and tested format that utilizes the benefits of instructional principles. *Strong Kids* is affordable, very feasible and acceptable to consumers; it can be implemented with a high degree of fidelity, conveys basic social and emotional concepts that are essential to promoting wellness and resilience, and can protect and even mitigate internalizing problems that are at risk of worsening. Studies to date using *Strong Kids* have provided valuable feedback and recommendations for users to incorporate in the successful implementation of the program (see Table 19.2).

Table 19.2 Strong Kids Planning and Implementation Recommendations Checklist

Considerations for Planning	Considerations for Implementation
☐ Build relationships with staff.	☐ Keep lessons short as needed (depending on student population).
☐ Identify at least two staff as leaders.	
☐ Use data for buy-in from teachers and administrators.	☐ Change the language and examples of the lessons to increase student interest and engagement (i.e., make the material meaningful for the group).
☐ Talk to teachers and administrative staff about the value of social and emotional learning.	☐ Build relationship with the class as a whole and individually, if possible.
☐ Logistics: Identify who will implement the lessons; how much will the teacher do? Teachers prefer another person to teach the lessons. When to implement? How much time will be utilized for the lessons?	☐ Change the structure of lessons, allowing for recreational activities. Either lesson and then a game or desired activity or game, lesson, game (if working with higher-needs population).
☐ Schedule fidelity checks in advance (other teachers, university researchers, if available).	☐ Review the rules and encourage students to do their best or to do better than the last session, if applicable.
☐ Schedule in-service trainings.	☐ Review lesson concepts throughout the week.
☐ Provide support throughout process.	☐ Provide a graduation-like activity at the end of implementation.
☐ Have an outline of the schedule.	
☐ Screen students for the program.	☐ Implement a behavior-management plan.
☐ Ask teachers about student strengths and behavioral needs.	☐ Ask another staff member (guidance counselor, social worker, intern, teacher, paraprofessional) to cofacilitate or help out during lessons.
☐ Principal briefly talks with students and teachers prior to starting the program.	
☐ Be aware of system issues (e.g., absenteeism, teacher turnover rate).	
☐ Get parents involved when possible.	

SUMMARY

The academic, social, and overall life stressors currently faced by school-aged children may place some at increased risk for mental health problems. Academic participation and performance may be affected by social and emotional problems and overall development and productivity may be hindered. Without a proactive focus on building resilience, along with appropriate identification, support, and intervention, many students may be at risk for depression, anxiety, school dropout, substance use and abuse, social difficulties, conduct problems, and aggression/violence. Schools are ideal venues in which to implement prevention and intervention programming because young children and adolescents spend a significant portion of their day in an educational setting. Ideally, schools can be a place where students succeed academically and socially, reach their full potential as active learners, and develop resilience and healthy emotional skills for lifelong success. These goals are possibilities for *all* students when a preventative, resilience-skill–based, continuum model of support is applied in schools.

Social and emotional learning (SEL) is a proactive framework for addressing students' mental health needs in schools. Research on SEL programming has demonstrated promising results for teaching students essential social and emotional skills to deal with life's adversities while promoting resilient behaviors. SEL has been found to be beneficial for both teachers and students when integrated into classrooms through effective instructional methods. According to CASEL (2012), SEL includes five primary areas of skill development: self-management (managing emotions and behaviors to achieve goals), self-awareness (recognizing emotions and values as well as strengths and weaknesses), responsible decision making (making ethical and constructive choices about personal and social behavior), relationship skills (forming positive relationships, working in teams, dealing effectively with conflict), and social awareness (showing understanding and awareness of others). Current research suggests that SEL can have positive effects on mental health, achievement performance, and social and emotional development. Importantly, SEL supports an interactive environment for positive learning in ethnically and culturally diverse student populations.

Many evidence-based SEL programs exist; this chapter focused on *Strong Kids* as an example for promoting SEL in schools to build resilience. The *Strong Kids* programs are innovative, socially valid, easy to use and low cost and produce positive outcomes in students. *Strong Kids* is adaptable for a continuum of support for various levels of need. The programs are semiscripted, with sample activities and worksheets for students to build knowledge and skills. The program's foundation is based on basic principles of effective teaching, that is, a teach–model–practice approach to emotional development skills. Many empirical studies support the utility and efficaciousness of *Strong Kids* in various settings and populations (e.g., in classrooms, pullout, small groups, after-school programs, residential programs, and multicultural groups). For SEL or *Strong Kids* to be most valuable and effective, schools should strongly consider developing a shared vision for social and emotional learning across grades levels and schools within a district, provide staff development, develop a plan of action, support staff and students throughout implementation, measure and review fidelity of implementation, identify key players within teams, identify supports and resources available in school, and select measurement evaluations to determine outcomes.

Now is the time for schools to build resilience in our students. We can no longer wait until mental health interventions at a tertiary level are a "must." Schools can universally adopt prevention and intervention programming that can alter the trajectory of negative outcomes. Social and emotional learning is a proven model for fostering resilience and increasing the likelihood that *all* students have the knowledge and skills necessary to cope with life's challenges.

REFERENCES

Benson, P. L., & Scales, P. C. (2009). The definition and preliminary measurement of thriving in adolescence. *Journal of Positive Psychology, 4*, 85–104. doi:10.1080/17439760802399240

Bowlby, J. (1954). The effect of separation from the mother in early life. *Irish Journal of Medical Science, 29,* 121–126.

Caldarella, P., Christensen, L., Kramer, T. J., & Kronmiller, K. (2009). The effects of Strong Start on second-grade students' emotional and social competence. *Early Childhood Education Journal, 37,* 51–56. doi:10.1007/s10643-009-0321-4

Castro-Olivo S., & Merrell, K. (2012). Validating cultural adaptations of a school-based social-emotional learning program for use with Latino immigrant adolescents. *Advances in School Mental Health Promotion, 5,* 78–92. doi:10.1080/1754730X.2012.689193

Catalano, R.F., Fagan, A.A., Gavin, L.E., Greenberg, M.T., Irwin, C.E., Ross, D.A., & Shek, D.T. (2012). World-wide application of prevention science in adolescent health. *Lancet, 379*(9826), 1653–1664. doi:10.1016/S0140-6736(12)60238-4

Collaborative for Academic, Social, and Emotional Learning (CASEL). (2003). *SEL and academic performance research brief.* Retrieved from http://casel.org/publications/sel-and-academic-performance-research-brief/

Collaborative for Academic, Social, and Emotional Learning (CASEL). (2012). *Effective social and emotional learning programs: Preschool and elementary school edition.* Retrieved from http://casel.org/wp-content/uploads/CASEL_Guide.pdf

Cowen, E.L. (1994). The enhancement of psychological wellness: Challenges and opportunities. *American Journal of Community Psychology, 22,* 149–179.

Coyne, M.D., Kame'enui, E.J., & Carnine, D.W. (2006). *Effective teaching strategies that accommodate diverse learners* (3rd ed.). Upper Saddle River, NJ: Pearson/Prentice-Hall.

Doll, B., Jones, K., Osborn, A., Dooley, D., & Turner, A. (2011). The promise and the caution of resilience models for schools. *Psychology in the Schools, 48,* 652–659. doi:10.1002/pits.20588

Doll, B., & Lyon, M.A. (1998). Implications for the delivery of educational and mental health services in schools. *School Psychology Review, 27,* 348–363.

Doll, B., Zucker, S., & Brehm, K. (2004). *Resilient classrooms: Creating healthy environments for learning.* New York, NY: Guilford.

Durlak, J.A., Weissberg, R.P., Dymnicki, A.B., Taylor, R.D., & Schellinger, K.B. (2011). The impact of enhancing students' social and emotional learning: A meta-analysis of school-based universal interventions. *Child Development, 82,* 405–432. doi:10.1111/j.1467-8624.2010.01564.x

Elias, M.J., Zins, J.E., Graczyk, P.Q., & Weissberg, R.P. (2003). Implementation, sustainability, and scaling up of social-emotional and academic innovations in public schools. *School Psychology Review, 32,* 303–319.

Elias, M.J., Zins, J.E., Weissberg, R.P., Frey, K.S., Greenberg, M.T., Haynes, N.M., . . . Shriver, T.P. (1997). *Promoting social and emotional learning: Guidelines for educators.* Alexandria, VA: Association for Supervision and Curriculum Development.

Faust, J.J. (2006). *Preventing depression and anxiety: An evaluation of a social-emotional curriculum.* Unpublished education specialist project, University of Wisconsin, Whitewater.

Feuerborn, L.L. (2004). *Promoting emotional resiliency through classroom instruction: The effects of a classroom-based prevention program.* Unpublished doctoral dissertation, University of Oregon, Eugene.

Garmezy, N., Masten, A.S., & Tellegen, A. (1984). The study of stress and competence in children: A building block for developmental psychopathology. *Child Development 55,* 97–111. http://www.jstor.org/stable/1129837

Greenberg, M.T., Weissberg, R.P., O'Brien, M.T., Zins, J.E., Fredericks, L., Resnik, H., & Elias, M.J. (2003). Enhancing school-based prevention and youth development through coordinated social, emotional, and academic learning. *American Psychologist, 58,* 466–474. Retrieved from http://casel.org/wp-content/uploads/2011/04/AmericanPsychologist2003.pdf

Gueldner, B.A., & Merrell, K.W. (2011). The effectiveness of a social and emotional learning program with middle school students in the general education setting and the effect of consultation on student outcomes. *Journal of Educational and Psychological Consultation, 21,* 1–27. doi:10.1080/10474412.2010.522876

Harlacher, J.E., & Merrell, K.W. (2010). Evaluating the follow-up effect of Strong Kids on social and emotional outcomes. *Journal of Applied School Psychology, 26,* 212–229. doi:10.1080/15377903.2010.495903

Harlow, H.F., & Woolsey, C.N. (Eds.). (1958). *Biological and biochemical bases of behavior.* Madison, WI: University of Wisconsin Press.

Hermann, H., Steward, D.E., Diaz-Granados, N., Berger, E.L., Jackson, B., & Yuen, T. (2011). What is resilience? *Canadian Psychiatry, 56,* 258–265.

Isava, D.M. (2006). *An investigation of the impact of a social-emotional learning curriculum on problem symptoms and knowledge gains among adolescents in a residential treatment center.* Unpublished doctoral dissertation, University of Oregon, Eugene.

Kramer, T.J., Caldarella, P., Christensen, L., & Shatzer, R.H. (2010). Social-emotional learning in kindergarten classrooms: Evaluation of the Strong Start curriculum. *Early Childhood Education Journal, 37,* 303–398. doi:10.1007/s10643-009-0354-8

Levitt, V.H. (2009). *Promoting social-emotional competency through quality teaching practices: The impact of consultation on a multidimensional treatment integrity model of the Strong Kids program.* Unpublished doctoral dissertation, University of Oregon, Eugene.

Lorion, R. P. (2000). Theoretical and evaluation issues in the promotion of wellness and the protection of "well enough." In D. Cicchetti, J. Rappaport, I. Snadler, & R. P. Weissberg (Eds.), *The promotion of wellness in children and adolescents* (pp. 1–27). Washington, DC: CWLA.

Marchant, M., Brown, M., Caldarella, P., & Young, E. (2010a). Effects of Strong Kids curriculum on students with internalizing behaviors: A pilot study. *Journal of Evidence-Based Practices for Schools, 11*, 124–143.

Marchant, M., Brown, M., Caldarella, P., & Young, E. (2010b). Internalizing behavior problems: Strong Kids curriculum responds to the hidden challenge. *Journal of Evidence-Based Practices for Schools, 11*, 144–148.

Masten, A. A., & Coatsworth, J. D. (1998). The development of competence in favorable and unfavorable environments: Lessons from research on successful children. *American Psychologist, 53*, 205–220. Retrieved from http://positiveemotions.gr/library_files/M/Masten_Coatsworth_Development_1998.pdf

Masten, A. S., & Obradovic, J. (2006). Competence and resilience in development. *Annals of the New York Academy of Sciences, 1094*, 13–27. doi:10.1196/annals.1376.003

Merrell, K. W. (2010). Linking prevention science and social-emotional learning: The Oregon Resiliency Project. *Psychology in the Schools, 47*, 55–70. doi:10.1002/pits.20451

Merrell, K. W., & Buchanan, R. (2006). Intervention selection in school-based practice: Using public health models to enhance systems capacity of schools. *School Psychology Review, 35*, 167–180. Retrieved from http://www.nasponline.org/publications/spr/index.aspx?vol=35&issue=2

Merrell, K. W., Carrizales, D., Feuerborn, L., Gueldner, B. A., & Tran, O. K. (2007a). *Strong Kids—Grades 3–5: A social and emotional learning curriculum.* Baltimore, MD: Paul H. Brookes.

Merrell, K. W., Carrizales, D., Feuerborn, L., Gueldner, B. A., & Tran, O. K. (2007b). *Strong Kids—Grades 6–8: A social and emotional learning curriculum.* Baltimore, MD: Paul H. Brookes.

Merrell, K. W., Carrizales, D., Feuerborn, L., Gueldner, B. A., & Tran, O. K. (2007c). *Strong Teens—Grades 9–12: A social and emotional learning curriculum.* Baltimore, MD: Paul H. Brookes.

Merrell, K. W., & Gueldner, B. A. (2010). *Social and emotional learning in the classroom: Promoting mental health and academic success.* New York, NY: Guilford.

Merrell, K. W., Juskelis, M. P., Tran, O. K., & Buchanan, R. (2008). Social and emotional learning in the classroom: Impact of Strong Kids and Strong Teens on students' social-emotional knowledge and symptoms. *Journal of Applied School Psychology, 24*, 209–224. doi:10.1080/15377900802089981

Merrell, K. W., Parisi, D., & Whitcomb, S. (2007). *Strong Start—Grades K–2: A social and emotional learning curriculum.* Baltimore, MD: Paul H. Brookes.

Merrell, K. W., Whitcomb, S., & Parisi, D. (2009). *Strong Start—Pre–K: A social and emotional learning curriculum.* Baltimore, MD: Paul H. Brookes.

Myers, C. L., & Holland, K. L. (2000). Classroom behavioral interventions: Do teachers consider the function of the behavior? *Psychology in the Schools, 37*, 271–280. doi:10.1002/(SICI)1520-6807(200005)37:3

Nakayama, N. J. (2008). *An investigation of the impact of the Strong Kids curriculum on social-emotional knowledge and symptoms of elementary-aged students in a self-contained special education setting.* Unpublished doctoral dissertation, University of Oregon, Eugene.

National Alliance on Mental Illness (NAMI). (2010). *Facts on children's mental health in America.* Retrieved from http://www.nami.org/Template.cfm?Section=federal_and_state_policy_legislation&template=/Content Management/ContentDisplay.cfm&ContentID=43804

National Association for the Education of Young Children. (2009). *Developmentally appropriate practice in early childhood programs serving children from birth through age 8.* Washington, DC: NAEYC.

Pellegrino J. W., & Hilton, M. L. (Eds.). (2012). *Education for life and work: Developing transferable knowledge and skills in the 21st century.* Washington, DC: National Academies Press, Board on Testing and Assessment and Board on Science Education, Division of Behavioral and Social Sciences and Education.

Pianta, R. C., & Walsh, D. J. (1998). Applying the construct of resilience in schools: Cautions from a developmental systems perspective. *School Psychology Review, 27*, 407–417.

Ragozzino, K., Resnik, H., O'Brien, M. U., & Weissberg, R. (2003). Promoting academic achievement through social and emotional learning. *Educational Horizons, 81*, 169–171.

Rutter, M. (1985). Resilience in the face of adversity: Protective factors and resistance to psychiatric disorder. *British Journal of Psychiatry, 147*, 598–611.

Rutter, M. (1987). Psychosocial resilience and protective mechanisms. *American Journal of Orthopsychiatry, 57*, 316–331. doi:10.1111/j.1939-0025.1987.tb03541.x

Sameroff, A.J. (1995). General systems theories and developmental psychopathology. In D. Cicchetti & O. Cohen (Eds.), *Developmental psychopathology: Theory and methods* (pp. 659–695). New York, NY: Wiley.

Spitz, R.A., & Wolf, K.M. (1946). Anaclitic depression: An inquiry into the genesis of psychiatric conditions in early childhood. *Psychoanalytic Study of the Child, 2,* 313–342.

Stoiber, K.C. (2011). Translating knowledge of social-emotional learning and evidence-based practice into responsive school innovations. *Journal of Educational and Psychological Consultation, 21,* 46–55. doi:10.1080/10474 412.2011.549039

Tran, O.K. (2007). *Promoting social and emotional learning in schools: An investigation of massed versus distributed practice schedules and social validity of the Strong Kids curriculum in late-elementary-aged students.* Unpublished doctoral dissertation, University of Oregon, Eugene.

Tran, O.K., & Merrell, K.W. (2010). Promoting student resilience: Strong Kids social and emotional learning curriculum (pp. 275–287). In B.J. Doll (Ed.), *Handbook of youth prevention science.* Mahwah, NJ: Erlbaum.

Weissberg, R.P., Caplan, M., & Harwood, R.L. (1991). Promoting competent young people in competence-enhancing environments: A systems-based perspective on primary prevention. *Journal of Consulting and Clinical Psychology, 59,* 830–841. doi:10.1037/0022-006X.59.6.830

Weissberg, R.P., Caplan, M., & Sivo, P.J. (1989). A new conceptual framework for establishing school-based social competence promotion programs. In L.A. Bond & B.E. Compas (Eds.), *Primary prevention and promotion in schools* (pp. 255–296). Newbury Park, CA: Sage.

Weissberg, R.P., Walberg, H.J., O'Brien, M.U., & Kuster, C.B. (Eds.). (2003). *Long-term trends in the well-being of children and youth.* Washington, DC: Child Welfare League of America Press.

Werner, E.E. (1993). Risk, resilience, and recovery: Perspective from the Kauai Longitudinal Study. *Development and Psychopathology, 5,* 503–515. doi.org/10.1017/s095457940000612x

Werner, E.E., & Smith, R.S. (1977). *Kauai's children come of age.* Honolulu, HI: University of Hawaii Press.

Whitcomb, S.A., & Merrell, K.W. (2012). Understanding implementation and effectiveness of *Strong Start K–2* on social-emotional learning. *Early Childhood Education Journal, 40,* 63–71. doi:10.1007/s10643-011-0490-9

Zimmerman, M.A., & Arunkumar, R. (1994). Resiliency research: Implications for schools and policy. *Social Policy Report, 8,* 1–8.

Zins, J.E., Bloodworth, M.R., Weissberg, R.P., & Walberg, H.J. (2004). The scientific base linking social and emotional learning to school success. *Building academic success on social and emotional learning: What does the research say?* New York, NY: Teachers College.

Zins, J.E., & Elias, M. (2006). Social and emotional learning: Promoting the development of all students. *Journal of Educational and Psychological Consultation, 17,* 233–255. doi:10.1080/10474410701413152

CHAPTER SUMMARY: RESILIENCE

- Social and emotional learning is a proactive, prevention, and intervention approach that is strength based.
- *Strong Kids* curricula are semiscripted, easy-to-use programs in schools and classrooms with applicable skills for social and emotional development.
- Resilience can be taught so students can maximize and build on current strengths.
- Social and emotional learning is effective and correlated with positive outcomes, such as academic, behavioral, and social success.
- *Strong Kids* effectiveness studies support its use in schools and in various settings and populations to address mental health needs.
- Select an evidence-based SEL program that fits the needs of the school—consider conducting a school needs assessment.
- The Collaborative, Academic, Social and Emotional Learning (CASEL) website, http://casel.org/, provides valuable resources and research on SEL.
- SEL and *Strong Kids* are ideal in a three-tiered continuum support model (primary, secondary, tertiary) of mental health prevention and intervention.

SUGGESTED READINGS: RESILIENCE

Durlak, J.A., Weisberg, R.P., Dymnicki, A.B., Taylor, R.D., & Schellinger, K.B. (2011). The impact of enhancing students' social and emotional learning: A meta-analysis of school-based universal interventions. *Child Development, 82*, 405–432.

This article presents the largest meta-analysis study to date, examining more than 200 school-based social and emotional learning (SEL) programs in grades kindergarten through high school. The study found that students who participated in SEL had significant improvements in social and emotional skills, attitudes, behavior, and academic performance. Recommended practices for successful implementation are discussed.

Greenberg, M.T., Weissberg, R.P., O'Brien, M.T., Zins, J.E., Fredericks, L., Resnik, H., & Elias, M.J. (2003). Enhancing school-based prevention and youth development through coordinated social, emotional, and academic learning. *American Psychologist, 58*, 466–474. Retrieved from http://casel.org/wp-content/uploads/2011/04/AmericanPsychologist2003.pdf

This article discusses the challenges for school systems providing appropriate and adequate mental health supports for students. The authors present analyses of exemplary, comprehensive SEL-based prevention programming that targets positive youth development, mental health, drug use, antisocial behavior, and academic performance. The authors conclude with the need for evidence-based practices, accountability, and coordinated and comprehensive approaches to ensure that no child is left behind and that all students can reach their full potential.

Merrell, K.W., Carrizales, D., Feuerborn, L., Gueldner, B.A., & Tran, O.K. (2007a). *Strong Kids—Grades 3–5: A social and emotional learning curriculum.* Baltimore, MD: Paul H. Brookes.

As part of the *Strong Kids* social emotional learning curriculum that spans prekindergarten through Grade 12, *Strong Kids—Grades 3–5*, is a 12-lesson program that teaches topics essential to building resilience in school-age children. Lessons include understanding feelings, dealing with anger, principles of cognitive therapy that aid "clear thinking," applying learned optimism to life situations, stress-reduction strategies, and goal setting. Language and practice activities are developmentally appropriate for students in third through fifth grade, lessons are scripted for ease of use, and tips are provided for planning and implementation.

Merrell, K.W., & Gueldner, B.A. (2010). *Social and emotional learning in the classroom: Promoting mental health and academic success.* New York, NY: Guilford.

This book is an excellent resource to anyone considering or currently implementing social and emotional learning (SEL) in schools. It reviews the principles of SEL and the relations among social and emotional health and academic achievement. Selected programs are reviewed to give readers ideas for programming that might meet their goals. Step-by-step and practical strategies are provided to aid SEL delivery and make adaptations for specific populations, such as multicultural and special education settings. Those interested in assessing outcomes will appreciate the chapter on assessment and evaluation to monitor fidelity of implementation and student outcomes. The authors are mindful of the "big picture" as they discuss challenges to and solutions for working within large organizations, promoting and sustaining change, and gaining the support of essential stakeholders.

Tran, O.K., & Merrell, K.W. (2010). Promoting student resilience: Strong Kids social and emotional learning curriculum (pp. 275–287). In B.J. Doll (Ed.), *Handbook of youth prevention science.* Mahwah, NJ: Erlbaum.

The authors present a discussion of a prevention and early intervention framework for children's social and emotional problems in school. Students' increasing need for mental health services is emphasized with consideration for social and emotional learning as a universal model to support students' mental health needs. Strong Kids social and emotional learning curriculum is discussed as a schoolwide and classwide intervention tool to promote student resilience.

20

SCHOOL CLIMATE
Definition, Measurement, and Application

Keith J. Zullig, Department of Social and Behavioral Sciences, School of Public Health, West Virginia University, Morgantown, West Virginia, USA

Molly R. Matthews-Ewald, Behavioral Medicine, Pennington Biomedical Research Center, Baton Rouge, Louisiana, USA

INTRODUCTION AND THEORY BASE

As Cohen, McCabe, Michelli, and Pickeral (2009) note, there is no one universal definition of school climate. However, these researchers refer to school climate as ". . . the quality and character of school life" (p. 182) because of its inclusiveness of the school physical environment, as well as the variety of social factors that can facilitate learning and achievement. A broad definition of a positive school climate encompasses the norms, values, relationships, and organizational structures that facilitate appropriate youth learning and development. Further, a positive school climate should provide feelings of safety socially, emotionally, and physically. We believe Cohen and colleagues' (2009) definition of school climate is the most comprehensive and will hold this definition throughout the duration of this chapter.

Historical Perspective

School climate first appeared in the literature more than 100 years ago, mentioned by Perry (1908), who examined school climate as it relates to student learning. The study of school climate as we know it, however, accelerated in the 1950s led by Halpin and Croft (1963), who sought to understand the relation between school climate and child development and learning. Anderson (1982) noted that studies of school climate emerged from organizational climate research and school effects research, from which research measures and methods were borrowed. In the 1990s, Haynes, Emmons, and Ben-Avie (1997) posited that failure in inner-city students was not a function of cognitive ability and argued that researchers should examine the social and physical context (i.e., school climate) in which students are asked to learn. This, of course, stands at odds with modern U.S. educational policy, which dictates primarily measurement of reading and mathematical skill.

DIMENSIONS OF SCHOOL CLIMATE

Although broad consensus of a definition of school climate is difficult, what is clear is that researchers have moved away from an exclusive physical environment focus, such as mold and indoor air quality (Anderson, 1982), to viewing school climate as a measure of subjective school experience (Cohen, 2006). As such, researchers nearly universally agree that school climate is composed of four overarching aspects of school life, with subcategories for each. These four aspects include (a) safety, (b) relationships, (c) instruction and learning, and (d) environmental-structural.

Safety

Safety within a school encompasses both physical and socioemotional safety and has been shown to promote or complicate a student's motivation to learn (Goodenow & Grady, 1993) and ultimately academic achievement (Sherblom, Marshall, & Sherblom, 2006). Physical safety includes having a clear plan for addressing violence and everyone in the school feeling physically safe, whereas socioemotional safety refers to teaching conflict resolution and the manner with which aggressive behavior, such as bullying, is viewed and subsequently addressed. Fortunately, most students are not exposed to physical violence (Mayer & Furlong, 2010), but this is counterbalanced by high exposure to bullying behavior in schools. Bullying behavior is a public health concern, and studies have implicated aggressive behavior as problematic for both adolescent victims and perpetrators (Boulton, Trueman, & Murray, 2008; Hawker & Boulton, 2000; Roland, 2002), where psychological well-being and prosocial skills are adversely impacted.

Relationships

Relationships within a school are also important to school climate and generally include respect for diversity, school community and collaboration, morale, and how connected students feel to their school. Of all the various relationships that involve students, none are more important to academic success than teacher–student relationships (Doll et al., 2009). This is likely because students find emotional security with their teachers and internalize teachers' values as their own (Pianta, 1999), spurring student engagement and appropriate behavior. For example, research has shown that teachers' academic or emotional support and monitoring (Thuen & Bru, 2000), approval and disapproval (Nafpaktitis, Mayer, & Butterworth, 1985), and reinforcement delivery (Austin & Soeda, 2008) play key roles in promoting students' abilities to follow direction and concentrate on individual or group work tasks.

Similar to teacher–student relationships, peer relationships spur participation and interest in learning, enhance psychological well-being, and bolster academic success (Wentzel & Caldwell, 1997; Wentzel & Watkins, 2002). School connectedness is also strongly related to student academic and health outcomes (McNeely, Nonemaker, & Blum, 2002) and risk behaviors (Catalano, Haggerty, Oesterle, Fleming, & Hawkins, 2004; Karcher, 2002; Kirby, 2001). The United States Centers for Disease Control and Prevention (2009) defines *school connectedness* as "the belief by students that adults and peers in the school care about their learning as well as about them as individuals." Greater school attachment, which ultimately improves teacher–student and peer relationships, is fostered by a positive school climate (Blum, McNeely, & Rinehart, 2002; Goodenow & Grady, 1993).

Instruction and Learning

Quality and creativity of instruction; social, emotional, and ethical learning; professional development; and leadership all comprise effective instruction and learning. Western educators have sometimes undervalued creative students because they associate creative students with impulsive and disruptive behavior and nonconformity (Dawson, 1997; Scott, 1999), and, therefore, fail to see the importance and significance of fostering creative classroom environments. However, when creativity is defined and structured through the lens of "novel and personally meaningful interpretations of experiences, actions, and events" as suggested by Beghetto and Kaufman (2007), research shows that supportive teacher feedback cultivates student confidence in the translation of creativity to real-world innovations (Beghetto, 2006). The encouragement of active, creative, and collaborative learning through real-world projects then promotes civic education and encourages student interaction (Ghaith, 2003; Wentzel & Watkins, 2002). Furthermore, evidence-based social and emotional learning programs have resulted in notable gains in achievement tests, as well as increasing an academic emphasis within students (Battistich, Schaps, & Wilson, 2004; Bradshaw, Koth, Thornton, & Leaf, 2009; Elias & Haynes, 2008). Finally, research demonstrates that when teachers feel supported by their principals and peers, they are more committed to their profession (Singh & Billingsley, 1998). This implies that school leadership influences school climate by setting the tone and affording teachers the ability to foster cooperative learning environments that have been shown to be essential to problem solving (Meloth & Deering, 1992). Research has also shown that students in a supportive, collaborative school environment will succeed academically (Haynes et al., 1997).

Environmental-Structural

The fourth component of school climate is the institutional environment, or the environmental-structural dimension. This dimension includes aspects of the physical environment such as cleanliness of the school and appropriate space and materials conducive to learning. In a mixed-methods study, one of the main contributing factors to students' higher levels of satisfaction with school was the physical school environment (Mok & Flynn, 1997). Students reported that cleanliness and spacious rooms were necessary for a comfortable physical school environment. However, other environmental aspects that may be important could be classroom layout, curricular offerings, activity schedules (Conroy & Fox, 1994), and even smaller school size (McNeely et al., 2002). While downsizing schools is not feasible in many circumstances, the creation of smaller learning communities as an alternative has also been shown to enhance student learning environments (Cotton, 2001).

RELATIONS WITH STUDENT BEHAVIOR

School climate is related with students' behavior. Stewart (2003) examined social bonds and student misbehavior as they related to school climate using multilevel analysis at both the individual student level and the school level. Utilizing data from the National Center for Educational Statistics (NCES), he found that school misbehavior was significantly and inversely related to most of the examined school-level school climate factors, including school attachment, school commitment, belief in school rules, positive peers, and parental school involvement. These five factors, in addition to student GPA, family income, gender, ethnicity, school size, and school location, accounted for almost 17% of the variance in school misbehavior. Wilson (2004) examined school climate and school connectedness as they relate to in-school behavior among middle and high school students and found, similarly to Stewart (2003), that as school climate improved, relational aggression decreased. In addition, highly connected students in both positive and negative school climates were more likely to experience decreased levels of victimization, suggesting that school connectedness has a protective effect independent of school climate.

Brooks, Magnusson, Spencer, and Morgan (2012) examined predictors of adolescents' engagement in risky behaviors such as substance use and sexual activity. Specifically, these researchers examined a variety of factors that were found to be negatively related to engagement in risky health behaviors, including (a) sense of belonging with family, school, and neighborhood; (b) personal autonomy with family, people, and school; (c) social networking with neighborhood; and (d) social support from father, mother; and peers. Of the three groups of factors (family, school, community/neighborhood), school-related and community-related factors were more influential in predicting risky health behaviors than the family-related factors (Brooks et al., 2012). Thus, increases in school connectedness appear to be inversely related to risky health behaviors.

Loukas, Suzuki, and Horton (2006) examined school connectedness as a mediator of school climate. These researchers examined perceived school climate in children aged 10 to 14 years via four components: (a) cohesion, (b) friction, (c) student competition, and (d) total class satisfaction. Three additional variables, including (a) school connectedness, (b) conduct problems, and (c) depressive symptoms were also examined. These researchers found that their model of school connectedness mediated the relation between conduct problems and depressive symptoms and perceived cohesion, friction, and total class satisfaction. This research highlighted the need to assess school connectedness as a component of perceived school climate among young adolescents.

Kidger, Araya, Donovan, and Gunnell (2012) conducted a literature review to understand the school environment's (including school climate) impact on the emotional health of adolescents. Articles were included in their review if they (a) were controlled trial or cohort designs, (b) included children aged 11 to 18 years, (c) used emotional health as the outcome, and (d) had the school environment as the exposure or an intervention. Among the 39 articles that met these criteria, Kidger and colleagues (2012) concluded that perceived positive school climate is related to a decrease in suicidal behavior; however, several studies found that as positive school climate increased, there were small but significant increases in depression, especially in smaller schools when compared to larger schools. The authors speculated that this surprising finding was perhaps because greater social facilitation led to greater student expressiveness of emotional distress.

MEASUREMENT APPROACHES AND ISSUES

The measurement of school climate has also varied widely over time. Often instruments may have limited or no evidence of validity and reliability. Emphasis is placed on student self-report instrumentation here because adult and adolescent reports of the same phenomena have been shown to be moderately correlated at best (Ellert, Ravens-Sieberer, Erhart, & Kurth, 2011; Sundblad, Saartok, & Engström, 2006; Waters, Stewart-Brown, & Fitzpatrick, 2002). Frieberg (1998) examined the use of three different measurement tools to assess school climate: (a) ambient noise checklists, (b) student concerns surveys, and (c) entrance and exit interviews. The *Cafeteria Ambient Noise Checklist* developed by Frieberg identifies various sources of noises within a school's cafeteria, including sounds arising from adults speaking to children across the room and the clanking of pots and pans in the kitchen. The goal of identifying unnecessary noises within the cafeteria stems from the relation between stress and noise levels. Thus, reducing cafeteria noise was thought to reduce stress levels among children, thereby increasing children's well-being and school climate.

Frieberg (1998) suggested that student concerns about the transition from elementary school to middle school and from middle school to high school may elicit unnecessary stress for youth, thereby impacting school climate. To measure student concerns, a 30-item survey using a four-point response scale was developed. Questions specifically examined individual students' greatest concerns when moving from their current school to the next level of schooling. In turn, teachers and administrators were able to make data-driven decisions based on these surveys to address some of the greatest concerns for their students, which led to students gaining a sense of belonging within their school. However, psychometric properties were not reported.

Stewart (2003) assessed school climate with both student-level and school-level variables. Student-level variables included school attachment, school involvement, school commitment, belief in school rules, association with positive peers, and parental school involvement. Student demographic variables and students' grade point averages (GPAs) were included as controls. School-level variables included school social problems, school cohesion, and a series of school demographic variables. Discussed in more detail in this chapter (*Relations with Student Behaviors* section), results from this study utilizing data from the National Center for Educational Statistics (NCES) indicated that school misbehavior was significantly and inversely related to many school climate factors, including school attachment, school commitment, belief in school rules, positive peers, and parental school involvement. As these were data had already been collected through the National Education Longitudinal Study of 1988 (NELS:88), sponsored by the National

Center for Education Statistics (NCES), Stewart (2003) did not assess the validity and reliability of the measures. The NELS:88 gathered information to characterize schools as a whole, including measures on students, school administrators, parents, and teachers, but few of the questions were pertinent to school climate.

The NCES (McLaughlin, Cohen, & Lee, 1997) reported on the validity of the school climate measures from baseline to the first and second follow-up time points and found adequate convergent validity ($r = .30$ to $.44$). Other analyses of validity by Kaufman, Rasinski, Lee, and West (1991) compared student responses with their parent responses and found moderate to high correlations with demographic variables (rs ranged from .41 to .85) but low to moderate correlations with selected school variables (rs ranged from .08 to .51). Examining reliability, it was found that the NELS:88 scale for school problems and teacher quality both had adequate reliability (.92 and .76, respectively). Although the NELS:88 demonstrated characteristics of reliability and validity, assessing school climate in this way may not be feasible (for these measures, see http://nces.ed.gov/surveys/nels88/questionnaires.asp). Brooks and colleagues (2012) utilized a series of questions to assess adolescents' sense of belonging among their family, school, and neighborhood, autonomy in relation to family, peers, and school, neighborhood social networking, and social support via communication with mother, father, teachers, and peers. The questions regarding communication with mother and father were derived from adolescents' reports of the degree of difficulty they had talking with their parents; however, psychometric properties of these questions were not reported.

The use of psychometrically sound measures has been particularly lacking in school climate research. For instance, a survey conducted by the National Center for Emotional Education with 40 principals, superintendents, state department of education, and national-level leaders revealed that among those who used school climate measures, more than one third had used homemade instruments that were not psychometrically supported (MMS Education, 2006). This in itself is problematic, but more problematic is the lack of available measurement tools that (a) are low burden and practical to administer, (b) offer psychometric support, (c) are designed to be used for universal assessment, and (d) are free or inexpensive to use.

Given these challenges, Zullig, Koopman, Patton, and Ubbes (2010) initiated a study to (a) review the most widely historically cited self-report (i.e., subjective) of school climate measures and (b) develop a low-burden, psychometrically sound measure that is free to the public and designed for universal assessment. Their review included the *California School Climate and Safety Survey* (CSCSS; Furlong, Morrison, & Boles, 1991; Furlong et al., 2005), the U.S. Department of Education's (1988) *National Longitudinal Study Student Questionnaire* (NELS), the National Association of Secondary School Principals' *Comprehensive Assessment of School Environments* (CASE, 1987), the San Diego County Office of Education's (1984) *Effective Schools Student Survey* (ESSS), and the *School Development Program* (SDP; Haynes, Emmons, & Ben-Avie, 2001). Of these measures, only the SDP, CASE, and CSCSS reported any psychometric data. The SDP reported internal consistency estimates but no validity data. The SDP had an average internal consistency of .79, with alpha coefficients ranging from .59 to .96. The CASE reported only internal consistency estimates with alpha coefficients ranging from .67 to .92 for each of the subscales. The CASE also reported that factor analytic validity testing had been performed, but those results are not available to the user. Notably, only the CSCSS was published in a peer-reviewed journal (Furlong et al., 2005).

This is not to suggest that other potentially useful school climate measures are not available. For example, the *Comprehensive School Climate Inventory* (CSCI) developed by the National School Climate Center has undergone several independent evaluations and demonstrated preliminary reliability and validity estimates from one pilot test of approximately 27,000 students. However, it is not offered free of charge and still has not been published in a peer-reviewed journal. The CSCSS also has a newer 10-item version of its scale (called the CSCSS-PM; Rebelez & Furlong, 2013) that may be suitable for some by use of three factors: Unsafe Student Behaviors (fights on campus, stealing things, bullying, weapons at school); Climate (respect from teachers, teachers are fair, treated fairly); and Unsafe Campus Conditions (crime on campus, crime in community, school ruined by gang activity). However, we note some of these behaviors are captured by national surveys like the Centers for Disease Control and Prevention's Youth Risk Behavior Survey.

For these reasons, the publically available and free-to-use School Climate Measure (SCM) developed by Zullig and colleagues (2010) was included in the PhenXToolkit (see Hamilton et al., 2011, for a review) as its measure of school climate. The PhenX-Toolkit was funded by the National Human Genome Research Institute to compose a core set of high-quality, well-established, low-burden measures intended for use in large-scale genomic studies. The SCM contains 39 items spread among eight scales measuring dimensions of school: Positive Student–Teacher Relationships (9 items), School Connectedness (6 items), Academic Support (6 items), Order and Discipline (7 items), School Physical Environment (4 items), School Social Environment (2 items), Perceived Exclusion/Privilege (3 items), and Academic Satisfaction (2 items). All items use the same Likert response option format: (*strongly disagree* = 1 . . . *strongly agree* = 5). The full instrument can be viewed free of charge on the companion website for this *Handbook* chapter.

The SCM psychometric properties are presented in two studies. The first study was conducted with 2,049 largely White students from Ohio (Zullig et al., 2010) whereas the second, conducted in partnership with the Arizona Department of Education, utilized a sample of 21,082 students of which 49% were non–White Hispanic (Zullig et al., 2014).

The first study by Zullig and colleagues (2010) randomly split the sample into exploratory and confirmatory samples and subjected the two halves to factor analytic and structural equation modeling techniques. Structural equation modeling revealed that the fully correlated model was found to fit the data well in the exploratory sample: $\chi^2 = 1166.78$ ($df = 674$, $p < .0001$), CFI = .95, TLI = .94, RMSEA = .04, goodness-of-fit index (GFI) = .91. The fully correlated factor structure was then fit to the confirmatory sample. The model also fit the data well: $\chi^2 = 1245.37$ ($df = 674$, $p < .0001$), CFI = .95, TLI = .95, RMSEA = .04. Overall, the GFI was .91. Exploratory and confirmatory factor analysis results confirmed an eight-factor solution (loadings with absolute values > .40). Item factor loadings ranged from .42 to .87. Coefficient alphas ranged from .65 to .91.

The second study (Zullig et al., 2014) was a replication and extension study. In this study, confirmatory factor analysis was performed and factor loadings ranged from .45 to .92. Structural equation models also fit the data well: $\chi^2 = 14325$ ($df = 293$, $p < .001$),

CFI = .95, TLI = .95, RMSEA = .05. The goodness-of-fit index was .94. Coefficient alphas ranged from .82 to .93. In addition, large effect sizes were demonstrated between the SCM constructs and U.S. Centers for Disease Control and Prevention Youth Risk Behavior school safety items and self-reported grade point average (GPA), most notably between academic support, weapon carrying at school ($d = .77$), being threatened or injured by a weapon at school ($d = .61$), feeling safe at school ($d = .66$), and GPA ($f = .40$). These analyses revealed that greater perceptions of a positive school climate were significantly associated with greater (and practically important) perceptions of school safety.

EDUCATIONAL APPLICATIONS

All school climate research demonstrates the importance of the connection between students and their school. This is not a surprising finding given that research suggests the classroom teacher is the most important figure in shaping student learning, followed closely by the school principal (Wallace Foundation, 2006). Positive student–teacher relationships are highly correlated with other climate factors, including perceptions of academic outcomes and school connectedness. As suggested by previous research, these and other climatic factors affect student motivation to learn (Eccles et al., 1993). School leaders set the tone and the expectations for behavior, which then affect faculty and staff and subsequently classroom learners.

Gottfredson, Gottfredson, Payne, and Gottfredson (2005) examined school climate in relation to teacher victimization, student victimization, and student misbehavior among a group of secondary students and teachers across the United States. School climate was measured via six different scales encompassing fairness of rules, clarity of rules, organizational focus, morale, planning, and administrative leadership. It was found that 46% of the variance in student delinquency was explained by school climate factors.

Schools serve as places for social development (Whitney, Rivers, Smith, & Sharp, 1994), and acts of violent and aggressive behavior unfortunately often occur at school (Whitney & Smith, 1993). Although less is known about their academic impact, noteworthy among successful school-based bullying interventions (Black & Jackson, 2007; Black & Washington, 2008) are the modification of the school climate, including but not limited to increased teacher involvement and supervision and clear order and disciplinary policies to improve the nature of relationships among teachers, students, and their school. This, in turn, may influence and improve perceptions of academic support, and emergent school climate research suggests that academic performance may also be significantly associated with improvements in academic support.

Although educational policy for the past decade (in the United States at least) has been driven primarily by the measures of reading and mathematical skill as mandated by No Child Left Behind (NCLB), school climate can affect student social, behavioral, and learning outcomes and that by addressing organizational processes and social relationships, positive behavioral change can occur (Flay, 2000; Moon et al., 1999; Patton et al., 2006). For instance, Hoy and Hannum (1997) found the most important school climate variables influencing student achievement were a serious and orderly learning environment (Academic Emphasis), teachers displaying a commitment to their students (Teacher Affiliation), and an adequate supply and material support for teaching

(Resource Support), even after controlling for socioeconomic circumstances. Moreover, a recent systematic review of interventions targeting school climate factors also suggested that school relationships and teacher support can positively impact student emotional health (Kidger et al., 2012). As such, many U.S. states have policies that directly or indirectly address school climate. To search individual state policies, we recommend the U.S. National School Climate Center's useful database (http://www.schoolclimate.org/climate/database.php).

Whole-School Versus Targeted Approaches

There is some debate about the relative value of universal, schoolwide approaches versus interventions geared toward specific classrooms or students. Schools are considered microcosms of the broader society and culture, and because schools are the only true setting in which nearly all children participate and function as environments for social development, they provide natural settings in which to study a range of adolescent behaviors. On one side, there are successful examples of schoolwide approaches such as the Positive Action program (Beets et al., 2009; Snyder et al., 2010), which has shown effectiveness to reduce substance use, including tobacco (Flay, 2009), but also violent and aggressive behavior, sexual activity, absenteeism, and suspensions while concurrently improving reading and math standardized test scores. Based on roughly 140 lessons taught by teachers over the course of an academic year, Positive Action operates on the principle that one feels good about oneself when taking positive action (e.g., eating a balanced diet, sleeping regularly, reading for fun, doing homework) and poorly about oneself when taking negative action.

Providing students a safe learning environment must be a top priority for schools because students who do not feel curious, potentially owing to safety concerns at school (being bullied or threatened), cannot learn as effectively. However, three meta-analyses have provided conflicting evidence on schoolwide bullying interventions. For example, Ttofi and Farrington (2011) suggest overall positive outcomes with average decreases in bullying and victimization ranging from 20 to 23% and 17 to 20%, respectively, while another suggested largely nonsignificant findings on self-reported victimization and bullying outcomes (Smith, Schneider, Smith, & Ananiadou, 2004). A third meta-analysis suggested modest improvements in student social competence, self-esteem, peer acceptance, and teacher knowledge of bullying prevention, efficacy of intervention skills, and responses to bullying (Merrell, Gueldner, Ross, & Isava, 2008). A fourth systematic review suggested teacher support and school connectedness could improve student emotional health (Kidger et al., 2012).

A common criticism of schoolwide approaches is that they are difficult to implement, and this viewpoint is supported by the relative dearth of quality experimental studies. Positive Action requires teachers of every grade to focus on the same topic at age-appropriate levels to reinforce concepts throughout school, yet the evidence of schoolwide bullying prevention and safety interventions is mixed at best. These findings can be explained by at least the lack of well-designed intervention studies. For instance, the Smith and colleagues (2004) review included only 14 studies that met their inclusionary criteria, 16 for Merrell and colleagues (2008), and only 5 for Kidger and colleagues

(2012). Thus, there is a clear need for additional research and well-designed experimental studies before conclusions can be made about the impact of schoolwide efforts.

Conversely, the role of the teacher (and indirectly school administration and relationships among students) and how connected students feel to their school seem to be common threads in creating a positive school climate regardless of approach. Positive student–teacher relationships by far explained the greatest amount of variance in the two studies conducted by Zullig and colleagues (2010, 2014), followed by school connectedness. While still important, the other domains explained less variance in the model, but one can look at the evidence and hypothesize that other aspects of school climate and life are driven by teacher and administrator actions that foster positive relationships with students that lead to cooperative learning environments, which drive feelings of connectedness and satisfaction with schooling, and, in turn, foster increased academic performance. It is, therefore, our judgment that creating, monitoring, and maintaining a positive school climate is a universal, schoolwide endeavor that creates the necessary conditions for additional targeted interventions as needed. This judgment is supported by multiple federal Safe and Supportive Schools School Climate Grant activities through which 11 U.S. states are measuring school safety at the building level to create safe learning environments supportive of academic improvement (National Center on Safe Supportive Learning Environments, n.d.).

Targeted interventions can address identified gaps in the school climate. For example, in cases in which deficiencies are identified among teachers and students in classroom management, it is not enough to look at why learning is or is not interesting. Rather, it seems more appropriate to examine the variety of goals or values students bring into the classroom and why they are attractive to them (Hofer, 2007) and to assist students in synthesizing those potentially conflicting goals concurrently (Sansone & Morgan, 1992). If, through monitoring school climate, perceptions of order and discipline appear low, several effective strategies can be implemented. For example, the posting of rules and consistent enforcement of those rules by teachers, staff, and adult monitors can engage students in activities that have the potential not only to reduce incident density of peer victimization (Black & Jackson, 2007; Black & Washington, 2007; Wolak, Mitchell, & Finkelhor, 2007) but also to increase social competence and self-esteem (Merrell et al., 2008), emotional health (Kidger et al., 2012), and academic achievement (Snyder et al., 2010).

CONCLUSION

Student achievement is not only a product of classroom instruction. Rather, instruction is one factor in high achievement, along with other factors such as interpersonal relationships, order within the school, and students' willingness to learn (Hoy & Hannum, 1997). These other nonacademic factors are commonly incorporated within the overarching construct of school climate.

Schools will continue to be held accountable and opt to make informed data-driven decisions for school improvement, despite states being granted waivers from No Child Left Behind (Cable News Network, 2012). Therefore, as schools continue to search for innovative ways to help students increase their academic performance and well-being, a measurement of school climate may assist school personnel to effectively guide systemic efforts to improve school climate, student well-being, and academic performance. Recent research (Zullig, Huebner, & Patton, 2011) suggests school climate is significantly associated with levels of student-reported well-being (i.e., school satisfaction) and that these relations were invariant across demographic variables and academic performance levels. Taken together, measures of school climate and student well-being might be incorporated into systemwide interventions such as the evidence-based schoolwide aforementioned Positive Action program and Positive Behavior Support Program, which support the integration of data-based decision making and measureable outcomes for both teacher and student improvement (Bohanon, et al., 2006; Sugai & Horner, 2006). However, it is suggested here that the creation of a positive school climate by itself will reduce some adolescent negative health behaviors associated with school climatic factors and increase academic achievement at the same time without necessarily employing specific (and potentially expensive) programs.

REFERENCES

Anderson, C. S. (1982). The search for school climate: A review of the research. *Review of Educational Research, 52*, 368–420. doi:10.3102/00346543052003368

Austin, J. L., & Soeda, J. M. (2008). Fixed-time teacher attention to decrease off-task behaviors of typically developing third graders. *Journal of Applied Behavior Analysis, 41*, 279–283. doi:10.1901/jaba.2008.41-279

Battistich, V., Schaps, E., & Wilson, N. (2004). Effects of an elementary school intervention on students' "connectedness" to school and social adjustment during middle school. *Journal of Primary Prevention, 24*, 243–262. doi:10.1023/B:JOPP.0000018048.38517.cd

Beets, M. W., Flay, B. R., Vuchinich, S., Snyder, F. J., Acock, A., Li, K., . . . Durlak, J. (2009). Use of a social and character development program to prevent substance use, violent behaviors, and sexual activity among elementary school students in Hawaii. *American Journal of Public Health, 99*, 1438–1445. doi:10.2105/AJPH.2008.142919

Beghetto, R. A. (2006). Creative self-efficacy: Correlates in middle and secondary students. *Creativity Research Journal, 18*, 447–457. doi:10.1207/s15326934crj1804_4

Beghetto, R. A., & Kaufman, J. C. (2007). Toward broader conception of creativity: A case for "mini-c" creativity. *Psychology of Aesthetics, Creativity, and the Arts, 1*, 13–79. doi:10.1037/1931-3896.1.2.73

Black, S. A., & Jackson, E. (2007). Using bullying incident density to evaluate the Olweus bullying prevention programme. *School Psychology International, 28*, 623–638. doi:10.1177/0143034307085662

Black, S. A., & Washington, E. (2008). Evaluation of the Olweus Bully Prevention Program in nine urban schools: Effective practices and next steps. *Educational Research Services Spectrum, 26*, 7–19. Retrieved from http://www.eric.ed.gov

Blum, R. W., McNeely, C. A., & Rinehart, P. M. (2002). *Improving the odds: The untapped power of schools to improve the health of teens*. Minneapolis, MN: University of Minnesota, Center for Adolescent Health and Development.

Bohanon, H., Penning, P., Carney, K. L., Minnis-Kim, M. J., Anderson-Harriss, S., Moroz, K. B., . . . Piggot, T. D. (2006). Schoolwide application of positive behavior support in an urban high school: A case study. *Journal of Positive Behavior Interventions, 3*, 131–145. doi:10.1177/10983007060080030201

Boulton, M. J., Trueman, M., & Murray, L. (2008). Associations between peer victimization, fear of future victimization and disrupted concentration on class work among junior school pupils. *British Journal of Educational Psychology, 67*, 473–489. doi:10.1348/000709908X320471

Bradshaw, C., Koth, C., Thornton, L., & Leaf, P. (2009). Altering school climate through school-wide positive behavioral interventions and supports: Findings from a group-randomized effectiveness trial. *Prevention Science, 10*, 100–115. doi:10.1007/s11121-008-0114-9

Brooks, F. M., Magnusson, J., Spencer, N., & Morgan, A. (2012). Adolescent multiple risk behaviour: An asset approach to the role of family, school and community. *Journal of Public Health, 34*(S1), i48–i56. doi:10.1093/pubmed/fds001

Cable News Network (CNN). (2012). 10 States freed from some "No Child Left Behind" requirements. Retrieved from http://articles.cnn.com/2012-02-09/politics/politics_states-education_1_waivers-flexibility-standards?_s=PM:POLITICS

Catalano, R. F., Haggerty, K. P., Oesterle, S., Fleming, C. B., & Hawkins, J. D. (2004). The importance of bonding to schools for healthy development: Findings from the social development research group. *Journal of School Health, 74*, 252–262. doi:10.1111/j.1746-1561.2004.tb08281.x

Centers for Disease Control and Prevention. (2009). *School connectedness: Strategies for increasing protective factors among youth.* Retrieved from http://www.cdc.gov/HealthyYouth/AdolescentHealth/pdf/connectedness.pdf

Cohen, J. (2006). Social, emotional, ethical, and academic education: Creating a climate of learning, participation in democracy, and well-being. *Harvard Educational Review, 76*, 201–237. Retrieved from http://her.hepg.org

Cohen, J., McCabe, E. M., Michelli, N. M., & Pickeral, T. (2009). School climate: Research, policy, practice, and teacher education. *Teachers College Record, 111*, 180–213. Retrieved from http://www.tcrecord.org/library/Issue.asp?volyear=2009&number=1&volume=111

Comprehensive Assessment of School Environments (CASE). (1987). *School climate survey.* Reston, VA: National Association of Secondary School Principals.

Conroy, M. A., & Fox, J. J. (1994). Setting events and challenging behaviors in the classroom: Incorporating contextual factors into effective intervention plans. *Preventing School Failure, 38*, 29–34. doi:10.1080/1045988X.1994.9944311

Cotton, K. (2001). *New small learning communities: Findings from recent literature.* Portland, OR: Northwest Regional Education Laboratory.

Dawson, V. L. (1997). In search of the wild bohemian: Challenges in the identification of the creativity gifted. *Roeper Review, 19*, 148–152. doi:10.1080/02783199709553811

Doll, B., Kurien, S., LeClair, C., Spies, R., Champion, A., & Osborn, A. (2009). The ClassMaps Survey: A framework for promoting positive classroom environments. In R. Gilman, E. S. Huebner, & M. J. Furlong (Eds.), *Handbook of positive psychology in schools* (pp. 149–160). New York, NY: Taylor & Francis.

Eccles, J. S., Wigfield, A., Midgley, C., Reuman, D., MacIver, D., & Feldlaufer, H. (1993). Negative effects of traditional middle schools on students' motivation. *Elementary School Journal, 9*, 553–574. Retrieved from http://www.jstor.org

Elias, M. J., & Haynes, N. M. (2008). Social competence, social support, and academic achievement in minority, low-income, urban elementary school children. *School Psychology Quarterly, 23*, 474–495. doi:10.1037/1045-3830.23.4.474

Ellert, U., Ravens-Siberer, U., Erhart, M., & Kurth, B. M. (2011). Determinants of agreement between self-reported and parent-assessed quality of life for children in Germany—results of the German Health Interview and Examination Survey for Children and Adolescents (KiGGS). *Health and Quality of Life Outcomes, 9*, 102. doi:10.1186/1477-7525-9-102

Flay, B. R. (2000). Approaches to substance use prevention utilizing school curriculum plus environmental social change. *Addictive Behaviors, 25*, 861–885. doi:10.1016/S0306-4603(00)00130-1

Flay, B. R. (2009). School-based smoking prevention programs with the promise of long-term effects. *Tobacco Induced Diseases, 26*, 6–23. doi:10.1186/1617-9625-5-6

Frieberg, J. (1998). Measuring school climate: Let me count the ways. *Educational Leadership, 56*, 22–26. Retrieved from http://www.jstor.org

Furlong, M. J., Greif, J. L., Bates, M. P., Whipple, A. D., Jimenez, T. C., & Morrison, R. (2005). Development of the California School Climate and Safety Survey–Short Form. *Psychology in the Schools, 42*, 137–149. doi:10.1002/pits.20053

Furlong, M. J., Morrison, G. M., & Boles, S. (1991, April). *California School Climate and Safety Survey.* Paper presented at the annual meeting of the California Association of School Psychologists, Los Angeles, CA.

Ghaith, G. (2003). The relationship between forms of instruction, achievement and perceptions of classroom climate. *Educational Research, 45*(1), 83–93. doi: 10.1080/0013188032000086145

Goodenow, C., & Grady, K. E. (1993). The relationship of school belonging and friends' values to academic motivation among urban adolescent students. *Journal of Experimental Education, 62*, 60–71. doi:10.1080/00220973.1993.9943831

Gottfredson, G. D., Gottfredson, D. C., Payne, A. A., & Gottfredson, N. C. (2005). School climate predictors of school disorder: Results from a national study of delinquency prevention in schools. *Journal of Research in Crime and Delinquency, 42*, 412–444. doi:10.1177/0022427804271931

Halpin, A. W., & Croft, D. B. (1963). *The organizational climate of schools.* Chicago, IL: Midwest Administration Center of the University of Chicago.

Hamilton, C. L., Strader, L. C., Pratt, J. G., Maiese, D., Hendershot, T., Kwok, R. K., . . . Haines, J. (2011). The PhenX Toolkit: Get the most from your measures. *American Journal of Epidemiology, 174*, 253–260. doi:10.1093/aje/kwr193

Hawker, D.S., & Boulton, M.J. (2000). Twenty years' research on peer victimization and psychosocial maladjustment: A meta-analytic review of cross-sectional studies. *Journal of Child Psychology and Psychiatry, 41*, 441–455. doi:10.1111/1469-7610.00629

Haynes, N.M., Emmons, C., & Ben-Avie, M. (1997). School climate as a factor in student adjustment and achievement. *Journal of Educational and Psychological Consultation, 8*, 321–329. doi:10.1207/s1532768xjepc0803_4

Haynes, N.M., Emmons, C., & Ben-Avie, M. (2001). *The School Development Program: Student, staff, and parent school climate surveys*. New Haven, CT: Yale Child Study Center.

Hofer, M. (2007). Goal conflicts and self-regulation: A new look at pupils' off-task behavior in the classroom. *Educational Research Review, 2*, 28–38. doi:10.1016/j.edurev.2007.02.002

Hoy, W.K., & Hannum, J.W. (1997). Middle school climate: An empirical assessment of organizational health and student achievement. *Educational Administration Quarterly, 33*, 290–311. doi:10.1177/0013161X97033003003

Karcher, M. (2002). The cycle of violence and disconnections among rural middle school students: Teacher disconnectedness as a consequence of violence. *Journal of School Violence, 1*, 33–51. doi:10.1300/J202v01n01_03

Kaufman, P., Rasinski, K.A., Lee, R., & West, J. (1991, September). *Quality of the responses of eighth-grade students in NELS:88* (NCES 91–487). Washington, DC: U.S. Department of Education.

Kidger, J., Araya, R., Donovan, J., & Gunnell, D. (2012). The effect of the school environment on the emotional health of adolescents: A systematic review. *Pediatrics, 129*, 1–25. doi:10.1542/peds.2011-2248

Kirby, D. (2001). Understanding what works and what doesn't in reducing adolescent risk-taking. *Family Planning Perspectives, 33*, 276–281. Retrieved from http://www.jstor.org

Loukas, A., Suzuki, R., & Horton, K.D. (2006). Examining school connectedness as a mediator of school climate effects. *Journal of Research on Adolescents, 16*, 491–502. doi:10.1111/j.1532-7795.2006.00504.x

Mayer, M.J., & Furlong, M.J. (2010). How safe are our schools? *Educational Researcher, 39*, 16–26. doi:10.3102/0013189X09357617

McLaughlin, D.H., Cohen, J., & Lee, R. (1997, March). *NELS:88 survey item evaluation report* (NCES 97–052). Washington, DC: U.S. Department of Education.

McNeely, C.A., Nonemaker, J.M., & Blum, R.W. (2002). Promoting student connectedness to school: Evidence from the National Longitudinal Study of Adolescent Health. *Journal of School Health, 72*, 138–146. doi:10.1111/j.1746-1561.2002.tb06533.x

Meloth, M.S., & Deering, P.D. (1992). Effects of two cooperative conditions on peer-group discussions, reading comprehension, and metacognition. *Contemporary Educational Psychology, 17*, 175–193. doi:10.1016/0361-476X(92)90057-6

Merrell, K.W., Gueldner B.A., Ross, S.W., & Isava, D.M. (2008). How effective are school bullying intervention programs? A meta-analysis of intervention research. *School Psychology Quarterly, 23*, 26–42. doi:10.1037/1045-3830.23.1.26

MMS Education. (2006, April). *Summary of findings: Interviews with educational leaders about school climate and school climate surveys*. Paper prepared for the Center for Social and Emotional Education, New York.

Mok, M., & Flynn, M. (1997). Does school size affect quality of school life? *Issues in Educational Research, 7*, 69–86. Retrieved from http://www.iier.org.au/iier7/mok.html

Moon, A.M., Mullee, M.A., Rogers, L., Thompson, R.L., Speller, V., & Roderick, P. (1999). Helping schools become health promoting environments: An evaluation of the Wessex Health Schools Award. *Health Promotion International, 14*, 111–122. doi:10.1093/heapro/14.2.111

Nafpaktitis, M., Mayer, G.R., & Butterworth, T. (1985). Natural rates of teacher approval and disapproval and their relation to student behavior in intermediate school classrooms. *Journal of Educational Psychology, 3*, 362–367. doi:10.1037/0022-0663.77.3.362

National Center on Safe Supportive Learning Environments (n.d.). *Safe and supportive schools grantees*. Retrieved from http://www.ed.gov/news/press-releases/us-department-education-awards-388-million-safe-and-supportive-school-grants

Patton, G.C., Bond, L., Carlin, J.B., Thomas, L., Butler, H., Glover, S., . . . Bowes, G. (2006). Promoting the social inclusion in schools: A group-randomized trial of effects on student health risk behavior and well-being. *American Journal of Public Health, 96*, 1582–1587. doi:10.2105/AJPH.2004.047399

Perry, A. (1908). *The management of a city school*. New York, NY: Macmillan.

Pianta, R.C. (1999). *Enhancing relationships between children and teachers*. Washington, DC: American Psychological Association.

Rebelez, J., & Furlong, M.J. (2013). Danger, climate, and safety at school: Psychometric support for an abbreviated version of the California School Climate and Safety Survey. *International Journal of School and Educational Psychology, 1*, 154–165. doi:10.1080/21683603.2013.819306

Roland, E. (2002). Aggression, depression, and bullying others. *Aggressive Behavior, 28,* 198–206. doi:10.1002/ab.90022

San Diego County Office of Education. (1984). *San Diego County effective schools program.* San Diego, CA: Author. (ERIC Document Reproduction Service No. ED239337).

Sansone, C., & Morgan, C. (1992). Intrinsic motivation and education: Competence in context. *Motivation and Emotion, 16,* 249–270. doi:10.1007/BF00991654

Scott, C.L. (1999). Teachers' biases toward creative children. *Creativity Research Journal, 12,* 321–337. doi:10.1207/s15326934crj1204_10

Sherblom, S., Marshall, J.C., & Sherblom, J.C. (2006). The relationship between school climate and math and reading achievement. *Journal of Research in Character Education, 4,* 19–31. Retrieved from http://www.ebscohost.com

Singh, K., & Billingsley, B.S. (1998). Professional support and its effects on teachers' commitment. *Journal of Educational Research, 91,* 229–239. doi:10.1080/00220679809597548

Smith, J.D., Schneider, B.H., Smith, P.K., & Ananiadou, K. (2004). The effectiveness of whole-school antibullying programs: A synthesis of evaluation research. *School Psychology Review, 33,* 547–560. Retrieved from http://www.ebscohost.com

Snyder, F., Vuchinich, S., Acock, A., Washburn, L., Beets, M., & Li, K. (2010). Impact of the *Positive Action* program on school-level indicators of academic achievement, absenteeism, and disciplinary outcomes: A matched-pair, cluster randomized, controlled trial. *Journal of Research on Educational Effectiveness, 3,* 26–55. doi:10.1080/19345740903353436

Stewart, E.A. (2003). School social bonds, school climate, and school misbehavior: A multilevel analysis. *Justice Quarterly, 20,* 575–604. doi:10.1080/07418820300095621

Sugai, G., & Horner, R.R. (2006). A promising approach for expanding and sustaining school-wide positive behavior support. *School Psychology Review, 35,* 245–259. Retrieved from http://www.brokersofexpertise.netwww.myboe.orgwww.myboe.orgwww.myboe.orgwww.myboe.orgwww.myboe.orgwww.myboe.orgwww.myboe.orgwww.myboe.org/cognoti/content/file/resources/documents/08/08d88012/08d88012b8f0a8bc8d93783ba791425c9208d5c8/spr352sugai.pdf

Sundblad, G.M.B., Saartok, T., & Engström, L.-M.T. (2006). Child–parent agreement on reports of disease, injury, and pain. *BMC Public Health, 6,* 276. doi:10.1186/1471-2458-6-276

Thuen, E., & Bru, E. (2000). Learning environment, meaningfulness of schoolwork and on-task-orientation among Norwegian 9th grade students. *School Psychology International, 21,* 393–413. doi:10.1177/0143034300214004

Ttofi, M.M., & Farrington, D.P. (2011). Effectiveness of school-based programs to reduce bullying: A systematic and meta-analytic review. *Journal of Experimental Criminology, 7,* 27–56. doi:10.1007/s11292-010-9109-1

U.S. Department of Education. (1988). *National Education Longitudinal Study school questionnaire, NELS:88, first follow-up.* Washington, DC: National Center for Education Statistics.

Wallace Foundation. (2006). *Leadership for learning: Making the connections among state, district and school policies and practices.* New York, NY: Author.

Waters, E., Stewart-Brown, S., & Fitzpatrick, R. (2002). Agreement between adolescent self-report and parent reports of health and well-being: Results of an epidemiological study. *Child: Care, Health, and Development, 29,* 501–509. doi:10.1046/j.1365-2214.2003.00370.x

Wentzel, K.R., & Caldwell, K. (1997). Friendships, peer acceptance, and group membership: Relations to academic achievement in middle school. *Child Development, 68,* 1198–1209. doi:10.2307/1132301

Wentzel, K.R., & Watkins, D.E. (2002). Peer relationships and collaborative learning as contexts for academic enablers. *School Psychology Review, 31,* 366–367. Retrieved from http://www.nasponline.org/publications/spr/abstract.aspx?ID=1618

Whitney, I., Rivers, I., Smith, P.K., & Sharp, S. (1994). The Sheffield Project: Methodology and findings. In P.K. Smith & S. Sharp (Eds.), *School bullying: Insights and perspectives* (pp. 20–56). London, UK: Routledge.

Whitney, I., & Smith, P.K. (1993). A survey of the nature and extent of bullying in junior/middle and secondary schools. *Educational Research, 34,* 3–25. doi:10.1080/0013188930350101

Wilson, D. (2004). The interface of school climate and school connectedness and relationships with aggression and victimization. *Journal of School Health, 74,* 293–299. doi:10.1111/j.1746-1561.2004.tb08286.x

Wolak, J., Mitchell, K.J., & Finkelhor, D. (2007). Does online harassment constitute bullying? An exploration of online harassment by known peers and on-line contacts. *Journal of Adolescent Health, 41,* S51–S58.

Zullig, K.J., Collins, R., Ghani, N., Patton, J.M., Huebner, E.S., & Ajamie, J. (2014). Psychometric support of the School Climate Measure in a large, diverse sample of adolescents: A replication and extension. *Journal of School Health, 84,* 82–90.

Zullig, K. J., Huebner, E. S., & Patton, J. M. (2011). Relationships among school climate domains and school satisfaction: Further validation of the School Climate Measure. *Psychology in the Schools, 48,* 133–145. doi:10.1002/pits.20532

Zullig, K. J., Koopman, T. M., Patton, J. M., & Ubbes, V. A. (2010). School climate: Historical review, instrument development, and school assessment. *Journal of Psychoeducational Assessment, 28,* 139–152. doi:10.1177/0734282909344205

CHAPTER SUMMARY: SCHOOL CLIMATE

- Schools serve as places for social development.
- Student achievement is not only a product of classroom instruction.
- School climate as a measure of subjective school experience relates to academic and nonacademic factors.
- Four overarching areas compose a school's climate: (a) safety, (b) relationships, (c) instruction and learning, and (d) environmental-structural.
- All school climate research demonstrates the importance of the connection between students and their school.
- The measurement of school climate has been difficult, but some emerging instruments demonstrate adequate psychometric properties.
- Many U.S. states have policies that directly or indirectly address school climate.
- Creating, monitoring, and maintaining a positive school climate should be considered a universal, schoolwide endeavor that creates the necessary conditions for additional targeted interventions as needed.
- Measures of school climate might be incorporated into systemwide interventions designed to improve academic and nonacademic factors.

SUGGESTED READINGS: SCHOOL CLIMATE

Catalano, R. F., Haggerty, K. P., Oesterle, S., Fleming, C. B., & Hawkins, J. D. (2004). The importance of bonding to schools for healthy development: Findings from the social development research group. *Journal of School Health, 74,* 252–262. doi:10.1111/j.1746-1561.2004.tb08281.x

While much literature has shown school connectedness is related to multiple adolescent outcomes, this article is presented here because it incorporates two longitudinal studies, which allows cause-and-effect conclusions.

Cohen, J., McCabe, E. M., Michelli, N. M., & Pickeral, T. (2009). School climate: Research, policy, practice, and teacher education. *Teachers College Record, 111,* 180–213. Retrieved http://www.scrc.schoolclimate.org/pdf/School-Climate-Paper-TC-Record.pdf

This seminal article examines the empirical research that suggests a relation between school climate and multiple academic and nonacademic factors. It also examines policy implications and provides a series of recommendations to improve adolescent development and learning.

Gottfredson, G. D., Gottfredson, D. C., Payne, A. A., & Gottfredson, N. C. (2005). School climate predictors of school disorder: Results from a national study of delinquency prevention in schools. *Journal of Research in Crime and Delinquency, 42,* 412–444. doi:10.1177/0022427804271931

This study provided national estimates of crime and violence occurring in and around schools in the United States. Using a complex sampling design, a total of 254 secondary schools were included in this study, which showed that school climate explained a significant percentage of the variance of delinquency and victimization.

Kidger, J., Araya, R., Donovan, J., & Gunnell, D. (2012). The effect of the school environment on the emotional health of adolescents: A systematic review. *Pediatrics, 129,* 1–25. doi:10.1542/peds.2011-2248

This systematic review of the school environment on adolescent emotional health suggests school-level variables display limited evidence of impacting mental health with the exception of teacher support and school connectedness.

Zullig, K.J., Koopman, T.M., Patton, J.M., & Ubbes, V.A. (2010). School climate: Historical review, instrument development, and school assessment. *Journal of Psychoeducational Assessment, 28,* 139–152. doi:10.1177/0734282909344205

This was the first study to balance historical precedent (what to measure) and modern scale-development procedures (e.g., structural equation modeling) into a single attempt to measure school climate.

21

ENGAGING STUDENTS IN SCHOOL CLIMATE IMPROVEMENT
A Student Voice Strategy

Meagan O'Malley, Adam Voight, and Jo Ann Izu, Health and Human Development Program, WestEd, San Francisco, California, USA

INTRODUCTION

The recent occurrence of several high-profile episodes of violence committed by young people in school and local community settings has reinvigorated a national conversation around the need for prevention strategies that reduce or eliminate experiences that hasten youths' feelings of isolation and alienation from peers and adults within their communities. School climate improvement strategies seek to prevent violent, aggressive, and uncivil experiences at school through the cultivation of environments that foster positive interpersonal experiences for youth. These school climate improvement strategies are heterogeneous in nature; some strategies, such as social and emotional learning (SEL) approaches (Greenberg et al., 2003), seek to improve students' ability to regulate internal emotional states and to use communication strategies to prevent and/or intervene with peer conflicts, while other systems-level strategies, such as positive behavior intervention and supports (PBIS; Sugai & Horner, 2002), aim to create transparent and consistent behavioral reinforcement systems within schools in order to help reduce the use of punitive control structures that cultivate toxic climates. Youth voice strategies complement SEL and PBIS-type approaches for school climate improvement by positioning students as agents of school leadership and change, recognizing that students *want* to attend safe and civil schools and that, with adult support and encouragement, they can take action to propel positive school environments.

The purpose of this chapter is to introduce readers to a youth voice activity, called the Student Listening Circle (SLC), which is designed to catalyze student-driven school climate improvement. The chapter begins with an overview of the SLC and goes on to describe the results of a recent study of students' responses from SLCs conducted in comprehensive high schools throughout the state of California during the winter of 2011 to 2012. The chapter closes with a discussion of future directions for SLC-related practice and research, as well as an outline of practical considerations for conducting an SLC.

THE STUDENT LISTENING CIRCLE

The Student Listening Circle (SLC), a youth voice activity, is conducted using the format of a modified youth focus group and is designed for the purpose of catalyzing student-driven improvements to the school context. Benard and colleagues (2004, 2009) originally developed SLCs to apply insights from resilience research to school settings. Benard and colleagues developed the SLC in an effort to move schools toward an asset-oriented lens, wherein the strengths of students, staff, and the organization are underscored and buttressed. Drawing on two decades of research with youth in adverse life situations, Benard and Slade (2009) sought to inform school community members about the protective processes that encourage young people to develop into competent, productive adults (Werner & Smith, 1992, 2001).

Among the studies that guided the development of the SLC is the Kauai Longitudinal Study (KLS; Werner & Smith, 1992, 2001), wherein Werner and her colleagues identified protective factors that moderated the relation between early life stressors (e.g., being born into poverty, experiencing perinatal stress, and/or living in distressed family environments) and otherwise expected deleterious developmental outcomes. Protective factors include characteristics of individual young people (e.g., positive self-concept, prosocial disposition) and characteristics of youths' environments (e.g., close bonds with caring adults, engagement in extracurricular hobbies and interests) that help buffer against the effects of experienced life stressors (Masten & Coatsworth, 1998; Werner & Smith, 1992). Researchers succeeding Werner and her colleagues provided ample evidence supporting the influence of these internal, family, community, and school-level protective factors on the healthy adaptation of youth to their complex and multidimensional social environments (e.g., Resnick, Harris, & Blum, 1993; Roeser, Eccles, & Sameroff, 2000; for review, see Masten, Cutuli, Herbers, & Reed, 2009). SLCs make use of these findings by creating opportunities for students to, at once, bolster their internal assets through participation in collaborative problem solving and strengthen their schools' ecological resources by working with peers and adults to improve school climate.

Context and Competence: Theoretical Foundations

The SLC is grounded in an ecological model of change that targets for intervention the intersection between school community members and their shared contexts (i.e., shared spaces within the school setting, such as classrooms and hallways; see Figure 21.1). The ecological model is informed by theoretical developments in the field of developmental psychology, including ecological systems theory (EST; Bronfenbrenner, 1979, 1992).

EST offers a taxonomy describing nested contextual systems that, despite their increasing distance from the immediate experience of the child, nevertheless exert an effect on her development. According to EST, the *microsystem*—the most proximal system to the child—includes settings wherein face-to-face interactions occur between the child and others, such as the home and classroom. One step removed is the *mesosystem*, defined by the overlap of microsystems. A child's mesosystem may include the relations between his home and school, for example, with some children profiting from bolstered physical and interpersonal resources resulting from highly engaged parents. The *exosystem* does not include the child herself, but nevertheless exerts influence on her developmental trajectory by shaping variables within her microsystem. Parents' work environments are often cited as exosystems for children because they frequently influence parents' behavior at home. Another example of an exosystem for a student would be his teachers' experience of collegial relationships at work. Though the student himself does not experience these staff relationships, they indirectly influence him through his teacher, who transfers her experience into the classroom space. The pattern of micro-, meso-, and exosystems shared within any group of people represents the most distal system, the *macrosystem*. Cultures can constitute macrosystems, but so can social classes, religious groups, and neighborhoods. Schools typically serve communities of students and families who develop within multiple, overlapping macrosystems.

Having generally accepted ecological models, scholars in human development–related fields have turned their attention to explaining the processes that shape development within these nested systems. *Self-organization* (Thelen & Smith, 1998) or *adaptation* (Sameroff, 2000) is the process whereby the child adapts his own internal (i.e., thoughts and mood) and/or external (i.e., behavior) state to the constraints and opportunities provided within his environmental systems. Additionally, the concept of a *transaction* explains that interactions between the child and his contexts are bidirectional in nature, influencing one another dynamically over time (Sameroff, 2000). From these theoretical concepts, we infer that students in schools are engaging in an ongoing process of adaptation to a multiplicity of environmental influences, some of which are immediately known to them and others that they themselves cannot identify but that nevertheless shape their presentation in the classroom and other school contexts.

Shaping the Context: Empowering Students

While ecological theory is most commonly used to understand how environments affect individual development, its transactional nature implies that agentic human action has the potential to influence and change settings as well. Bronfenbrenner (1979) himself, the pioneer of EST, writes: "Development is defined as the person's evolving conception of the ecological environment, and his relation to it, as well as the person's growing capacity to discover, sustain, or alter its properties" (p. 9). In the context of schools, this implies that students' development is shaped by their schools (e.g., the teaching and learning experience, discipline policies, the physical space), and that students have the ability to, in turn, influence their schools (notated with the outward-pointing arrows in Figure 21.1).

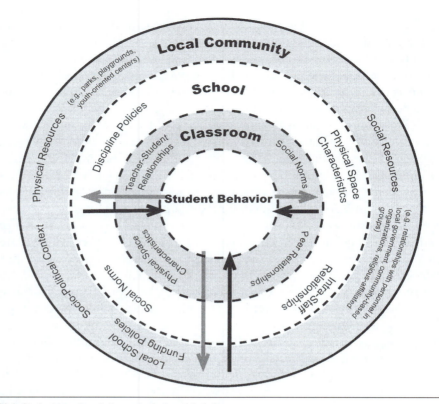

Figure 21.1 Student learning circles ecological model of change.

One way in which students are able to make a difference in their schools is through student voice. Student voice refers to efforts to involve young people in collaborative decision making and problem solving with adults (Camino, 2000; O'Donoghue, Kirshner, & McLaughlin, 2002). It is motivated both by the notion that democratic participation is a key mission of public education and should thus be modeled in school decision making and by the notion that students have unique experiences and perspectives on schooling that make them special experts. Student voice initiatives can take different forms and involve varying degrees of student control and power. An example of student voice that involves limited student control and power is a student survey that allows students to give feedback on school climate and teacher effectiveness. Here, the parameters of "conversation" are set in advance, and students may have little say in how the results of such surveys are used. On the other end of the spectrum are youth-led organizing initiatives in which student groups identify and research issues of importance and develop action plans to pressure decision makers for change. In the middle are activities such as service learning, student government, and students participating on adult boards and committees.

Using the SLC for School Climate Improvement

Research exploring the pathways through which Student Listening Circles affect students' global experiences at school is in its infancy. Until findings are available that compare outcomes for SLC participants and nonparticipants, determination of the SLC's optimal use, including timing and frequency, is based on experience and conjecture. Nevertheless, research regarding other student-voice initiatives has examined the two primary paths through which the SLC is believed to impact student, staff, and school outcomes: by building social support networks and by bolstering opportunities for student voice. These proposed pathways provide a rough guide for practitioners to make decisions about how and when to use the SLC in their schools.

First, the SLC is believed to lead to improved student outcomes by building students' sense that they belong at school—that they are members of a supportive school social network. Students' perception of social support at school has been linked to a number of positive youth outcomes, including improved academic performance (Jia, et al., 2009; Niehaus, Rudasill, & Rakes, 2012), improved mental health and self-esteem (Jia et al., 2009; Shochet, Dadds, Ham & Montague, 2006; Suldo, McMahon, Chappel, & Loker, 2012), increased willingness to seek help when faced with threats of violence (Eliot, Cornell, Gregory, & Fan, 2010), and reduced frequency of disruptive behaviors (Want, Selman, Dishion, & Stormshak, 2010).

Giving students voice in school improvement, the second hypothesized mechanism of change for the Student Listening Circle, has been shown to improve teaching and learning and overall teacher–student relationships (Fielding, 2001; Mitra, 2003; Soo Hoo, 1993). It also confers benefits to the student participants. Students who have the opportunity to contribute to school improvement enjoy better relationships with teachers and increased academic motivation as a result (Ames, 1992; Eccles, Wigfield, & Schiefele, 1998; Lee & Zimmerman, 1999). Further, when students are tapped to provide input into curriculum and instruction decisions, they may experience an increase in achievement (Oldfather, 1995; Rudduck & Flutter, 2000). Giving young people the opportunity to tackle issues of importance to them, in partnership with supportive adults, appears to be an instrument of individual and organizational growth. That is to say, it helps build both internal assets and environmental assets.

Based on the hypothesized mechanisms of change, there exist two potential uses for the SLC. First, the SLC can be viewed as a data-gathering tool to guide intervention, with the target of intervention being the larger school context. From this school change framework, the SLC would be best implemented once or twice during the school year to collect information that informs school improvement decisions. Presumably, the information gathered from different SLCs within the same school will not vary too much, so conducting multiple SLCs would not be the best use of participants' time. Instead, the time of SLC participants, including school leaders, could be better spent implementing the students' improvement suggestions uncovered in the initial SLC. Because research has not yet provided insight into whether and how the SLC works at the individual level (i.e., whether the SLC shifts internal beliefs and attitudes), practitioners are urged to implement the SLC from this school change framework.

From an alternative and untested perspective, the SLC could be viewed as an intervention itself, with the target of the intervention being the student and adult participants. Operating within this framework, more SLCs would presumably be better because the intervention is able to reach more school community members. Until research is conducted to understand how the SLC acts as an individual-level intervention, practitioners are encouraged to employ caution when choosing to operate from this framework.

LETTING STUDENTS SPEAK: THEMES FROM SLCS

The recognition that meaningful participation and engagement at school encourages social well-being, belonging, and a sense of agency in young people has influenced policy in human services and education. Recognizing the need for attention to these nonacademic dimensions of learning, the U.S. Department of Education's Office of Safe and Healthy Students (OSHS) recently issued $38.8 million in Safe and Supportive Schools (SSS or S3) grants to 11 states. The purpose of the S3 grant is to use school climate data to inform the selection and implementation of evidence-based programs to improve the developmental opportunities offered within the comprehensive high school setting. Because of its asset focus and its reliance on the school context as the unit of change, the SLC has been incorporated as a data-gathering and youth-action tool by 58 S3-funded comprehensive high schools in California. Data collected from SLCs were used to complement insights from quantitative school climate data collected via the California Healthy Kids Survey and its staff and parent partner surveys (WestEd, 2012). Together, these multiple sources of data were used to drive grantees' selection of evidence-based policies, programs, and practices for school climate improvement.

The study described in the remainder of this chapter identifies themes from a selection of student responses from SLCs facilitated in 31 S3-funded comprehensive high schools throughout California during the winter of 2011 to 2012. Two major phases constituted the SLCs conducted for this study: Data Gathering and Solution Planning. During Data Gathering, students were provided an opportunity to communicate authentic, uncensored messages about their school experiences while adults listened carefully. Importantly, there was no dialogue during this time; students spoke and adults listened. Participating students answered the following prompts:

1. How do you know when an adult at school cares about you? What do they say and do?
2. How do you know when an adult at school believes in you? What do they say and do?
3. What makes your classes engaging or interesting to you?
4. If you could change or improve one thing at school, what would it be?
5. What could you do at your school that would make a difference?
6. What are your hopes and dreams and how can adults at school help you achieve them?

After writing open-ended responses to these questions, students discussed their responses in an adult-facilitated forum of peers. After practicing their answers to the prompts in a safe environment with peers and a trained adult facilitator, students joined a room with school adults, sat in a circle facing each other with adults seated in a concentric circle on their perimeter, and proceeded to provide their rehearsed responses to each of the aforementioned prompts.

Following Data Gathering, the Solution Planning phase provided a structured opportunity for productive, solution-oriented dialogue between students and staff about improving the school context. Students and adults joined a single circle in order to reflect on what they experienced. They then moved into small groups, wherein they were asked to begin to generate ideas to address themes within students' responses.

In every case, the product of the SLC was agreement on two to four concrete, achievable, time-limited action steps. In some cases, such as groups that had agreed upon broad and/or distal goals (e.g., painting the school), SLC time limitations required that the facilitator follow-up with members of the school leadership after the conclusion of the SLC in order to further hone the ideas into more proximally achieved parts (e.g., obtain bids for painting the front wing of the school).

Methods for the Present Study

To learn more about insights on school climate proffered by student voice, students' responses to these questions were analyzed using a sample of 10 S3-funded schools. These 10 schools were selected through a stratified randomization process that ensured representation of urban, suburban, and rural schools (as defined by the California State Department of Education).

Students wrote their responses to the six SLC questions on forms that they then used to guide their open discussion. These written responses were compiled into a database and analyzed to uncover general themes. The analysis involved a two-step qualitative coding procedure. The first step in this process involved coding—or giving a label to—each individual idea or concept noted in students' responses. For example, in response to question 1 ("How do you know when an adult at school cares about you?"), a student might have said, "when they greet me by name when I come into the classroom and when they help me with my homework after school." The idea of greeting the student by name and the idea of helping with homework after school would each be coded separately.

The second step involved grouping each of these coded concepts into themes. In some cases, this was straightforward, such as when multiple codes were given the exact same name. In other cases, it required more discussion on the part of the research team. From there, we used a "constant comparative" procedure that examines one code at a time in each thematic category and compared it to all other pieces of data in that category and related categories with the goal of integrating categories where there was sufficient overlap or creating new ones where there was sufficient difference. For example, for question 5 ("What could you do at your school that would make a difference?"), the decision was made to combine *peer support groups* and *peer relationship building* into the same thematic category, as there was overlap in the types of responses included in each category.

The end result of this analysis was a parsimonious group of themes related to each of the questions that students were asked in SLCs. These themes provided insight into how students understand school climate and potential intervention priorities.

Included below are the response themes for four SLC response prompts. Although the items "How do you know when an adult at school believes in you? What do they say and do?" and "How do you know an adult at school cares about you? What do they say and do?" were asked separately, the degree of overlap in students' responses warranted collapsing the included thematic summary. Also, students' responses to the question, "What are your hopes and dreams and how can adults at school help you achieve them?" are not described because students' responses were often too narrow and/or too broad to inform decisions beyond those made at their particular schools. This trend is reflected in the following responses: (a) "My goal is to graduate and go to college and my dream is to be a police officer and I would need for my teachers to help me continue doing good in school" and (b) "My goals and dreams are to join the military or Cal fire. . . [Adults can help by being] supportive of me and my goals/dreams."

Student Voice Themes for School Climate Improvement

Caring Relationships and High Expectations

Students responses to the two questions, "How do you know when an adult at school cares about you?" and "How do you know when an adult at school believes in you?" fell into four general themes: (a) attention to the personal connection, (b) commitment to student learning, (c) expectations for behavior and success, and (d) encouragement and motivation to succeed.

Simple but genuine interactions about student lives outside the confines of the classroom build personal connections with students that they commonly view as caring. In addition to greeting students and knowing them by name, taking time to ask about their day, weekend, or holiday break was commonly mentioned as evidence that adults at school care. The students also remarked that it was not just what adults said, but how they said it, that made a difference—positive, "polite," welcoming tones and facial expressions, and an open, nonjudgmental attitude communicated caring. As one student explained, "The way I know adults care is by their way of speaking to me. They always [speak] with a smile and [are] always open to my opinions." Listening attentively, and responding "in more than one or two words" conveyed a personal interest in students which some described as acting like a friend or peer. One student said she knows adults care "When a teacher actually gets on your level and [has a conversation] with you as [though] they were one of your peers."

Noticing changes in student attitude and behavior also conveyed caring. For example, teachers who consistently noticed when students were sad, frustrated, or having a bad day and took the time to ask students about it were described as caring. This "checking in" at a personal level conveyed responsiveness to student attitudes and experiences that may have led to stronger connections. "When an adult cares," one student claimed, "you can tell because they are the people that you know you can go to for advice." Caring adults were also described as those who were interested in students' personal lives and experiences and who were willing to share their own.

For some students, "checking in" academically on a one-to-one basis was also a sign of caring. Adults who took the time to have one-to-one conversations about student work—whether in regard to grades, missed assignments, or accomplishments—and gave feedback to students on ways they could improve or meet their goals and deadlines were described as caring. For example, one student noted, "The adults that care in my school check on me, they come ask me how my day is when they see me, they also check on my grades and behavior in and around campus."

On a similar note, adult commitment to student learning is another major theme. Teachers who offered to help students outside of class and who took the time to provide extra help, tutoring, or study sessions at lunch or after school were commonly described as caring. Several students reported caring teachers are ones who ensure students actually learned the concepts and material. "They don't leave you behind while teaching" is how one student described it. Caring adults, as another student indicated, ". . .teach the way students learn and [are] not constantly forcing them to learn how teachers teach."

Having high expectations for student behavior and success is a third aspect of caring and belief in student potential. Students noted that holding them accountable to certain academic standards such as going to class, participating, and staying focused and on track ("tell me 'don't fool around'") showed both caring and belief in students. As one student indicated, "They keep bugging me to do my work, come to class on time and believe I can do better." Interest in and affirmation of student success is another way students know adults care and believe in them. As these students noted,

"This is how I know if they believe in me—They will never give me up for failure. They will always tell me to go for the 3.0 [GPA] because they know I can get it."

"I know adults believe in me because they pull me aside and tell me, 'Why do [you] have a bad grade in this class? You can do better.' And that makes me feel like they believe in me."

Finally, students pointed to encouragement and motivation to succeed as another way they know adults care and believe in them. Students indicated that praise and reminders of what they and other students have accomplished in the past offer hope and optimism that they can succeed at the task at hand. Examples they gave include encouraging perseverance through statements like, "Don't give up; you almost got it" or simply "You can do it." Pushing students to optimize achievement by working harder, doing their best, and completing the assignments is another form of encouragement noted by students. Similarly, challenging students to take on classes and tasks that they typically avoid or to "do things outside the norm" while communicating adults' faith that they can complete them is how students knows adults believe in them.

Engaging Learning Opportunities

To the question, "What makes your classes engaging or interesting to you?" students answered according to four general themes, which we have labeled: (a) variety in instructional tools and techniques, (b) opportunities for self-expression and self-direction, (c) real-world applications, and (d) teacher attitudes and beliefs.

Most frequent were requests for engaging instructional tools and techniques. Students noted that they find classes to be most engaging when teachers use a variety of pedagogical tools, including instructional games, hands-on activities, and diversity in media, such as videos and computer software. To engage more deeply with the content, students noted labs, projects, class dialogues, and small-group work opportunities to be useful. Finally, students responded that they value opportunities to review course content in experiential, creative ways such as playing quiz games.

Second to engaging instructional tools were requests for opportunities for self-expression and self-direction. Students noted that classes are engaging when there are opportunities to make choices, such as selecting where to sit or selecting learning activities. As in other SLC item responses discussed herein, students requested opportunities to express their personal opinions and beliefs and to hear the opinions and beliefs of others. In one example, a student responded, "some [classes] require participation from the students and it's interesting to hear others' opinions. It'd be better to have more people involved. Voluntary sharing of inner opinions with a group of peeps."

Additionally, students consistently reported the need to engage in material through real-world applications. They asked for teachers to provide examples for how the material could be used in future professional and personal life and to illustrate material using examples that students could connect to their own lived experiences. Students at the high school level are pondering the world, thinking about what opportunities life outside of high school has to offer them and what skills they may need to adapt to new life demands.

Finally, students often supplemented their answers by noting that, in addition to developmentally appropriate pedagogical tools and techniques, teacher attitudes and behaviors can support an engaging learning environment. Specifically, students noted that they find that they are most engaged in their courses when their teachers are fun, positive, and personally interested in the course material.

Improving Your School

The question, "What could you do at your school that would make a difference?" gave students an open-ended opportunity to talk about their priorities for school improvement. Their responses fell into four general themes: (a) the physical environment/resources, (b) staff–student rapport, (c) student peer relationships, and (d) school rules and policies.

The most commonly mentioned target for improvement was the physical environment, including food options. Students described school campuses that were drab, littered, and generally unclean. One student claimed, "Every day I hear people say that this campus is dirty and disgusting. There is trash everywhere. The things we do have are outdated, like in the quad area." The cleanliness of bathrooms was a particular concern. As for food, students claimed that they would prefer more variety in lunch offerings or the ability to leave campus for lunch.

Regarding staff–student relationships, many students voiced concern about the disposition of some adults in the school. Students wished that administrative staff, in particular, were more friendly, helpful, and welcoming. They expressed a desire for more enthusiasm and positivity on the part of teachers and counselors. Some felt that an improvement in staff attitudes toward students was necessary. There was also an acknowledgment that students need to be more respectful of adults in school, especially regarding attentiveness in class.

Additionally, students pointed to peer relationships as an area for improvement. There was a concern over violence and racism among students. To combat this, students recommended more opportunities for students to build prosocial relationships, with one student stating, "Many kids don't know each other very well, and we only know what we infer. If we had a day or two to get to know each other I think that would help." Students expressed a desire for more mutual helping and connectedness in the student body.

Lastly, many students felt that some school policies were too restrictive. Special attention was given to dress codes, bans on the use of portable electronics, discipline policies, and scheduling. Student felt that dress codes prevented them from expressing themselves. In terms of electronics, students felt it would be fair to be able to use them between classes. "At lunch we're doing it anyway, so why is it bad if we [use electronics] when we're not in class?" said one student. Another student wished that teachers would be more consistent in enforcing discipline policies. Finally, for students who had jobs, there was some frustration over the inability of schools to accommodate work schedules.

Students Make a Difference

Students' responses to the question "What could you do at your school that would make a difference?" fell into three thematic categories: (a) prosocial peer interactions, (b) positive norm-encouraging behavior, and (c) community events and activities. Overall, students' responses to this item suggested that not only do students want to contribute to their school environments, but they also have a variety of creative, youth-appropriate ideas for how to do so.

Most commonly, students responded that they could make a difference at school by helping and connecting with other students. For these participants, ideas for helping and connecting with other students were expressed with a variety of textures, such as mentoring subpopulations and/or groups of students with traditionally less power within the school, such as underclassmen, students with disabilities, and/or students who are learning English as a second language; tutoring students in academics; building friendships across subgroups or "cliques"; making conversation with students they don't already know; and providing peer counseling.

Second to prosocial peer interactions, students responded that they could make a difference at their school by encouraging positive norm-following behavior. For example, they mentioned encouraging other students to follow school rules, "stop bullying and put downs," "respect each other," and "be themselves."

Finally, students indicated that they could help by hosting and encouraging participation in school community events and activities. Ideas included advertising activities and programs on campus, starting student clubs, and volunteering to perform community service on campus (e.g., volunteering at the library, picking up trash). In other words, students indicated that they were looking for opportunities to conduct student-led initiatives that weave peers into the school's social fabric.

ILLUSTRATING STUDENT-DRIVEN SCHOOL CLIMATE IMPROVEMENT

The following is an example of how one high school used the SLC process to inform changes to their school environment.

On a Saturday morning in April 2012, a comprehensive high school in California held a SLC. Twenty-seven people (8 students and 19 adults) participated. A diverse group of adults (parents, staff, school administrators, school-based health center staff, and community-based organization staff) and students were represented. Issues that arose during the SLC included the need for better schoolwide communication, more adult involvement in school activities, a wider range of strategies to engage students in learning, more opportunities for student voices to be heard, and in particular, more activities and opportunities to "break boundaries" between the cliques and divisions in this racially and economically diverse school and community.

The group decided to address three of the SLC's suggestions, with at least one student and one adult taking responsibility for moving the work forward in each area:

1. Develop more opportunities to hear students by forming a committee to plan and conduct a series of listening circles with strategies to share the results with more adults.
2. Form a diversity committee to examine communication and breaking the status quo.
3. Form a committee to coordinate club outreach and communication.

In less than a month (and with the close of school just weeks away), changes were already being put in place. While work to coordinate club outreach and communication had just begun, improvement efforts in other areas were well underway. Announcing his commitment to student voice at the circle, the principal, along with student and adult SLC participants, shared the results of the SLC at the next staff meeting. In addition, several students were invited to participate in a panel to talk about their perspectives on school issues at the school board meeting held at the high school. Another SLC involving students who participate in the Life Skills for Peace program was planned to take place before school ended to ensure more diversity in the voices heard.

Similarly, the adult and student responsible for communication and breaking the status quo met at least twice to develop a survey regarding cliques and belonging or "fitting in" issues on campus, and to plan a Mix It Up Day for the fall. They hoped to use the survey to identify students for an ongoing committee to look at issues of cliques and ethnic/racial tensions on campus.

FUTURE DIRECTIONS IN SLC

Future directions for the SLC follow two major courses: improvements to practice and improvements in research. Practice-related improvements include building systematic opportunities for students to participate in the planning and follow-up stages of the SLC. Related to planning, it is notable that the questions that were asked in this SLC process were selected by SLC adult facilitators based on what research has suggested are the building blocks of resilience in youth. Given that the parameters of the constructs tapped are constricted by the questions being asked, there is no way to be sure that all potential dimensions of school climate relevant to students were tapped with the current set of questions. Working with a group of students in advance to determine the content and wording of items being used at their school could strengthen the SLC process. One potential way to organize this discussion is to ask the students to review existing school climate data (e.g., student, staff, and parent perception data [school climate surveys], behavioral incidence data, and suspension/expulsion data) and discuss what they believe to be the school's greatest strengths and challenges. This discussion could naturally lead to a determination of the school climate areas that the students would like to explore more deeply via the SLC. Moreover, there is currently no systematic follow-up to the SLC; instead, the process leaves schools to independently and idiosyncratically implement SLC-generated solutions. A more systematic approach could help ensure that solution ideas become reality.

Table 21.1 Steps for Conducting a Student Listening Circle

Phase I: Planning

1. **Obtain administrator buy-in.** It is critical to gauge school administrator readiness and support before proceeding with the SLC to ensure that key school leaders value and intend to act upon student voice. Some school leaders are ready to share their power, while others may be initially skeptical or, alternatively, entirely opposed to the idea. Do not proceed with the SLC unless key school leaders are supportive of the approach.

2. **Select and recruit student participants.** Students recruited to participate in the SLC should represent a cross-section of the school community, both in terms of age, gender, and race/ethnicity and in terms of school engagement and current academic achievement. The SLC is best run with no less than five and no more than eight students.

3. **Obtain parent/guardian consent.** Consent is recommended, as participating students may be missing instructional time.

4. **Select and recruit adult participants.** Adults recruited to participate in the SLC should be advocates for student voice. This is not the time to invite skeptical staff, as they may undermine the emotionally safe experience for students. A ratio of two adults per participating student is recommended. As with students, the adult participants should represent a cross-section of the school. Recommended participants include school leadership, instructional staff, counselors and school psychologists, certificated staff members, school security personnel, and parents.

5. **Locate appropriate space.** Two rooms will need to be located. The first room will need to be large enough to hold all SLC participants, adults and students. This room should have a reduced number of doors and doors should be able to be locked while the SLC is being conducted to avoid disruptions. Large tables in the room should be able to be moved to the perimeter of the room to allow space for two concentric circles of chairs. Midsized rooms are best; cafeterias and other very large spaces are not recommended.

Phase II: Implementation

6. **Brief adults and students.** Review SLC Agreements (Table 21.2), discuss the purpose of the SLC, and describe the expected flow of the day.

7. **Prepare adults.** Re-review adult agreements; discuss existing school climate data (e.g., student/staff perception data from school climate surveys, behavioral incidence data, suspension and expulsion data), paying special attention to disparities across student groups; and discuss current practices in school climate improvement (e.g., school policies, evidence based programs, day-to-day practices).

8. **Prepare students.** Coach students through their answers to each SLC question. Facilitator provides feedback and encourages students to share all of their ideas while actively listening to and reflecting their answers, and, when needed, assisting them to reframe responses in constructive, solution-focused ways.

9. **Conduct Student Listening Circle.** Students are asked to sit in center circle, facing one another. The facilitator sits in the center circle with the students. Adult participants sit in a concentric circle outside of the student circle. Every student answers every question in the same order that has been practiced in the student preparation, while adults listen quietly.

(Continued)

Table 21.1 (Continued)

Phase III: Synthesis and Solution Planning

10. **Adult reflection.** Students and adults are asked to join a single circle. Facilitator asks adults, "What did it feel like to listen to students? What did you hear the students say?" It is important that the facilitator remind the adults that this is not a time to defend the school or to commit to action but only to reflect on what the experience was like for them and what they learned from the students.

11. **Student reflection.** Facilitator asks the students, "What did it feel like to be listened to?" Students are reminded that this is the time to thank the adults, but not to add additional critiques of the school or school personnel. Students are asked to acknowledge that adults listened and/or revise any miscommunicated statements.

12. **Paired solution planning.** Facilitator asks the students to partner with adults in small groups (e.g., two adults and one student per small group) to consider at least two action steps based on a theme that emerged in the students' responses. Facilitator leads small groups through a share-out around each theme that emerged.

Phase IV: Follow-Up

13. **Reconvene adults and students to discuss progress on action steps.** Revise action steps if necessary.

Table 21.2 Student Listening Circle Agreements

Adults agree to:

- Turn off cell phones and other electronics. No phone calls, e-mails, or texts!
- Stay for the *entire* Listening Circle.
- Be silent during the Listening Circle.
- Commit to a plan of action that reflects the youths' perspectives.
- Keep comments offered by students anonymous when reporting to staff, parents, or community members.
- Avoid approaching Listening Circle students for clarification outside of preplanned, structured follow-up activities.

Students agree to:

- Turn off cell phones and other electronics. No phone calls, emails, or texts.
- Focus on what you do like, want, and need.
- When referring to specific people, only use names for positive comments.
- Be respectful of each other.
- Be mindful of time.
- Speak one at a time.
- Speak your truth!

Though the anecdotal evidence for the SLC process is strong (e.g., one school adult called it "the most powerful data-gathering tool" he had ever seen), there is little empirical research on the SLC. Validating the SLC as an impactful school climate intervention will require thoughtful study of both the ingredients that predict high SLC quality, such as administrators' orientation toward youth voice activities and student and adult participant characteristics; as well as the adult and student psychological, social, and behavioral outcomes that result from participation in the SLC. Deeper study of the process by which the SLC influences change in the school environment is also warranted. Of particular interest to these authors is the process by which participants in the SLC influence nonparticipants through social action and behavior and how the accumulation of influence results in lasting change to the school's social norms.

Included in Table 21.1 are the broad steps for conducting a best-practice Student Listening Circle in a high school setting. For a detailed description of each step, including nuances and problem-solving strategies, review Burgoa and Izu (2010).

REFERENCES

Ames, C. (1992). Classrooms: Goals, structures, and student motivation. *Journal of Educational Psychology, 84*, 261–271. doi:10.1037/0022-0663.84.3.261

Benard, B. (2004). *Resiliency: What we have learned.* San Francisco, CA: WestEd.

Benard, B., & Slade, S. (2009). Listening to students: Moving from resilience research to youth development practice and school connectedness. In R. Gilman, E.S. Huebner, & M.J. Furlong (Eds.), *Handbook of positive psychology in schools* (pp. 353–370). New York, NY: Routledge.

Bronfenbrenner, U. (1979). *The ecology of human development: Experiments by nature and design.* Cambridge, MA: Harvard University Press.

Bronfenbrenner, U. (1992). Ecological systems theory. In R. Vasta (Ed.), *Six theories of child development* (pp. 187–250). Philadelphia, PA: Jessica Kingsley.

Burgoa, C., & Izu, J. (2010). *Guide to a student-family-school-community partnerships.* San Francisco, CA: WestEd. Available from http://chks.wested.org/resources/StudentFamilySchoolCommunity.pdf

Camino, L. (2000). Youth–adult partnerships: Entering new territory in community work and research. *Applied Developmental Science, 4*, 11–12. doi:10.1207/S1532480XADS04Suppl_2

Eccles, J., Wigfield, A., & Schiefele, U. (1998). Motivation to succeed. In W. Damon & N. Eisenberg (Eds.), *Handbook of child psychology, Vol. 3: Social, emotional and personality development* (pp. 1017–1094). New York, NY: Wiley.

Eliot, M., Cornell, D., Gregory, A., & Fan, X. (2010). Supportive school climate and student willingness to seek help for bullying and threats of violence. *Journal of School Psychology, 48*, 533–553. doi:10.1016/j.jsp.2010.07.001

Fielding, M. (2001). Students as radical agents of change. *Journal of Educational Change, 2*, 123–141. doi:10.1023/A:1017949213447

Greenberg, M., Weissberg, R., Utne O'Brien, M., Zins, J., Fredericks, L., Resnik, H., & Elias, M. (2003). Enhancing school-based prevention and youth development through coordinated social, emotional, and academic learning. *American Psychologist, 58*, 466–474. doi:10.1037/0003-066X.58.6-7.466

Jia, Y., Way, N., Ling, G., Yoshikawa, H., Chen, X., Hughes, D. . . . Lu, Z. (2009). The influence of student perceptions of school climate on socioemotional and academic adjustment: A comparison of Chinese and American adolescents. *Child Development, 80*, 1514–1530. doi:10.1111/j.1467-8624.2009.01348.x

Lee, L., & Zimmerman, M. (1999). Passion, action and a new vision for student voice: Learnings from the Manitoba School Improvement Program. *Education Canada, 39*, 34–35.

Masten, A., & Coatsworth, J. (1998). The development of competence in favorable and unfavorable environments: Lessons from research on successful children. *American Psychologist, 53*, 205–220. doi:10.1037/0003-066X.53.2.205

Masten, A.S., Cutuli, J.J., Herbers, J.E., & Reed, M.J. (2009). Resilience in development. In S. Lopez & C. Snyder (Eds.), *The Oxford handbook of positive psychology* (2nd ed., pp. 117–132). New York: Oxford University Press.

Mitra, D.L. (2003). Student voice in school reform: Reframing student–teacher relationships. *McGill Journal of Education, 38*, 289–304.

Niehaus, K., Rudasill, K., & Rakes, C. (2012). A longitudinal study of school connectedness and academic outcomes across sixth grade. *Journal of School Psychology, 50*, 443–460. doi:10.1016/j.jsp.2012.03.002

O'Donoghue, J.L., Kirshner, B., & McLaughlin, M. (2002). Introduction: Moving youth participation forward. *New Directions for Youth Development, 96*, 15–26. doi:10.1002/yd.24

Oldfather, P. (1995). Songs "come back most to them": Students' experiences as researchers. *Theory Into Practice, 34*, 131–137. doi:10.1080/00405849509543670

Resnick, M., Harris, L., & Blum, R. (1993). The impact of caring and connectedness on adolescent health and well-being. *Journal of Pediatrics and Child Health, 29,* S3–S9. doi:10.1111/j.1440-1754.1993.tb02257.x

Roeser, R.W., Eccles, J.S., & Sameroff, A. (2000). School as a context of early adolescents' academic and social-emotional development: A summary of research findings. *Elementary School Journal, 100,* 443–471.

Rudduck, J., & Flutter, J. (2000). Pupil participation and pupil perspective: "Carving a new order of experience." *Cambridge Journal of Education, 30,* 75–89. doi:10.1080/03057640050005780

Sameroff, A.J. (2000). Developmental systems and psychopathology. *Development and Psychopathology, 12,* 297–312.

Shochet, I., Dadds, M., Ham, D., & Montague, R. (2006). School connectedness is an underemphasized parameter in adolescent mental health: Results of a community prediction study. *Journal of Clinical Child & Adolescent Psychology, 35,* 170–179.

Soo Hoo, S. (1993). Students as partners in research and restructuring schools. *Educational Forum, 57*(Summer), 386–393.

Sugai, G., & Horner, R. (2002). The evolution of discipline practices: School-wide positive behavior supports. *Child & Family Behavior Therapy, 24,* 23–50.

Suldo, S., McMahon, M., Chappel, A., & Loker, T. (2012). Relationships between perceived school climate and adolescent mental health. *School Mental Health, 4,* 69–80.

Thelen, E., & Smith, L. (1998). Dynamic systems theory. In W. Damon & R. Lerner (Eds.), *Handbook of child psychology V: Theoretical models of human development* (pp. 258–312). Hoboken, NJ: Wiley.

Want, M., Selman, R., Dishion, T., & Stormshak, E. (2010). A tobit regression analysis of the covariation between middle school students' perceived school climate and behavioral problems. *Journal of Research on Adolescence, 20,* 274–286.

Werner, E., & Smith, R. (1992). *Overcoming the odds: High-risk children from birth to adulthood.* Ithaca, NY: Cornell University Press.

Werner, E., & Smith, R. (2001). *Journeys from childhood to midlife: Risk, resilience, and recovery.* Ithaca, NY: Cornell University Press.

WestEd. (2012). *The California Healthy Kids Survey.* San Francisco, CA: WestEd. Available from http://chks.wested.org/

CHAPTER SUMMARY STUDENT VOICE

- The Student Listening Circle (SLC) is two-phase student voice activity wherein students are first provided a structured opportunity to give authentic, uncensored feedback about their school experiences to school adults and then provided a space to engage in a productive dialogue with school adults about improving the school context.

- Student voice strategies complement SEL and PBIS-type school strategies by targeting students as agents of self-discipline, leadership, and organizational change.

- The SLC is grounded in an ecological model of change that targets for intervention the intersection between school community members and their shared contexts (i.e., shared spaces within the school setting, such as classrooms and hallways; see Figure 21.1).

- The SLC relies on the proposition that democratic participation is a key mission of public education and should thus be modeled in school decision making and by the notion that students have unique experiences and perspectives on schooling that make them special experts.

- The SLC is believed to lead to improved student academic, social, and emotional outcomes by building students' sense that they belong to a supportive school social network consisting of peers and adults and by bolstering students' sense of agency and control of resources in their school environment.

- Results of a thematic analysis of students' responses from 10 SLCs conducted in rural, suburban, and urban schools throughout California in winter of 2011 to 2012 indicate:

  o Simple but genuine interactions suggest to students that adults at school care about and believe in them. According to students, adults at school demonstrate they care when they check in about students' personal lives outside the confines of the classroom; notice changes in students' attitudes and behavior; and carefully monitor students' academic performance, regardless of students' perceived effort.

  o Students perceive their classes to be engaging and motivating when adults employ a variety of instructional tools and techniques, include ample opportunities for self-expression and self-direction, and connect lessons to real-world applications.

  o Students' primary school improvement concerns relate to their day-to-day experiences, including most prominently the cleanliness of the school environment and the quality of available food; the quality of interactions with school personnel, including administrative and counseling office staff members; lack of perceived rationale for and/or restrictiveness of some school rules; and the quality of interactions with peers on campus.

  o Not only do students want to contribute to their school environments, but they have a variety of creative, youth-appropriate ideas for how to do so. Students are motivated to contribute by helping and connecting with other students both socially and academically and by leading school community events and activities.

- Future research is needed to determine the effects that participating in an SLC may have on adult and student psychological, social, and behavioral outcomes.

SUGGESTED READINGS: STUDENT VOICE

Goldstein, S., & Brooks, R.B. (2013). *Handbook of resilience in children* (2nd ed.). New York, NY: Springer.

Chapters within this handbook provide an overview of contemporary research on resilience in children.

Kirshner, B., O'Donoghue, J., & McLaughlin, M. (2003). Youth participation: Improving institutions and communities. *New directions for youth development: Theory, practice and research, 96* (winter).

This volume offers an assessment of the field of Youth Development. Included chapters describe efforts to increase youth participation in schools and other community settings.

Mitra, D. (2008). *Student voice in school reform: Building youth–adult partnerships that strengthen schools and empower youth.* Albany, NY: State University of New York Press.

This book describes the story of one high school in the San Francisco Bay Area in which educators implemented measures to bolster student voice on campus. The school's narrative is couched in a discussion of research on youth voice.

Preble, B., & Gordon, R. (2011). *Transforming school climate and learning: Beyond bullying and compliance.* Thousand Oaks, CA: Corwin Press.

This book describes the authors' proposed process for improving school climate, from school climate data use through youth participation strategies.

Zullig, K.J., Koopman, T.M., Patton, J.M., & Ubbes, V.A. (2010). School climate: Historical review, instrument development, and school assessment. *Journal of Psychoeducational Assessment, 28,* 139–152. doi:10.1177/0734282909344205

This research article provides a contemporary introduction to the study of school climate, including defining features and measurement of student perceptions.

22

POSITIVE PSYCHOLOGY AND SCHOOL DISCIPLINE

George G. Bear, School of Education, University of Delaware, Newark, Delaware, USA

Maureen A. Manning, Department of Psychology, Towson University, Towson, Maryland, USA

INTRODUCTION

During the past several decades, the term *positive* has been utilized on an increasing basis to describe many approaches to classroom management and school discipline. In fact, among the multiple models of classroom management and school discipline available (see Charles, 2010), the term *positive* appears in the title of two popular, and perhaps *the* most popular, models: *Positive Discipline* (Nelsen, Lott, & Glenn, 2000) and *Assertive Discipline: Positive Behavior Management for Today's Classroom* (Canter, 2010). It also appears in the title of the most rapidly growing general approach to school discipline, the schoolwide positive behavioral interventions and supports (SWPBIS) approach (Sugai & Horner, 2009; Sugai et al., 2010; also see www.pbis. org). Another widespread general approach is social and emotional learning (SEL). Although this approach does not include *positive* in its title, when evaluated within the framework of positive psychology, SEL appears to be the most positive of the four models and approaches. In this chapter, we present guiding principles of positive psychology applied to school discipline. Next, we briefly review the core features of the four popular models and approaches to school discipline cited. We then critique the four models and approaches as to the extent to which each is consistent with the guiding principles.

GUIDING PRINCIPLES OF POSITIVE PSYCHOLOGY
APPLIED TO SCHOOL DISCIPLINE

When applied to the school setting, positive psychology has been termed *positive education* and defined as the teaching of skills that promote academics and skills that enhance well-being (Seligman, Ernst, Gillham, Reivich, & Linkin, 2009). Positive psychology entails the development of character strengths and virtues that address the *why* and *how* of good character (Peterson & Seligman, 2004). This includes the development of emotions and thought processes that underlie and support strengths and virtues of good character. Since the onset of American education, the development of character strengths and virtues, especially those associated with self-discipline, has been a primary aim of school discipline (Bear, 2005). Thus, the relation of positive psychology to school discipline is well founded. From the framework of positive psychology, five basic principles can be used to guide positive school discipline, as described in the following sections.

The Primary Aim of Positive School Discipline Is the Development of Character Strengths and Virtues of Self-Discipline

Self-discipline refers to students inhibiting inappropriate behavior and exhibiting prosocial behavior under their own volition, reflecting the internalization of the values, standards, beliefs, and attitudes of their parents, teachers, peers, and others in society. When used within the context of *school discipline*, the term *self-discipline* highlights the need for schools to view the development of self-regulated behavior rather than the use of external discipline as their primary aim (Bear, 2005). Among the character strengths and virtues identified by Peterson and Seligman (2004) as being central to mental health and emotional well-being, self-regulation, social intelligence, citizenship, fairness, authenticity, and kindness are most directly related to self-discipline. They underlie what Kochanska (2002) refers to as *committed* compliance and Brophy (1996) terms *willing* compliance, which is motivated by a sense of pride and autonomy (in contrast to *situational* or *grudging* compliance, which is motivated by external rewards and punishment).

Research shows that character strengths associated with self-discipline are related to greater supportive relations with teachers and peers and a more positive school climate, foster academic achievement, and promote self-worth and overall emotional well-being (Bear, 2012a; Bear, Manning, & Izard, 2003). However, it is important to note that each character strength and virtue also has traditionally been "morally valued in its own right, even in the absence of obvious beneficial outcomes" (Peterson & Seligman, 2004, p. 19).

School Discipline Should Help Children Meet Three Basic Human Needs: The Need for Competence, the Need for Belongingness, and the Need for Autonomy

In positive psychology, the needs for competence, belongingness, and autonomy are viewed as critical to self-determination, intrinsic motivation, and overall personal and social well-being (Ryan & Deci, 2000, 2006). The three needs are interrelated and related closely to the character strengths and virtues listed earlier. Each builds upon and supports the others. For example, kindness and authenticity enhance social belonging, self-regulation enhances autonomy, and social intelligence enhances competence (particularly social competence).

School Discipline Should Focus on Developing Emotions, Thoughts, and Behaviors That Reflect Character Strengths and Virtues

From the perspective of positive psychology, learning *why* and *how* with respect to behavior—how to decide and choose what one should do and the reasons why—is of equal if not greater importance than learning *what* to do. In a given social context, *not* complying with and questioning authority rules can reflect a character strength. As such, students should learn that "good" behavior is not necessarily behavior that is rewarded. Although emotions, cognitions, and actions are targeted in positive psychology, emotions receive greatest emphasis, especially *moral emotions* (as seen in virtues) and *positive emotions* (Kristja'nsson, 2012).

Several robust areas of research and theory have identified a variety of cognitive processes and emotional mechanisms that mediate, support, enhance, or augment prosocial behavior and antisocial behavior, and thus should be targeted in programs designed to develop character strengths of self-discipline (see Bear, 2010, for a recent review). For example, research indicates substantial overlap between emotional intelligence and positive psychology, with the two constructs sharing an emphasis on character traits, virtues, and skills such as optimism, autonomy, emotion regulation, problem solving, self-acceptance based on genuine self-awareness, and the capacity for empathy and positive social interactions (Bar-On, 2010). Likewise, research in the area of moral reasoning (Manning & Bear, 2002, 2011; Stams et al., 2006) indicates that when asked why they should not engage in behaviors that harm others, aggressive and antisocial children, including bullies and juvenile delinquents, are much more likely to respond with self-centered reasons such as: "You might get caught" or "You'll get in trouble." In comparison, children with few if any behavior problems are more likely to focus on the impact of their behavior on others and issues of fairness.

Greater Emphasis Should Be Placed on Using Positive Techniques for Developing Self-Discipline, Preventing Misbehavior, and Meeting Children's Basic Needs Than on Correcting Misbehavior

Each of the listed guiding principles concerns the primary *aims* of school discipline from a positive psychology framework. The present principle and the following one concern the *means* for attaining these aims. Just as the previous aims are viewed as positive, so too should be the means for achieving them. Thus, emphasis is placed on the use of strategies and techniques for developing, strengthening, or increasing what is desired (e.g., character strengths) and preventing what is not desired. However, in light of research on the effectiveness of sanctions and punishment in deterring misbehavior and promoting safety and learning (Bear, 2012b; Cornell & Mayer, 2010; Gottfredson, 2001), schools should not forgo the reasonable use of such measures. As emphasized by Seligman, Steen, Park, and Peterson (2005), the intent of positive psychology is not simply to replace effective practices for addressing individual weaknesses with effective practices for promoting strengths. Nor is it the intention of positive psychology to necessarily replace reasonable forms of punishment with positive alternatives, but rather to minimize the need for the use of punishment.

In positive psychology, the limitations of rewards and praise, but particularly the former, are well recognized (see Brophy, 1981; Hattie & Timperley, 2007, for limitations). The one limitation that has been subject of ongoing debate among researchers is the effect of rewards and praise, especially the former, on intrinsic motivation (see Akin-Little, Eckert, Lovett, & Little, 2004; Deci, Koestner, & Ryan, 2001). It is beyond the scope of this chapter to cover that debate. However, it should be noted that research shows that although praise and rewards are generally effective in increasing desired behavior, they may be detrimental to intrinsic motivation under some, albeit limited, circumstances. The circumstances under which this is most likely to occur are when they are used in a controlling (rather than informational) manner—to elicit situational versus committed compliance or to get students to engage in behaviors that they already enjoy doing.

Programs and Techniques for Positive School Discipline Should Be Based on Theory and Empirical Evidence as to Their Effectiveness

In the field of mental health, many *positive* therapies and interventions have been proposed and implemented with the intended purpose of enhancing personal well-being and happiness and were later found to be ineffective (Petersen & Seligman, 2004). The same holds true with respect to many positive-oriented programs in education designed to develop character strengths and reduce behavior problems. Noteworthy among them are values clarification (Raths, Harmin, & Simon, 1966), which was popular in the 1960s and 1970s, and the self-esteem movement, which was popular in the early 1990s (California Task Force to Promote Self-Esteem and Personal and Social Responsibility, 1990). Each was shown to be ineffective. To prevent this from happening in the new field of positive psychology, interventions are to be supported by theory and empirical research, especially research on the study of positive emotions, positive character, and positive institutions (Seligman & Csikszentmihalyi, 2000).

POPULAR MODELS AND APPROACHES TO SCHOOL DISCIPLINE

In this section, we present a brief summary of the defining features of what are perhaps the most popular models and approaches to classroom management and school discipline: Positive Discipline, Assertive Discipline, SWPBIS and SEL.

Positive Discipline

The philosophy and techniques of this model draw heavily from the writings of Rudolph Dreikurs (Dreikurs, 1968; Dreikurs & Cassel, 1972; Dreikurs & Grey, 1968). Core principles of Positive Discipline, particularly those that its developers are likely to argue are consistent with positive psychology, are presented as follows.

School Discipline Should Be Student Centered and Responsive to the Individual Needs and Goals of Students

Positive Discipline asserts that although the classroom environment, especially the classroom teacher, clearly influences student behavior, behavior is determined primarily by an individual student's needs, goals, values, and beliefs. Social belonging is viewed as the foremost need and goal, the primary motivator of behavior, and central to self-esteem, happiness, and success in all areas of life. Accordingly, school discipline must strengthen rather than harm self-esteem, happiness, and social belonging.

The Foremost Aim of Discipline Is the Development of Self-Discipline

Dreikurs argued that all individuals cherish a sense of autonomy, or self-determination, and that self-discipline is necessary for an individual to function successfully in a democratic society (Dreikurs & Cassel, 1972). In developing self-discipline, Positive Discipline prescribes that teachers foster students' self-perceptions of personal competence, social belonging, and autonomy and develop students' intrapersonal skills, interpersonal judgment, and systemic skills (e.g., responsibility, responding to consequences).

A Positive Approach Is Democratic and Caring, With Emphases on a Positive Classroom Climate, Encouragement, and Classroom Meetings

Following Dreikurs (1968; Dreikurs & Cassel, 1972), Nelsen and colleagues (2000) highlight the importance of a *democratic and caring classroom climate* in which teacher–student and student–student relations are supportive, caring, and mutually respectful and in which students are actively engaged in democratic decision making. *Encouragement*, defined by Dreikurs (Dreikurs & Grey, 1968) as unconditional love (but not to be equated with praise or reinforcement), is viewed as the "foundation" of Positive Discipline (Nelsen et al., 2000, p. 161). *Classroom meetings* are seen as a core element of a democratic, caring, and encouraging classroom climate.

Punishment, Rewards, and Praise Should Not Be Used

Punishment, rewards, and praise are perceived as being detrimental to developing self-discipline and teacher–student relations and as primary sources of misbehavior. Nelsen and colleagues (2000) state that "*Any form* [italics added] of punishment or permissiveness is both disrespectful and discouraging" and that "Punishment has no place in the Positive Discipline classroom" (p. 117). Rewards and praise are viewed nearly as harshly as punishment. Nelsen and colleagues (2000) argue that rewards and punishment encourage teachers, not students, to be responsible for student behavior, foster long-term negative effects, and fail to teach self-discipline.

In Correcting Misbehavior, Teachers Should Use a Variety of Positive Discipline Classroom Management Tools

In preventing and correcting misbehavior, teachers are advised to be kind and firm, follow classroom routines, redirect behavior, offer limited choices, avoid arguments and punishment, encourage problem solving and self-reflection, discuss the disciplinary issue in a class meeting, and foster individual and group responsibility. Greatest emphasis, however, is on use of encouragement. That is, the primary role of the teacher in correcting misbehavior is to encourage students to apply their strengths and skills while also providing necessary supports to help students be successful. When encouragement is insufficient, teachers are advised to use *natural consequences, logical consequences, and solutions,* as well as a variety of additional positive discipline management tools. Those tools include positive time-out, which is a form of time-out that is neither punitive nor "humiliating" (Nelson et al., 2000, p. 176) but helps students to calm down, reflect upon their behavior, and "feel better" (Nelson et al., 2000, p. 212). When behavior problems continue to occur, teachers are advised to hold a conference with parents in which the student is to attend and to be actively involved.

Assertive Discipline: A Positive Behavior Management for Today's Classroom

Assertive Discipline was first introduced in 1976 with the subtitle *A Take Charge Approach for Today's Educator* (Canter, 1976). Since 1976, three newer and much less strident versions of *Assertive Discipline* have been published (Canter, 2010; Canter & Canter, 1992, 2001). The primary techniques of Canter's (2010) model of *Assertive Discipline: Positive Behavior Management for Today's Classroom* are summarized in the context of what Canter would likely argue are its positive principles.

A Positive Approach Is Teacher Centered, With the Teacher Providing Structure and Support

Although both structure and support are viewed as being important in classroom management, structure is primary in Assertive Discipline. Reflecting a greater emphasis on structure than support, teachers are advised to (a) develop and maintain an assertive teacher voice (to "say what they mean and mean what they say"; Canter, 2010, p. 9), (b) hold high expectations (to "expect 100 percent compliance with your directions 100 percent of the time," p. 15), (c) develop a classroom discipline plan (consisting of 3–5 classroom rules, positive support strategies, and a hierarchy of corrective actions), and (d) directly teach responsible behavior. *Positive support strategies* teach and reinforce students' compliance with the classroom discipline plan and prevent behavior problems. They include classwide rewards, which are monitored with points on the board.

Students Learn Responsible Behavior and Self-Management by the Direct Teaching of Policies, Procedures, Rules, and Corrective Actions

Self-discipline, or what is referred to as responsible behavior and self-management of behavior, means knowing and obeying the rules and demonstrating compliance (i.e., situational compliance) to teachers' expectations. Consistent with a behavioral model of learning, it is understood that nearly all behavior is learned and that direct instruction, positive reinforcement, and punishment explain the bulk of the learning process. Teachers are to develop a responsible behavior curriculum in which specific observable and desired behaviors are targeted. Following a direct instruction approach, teachers explain the behavior, model the behavior, check for student understanding, and allow for student practice (with positive feedback given for responsible behavior).

Canter (2010) offers the *Behavior Management Cycle* as a method of motivating students to follow directions, which consists of three steps: (a) clearly communicate explicit directions, (b) utilize *behavioral narration* to support students who follow directions, and (c) take corrective action with students who fail to comply. Behavioral narration consists of "repeating your directions to the students by describing the behavior of those students who are following your directions" (Canter, 2010, p. 64).

Schoolwide Positive Behavioral Interventions and Supports (SWPBIS)

The SWPBIS approach has much in common with Assertive Discipline, sharing the same behavioral framework and many behavioral strategies and techniques (although different terms are often used). The commonalities between the two are seen in Canter (2010) devoting a new chapter in his book on establishing *schoolwide* Assertive Discipline, in which he cites research studies and articles on SWPBIS (while never mentioning SWPBIS by name).

Compared to Assertive Discipline, the SWPBIS approach places significantly greater emphasis on schoolwide system change. This includes the implementation of a three-tiered system of supports (universal, selective, indicated) to prevent problems, reduce existing problems, and improve the *social culture* of the school. Five defining features of SWPBIS are consistently identified in the literature (e.g., Horner, Sugai, Todd, & Lewis-Palmer, 2005; Sugai & Horner, 2009; Sugai et al., 2010), as described briefly in the following sections.

Operationally Defined and Valued Outcomes

Key academic and behavioral outcomes, defined in observable and measurable terms, are targeted for intervention and regularly evaluated. The most common outcome measures include office disciplinary referrals (ODRs) and suspension data; however, attendance, school climate, and academic achievement have also been assessed (e.g., Horner et al., 2009).

Ongoing Collection and Use of Data for Decision Making

School teams are encouraged to review ODRs on a routine basis (i.e., at least quarterly), carefully examining the average number of ODRs per day and per staff member and by location, problem behavior, student, and time of day (Sugai et al., 2010). These data are analyzed by staff using the principles of functional behavioral analysis, and interventions are implemented to address areas of concern.

Systems Change

SWPBIS emphasizes the importance of team-based selection and implementation of research-validated practices, data-based decision making, administrative and team leadership, staff commitment, communication and information systems, adequate personnel and time, and budgeted support for SWPBIS. These features are found in most school reform efforts, but a notable difference is the emphasis placed in SWPBIS on the composition of the leadership team. The leadership team is to be composed of at least two individuals with expertise and experience in behavioral theory, applied behavior analysis, function-based behavior intervention planning and support, direct social skills instruction, and principles of reinforcement (Sugai et al., 2010).

Research-Validated Practices

According to Sugai et al. (2010), "research validated refers to studies that directly and systematically examine whether a functional relationship exists between the accurate implementation of a practice and important changes in the behavior or performance of the recipients of the practice" (p. 15). SWPBIS schools are characterized by four major research-validated practices: clearly defined behavioral expectations, direct teaching of behavioral expectations, reinforcement of appropriate behavior, and a recognition/reward system for responding to inappropriate behavior.

Foundations in Applied Behavior Analysis and Biomedical Sciences

The principles of applied behavior analysis (ABA) are evident throughout each of the four defining features outlined previously (Dunlap, Sailor, Horner, & Sugai, 2009; Sugai & Horner, 2009). According to Sugai and colleagues (2010), SWPBIS is grounded not only in ABA but also in *biomedical science* (Sugai et al., 2010). It is unclear, however, what they mean by this term, as they fail to define or explain it (Bear, Whitcomb, Elias, & Blank, in press).

Social and Emotional Learning (SEL)

Assuming an ecological-developmental systems perspective, the SEL approach is based on theory and research in a variety of fields that share this perspective, including prevention and resilience, positive youth development, social-cognitive theory, emotional development, and positive psychology (Osher, Bear, Sprague, & Doyle, 2010). The SEL approach seeks to enhance students' social, emotional, and moral development and promote positive mental health and well-being (Durlak, Weissberg, Dymnicki, Taylor, & Schellinger, 2011). SEL programs target how children *think, feel,* and *act*. As such, they are intended not only to promote socially and morally responsible behavior but also to develop the social cognitive and emotional processes that underlie such behavior. Five core social and emotional competencies are targeted in SEL programs: (a) self-awareness, (b) self-management of emotions and behavior, (c) social awareness, (d) relationship skills, and (e) responsible decision making at school, at home, and in the community (Collaborative for Academic, Social, and Emotional Learning [CASEL], 2013). These competencies are developed within the context of the following basic strategies commonly found in SEL programs (see Bear, 2005, 2010; Durlak et al., 2011; Elias et al., 1997; Zins & Elias, 2006).

Evidenced-Based Curriculum Lessons

Lessons are developmentally appropriate, evidence based, and consistent with the acronym SAFE (Durlak et al., 2011). That is, they are sequenced (step-by-step lessons are taught within and across school years), active (students play an active rather than passive role in learning), focused (sufficient time is focused on skill development), and explicit (the lessons' goals are clearly articulated). Lessons are based on unifying themes, such as empathy, social problem solving, emotion regulation, responsibility, and respect (see the CASEL website at www.CASEL.org for a review of more than 80 SEL curriculum programs).

Positive Classroom and School Climates

Emphasis is placed on building and maintaining a caring climate that meets students' needs: Students feel good about themselves, feel attached or connected with others, and are actively engaged. In light of ample research showing the importance of positive teacher–student relationships in developing SEL competencies and preventing behavior problems (Hamre & Pianta, 2006), teacher–student relationships receive primary attention. However, other commonly recognized aspects of school climate also are targeted, including student–student relationships, school–home relationships, safety, clear and fair expectations and rules, respect for diversity, and student engagement.

Ample Opportunities for Students to Apply and Practice SEL Skills

Students are taught SEL skills directly and indirectly and are expected to apply them throughout the school day, as well as at all other times. Frequent opportunities are provided for them to do so. This includes service learning, class meetings, student government, peer-assisted learning, peer mediation, and sports and extracurricular activities (see Bear, 2010; Elias, Wang, Weissberg, Zins, & Walberg, 2002; Elias et al., 1997; Zins & Elias, 2006).

An Authoritative Approach to Discipline

Discipline is consistent with the dual meanings of the term discipline and with the dual aims of school discipline: the short-term management and correction of student behavior and the long-term development of self-discipline. Guided by an evidence-based authoritative approach to discipline (Baumrind, 1996, 2012; Brophy, 1996; Gregory et al., 2010), demandingness (also referred to as structure) and responsiveness (also referred to as support) receive equal emphasis. Thus, a developmentally appropriate discipline system is in place with fair expectations, rules, and consequences (including forms of punishment), but it coexists with an emphasis on adults being responsive to students' social and emotional needs, which include demonstrating caring and support. Teachers clearly recognize that most discipline problems can be prevented but also understand that at times correction is needed. Disciplinary encounters are viewed as opportunities to teach and develop SEL competencies, and it is understood that teachers and school staff, students (individually and collectively), parents, and the community share responsibility for student behavior and the school climate.

Additional Supportive Systems and Services

Although this element often receives less emphasis than the other elements, it is recognized that the other elements are not always sufficient for preventing and correcting behavior problems and developing self-discipline. Thus, additional supports and services are needed, especially for those students with serious or chronic behavior problems.

This includes services at the indicated and selected levels of prevention and intervention, such as individual and small-group counseling, booster sessions from the SEL curriculum, additional social skills or anger management training, consultation to teachers from a mental health specialist, crisis intervention, and supports to parents (e.g., Conduct Problems Prevention Research Group, 2011).

ARE THEY POSITIVE?

In this section, we present a brief critique of the four models and approaches presented previously while answering "Are they positive?" Clearly, each one is *positive*, and presents itself as such, from the narrow perspective of equating positive with an emphasis on the use of alternatives to punishment rather than the use of punishment (especially suspension), valuing prevention over correction, and striving to create safe schools. From the framework of positive psychology, those criteria are insufficient for a program to be considered truly *positive*. Instead, to be judged positive from the perspective of positive psychology, a program must be consistent with the guiding core principles of positive psychology applied to school discipline, as presented previously. Those principles are repeated here, with comments as to the extent to which each model or approach is consistent with them.

The Primary Aim of Positive Classroom Discipline Is the Development of Character Strengths and Virtues of Self-Discipline

In too many schools, the techniques and strategies of school discipline most commonly used are not designed to develop character strengths and self-discipline but to attain situational compliance. The aim is short term and teacher centered, achieved by adults managing and correcting student behavior. Assertive Discipline and SWPBIS share this aim. Canter makes it very clear that the aim of Assertive Discipline is to provide teachers with behavioral techniques to take charge of, or control, student behavior. The SWPBIS approach is less clear as to its primary aim. Other than preventing behavior problems, its historical roots clearly indicate that the techniques of positive behavioral supports were designed to manage and control the behavior of individuals with serious behavior problems, especially those with disabilities (Bear et al., in press; Dunlap, Sailor, Horner, & Sugai, 2009). To be sure, responsibility and respect are among the behavioral expectations in many SWPBIS programs, but when one examines what is actually taught, it becomes clear that these expectations often translate into acts of compliance to the expectations and rules of adults (Bear, 2010; Bear et al., in press). Thus, in both Assertive Discipline and SWPBIS, compliance, and particularly situational compliance rather than self-discipline, appears to be the primary aim.

In contrast to Assertive Discipline and SWPBIS, Positive Discipline and SEL place greater emphasis on developing self-discipline and thus are more congruent with positive psychology. However, although Positive Discipline aims to develop self-discipline, the model fails to provide educators with sufficient understanding and guidance in achieving that aim. The program is overly ambitious in its goals and lacks theory and research to help educators achieve them. For example, Positive Discipline fails to cite research on children's cognitions and emotions supporting its recommended techniques for fostering self-discipline. In contrast, the SEL approach clearly articulates its goals and techniques for achieving them, including evidence-based techniques that teach students character strengths and virtues related to self-discipline.

In Addition to Developing Character Strengths and Virtues, Programs Should Help Children Meet Three Basic Human Needs: The Need for Autonomy, the Need for Belongingness, and the Need for Competence

Whereas Positive Discipline and SEL recognize the critical importance of the needs for autonomy, belongingness, and competence, Assertive Discipline and SWPBIS fail to do so, particularly with respect to autonomy and belongingness. In Assertive Discipline and SWPBIS, social cognitions and emotions shown to be related to autonomy, belongingness, and competence receive little, if any, attention. Whereas Assertive Discipline and SWPBIS give too little attention to these areas, Positive Discipline places too much emphasis on the role of self-esteem in student behavior. This is seen in its advice to educators not to use punishment and rewards because they harm self-esteem. Such advice is simply inconsistent with research on the effectiveness of punishment and rewards when used strategically and wisely (see Bear, 2010, for a review of the research). Moreover, school discipline programs, such as Positive Discipline, that place their focus primarily on personal happiness might foster self-esteem but are unlikely to foster self-discipline. Students can be quite happy when they misbehave (especially when they don't get caught). Although self-esteem and happiness are important in their own right, there is a lack of research supporting the idea that happiness and positive self-esteem per se prevent behavior problems and thus should be a primary focus in school discipline (Manning, Bear, & Minke, 2006).

Greater Emphasis Should Be Placed on Using Positive Techniques for Developing Self-Discipline, Preventing Misbehavior, and Meeting Children's Basic Needs Than on Correcting Misbehavior

As noted above, compared to Assertive Discipline and SWPBIS, Positive Discipline and SEL place greater emphasis on developing self-discipline and meeting students' needs for competence, belongingness, and autonomy. They also place less emphasis on correcting misbehavior than on those aims. All four favor prevention over correction. They share many of the same techniques for prevention and correction. For example, all four emphasize teacher–parent communication, motivating instruction, and the use of a variety of common techniques of classroom management for preventing and correcting misbehavior (e.g., redirection, physical proximity, positive reinforcement), although often they differ in what they call those techniques (e.g., natural and logical consequences instead of punishment, positive support instead of praise).

All four models and approaches criticize the use of punishment, but each uses it. This is particularly true when punishment is defined, as is common in psychology, as anything that reduces the frequency of a behavior and is generally viewed as aversive by the individual to whom it is applied (Alberto & Troutman, 2008). When these conditions apply, punishment includes natural and logical consequences in Positive Discipline (and many SEL programs) and corrective actions in Assertive Discipline and SWPBIS (e.g., time-out, referral to the office). Although all four use punishment, they recognize the many limitations to its use and thus prefer more positive alternatives for strengthening desired behaviors.

Greater differences between models and approaches are found in the recommended use of praise and rewards. As noted previously, whereas praise and rewards, and especially the latter, are generally effective in teaching new skills and managing behavior, they have their limitations. Although Positive Discipline ignores research on the effectiveness of the use of praise and rewards, recommending that they not be used, Assertive Discipline and SWPBIS largely ignore the limitations of the systematic use of tangible rewards, recommending that tokens and rewards be used widely and in a similar manner across all age levels to teach and reinforce students for following adults' expectations and rules. In contrast, in the SEL approach, praise and rewards are used, but rewards more sparingly. In recognition of their limitations, praise and rewards are used more strategically, with consideration of factors that determine how and when they might be effective or detrimental (see Bear, 2010, for specific strategies). Perhaps most importantly, however, those following the SEL approach are cognizant of the thoughts and reasoning they may be reinforcing with their use of praise and rewards, preferring to reinforce the intentions and reasons behind a prosocial behavior instead of the observed acts of compliance per se.

Although compliance should *not* be the primary aim of school discipline, compliance *is* important in classroom management and school discipline, as well as in developing self-discipline (Bear, 2005, 2010). A strength of both Assertive Discipline and SWPBIS is that they provide the structure often necessary for compliance. In this manner, they address a general weakness of positive psychology (especially with respect to school discipline), which its emphasis on increasing positive behaviors at the expense of directing much less attention to decreasing negative behaviors (Huebner, Gilman, & Furlong, 2009; Kristja'nsson, 2012). Indeed, with respect to comprehensive school discipline, a lack of recognition of the effectiveness of punishment in correcting behavior problems and sound guidance on its limited use may well be viewed as limitations of Positive Discipline and SEL.

Where Assertive Discipline and SWPBIS are especially lacking is in placing equal emphasis on support *and* responsiveness with respect to meeting the social and emotional needs of students. This includes the dearth of student-centered techniques for developing social and emotional assets, character strengths, and virtues of self-discipline. Instead of providing teachers with guidance for developing those qualities and assets, teachers are simply told that over time, self-discipline, or self-management, will automatically emerge as a result of the direct teaching and positive reinforcement of acts of compliance.

Programs and Techniques for Positive School Discipline Should Be Based on Theory and Empirical Evidence as to Their Effectiveness

In general, Positive Discipline and Assertive Discipline cite little research to support their recommended practices and no research demonstrating the effectiveness of their model compared to other models. When the developers cite supporting research, few of the studies are published ones, and none would be considered by most researchers as meeting minimal standards of scientific rigor. To be fair, although they fail to reference supporting research, their developers are correct in claiming that research supports many of their techniques, including techniques in Assertive Discipline for managing and correcting misbehavior, techniques in Positive Discipline for developing self-discipline, and techniques in both for preventing misbehavior.

With respect to the SWPBIS approach, and compared to the previous two models, research is much greater in both quantity and quality. In brief, the strongest and most frequently reported evidence of the effectiveness of the SWPBIS approach is in reducing ODRs and suspensions; evidence that it promotes academic achievement and a positive school climate is weak; and evidence that it promotes other positive outcomes, such as prosocial behavior and the development of social cognitions and emotions associated with self-discipline, is practically nonexistent (see Bear, 2010, 2012, and Osher et al., 2010, for reviews of the research on SWPBIS). Another limitation of research on SWPBIS is that it is largely limited to research conducted in the fields of special education and applied behavior analysis, often by its own developers, in which the theory and research of others in the areas of developmental psychology and educational psychology, particularly research on children's social cognitions and emotions, are ignored.

In contrast, the goals of SEL are linked to theory and research as to their importance, and the techniques and programs are generally supported by research as to their effectiveness (Bear, 2010; Bear et al., in press; Osher et al., 2010). In a recent meta-analysis of the research literature, which included 213 studies of universal-level SEL programs and 270,034 students, Durlak and colleagues (2011) found that SEL programs improved a variety of social and emotional skills, including emotion regulation, perspective taking, and social problem solving; were associated with more favorable attitudes toward self and others, including self-esteem, self-efficacy, self-perceptions of relations with teachers, and liking of school; and increased both academic achievement and prosocial behavior. SEL programs also led to fewer conduct problems—including classroom disruption, noncompliance, aggression, and bullying—and less emotional distress.

CONCLUSION

Positive Discipline (Canter, 2010) and Assertive Discipline (Nelsen et al., 2001) present two contrasting models of school discipline, each claiming to be a positive model. Positive Discipline is student centered, emphasizing practices that promote the development of cognitions and emotions related to self-discipline and meeting students' basic needs. To achieve those aims and prevent misbehavior, it strongly opposes the use of rewards, praise, and punishment and relies heavily on close teacher–student relations, class meetings, and positive behavior management tools, especially encouragement. In contrast, Assertive Discipline is teacher centered, emphasizing the direct teaching of rules and use of corrective actions, albeit within the context of teachers' positive support. Rewards and punishment are critical components of the model and are viewed as serving not only to correct behavior problems but also as preventing them and helping to develop self-management. Although Positive Discipline fits within the framework of positive psychology much more so than does Assertive Discipline, it has many of the same short-comings as Assertive Discipline. First, both programs fail to draw from recent research and theory in the areas of positive emotions, positive character, and positive institutions. Second, they lack evidence demonstrating that the programs can be implemented with integrity and lead to positive outcomes.

In many ways, the SWPBIS and SEL approaches present similar contrasts. Assertive Discipline and SWPBIS share many of the same strategies and techniques, as do Positive Discipline and SEL. The major differences between the two models and two general approaches are that the two approaches (i.e., SWPBIS and SEL) are supported by much more research as to their effectiveness. The outcomes generally measured in the two approaches differ, however, with SWPBIS focusing primarily on measures of situational compliance and SEL including a greater variety of outcomes that are much more consistent with the guiding principles of positive psychology.

If educators' aim is to elicit situational compliance via teacher-centered techniques of prevention and correction, they may prefer Assertive Discipline and SWPBIS. If their aim is the long-term development of self-discipline, then they may prefer Positive Discipline. The latter aim is most consistent with positive psychology. Both goals are important components of a comprehensive approach to school discipline. Achieving both aims necessitates a combination of teacher-centered and student-centered techniques, with a balance of demandingness and responsiveness (i.e., an authoritative approach). As seen in Table 22.1, SEL comes closest to offering a comprehensive approach and one most consistent with positive psychology. Nevertheless, compared to SEL, Assertive Discipline and SWPBIS offer a greater number of specific behavioral techniques often of value in the correction of behavior problems, particularly for those students with serious and chronic behavior problems. It is for this reason, and in recognition of other strengths of SWPBIS (see Bear, 2010; Bear et al., in press), that it is recommended that educators who desire a more comprehensive approach to school discipline should draw from the strategies and techniques of SWPBIS, particularly in preventing and correcting behavior problems and when the techniques of SEL are insufficient.

REFERENCES

Akin-Little, K.A., Eckert, T.L., Lovett, B.J., & Little, S.G. (2004). Extrinsic reinforcement in the classroom: Bribery or best practice. *School Psychology Review, 33*, 344–362.

Alberto, P.A., & Troutman, A.C. (2008). *Applied behavior analysis for teachers* (8th ed.). Upper Saddle River, NJ: Prentice Hall.

Bar-On, R. (2010). Emotional intelligence: An integral part of positive psychology. *South African Journal of Psychology, 40*, 54–62.

Baumrind, D. (1996). The discipline controversy revisited. *Family Relations, 45*, 405–414. doi:10.2307/585170

Baumrind, D. (2012). Authoritative parenting revisited: History and current status. In R.E. Larzelere, A.S. Morris, & A.W. Harrist (Eds.), *Authoritative parenting: Synthesizing nurturance and discipline for optimal child development* (pp. 11–34). Washington, DC: American Psychological Association.

Bear, G. G. (with A. Cavalier & M. Manning). (2005). *Developing self-discipline and preventing and correcting misbehavior.* Boston, MA: Allyn & Bacon.

Bear, G. G. (2010). *School discipline and self-discipline: A practical guide to promoting prosocial student behavior.* New York, NY: Guilford.

Bear, G. G. (2012a). Both suspension and alternatives work, depending on one's aim. *Journal of School Violence, 2,* 174–186. doi:10.1080/15388220.2012.652914

Bear, G. G. (2012b). Self-discipline as a protective asset. In S. Brock & S. Jimerson (Eds.), *Best practices in crisis prevention and intervention in the schools* (2nd ed., pp. 27–54). Bethesda, MD: National Association of School Psychologists.

Bear, G. G., Manning, M. A., & Izard, C. (2003). Responsible behavior: The importance of social cognition and emotion. *School Psychology Quarterly, 18,* 140–157. doi:10.1521/scpq.18.2.140.21857

Bear, G. G., Whitcomb, S., Elias, M., & Blank, J. (in press). SEL and school-wide positive behavioral interventions and supports. In J. Durlak, T. Gullotta, C. Domitrovich, P. Goren, & R. Weissberg (Eds.), *Handbook of social and emotional learning.* New York, NY: Guilford.

Brophy, J. E. (1981). On praising effectively. *Elementary School Journal, 81,* 269–278. doi:10.3102/00346543051001005

Brophy, J. E. (1996). *Teaching problem students.* New York, NY: Guilford.

California Task Force to Promote Self-Esteem and Personal and Social Responsibility. (1990). *Toward a state of esteem: The final report of the California Task Force to Promote Self-Esteem and Personal and Social Responsibility.* Sacramento, CA: Author.

Canter, L. (1976). *Assertive discipline: A take charge approach for today's educator.* Santa Monica, CA: Lee Canter and Associates.

Canter, L. (2010). *Assertive discipline: Positive behavior management for today's classroom.* Bloomington, IN: Solution Tree Press.

Canter, L., & Canter, M. (1992, 2001). *Assertive discipline: Positive behavior management for today's classroom.* Santa Monica, CA: Canter and Associates.

Charles, C. M. (2010). *Building classroom discipline* (10th ed.). New York, NY: Pearson.

Collaborative for Academic, Social, and Emotional Learning (CASEL). (2013). *CASEL guide: Effective social and emotional programs, preschool and elementary edition.* Retrieved from http://casel.org/publications

Conduct Problems Prevention Research Group. (2011). The effects of the Fast Track preventive intervention on the development of conduct disorder across childhood. *Child Development, 82,* 331–345. doi:10.1111/j.1467-8624.2010.01558.x

Cornell, D., & Mayer, M. J. (2010). Why do school order and safety matter? *Educational Researcher, 39,* 7–15. doi:10.3102/0013189X09357616

Deci, E. L., Koestner, R., & Ryan, R. M. (2001). Extrinsic rewards and intrinsic motivation in education: Reconsidered once again. *Review of Educational Research, 71,* 1–27. doi:10.3102/00346543071001001

Dreikurs, R. (1968). *Psychology in the classroom: A manual for teachers.* New York, NY: Harper & Row.

Dreikurs, R., & Cassel, P. (1972). *Discipline without tears: What to do with children who misbehave.* New York, NY: Hawthorn Books.

Dreikurs, R., & Grey, L. (1968). *Logical consequences: A handbook of discipline.* New York, NY: Meredith Press.

Dunlap, G., Sailor, W., Horner, R. H., & Sugai, G. (2009). Overview and history of positive behavior support. In W. Sailor, G. Dunlap, G. Sugai, & R. Horner (Eds.), *Handbook of positive behavior support* (pp. 3–16). New York, NY: Springer.

Durlak, J. A., Weissberg, R. P., Dymnicki, A. B., Taylor, R. D., & Schellinger, K. B. (2011). The impact of enhancing students' social and emotional learning: A meta-analysis of school-based universal interventions. *Child Development, 82,* 474–501. doi:10.1111/j.1467-8624.2010.01564.x

Elias, M. J., Wang, M. C., Weissberg, R. P., Zins, J. E., & Walberg, H. J. (2002). The other side of the report card: Student success depends on more than test scores. *American School Board Journal, 189*(11), 28–30. Retrieved from http://casel.org/wp-content/uploads/otherside.pdf

Elias, M. J., Zins, J. E., Weissberg, R. P., Frey, K. S., Greenberg, M. T., Haynes, N., . . . Shriver, T. P. (1997). *Promoting social and emotional learning: Guidelines for educators.* Alexandria, VA: Association for Supervision and Curriculum Development.

Gottfredson, D. (2001). *Schools and delinquency.* New York, NY: Cambridge University Press.

Gregory, A., Cornell, D., Fan, X., Sheras, P., Shih, T., & Huang, F. (2010). Authoritative school discipline: High school practices associated with lower student bullying and victimization. *Journal of Educational Psychology, 102,* 483–496. doi:10.1037/a0018562

Hamre, B.K., & Pianta, R.C. (2006). Student–teacher relationships. In G.G. Bear & K.M. Minke (Eds.), *Children's needs III: Development, prevention, and intervention* (pp. 59–71). Bethesda, MD: National Association of School Psychologists.

Hattie, J., & Timperley, H. (2007). The power of feedback. *Review of Educational Research, 77,* 81–112. doi:10.3102/003465430298487

Horner, R.H., Sugai, G., Smolkowski, K., Eber, L., Nakasato, J., Todd, A.W., & Esperanza, J. (2009). A randomized, wait-list controlled effectiveness trial assessing School-Wide Positive Behavior Support in elementary schools. *Journal of Positive Behavior Interventions, 11,* 133–144. doi:10.1177/1098300709332067

Horner, R.H., Sugai, G., Todd, A.W., & Lewis-Palmer, T. (2005). Schoolwide behavior support. In L.M. Bambara & L. Kern (Eds.), *Individualized supports for students with problem behaviors: Designing positive behavior plans* (pp. 359–390). New York, NY: Guilford.

Huebner, E.S., Gilman, R., & Furlong, M.J. (2009). A conceptual model for research in positive psychology in children and youth. In R. Gilman, E.S. Huebner, & M.J. Furlong (Eds.), *Handbook of positive psychology in schools* (pp. 3–8). New York, NY: Routledge.

Kochanska, G. (2002). Committed compliance, moral self, and internalization: A mediational model. *Developmental Psychology, 38,* 339–351. doi:10.1037/0012-1649.38.3.339

Kristja'nsson, K. (2012). Positive psychology and positive education: Old wine in new bottles? *Educational Psychologist, 47,* 86–105. doi:10.1080/00461520.2011.610678

Manning, M.A., & Bear, G.G. (2002). Are children's concerns about punishment related to their aggression? *Journal of School Psychology, 40,* 523–539. doi:10.1016/S0022-4405(02)00123-1

Manning, M.A., & Bear, G.G. (2011). Moral reasoning and aggressive behavior: Concurrent and longitudinal relations. *Journal of School Violence, 11,* 258–280. doi:10.1080/15388220.2011.579235

Manning, M.A., Bear, G.G., & Minke, K.M. (2006). Self-concept and self-esteem. In G.G. Bear & K.M. Minke (Eds.), *Children's needs III: Development, prevention, and intervention* (pp. 341–356). Bethesda, MD: National Association of School Psychologists.

Nelsen, J.D., Lott, L., & Glenn, H.S. (2000). *Positive discipline in the classroom: Developing mutual respect, cooperation, and responsibility in your classroom* (3rd ed.). New York, NY: Three Rivers.

Osher, D., Bear, G.G., Sprague, J.R., & Doyle, W. (2010). How can we improve school discipline? *Educational Researcher, 39,* 48–58. doi:10.3102/0013189X09357618

Petersen, C., & Seligman, M.E.P. (2004). *Character strengths and virtues: A handbook and classification.* Washington, DC: American Psychological Association.

Raths, L., Harmin, M., & Simon, S. (1966). *Values and teaching.* Columbus, OH: Charles E. Merrill.

Ryan, R.M., & Deci, E.L. (2000). Self-determination theory and the facilitation of intrinsic motivation, social development, and well-being. *American Psychologist, 55,* 68–78. doi:10.1037/0003-066X.55.1.68

Ryan, R.M., & Deci, E.L. (2006). Self-regulation and the problem of human autonomy: Does psychology need choice, self-determination, and will? *Journal of Personality, 74,* 1557–1585. doi:10.1111/j.1467-6494.2006.00420.x

Seligman, M.E.P., & Csikszentmihalyi, M. (Eds.). (2000). Positive psychology: An introduction. *American Psychologist, 55,* 5–14. doi:10.1037/0003-066X.55.1.5

Seligman, M.E.P., Ernst, R.M., Gillham, J., Reivich, K., & Linkin, M. (2009). Positive education: Positive psychology and classroom interventions. *Oxford Review of Education, 35,* 293–311. doi:10.1080/03054980902934563

Seligman, M.E.P., Steen, T.A., Park, N., & Peterson, C. (2005). Positive psychology progress: Empirical validation of interventions. *American Psychologist, 60,* 410–421. doi:10.1037/0003-066X.60.5.410

Stams, G.J., Brugman, D., Dekovic, M., van Rosmalen, L., van der Laan, P., & Gibbs, J.C. (2006). The moral judgment of juvenile delinquents: A meta-analysis. *Journal of Abnormal Child Psychology, 34,* 697–713. http://dx.doi.org/10.1007/s10802-006-9056-5

Sugai, G., & Horner, R.H. (2009). Defining and describing schoolwide positive behavior support. In W. Sailor, G. Dunlap, G. Sugai, & R. Horner (Eds.), *Handbook of positive behavior support* (pp. 307–326). New York, NY: Springer.

Sugai, G., Horner, R.H., Algozzine, R., Barrett, S., Lewis, T., Anderson, C., . . . Simonsen, B. (2010). *School-wide positive behavior support: Implementers' blueprint and self-assessment.* Eugene, OR: University of Oregon. Retrieved from www.pbis.org

Zins, J.E., & Elias, M.J. (2006). Social and emotional learning. In G.G. Bear & K.M. Minke (Eds.), *Children's needs III: Development, prevention, and intervention* (pp. 1–13). Bethesda, MD: National Association of School Psychologists.

CHAPTER SUMMARY: SCHOOL DISCIPLINE

Table 22.1 Strengths and Weaknesses of Models and Approaches to School Discipline

Principle of Positive Psychology	Positive Discipline	Assertive Discipline	SWPBIS	SEL
Primary aim of developing self-discipline	√	√–	√–	√+
Targets emotions, cognitions, and behavior	√	√–	√–	√+
Aim of meeting three basic needs of competence, belongingness, and autonomy	√	√–	√–	√
Emphasis on prevention and positive techniques	√+	√	√+	√+
Provides structure for managing and correcting misbehavior	√–	√+	√+	√
Supported by research on its effectiveness[a]	√–	√–	√	√+

Note. √+ = Major strength of model or approach. √ = Meets criteria, neither major strength nor weakness. √– = Weakness of model or approach.

[a] Effectiveness pertains to outcomes valued in positive psychology.

SUGGESTED READINGS: SCHOOL DISCIPLINE

Bear, G.G. (2010). *School discipline and self-discipline: A practical guide to promoting prosocial student behavior.* New York, NY: Guilford.

Presents evidence-based and practical strategies and techniques for achieving the dual aims of school discipline: creating safe and orderly schools and developing self-discipline.

Canter, L. (2010). *Assertive discipline: Positive behavior management for today's classroom.* Bloomington, IN: Solution Tree.

In this most recent version of *Assertive Discipline,* Canter offers a wide range of basic behavioral techniques of managing and controlling student behavior.

Durlak, J.A., Weissberg, R.P., Dymnicki, A.B., Taylor, R.D., & Schellinger, K.B. (2011). The impact of enhancing students' social and emotional learning: A meta-analysis of school-based universal interventions. *Child Development, 82,* 474–501. doi:10.1111/j.1467-8624.2010.01564.x

Presents a meta-analysis of 213 studies of universal-level SEL programs. SEL programs were found to have number of positive outcomes. Key features of effective programs are discussed.

Nelsen, J. D., Lott, L., & Glenn, H. S. (2000). *Positive discipline in the classroom: Developing mutual respect, cooperation, and responsibility in your classroom* (3rd ed.). New York, NY: Three Rivers.

Based on the earlier work of Dreikurs, the authors present a model of classroom management that emphasizes the development of self-discipline and other aspects of positive psychology.

Sugai, G., Horner, R. H., Algozzine, R., Barrett, S., Lewis, T., Anderson, C., . . . Simonsen, B. (2010). *School-wide positive behavior support: Implementers' blueprint and self-assessment.* Eugene, OR: University of Oregon. Retrieved from www.pbis.org

This official blueprint presents the key features and characteristics of the Sugai and Horner behavioral approach to SWPBIS.

23

UNDERSTANDING AND PROMOTING SCHOOL SATISFACTION IN CHILDREN AND ADOLESCENTS

Shannon M. Suldo, Lisa P. Bateman,
and Cheryl D. Gelley, Department of Psychological
and Social Foundations, University of South Florida,
Tampa, Florida, USA

INTRODUCTION

Although children spend the majority of their time outside of the home in school, students' happiness at school is often a neglected factor in the educational system. This increasingly sole attention to academic achievement is a likely byproduct of the current era of accountability. Nevertheless, research has demonstrated that a significant portion of students' global satisfaction with life is affected by their experiences in and satisfaction with school (Baker, Dilly, Aupperlee, & Patil, 2003). Noddings (2003) argues, "Happiness and education are, properly, intimately related: Happiness should be an aim of education, and a good education should contribute significantly to personal and collective happiness" (p. 1). In addition to the psychological implications of school satisfaction, it has been reasoned that students learn best when they are happy because they "seize their educational opportunities with delight, and they will contribute to the happiness of others" (Noddings, 2003, p. 261). Accordingly, this chapter summarizes the predictors and outcomes of students' positive appraisals of their schooling and concludes with implications for future research and practice.

DEFINITIONS AND THEORY BASE

In the first edition of this handbook, Baker and Maupin (2009) conveyed that school satisfaction refers to a student's subjective cognitive appraisal of the quality of his or her school life. School satisfaction is perhaps best understood in the larger context of wellness indicators. In brief, global life satisfaction, a common indicator of happiness, refers to one's cognitive appraisal of the overall quality of his or her life (see Gilman and Huebner, this edition). When making such overall judgments of personal well-being, individuals vary in which aspects of their lives they consider most; for example, some people emphasize financial status while others weigh relationship qualities most heavily. The domains deemed to be most salient to global life satisfaction are largely a function of one's developmental level. Early investigations of the areas of life that influence global life satisfaction appraisals among American youth implicated five core domains: family, friendships, living environment, self, and school (Huebner, 1994). Satisfaction in each domain is empirically linked to global life satisfaction (Seligson, Huebner, & Valois, 2003). Recent research on the Personal Wellbeing Index (PWI) among Australian adolescents confirmed that the School Children form of the PWI differs from the Adult form in the necessary inclusion of school as a contributing domain to global life satisfaction (Tomyn & Cummins, 2011). Specifically, Australian adolescents' satisfaction with school predicted their global life satisfaction above and beyond the contributions of the other seven domains of life (e.g., health, safety, achievements, future security) historically assessed with the PWI. School satisfaction appears to be a particularly strong contributor of life satisfaction among some subgroups of youth, including Korean secondary students (Park & Huebner, 2005), gifted American middle school students (Ash & Huebner, 1998), adolescent Norwegian girls (Danielson, Samdal, Hetland, & Wold, 2009), and adolescent boys in urban schools (Vera et al., 2012).

MEASUREMENT APPROACHES AND ISSUES

The growing literature base on school satisfaction among students in different school levels and from diverse cultures has used a variety of student self-report surveys to assess this inherently subjective construct. The earliest multi-item measure of school satisfaction came from the Quality of School Life Scale (QSL; Epstein & McPartland, 1976). The QSL includes a five-item Satisfaction with School scale (e.g., "The school and I are like: Good Friends, Friends, Distant Relatives, Strangers, or Enemies"), in addition to two scales tapping students' commitment to classwork and teacher–student relationship quality. A more commonly used alternative is the eight-item School Satisfaction scale of the Multidimensional Students' Life Satisfaction Scale (MSLSS; Huebner, 1994). Students rate the extent to which they agree with statements like "I look forward to going to school" and "There are many things about school I don't like." The school satisfaction scales of the MSLSS and QSL both have acceptable psychometric properties. Most studies reviewed in this chapter used the MSLSS School Satisfaction scale (e.g., Baker, 1998; Ferguson, Kasser, & Jahng, 2010; Hui & Sun, 2010; Torsheim et al., 2012; Vera et al., 2012) and a few used items from the QSL (e.g., Okun, Braver, & Weir, 1990; Verkuyten & Thijs, 2002).

In contrast to analyzing composite scores, some researchers have relied on a one-item indicator of school satisfaction in which students are asked to make a global judgment of their happiness with their schooling experiences (e.g., how much students "like school at the present," as used in Wachs, 2012). Case in point, the Brief Multidimensional Students' Life Satisfaction Scale (BMSLSS; Seligson et al., 2003) contains one item that gauges students' satisfaction with school. Students respond to the item "I would describe my satisfaction with my school experience as. . ." on a 7-point scale from *terrible* to *delighted*. The BMSLSS school item was analyzed in the report of mean levels of middle school students' school satisfaction by Huebner, Valois, Paxton, and Drane (2005). In another example, a single item on the 2005–2006 Health Behavior in School-aged Children (HBSC) survey asks students to indicate how much they like school (i.e., "How do you feel about school at present?") on a 4-point scale from *I like it a lot* to *I don't like it at all*. The HBSC is supported by the World Health Organization and administered every 4 years to adolescents (ages 11–15) throughout North America (Canada, United States), Israel, and Europe (e.g., Norway, Romania). Studies cited in this chapter that examined the HBSC school satisfaction item include Freeman, Samdal, Băban, and Bancila (2012) and Danielsen, Breivik, and Wold (2011). Danielsen and colleagues provided some support for the construct validity of this single item indicator by finding it loaded strongly on a factor composed of several items of the MSLSS School Satisfaction scale.

Beyond the MSLSS, QSL, and single-item indicators, other studies have created composite scores of multiple items tapping general school satisfaction that were designed for use in large-scale, cross-national studies. For example, some research cited in this chapter analyzed a composite school satisfaction variable composed of additional/optional items on an earlier administration of the HBSC (e.g., five items reflecting enjoyment of school and school activities from the 2001–2002 survey; Hoff, Anderson, & Holstein, 2010). In another example, Randolph, Kangas, and Ruokamo (2009) developed the six-item Children's Overall Satisfaction with Schooling Scale (COSSS) for use with Finnish and Dutch children ages 7 to 12. Four items reflect general school satisfaction (e.g., "I like to go to school") that are conceptually aligned with the QSL Satisfaction with School scale, while two pertain to satisfaction with school learning (e.g., "Learning is fun"), akin to the QSL Commitment to Classwork scale. The COSSS was utilized by the measure developers (Randolph et al., 2010) in a study of intrapersonal and environmental predictors of school satisfaction in the intended populations.

REVIEW OF KEY RESEARCH STUDIES

Key Research With Children and Adolescents (Ages 5–18)

Large-scale studies suggest that most students report positive levels of school satisfaction, although a sizable minority of middle and high school students are dissatisfied with their schooling experiences (Huebner, Drane, & Valois, 2000; Huebner et al., 2005). Factors that contribute to how students judge the quality of their school life include an array of intrapersonal variables and environmental contexts within and outside of school.

Intrapersonal Factors

School satisfaction tends to vary as a function of many student factors somewhat outside the direct realm of school, including students' cognitive patterns (i.e., perceptions of their abilities and control over their circumstances) and personal characteristics. Regarding the latter category, although research to date has not supported differences in school satisfaction between students of different socioeconomic levels (Huebner, Ash, & Laughlin, 2001), demographic features such as age and gender matter.

Age

Throughout the world, school satisfaction tends to decline as students age. Even within samples of elementary school children, younger Finnish and Dutch children reported greater school satisfaction than their older peers (Randolph, Kangas, & Ruokamo, 2010). Studies of American students have found an inverse relationship between age and school satisfaction among students in Grades 1 through 8 (Okun, Braver, & Weir, 1990), and lower mean levels of school satisfaction among high school students as compared to middle school students (DeSantis King, Huebner, Suldo, & Valois, 2006; Elmore & Huebner, 2010). This trend for decreasing mean levels of school satisfaction has also been observed among Chinese students in Grades 3 through 6 (Hui & Sun, 2010). In a large sample of Norwegian adolescents, 15-year-old boys and girls reported lower school satisfaction than 13-year-old students of the same gender (Danielsen et al., 2011).

Gender

Across developmental levels and countries, girls tend to be happier with school. With regard to children, European girls (median age of 10) from three elementary schools reported greater school satisfaction than their male classmates (Randolph et al., 2010). Adolescent females have also reported slightly higher mean levels of school satisfaction than their same-age male peers in large samples of youth from the United States (DeSantis King et al., 2006; Huebner et al., 2000; Huebner et al., 2005), Norway (Danielson et al., 2009), and Ireland (Gilman et al., 2008).

Cognitive Variables

The internal variables that co-occur most strongly with greater school satisfaction involve positive self-views, such as high self-esteem (Karatzias, Power, Flemming, Lennan, & Swanson, 2002; Vera et al., 2012) and confidence in one's academic and social abilities (Briones & Taberno, 2012). An internal locus of control has also been identified as a correlate of school satisfaction, with students who perceive less control over their lives tending to be less satisfied with school (Huebner et al., 2001; Huebner & Gilman, 2006).

Key Research on Classroom Context

Aspects of the classroom environment that have been investigated in relation to students' school satisfaction include demographic features of the classroom composition, curricula tailored to student ability level, and interpersonal relationships at school. These contextual variables influence the frequency with which students experience positive emotions during the school day. Early research found that such emotional and social experiences at school were among the strongest correlates of students' school satisfaction (Epstein & McPartland, 1976). More recent research with adolescents from the United States (Lewis, Huebner, Reschly, & Valois, 2009) and Scotland (Karatzias et al., 2002) clarified that students' school satisfaction appears particularly tied to how often they experience joy and other such positive emotions at school, as positive affect accounts for much more variance in school satisfaction than frequency of negative affect while at school (although both types of emotional experiences are significant predictors).

Classroom Composition

Clarifying early research that did not find a linear association between school satisfaction and class size among elementary school students (Verkuyten & Thijs, 2002), a more recent study of the same age group suggested that a moderate-sized class is associated with the highest school satisfaction (Randolph et al., 2010). Specifically, elementary school students in classes of around 20 students reported greater school satisfaction than students in classes that were particularly small (i.e., fewer than 15 students) or large (i.e., more than 25 students). In contrast, school satisfaction does not seem to be affected by the gender or ethnic makeup of a classroom (Verkuyten & Thijs, 2002). Case in point, Randolph and colleagues (2010) found that a higher proportion of students in the class that were the same gender as the participating student was unrelated to elementary school students' school satisfaction.

Academic Program

School satisfaction varies as a function of the match between a specialized curriculum and students' cognitive abilities. For example, greater school satisfaction has been found among American high school students with diagnosed mild cognitive disabilities who received special education services (as compared to their typically developing peers in regular education; Brantley, Huebner, & Nagle, 2002). Among students identified as academically and intellectually gifted, greater school satisfaction has been reported by Israeli students in junior high school served in special classes for the gifted (as compared to their gifted peers served in regular mainstream classes; Zeidner & Schleyer, 1999) and by academically gifted Korean students served in specialized science-oriented high schools (as compared to their gifted peers served in traditional high schools; Jin & Moon, 2006).

Key Research on In-Class Relationships

Greater perceptions of social support from people at school (i.e., classmates and especially teachers) consistently relate to higher levels of school satisfaction, from teenagers in European countries (Danielsen et al., 2009, 2011) to middle and high school students in the United States (DeSantis King et al., 2006). These supportive relationships likely engender a climate of care that facilitates students' positive appraisals of their schooling experiences. In Baker's (1998) seminal study of intrapersonal and environmental predictors of school satisfaction among low-income, urban, African-American elementary school students, children's perceived quality of their classroom's social climate (including perceptions of teacher care and fairness) emerged as the strongest correlate of their school satisfaction. In fact, this aspect of relationship quality (i.e., classroom social climate) distinguished students with the lowest school satisfaction more than objective indicators of teacher behavior (i.e., observed frequency of negative or positive teacher–student interactions) or student perceptions of general social support at school (Baker, 1999).

Students' satisfaction with school is particularly tied to their perceptions of student–teacher relationship quality (Whitley, Huebner, Hills, & Valois, 2012), often indicated by perceived social support from teachers (Hui & Sun, 2010; Tomyn & Cummins, 2011). Case in point, a recent analysis of data from more than 23,000 students (in Grades 8 and 10) from seven countries found that teacher support was at least twice as strong a predictor of school satisfaction as classmate support in all contexts, from North American to European countries (Torsheim et al., 2012). Beyond perceived support, teacher characteristics such as promotion of student autonomy, personality, and even gender play a role in students' school satisfaction. Regarding autonomy support, teenagers from collectivist and individualistic societies alike reported greater school satisfaction when they perceived their teachers were more receptive to students' points of view and feelings and afforded students choice and options in class (Ferguson et al., 2010). Among elementary school students in Finland and the Netherlands, the strongest classroom factor associated with school satisfaction was greater teacher likeability; students who reported greater school satisfaction agreed more with the statement "my teachers are nice" (Randolph et al., 2010). Randolph and colleagues also found a preliminary effect of teacher gender, in that elementary school boys and girls alike who had male teachers reported greater school satisfaction. In that study, 47% of teachers were male; it is unknown if teacher gender would relate to school satisfaction in societies such as the United States, where there are roughly twice as many female teachers as male teachers in preK–through sixth-grade classrooms (National Education Association, 2010).

Regarding the particular influence of relationships with classmates, students who feel more attached to their peers report greater school satisfaction, even 1 year later (Elmore & Huebner, 2010). In contrast, peer victimization (i.e., name calling, social exclusion) has been indirectly linked to lower school satisfaction in Dutch elementary school students, primarily via a negative association with perceived social competence (Verkuyten & Thijs, 2002). A direct association between peer victimization and school satisfaction was observed in students from German secondary schools; students who reported liking school a lot were 3 to 10 times less likely to be involved in traditional bullying (i.e., repeated acts of aggression) or cyberbullying (i.e., a form of bullying using information and communication technologies), either as victims or perpetrators or both, as compared to their peers with moderate to low levels of school satisfaction (Wachs, 2012).

Social relationships in the classroom fall under the broader umbrella of school climate. Zullig, Huebner, and Patton (2011) found that the combined influence of students' perceptions of eight dimensions of school climate accounted for approximately one third of the variance in their school satisfaction. Within this sample of more than 2,000 American middle and high school students, school satisfaction was uniquely associated with five dimensions of school climate, specifically student perceptions of academic support, student–teacher relationships, school connectedness, academic satisfaction, and order and discipline. With respect to the latter dimension, elementary school children who perceive a more disciplined and academically oriented classroom environment also experience greater school satisfaction (Verkuyten & Thijs, 2002). Other aspects of school climate that co-occur with greater school satisfaction include parent involvement in schooling (Suldo, Shaffer, & Riley, 2008) and perceived safety at school (Tomyn & Cummins, 2011).

Key Research on Events and Environments Outside of School

Students' school satisfaction appears influenced not only by the classroom context but also by their relationships with significant others (i.e., family) and the number and type of stressors in their lives. For example, lower school satisfaction has been observed among students who experience more stressors (chronic strains as well as acute, major events) and fewer resources in areas of life beyond school, namely related to family and friends (Huebner & McCullough, 2000; Huebner et al., 2001). Family relationships in particular are among the largest environmental correlates of school satisfaction. For instance, American students who reported greater perceptions of attachment to their parents reported higher levels of school satisfaction concurrently and 1 year later (Elmore & Huebner, 2010). Other aspects of the parent–child relationship that have emerged as moderate correlates of school satisfaction include perceived social support (Danielsen et al., 2009; DeSantis King et al., 2006) and parental promotion of adolescent autonomy (Ferguson et al., 2010). In general, youth who are more satisfied with their family life (for various reasons personally important to them) are also moderately more likely to report satisfaction with school (Vera et al., 2012; Whitley et al., 2012).

Perhaps in part because many stressors pertinent to youth occur in the family context, multiple studies have found that students who experience more frequent stressors tend to also report lower school satisfaction. Case in point, in Baker's (1998) study of urban elementary school children, stress emerged as a greater contributor (in terms of total indirect and direct effects) to students' school satisfaction than other known interpersonal correlates, including family satisfaction and social support at school. Correlational studies of American high school students yielded small to moderate inverse relationships between school satisfaction and the frequency with which students incurred adverse major and chronic stressors (Huebner et al., 2001; Huebner & McCullough, 2000). Similarly, Scottish adolescents who reported less stress also reported moderately greater satisfaction with the quality of their schooling experiences (Karatzias et al., 2002). In sum, stress inside and beyond the family generally contributes to diminished school satisfaction.

A thorough understanding of the previously summarized intrapersonal and environmental correlates of school satisfaction is in part justified by the multiple benefits associated with liking school. Specifically, students who are more satisfied with school evidence superior academic adjustment and health.

RELATIONS WITH EDUCATIONAL OUTCOMES

Accumulating evidence suggests that liking school is not synonymous with performing well at school in terms of grades earned or academic skills acquired. The literature reviewed next illustrates rather weak (but generally positive) associations between school satisfaction and objective indicators of academic success but stronger associations with in-school behavior and academic attitudes and motivation that are facilitative of continued learning.

Academic Achievement

Some examinations of American adolescents in middle and high school identified small but statistically significant, positive correlations between school satisfaction and students' grade point averages (GPA; Lewis et al., 2009; Suldo et al., 2008). In contrast, another study of the same population found minimal (and sometimes inverse) associations between middle school students' school satisfaction and objective indicators of their academic achievement, including final-quarter grades earned in classes and performance on a statewide test of student mastery of grade-level content standards (Whitley et al., 2012). Academic performance may be more tied to school satisfaction among younger students, as one study yielded a moderate, positive association between school satisfaction and math skills among Norwegian elementary school students (Cock & Halvari, 1999).

In-School Behavior

Accumulating evidence supports that school satisfaction is tied to better in-school behavior in terms of compliance with school rules and academic engagement. An early examination of the in-class behavior of urban at-risk elementary school children found that those students who reported low school satisfaction (i.e., in the bottom quartile of the school sample) experienced more negative verbal reprimands from their teacher about their classroom behavior, as well as self-reported getting in trouble more at school, compared to their peers with high school satisfaction (i.e., in the top quartile; Baker, 1999). Regarding engagement, a longitudinal study found that students in kindergarten who reported liking school had greater classroom participation, which, in turn, predicted better achievement (Ladd, Buhs, & Seid, 2000). Analyses further suggested that gains in achievement were most likely a consequence of high initial school satisfaction rather than a competing pathway in which high initial participation and achievement would cause children to like school more (Ladd et al., 2000).

These positive associations between school satisfaction and in-school behavior extend beyond the elementary school years. American high school students who were more satisfied with school also reported fewer disruptive behaviors at school, such as cheating, fighting, and skipping class (Suldo et al., 2008). Australian adolescents with greater school satisfaction report greater satisfaction with their behavior at school (Tomyn & Cummins, 2011). Regarding the lasting benefits of school satisfaction, Elmore and Huebner's (2010) longitudinal study of American middle school students found school satisfaction predicted subsequent behavioral engagement at school; students with greater school satisfaction reported less withdrawal in the classroom, academic resistance, and aggressive classroom behavior 1 year later.

Adaptive Academic Attitudes and Beliefs

Students who experience greater school satisfaction also report substantially greater intrinsic motivation for completion of schoolwork (i.e., completing homework and working in class due to enjoyment rather than only to avoid punishment or negative feelings like guilt; Cock & Halvari, 1999) and academic initiative (i.e., goal setting, concentration, and challenge seeking in one's schoolwork; Danielson et al., 2011). Such mindsets are important in that self-regulated learning is essential in societies that prize self-directed lifelong learning. Danielson and colleagues found that the facilitative effect of school satisfaction on academic initiative was both direct and indirect, through positive associations with increased academic competence (specifically, perceptions of one's schoolwork performance relative to the performance of classmates). Perceived academic competence is another salient academic attitude, as confidence in one's ability to succeed in a task is a prerequisite for approaching the challenge. Students with greater school satisfaction tend to feel more confident about their academic abilities, as indicated by mostly moderate correlations between school satisfaction and perceived academic competence among samples of children (Baker, 1998; Huebner, 1994; Verkuyten & Thijs, 2002) and adolescents (Danielsen et al., 2009; Huebner & McCullough, 2000) from multiple cultures.

RELATIONS WITH MENTAL AND PHYSICAL HEALTH OUTCOMES

In addition to experiencing enhanced academic adjustment, students who like school more also evidence superior psychological functioning. Case in point, Huebner and Gilman (2006) compared the outcomes of three groups of American adolescents: students with the lowest 20% of school satisfaction scores, students with the highest 20% of scores, and a comparison sample of students in the average range of school satisfaction (middle 30% of scores). The subgroup with very high school satisfaction reported the highest global life satisfaction and hope, as well as the lowest rates of clinical levels of psychopathology. In contrast, very low school satisfaction was associated with greater rates of anxious and depressive symptoms. The link between school satisfaction and mental health appears to at least partially explain the effect of some social contexts on psychopathology. DeSantis King and colleagues (2006) found that adolescents who perceived more social support had higher school satisfaction, which, in turn, predicted lower rates of internalizing and externalizing behavior problems. Whereas low school satisfaction may be a risk factor for mental health problems, students who like school are generally happier with their lives (Salmela-Aro & Tynkkynen, 2010; Shin, Morgan, Buhin, Truitt, & Vera, 2010), consistent with the theoretical link between school satisfaction and global life satisfaction.

Examinations of large samples of youth in Denmark suggest a link between school satisfaction and better physical health, as indicated by adaptive health choices. Specifically, Danish students who liked their school were more likely to discuss health-related issues with their parents and to follow the health advice of their school nurse (Borup & Holstein, 2006), as well as less likely to use marijuana repeatedly (Hoff, Anderson, & Holstein, 2010). More studies are needed to determine associations between school satisfaction and other indicators of health, such as frequency of illness and physical fitness. The existing research suggests that school satisfaction is linked to better choices that facilitate physical health, in addition to superior academic and psychological well-being.

DIVERSITY CONSIDERATIONS

The growing body of literature on school satisfaction now includes youth from multiple continents. These studies afford examinations of differences in mean levels and correlates of school satisfaction among and between students from different countries in North America, Europe, and Asia. For instance, a cross-national study of two collectivist and two individualist cultures indicated lower levels of school satisfaction among South

Korean students and greater school satisfaction among Chinese students, with the school satisfaction means of Irish and American students in the middle (Gilman et al., 2008). Other research indicates remarkable similarity in the predictors of school satisfaction across adolescents from different cultures/countries, likely because most all teenagers are striving for independence. These studies imply that mean differences in school satisfaction likely reflect mean differences in the extent to which countries provide opportunities for adolescents to experience relatedness, autonomy, and competence (Ferguson, Kasser, & Jahng, 2010; Freeman, Samdal, Baban, & Bancila, 2012). Case in point, in a study with approximately 100 high-school-age students from each of three countries (Denmark, Korea, United States), the lower level of school satisfaction reported by the Korean sample appeared to largely reflect the lower perceptions of autonomy support offered by parents and particularly teachers in that country (Ferguson et al., 2010). Even among individualistic cultures, greater school satisfaction was evidenced in the country in which youth perceived greater parent support for autonomy (i.e., Denmark, whose culture particularly values egalitarian relationships and de-emphasizes hierarchical interactions). In line with the positive link between perceived autonomy support and school satisfaction in Korean students, the researchers concluded that their findings contradict the notion that autonomy support is unimportant in collectivistic cultures and assert that "when [any] adolescents felt controlled by their parents and teachers, and felt that these authorities treated the adolescents' own experiences and choices as relatively unimportant, they reported lower satisfaction with school" (Ferguson et al., 2010, p. 658). Regarding the universal importance of relatedness to adolescents' school satisfaction, research with large samples of teenagers in North America (Canada) and Europe (Norway and Romania) has indicated moderate to large correlations between school satisfaction and school climate in particular (i.e., as reflected in student perceptions of teacher support and school pressure) and to a lesser extent perceived classmate support (Freeman et al., 2012).

An emerging cultural consideration pertains to the possibly unique school satisfaction appraisals of students new to their present country. To date, research with different cultural groups in Spain (i.e., South American, African, and native Spanish students) suggests that immigrant adolescents' school satisfaction is not necessarily at risk, as greater satisfaction with schooling and the learning process was reported by immigrant students (particularly those born in Africa; Briones & Taberno, 2012).

EDUCATIONAL APPLICATIONS

Given the modest associations between academic performance and school satisfaction, the current near-exclusive focus on students' academic learning is unlikely to simultaneously influence positive affect pertinent to schooling. Instead, a dual focus on educational achievement as well as students' emotional experiences at and about school is needed to ensure complete academic functioning (both academic performance and school satisfaction). Importantly, there are no known negative consequences (in terms of achievement or interpersonal relationships) of having extremely elevated school satisfaction; instead, associations between school satisfaction and desirable outcomes, such as positive student–teacher relationships, increase linearly through the highest level of school satisfaction (Whitley et al., 2012). Thus, there appears to be no harm in attempting to improve students' happiness with their schooling experiences, only enhanced functioning to be gained.

Support Adolescents' Strivings for Relatedness, Competence, and Autonomy

The desire for relatedness and competence in the classroom might best be addressed by enhancing students' interpersonal connections at school and providing appropriately challenging academic experiences, as discussed in the subsequent sections. Regarding autonomy, Ferguson and colleagues (2010) summarize that greater well-being follows from perceiving that caregiving adults (including teachers) consider a student's perspective and permit the student as much choice as possible. Indeed, intrinsically motivated reasons for both independent and dependent (i.e., collaborative, compliant) decision making are related to greater well-being and less problem behavior among adolescents, whereas motives related to pressure from others are related to less positive adjustment (Van Petegem, Beyers, Vansteenkiste, & Soenens, 2012). Accordingly, rather than focusing solely on allowing adolescents complete freedom of choice (independent decision making), youth autonomy may be best promoted through considering motives involved in decisions pertinent to schooling. Students whose activities are in line with their personal ideals and desires (rather than result from adults' coercion) are likely to experience greater satisfaction with school, including when they are complying with adults' suggestions that are consistent with their beliefs.

Enhance Students' Interpersonal Connections at Schools

Correlational research suggests that fostering a positive classroom climate, complete with strong interpersonal bonds between students and teachers, as well as among students, may hold the most potential for facilitating children's school satisfaction. Regarding student–teacher relationships, school administrators may want to expand the dangerously exclusive focus on teachers' instructional skills and heed the concluding suggestion of Randolph and colleagues (2010) to strive to employ teachers who are "nice and likeable" (p. 203). This benign recommendation is underscored by the growing number of charter schools achieving success with historically at-risk students through embracing an educational philosophy that emphasizes teachers' personal traits, including forming strong relationships with children and their families, communicating high expectations for all children's learning, and frequently expressing joy and warmth (Mathews, 2009). Students themselves can contribute to the promotion of positive student–teacher relationships by becoming actively involved in their schooling. Students' thoughts and behaviors become egocentric when they are not actively involved in their own care (Ferreira & Bosworth, 2001), underscoring the value of opportunities for students to build caring relationships with peers, teachers, and the community through service learning projects, classroom responsibilities, and collaborative learning activities.

At the schoolwide level, positive peer relationships can be facilitated through direct teaching of social skills in addition to a proactive, preventative approach to peer victimization. Encouraging involvement in school clubs, sports, and other elective after-school activities may also facilitate bonds between students outside the classroom. Indeed, cross-sectional research indicates that students involved in more structured extracurricular activities during middle or high school have somewhat higher school satisfaction (Huebner & Gilman, 2006).

Arrange Classroom Conditions to Foster Positive Emotions

Classrooms that are moderate in size (for instance, roughly 20 students at the elementary level) and that provide access to curricula and expectations appropriately matched to students' cognitive abilities and goals may be ideal in terms of facilitating children's school satisfaction. There is particularly strong support for the latter recommendation when applied to high-achieving and gifted adolescents (Jin & Moon, 2006; Zeidner & Schleyer, 1999). At a minimum, school satisfaction is unlikely to be diminished by increasing talented students' academic demands and expectations. Research with American high school students found comparable levels of school satisfaction between high-achieving students in academically rigorous college preparatory programs as compared to their typically achieving peers in general education (Suldo & Shaunessy-Dedrick, 2013).

Consider Children's Contexts Outside of Schools

Children in classrooms come from home circumstances that vary widely in terms of stability and stress. Stressors some children face range from chronic tension (e.g., family conflict, illness, poverty) to major household changes resulting from adults' legal, economic, and interpersonal problems. Insurmountable evidence supports a linear association between greater environmental stress during childhood (e.g., experiences of child abuse, household dysfunction associated with domestic violence, and mentally ill and/or imprisoned parents) and risk for deleterious health outcomes throughout adulthood (Felitti et al., 1998). Clearly, the effects of stress endure beyond the child's daily exit from the home. Given that children who incur greater stress appear at risk for diminished school satisfaction, educators have an even greater rationale for enacting formal mechanisms to identify students incurring environmental stressors and refer these students for targeted supports (e.g., psychological services, school-based mentoring relationships).

Attend to the School Satisfaction of Boys in Particular

Boys appear at risk for experiencing diminished school satisfaction. Randolph and colleagues (2010) provide a compelling discussion of these mean differences resulting from either (a) the mismatch between typical expectations for classroom behavior and the behavioral activity level of boys (whereas girls benefit from the match between traditional gender roles that emphasize compliance) and/or (b) girls' traditional emphasis on relatedness (vs. independence), which may allow them to capitalize more on facilitative peer and teacher relationships available in the classroom context. Vera and colleagues (2012) encourage educators to promote experiences particularly likely to enhance school belonging for boys, such as participation in sports teams or clubs. Other strategies likely to appeal to boys' preference for independence include the provision of additional leadership opportunities as well as input in class activities when possible.

DIRECTIONS FOR FUTURE RESEARCH

The growing body of research on school satisfaction made possible the aforementioned recommendations for where educators may focus their attempts to systematically improve students' satisfaction with their schooling experiences. Next steps for research involve moving the school satisfaction literature beyond the identification of correlates. Intervention or longitudinal observational studies are needed to document which educational strategies are responsible for elevations in students' school satisfaction, as well as identify causal mechanisms of change. For instance, research is needed to determine if students' school satisfaction changes as a function of their engagement in after-school activities and if strengthened interpersonal connections or pride in one's school mediate associations between activity involvement and school satisfaction. Similarly, studies that identify the extent to which changes in school satisfaction covary with changes in academic performance would help elucidate the interrelationships between these two crucial student outcomes.

REFERENCES

Ash, C., & Huebner, S. (1998). Life satisfaction reports of gifted middle-school children. *School Psychology Quarterly, 13,* 310–321. doi:10.1037/h0088987

Baker, J.A. (1998). The social context of school satisfaction among urban, low-income, African-American students. *School Psychology Quarterly, 13,* 25–44. doi:10.1037/h0088970.

Baker, J.A. (1999). Teacher–student interaction in urban at-risk classrooms: Differential behavior, relationship quality, and student satisfaction with school. *Elementary School Journal, 100,* 57–70. doi:10.1086/461943

Baker, J.A., Dilly, L.J., Aupperlee, J.L., & Patil, S.A. (2003). The developmental context of school satisfaction: Schools as psychologically healthy environments. *School Psychology Quarterly, 18,* 206–221.

Baker, J.A., & Maupin, A.N. (2009). School satisfaction and children's positive school adjustment. In R. Gilman, E.S. Huebner, & M.J. Furlong (Eds.), *Handbook of positive psychology in the schools* (pp. 189–196). New York, NY: Routledge.

Borup, I., & Holstein, B. (2006). Does poor school satisfaction inhibit positive outcome of health promotion at school? A cross-sectional study of schoolchildren's response to health dialogues with school health nurses. *Journal of Adolescent Health, 38,* 758–760. doi:10.1016/j.jadohealth.2005.05.017

Brantley, A., Huebner, S., & Nagle, R. (2002). Multidimensional Life Satisfaction reports of adolescents with mild mental disabilities. *Mental Retardation, 40,* 321–329. doi:10.1352/0047-6765(2002)040<0321:MLSROA> 2.0.CO;2

Briones, E., & Tabernero, C. (2012). Social cognitive and demographic factors related to adolescents' intrinsic satisfaction with school. *Social Psychology of Education, 15,* 219–232. doi:10.1007/s11218-012-9176-4

Cock, D., & Halvari, H. (1999). Relations among achievement motives, autonomy, performance in mathematics, and satisfaction of pupils in elementary school. *Psychological Reports, 84,* 983–997. doi:10.2466/PR0.84.3.983-997

Danielsen, A., Breivik, K., & Wold, B. (2011). Do perceived academic competence and school satisfaction mediate the relationships between perceived support provided by teachers and classmates, and academic initiative? *Scandinavian Journal of Educational Research, 55,* 379–401. doi:10.1080/00313831.2011.587322

Danielsen, A., Samdal, O., Hetland, J., & Wold, B. (2009). School-related social support and students' perceived life satisfaction. *Journal of Educational Research, 102,* 303–318.

DeSantis King, A., Huebner, S., Suldo, S., & Valois, R. (2006). An ecological view of school satisfaction in adolescence: Linkages between social support and behavior problems. *Applied Research in Quality of Life, 1,* 279–295. doi:10.1007/s11482-007-9021-7

Elmore, G., & Huebner, S. (2010). Adolescents' satisfaction with school experiences: Relationships with demographics, attachment relationships, and school engagement behavior. *Psychology in the Schools, 47,* 525–537. doi:10.1002/pits.20488

Epstein, J., & McPartland, J. (1976). The concept and measurement of the quality of school life. *American Educational Research Journal, 13,* 15–30. doi:10.2307/1162551

Felitti, V. J., Anda, R. F., Nordenberg, D., Williamson, D. F., Spitz, A. M., Edwards, V., . . . Marks, J. S. (1998). Relationship of childhood abuse and household dysfunction to many of the leading causes of death in adults: The Adverse Childhood Experiences (ACE) Study. *American Journal of Preventive Medicine, 14,* 245–258.

Ferguson, Y., Kasser, T., & Jahng, S. (2010). Differences in life satisfaction and school satisfaction among adolescents from three nations: The role of perceived autonomy support. *Journal of Research on Adolescence, 21,* 649–661. doi:10.1111/j.1532-7795.2010.00698.x

Ferreira, M. M., & Bosworth, K. (2001). Defining caring teachers: Adolescents' perspectives. *Journal of Classroom Interaction, 36,* 24–30.

Freeman, J., Samdal, O., Băban, A., & Bancila, D. (2012). The relationship between school perceptions and psychosomatic complaints: Cross-country differences across Canada, Norway, and Romania. *School Mental Health, 4,* 95–104. doi:10.1007/s12310-011-9070-9

Gilman, R., Huebner, S., Tian, L., Park, N., O'Byrne, J., Schiff, M., . . . Langknecht, H. (2008). Cross-national adolescent multidimensional life satisfaction report: Analyses of mean scores and response style differences. *Journal of Youth and Adolescence, 37,* 142–154. doi:10.1007/s10964-007-9172-8

Hoff, D., Anderson, A., & Holstein, B. (2010). Poor school satisfaction and number of cannabis-using peers within school classes as individual risk factors for cannabis use among adolescents. *School Psychology International, 31,* 547–556. doi:10.1177/0143034310382870

Huebner, E. S. (1994). Preliminary development and validation of a multidimensional life satisfaction scale for children. *Psychological Assessment, 6,* 149–158. doi:10.1037/10403590.6.2.149

Huebner, E. S., Ash, C., & Laughlin, J. (2001). Life experiences, locus of control, and school satisfaction in adolescence. *Social Indicators Research, 55,* 167–183. doi:10.1023/A:1010939912548

Huebner, E. S., Drane, W., & Valois, R. (2000). Levels and demographic correlates of adolescent life satisfaction reports. *School Psychology International, 21,* 281–292. doi:10.1177/0143034300213005

Huebner, E. S., & Gilman, R. (2006). Students who like and dislike school. *Applied Research in Quality of Life, 1,* 139–150. doi:10.1007/s11482-006-9001-3

Huebner, E. S., & McCullough, G. (2000). Correlates of school satisfaction among adolescents. *Journal of Educational Research, 93,* 331–335. doi:10.1080/00220670009598725

Huebner, E. S., Valois, R., Paxton, R., & Drane, W. (2005). Middle school students' perceptions of quality of life. *Journal of Happiness Studies, 6,* 15–24. doi:10.1007/s10902-004-1170-x

Hui, E., & Sun, R. (2010). Chinese children's perceived school satisfaction: The role of contextual and intrapersonal factors. *Educational Psychology, 30,* 155–172. doi:10.1080/01443410903494452

Jin, S., & Moon, S. (2006). A study of well-being and school satisfaction among academically talented students attending a science high school in Korea. *Gifted Child Quarterly, 50,* 169–184. doi:10.1177/001698620605000207

Karatzias, A., Power, K., Flemming, J., Lennan, F., & Swanson, V. (2002). The role of demographics, personality variables and school stress on predicting school satisfaction/dissatisfaction: Review of the literature and research findings. *Educational Psychology, 22,* 33–50. doi:10.1080/01443410120101233

Ladd, G., Buhs, E., & Seid, M. (2000). Children's initial sentiments about kindergarten: Is school liking an antecedent of early classroom participation and achievement? *Merrill-Palmer Quarterly, 46,* 255–279.

Lewis, A., Huebner, E. S., Reschly, A., & Valois, R. (2009). The incremental validity of positive emotions in predicting school functioning. *Journal of Psychoeducational Assessment, 27,* 397–408. doi:10.1177/0734282908330571

Mathews, J. (2009). *Work hard. Be nice: How two inspired teachers created the most promising schools in America.* Chapel Hill, NC: Algonquin.

National Education Association. (2010). *Status of the American public school teacher: 2005–2006* (Item No. 3259–200). Retrieved from http://files.eric.ed.gov/fulltext/ED521866.pdf

Noddings, N. (2003). *Happiness and education.* New York, NY: Cambridge University Press.

Okun, M. A., Braver, M. W., & Weir, R. M. (1990). Grade level differences in school satisfaction. *Social Indicators Research, 22,* 419–427. doi:10.1007/BF00303835

Park, N., & Huebner, S. (2005). A cross-cultural study of the levels and correlates of life satisfaction among adolescents. *Journal of Cross-Cultural Psychology, 36,* 444–456. doi:10.1177/0022022105275961

Randolph, J. J., Kangas, M., & Ruokamo, H. (2009). The preliminary development of the Children's Overall Satisfaction with Schooling Scale (COSSS), *Child Indicators Research, 2,* 79–93. doi:10.1007/s12187-008-9027-1

Randolph, J. J., Kangas, M., & Ruokamo, H. (2010). Predictors of Dutch and Finnish children's satisfaction with schooling. *Journal of Happiness Studies, 11,* 193–204. doi:10.1007/s10902-008-9131-4

Salmela-Aro, K., & Tynkkynen, L. (2010). Trajectories of life satisfaction across transition to post-compulsory education: Do adolescents follow different pathways? *Journal of Youth and Adolescence, 39,* 870–881. doi:10.1007/s10964-009-9464-2

Seligson, J.L., Huebner, E.S., & Valois, R.F. (2003). Preliminary validation of the Brief Multidimensional Students' Life Satisfaction Scale (BMSLSS). *Social Indicators Research, 61,* 121–145. doi:10.1023/A:1021326822957

Shin, R., Morgan, M., Buhin, L., Truitt, T., & Vera, E. (2010). Expanding the discourse on urban youth of color. *Cultural Diversity and Ethnic Minority Psychology, 16,* 421–426. doi:10.1037/a0018693

Suldo, S., Shaffer, E., & Riley, K. (2008). A social-cognitive-behavioral model of academic predictors of adolescents' life satisfaction. *School Psychology Quarterly, 23,* 56–69. doi:10.1037/1045-3830.23.1.56

Suldo, S.M., & Shaunessy-Dedrick, E. (2013). The psychosocial functioning of high school students in academically rigorous programs. *Psychology in the Schools, 50,* 823–843. doi: 10.1002/pits

Tomyn, A.J., & Cummins, R.A. (2011). The subjective wellbeing of high-school students: Validating the Personal Wellbeing Index–School Children. *Social Indicators Research, 101,* 405–418. doi:10.1007/s11205-010-9668-6

Torsheim, T., Samdal, O., Rasmussen, M., Freeman, J., Griebler, R., & Dür, W. (2012). Cross-national measurement invariance of the Teacher and Classmate Support Scale. *Social Indicators Research, 105,* 145–160. doi:10.1007/s11205-010-9770-9

Van Petegem, S., Beyers, W., Vansteenkiste, M., & Soenens, B. (2012). On the association between adolescent autonomy and psychosocial functioning: Examining decisional independence from a self-determination theory perspective. *Developmental Psychology, 48,* 76–88. doi:10.1037/a0025307

Vera, E.M., Moallem, B.I., Vacek, K.R., Blackmon, S., Coyle, L.D., Gomez, K.L., . . . Steele, C.J. (2012). Gender differences in contextual predictors of urban, early adolescents' subjective well-being. *Journal of Multicultural Counseling and Development, 40,* 174–183. doi:10.1002/j.2161-1912.2012.00016.x

Verkuyten, M., & Thijs, J. (2002). School satisfaction of elementary school children: The role of performance, peer relations, ethnicity and gender. *Social Indicators Research, 59,* 203–228. doi:10.1023/A:1016279602893

Wachs, S. (2012). Moral disengagement and emotional and social difficulties in bullying and cyberbullying: Differences by participant role. *Emotional and Behavioural Difficulties, 17,* 347–360. doi:10.1080/13632752.2012.704318

Whitley, A.M., Huebner, E.S., Hills, K.J., & Valois, R.F. (2012). Can students be too happy in school? The optimal level of school satisfaction. *Applied Research in Quality of Life, 7,* 337–350. doi:10.1007/s11482-012-9167-9

Zeidner, M., & Schleyer, E. (1999). The effects of educational context on individual difference variables, self-perceptions of giftedness, and school attitudes in gifted adolescents. *Journal of Youth and Adolescence, 28,* 687–703. doi:10.1023/A:1021687500828

Zullig, K., Huebner, S., & Patton, J. (2011). Relationships among school climate domains and school satisfaction. *Psychology in the Schools, 48,* 133–145. doi:10.1002/pits.20532

CHAPTER SUMMARY: SCHOOL SATISFACTION

- Students who like school have better psychological functioning, including greater overall well-being and fewer symptoms of mental health problems.
- Students who like school also demonstrate better academic adjustment. They are more compliant and engaged at school and hold more adaptive beliefs that facilitate learning.
- Most students report at least mildly positive perceptions of their schooling experiences.
- Factors that contribute to differences in students' school satisfaction include a host of intrapersonal characteristics and environmental contexts within and outside of school.
- Older students and boys are at particular risk for liking school less.
- Elevated school satisfaction is most closely tied to positive interpersonal connections at school, especially student–teacher relationships.
- Most correlates of school satisfaction appear robust across cultures.
- Recommendations for enhancing students' school satisfaction include supporting adolescents' need for autonomy, enhancing students' interpersonal connections at school, adapting classroom conditions to foster positive emotions, and considering students' experiences outside of school.

SUGGESTED READINGS: SCHOOL SATISFACTION

Baker, J.A., Dilly, L.J., Aupperlee, J.L., & Patil, S.A. (2003). The developmental context of school satisfaction: Schools as psychologically healthy environments. *School Psychology Quarterly, 18,* 206–221. doi:10.1521/scpq.18.2.206.21861

This article contains a thought-provoking discussion of how to operationalize positive adjustment in students. The comprehensive literature review summarizes aspects of the school ecology that influence school satisfaction, as well as the salient student-level correlates.

Edwards, O., & Ray, S. (2008). An attachment and school satisfaction framework for helping children raised by grandparents. *School Psychology Quarterly*, *23*, 125–138. doi:10.1037/1045-3830.23.1.125

This manuscript describes the unique experiences and needs of children and caregivers in families headed by grandparents. It provides extensive guidance for school-based mental health professionals who are interested in promoting the school satisfaction of this particular subgroup of students.

Ervasti, J., Kivima, M., Puusniekka, R., Luopa, P., Pentti, J., Suominens, S., . . . Virtanen, M. (2012). Students' school satisfaction as predictor of teachers' sickness absence: A prospective cohort study. *European Journal of Public Health, 22,* 215–219. doi:10.1093/eurpub/ckr043

This large-scale study of 90 Finnish schools illustrates that consequences of students' school satisfaction extend beyond personal risk or benefit to also impacting teachers' well-being. Findings indicated that teachers at schools with relatively low mean levels of school satisfaction were absent more from work due to mental health reasons, particularly stress related.

Froh, J.J., Sefick, W.J., & Emmons, R.A. (2008). Counting blessings in early adolescents: An experimental study of gratitude and subjective well-being. *Journal of School Psychology, 46,* 213–233. doi:10.1016/j.jsp.2007.03.005

This study provides an example of a classroom-based intervention experimentally shown to have a lasting, positive impact on children's school satisfaction. Middle school students who participated daily for 2 weeks in a writing activity designed to promote grateful thinking experienced gains in school satisfaction, whereas students who wrote about hassles and students in a control condition did not show changes in school satisfaction.

24

INNOVATIVE MODELS OF DISSEMINATION FOR SCHOOL-BASED INTERVENTIONS THAT PROMOTE YOUTH RESILIENCE AND WELL-BEING

Amy Kranzler, Rutgers, The State University of New Jersey, Piscataway, New Jersey, USA

Lauren J. Hoffman, Graduate School of Applied and Professional Psychology, Rutgers University, Piscataway, New Jersey, USA

Acacia C. Parks, Psychology Department, Hiram College, Hiram, Ohio, USA

Jane E. Gillham, Psychology Department, Swarthmore College, Swarthmore, Pennsylvania, USA

INTRODUCTION

Positive psychology and well-being interventions have flourished in the past decade (Parks & Biswas-Diener, 2013; Seligman, Steen, Park, & Peterson, 2005). Effective programs have been developed to build resilience and increase positive variables such as subjective well-being, positive emotion, individual strengths, positive relationships, and a sense of fulfillment and meaning among youth. Programs such as the Penn Resiliency Program (PRP; Gillham, Reivich & Jaycox, 2008) and the high school Positive Psychology Program (PPP; Gillham et al., 2013; Seligman, Ernst, Gillham, Reivich, & Linkins, 2009) have been found to improve factors related to students' resilience and well-being when evaluated as school-based programs. Yet, despite this exciting progress, these programs are not reaching the vast number of youth who might benefit most from them. In this chapter, we discuss the prevalence of depression in school-aged youth and the importance of school-based resilience and well-being interventions. We then describe the PRP and PPP and review some of the challenges that prevent broad implementation of these programs despite apparent need for them. We conclude by describing two novel methods of program implementation that can be replicated at schools across the country. The first employs undergraduates in the context of university–community partnerships. The second integrates well-being program activities and concepts into academic courses. Both methods constitute innovative strategies to impact the large number of adolescents who might benefit from these programs.

RESILIENCE AND WELL-BEING INTERVENTIONS

Resilience refers to a person's ability to respond effectively to major adversity, as well as their positive adaptation in response to daily stressors (e.g., academic and peer pressures) and common life transitions (e.g., the transition to high school; Gillham et al., 2013). There is increasing recognition of the importance of interventions that teach youth resilience skills (e.g., Greenberg et al., 2003). Generally, prevention programs that target youth at high risk have been shown to be beneficial (Horowitz & Garber, 2006; Stice, Shaw, Bohon, Marti, & Rohde, 2009). However, given the frequency of exposure to adversity or significant stressors during adolescence, there is also a great need for universal prevention programs that provide all youth with the social and emotional skills they need to effectively respond to these challenges and continue to thrive. While resilience refers specifically to a child's ability to respond to challenges and setbacks, well-being is a somewhat broader construct that includes many positive variables such as a child's positive behavior, positive relationships, achievement, emotional well-being, engagement in school, and sense of meaning and fulfillment. Importantly, there is often overlap between these constructs, with resilience constituting continued well-being in the face of stressors and well-being often increasing one's capacity for resilience.

Programs that promote youth resilience and well-being often utilize one of two approaches. The first approach focuses on *prevention*, seeking to help youth avert downward spirals by building resilience and adaptive coping skills. Interventions such as depression prevention programs exemplify this model by preparing youth to respond effectively to environmental and emotional stressors that are commonly associated with negative outcomes, such as depression. These programs often teach youth skills such as problem solving, adaptive coping, and social and emotional competence to prepare them to deal with difficult emotions and life events and continue to thrive. In the second approach, the focus is on the *promotion* of positive upward spirals in youth by increasing positive experiences and positive emotions and helping youth develop and use their individual strengths. This approach is based on research suggesting that enhancing youth capacity for positive emotions improves problem solving (Fredrickson, 2001), and increasing their positive resources and use of individual strengths (e.g., teamwork, humor, creativity) serves to promote resilience and prepare them to better respond to stressors

(Gillham et al., 2013). Many programs incorporate elements from both approaches, with varying emphases placed on each. Below, we describe two programs that exemplify these different emphases—PRP primarily uses a prevention approach, while PPP emphasizes a promotion approach.

THE PENN RESILIENCY PROJECT (PRP)

A surprisingly large percentage of youth are exposed to some form of adversity such as exposure to violence, poverty, parental depression, death of a parent, abuse, or neglect. In addition to these external stressors, many children and adolescents struggle with psychological difficulties. Depression is currently one of the most prevalent and debilitating psychological disorders among children and adolescents and is therefore an important target for prevention efforts.

By the end of middle school, as many as 9% of youth experience unipolar depression (Garrison, Schluchter, Schoenback, & Kaplan, 1989). Research shows that the peak increase in overall rates of depression occurs in mid-adolescence, particularly between ages 15 and 18 (Hankin et al., 1998). This stark increase in such a short period of time suggests that middle to late adolescence may be a critical time for heightened vulnerability for depression. Even more adolescents suffer from subclinical but disruptively high levels of depressive symptoms (Kessler, Avenevoli, & Merikangas, 2001; Peterson, Compas, Brooks-Gunn, Stemmler, & Grant, 1993). These rates are especially problematic in light of research suggesting that adolescent depression and depressive symptoms are associated with increased risk of smoking (Covey, Glassman, & Stetner, 1998), drug use, academic difficulties, and suicide (Fergusson, Horwood, Ridder, & Beautrais, 2005; Gotlib, Lewinsohn, & Seeley, 1995). Further, adolescent depression predicts future academic failure, marital difficulties, interpersonal relationship problems, unemployment, and legal problems (Kessler et al., 2003). Depression is also often recurrent, with adolescent depression typically predicting future episodes throughout the lifespan (Kim-Cohen et al., 2003).

In response to these alarming rates and implications of adolescent depression, there has been a movement in the past 15 years toward the development of depression prevention programs for adolescents (Horowitz & Garber, 2006). As one such program, the Penn Resiliency Program (PRP) emphasizes the *prevention* approach to resilience by employing cognitive-behavioral techniques to prevent symptoms of depression and promote resilience in early adolescence (Gillham, Reivich, Jaycox, & Seligman, 1995; Jaycox, Reivich, Gillham, & Seligman, 1994). Based on the cognitive-behavioral model of depression, which focuses on negative or maladaptive patterns of thinking and coping, the program teaches both cognitive techniques and social-problem-solving skills for handling problems that are common during adolescence (Gillham, Brunwasser, & Freres, 2008). PRP's cognitive component teaches adolescents to understand the link between beliefs and emotions, to challenge negative cognitions, and to decatastrophize, while the social-problem-solving component teaches assertiveness, relaxation, and problem-solving techniques. Like many other depression prevention programs, PRP utilizes cartoons, role-play skits, interactive and group exercises, and group discussion to make the curriculum content concrete and engaging for younger participants. The curriculum is designed to be modular and can be broken down into 12 segments and taught in 60- to 90-minute blocks. Table 24.1 presents an overview of each lesson.

Table 24.1 Penn Resiliency Project (PRP) Overview

Lesson	Topic	Description
1	**Link Between Thoughts and Feelings**	• Welcome students to program • Build group cohesion • Introduce automatic thoughts; discuss "self-talk" associated with recent events • Use cartoons to demonstrate link between activating events, thoughts, and emotional consequences
2	**Thinking Styles**	• Use skits to highlight optimistic vs. pessimistic thinking styles • Help students generate alternatives to the initial, explanatory style-driven thoughts
3	**Challenging Beliefs: Alternatives and Evidence**	• Use "Sherlock and Merlock Holmes" story (comparing skilled and unskilled detectives) to introduce skill of searching for evidence behind thoughts • Play File Game in which each student searches through a portfolio about a fictitious child, which contains letters, report cards, awards, diary entries, etc. Students use information in portfolio to evaluate accuracy of fictitious child's automatic thoughts
4	**Evaluating Thoughts and Putting Them in Perspective**	• Use Chicken Little story to introduce concept of catastrophizing • Help students differentiate worst-case, best-case, and most likely outcomes • Play Real-Time Resilience: The Hot Seat to teach students to use cognitive skills in real time. This skill is practiced throughout the rest of the program
5	**Review of Lessons 1–4**	Review cognitive skills and apply to relevant student experiences
6	**Assertiveness and Negotiation**	• Use skits to illustrate three interaction styles: aggression, passivity, and assertiveness • Discuss the consequences of each type of behavior • Learn a four-step approach to assertiveness • Practice assertiveness and negotiation skills
7	**Coping Strategies**	• Introduce a variety of behaviorally oriented techniques to help students cope with stressful situations or difficult emotions • Practice controlled breathing, muscle relaxation, and positive imagery • Encourage students to seek support from family members and friends
8	**Graded Task and Social Skills Training**	• Highlight all-or-nothing-thinking associated with procrastination • Apply cognitive skills to procrastination and avoidance of projects and chores • Students discuss ways to break large projects into smaller, more manageable steps
9	**Decision Making and Review of Lessons 6–8**	• Review and practice relaxation techniques and assertiveness strategies covered in Lessons 6 through 8 • Introduce technique for decision making in which children generate pros and cons for different actions • Apply this technique to examples from students' lives

Lesson	Topic	Description
10	**Social Problem Solving**	• Teach five-step approach to problem solving • Step 1: stop and think about problems (i.e., gather evidence for and against belief, consider interpretations, take perspective) • Step 2: determine goal • Step 3: generate variety of possible solutions • Step 4: use decision-making techniques to choose course of action • Step 5: evaluate outcome
11 & 12	**Social Problem Solving Continuation & Review of PRP**	• Apply five-step problem-solving technique to difficult interpersonal situations in students' lives • Review entire program • Celebrate end of program with party

Since its development in the 1990s, PRP has been well researched, with more than 19 controlled studies measuring its effects in a variety of socioeconomic and demographic settings (Brunwasser, Gillham, & Kim, 2009). In total, the program has reached more than 2,000 youths in the United States, Australia, the United Kingdom, and China. Most implementations of PRP are school based and are led by research team members or school personnel. A review of PRP trials found that the program significantly reduces symptoms of depression for at least 1 year following program participation (Brunwasser et al., 2009). In several studies, these effects were even longer lasting, with symptom reduction up to 2 years after the program (Gillham et al., 1995). The program also improves cognitions related to depression, such as pessimistic explanatory style, hopelessness, and negative automatic thoughts (Cardemil, Reivich, & Seligman, 2002; Gillham et al., 1995; Yu & Seligman, 2002). Importantly, Horowitz and Garber (2006) found that PRP was the only curriculum of 30 such programs they reviewed to prevent (rather than simply treat) an elevation of depressive symptoms. Together, these findings suggest that there is promise for the Penn Resiliency Program as a school-based prevention program to build resilience and well-being among adolescents.

However, despite research suggesting its effectiveness, PRP is not currently implemented in a large number of schools, and the important skills it teaches do not reach the vast number of youth that might benefit from them. Given the prevalence of psychological disorders in children, it is not enough to develop intervention programs such as PRP and demonstrate their efficacy with small groups of adolescents in tightly controlled research studies. Rather, it is also necessary to focus on the development of effective methods for the wide-scale dissemination of these programs (Kazdin, 2008). Indeed, of the estimated 15 million children with psychiatric disorders, only 34% receive treatment (Kazdin, 2008). Novel models of dissemination must be developed with an emphasis on cost effectiveness and accessibility so that we might begin to meaningfully impact the burden of mental health in our nation (Kazdin, 2008; Kazdin & Blase, 2011). Schools serve as critical locations for well-being programs, with the potential to reach large numbers of youth who might otherwise not receive services. Thus, the next important step for PRP and for other well-being programs is to develop a model to integrate programming into schools in a way that is sustainable and scalable.

School-Based Programs: Challenges and Unique Opportunities

Integrating resilience and well-being into schools offers both advantages and challenges. School-based programs are particularly promising because they enable families to obtain services for emotional and behavioral health problems without the financial and logistical challenges that often impede such efforts. As such, 75% of all American youth who receive mental health services do so in a school setting, making schools the largest provider of mental health care for youth (Burns et al., 1995; Rones & Hoagwood, 2000). Further, universal school-based programs are less stigmatizing and limit the shame and discomfort youth frequently associate with obtaining mental health services (Offord, Kraemer, Kazdin, Jensen, & Harrington, 1998). Additionally, although school-based mental health programs have historically focused on individual assessment and intervention, the expansion of mental health programming in schools allows for broader health promotion and problem prevention.

Sedlak (1997) highlighted the historically "uneasy alliance" between mental health providers and schools, citing the conflicting goals (nonacademic vs. academic) of mental health providers and educators. However, growing research emphasizes that these goals are not truly incompatible, and schools are best suited to meet their educational goals by simultaneously promoting students' academic, social, and emotional learning (Elias et al., 1997). In fact, research by Wang, Haertel, and Walberg (1997) demonstrated that social and emotional factors were among the most influential factors on learning in school. Research also demonstrates that positive mood enhances attention and creative thinking, and increases in well-being produce increases in learning and engagement in school (Seligman et al., 2009). Furthermore, increases in the use of skills related to well-being, such as self-regulation and optimism, also enhance school performance (Duckworth & Seligman, 2005; Schulman, 1995). Conversely, social-emotional difficulties are consistently reported as significant barriers to learning. For example, children's feelings of sadness or anger often impact the way in which they perceive their academic competence (Cole, 1991; Nolen-Hoeksema, Girgus, & Seligman, 1986), which, in turn, leads to poor academic performance (Eccles et al., 1993). Similarly, depressive symptoms are associated with measurable impairments in academic performance and reduced problem-solving skills (Blechman, McEnroe, Carella, & Audette, 1986; Kovacs, 1989). Given the interdependent nature of academic and emotional success, it is in the mutual interests of mental health providers and educators to strive for program integration and to form interdisciplinary goals that simultaneously address the academic, behavioral, social, and emotional well-being of students.

Still, several challenges currently limit the seamless integration of well-being programs into schools. Schools' staffs are often already stretched thin, with teachers, guidance counselors, and other school personnel often unable to take on additional responsibilities. Existing mental health staff in the building are often concerned with higher-profile issues such as violence, drug use, pregnancy, and truancy, and, therefore, focus almost exclusively on individual treatment and assessment. When asked to cite the main barriers to mental health service delivery in their schools, school psychologists most commonly reported difficulties managing overwhelming caseloads, as well as insufficient training and lack of support from administration and school personnel (Suldo, Friedrich, & Michalowski, 2010). It is unsurprising, therefore, that schools often lack the funding, personnel, and organizational capacity to effectively implement positive prevention programs within the school setting (Weist, Goldstein, Morris, & Bryant, 2003).

Innovative Methods of Dissemination

In light of these challenges, there is a need for new models that allow for the wide-scale implementation of programs designed to promote well-being in youth. We discuss here two novel and scalable models of implementation. One promising model employs university–community partnerships to increase dissemination of effective programs, such as the Penn Resiliency Project. Another model incorporates positive psychology concepts into academic courses, employing teachers to disseminate these concepts in the context of classroom discussions and assignments. Both models, though dramatically different in approach, provide a low-cost and sustainable method of dissemination of important social and emotional well-being skills for youth.

University–Community Partnerships

By employing undergraduate psychology students as service providers, university–community partnerships can provide an invaluable resource in the process of disseminating positive interventions to community youth. There has been increasing recognition of a "person-power" problem in the mental health field and the reality that many more people are needed to provide the treatment and prevention programs that are sorely needed (Kazdin & Blase, 2011). As such, the field is increasingly expressing a renewed perspective on the value of paraprofessional and/or nonprofessional treatments and their potential for wide-scale, low-cost delivery (e.g., Christensen & Jacobson, 1994). Such paraprofessionals have included nurses, clergy, teachers, and graduate students. In a meta-analysis of 42 studies, Durlak (1979) reported that the majority of studies found no differences in effectiveness between professional and paraprofessional therapists, and in some studies paraprofessionals actually outperformed professionals. Durlak (1979) concluded that "professional mental health education, training, and experience do not appear to be necessary prerequisites for an effective helping person" (p. 80). Similarly, in a meta-analysis of child psychotherapy, there was no difference in treatment outcomes between professionals and trained graduate students (Weisz, Weiss, Han, & Granger, 1995). Together, these studies suggest that nonprofessionals can provide effective treatments.

Undergraduate psychology students provide particular promise as alternative service providers for several reasons. First, while undergraduates are clinically inexperienced, they have the time to receive extensive supervision and training. This is significant in light of a review of PRP, suggesting that the program was often ineffective when leaders received minimal or insufficient training (Gillham et al., 2007). As such, undergraduates might serve as effective leaders because the context of a college-level course enables them to be properly trained and supervised. Indeed, in a recent study, trained undergraduates were found to be effective group leaders of an eating disorder prevention program (Becker, Smith, & Ciao, 2006). Second, undergraduates might offer unique advantages as leaders of positive interventions with youth. Research on undergraduate mentoring programs such as the Big Brothers/Big Sisters program suggests that undergraduates are effective mentors and role models for youth. Undergraduates might better remember the world and challenges of adolescent life, giving them a unique advantage as group leaders in their ability to create positive relationships and build rapport with youth. In our experiences in schools, youth have looked forward to their relationships with their undergraduate group leaders and have expressed little resistance to the idea of additional after-school programming. Lastly, preliminary research suggests that undergraduates themselves might benefit from teaching youth resilience skills, as they begin to incorporate the skills and techniques into their own lives. For these reasons, undergraduates stand to serve as important leaders, opening up a promising new possibility for dissemination models.

Using the University–Community Partnership Model for Resilience Interventions

Within this model, advanced undergraduates enroll in an upper-level psychology course in which they are taught the research and theory behind well-being programs like PRP. As part of their coursework, undergraduates are then trained and supervised to teach the intervention to youth at local schools. Undergraduate leaders receive ongoing supervision and training throughout the semester as they implement prevention programs as part of after-school programming.

This model was successfully implemented for several years at both the University of Pennsylvania and Swarthmore College. In both institutions, undergraduates enrolled in a credit-bearing psychology course. As part of their coursework, undergraduates were trained to teach the Penn Resiliency Program (PRP) curriculum to local youth. In one implementation, undergraduates were also trained to teach lessons from the high school Positive Psychology Program (described later in this chapter) to youth as part of the intervention, including skills such as savoring, identifying character strengths, and gratitude. Positive interventions such as PRP and PPP are particularly well suited for this model, because they include structured and modular curricula, including a group leader's manual and workbooks for students. The PRP curriculum includes detailed lesson plans that outline each lesson's activities, discussion questions, and main points. The curriculum also includes an example script to serve as a model for running groups. This provides inexperienced undergraduates with structure and guidance to effectively implement the program.

In terms of logistics, there are different possibilities for the implementations of these programs. At the University of Pennsylvania, undergraduates commuted to local schools, where they implemented the program as part of an existing after-school program. At Swarthmore College, undergraduates have worked in area schools and, some years, local youth were invited to the college campus to participate in the program. Other schedules and structures might also be effective depending on the needs of each school, such as a lunchtime intervention or sessions held during a health education course.

Undergraduate Course Structure

In the first class sessions of the term, undergraduates are introduced to the central ideas and research findings in the field of positive psychology. As preparation for the intervention, they are assigned readings from Seligman's (1991) *Learned Optimism* text or Reivich and Shatté's (2003) *Resilience Factor* as well as several articles discussing the development and effectiveness of the Penn Resiliency Program (e.g., Gillham et al., 2007). These readings help familiarize students with both the fundamental and the current work in the relevant field.

Following these initial sessions, classes focus on training students to deliver the program. Students are first provided with a general overview of the program and its structure and focus on general skills necessary for working with youth in school settings. Then they receive focused training on each week's session. Each class session is split between reflecting on the previous session and preparing students for the week's upcoming lesson. Undergraduates are invited to voice challenges and difficulties they encountered in the previous week and receive guidance and support from the course instructor as well as their classmates. The course instructor initially provides a brief review of the next lesson plan with undergraduates, noting challenging areas and points of emphasis. In between classes, undergraduates are asked to practice teaching the following week's lesson in small groups or pairs, and during the next class the instructor describes the lesson in greater depth and provides coaching and feedback to in-class practice. At this time, the instructor also answers any questions undergraduates have to ensure that they feel adequately prepared for each week's session.

In addition, undergraduates are asked to reflect on and record their experience through weekly journal entries. These entries are often shared and discussed during course time to facilitate class discussions and help students process their experience. At the end of the course, students are asked to produce a final paper, incorporating both their own personal reflections on the experience as well as an analysis of any data (e.g., anonymous feedback surveys) collected from youth and undergraduates involved in the program. Together, these components of the course provide students with guidance and structured reflection, enabling them to successfully implement the program while simultaneously fostering their own personal growth.

Intervention Implementation

Another benefit of university–community partnerships is the flexible nature of undergraduate schedules. As such, undergraduate-led interventions can be implemented during the school day or as part of an existing after-school program, depending on the needs of each school and community. In this way, instead of overwhelming school personnel with additional scheduling conflicts, previous implementations of this model have capitalized on undergraduate flexibility, working with each school to develop a feasible schedule for the program. Undergraduates who enroll in the course are then informed of the intervention schedule and commit to running weekly intervention sessions throughout the term.

Sessions are held once a week for a total of eight 90-minute sessions. During this time, undergraduates often facilitate a group activity and then break into smaller groups, with two undergraduates and two youth working together in each small group. While this structure is unessential, we found it effective in that the small groups facilitate a mentorship-type relationship between undergraduates and youth, while the presence of small groups of youth helped increased comfort levels. In other implementations, it has been effective for two or three undergraduates to colead larger groups of youth in the PRP curriculum.

Table 24.2 Penn Resiliency Project (PRP) Feedback from Youth Participants and Undergraduate Leaders

Item	Responding At Least "Mostly True"
Undergraduate leader feedback	
I liked teaching the after school groups.	82%
I felt prepared to lead the sessions each week.	82%
The training I received prepared me to deliver the program to children.	65%
I think the after school program was helpful to the 5th-8th graders who participated.	53%
Youth participant feedback	
I learned a lot from the program that will help me feel happier in my life.	79%
I liked the program.	84%
I think my group leaders helped me.	95%
I liked my group leaders.	90%
I'm glad I was part of this program.	79%

During our first implementation of this course at the University of Pennsylvania, we collected feedback surveys from youth and undergraduates. Findings from these surveys suggested that the program was beneficial for both youths and undergraduates. The majority of the youth participants cited using skills (e.g., noticing self-talk, acting assertively, and challenging all-or-nothing thinking) in their daily lives following participation in PRP. Youths and undergraduates were asked to rate how true each item was; responses ranged from *not true* (0) to *very true* (4). Table 24.2 highlights feedback from youth participants and undergraduate leaders at the University of Pennsylvania. This initial feedback suggested that youths generally liked the program, felt that they learned skills, and liked their undergraduate group leaders. In addition, the majority of undergraduate leaders enjoyed running the groups, felt prepared to lead groups, and felt the youths benefited from them. While more research is needed on the efficacy of this model, this feedback is promising and suggests the acceptability of undergraduate service providers for both youth and undergraduates.

Summary of the University–Community Partnership Model

In universities around the country, undergraduates already offer important services to youth, in the context of tutoring and mentoring programs such as Big Brothers/Big Sisters. Our work suggests that with proper training, supervision, and guidance, undergraduates can similarly be effective service providers for resilience and well-being interventions such as the PRP and PPP. While further research is needed to determine whether groups led by undergraduates can produce the same benefits as those observed in previous research on PRP and PPP, our experiences and preliminary data suggest that undergraduates can successfully teach youths the skills included in these curricula that have been shown to effectively prevent depression and increase well-being. Our initial experiences suggest that this model is both feasible and acceptable to the schools, youth, parents, universities, and undergraduates involved. If this model is replicated, universities could employ undergraduate psychology majors to deliver these programs in local schools throughout the country. As the importance of these school-based resilience and well-being interventions becomes increasingly recognized, the university–community partnership offers a unique model for a sustainable and scalable dissemination of these programs.

EMBEDDING WELL-BEING INTERVENTIONS IN THE CURRICULUM: THE POSITIVE PSYCHOLOGY PROGRAM

The Positive Psychology Program (PPP; Gillham et al., 2013; Seligman et al., 2009) provides a second innovative model of dissemination consisting of positive psychology lessons that can be embedded in existing high school curricula, such as a language arts curriculum. In this way, classroom teachers can function as service providers for this well-being intervention. In addition to discussion and activities, concepts are conveyed through writing and reading assignments, and youths are exposed to these concepts while simultaneously developing academic skills. While the PPP is composed of specific lesson plans, teachers are also encouraged to incorporate positive psychology concepts into their existing lessons, allowing for an integration of social-emotional and academic goals.

Positive Psychology Curriculum

The PPP curriculum emphasizes the *promotion* approach to resilience and well-being by helping students identify and use their strengths, develop an increased capacity for positive emotions, develop close relationships, and engage in activities that are meaningful to them. Research has shown that interventions that use this promotion model improve life satisfaction and reduce depression (Seligman et al., 2005; Seligman, Rashid, & Parks, 2006; Sin & Lyubomirsky, 2009).

The curriculum is composed of 20 to 25 lessons taught over the course of the ninth-grade school year. Lessons involve discussions of positive psychology concepts and skills (e.g., identifying character strengths) and an in-class activity. In addition, the lessons include homework assignments that encourage participants to practice and apply skills that they learn in their own lives, and a follow-up journal reflection. Table 24.3 highlights the content of each lesson. In addition, teachers are encouraged to weave positive psychology concepts into their regular lesson plans. For example, many teachers encourage their students to consider the character strengths exhibited by the characters in the works of literature they assign as course readings.

As shown in Table 24.3, lessons include cognitive skills taught in the Penn Resiliency Program, as well as skills specifically designed to increase positive experiences and promote upward spirals such as savoring, gratitude, identifying and developing strengths, putting strengths to use, exhibiting kindness, and increasing meaning and purpose. While teachers must make some adjustments to their curriculum, the skills are embedded in a language arts curriculum and taught through writing assignments, class discussions, and journal reflections. For example, to encourage youth to examine what it means to live a meaningful life, teachers assign relevant passages from literature that represent the reflections of different writers, philosophers, politicians, spiritual leaders, and comedians about the meaning of life. Students then reflect about their own perspective on cultivating meaning and complete a written dialogue with their parents on the topic in the context of a "meaning journal." In this way, youths are simultaneously developing skills in both writing and literature as they discuss the concept of cultivating life meaning.

Table 24.3 Positive Psychology Program (PPP) Overview

Lesson	Topic	Description

1	**Introductory Lesson: The Three Paths to Happiness**
	Suggested class time: 80 min
		• Discuss history and mission of positive psychology
		• Use related songs and poems to introduce the "three paths to happiness"
		  o *The Pleasant Life* (increasing pleasure and positive emotion)
		  o *The Good Life* (increasing gratification through using one's signature strengths)
		  o *The Meaningful Life* (finding a connection with and using one's signature strengths in the service of something larger than oneself)

2	**Sensory Savoring** Suggested class time: 60 min	• Define *Savoring, Absorption*, and *Sharpening Perceptions* • Assign students to complete *Personal Savoring Survey* • Complete *Savoring Exercise With Fruit*; students practice using the concepts of absorption and sharpening perceptions to feel, smell, and taste piece of fruit • Assign *Savoring Assignment* homework
3	**Savoring Beyond the Senses** Suggested class time: 40 min	• Introduce the need to appreciate meaningful events, people, or places in one's life • Discuss difference between *cultural artifacts* and *personal artifacts* • Ask students to present on a chosen personal artifact • Assign *Personal Artifact* homework
4	**Countering the Negativity Bias (Counting Our Blessings)** Suggested class time: 90 min	• Discuss tendency to focus on negative rather than positive aspects of life • Introduce concept of actively recalling and analyzing good events to build pleasant memories, gratitude, and optimism • Complete in class *Blessings Worksheet* and assign Blessings Daily Log
5	**Expressing Gratitude (Gratitude Letter/ Visit)** Suggested class time: 90 min	• Introduce the strength of feeling appreciative for good things that others do for us • Discuss the importance of openly expressing gratitude • Have students complete *Personal Gratitude List* in which they describe helpful people in their lives • Assign *Gratitude Letter and Visit* in which students express gratitude to an important person in their lives
6	**Optimism Lessons: ABC Model** Suggested class time: 80 min	• Introduce the ABC model and help students identify the link between self-talk and consequent feelings and behaviors • Examine common belief–emotion connections • Discuss optimism as tendency to take a hopeful view • Assign *ABC Worksheet*
7	**Optimism Lessons: Generating Alternatives** Suggested class time: 80 min	• Introduce three explanatory styles: Me versus Not Me; Always versus Not Always; and Everything versus Not Everything • Practice identifying beliefs according to thinking style • Have students work in pairs to generate alternative, more accurate beliefs • Assign *Generating Alternatives Worksheets*
8	**Optimism Lessons: Evaluating Evidence** Suggested class time: 80 min	• Discuss need to look for evidence that supports and refutes each belief generated • Break students into small groups to complete the File Game activity in which students sift through materials (e.g., awards, diary entries, photos, report cards) about a fictitious child and are instructed to use the information to evaluate accuracy of the child's negative self-talk • Practice looking for evidence in a situation in students' own lives using the *Getting More Accurate* worksheet

Lesson	Topic	Description
9	**Optimism Lessons: Real-Time Resilience** Suggested class time: 80 min	• Describe Real-Time Resilience: responding to negative beliefs in real time so one can remain optimistic and focused on task • Practice with one student acting out negative beliefs and one student generating accurate alternatives or using evidence • Discuss common pitfalls to real-time resilience: *dismissing the grain of truth, minimizing the situation, rationalizing or excusing one's contribution to a problem* • Assign *Real-Time Resilience Reflection* worksheet
10	**Strengths: Identifying Strengths** Suggested class time: 80 min	• Examine differences between character strengths and talents • Describe each character strength and ask students to write their top five strengths
11	**Strengths in Context** Suggested class time: 130 min	• Watch *Whats Eating Gilbert Grape* movie and ask students to pay attention to character strengths of each character • Assign *Strengths Analysis* homework for students to describe how characters in the movie used strengths
12	**Strengths Narrative** Suggested class time: 30 min	• Students write strengths narrativesthat describe specific events in their lives that demonstrate use of a particular character strength • Ask volunteers to read their narratives aloud while other students in the class attempt to identify the strength exemplified
13	**Family Tree of Strengths** Suggested class time: 30 min	• *Use Family Tree of Strengths* worksheet todiscuss ways in which family members use strengths in the service of something greater than themselves • Assign *Family Tree of Strengths Interview* and *Written Reflection* in which students interview family members about their use of character strengths
14	**Developing a Target Strength** Suggested class time: 50 min	• Discuss strengths that students may like to develop • Create an *Action Plan* for developing one of those strengths
15	**Five Kindnesses in One Day** Suggested class time: 30 min	• Examine ways in which students can complete small acts of kindness throughout the day • Assign *Kindness Reports* to log opportunities for kindness that arise throughout the week
16	**Examining Meaning** Suggested class time: 80 min	• Discuss what it means to live a meaningful and purposeful life • Introduce connection between such a life and happiness • In groups, students read excerpts of passages and/or quotations and reflect on their understanding and agreement with the message • Assign *Meaning Reflection* homework in which students are instructed to write letters that explore various perspectives on meaning and purpose
17	**Culminating Lesson** Suggested class time: 80 min	• Before this lesson, ask students to bring to class some object that shows how the course has impacted them • Students present their object and discuss experiences participating in the program • Review what was learned about strengths and meaning
	Weekly Maintenance	• Set aside first 10 to 15 minutes of one day each week for journal reflection, class discussion, or review of homework exercises • Encourage repeated practice and habituation of skills and concepts

This program is still in the early stages of evaluation, but initial findings suggest that the program increases social skills (e.g., cooperation, assertiveness, empathy) and students' reports of enjoyment and engagement in school while improving language arts achievement through the 11th grade (Gillham et al., 2013; Seligman et al., 2009). Thus, this program may provide an effective method of teaching well-being and resilience to high school students within the context and structure of an adapted language arts course.

CONCLUSION

There is increasing recognition of the link between children's academic and emotional success. In order to create schools that foster achievement, resilience, and well-being among today's youth, we must be conscious of the cognitive, emotional, and behavioral skills they need to meet the challenges they will face in school and in the real world. Interventions that promote adolescent well-being such as the Penn Resiliency Project and the Positive Psychology Program offer effective ways to help youth recognize their unique strengths, develop resilience, and experience meaning and purpose. With the development of these programs, we are poised to effect lasting change in the quality of these children's lives. However, innovative strategies such as those described here are needed to ensure that these programs reach the many youth that might benefit from them. Future research should continue to evaluate these and other models for the dissemination of positive interventions in schools.

REFERENCES

Becker, C.B., Smith, L.M., & Ciao, A.C. (2006). Peer-facilitated eating disorder prevention: A randomized effectiveness trial of cognitive dissonance and media advocacy. *Journal of Counseling Psychology, 53*, 550–555. doi:10.1037/0022-0167.53.4.550

Blechman, E.A., McEnroe, M.J., Carella, E.T., & Audette, D.P. (1986). Childhood competence and depression. *Journal of Abnormal Psychology, 95*, 223–227. doi:10.1037//0021-843X.95.3.223

Brunwasser, S.M., Gillham, J.E., & Kim, E.S. (2009). A meta-analytic review of the Penn Resiliency Program's effect on depressive symptoms. *American Psychological Association, 77*, 1042–1054. doi:10.1037/a0017671

Burns, B.J., Costello, E.J., Angold, A., Tweed, D., Stangl, D., Farmer, E.M., & Erkanli, A. (1995). Children's mental health services use across service sectors. *Health Affairs, 14*, 147–159. doi:10.1377/hlthaff.14.3.147

Cardemil, E.V., Reivich, K.J., & Seligman, M.E.P. (2002). The prevention of depressive symptoms in low-income minority middle school students. *Prevention and Treatment, 5*, Article 8. doi:10.1037//1522-3736.5.1.58a

Christensen, A., & Jacobson, N. (1994). Who (or what) can do psychotherapy: The status and challenge of nonprofessional therapies. *Psychological Science, 5*, 8–14. doi:10.1111/j.1467-9280.1994.tb00606.x

Cole, D.A. (1991). Preliminary support for a competency-based model of child depression. *Journal of Abnormal Psychology, 100*, 181–190.

Covey, L.S., Glassman, A.H., & Stetner, F. (1998). Cigarette smoking and major depression. *Journal of Addictive Diseases, 17*, 35–46. doi:10.1300/J069v17n01_04

Duckworth, A.L., & Seligman, M.E.P. (2005). Self-discipline outdoes IQ in predicting academic performance of adolescents. *Psychological Science, 16*, 939–944. doi:10.1111/j.1467-9280.2005.01641.x

Durlak, J. (1979). Comparative effectiveness of paraprofessional and professional helpers. *Psychological Bulletin, 86*, 80–92. doi:10.1037//0033-2909.86.1.80

Eccles, J.S., Midgley, C., Wigfield, A., Buchanan, C.M., Reuman, D., Flanagan, C., & Mac Iver, D. (1993). Development during adolescence: The impact of stage-environment fit on young adolescents' experiences in schools and in families. *American Psychologist, 48*, 90–101. doi:10.1037/0003-066X.48.2.90

Elias, M.J., Zins, J.E., Weissberg, R.P., Frey, K.S., Greenberg, M.T., Haynes, N.M., . . . Shriver, T.P. (1997). *Promoting social and emotional learning: Guidelines for educators.* Alexandria, VA: Association for Supervision and Curriculum Development.

Fergusson, D. M., Horwood, L., Ridder, E. M., & Beautrais, A. L. (2005). Subthreshold depression in adolescence and mental health outcomes in adulthood. *Archives of General Psychiatry, 62,* 66–72. doi/10.1001/archpsyc.62.1.66

Fredrickson, B. L. (2001). The role of positive emotions in positive psychology: The broaden-and-build theory of positive emotions. *American Psychologist, 56,* 218–226. doi/10.1037//0003-066X.56.3.218

Garrison, C. Z., Schluchter, M. D., Schoenback, V. J., & Kaplan, B. K. (1989). Epidemiology of depressive symptoms in young adolescents. *Journal of the American Academy of Child and Adolescent Psychiatry, 28,* 343–351. doi/10.1097/00004583-198905000-00007

Gillham, J. E., Abenevoli, R. M., Brunwasser, S. B., Linkins, M., Reivich, K. J., & Seligman, M. E. P. (2013). Resilience education. In S. A. David, I. Boniwell, & A. C. Ayers (Eds.), *The Oxford handbook of happiness* (pp. 609–630). Oxford, UK. Oxford University Press.

Gillham, J. E., Brunwasser, S. M., & Freres, D. R. (2008). Preventing depression in early adolescence. In J. R. Z. Abela & B. L. Hankin (Eds.), *Handbook of depression in children and adolescents.* New York, NY: Guilford.

Gillham, J. E., Reivich, K. J., & Jaycox, L. H. (2008). *The Penn Resiliency Program* (also known as *The Penn Depression Prevention Program* and *The Penn Optimism Program*). Unpublished manuscript, University of Pennsylvania.

Gillham, J. E., Reivich, K. J., Jaycox, I. H., & Seligman, M. E. P. (1995). Preventing depressive symptoms in schoolchildren: Two-year follow-up. *Psychological Science, 6,* 343–351. doi/10.1111/j.1467-9280.1995.tb00524.x

Gotlib, I. H., Lewinsohn, P. M., & Seeley, J. R. (1995). Symptoms versus a diagnosis of depression: Differences in psychosocial functioning. *Journal of Consulting and Clinical Psychology, 63,* 90–100. doi/10.1037//0022-006X.63.1.90

Greenberg, M. T., Weissberg, R. P., O'Brien, M. U., Zins, J. E., Fredericks, L., Resnik, H., & Elias, M. J. (2003). Enhancing school-based prevention and youth development through coordinated social, emotional, and academic learning. *American Psychologist, 58,* 466–474. doi/10.1037/0003-066X.58.6-7.466

Hankin, B. L., Abramson, L. Y., Moffitt, T. E., Silva, P. A., McGee, R., & Angell, K. E. (1998). Development of depression from preadolescence to young adulthood: Emerging gender differences in a 10-year longitudinal study. *Journal of Abnormal Psychology, 107,* 128–140. doi/10.1037//0021-843X.107.1.128

Horowitz, J. L., & Garber, J. (2006). The prevention of depressive symptoms in children and adolescents: A meta-analytic review. *Journal of Consulting and Clinical Psychology, 74,* 401–415. doi/10.1037/0022-006X.74.3.401

Jaycox, L., Reivich, K., Gillham, J., & Seligman, M. (1994). Prevention of depressive symptoms in school-children. *Behavior Research and Therapy, 38,* 801–816. doi/10.1016/0005-7967(94)90160-0

Kazdin, A. E. (2008). Evidence-based treatments and delivery of psychological services: Shifting our emphases to increase impact. *Psychological Services, 5,* 201–215. doi/10.1037/a0012573

Kazdin, A. E., & Blase, S. (2011). Rebooting psychotherapy research and practice to reduce the burden of mental illness. *Perspectives on Psychological Sciences, 6,* 21–37. doi/10.1177/1745691610393527

Kessler, R. C., Avenevoli, S., & Merikangas, K. R. (2001). Mood disorders in children and adolescents: An epidemiologic perspective. *Biological Psychiatry, 49,* 1002–1014. doi/10.1016/S0006-3223(01)01129-5

Kessler, R. C., Berglund, P., Demler, O., Jin, R., Koretz, D., Merikangas, K. R., . . . Wang, P. S. (2003). The epidemiology of major depressive disorder: Results from the National Comorbidity Survey replication (NCS-R). *Journal of American Medical Association, 23,* 3095–3105. doi/10.1016/S0006-3223(01)01129-5

Kim-Cohen, J., Caspi, A., Moffitt, T. E., Harrington, H., Milne, A. J., & Poulton, R. (2003). Prior juvenile diagnoses in adults with mental disorder: Developmental follow-back of a prospective-longitudinal cohort. *Archives of General Psychiatry, 60,* 709–717. doi/10.1001/archpsyc.60.7.709

Kovacs, M. (1989). Affective disorders in children and adolescents. *American Psychologist, 44,* 209–215. doi/10.1037//0003-066X.44.2.209

Nolen-Hoeksema, S., Girgus, J. S., & Seligman M. E. P. (1986). Learned helplessness in children: A longitudinal study of depression, achievement, and explanatory style. *Journal of Personality and Social Psychology, 51,* 435–442. doi/10.1037//0022-3514.51.2.435

Offord, D. R., Kraemer, H. C., Kazdin, A. E., Jensen, P. S., & Harrington, R. (1998). Lowering the burden of suffering from child psychiatric disorder: Trade-offs among clinical, targeted, and universal interventions. *Journal of the American Academy of Child & Adolescent Psychiatry, 37,* 686–694. doi/10.1097/00004583-199807000-00007

Parks, A. C., & Biswas-Diener, R. (2013). Positive interventions: Past, present and future. In T. Kashdan & J. Ciarrochi (Eds.), *Bridging acceptance and commitment therapy and positive psychology: A practitioner's guide to a unifying framework.* Oakland, CA: New Harbinger.

Peterson, A. C., Compas, B. E., Brooks-Gunn, J., Stemmler, M. Y S., & Grant, K. E. (1993). Depression in adolescence. *American Psychologist, 48,* 155–168. doi/10.1037//0003-066X.48.2.155

Reivich, K., & Shatté, A. (2003). *The resilience factor: 7 keys to finding your inner strength and overcoming life's hurdles.* New York, NY: Broadway books.

Rones, M., & Hoagwood, K. (2000). School-based mental health services: A research review. *Clinical Child and Family Psychology Review, 3,* 223–241.

Schulman, P. (1995). Explanatory style and achievement in school and work. In G.M. Buchanan & M.E.P. Seligman (Eds.), *Explanatory style* (pp. 159–171). Hillsdale, NJ: Erlbaum.

Sedlak, M. (1997). The uneasy alliance of mental health services and the schools: An historical perspective. *American Journal of Orthopsychiatry, 67,* 349–362. doi/10.1037/h0080238

Seligman, M. (1991). *Learned optimism.* New York, NY: Knopf.

Seligman, M.E.P., Ernst, R.M., Gillham, J., Reivich, K., & Linkins, M. (2009). Positive education: Positive psychology and classroom interventions. *Oxford Review of Education, 35,* 293–311. doi/10.1080/03054980902934563

Seligman, M.E.P., Rashid, T., & Parks, A.C. (2006). Positive psychotherapy. *American Psychologist, 61,* 774–788. doi/10.1037/0003-066X.61.8.774

Seligman, M.E.P., Steen, T.A., Park, N., & Peterson, C. (2005). Positive psychology progress: Empirical validation of interventions. *American Psychologist, 60,* 410–421. doi/10.1037/0003-066X.60.5.410

Sin, N.L., & Lyubomirsky, S. (2009). Enhancing well-being and alleviating depressive symptoms with positive psychology interventions: A practice-friendly meta-analysis. *Journal of Clinical Psychology, 65,* 467–487. doi/10.1002/jclp.20593

Stice, E., Shaw, H., Bohon, C., Marti, C.N., & Rohde, P. (2009). A meta-analytic review of depression prevention programs for children and adolescents: Factors that predict magnitude of intervention effects. *Journal of Consulting and Clinical Psychology, 77,* 486–503. doi/10.1037/a0015168

Suldo, S.M., Friedrich, A., & Michalowski, J. (2010). Personal and systems-level factors that limit and facilitate school psychologists' involvement in school-based mental health services. *Psychology in the Schools, 47,* 354–373. doi/10.1002/pits.20475

Wang, M.C., Haertel, G.D., & Walberg, H.J. (1997). Toward a knowledge base for school learning. *Review of Educational Research, 63,* 249–294. doi/10.2307/1170546

Weist, M.D., Goldstein, A., Morris, L., & Bryant, T. (2003). Integrating expanded school mental health programs and school-based health centers. *Psychology in the Schools, 40,* 297–308. doi/10.1002/pits.10089

Weisz, J.R., Weiss, B., Han, S.S., & Granger, D.A. (1995). Effects of psychotherapy with children and adolescents revisited: A meta-analysis of treatment outcome studies. *Psychological Bulletin, 117,* 450–468. doi/10.1037//0033-2909.117.3.450

Yu, D.L., & Seligman, M.E.P. (2002). Preventing depressive symptoms in Chinese children. *Prevention and Treatment, 5,* Article 9. doi/10.1037//1522-3736.5.1.59a

CHAPTER SUMMARY: INNOVATIVE DISSEMINATION MODELS

- A large percentage of youth are exposed to some form of adversity (e.g., exposure to violence, poverty, parental depression, death of a parent, abuse, or neglect) or psychological difficulty (e.g., depression) by the end of middle school.
- Despite increasing recognition of the importance of school-based resilience and well-being interventions, wide-scale implementation has not yet been achieved.
- With these programs, as with all school-based interventions, limitations in school and clinical resources limit opportunities for dissemination.
- Innovative models of dissemination are needed in order to ensure these programs reach the large number of youth who may benefit from them.
- University–community partnerships offer one promising new model of dissemination, employing undergraduates as program leaders in the context of service-learning university courses.
- A second promising model involves the integration of well-being concepts into lessons that can be embedded in existing academic courses such as a high school language arts curriculum. In this model, teachers disseminate the intervention and are encouraged to weave concepts from the curriculum into their existing lesson plans.
- Results from early implementations of both of these models suggest that they constitute promising new methods of wide-scale dissemination.

- These models can be replicated and implemented at schools around the country as a way of teaching youth important skills without sacrificing extensive school time or resources.
- For more information about the Penn Resiliency Program and Positive Psychology curriculum materials, contact info@pennproject.org.

SUGGESTED READINGS: INNOVATIVE DISSEMINATION MODELS

Gillham, J.E., Abenevoli, R.M., Brunwasser, S.B., Linkins, M., Reivich, K.J., & Seligman, M.E.P. (2013). Resilience education. In S.A. David, I. Boniwell, & A.C. Ayers (Eds.), *Handbook of happiness*. Oxford, UK: Oxford University Press.

This chapter highlights the potential for schools to promote resilience and social and emotional well-being in children. The authors provide a comprehensive overview of current research on resilience and describe a rationale for integrating resilience into educational practices. They provide detailed overviews of two types of well-being interventions: one that teaches problem-solving and coping skills and one that aims to increase positive emotion, personal strengths, and a sense of meaning and fulfillment.

Kranzler, A., Parks, A.C., & Gillham, J. (2011). Illustrating positive psychology concepts through service learning: Penn teaches resilience. *Journal of Positive Psychology, 6,* 482–486. doi/10.1080/17439760.2011.634829

The authors provide a more detailed description of the university–community partnership model for dissemination of resilience interventions. Information is provided about the logistics of implementing a service-learning course, and recommendations for replication of this model at other institutions are made. The authors also provide insights into the strengths and challenges of the model.

Parks, A.C., & Biswas-Diener, R. (2013). Positive interventions: Past, present and future. In T. Kashdan & J. Ciarroch (Eds.), *Bridging acceptance and commitment therapy and positive psychology: A practitioner's guide to a unifying framework*. Oakland, CA: New Harbinger.

Parks and Biswas-Diener provide a comprehensive review of positive interventions. They include a description of what constitutes a positive intervention and describe different types of positive interventions. They also review evidence of the effectiveness of these interventions and considerations for their implementation. This article provides a helpful overview and update of the current state of positive interventions as well as a look toward future directions in this area.

Seligman, M.E.P., Ernst, R.M., Gillham, J., Reivich, K., & Linkins, M. (2009). Positive education: Positive psychology and classroom interventions. *Oxford Review of Education, 35,* 293–311. doi/10.1080/03054980902934563

This article provides a definition of "positive education:" the integration of both the skills of well-being and the skills of achievement within the school setting. The authors describe an evidence-based rationale for teaching skills that increase resilience, positive emotion, engagement, and meaning with school-aged children. The article summarizes research findings from trials examining the effectiveness of two well-being programs (PRP & PPP) that have been implemented in schools. They conclude with a thorough description of the development and implementation of a schoolwide well-being program piloted in Australia.

Section IV
School-Based International Perspectives

25

POSITIVE EDUCATION
An Australian Perspective

Suzy Green, The Positivity Institute, Sydney, NSW, Australia

INTRODUCTION

Within Australia, there is increasing recognition that schools are important locations for the adoption of positive psychology, particularly in regard to student well-being. This is not unique to Australia, and it should be noted that this recognition is gaining increasing acknowledgment globally. For example, Gill (2009) argued that "human flourishing should be the core aim of education, and that education ought to be directed at the child as a whole, nurturing their diverse qualities and virtues as well as their inner integrity and harmony" (p. 6). Huitt (2010) also acknowledged the paradigm change occurring in education whereby schools are now being seen as institutions whose role extends beyond academic competence to preparing the whole child (Huitt, 2010).

Nevertheless, what appears to be unique to Australia is the increasing interest in the field of "positive education" and in the creation and implementation of large-scale, customized, and strategic positive education programs (PEPs). The creation of these programs was primarily driven by the strong interest in the Australian educational community, stimulated by media coverage surrounding the first large-scale strategic positive education program implemented in Victoria, Australia (the Geelong Grammar Positive Education Program; Seligman, Ernst, Gillham, & Linkins, 2009).

This chapter aims to provide an introduction to and overview of the emerging field of positive education and positive education programs within Australia. An expanded definition of positive education will also be proposed that integrates the application of positive psychology and other well-being sciences (such as coaching psychology and its applied discipline, evidence-based coaching). The chapter also includes a review of research on evidence-based coaching programs in schools. Finally, issues pertinent to the strategic and appropriate implementation of larger-scale positive education programs in schools are discussed.

WHAT IS POSITIVE EDUCATION?

Seligman and colleagues (Seligman et al., 2009) defined positive education as "education for both traditional skills and for happiness" with a focus on the use of classroom interventions that teach resilience, positive emotions, engagement, and meaning to schoolchildren. However, Seligman and colleagues (2009) also acknowledged, "there is much more to positive education than simple stand-alone courses" (p. 305) with the suggestion of the need for embedding and living positive psychology.

In Australia, there is an increasing recognition that positive education is more than the provision of "well-being classes." Green, Oades, and Robinson (2011) have provided an alternative definition of positive education as being simply applied positive psychology in education. This definition allows for positive education to be viewed more broadly in terms of its application not only to students but also to staff and whole communities. This definition also expands the scope and application of positive education beyond "school," placing it in a broader educational context that includes early childhood education and higher education—that is, education from the cradle to the grave. Currently, the focus of positive psychology in education has been at the primary and secondary school levels; however, there is increasing interest in the adoption of positive psychology in early childhood (Armstrong, Missall, Shaffer, & Jojnoski, 2009) and in higher education (Oades, Robinson, Green, & Spence, 2011). As such, an expanded definition allows for further exploration of applied positive psychology in broader educational settings.

While the Green and colleagues (2011) definition appears sufficient, the author proposes a newer and refined definition of positive education. It is suggested that positive education be defined as "the application of well-being science into an educational setting aimed at increasing the resilience and well-being of students, staff, and whole-school community." This definition expands on Seligman's initial definition, which focused on learning the skills of "happiness" through the teaching of positive psychology. This is an important point for three primary reasons: (a) the increasing use of the term "well-being" in place of "happiness"; (b) the increasing recognition that well-being effects may be created both explicitly (through teaching) and implicitly (through experiencing); and (c) the increasing application of other well-being sciences in educational settings (e.g., evidence-based coaching and neuroscience).

First, in Seligman's 2011 book titled *Flourish*, he notes that he detests the word "happiness" and claims it is an "unworkable term for science (p. 9) and goes on to suggest "the topic of positive psychology is well-being" (p. 13). Second, the explicit/implicit denotation is important for positive education and for positive education programs, which require a combination of both to be successful. The explicit approach occurs through the teaching and learning of positive psychology and primarily occurs through stand-alone classes on positive psychology, whereas the implicit approach occurs through experiencing it and living it. The implicit approach can occur in a variety of ways, including cocurricular activities often experiential in nature (e.g., education and sports) in addition to the whole-school environment, which can be created to prime for positive or negative affect (Bargh & Morsella, 2008). Furthermore, school culture can similarly have both a positive or negative effect on well-being. Third, there is increasing interest in the application of alternate well-being sciences in educational settings such as evidence-based coaching and neuroscience and, hence, there is a need to refer to and include other fields of research and practice relating to well-being, in addition to positive psychology.

Why Positive Education?

Like many other westernized societies, Australian schools have aimed for academic excellence as primary evidence for their success. Nevertheless, paralleling similar stances in other nations, a growing number of Australian schools acknowledge the need to develop students in a more holistic way, with a stronger focus on well-being. In addition, there is a growing recognition of the need for schools to focus on teacher and staff well-being (Grant, Green, & Rynsaardt, 2010). For example, within Australia in recent years, an increasing number of both independent and state schools have made commitments to whole-school positive education programs that aim to help students, staff, and whole-school communities flourish psychologically, socially, and academically.

The increasing focus on well-being in schools is a proactive approach to the increasing rates of psychological distress in both school students and staff. Norrish and Vella-Brodrick (2009) quote a national survey investigating a range of mental health issues in a stratified, random sample of 4,500 Australian youths (ages 4–17 years), whereby 14% of those surveyed had mental health problems (Sawyer et al., 2000). They go on to note that while this high prevalence rate is cause for concern, the number of adolescents who are not flourishing may be higher still.

Many schools consider and commence proactive positive education programs as a means to reduce the incidence of mental distress in youths. However, there is a simultaneous desire to enhance well-being and functioning beyond the absence of psychological distress. According to Benson and Scales (2009), adequate functioning in adolescents (e.g., the absence of serious behavioral, psychological, and emotional problems) does not necessarily equate with thriving. Norrish and Vella-Brodrick (2009) suggest that psychologists and other health professionals have an important role in researching and communicating how well-being can be enhanced and how individuals can thrive and flourish (Seligman & Csikszentmihalyi, 2000). Wyn (2007) also argues that "While older educational agendas such as literacy and numeracy remain significant . . . education is increasingly important for its role in assisting young people to develop the capacities and skills that will enable them to live well and that will enable social cohesion" (p. 35).

In addition, there are real opportunities to increase teacher well-being through the provision of whole-school positive education programs. This is particularly important given statistics highlighting significant levels of teacher stress (Kyriacou, 1987, 2001; Wiley 2000). Grant and colleagues (2010) suggested some of the key challenges facing high school teachers, in particular, include stress, lack of resources, increased scrutiny and evaluation from key stakeholders, dealing with a cumbersome bureaucratic system, dealing constructively with a diverse student population, and the need to display positive leadership behaviors while under pressure (MacKenzie & Marnik, 2008). In addition, a key challenge facing the secondary school sector is the retention of teaching staff (Quartz & The TEP Research Group, 2003).

With a greater focus on the enhancement of well-being in schools, there is also increasing recognition of the need for scientific research. Research can support scientifically grounded well-being initiatives in playing a crucial preventative role in reducing depression, anxiety, and stress within the school environment (Neil & Christensen, 2007). While the foundation of positive education is rooted firmly in science, as will be highlighted in the following sections, there is a pressing need for further research on school-wide programs that aim to increase well-being, particularly on whole-school positive education programs. At this time, there have been no peer-reviewed publications on the effects of such programs such as Geelong Grammar School.

The Foundations of Positive Education

It should be acknowledged that the interest in the promotion of mental health and well-being in schools is not new. There has been significant interest in promoting mental health in schools including the creation and implementation of a variety of mental health programs in schools over the past two decades. Weare (2010) also acknowledged this significant growth of research and good practice and claims activities operate under a variety of headings, including "social and emotional learning," "emotional literacy," "emotional intelligence," "resilience," "life skills," and character education." Systematic reviews of interventions, using the most rigorous and exacting criteria, are repeatedly demonstrating definitively that well-designed and well-implemented interventions are effective (Adi, Killoran, Janmohamed, & Stewart-Brown, 2007; Shucksmith, Summerbell, Jones, & Whittaker, 2007).

Many of these approaches have fallen under the umbrella of "mental health promotion" more broadly and often with the explicit aim of reducing psychological distress and mental illness in the student population. While some interventions explicitly suggest their aim is to increase well-being, it is the author's understanding they have not been in the main explicitly identified as positive psychology approaches or interventions.

In Australia, similarly, there is a long history of well-being interventions; however, there has been a shift in focus over time. McGrath (2009) noted that the initial focus was on self-esteem in the 1970s, which moved to social skills programs in the early 1990s and then to resilience programs in the early 2000s. McGrath (2009) suggested from then on there has been a strong focus on antibullying initiatives, values programs, and student well-being initiatives, including social and emotional learning programs.

With the emergence of the field of positive psychology, there has been increasing recognition of the potential beneficial applications of positive psychology to schools with the explicit aim of increasing well-being. In one of the earliest publications on this topic, titled "Positive Psychology Goes to School," the authors suggested that schools might serve as the nexus between the movement in positive psychology searching to promote positive human development and the institutions that could serve as the vehicle for positive youth development (Clonan, Chafouleas, McDougal, & Riley-Tillman, 2004).

While there has been increasing interest in the application of positive psychology in school settings (i.e., the first edition of the *Handbook of Positive Psychology in Schools* was published in 2009) as noted previously, it was Seligman who formally named the field of positive education in 2009 (Seligman et al., 2009). Seligman's own interest in education began with rigorous research aimed at solving the question, "Can well-being be taught in schools?" Seligman and colleagues (2009) identify both the Penn Resilience Program (PRP; Brunwasser, Gillham, & Kim, 2009) and Strathhaven Positive Psychology Curriculum (Seligman et al., 2009) as two evidence-based approaches that give support to a positive response to this question. The PRP is designed to prevent depression and, hence, falls under the prevention banner. Seligman and colleagues (2009) note that PRP is one of the most widely researched programs designed to prevent depression in young people, quoting more than 17 studies conducted over 20 years, which provided evidence for its use in reducing depression. The Strathhaven program has a stronger focus on the promotion of well-being. Seligman and colleagues (2009) suggest the major goals of this program are to (a) help students identify their signature character strengths and (b) increase students' use of these strengths in their day-to-day lives. This program has also been scientifically evaluated and shown to increase students' enjoyment and engagement in school and their social skills.

In Australia, many schools continue to offer stand-alone programs like PRP and Strathhaven focused on resilience and well-being (e.g., Bounce Back and You Can Do It) and, hence, might consider themselves to be offering programs that fall under the umbrella of positive education. However, they are in the main not whole-school programs that use an integrated and strategic approach for both students and staff and that aim to enable the school as a positive institution.

As noted earlier, a newer and broader definition of positive education includes applications of well-being science to not only students but staff and whole-school communities. As such, schoolwide positive education programs provide well-being initiatives and programs for students, staff, and parents. In addition, these positive education programs are strategic in nature, integrate many well-being initiatives and programs already in place, and involve whole-school engagement with the aim of creating a positive school climate.

It has also been argued recently that the other differentiating factor of positive education programs compared to traditional approaches to well-being enhancement is that of the inclusion of coaching psychology and its applied form, evidence-based coaching, as a core component of a positive education program (Green, Oades, & Robinson, 2012).

COACHING PSYCHOLOGY AND EVIDENCE-BASED COACHING

First, it is important to clarify what is meant by the terms *coaching psychology* and *evidence-based coaching*. According to Grant (2007), coaching psychology is the "systematic application of behavioral science [within the coaching context] to the enhancement of life experience, work performance and well-being of individuals, groups and organizations" (Grant, 2007, p. 23). Evidence-based coaching is an applied discipline (as it is focused on how knowledge is used). Grant and Stober (2006) define *evidence-based coaching* as "the intelligent and conscientious use of *best current knowledge* integrated with practitioner expertise in making decisions about how to deliver coaching" (p. 6, italics in original), with "best current knowledge" defined as "up-to-date information from relevant, valid research, theory and practice" (Grant & Stober, 2006, p. 6). It represents a broader perspective on coaching, as its practice can potentially be informed by knowledge drawn from multiple disciplines (e.g., psychology, sociology, adult learning, education, organizational behavior, and business management; Green & Spence, in press).

Evidence-Based Coaching as a Positive Psychology Intervention

Evidence-based coaching underpinned by the field of coaching psychology, similar to positive psychology, is also concerned with optimal functioning and well-being enhancement. Its focus, however, is on understanding and applying relevant psychological theories and techniques to a collaborative relationship to enhance goal attainment and increase self-regulation for the normal, nonclinical population (Grant, 2007).

Coaching psychology has been defined as an applied positive psychology (Interest Group in Coaching Psychology, Australian Psychological Society), whereby coaching (including the methodology and relationship) provides the opportunity for the application of positive psychology research, such as strengths identification and use (Linley, Nielson, Gillett, & Biswas-Diener, 2010). The role of positive psychology in coaching has also been discussed previously; however, further research in regard to its specific applications is needed (Biswas-Diener & Dean, 2007; Kauffman, 2006; Linley & Harrington, 2005).

Evidence-Based Coaching in Schools

Coaching is increasingly being utilized in schools with growing interest. One recent publication, titled "Coaching in Education" (van Nieuwerburgh, 2012), provided examples of coaching applications in schools in Australia, the United Kingdom, and the United States of America. In addition, there is increasing global sophistication involved in training and education in coaching generally and also more specifically in regard to coaching in the education sector. For example, the University of East London's Coaching Psychology Unit offers students a dedicated module on "Coaching and Mentoring in Education" and in 2010 held an International Conference on Coaching and Positive Psychology in Education.

Research conducted in Australia at the University of Sydney has given preliminary support for the use of evidence-based coaching in educational settings for students and staff. For example, Green and colleagues (2007) conducted a randomized waitlist control group study of evidence-based life coaching with an adolescent population. Participants were randomly assigned to receive either a 10-week cognitive-behavioral solution-focused life coaching (CB-SF) program or a wait-list control. Fifty-six female senior high school students (mean age = 16 years) were randomly allocated to an individual life-coaching group or to a wait-list control group. Participants were randomly assigned to a teacher-coach (who had been trained in the use of an evidence-based coaching [EBC] model and techniques), and they met one on one for 10 sessions over two school terms. Each coaching session involved the setting of session goals, followed by a discussion of what was going on in the student's life. A primary aim of coaching was to raise awareness of personal circumstances and use that awareness to identify resources that could be utilized to move toward personal goals. Students were also assisted to systematically work through the self-regulatory cycle of setting goals, developing (self-generated) action plans, and then monitoring and evaluating progress. The findings indicated that student coachees (compared to controls) experienced significant increases in cognitive hardiness and hope and a significant decrease in levels of depression, which suggested that evidence-based life coaching might be an effective intervention for high school students.

Madden, Green, and Grant (2011) also conducted a pilot study by utilizing strengths-based coaching for primary school boys in a within-subject design study. Thirty-eight Year 5 male students (mean age 11 years) participated in a strengths-based coaching program as part of their personal development/health program at an independent, private primary school in Sydney, Australia. Participants were randomly allocated to groups of four or five, with each group receiving eight coaching sessions over two school terms. The Youth Values in Action survey was used to highlight participants' character strengths, and the participants were coached in identifying personally meaningful goals and in being persistent in their goal striving, as well as finding novel ways to use their signature strengths. They also completed a "letter from the future" that involved writing about themselves at their best. The strengths-based coaching pilot program was associated with significant increases in the students' self-reported levels of engagement and hope. Thus, strengths-based coaching programs might be considered as a potential mental health prevention and promotion intervention in a primary school setting to increase students' well-being and may also form an important part of an overall positive education program.

In another study, Grant and colleagues (2010) studied the impact of developmental coaching on teachers. A randomized controlled (pretest-posttest) design was used to explore the impact of coaching on goal attainment, workplace well-being, resilience, and leadership styles. Participants were 44 high school teachers who were randomly assigned to either a 20-week CB-SF coaching intervention or a wait-list control group. Participants in the coaching group received multirater (i.e., 360-degree) feedback on their leadership behaviors and, with the help of a professional coach, attempted to use that feedback to develop more of a positive, constructive leadership style (by, for example, disputing self-limiting beliefs or displaying greater empathy). The findings indicated that the coaching participants reported significant increases in goal attainment, well-being, and resilience. They also had significant reduction in stress in comparison to the wait-list control group. Coaching also appeared to enhance dimensions of constructive leadership (e.g., achievement, humanistic–encouraging) while reducing self-reported aggressive/defensive and passive/defensive styles. These findings suggested that coaching, as a professional development methodology, has great potential to contribute to the professional development and well-being of teachers in an educational setting.

SCHOOL-BASED POSITIVE PSYCHOLOGY
INTERVENTIONS IN AUSTRALIA

There are an increasing number of school-based positive psychology interventions (PPIs) being created and utilized in Australian schools in an attempt to teach and enhance well-being of students. Such interventions are defined as initiatives that explicitly aim to enhance well-being or build competence within the school context. These programs can be divided into single-component PPIs that focus on one key construct such as hope (Marques, Lopez, & Pais-Ribeiro, 2011) or gratitude (Froh, Sefick, & Emmons, 2008) or multicomponent PPIs that integrate several key positive psychology concepts into a comprehensive approach.

Unfortunately, while there has been substantial research into school-based programs that aim to prevent or treat mental distress, pathology, or risk behaviors (see Neil & Christensen, 2007; Spence & Shortt, 2007), studies investigating the effectiveness of school-based PPIs to promote well-being are less common. Nevertheless, PPIs focused on building capabilities and strengths (versus approaches that aim to alleviate problems or fix deficits) are inherently attractive to educational professionals due to their constructive and holistic focus.

Positive Education Programs: Strategic Integration of Positive Psychology and Coaching Psychology

Green and colleagues (2012) have argued for the integration of coaching psychology and positive psychology in the school setting to facilitate student, staff, and whole-school optimal functioning and well-being. While both positive psychology and coaching psychology can be utilized to enhance well-being and optimal functioning, they suggested that both approaches have primarily been applied independently of each other and require further integration. For example, schools that may utilize single- or multicomponent PPIs may not have even considered coaching or be mindful of what it has to offer a school, believing it to be primarily utilized in organizational settings. Similarly, a school implementing coaching for academic performance or for the broader purposes of enhancing well-being, such as the Madden and colleagues (2011) study, might not have considered also offering class- or group-based PPIs.

Given research support that both positive psychology and coaching psychology approaches lead to increased well-being, it might not be necessary to utilize both approaches simultaneously. However, Green and colleagues (2012) suggested that "whilst a school may choose to select either approach as a means to create enhanced well-being and optimal functioning for both students and staff, it would behoove school leadership to consider how a strategic integration of both approaches may provide the best overall approach, particularly in terms of sustainability" (p. 124). They further argue that any training in positive psychology principles could be enhanced through the use of coaching to support the transfer of training and sustain application in daily life. For example, if a student was learning about strengths, that student could then set a personal goal to leverage that character strength. The student then takes ownership of the goal, with the learning becoming more personalized. If coaching was offered on a continuing basis to the student (either individually or in a group), there is opportunity to offer ongoing support and track progress of that goal. Green and colleagues (2012) suggested that "goals can be set in regard to the application of any positive psychology concept including gratitude, kindness, forgiveness etc." (p. 125). In this manner, they argue, positive psychology is brought to life when the concepts are applied meaningfully and practically to a student's academic or personal life, drawing on the goal-setting and goal-striving methodologies of coaching.

As such, the author would argue that positive education programs incorporate both training in and implementation of positive psychology and coaching psychology/ evidence-based coaching. For example, in positive education programs created and implemented at Knox Grammar School and Loreto Kirribilli in New South Wales, all staff undergo 3 days of introductory training in both positive psychology and coaching psychology, with advanced master classes offered to ensure ongoing knowledge and skill is maintained and developed. In addition, at Knox Grammar School, individual coaching is available through academic mentoring/coaching programs for senior high school students, and all mentors (traditionally the tutor role) utilize a coaching approach in their mentor class, which is where positive psychology is brought to life for students.

As part of the positive education program, Knox Grammar places particular emphasis on "positive relationships in action" through a teacher–student mentor program. The mentoring program adopts the principles of positive psychology. Mentors provide a structured framework for group interaction based on understanding/knowing each other, respect, encouragement, safety, inclusion, and equal opportunities for participation with the ability to customize the program according to what is appropriate to their own styles/abilities and the needs/desires of the students. Each mentor receives a mentor pack that includes a handbook, pocket reminder, positive-education-in-a-nutshell sheet, training program, positive education staff interest areas, and reading list. A key motto of the mentoring program at Knox is "Meet them where they are, not where you want them to be" (personal communication with Steve Zolezzi, Head of Positive Education, Knox Grammar School). Furthermore, staff professional development at Knox Grammar is underpinned by a coaching approach, highlighted by Jim Knight's instructional coaching (Knight, 2007) approach.

At Loreto Kirribilli, the creation of a customized positive education curriculum to be offered during pastoral-care class time is also underway. While this program will be underpinned by the science of positive psychology, the teachers who facilitate the positive education class will utilize a coaching approach that is more about asking than telling and utilizes a goal-setting approach to ensure the learning is made personally meaningful as all students reflect on how the concepts of positive psychology can be applied to their own lives. A primary aim of coaching is to raise awareness of personal circumstances and use that awareness to identify resources that can be utilized to move toward personal goals. In coaching, students are assisted to systematically work through the self-regulatory cycle of setting goals, developing (self-generated) action plans, and then monitoring and evaluating progress. As such, it is suggested that schools consider carefully how applications of both positive psychology and coaching psychology, under the umbrella of a strategic, integrated, and customized positive education program, could help create and enable well-being for students and staff.

FUTURE RESEARCH AND IMPLICATIONS

Future research is required on school-based PPIs and evidence-based coaching in schools. In addition to supporting the use of both PPIs and evidence-based coaching in schools, further research will yield a more sophisticated understanding of the benefits of the two approaches for students with different needs and characteristics, potentially enabling the targeting of interventions for maximum effect. In an attempt to resolve some of these questions, the author and her colleagues are currently undertaking comparative research on these two fields involving a randomized controlled trial with senior high schools students in Sydney, Australia (Harvard University, Institute of Coaching Grant, 2011). This research will involve the comparison of a cognitive-behavioral solution-focused (CB-SF) coaching intervention and a positive psychology intervention (PPI) in enhancing well-being within a general adolescent population. Both interventions will be teacher facilitated. Senior high school students (including males and females) from two Sydney selective high schools are participating in the study.

More importantly, research is required on how these two complementary fields might be more closely integrated under the umbrella of positive education. Larger-scale positive education initiatives, such as those currently being conducted at Knox Grammar School and Loreto Kirribilli in Sydney, Australia, are utilizing and combining both approaches in an attempt to increase student, staff, and whole-school well-being (Green et al., 2011). Independent scientific evaluation will provide further support for these types of programs.

It is also important to note that PPIs and evidence-based coaching interventions are usually aimed at nonclinical populations. Mental health screening is not, to the author's knowledge, widely undertaken prior to commencement of a PPI, with an underlying assumption that those undergoing such interventions primarily fall within the nonclinical range. This is particularly so in regard to coaching, whereby many coaches assume that those wanting to engage a coach are absent of psychological distress. Fortunately, this assumption has been questioned by three scientific studies showing that 25 to 52% of people attending for coaching interventions present with significantly high levels of psychological distress as assessed by the Brief Symptom Inventory (Derogatis & Melisaratos, 1983; see also Green, Oades, & Grant, 2006; Kemp & Green, 2010; Spence & Grant, 2007). It has been suggested previously that these mental health or screening issues have not yet been raised or discussed adequately within the positive psychology literature or in terms of screening for PPIs (Green & Norrish, 2013). As such, there are real concerns that such interventions may lead to negative outcomes. Green and colleagues (2011) highlight this issue and provide the example of a student who undertakes a strengths-based coaching intervention and might fail to apply her strengths sufficiently or achieve her goals due to an underlying clinical disorder such as depression. This could potentially worsen the clinical disorder rather than improving the child's well-being.

Overall, the understanding of the impact of PPIs on adolescents that fall within the clinical population is limited. As such, a priority for both research and the application of positive education is a greater understanding of the experience of students with symptoms of mental illness and how such students can be supported to obtain the help and support they need without excluding them from schoolwide well-being practices. It is argued that positive education initiatives will work best when efforts to promote well-being and efforts to treat mental ill health are applied in an complementary, integrated, and sustained way (Norrish & Vella-Brodrick, 2009).

As previously mentioned, positive education includes both explicit, structured education and implicit practices that support key learning in more informal ways. For example, students might explore their character strengths as part of a positive education program—this learning could then be supported and developed implicitly via schoolwide practices such as exploring strengths at assemblies, educating parents on the importance of strengths, or creating a school culture in which the strengths language is used frequently (Fox-Eades, 2008). Similarly, the goal-setting strategies students learn as part of a coaching program might be developed by opportunities for students to set and work toward their goals in various classes and extracurricular activities. It is proposed that student learning is greatest when key messages are reinforced across numerous levels of the school environment and when core ideas are communicated between school staff, families, and the wider community (Weare, 2000).

While the whole-school approach is potentially the most powerful in terms of promoting student well-being, it is also inherently more challenging to measure via rigorous research techniques such as randomized controlled trials, as it requires the manipulation of naturally occurring factors and the pervasiveness of the approach precludes the creation of control groups. Balancing the importance of rigorous research techniques with ecological factors such as the importance of the schoolwide practices that support and deepen learning is one of the greatest challenges of positive education moving forward.

The Future of Positive Education

As more schools consider applications of positive psychology and look to create customized positive education programs, it will be important that those positive education pioneers such as Geelong Grammar and Knox Grammar live the spirit of positive psychology and share their knowledge and experiences. This can be done through dissemination of research findings and by providing opportunities for other schools to engage in conversations that inspire them to consider the creation and implementation of their own positive education programs. For example, Geelong Grammar holds regular Positive Education Visitor Days. These Visitor Days provide visiting institutions an overview of the school's journey with positive psychology and positive education. In addition, Knox Grammar School sponsored the First Australian Positive Education Conference in 2013, which provided opportunities for both scientists (conducting research on positive education) and practitioners (the educational pioneers) to showcase their work. It is acknowledged that not all schools have the resources (financial or otherwise) to provide extensive training by external consultants. It is the author's suggestion, though, that this should not prevent schools from investing time and energy in reviewing what positive education has to offer and to learn from those that have gone before, such as Geelong Grammar and Knox Grammar. For some schools, it may be as simple as conducting a well-being audit, utilizing an appreciative inquiry approach (Cooperrider & Srivastva, 1987) to identify what's working well, investigating what other schools are doing that might also be beneficial, and considering implementation of their own program.

In addition, to assist with the creation of positive education programs, many schools in Australia are creating positive education program teams (PEP teams), which consist of school staff who are intrinsically motivated to learn and apply the principles of positive psychology. A leader, identified as the head of positive education (HOPE), works with this team to create and implement the school's customized positive education program. One option to enhance the successful outcomes of the team might be to engage a positive education coach to work with the leader and/or the team to keep their focus on accountable outcomes over an extended period and to provide expertise and resources from positive education.

CONCLUSION

It has been argued that positive education programs have much to offer schools by not only enhancing well-being but also improving the optimal functioning of students, staff, and whole-school communities. It has been suggested that both positive psychology and coaching psychology underpin positive education and should be strategically integrated under the banner of a positive education program.

In conclusion, we concur with Clonan and colleagues (2004), who note that "no two school systems would implement positive school psychology in an identical fashion" (p. 105). In terms of positive education programs, it is recommended that educators create programs that meet the individualized needs of their school, building on what is already working well. It is also noted there is a pressing need for further research to support the widespread adoption of positive education programs in schools in Australia and globally to increase the overall flourishing of students, staff, and whole-school communities.

REFERENCES

Adi, Y., Killoran, A., Janmohamed, K., & Stewart-Brown, S. (2007) *Systematic review of the effectiveness of interventions to promote mental wellbeing in primary schools: Universal approaches which do not focus on violence or bullying.* London, UK: National Institute for Clinical Excellence.

Armstrong, K.H., Missall, K.N., Shaffer, E.I., & Jojnoski, R.L. (2009). Promoting positive adaptation during the early childhood years. In R. Gilman, E.S. Huebner, & M.J. Furlong (Eds.), *Handbook of positive psychology in schools* (pp. 339–352). New York, NY: Routledge.

Bargh, J.A., & Morsella, E. (2008). The unconscious mind. *Perspectives on Psychological Science, 3,* 73–79.

Benson, P.L., & Scales, P.C. (2009). The definition and preliminary measurement of thriving in adolescence. *Journal of Positive Psychology, 4,* 85–104. doi:10.1080/17439760802399240

Biswas-Diener, R., & Dean, B. (2007). *Positive psychology coaching: Putting the science of happiness to work for your clients.* Hoboken, NJ: Wiley.

Brunwasser, S.M., Gillham, J.E., & Kim, E.S. (2009). A meta-analytic review of the Penn Resiliency Program's effects on depressive symptoms. *Journal of Consulting and Clinical Psychology, 77,* 1042–1054. doi:10.1037/a0017671

Clonan, S.M., Chafouleas, S.M., McDougal, J.L., & Riley-Tillman, T.C. (2004). Positive psychology goes to school: Are we there yet? *Psychology in the Schools, 41,* 101–110. doi:10.1002/pits.10142

Cooperrider, D.L., & Srivastva, S. (1987) Appreciative inquiry in organizational life. In R.W. Woodman & W.A. Pasmore (Eds.), *Research in organizational change and development* (Vol. 1, pp. 129–169). Stamford, CT: JAI.

Derogatis, L.R., & Melisaratos, N. (1983). The Brief Symptom Inventory: An introductory report. *Psychological Medicine, 13,* 595–605. doi:10.1017/S0033291700048017

Fox-Eades, J. (2008). *Celebrating strengths: Building strengths-based schools.* Coventry, UK: CAPP.

Froh, J.J., Sefick, W.J., & Emmons, R.A. (2008). Counting blessings in early adolescents: An experimental study of gratitude and subjective well-being. *Journal of School Psychology, 46,* 213–233. doi:10.1016/j.jsp.2007.03.005

Gill, S. (2009). *Monitoring and promoting well-being in education principles and possible approaches to child well-being indicators.* Working paper, Education for Well-Being Europe Consortium, July 2009.

Grant, A.M. (2007). Past, present and future: The evolution of professional coaching and coaching psychology. In S. Palmer & A. Whybrow (Eds.), *Handbook of coaching psychology* (pp. 23–39). New York, NY: Routledge.

Grant, A.M., Green, L.S., & Rynsaardt, J. (2010). Developmental coaching for high school teachers: Executive coaching goes to school. *Consulting Psychology Journal: Practice & Research, 62,* 151–168. doi:10.1037/a0019212

Grant, A.M., & Stober, D.R. (2006). Introduction. In D.R. Stober & A.M. Grant (Eds.), *Evidence based coaching handbook: Putting best practices to work for your clients.* Hoboken, NJ: Wiley.

Green, L. S., Grant, A. M., & Rynsaardt, J. (2007). Evidence-based coaching for senior high school students: Building hardiness and hope. *International Coaching Psychology Review, 2,* 24–31.

Green, L. S., & Norrish, J. M. (2013). Enhancing well-being in adolescents: Positive psychology and coaching psychology interventions in schools. In C. Proctor & P. A. Linley (Eds.), *Research, applications and interventions for children and adolescents: A positive psychology perspective.* New York: Springer. doi:10.1007/978-94-007-6398-2_13

Green, L. S., Oades, L. G., & Grant, A. M. (2006). Cognitive-behavioural, solution focused life coaching: Enhancing goal striving, well-being and hope. *Journal of Positive Psychology, 1,* 142–149. doi:10.1080/17439760600619849

Green, L. S., Oades, L., & Robinson, P. (2011). Positive *education: Creating flourishing students, staff and schools, InPsych, the Bulletin of the Australian Psychological Society,* April. Available from http://www.psychology.org.au/publications/inpsych/2011/april/green/

Green, L. S., Oades, L. G., & Robinson, P. L. (2012). Positive education programmes: Integrating coaching and positive psychology in schools. In C. van Nieuwerburgh (Ed.), *Coaching in education: Getting better results for students, teachers and parents* (pp. 115–132). London, UK: Karnac.

Green, L. S., & Spence, G. B. (in press). Evidence-based coaching as a positive psychology intervention, In A. C. Parks (Ed.), *The Wiley-Blackwell handbook of positive psychological interventions.*

Harvard University, Institute of Coaching Grant. (2011). *Enhancing well-being and self-regulation in a general adolescent population: Comparing evidence-based coaching and positive psychology interventions.* Investigators: L. S. Green, A. Norrish, D. Vella-Brodrick, & A. M. Grant. Boston, MA.

Huitt, W. (2010). Analyzing paradigms used in education and schooling. *Educational Psychology Interactive.* Valdosta, GA: Valdosta State University. Retrieved from http://www.edpsycinteractive.org/topics/intro/paradigm.html

Kauffman, C. (2006). Positive psychology: The science at the heart of coaching. In D. R. Stober & A. M. Grant (Eds.), *Evidence-based coaching handbook: Putting best practices to work for your clients* (pp. 219–253). Hoboken, NJ: Wiley.

Kemp, T., & Green, L. S. (2010). *Executive coaching for the normal "non-clinical" population: Fact or fiction?* Paper presented at the Fourth Australian Conference on Evidence-Based Coaching, University of Sydney.

Knight, J. (2007). *Instructional coaching: A partnership approach to improving instruction.* Thousand Oaks, CA: Corwin.

Kyriacou, C. (1987). Teacher stress and burnout: An international review. *Educational Research, 29,* 146–152. doi:10.1080/0013188870290207

Kyriacou, C. (2001). Teacher stress: Directions for future research. *Educational Review, 53,* 28–35. doi:10.1080/00131910120033628

Linley, P. A., & Harrington, S. (2005). Positive psychology and coaching psychology: Perspectives on integration. *The Coaching Psychologist, 1*(1), 13–14.

Linley, P. A., Nielsen, A. M., Gillett, R., & Biswas-Diener, R. (2010). Using signature strengths in pursuit of goals: Effects on goal progress, need satisfaction, and well-being, and implications for coaching psychologists. *International Coaching Psychology Review, 5,* 8–17.

MacConville, R. (2008). *Teaching happiness: A ten-step curriculum for creating positive classrooms.* London, UK: Optimus Education.

MacKenzie, S. V., & Marnik, G. F. (2008). Rethinking leadership development: How school leaders learn in action. *Schools: Studies in Education, 5,* 183–204.

Madden, W., Green, S., & Grant, A. (2011). A pilot study evaluating strengths-based coaching for primary school students: Enhancing engagement and hope. *International Coaching Psychology Review, 61,* 71–83.

Marques, S. C., Lopez, S. J., & Pais-Ribeiro, J. L. (2011). "Building Hope for the Future": A program to foster strengths in middle-school students. *Journal of Happiness Studies, 12,* 139–152. doi:10.1007/s10902-009-9180-3

McGrath, H. (2009). *An evidence-based positive psychology approach to student wellbeing.* Paper presented at the First Australia Positive Psychology in Education Symposium, University of Sydney.

Neil, A. L., & Christensen, H. (2007). Australian school-based prevention and early intervention programs for anxiety and depression: A systematic review. *Medical Journal of Australia, 186,* 305–308.

Norrish J. M., & Vella-Brodrick D. A. (2009) Positive psychology and adolescents: Where are we now? Where to from here? *Australian Psychologist, 1,* 1–9. doi:10.1080/00050060902914103

Oades, L. G., Robinson, P., Green, L. S., & Spence, B. B. (2011). Towards a positive university. *Journal of Positive Psychology, 6,* 432–439.

Quartz, K. H., & The TEP Research Group. (2003). "Too angry to leave": Supporting new teachers' commitment to transform urban schools. *Journal of Teacher Education, 54,* 99–111.

Sawyer, M. G., Arney, F. M., Baghurst, P. A., Clark, J. J., Graetz, B. W., Kosky, R. J., . . . Zubrick, S. R. (2000). *The mental health of young people in Australia.* Mental Health and Special Programs Branch, Commonwealth Department of Health and Aged Care. Canberra, ACT, AU: Available from http://www.health.gov.au/internet/publications/publishing.nsf/Content/mental-pubs-m-young-toc

Seligman, M.E.P. (2011). *Flourish*. New York, NY: Simon & Schuster.

Seligman, M.E.P., & Csikszentmihalyi, M. (2000). Positive psychology: An introduction. *American Psychologist*, *55*, 5–14. doi:10.1037//0003-066X.55.1.5

Seligman, M., Ernst, R., Gillham, K., & Linkins, M. (2009). Positive education: Positive psychology and classroom interventions. *Oxford Review of Education, 35*, 293–311. doi:10.1080/03054980902934563

Seligman, M.E.P, Park, N., & Peterson, C. (2004). The Values In Action (VIA) classification of character strengths. Ricerche di Psicologia. *Special Positive Psychology, 27*(1), 63–78.

Shucksmith, J., Summerbell, C., Jones, S., & Whittaker, V. (2007). *Mental wellbeing of children in primary education (targeted/indicated activities)*. London, UK: University of Teesside, School of Health and Social Care. Available from http://www.nice.org.uk/nicemedia/pdf/MentalWellbeingChildrenReview.pdf

Spence, G.B., & Grant, A.M. (2007). Professional and peer life coaching and the enhancement of goal striving and well-being: An exploratory study. *Journal of Positive Psychology, 2*, 185–194. doi:10.1080/17439760701228896

Spence, S.H., & Shortt, A.L. (2007). Research review: Can we justify the widespread dissemination of universal, school-based interventions for the prevention of depression among children and adolescents? *Journal of Child Psychology and Psychiatry, 48*, 526–542. doi:10.1111/j.1469-7610.2007.01738.x

van Nieuwerburgh, C. (2012). *Coaching in education: Getting better results for students, teachers and parents*. London, UK: Karnac.

Weare, K. (2000). *Promoting mental, emotional and social health. A whole school approach*. London, UK: Routledge. doi:10.4324/9780203270059

Weare, K. (2010). Mental health and social and emotional learning: Evidence, principles, tensions, balances. *Advances in School Mental Health Promotion, 3*(1), 5–7.

Wiley, C. (2000). A synthesis of research on the causes, effects and reduction strategies of teacher stress. *Journal of Instructional Psychology, 27*(2), 80–87.

Wyn, J. (2007). Learning to become somebody well: Challenges for educational policy. *Australian Educational Researcher, 34*(3), 35–52. doi:10.1007/BF03216864

Yeager, J.M., Fisher, S.W., & Shearon, D.N. (2011). *Smart strengths: Building character, resilience and relationships in youth*. New York, NY: Kravis.

CHAPTER SUMMARY: AUSTRALIA

- In Australia, there is increasing recognition that schools are important locations for the adoption of positive psychology, particularly in regard to student well-being.
- Unique to Australia is the increasing interest in the field of "positive education" and in the creation and implementation of large-scale, customized, and strategic positive education programs (PEPs), for example, Geelong Grammar School and Knox Grammar School.
- The author proposes a newer and refined definition of positive education being "the application of well-being science into an educational setting aimed at increasing the resilience and well-being of students, staff, and whole school community."
- There is an increasing recognition that positive education is more than the provision of well-being classes and that implicit approaches are also required. Implicit approaches include cocurricular activities often experiential in nature (e.g., education and sports), the school environment (created to prime for positive or negative affect), and the creation of a whole-school positive climate.
- Strategic positive education programs incorporate evidence-based coaching as a core component. Training in positive psychology principles can be enhanced through the use of evidence-based coaching to support the transfer of training.

- In terms of PEPs, it is recommended that schools create customized programs that meet the individualized needs of their school, building on what is already working well.

RECOMMENDED READINGS: AUSTRALIA

Fox-Eades, J. (2008). *Celebrating strengths: Building strengths based schools.* Coventry, UK: CAPP.

This book provides an overview of strengths applications in school settings drawing primarily from the Seligman and Peterson (2004) Values in Action Classification of Strengths.

Knight, J. (2007). *Instructional coaching: A partnership approach to improving instruction.* Thousand Oaks, CA: Corwin.

This book provides an introduction to instructional coaching being an innovative professional development strategy that facilitates change, improves instruction, and transforms school culture.

MacConville, R. (2008). *Teaching happiness: A ten-step curriculum for creating positive classrooms.* London, UK: Optimus Education.

This book translates key concepts from positive psychology into a practical, 10-session curriculum, which is suitable for both primary- and secondary-aged pupils.

van Nieuwerburgh, C. (2012). *Coaching in education: Getting better results for students, teachers and parents.* London, UK: Karnac.

This edited book provides a broad and thorough overview of the applications of coaching in the education sector, including coaching for students, educators, and parents.

Yeager, J.M., Fisher, S.W., & Shearon, D.N. (2011). *Smart strengths: Building character, resilience and relationships in youth.* New York, NY: Kravis.

This book is a user-friendly text that provides an overview of the application of strengths in school settings, including activities, resources, and examples.

26

ENHANCING WELL-BEING IN YOUTH
Positive Psychology Interventions for Education in Britain

Carmel Proctor, Positive Psychology Research Centre,
Guernsey, Great Britain

INTRODUCTION

Within the U.K., there is a growing concern about the well-being of children and adolescents. For example, a comprehensive assessment of the lives and well-being of children and adolescents in economically advanced nations conducted by UNICEF in 2007 lists the U.K. at the bottom of a list of 21 developed nations on five dimensions (i.e., material and educational well-being, family and peer relationships, behaviors and risks, subjective well-being) of assessed child well-being (UNICEF, 2007). The Every Child Matters (DfES, 2004) agenda stressed schools' responsibility to promote students' well-being (Challen, Noden, West, & Machin, 2011). The Children Act 2004 "[i]ncludes duties to improve well-being and to safeguard and promote the welfare of children and young people" (DfES, 2004, p. 20) until they are 19. Moreover, research on trends in adolescent mental health indicate that the number of children with emotional and behavioral problems in the U.K. substantially increased during a 25 year (1974–1999) period (Collishwa, S., Maughan, B., Goodman, & Pickles, 2004).

The overall state of children's well-being with the U.K. was recently published in *The Good Childhood Report 2012* (The Children's Society, 2012), the first in a series of annual reports on well-being data collected since 2005. This report indicated that although most children are happy with their lives as a whole, approximately 1 in 11 (9%) are not. This equates to approximately half a million children in the U.K. between the ages of 8 and 15 who have low well-being at any given time. Moreover, this research suggests that children's well-being does not vary much according to individual or family characteristics, that there are few differences in well-being for boys and girls and for children living in different types of households, and that well-being declines with age, with approximately

4% of children aged 8 years having low well-being compared to 14% of adolescents aged 15 years—findings that are consistent with those reported in the literature (see Gilman & Huebner, 2003; Proctor, Linley, & Maltby, 2009, for reviews). Furthermore, these factors have been found to account little for the wide variations that exists.

The research reported in *The Good Childhood Report 2012* was generated by the Children's Society, a charitable organization that campaigns and conducts research on children's well-being in an effort to influence policy and improve child protection. Data presented were gathered using their Good Childhood Index, which includes measurement of overall well-being in 10 key areas: family, home, money and possessions, friendships, school, health, appearance, time use, choice and autonomy, and the future. The reported research findings not only shed light on the state of well-being among Britain's young people but are also in keeping with findings reported in the research literature, suggesting the generalizability of the results. In the paragraphs that follow, these results are summarized and examples of corresponding research literature are presented (see The Children's Society, 2012).

WHAT AFFECTS CHILDREN'S WELL-BEING IN BRITAIN?

While all the included aspects are important, similar to findings reported in the literature (see Proctor et al., 2009, for a review), results indicated that children's relationship with parents is the most important component of well-being, irrespective of family structure, and that stability of family structure is of utmost importance; those who experience a change in family structure were found to be twice as likely to experience low well-being (cf. Demo & Acock, 1996; Greenberg, Siegel, & Leitch, 1983; Grossman & Rowat, 1995).

The home environment also plays a critical role, with safety, poverty, and frequent moves having an adverse impact on children's well-being (cf. Brown & Orthner, 1990; Homel & Burns, 1989). Related to these findings, lack of money and possessions also adversely impacts well-being, with children living in the poorest 20% of households having much lower well-being than average; above average there is little difference in levels of well-being (cf. Wilson et al., 1997). Friends also appear to play an important role in well-being, with number and quality of relationships having an impact. For example, 6% of children reported they felt they did not have enough friends, which was linked to lower well-being, and those who experience bullying are six times more likely to have low well-being than those who have not been bullied at all (cf. Asher & Hopmeyer, 1997; Diener et al., 2010; Flouri & Buchanan, 2002; Rigby, 2000). Satisfaction with school, schoolwork, and safety at school are also important aspects, with 80% reporting that doing well at school is very important and 7% reporting that they feel unsafe at school (cf. Park, 2005; Valois, Paxton, Zullig, & Huebner, 2006). Children's well-being is also related to their physical health, with those who rate their health as "very bad" being more likely than those who are happy with their health to be living in poor households (cf. Zullig, Valois, Huebner, & Drane, 2005). Satisfaction with appearance is also an important factor, one that increases with age, with 32% of boys and 56% of girls being worried about appearance by the age of 15; children who are unhappy with their appearance are also much more likely to be the victims of bullying (cf. Blom-Hoffman, Edwards George, & Franko, 2006; Valois, Zullig, Huebner, & Drane, 2003).

Results also indicated that children who feel they spend too little time with family and friends or too little time with friends and too much time with family experience low well-being. Also, decreased feelings of autonomy were found to be related to low well-being, suggesting a mismatch between children's wishes and expectations and experience of choice. Finally, although most young children report that they feel positive about their future, 10% do not. Moreover, girls are less likely than boys to be optimistic, and children tend to feel less positive as they grow older; also there is a link between poverty and expectations, with only 40% of children from poor households indicating that they hope to go to university.

Overall, the report notes six key themes to their research findings and suggests that decision makers in Parliament, central government, and local areas use these six priority areas as a checklist in assessing any given policy on children's well-being. On the top of the list of "what children need" is "the conditions to learn and develop," which includes having opportunities for free play, a high-quality and appropriate education, and positive relationships with teachers. Second on the list is "a positive view of themselves and an identity that is respected," which includes being comfortable with their appearance, being physically and mentally healthy, and being respected and valued for who they are. In keeping with the Department of Education's Every Child Matters agenda, schools are an ideal places for initiatives to satisfy these two top priorities.

PROMOTING POSITIVE WELL-BEING IN SCHOOLS

Recently researchers of positive psychology have asked, "Should well-being be taught in school?" (Seligman, Ernst, Gillham, Reivich, & Linkins, 2009, p. 294). According to Seligman and colleagues (2009), the answer is yes, not only because increased well-being is synergistic with better learning but also because increased well-being and happiness are outcomes that parents most want for their children. Moreover, although most young people report that they are happy, it is not necessarily the case that they are flourishing—that is, filled with positive emotion and functioning well psychologically and socially (Diener & Diener, 1996; Huebner, Drane, & Valois, 2000). Indeed, parents want more for their children than just the avoidance of negative behaviors (e.g., drug and alcohol abuse, violence, bullying, depression); they want their children to be happy and to thrive in all domains of life (Moore & Lippman, 2005). Unfortunately, however, as already noted, there are a significant number of children and adolescents who are unhappy and dissatisfied with life. Because healthy psychological states, such as happiness and well-being, are both the cause and consequence of diverse positive personal, behavioral, psychological, and social outcomes (Lyubomirsky, King, & Diener, 2005), it is vital to understand how to boost those who are languishing and unhappy to a more optimal state of functioning (Sin & Lyubomirsky, 2009) while protecting those with positive levels from diminishing.

Schools are ideal places for well-being initiatives, especially considering that children spend the majority of their weekday in school and much of their day-to-day interactions affecting their well-being occur while at school (Seligman et al., 2009). Indeed, national education strategies, such as the Social and Emotional Aspects of Learning (SEAL), have been implemented so that emotional and personal well-being can be taught overtly through existing curriculum courses such as Personal, Social, and Health Education (PSHE).

Driven in part by the positive psychology movement, attention is now turning to what might be done to make schools happy places (Linley & Proctor, in press; Noddings, 2003). Unfortunately, however, despite nationwide efforts to promote well-being among young people over the last decade, reports (e.g., as reviewed above) on the state of well-being within the U.K. suggest their effectiveness may be in question.

Concerns over the effectiveness of such nationwide efforts to promote well-being point to many of these initiatives being too prescriptive, with a focus on informing students what to do and what not to do instead of fostering good character through practicing and modeling moral behavior (Park & Peterson, 2009). A promising alternative to increasing well-being among young people in school is through positive psychology interventions (intentional activities that aim to cultivate positive feelings, behaviors, or cognitions; Sin & Lyubomirsky, 2009). Indeed, exploratory investigations into the teaching of well-being in school through the application of positive psychology interventions and theory have led to reliable improvements in students' well-being and life satisfaction (e.g., Proctor et al., 2011; for reviews see Seligman et al., 2009; Waters, 2011).

The remainder of this chapter reviews school-based positive psychology interventions in Britain, which are outside of the context of national well-being strategies implemented by the U.K. government and are not typically associated with positive psychology. In the section that follows, nine examples of curriculum-based programs implemented in Britain are reviewed in detail, including examples of interventions in Scotland and Ireland.

SCHOOL-BASED POSITIVE PSYCHOLOGY INTERVENTIONS

Positive psychology interventions (PPIs) have been successfully applied in educational settings and resulted in positive behavioral, social, psychological, and academic outcomes among adolescent students. Such interventions and strategies come in various diverse forms and include a wide array of activities. In general, however, PPIs can be conceptualized as either single-component PPIs that focus on one key strength, such as gratitude, or multicomponent PPIs that integrate several positive psychology concepts (Green & Norrish, 2013).

Examples of Curriculum-Based Single-Component PPIs

Making Listening Special

Making Listening Special is a project being run at the Milestone School in Gloucestershire. This project is part of the Listening to Young Children Strategy, which is committed to hearing the voices of young children and enabling these voices to shape services. Milestone School is a special school for children aged 2 to 16 years who have a mixture of special needs. The project uses teaching approaches adapted from *Gentle Teaching* (McGee & Menolascino, 1991), an approach to helping those with special needs that has an explicit focus on well-being (Fox Eades, Proctor, & Ashley, 2013). The project recognizes that children learn to be strong and independent from a base of secure relationships and that for children with autism and complex learning difficulties, creating a safe and secure environment is an important prerequisite to their learning (Thompson, 2009). The class group that took part included six reception children with autism and severe learning difficulties and involved three staff supporting the children at any one time. The project aimed to achieve the following outcomes for the children:

- To feel happy and safe within their new classroom environment—increasing confidence and self-esteem
- To feel like a valued member of the class group—wanting to be with others and feeling relaxed in interactions with others
- To feel a good sense of self-worth—increasing confidence in participation and cooperation
- To understand they are special and valued through the response of adults to their individual needs—feeling a sense of companionship, having a close circle of friends, and respecting others and being respected by others
- To feel inner contentment—feeling inner harmony, free from traumatic experiences
- To have meaningful daily activities—enjoying daily life and having daily activities that incorporate their special needs and interests
- To begin to experience daily structure—having daily routines and having their individual beliefs and rituals respected by others

The staff skillfully put the individual strengths and abilities of the students at the heart of student learning and created a personalized curriculum rather than making the students fit into an imposed curriculum. Assessment of the project was accomplished using a variety of methods, including photographs, observations, discussions with staff and parents, and school assessment procedures. Results indicated that teaching was enhanced by teacher development of the following abilities:

- Be engaged or "fully present" in all interactions with the children—being there for the children with clarity of mind and fully focused attention
- Be unconditionally accepting—value the children for who they are, which involves giving them space to be themselves
- "Let go" of assumptions and be open to listen. Allocate equal worth to the children and listening with the intent to understand
- Teach not only with mind but also with heart—teaching with love, kindness, and compassion
- Foster a sense of belonging, enabling the children to achieve inner states of harmony and ease
- Provide serenity of approach—giving time for reflection and being sensitive to the inner world of individual children's special needs
- Believing in the children—grounded in respects and understanding

In effectively achieving these outcomes in the classroom, the staff recognized the importance of the students as "experts" in their own lives and focused on individuals' preferred activities to increase positive emotions and improve learning (Fox Eades et al., 2013). Areas of difficulty were approached by drawing on individual strengths and by giving students choice. Overall outcomes included positive changes to both the individual classroom and the wider school environment.

Mindfulness

Mindfulness is an intentional self-regulated state of attention on the present moment involving an orientation that is characterized by curiosity, openness, and acceptance (Bishop et al., 2004). Mindfulness meditation is a form of meditation that involves acknowledgment and observation of constantly changing internal and external stimuli as they arise, thereby allowing one to relate opening with one's experience (Bishop et al., 2004). Huppert and Johnson (2010) examined the results of mindfulness training in a classroom setting among adolescent boys from two English private boys' schools. Students in the intervention group participated as part of their religious instruction classes and completed four mindfulness lessons over a 4-week period (Waters, 2011). Groups were compared on measures of mindfulness, resilience, and psychological well-being. Although differences between the two groups failed to reach significance, among the mindfulness group there was a significant positive association between outside-the-classroom individual mindfulness practice and improvements in psychological well-being and mindfulness (Huppert & Johnson, 2010). Overall, most students reported that they enjoyed and benefited from the training, and 74% indicated that they would like to continue to practice mindfulness in the future.

Examples of Curriculum-Based Multicomponent PPIs

Wellington College

Since 2006, Wellington College in Berkshire has been implementing a happiness and well-being course for their fourth- and fifth-form students; courses are also provided for their third- and lower sixth-form students. The aim of the course is to promote flourishing and excellence among young people by educating them on how to capitalize upon their strengths and potentialities (Wellington College, 2012). The course is based on six elements that serve to promote well-being:

1. Physical health—foundations of well-being and physical health
2. Positive relationships—relationships with other people
3. Perspective—building resilience and developing thinking skills to overcome adversity
4. Strengths—identifying character strengths and abilities and applying them in daily life
5. World—living sustainably and considering our place in the world
6. Meaning and purpose—exploring meaning making and our response to the questions life asks of us

Each strand contains examples of dispositions that can be explicitly taught and also reflected across the whole school community (Morris, 2013). During the first 3 years of school, students receive 1 hour every other week of well-being instruction. These lessons involve teaching the students skills and cognitive methods they can use to enhance their well-being in life. The students also benefit from a series of lectures from inspiring speakers designed to help them reflect on making the most of their lives. Moreover, mindfulness has been an integral part of the well-being program at Wellington since it began, and short meditations form part of the well-being lessons. Overall, the approach to teaching well-being at Wellington is one of activity or habituation, an approach most closely associated with Aristotle—that is, that happiness arises from doing things well, by striving for personal excellence. At Wellington they believe that schools should be "educating for happiness"; that is, they should be providing a formal curriculum that enables children to acquire, develop, and exercise their strengths and talents and foster their decision-making skills so that children can experience what makes them happy.

Celebrating Strengths

At the primary school level, Celebrating Strengths (Fox Eades, 2008) is an approach that takes a holistic school view of well-being. This approach is built on the belief that a flourishing classroom requires a flourishing teacher to create the conditions in which students will flourish. This program links the VIA (Values in Action; Peterson & Seligman, 2004) strengths to specific festivals and events throughout the school calendar and incorporates activities such as the strengths-based classroom (recognizing the strengths of all class members), victory logs (record books noting students' achievements), and celebrations (of "what went well") into the curriculum. The program structure includes three threads—strengths, festivals, and stories—and works at three levels: individual, class, and whole school. The teaching principles within Celebrating Strengths include using the environment to reinforce and highlight strengths and concepts, linking abstract concepts such as hope to durable traditions, exploring abstract concepts through philosophy for children, directly reinforcing strengths and concepts through exercises, and indirectly reinforcing strengths and concepts through stories. To fully imbed all aspects of the program takes approximately 3 years. An evaluation of this program has indicated several positive outcomes, including increases in children's self-confidence and motivation to achieve, improved behavior at home and school, and an overall positive impact on cognitive, emotional, and behavioral development (Govindji & Linley, 2008).

Strengths Gym

At the secondary school level, Strengths Gym (Proctor & Fox Eades, 2009a) is an approach constructed around the character strengths included in the VIA classification (Peterson & Seligman, 2004). The approach aims to combine a focus on the individual (e.g., through specific strengths-based activities) with a focus on the institution (e.g., by providing classroom lesson plans and applications across the curriculum; Fox Eades et al., 2013). The program involves students completing age-appropriate strengths-based exercises on each of the 24 VIA strengths.

The aim of the program is to encourage students to build their strengths, learn new strengths, and learn to recognize strengths in others. The course has three levels for implementation in the British school curriculum: Year 7, Year 8, and Year 9 (i.e., ages 11 to 14), and students are provided with a corresponding student booklet (Proctor & Fox Eades, 2009b, 2009c, 2009d) or worksheet (Proctor & Fox Eades, 2011) depending on which year they are in. The student booklets begin with a self-identification of each individual's top five strengths. Each booklet then presents 24 lessons, one for each of the 24 VIA strengths. Each lesson contains a definition of the strength being focused on and two "Strengths Builder" and one "Strengths Challenge" exercise. The exercises at each level are unique but designed to be equivalent and age appropriate. The program involves a three-stage learning process: (a) general understanding of strengths and development of a strengths vocabulary; (b) identification of own use of strengths; and (c) recognition and identification of use of strengths by others. Each booklet level concludes by providing students with the opportunity to list any strengths they found difficult but persisted to learn, space to write about things they are proud of accomplishing, and an opportunity to reevaluate their top 5 strengths after they have had a chance to learn about all 24 strengths (Proctor et al., 2011). The program includes a comprehensive teacher's manual (Proctor & Fox Eades, 2009a) containing flexible lesson plans enabling teachers to choose activities that suit the mood and the needs of their class. The manual was designed to provide teachers with as much flexibility as possible and enough material and options to cover all three levels of the course. Each strengths session in the manual contains the following elements: key features, definition, benefits, famous quotes, (philosophical) thinking questions, closing activities, display suggestions, PSHE curriculum links, strengths story, and applications across the curriculum. Results of a preliminary research study examining the impact of the program among 319 adolescent students aged 12 to 14 years by Proctor and colleagues (2011) revealed that students who participated in the program experienced significantly increased life satisfaction compared to adolescents who did not participate in the program, difference $= 0.18$, $t(14) = 2.20$, $p = .045$, $r_{effect} = 0.51$.

The U.K. Resilience Program (UKRP)

The UKRP is the U.K. implementation of the Penn Resiliency Program (PRP). A 3-year study of the UKRP began in 2007, led by the London School of Economics. During 2007, members of the PRP research team trained approximately 90 teachers to deliver an adapted version of the PRP curriculum to groups of students in three local authorities (South Tyneside, Hertfordshire, and Manchester; University of Pennsylvania, 2007). The PRP is an 18-lesson curriculum designed to prevent depression in young people. The major goal of the PRP curriculum is to increase students' ability to handle daily stressors and adolescent problems (Seligman et al., 2009). The PRP promotes optimism through realistic and flexible thinking techniques and teaches students assertiveness, creative brainstorming, decision making, relaxation, and coping and problem-solving skills (Seligman et al., 2009). In general, the program is an evidenced-based cognitive behavioral program developed within the positive psychology framework that helps students understand their thinking style and how it impacts on how they feel and what they do.

A central element to PRP is Albert Ellis's Activating-Belief-Consequences model—that beliefs (B) about an activating (A) event influence the consequent (C) feelings (Challen et al., 2011). Overall, the program aims to provide young people with the skills to be more resilient in dealing with situations in and out of school.

The UKRP was piloted among Year 7 students in 22 schools, with the aim of building resilience and promoting well-being. Teachers attend a 5- to 8-day training course on how to teach the program to young people. The nature of curriculum is such that adult-level cognitive behavior therapy skills are required. Thus, during the training teachers develop adult-level resilience skills before learning how to teach the program to students. A large-scale evaluation of the program was conducted by Challen and colleagues (2011) and a report of the findings commissioned by the U.K. government. The research consisted of both quantitative and qualitative elements.

The quantitative results indicated significant improvements in depression and anxiety scores, attendance rates, and attainment in English and math. Overall, the impact varied by student characteristics, with a larger impact for students (a) entitled to free school meals, (b) who had not attained the national targets at Key Stage 2, and (c) who had worse initial symptoms of depression or anxiety.

The qualitative results indicated that teachers were extremely positive about the ideas underlying the program and the training they had received, with most reporting that they used the skills themselves. The students were also positive about the program, and interviews for the First Interim Report suggested that students had applied PRP skills in real-life situations, with some interviewees showing a good understanding of elements of the program. In addition, return visits to nine of the case-study schools in autumn 2009 revealed that seven of the nine schools were continuing to deliver the UKRP to all Year 7 students

Overall, the key findings of the UKRP evaluations included: (a) significant short-term improvements in depression symptom scores, school attendance rates, and academic attainment in English; (b) larger impacts with increased participation (e.g., weekly larger than biweekly); (c) impacts lasting only as long as participation, with effects fading after 1 year, and with no impacts at 2 years; (d) no impacts of workshops on behavior scores or life satisfaction scores; and (e) students reporting generally positive appraisal of the program and that they used skills in real life circumstances. These findings are similar to those of the PRP, which has been demonstrated to reduce and prevent symptoms of depression in young people (for a review, see Seligman et al., 2009).

Haberdashers' Aske's Hatcham College

Through a unique partnership with the University of East London, the Haberdashers' Aske's Federation, principally sponsored by the Worshipful Company of Haberdashers, has developed its own well-being curriculum devised for Years 1 to 13 based on the research and theory of positive psychology. This program has been implemented at Haberdashers' Aske's Hatcham College in London. The aim in developing this program was to create a comprehensive positive psychology-based well-being curriculum that targets all of the major predictors and correlates of well-being, using individually tested interventions to enhance learning. In Years 1 to 9, the emphasis is on positive interventions, such as happiness, positive emotions, flow, resilience, achievement, positive relationships, and meaning. In Years 10 to 11, the emphasis is on positive education, such as enabling young people to reflect on and make choices about their well-being and development.

The program spans five different key stages, with different outcomes and focuses for each year group, and the weekly well-being lessons take the form of informal discussions, group work, practical exercises, and role play grounded in the latest positive psychological theory. Examples of the topics covered in Years 1 to 3 during the primary phase of the program include what is happiness, recognizing emotions, joy, just for fun, interest/curiosity, love, being calm and patient, sadness, anger, flow, good memories, savoring, celebrating, play, noticing good things and being thankful, hope, and mood boosting.

In Years 7 to 9, students participate in one form period of well-being per week, which is delivered by their form tutor. Some of the topics covered in this lower secondary phase of the program include key skills of well-being, measuring happiness, the effects of happiness, optimizing well-being, positive and negative emotions, managing feelings through minimizing negative emotions, enhancing positive emotions, getting on with others, resolving conflict, positive reminiscence, learning to breathe, mindfulness, meditation basics, the power of exercise, nutrition, sleep, and being in charge.

In Years 10 to 11, students also participate in one form period of well-being per week delivered by their form tutor. Some of the topics covered in this upper secondary phase of the program include self-awareness and acceptance, personal change, self-valuation (respect and esteem), feelings, emotions and moods, reasoning, creative thinking, beliefs, courage and confidence, worrying, security, aliveness, pleasure, learning, and death.

The effectiveness of the program has been assessed by standardized questionnaires, measuring self-actualization, global and multidimensional life satisfaction, and affect, administered at the beginning and end of each year. Initial results have been compared to a comparison school in which no well-being intervention took place. Results from data gathered during the first year of implementation (i.e., 2008–2009) have indicated significant increases in positive affect, satisfaction with friends, self, and family, self-actualization, and global life satisfaction and significant decreases in negative affect in comparison to students who did not receive the program.

Examples of Interventions in Scotland and Ireland

Bounce Back

Bounce Back is an Australian well-being and resilience program sponsored by the Young Foundation that has recently been trialed in 16 schools in Scotland. Bounce Back is based on the following acronyms:

- **B**ad times don't last. Things always get better. Stay optimistic.
- **O**ther people can help if you talk to them. Get a reality check.
- **U**nhelpful thinking makes you feel more upset. Think again.
- **N**obody is perfect—not you and not others.
- **C**oncentrate on the positives, no matter how small, and use laughter.
- **E**verybody experiences sadness, hurt, failure, rejection, and setbacks sometimes, not just you.
- **B**lame fairly—how much was due to you, to others, and to bad luck?
- **A**ccept the things you can't change, but try to change what you can first.
- **C**atastrophizing exaggerates your worries—don't believe the worst possible picture.
- **K**eep things in perspective—it's only one part of your life.

The program includes nine units (i.e., core values, people bouncing back, courage, looking on the bright side, emotions, relationships, humor, no bullying, success), which are repeated in each book with age-appropriate activities (for students in kindergarten to Grade 8). It uses children's literature and literacy activities, and the content is integrated across subject areas. Activities include circle time, cooperative learning, and educational games. The program is integrated with social emotional learning (SEL) and incorporates both positive psychology and cognitive behavior therapy techniques. The incorporated teaching strategies include literacy activities and games, thinking tools and activities, cooperative strategies, drama, multimedia and art, and numeracy activities. For example, a "blame fairly" activity can utilize the "attribution wheel," whereby students explore their attributional style (i.e., how they explain the bad events in their lives) and learn to improve optimistic thinking.

Evaluation of the program in Scotland included comparing quantitative and qualitative data collected before implementation of the program and at 18-month follow-up. Conclusions from the evaluation are as follows:

Students:

- Reported feeling more connected to their school
- Perceived school as a happier and kinder place where fewer students felt lonely or left out and more students were now accepted
- Perceived that they had more control over their feelings and actions
- Felt it increased their sense of confidence and their social skills

Teachers:

- Observed more positive relationships and interactions between students
- Felt more resilient and confident
- Reported more effective skills for dealing with challenging situations in their professional and personal lives
- Had higher levels of overall well-being

Overall results to date have been encouraging, and the program has been evaluated as having a positive impact on both students and teachers.

Blackrock College

In Ireland in 2012, an all-boys school, Blackrock College in Dublin, introduced a Leadership Values and Behavior Policy as part of its future strategic development. An integral part of this strategy was a training program in positive psychology for the 72 House Captains (school prefects from second to sixth year inclusive, aged between 13 and 18 years, approximately). The objective of this positive leadership and well-being program was to facilitate a basic understanding and to promote the creation of the necessary skills for positive leadership, specifically including self-awareness, character strengths, personal values and virtues, growth mind-set, love of learning, true grit and drive, courage and compassion, goals for growth, willpower and intrinsic motivation, self-regulation, self-control, effective decision making, and routine in the creation of authentic self-esteem and a healthy confidence that is necessary for quality leadership.

The aim was optimum engagement through participative interaction and energetic fun and was both task and team oriented, involving games and play designed to be challenging and promote creativity. Visual thinking was also engaged with short videos and illustrations that represent learning through visual senses and humor. Forum theatre or role play to replicate real-school-life scenarios was also utilized to ensure ongoing engagement through variety and novelty. This was also complemented by a popular session of guest speakers.

The learning from these multivaried sessions was concretely reinforced by debriefings and both small- and full-group discussions. In addition, all participants were given preparatory tasks, and ongoing assignments were reviewed and discussed in the next session/workshop. Preparatory tasks included online completion of the VIA-Youth (Peterson & Seligman, 2004) and an assessment of personal meaning. Assignments included prescribed book reviews and listing of top lessons. Positive active interventions were also included, such as expressing gratitude, cultivating optimism, committing to your goals, practicing random acts of kindness, learning to forgive, and savoring life's joys. Storyboard posters were also created displaying particular leadership events within the college, which were displayed on the college campus to enhance leadership awareness.

The Positive Leadership and Well-being Program is an individual strengths-based and positive-culture approach to enhancing leadership and personal potential. It is tailored to enhance the environment and culture in which "strength and truth," "fearless and bold," and a "creed of caring" can be nurtured and allowed to flourish. Overall, feedback on the program has been positive and encouraging and a solid start for future development at Blackrock College.

APPLYING POSITIVE PSYCHOLOGY INTERVENTIONS IN SCHOOLS: CONSIDERATIONS

In considering the application of positive psychology interventions in schools, several points are noteworthy for those wishing to implement or develop well-being programs. First, it is essential to have the support of the head teacher of the school. Second, consultants and others working with teachers and schools need to provide them with "positive psychoeducation"; that is, teachers require genuine insight into the techniques they will be implementing in order to maximize success. As noted in Waters's (2011) review of positive education interventions, most PPIs are implemented by teachers, and thus positive education training needs to be delivered to teachers. Indeed, teachers need to understand the positive psychology approach and value it in order to apply it. For example, research on the success of the PRP program indicated that training was essential, with variability in effectiveness being found to be related to the level of training and supervision that group leaders received (Gillham, Brunwasser, & Freres, 2007; Seligman et al., 2009).

One of the major stumbling blocks to providing adequate positive psychoeducation, however, is lack of funding and resources by the majority of schools who need these programs the most. Indeed, impressive positive outcomes of whole-school applications have been noted in the literature (e.g., Seligman et al., 2009); however, the schools being considered are often privately funded and thus have the ability and resources to implement schoolwide programs (e.g., Wellington College in Berkshire, Geelong Grammar School in

Australia). Therefore, materials supplied to teachers designed to enable them to implement positive psychology programs where training has not been or cannot be provided need to be informative and user friendly. Furthermore, the job of educational consultants is not to teach teachers how to teach but to provide them with the tools to implement positive psychology techniques in their teaching. Those working with schools need to consider what they can give that can be applied once they leave. In the school context, very little is "pure" positive psychology—most of what is taken away is adapted to suit the needs of the institution. Successful application in the school context involves adding positive psychology to existing techniques. For example, art teachers will respond well to creativity applications. Overall, the key is the infusion of positive psychology skills into established school subjects.

Third, schoolwide approaches are required in order that positive psychology becomes part of the wider school culture (Waters, 2011). In order to achieve this, teachers need to know how to implement the techniques across the curriculum and to be provided with ideas and suggestions on how to do this. Moreover, implementation of programs needs to extend throughout the whole school year. Research has indicated that longer interventions produce greater gains in well-being (Sin & Lyubomirsky, 2009). Unfortunately, however, many look to positive psychology for quick-fix remedies. Schools need to be reminded that PPI programs are a way of being and doing, not a quick remedy for unhappiness. Thus, interventions need to be built into the whole school curriculum and the focus extended throughout the year, with structure and consistency in order for integration and learning to occur among both staff and students.

Finally, research has indicated that a scattered approach, in which individuals practice multiple and varied PPI activities, is more effective than single approaches (Sin & Lyubomirsky, 2009). Therefore, where possible, schools need programs that include multiple activities and techniques for application across the curriculum. Indeed, a variety of PPIs have been found effective in increasing well-being that could be built into individual programs—for example, counting blessings and participating in self-guided gratitude exercises (Emmons & McCullough, 2003; Froh, Sefick, & Emmons, 2008), counting one's own acts of kindness for 1 week (Otake, Shimai, Tanaka-Matsumi, Otsui, & Frederickson, 2006), keeping a gratitude journal (Froh et al., 2008), writing down three good things that went well each day and using strengths in a new way every day for 1 week (Seligman, Steen, Park, & Peterson, 2005), mindfulness training (Huppert & Johnson, 2010), and meditation (Nidich et al., 2011) to name but a few. Teachers will be best placed to adapt these and many more applications to their classrooms.

CONCLUSION

Within the U.K., there is growing concern about the well-being of children and adolescents. Recent reports indicate that despite national strategies to increase well-being among Britain's young people, approximately half a million are unhappy at any given time. A major priority in addressing low levels of well-being among young people is through high-quality education, positive relationships with teachers, and fostering children's ability to have positive views of themselves. Recently positive psychology interventions are proving to be beneficial in aiding these endeavors through both independent application and application through existing strategies and curriculum courses. Applied techniques reviewed in this chapter include allowing those with special needs to become experts in their own lives, thereby enabling them to engage in preferred activities to increase positive emotions; increasing psychological well-being through mindfulness training and meditation; promoting flourishing and excellence through whole-school techniques and a community environment that focuses on teaching students how to capitalize on their strengths and potentialities; creating the conditions in which young students will flourish by linking personal strengths to festivals and celebrations throughout the year; providing lesson plans and activities that enable students to explore and identify with their strengths and learn how to apply these skills in their own lives to increase happiness; promoting optimism through realistic and flexible thinking techniques that focus on enabling students to handle daily stressors and problems; implementing positive education across the whole school, thereby enabling young people to reflect on and make choices about their well-being and development; using cognitive behavior therapy techniques alongside positive psychology application to facilitate resilience; and applying positive leadership to facilitate and promote well-being. Overall, these applications and interventions provide encouraging support for the continued development and application of positive psychology interventions in education.

REFERENCES

Asher, S. R., & Hopmeyer, A. (1997). Loneliness in childhood. In G. G. Bear, K. M. Minke, & A. Thomas (Eds.), *Children's needs II: Development, problems and alternatives* (pp. 279–292). Bethesda, MD: National Association of School Psychologists.

Bishop, S. R., Lau, M., Shapiro, S., Carlson, L., Anderson, N. D., Carmody, J., . . . Devins, G. (2004). Mindfulness: A proposed operational definition. *Clinical Psychology: Science and Practice, 11*, 230–241. doi:10.1093/clipsy.bph077

Blom-Hoffman, J., Edwards George, J. B., & Franko, D. L. (2006). Childhood overweight. In G. G. Bear & K. M. Minke (Eds.), *Children's needs III: Development, prevention and intervention* (pp. 989–1000). Bethesda, MD: National Association of School Psychologists.

Brown, A. C., & Orthner, D. K. (1990). Relocation and personal well-being among early adolescents. *Journal of Early Adolescence, 10*, 366–381. doi:10.1177/0272431690103008

Challen, A., Noden, P., West, A., & Machin, S. (2011). *UK Resilience Programme evaluation: Final report.* Retrieved from https://www.gov.uk/government/publications/uk-resilience-programme-evaluation-final-report

Children Act (2004). London, UK: HMSO.

Collishaw, S., Maughan, B., Goodman, R., & Pickles, A. (2004). Time trends in adolescent mental health. Journal of Child Psychology and Psychiatry, 45, 1350–1362. doi.1111/j.1469-7610.2004.00335.x

Demo, D. H., & Acock, A. C. (1996). Family structure, family process, and adolescent well-being. *Journal of Research on Adolescence, 6*, 457–488.

Department for Education and Skills (2004). *Every child matters: Change for children.* Nottingham, UK: DfES Publications.

Diener, E., & Diener, C. (1996). Most people are happy. *Psychological Science, 7*, 181–185. doi:10.1111/j.1467-9280.1996.tb00354.x

Diener, E., Wirtz, D., Tov, W., Kim-Prieto, C., Choi, D., Oishi, S., & Biswas-Diener, R. (2010). New well-being measures: Short scales to assess flourishing and positive and negative feelings. *Social Indicators Research, 97*, 143–156. doi:10.1007/s11205-009-9493-y

Emmons, R. A., & McCullough, M. E. (2003). Counting blessings versus burdens: An experimental investigation of gratitude and subjective well-being in daily life. *Journal of Personality and Social Psychology, 84*, 377–389. doi:10.1037/0022–3514.84.2.377

Flouri, E., & Buchanan, A. (2002). Life satisfaction in teenage boys: The moderating role of father involvement and bullying. *Aggressive Behavior, 28*, 126–133. doi:10.1002/ab.90014

Fox Eades, J. M. (2008). *Celebrating strengths: Building strengths-based school.* Coventry, UK: CAPP Press.

Fox Eades, J.M., Proctor, C., & Ashley, M. (2013). Happiness in the classroom. In S.A. David, I. Boniwell, & A.C. Ayers (Eds.), *Oxford handbook of happiness* (pp. 579–591). Oxford, UK: Oxford University Press.

Froh, J.J., Sefick, W.J., & Emmons, R.A. (2008). Counting blessings in early adolescents: An experimental study of gratitude and subjective well-being. *Journal of School Psychology, 46*, 213–233. doi:10.1016/j.jsp.2007.03.005

Gillham, J.E., Brunwasser, S.M., & Freres, D.R. (2007). Preventing depression early in adolescence: The Penn Resiliency Program. In J.R.Z. Abela & B.L. Hankin (Eds.), *Handbook of depression in children and adolescence* (pp. 309–332). New York, NY: Guilford.

Gilman, R., & Huebner, E.S. (2003). A review of life satisfaction research with children and adolescents. *School Psychology Quarterly, 18*, 192–205. doi:10.1521/scpq.18.2.192.21858

Govindji, R., & Linley, P.A. (2008, August). *An evaluation of Celebrating Strengths Prepared for North Lincolnshire Local Education Authority.* Coventry, UK: Centre for Applied Positive Psychology, University of Warwick.

Green, L.S., & Norrish, J.M. (2013). Enhancing well-being in adolescents: Positive psychology and coaching psychology interventions in schools. In C. Proctor & P.A. Linley (Eds.), *Research, applications and interventions for children and adolescents: A positive psychology perspective* (pp. 211–222). New York, NY: Springer.

Greenberg, M.T., Siegel, J.M., & Leitch, C.J. (1983). The nature and importance of attachment relationships to parents and peers during adolescence. *Journal of Youth and Adolescence, 12*, 373–386. doi:10.1007/BF02088721

Grossman, M., & Rowat, K.M. (1995). Parental relationships, coping strategies, received support and well-being in adolescents of separated or divorced and married parents. *Research in Nursing & Health, 18*, 249–261. doi:10.1002/nur.4770180308

Homel, R., & Burns, A. (1989). Environmental quality and the well-being of children. *Social Indicators Research, 21*, 133–158. doi:10.1007/BF00300500

Huebner, E.S., Drane, J.W., & Valois, R.F. (2000). Levels and demographic correlates of adolescent life satisfaction reports. *School Psychology International, 21*, 281–292. doi:10.1177/0143034300213005

Huppert, F.A., & Johnson, D.M. (2010). A controlled trial of mindfulness training in schools: The importance of practice for an impact on well-being. *Journal of Positive Psychology, 5*, 264–274. doi:10.1080/17439761003794148

Linley, P.A., & Proctor, C.L. (in press). Applied positive psychology: An introduction and applications in childhood and adolescence. In M. Salama & A.D. Fave (Eds.), *Positive psychology for all: Introduction, concepts, and applications in school age* (Vol. 1). Cairo, Egypt.

Lyubomirsky, S., King, L., & Diener, E. (2005). The benefits of frequent positive affect: Does happiness lead to success? *Psychological Bulletin, 131*, 803–855. doi:10.1037/0033-2909.131.6.803

McGee, J., & Menolascino, F.J. (1991). *Beyond gentle teaching: A nonaversive approach to helping those in need.* New York, NY: Plenum.

Moore, K.A., & Lippman, L.H. (2005). Introduction and conceptual framework. In K.A. Moore & L.H. Lippman (Eds.), *What do children need to flourish? Conceptualizing and measuring indicators of positive development* (pp. 1–10). New York, NY: Springer.

Morris, I. (2013). A place for well-being in the classroom? In C. Proctor & P.A. Linley (Eds.), *Research, applications and interventions for children and adolescents: A positive psychology perspective* (pp. 185–198). New York, NY: Springer.

Nidich, S., Mjasiri, S., Nidich, R., Rainforth, M., Grant, J., Valosek, L., . . . Zigler, R. (2011). Academic achievement and transcendental meditation: A study with at-risk urban middle school students. *Education, 131*, 556–564.

Noddings, N. (2003). *Happiness and education.* New York, NY: Cambridge University Press.

Otake, K., Shimai, S., Tanaka-Matsumi, J., Otsui, K., & Frederickson, B.L. (2006). Happy people become happier through kindness: A counting kindnesses intervention. *Journal of Happiness Studies, 7*, 361–375. doi:10.1007/s10902-005-3650-z

Park, N. (2005). Life satisfaction among Korean children and youth: A developmental perspective. *School Psychology International, 26*, 209–223. doi:10.1177/0143034305052914

Park, N., & Peterson, C. (2009). Strengths of character in schools. In R. Gilman, E.S. Huebner, & M.J. Furlong (Eds.), *Handbook of positive psychology in schools* (pp. 65–76). New York, NY: Routledge.

Peterson, C., & Seligman, M.E.P. (2004). *Character strengths and virtues: A classification and handbook.* Washington, DC: American Psychological Association.

Proctor, C., & Fox Eades, J. (2009a). *Strengths gym: Teacher's manual.* St. Peter Port, Guernsey: Positive Psychology Research Centre.

Proctor, C., & Fox Eades, J. (2009b). *Strengths gym: Year 7.* St. Peter Port, Guernsey: Positive Psychology Research Centre.

Proctor, C., & Fox Eades, J. (2009c). *Strengths gym: Year 8.* St. Peter Port, Guernsey: Positive Psychology Research Centre.

Proctor, C., & Fox Eades, J. (2009d). *Strengths gym: Year 9*. St. Peter Port, Guernsey: Positive Psychology Research Centre.

Proctor, C., & Fox Eades, J. (2011). *Strengths gym: Build and exercise your strengths!* St Peter Port, Guernsey: Positive Psychology Research Centre.

Proctor, C., Tsukayama, E., Wood, A. M., Maltby, J., Fox Eades, J.M., & Linley, P.A. (2011). Strengths Gym: The impact of a character strengths-based intervention on the life satisfaction and well-being of adolescents. *Journal of Positive Psychology, 6*, 377–388. doi:10.1080/17439760.2011.594079

Proctor, C.L., Linley, P.A., & Maltby, J. (2009). Youth life satisfaction: A review of the literature. *Journal of Happiness Studies, 10*, 583–630. doi:10.1007/s10902-008-9110-9

Rigby, K. (2000). Effect of peer victimization in schools and perceived social support on adolescent well-being. *Journal of Adolescence, 23*, 57–68. doi:10.1006/jado.1999.0289

Seligman, M.E.P., Ernst, R.M., Gillham, J., Reivich, K., & Linkins, M. (2009). Positive education: Positive psychology and classroom interventions. *Oxford Review of Education, 35*, 293–311. doi:10.1080/03054980902934563

Seligman, M.E.P., Steen, T.A., Park, N., & Peterson, C. (2005). Positive psychology progress: Empirical validation of interventions. *American Psychologist, 60*, 410–421. doi:10.1037/0003-066X.60.5.410

Sin, N.L., & Lyubomirsky, S. (2009). Enhancing well-being and alleviating depressive symptoms with positive psychology interventions: A practice-friendly meta-analysis. *Journal of Clinical Psychology, 65*, 467–487. doi:10.1002/jclp.20593

The Children's Society (2012). *The good childhood report 2012: A review of our children's well-being*. Available at http://www.childrenssociety.org.uk/what-we-do/research/well-being/publications

Thompson, J. (2009). *Making listening special*. Unpublished manuscript.

UNICEF (2007). *Child poverty in perspective: An overview of child well-being in rich countries (Innocenti Report Card 7)*. Retrieved from http://www.unicef-irc.org/publications/445

University of Pennsylvania. (2007). *Resilience research in children*. Retrieved from http://www.ppc.sas.upenn.edu/prpsum.htm

Valois, R.F., Paxton, R.J., Zullig, K.J., & Huebner, E.S. (2006). Life satisfaction and violent behaviors among middle school students. *Journal of Child and Family Studies, 15*, 695–707. doi:10.1007/s10826-006-9043-z

Valois, R.F., Zullig, K.J., Huebner, E.S., & Drane, J.W. (2003). Dieting behaviors, weight perceptions, and life satisfaction among public high school adolescents. *Eating Disorders: The Journal of Treatment & Prevention, 11*, 271–288. doi:10.1080/10640260390242506

Waters, L. (2011). A review of school-based positive psychology interventions. *The Australian Educational and Developmental Psychologist, 28*, 75–90. doi:10.1375/aedp.28.2.75

Wellington College. (2012). *Well-being*. Retrieved from http://www.wellingtoncollege.org.uk/well-being

Wilson, S.M., Henry, C.S., & Peterson, G.W. (1997). Life satisfaction among low-income rural youth from Appalachia. *Journal of Adolescence, 20*, 443–459. doi:10.1006/jado.1997.0099

Zullig, K.J., Valois, R.F., Huebner, E.S., & Drane, J.W. (2005). Adolescent health-related quality of life and perceived satisfaction with life. *Quality of Life Research, 14*, 1573–1584. doi:10.1007/s11136-004-7707-y

CHAPTER SUMMARY: BRITAIN

- Children's perception of their relationship with parents is the most important component of well-being, irrespective of family structure.
- Consistency and stability of family structure is vital to well-being.
- A safe and stable home environment is related to increased well-being.
- Cultivating good friendships along with spending quality time with both friends and family is associated with increased well-being.
- A major priority in addressing low levels of well-being among young people is through high-quality education, positive relationships with teachers, and fostering children's ability to have positive views of themselves.
- Teachers need to understand the positive psychology approach to apply it successfully.
- Successful application in the school context involves adding positive psychology to existing techniques.

- Schoolwide approaches are required in order that positive psychology becomes part of the ethos of the school.
- Interventions need to be applied throughout the whole school year in order for habituation to occur.
- Application of multiple and varied activities and techniques appears to be more effective than focusing on single activities.

SUGGESTED KEY READINGS: BRITAIN

Noddings, N. (2003). *Happiness and education*. New York, NY: Cambridge University Press.

> This is a truly excellent book for anyone interested in how happiness and education can coexist in the school system. The author argues that happiness should be the aim of education and that a good education should contribute significantly to happiness.

Proctor, C. L., Linley, P. A., & Maltby, J. (2009). Youth life satisfaction: A review of the literature. *Journal of Happiness Studies, 10*, 583–630. doi:10.1007/s10902-008-9110-9

> In order to understand how to lift those who are languishing, we must first understand what impacts their life satisfaction. This comprehensive review of the literature provides the foundations for exploration in this area.

Seligman, M. E. P., Ernst, R. M., Gillham, J., Reivich, K., & Linkins, M. (2009). Positive education: Positive psychology and classroom interventions. *Oxford Review of Education, 35*, 293–311. doi:10.1080/03054980902934563

> This review of positive psychology interventions in education is an excellent resource for those wishing to learn more about successful applications and their outcomes to date.

Sin, N. L., & Lyubomirsky, S. (2009). Enhancing well-being and alleviating depressive symptoms with positive psychology interventions: A practice-friendly meta-analysis. *Journal of Clinical Psychology, 65*, 467–487. doi:10.1002/jclp.20593

> This paper addresses the question of the effectiveness of positive psychology interventions through a meta-analysis of these interventions and provides a practical guide for their use by clinicians and others.

Waters, L. (2011). A review of school-based positive psychology interventions. *The Australian Educational and Developmental Psychologist, 28*, 75–90. doi:10.1375/aedp.28.2.75

> This paper reviews 12 school-based interventions designed to foster student well-being from a positive psychology perspective and offers advice and suggestions for those wishing to develop positive psychology interventions in schools.

27

APPLICATIONS OF POSITIVE PSYCHOLOGY TO SCHOOLS IN CHINA

Lili Tian, Zhaorong Li, Huan Chen, Mengmeng Han, Dushen Wang, Siyuan Huang, and Xiaoting Zheng, School of Psychology, South China Normal University, Shipai, Guangzhou, Guangdong, P. R. China

OVERVIEW OF ADOPTION OF POSITIVE PSYCHOLOGY IN CHINA

Positive psychology was introduced to China in the early 21st century. It has become one of the hottest fields of psychological research. Especially after 2007, the number of articles on positive psychology has risen rapidly (Fu, Yin, Wang, Tang, & Liao, 2012). In the course of research, Chinese scholars have not only begun paying attention to the academic studies on positive psychology, but they have also begun putting their findings into practice.

Academic Studies on Positive Psychology in China

In China, scholars from economics, management, education, sociology, psychology, and other fields are actively carrying on local studies about positive psychology. These studies can be organized into studies of positive subjective experiences, positive individual traits, and positive institutions (Seligman & Csikszentmihalyi, 2000).

At the level of subjective experiences, subjective well-being (SWB) is a particularly popular topic (Yan, Zheng, & Qiu, 2003). Scholars have studied the SWB of different groups, such as the elderly (R. Liu & Gong, 2000), adults (i.e., teachers and laid-off workers; Yang, 2003; H. Zhu, 2008), and children (L. Zheng & Tao, 2001). In addition to general SWB, domain-based SWB studies have been conducted, such as studies of the school SWB of students (Tian, 2008).

At the level of individual traits, research has mainly involved resilience (S. Zeng & Li, 2003), gratitude (C. Yu, Zhang, Li, & Xiao, 2010), and other subjects. The antecedents and consequences of these positive personality traits are also studied.

At the level of positive institutions, research has mainly involved studies of positive schools and government policy. These studies have addressed how to apply positive psychology concepts to building a harmonious campus (Fu et al., 2012), city, and society (Ren & Zhang, 2006). Among these applications to institutions, research on positive schooling has been the most frequent topic of research in China.

Beyond the studies focusing on the three aspects of Western positive psychology, Chinese scholars have proposed the construct of psychological suzhi within the context of quality-oriented education (D. Zhang & Wang, 2012). These scholars have developed a series of textbooks and measures of psychological suzhi and carried out experimental explorations of psychological suzhi education. All of these practical activities have promoted the further development of mental health education in China (D. Zhang, 2012).

Practical Applications of Positive Psychology in China

Based on the citedacademic research, Chinese professionals in various fields have actively put the research findings into practice. School is a particularly important environment for children and adolescents to form and develop their psychological characteristics; therefore, the concept of positive psychology has especially attracted Chinese educators' attention.

The positive psychology perspective has impacted Chinese education in two major ways. First, it provides a new perspective for daily classroom teaching and school counseling. That is, a major assumption of positive psychology is that teachers should respect all students, appreciate their individual differences, and help them become happy and healthy by fostering their inherent positive qualities.

Second, positive psychology deepens the content of daily classroom teaching and school counseling. Chinese school educators once only focused on the prevention and intervention of students' psychological problems, ignoring the development of students' potentials as well as the cultivation of psychological suzhi (Y. Liu & Xie, 2011). Now Chinese educators are beginning to place a greater emphasis on facilitating students' positive emotional experiences, cultivating students' positive personality characteristics, and creating a positive school atmosphere (Y. Shao, 2009). Based on the concepts, theory, and research findings associated with positive psychology, Chinese educators have implemented various positive psychology-based practices in the schools.

KEY RESEARCH STUDIES OF YOUTH POSITIVE PSYCHOLOGY IN CHINA

Based on the considerations of Chinese youth research status and cultural characteristics, this section mainly focuses on the following three topics: subjective well-being, resilience, and psychological suzhi.

Subjective Well-Being

Most Chinese psychologists have adopted Diener's (1984) conceptualization of SWB. In the Chinese context, scholars have confirmed the hierarchical, multidimensional structure of students' life satisfaction (Tao, Sun, Feng, Su, & Zhu, 2005; X. Zhang, He, & Zheng, 2004). In addition, applying the conception of SWB to adolescents' school lives in particular, Tian proposed a theoretical model of School Well-Being and developed the associated Adolescents' School Well-Being Scale (ASW-BS; Tian, 2008).

The Status of SWB

Chinese scholars have studied the relation between SWB and demographic variables (e.g., grade/age, gender, residence). Research has shown that the SWB level of Chinese adolescents is at the neutral point (Yue, Zhang, Huang, & Li, 2006). However, as their grade level increases, SWB decreases (X. Wang & Zhang, 2012a; S. Zhao, Cai, Zeng, & Chen, 2011). Findings on the relation between gender and Chinese students' SWB have been inconsistent (Long, 2010; S. Zhao et al., 2011). Because China is undergoing urbanization, scholars have also been particularly concerned about two special youth groups. One group is the left-behind children, whose parents go to the faraway city for jobs, leaving their children behind in the countryside without living together. Another group is the immigrant children, who live with their parents working in cities but have no fixed residence. Studies of these children have found that both groups report significantly lower SWB than those with stable families in the city (R. Wang & Zou, 2010; Y. Yu & Zhang, 2010); and the longer the children were left behind in the countryside, the lower their levels of SWB (L. Zhang, Shen, Wong, & Luo, 2011).

Antecedents of SWB

Chinese scholars have investigated the antecedents of individual differences in Chinese youths' SWB. The scholars have mainly focused on family factors (e.g., family structure and communication). The major findings have been that children from single-parent families view their lives less positively than those from intact families (Qi, Li, Chen, & Hao, 2008). Students in harmonious families have higher SWB compared with those suffering from frequent family quarrels (Shi & Yang, 2006). Moreover, researchers have found that positive parenting and good communication among family members have positive effects on students' SWB (D. Li et al., 2006; Long, 2010).

Concerning SWB and individual difference factors (e.g., personality, coping, self-concept), Chinese scholars have focused on personality and coping behavior. Studies of Chinese students' personality and SWB show that neuroticism is negatively correlated with SWB, while extraversion is positively correlated with SWB (R. Wang & Zou, 2008; X. Zhang, He, & Jia, 2007). Research on coping has found that active problem-solving strategies, cognitive retraining, and self-relaxation skills have positive effects on SWB (Yin, Gu, & Zhao, 2010; Yue et al., 2006). Chinese scholars have also conducted some research on the outcomes of SWB (e.g., mental health, school belonging), but they have paid more attention to the antecedents of SWB.

Resilience

In China, scholars have studied the antecedent factors of resilience (e.g., social support) as well as its protective effects. Following the Wenchuan earthquake, the protective effects of resilience on young victims received substantial attention.

Antecedents of Resilience

The antecedents of resilience have been studied (e.g., social support, relationship, and self-worth), with the most attention to social support. Research has revealed differential effects of social support across grades (Grade 3 to 5), with the influence of parent support increasing across time while the influence of school support is gradually declining (J. Wang et al., 2008). Another study has found that objective supports (such as social networks and financial aid) have positive effects on the development of children's resilience. Furthermore, those students who make good use of social supports have developed greater resilience (Z. Li, 2009).

Protective Effects of Resilience

In daily life, resilient students suffer less from academic stress (Cai, Liang, & Zhou, 2010), regulate burnout more effectively (P. Wang & Zhang, 2011), and experience less lasting adversity (Xi et al., 2011). In the case of the Wenchuan earthquake, scholars found that parental bonding and trait gratitude increased students' resilience, protecting adolescents from experiencing posttraumatic stress symptoms (S. Sun et al., 2012; Y. Zheng, Fan, Yu, & Luo, 2011). Also, resilience mediated the relation between post-earthquake negative life events and depression (Q. Zhu et al., 2012), fostering posttraumatic growth in youth victims (J. Zhang, Shi, Zhao, & Wang, 2012).

Psychological Suzhi

Psychological suzhi is a native academic conception proposed by Chinese scholars within the context of quality-oriented education (X. Wang & Zhang, 2012b). Psychological suzhi reflects the positive psychological traits that facilitate Chinese adolescents' positive adaptation to the Chinese school environment.

The theoretical model of psychological suzhi proposed by Dajun Zhang and Xinqiang Wang is currently the most accepted one (D. Zhang, 2010; D. Zhang, Wang, & Yu, 2011). They believe that psychological suzhi is an essential, stable, and implicit mental quality or characteristic, which forms through interactions between individuals and their environments (e.g., education and social activities). Psychological suzhi consists of cognition quality, personality quality, and adaptability, all of which can be further divided into 22 elements, such as curiosity, self-monitoring, independence, and stress adaptation (X. Wang & Zhang, 2012b). According to X. Wang and Zhang (2012b), *cognition quality* is "directly involved in the cognition of the objective reality" (p. 321); *personality quality* motivates and regulates individual cognition; and *adaptability* is "the habitual behavioral tendency reflecting the person's cognition quality and personality quality" (p. 321). According to the conclusion from D. Zhang and colleagues (2011), psychological suzhi is the multilevel self-regulation system including implicit psychological qualities and explicit adaptive behaviors.

The concept of psychological suzhi differs from the conceptualization of the six moral competencies and 24 character strengths proposed by Seligman and colleagues (Park & Peterson, 2006; Peterson & Seligman, 2004). Seligman's strengths of character refer to the entire set of positive traits that has emerged across cultures and history, which is important for individuals and the "good life." The character strengths consist of the core qualities valued by moral philosophers and religious thinkers, which reflect philosophy, religion, and other issues. The character strengths reflect presumably universal, positive psychological characteristics, applicable to individuals across all cultures and nations. However, the concept and theoretical structure of psychological suzhi is based on the Chinese culture, specifically as it relates to quality-oriented education. Psychological suzhi mainly reflects the cognition quality, personality quality, and adaptability that students would have, and it would influence their behavior as well (D. Zhang et al., 2011). Character strengths and psychological suzhi are thus different in terms of their conceptualization and range of application.

Status of Psychological Suzhi

Scholars have conducted several studies on the relation between psychological suzhi and demographic variables (e.g., grade/age, gender, academic achievement). For students from Grade 7 to Grade 12, research has found the level of suzhi increases across grade levels, but this trend is greatly influenced by the high pressure of entrance examinations that occur in Grades 9 and 12 (Feng, Zhang, & Fan, 2004). Analyses of gender differences have revealed that Chinese girls' overall psychological suzhi is higher than boys' (Feng et al., 2004). Consistent with theoretical expectations, one study demonstrated that schoolchildren's psychological suzhi varied across different academic achievement levels: Students in the highest achievement group showed the highest levels of psychological suzhi, while the students in the middle or bottom academic achievement groups showed the lowest levels of psychological suzhi (D. Zhang, Liu, & Guo, 2004).

The Cultivation of Psychological Suzhi

D. Zhang and colleagues (2011) have developed methods to infuse psychological suzhi training into conventional school courses (T. Zeng, Jiang, & Zhang, 2007). In light of this model, researchers have carried out a series of experiments and achieved some positive outcomes, such as enhancing students' capability of self-monitoring (D. Zhang et al., 2011) and self-efficacy (C. Wang & Zhang, 2007) and ameliorating students' difficulties in emotional regulation (J. Shao, Zhang, Wang, & Yi, 2010).

CROSS-NATIONAL AND CROSS-CULTURAL CONSIDERATIONS

Research Content

Research topics in cross-cultural research should have both commonality and comparability across cultures. In other words, psychological characteristics studied in cross-cultural research should be universal but can also be different as a result of cultural differences.

The distinction between Eastern and Western values is a widely accepted criterion for the classification of cultural types (Hofstede, 1980). Culture can be divided into collectivistic cultures and individualistic cultures (Hofstede, 1980). In the traditional Chinese culture, the values of collectivism emphasize the achievement of individual goals within the development of the family, society, and nation. In contrast, the values of individualism in Western cultures emphasize individual independence and capability. The differences in the two cultures support the development of different psychological characteristics of individuals. As an example, Chinese psychologist Guoshu Yang believes that although the construct of self-esteem is useful in both types of cultures, it differs in that it is individual oriented in individualistic societies, but it is collective oriented in collectivistic societies (X. Huang & Yin, 2012; Weng, Yang, & Xu, 2006). Previous research showed that, among low-self-esteem students, American students evaluated their individual traits more positively than Chinese students, while Chinese students evaluated their social traits more positively (Brown & Cai, 2010). For another example, self-modesty is regarded as an ideal moral pursuit and a positive strength in the Chinese culture. The Chinese traditional value system does not encourage individuals to try to control their environments, express themselves, or actualize their potentials. Rather, the traditional Chinese culture advocates for harmonious relations between people and their environments, sacrificing individual interests for the sake of the group (J. Hu & Huang, 2009; Lu, 2007) Self-modesty in the Chinese culture requires that individuals belittle themselves but praise others. However, the similar construct of humility, which is valued in individualistic cultures, has a different meaning. "Humility" in individualistic cultures emphasizes that individuals should be humble before God. Therefore, people are encouraged to express themselves and actualize their individual potentials. In a word, the Eastern-Western cultural differences yield different connotations for similar psychological characteristics. When conducting cross-cultural research, it is crucial to understand the differences in the meaning and value associated with various positive psychology constructs. Institutions (e.g., schools) embedded in different cultural contexts may define (and wish to promote) different "positive" emotions, character strengths, and institutional practices as part of varying definitions of the "good life."

The issues discussed above need to be addressed when both foreign and Chinese scholars conduct cross-national studies. As China is a multiethnic country, for example, "ethnic identity/national identity" is a popular cross-national research topic in China. Research has suggested that there are no significant differences in ethnic identity and national identity between Hui and Han high school students. Moreover, these two identities are both important predictors of self-esteem (Liang, Gao, & Wan, 2010). However, another study conducted with college students showed that minority ethnic students scored higher in ethnic identity than Han students (Gao, An, & Wan, 2011). Therefore, additional studies are needed to explore further whether there are significant differences in ethnic identity between minority students and Han students.

Beyond cross-cultural comparability of research topics, there are also other important issues that should not be neglected. For instance, the meaning of core concepts supporting theoretical frameworks should be comparable in cross-national and cross-cultural research.

Research Measurement

Cultural applicability should be considered when selecting research measures. In cross-cultural research, Chinese researchers often revise foreign scales and apply them in studies of Chinese youth (H. Li, Zhang, & Zhang, 2008; Shi & Tian, 2009). An important issue is that, when adopting measures from other countries, Chinese researchers should carefully consider whether the particular measures are applicable in the Chinese culture.

Research Methods

For the most part, self-report measures have been the primary method used by Chinese scholars in their cross-cultural research. For instance, Tian and colleagues completed a series of cross-cultural comparison studies on life satisfaction between Chinese and foreign middle school students (W. Liu, Tian, & Gilman, 2005; Tian, Liu, & Gilman, 2005) by using a Chinese version of the Multidimensional Students' Life Satisfaction Scale (MSLSS; Huebner, 1994). However, a potential shortcoming of such a method is that if the measure has psychometric limitations when applied in the new culture, the results may lack generalizability. For this reason, multimethod assessment is encouraged. Additional methods, such as the Day Reconstruction Method (DRM) or scenario stories method can be employed to supplement self-report methods in cross-cultural research. For example, Tian investigated Chinese senior high school students' daily rhythm patterns of affective experiences, corresponding to specific activities (e.g., attending class, doing exercise, having lunch at school), locations, and interactive partners in school lives using the DRM (Tian, 2010).

Research Results

Research conducted on similar participants from different cultural backgrounds can reveal the influences of culture on people's psychological experiences and daily behaviors. For example, Chinese researchers have compared the happiness of Chinese and American college students. The results showed that Chinese college students reported less positive affect and lower life satisfaction (Yan et al., 2003). Cultural differences may have influenced the interpretations of these results, however. Given that China is a collectivistic-oriented nation, it is important to understand that Chinese individuals do not value individual happiness to the same extent or in the same manner as American individuals (Yan et al., 2003). Such knowledge provides a different framework from which to interpret divergent research findings. For the reasons listed, cultural factors must be fully considered and understood when research is conducted in different cultural environments.

MEASUREMENT AND CONSIDERATIONS ISSUES APPLIED IN CHINA

In this section, the measurement of positive school psychology constructs in China and some relevant considerations issues are introduced.

Positive School Psychology Measures Applied in China

Measures of Positive Psychological Experience

Measures of positive school psychological experiences reflect two major areas of interest: general SWB and school well-being. General SWB includes life satisfaction, positive affect (PA), and negative affect (NA). Measurements of life satisfaction include the following: the Chinese version of the Multidimensional Students' Life Satisfaction Scale (MSLSS; Tian & Liu, 2005) originally developed by Huebner (1994), the Inventory of Subjective Life Quality for Child and Adolescent (ISLQ; Cheng, Gao, Peng, & Lei, 1998), and the Scale of Adolescent Students' Life Satisfaction (SASLS; X. Zhang et al., 2004). The Chinese version of MSLSS has good applicability for Chinese adolescents. The ISLQ can be applied to primary and secondary school students, with Chinese norms. Chinese scholars developed the SASLS to reflect Chinese adolescents' learning and living experiences.

The most frequently employed measures of PA and NA include the following: the Chinese Positive and Negative Affect Scale for Students (CPNASS; W. Chen & Zhang, 2004) based on Bradburn's Positive and Negative Affect Scale and the Chinese version of Hedonic Balance Scale (HBS; X. Zhang & Zheng, 2005) developed by Schimmack, Diener, and Oishi (2002). These scales have been found suitable for Chinese adolescents.

The main measure of school well-being is the Adolescent's School Well-Being Scale (ASW-BS), which was developed by Tian (2008) and reflects adolescents' school lives. This scale consists of students' school satisfaction, positive affect in school, and negative affect in school.

Measures of Positive Human Strengths

Measures of resilience include the Chinese version of Healthy Kids Resilience Assessment (HKRA), which was revised from the Resilience Youth Development Module (RYDM) subscale of the California Healthy Kids Survey (H. Li et al., 2008) and Resilience Scale for Adolescents (RSA; Y. Hu & Gan, 2008). Both are suitable for adolescents. Some dimensions of the revised HKRA are different from the original one but still fit the theoretical model, including external protective factors and resilience trait dimensions. Caring relationships in school and school high expectations from the original scale converged into a factor named "Teachers' care," which is similar to a RYDM factor that Hanson and Kim (2007) found and called "School Support." In addition, caring relationships at home and social high expectations converged into one factor named "Relatives' care." The reason may be that children equated caring relationships and high expectations from their teachers or relatives; therefore, both of them are regarded as emotional support and care. The RSA, developed by Chinese scholars, includes five factors: goal planning, help seeking, family support, affect control, and positive thinking.

Measures of gratitude include: the revised McCullough's GQ-6 (Hou & Zhang, 2009); the locally developed Adolescent Gratitude Scale (AGS; Wen, Zhang, Li, Yu, & Dai, 2010); and the Gratitude Questionnaire of Middle School Students (GQMSS; G. Zhao & Chen, 2006). All of these scales are suitable for adolescents. The revised GQ-6 assesses two dimensions of gratitude. The AGS includes five aspects of gratitude reflecting Chinese cultural values: motherland/society, parents, teachers, friends, and nature. The GQMSS consists of three dimensions reflecting students' moral values tendencies: people orientation, things orientation, and moral orientation.

Measures of Positive School Circumstance

Measures of school climate include the Perceived School Climate Inventory (PSCI; Ge & Yu, 2006) and My Class Inventory (MCI; Jiang, 2004), developed by Chinese scholars. They both evaluate three aspects of school climate: students' interpersonal relationships, academic pressure, and school management.

Measures of school belonging mainly include the revised Psychological Sense of School Membership Scale (PSSM; Hoi & Sammy, 2003), originally developed by Goodenow (1993), and Adolescent School Belonging Questionnaire (ASBQ; B. Zhou, Yang, & Chen, 2011). Both of these scales are suitable for middle school students. Hong Kong scholars revised the Chinese version of the PSSM by including belonging and rejection dimensions. The ASBQ measures students' school relationships and school management.

Measures of Psychological Suzhi

Chinese scholars have developed some measures of psychological suzhi, including the Mental Quality Scale of Adolescent Students(MQSAS; Feng et al., 2004) and Elementary School Students' Mental Quality (ESSMQ; D. Zhang et al., 2004). The MQSAS evaluates psychological suzhi through academic ability, personality, and adaptability; it is suitable for middle school students. The ESSMQ is composed of metacognition, personality, and adaptability subscales; it is suitable for primary students.

Measurement Issues

Applicability of Measurements

When international scales are used in China, the cultural applicability of measurements should be considered. First, universality must be considered, which means researchers should determine whether a particular variable is an essential psychological trait in the Chinese context. Second, specificity must be considered, which means researchers should know whether this variable has different meanings in the Chinese context. Finally, researchers should define the variable based on the Chinese culture and develop appropriate measurements consistent with the definition.

Measurement Equivalence

When international instruments are applied in China, measurement equivalence should be considered. There may be differences in the meaning and characteristics of various psychological constructs among individuals in different countries, cultures, and ethnic groups. The nature of the constructs and associated measures may vary if they are translated directly from the original foreign ones, such as the HKRA and GQ-6 mentioned earlier. Thus, the content and the function of the measures should be carefully evaluated for equivalence. In addition, when conducting cross-cultural studies, researchers should ensure that the measures are understood equally well and in similar ways across different culture contexts. This requires that the item content is familiar to respondents. Translations must be done in a manner that yields items with equivalent meaning (Kagitcibasi, Bond, & Smith, 2006). Therefore, "decentering" translation, which draws on the cultural knowledge of the translators to use phrases that have equivalent meaning in both languages (Kagitcibasi et al., 2006), and back-translation are recommended when scales are translated from a foreign language into Chinese.

Acquiescent Response Bias

When conducting cross-cultural comparisons, researchers should also consider the effects of acquiescent response bias—a tendency to respond in the affirmative to survey items irrespective of substantive content. If researchers are not aware of this possibility, differences in the scores of students across cultures may be misinterpreted to reflect cultural differences, when in fact the differences may reflect variations in acquiescence biases. Researchers can control or correct the acquiescence response bias, either by balancing items requiring positive and negative responses or by conducting within-subject standardization of scores. A study of acquiescent response bias covering 34 countries showed that participants from collectivistic-oriented countries reported the highest scores (Kagitcibasi et al., 2006). Since China is a collectivistic country, Chinese participants' responses are likely to exhibit higher levels of acquiescence response bias. Therefore, researchers should take this into consideration when designing and interpreting cross-cultural research.

EDUCATIONAL APPLICATIONS IN CHINA

The school is a primary context in which children and teenagers learn and interact with others. Chinese school professionals attach great importance to students' psychological health (Y. Huang, 2012). However, traditional Chinese psychological education was problem based, focusing on students' psychological problems. Students were viewed primarily in terms of their deficits, which needed remediation. This narrow, one-sided mode of psychological education seriously restricted the development of Chinese school education (D. Zhou, 2010).

The rise of positive psychology provides a new perspective for Chinese education. The research base in positive psychology regarding children's positive emotional experiences, positive traits, and positive institutions provides important implications for Chinese school professionals' daily classroom teaching and school counseling activities. However, at present, the translation of positive psychological science into education practices in Chinese primary and middle schools is still in the early stages.

Applications to Classroom Teaching

Classroom teaching is a bidirectional activity between teachers and students. Advocates of positive psychology argue that teachers should base their interactions with students on the theory and emerging research base associated with positive psychology to develop students' potentials and to promote comprehensive development (Q. Zhang & Tian, 2011).

Applications to Mental Health Class

Positive psychology is relevant to Chinese mental health classes, which are specially designed classes to promote students' positive mental health, particularly with respect to facilitating positive emotional experiences (C. Zhu, 2007), positive personality characteristics (Cao, 2011), and positive classroom atmospheres (J. Zhang, 2011). These classes are consistent with some applications of school-based mental health services in the United States. For example, Yichan Shao (2009) applied principles of positive psychology to a Chinese mental education classroom for middle school students. She designed specific class interventions. In the first few lessons, she taught students some theoretical knowledge to help students learn more about themselves and master some interpersonal techniques, which laid a good foundation for a positive and harmonious classroom atmosphere. Then she arranged some different class activities for students to appreciate the beauty and power of life. For instance, she told a story about a disabled entrepreneur to encourage students to learn to be more grateful and caring. After these class interventions, students reported increased gratitude, love, and courage.

Applications to Conventional Courses

The principles of positive psychology are not only infused into mental health classes but also into most other conventional courses. Some specific examples are as follows. First, Hui Zhang (2011) applied positive psychology theory to English teaching. She made full use of the students' spare time and created favorable English learning situations for students. She guided students to appreciate classical English movies and to carry out English story speech activities. These activities significantly improved students' motivation, enthusiasm, and sense of accomplishment in learning English. Second, Min Li (2011) applied positive psychology principles in music teaching. She arranged opportunities for students to feel, experience, and create beauty during music classes, which significantly enriched students' positive emotional experiences. Finally, Bin Sun (2008) also paid attention to students' positive experiences in the teaching of sports. He set individual (vs. group) goals for students according to their individual fitness levels and motor abilities. Every student thus reportedly enjoyed a sense of joy and pride related to their individual accomplishments.

Chinese scholars have also tried to develop students' psychological suzhi in some traditional courses, such as Chinese and mathematics. For example, an elementary Chinese teacher taught a Race-with-Time lesson and carried out a group discussion to (a) guide students to understand the author's point of view and (b) elaborate methods to alleviate the author's grief. Through the series of classroom activities, students improved the ability to regulate their emotions and develop their psychological suzhi (J. Shao et al., 2010). Moreover, Chinese scholars have attempted to combine the education of psychological suzhi with mathematics instruction in middle school. In one study, the teacher set up different levels of problems for different students according to their individual ability. When the students could answer the question, the teacher gave positive feedback and attributions for their good performance. When the students appeared to experience anxiety, the teacher gave the students more time to think about the question and offered some tips to help them. In this manner, the teacher made it possible for every student to experience success. The results revealed increased student academic self-efficacy, psychological health, and academic success (C. Wang & Zhang, 2007).

Applications to School Counseling

The application of positive psychology to school counseling mainly involves the following two aspects. First, it clarifies the nature and goals of school counseling. Positive psychology attaches great importance to the discovery and cultivation of the positive side of human nature. Therefore, school counselors operating from a positive psychology perspective should help students lay the foundation for life happiness as well as cultivate the positive psychological traits that facilitate healthy life-span development (Wu & Ma, 2008), in addition to helping "treat" psychological problems. Second, it broadens the methodological and population base of school counseling (Wu & Ma, 2008). Positive psychology research is dedicated to studying people's positive psychological characteristics, such as happiness, resilience, and optimism. Based on such research, some Chinese school counselors are developing practices that are related to facilitating students' needs for growth on the basis of the students' mental development, such as honesty (Wei, 2010), creativity (Tang & Guo, 2011), effective responses to negative pressure (H. Zheng, 2007), self-confidence (L. Li, Sun, Fu, Guo, & Li, 2012), and self-esteem and happiness (L. Liu & Wang, 2007).

In the field of individual psychological counseling, new models have emerged, such as short-term, solution-focused counseling (Fang, Liu, Zhang, & He, 2006). This approach emphasizes that counselors should act as consultants, who focus attention on the solution, rather than the problem, in an effort to help students through acknowledging and amplifying prior successful experiences and resources (J. Chen & Wang, 2008).

In addition to individual counseling, the principles of positive psychology have also been widely applied to the field of group counseling. For example, group counseling activities involving students reviewing previous successful experiences can strengthen their self-confidence (L. Li et al., 2012). Moreover, the group counseling activities of Self-Exploration and Interpersonal Communication help improve students' self-esteem and happiness (L. Liu & Wang, 2007). Finally, the class activities of Life Is So Good and Learn to Be Thankful can improve students' gratitude and SWB (Shi & Zhu, 2008).

CONCLUSION

In summary, positive psychology is alive and well in China. Chinese scholars are pursuing important research questions and revising and developing appropriate measures for local, cross-national, and cross-cultural studies of positive psychology. Many school professionals are enthusiastically applying positive psychology principles and practices in classroom teaching and school counseling.

REFERENCES

Brown, J. D., & Cai, H. (2010). Self-esteem and trait importance moderate cultural differences in self-evaluations. *Journal of Cross-Cultural Psychology, 41*, 116–123. doi:10.1177/0022022109349509

Cai, Y., Liang, B., & Zhou, Y. (2010). Relationship among stress of entrance examination, resilience and stress distress of middle school students. *Chinese Journal of Clinical Psychology, 2*, 180–182, 179

Cao, H. (2011). The enlightenment of positive psychology on school mental health education. *Folk Art and Literature, 9*, 176–177.

Chen, J., & Wang, Z. (2008). The enlightenment given by the sense-of-well-being research to school psychological consultation. *Psychological Science, 31*, 408–410.

Chen, W., & Zhang, J. (2004). Factorial and construct validity of the Chinese Positive and Negative Affect Scale for students. *Chinese Mental Health Journal, 18*, 763–765, 759.

Cheng, Z., Gao, B., Peng, J., & Lei, L. (1998). The Inventory of Subjective Life Quality for child and adolescent: Development, reliability, and validity. *Chinese Journal of Clinical Psychology, 6*, 11–16.

Diener, E. (1984). Subjective well-being. *Psychological Bulletin, 95*, 542–575. doi:10.1037/0033-2909.95.3.542.

Fang, J., Liu, X., Zhang, Y., & He, W. (2006). A new mode of counseling: Solution-focused brief counseling. *Psychological Science, 29*, 430–432.

Feng, Z., Zhang, D., & Fan, H. (2004). A study of the characteristics of the mental quality of adolescent students. *Psychological Science, 27*, 890–895.

Fu, Y., Yin, K., Wang, J., Tang, J., & Liao, J. (2012). Bibliometric analysis of the positive psychology in China. *Journal of Dali University, 11*(2), 93–96.

Gao, C., An, J., & Wan, M. (2011). On the relationship between the ethnic identity, acculturation and the psychological well-being of the multi-ethnic university students. *Contemporary Education and Culture, 3*(5), 106–113.

Ge, M., & Yu, Y. (2006). The development of junior high school students' Perceived School Climate Inventory. *Psychological Science, 29*, 460–464.

Goodenow, C. (1993). The psychological sense of school membership among adolescents: Scale development and educational correlates. *Psychology in the Schools, 30*, 79–90. doi:10.1002/1520–6807(199301)30:1<79::aid-pits2310300113>3.0.co;2-x

Hanson, T.L., & Kim, J.O. (2007). *Measuring resilience and youth development: the psychometric properties of the Healthy Kids Survey.* (Issues & Answers Report, REL 2007–No. 034). Washington, DC: U.S. Department of Education, Institute of Education Sciences, National Center for Education Evaluation and Regional Assistance, Regional Educational Laboratory West. Retrieved from http://ies.ed.gov/ncee/edlabs/regions/west/pdf/REL_2007034.pdf

Hofstede, G. (1980). *Culture's consequences: International differences in work-related values* (Vol. 5). Thousand Oaks, CA: Sage.

Hoi, Y.C., & Sammy, K.F.H. (2003). Mainland immigrant and Hong Kong local students' psychological sense of school membership. *Asia Pacific Education Review, 4*(1), 67–74. doi:10.1007/bf03025553

Hou, X., & Zhang, L. (2009). Applicability of GQ-6 in middle school students. *Educational Measurement and Evaluation, 2*(2), 37–39.

Hu, J., & Huang, X. (2009). Preliminary study on self-modesty: One significant behavioral style of Chinese. *Acta Psychologica Sinica, 41*, 842–852.

Hu, Y., & Gan, Y. (2008). Development and psychometric validity of the Resilience Scale for Chinese adolescents. *Acta Psychologica Sinica, 40*, 902–912. doi:0.3724/SP.J.1041.2008.00902

Huang, X., & Yin, T. (2012). On cultural differences in zi zun (self-esteem). *Journal of Psychological Science, 35*(1), 2–8.

Huang, Y. (2012). Strengthen the psychological education to promote physical and mental health. *Teaching Reference of Middle School Politics, 9*, 74–75.

Huebner, E.S. (1994). Preliminary development and validation of a multidimensional life satisfaction scale for children. *Psychological Assessment, 6*(2), 149–158. doi:10.1037/1040–3590.6.2.149

Jiang, G. (2004). Class environment in the Chinese school system: Structure and measurement. *Psychological Science, 27*, 839–843.

Kagitcibasi, C., Bond, M.H., & Smith, P.B. (2006). *Understanding social psychology across cultures: Living and working in a changing world.* Thousand Oaks, CA: Sage.

Li, D., Yu, M., Wang, C., Xie, X., Zhou, L., & Zhu, X. (2006). Self-disclosure and self-concealment in adolescence and the relationship between them and subjective well-being. *Psychological Development and Education, 22*(4), 83–90.

Li, H., Zhang, W., & Zhang, J. (2008). The Chinese version of Healthy Kids Resilience Assessment. *Studies of Psychology and Behavior, 6*(2), 98–102, 111.

Li, L., Sun, H., Fu, Y., Guo, Y., & Li, J. (2012). Experimental research on the effect of group instruction in improving the level of college students' self-confidence, acceptance of others and self consistency and congruence. *China Journal of Health Psychology, 20*, 705–707.

Li, M. (2011). *Research of primary school music teaching under the concept of positive psychology* (master's thesis). Shandong Normal University.

Li, Z. (2009). Relationship between ego-resiliency and social support of parent-absent children. *China Journal of Health Psychology, 17*, 440–442.

Liang, J., Gao, C., & Wan, M. (2010). The influence of ethnic identity, national identity on Hui and Han middle school students' self-esteem. *Contemporary Education and Culture, 2*(6), 63–67.

Liu, L., & Wang, X. (2007). Effects of group counseling on sense of security, self-esteem and psychological well-being of university students. *Chinese Journal of Behavioral Medicine Science, 16*, 642–643.

Liu, R., & Gong, Y. (2000). Research on subject well-being and its influence factors among old people. *Chinese Journal of Clinical Psychology, 8*(2), 73–78.

Liu, W., Tian, L., & Gilman, R. (2005). A cross-cultural study on life satisfaction between Chinese and American middle school students. *Chinese Mental Health Journal, 19*(5), 29–31.

Liu, Y., & Xie, G. (2011). Positive psychology and college mental health education. *Journal of Higher Education Management, 5*(1), 82–85.

Long, L. (2010). Relationship between subjective well-being and parenting mode of junior school students. *Science of Social Psychology, 25*(7), 25–28.

Lu, L. (2007). Individual and social-oriented self views: Conceptual analysis and empirical assessment. *US-China Education Review, 4*(2), 1–23.

Park, N., & Peterson, C. (2006). Character strengths and happiness among young children: Content analysis of parental descriptions. *Journal of Happiness Studies, 7*, 323–341. doi:10.1016/j.adolescence.2006.04.011

Peterson, C., & Seligman, M. E. P. (2004). *Character strengths and virtues: A handbook and classification*. Oxford, UK: Oxford University Press.

Qi, L., Li, Y., Chen, Y., & Hao, J. (2008). Subjective well-being of divorced children and its influencing factors. *Psychological Research, 1*(2), 62–65.

Ren, J., & Zhang, Y. (2006). Positive psychology movement and its revelation to building a harmonious society in China. *Academic Forum, 12*, 67–71.

Schimmack, U., Diener, E., & Oishi, S. (2002). Life satisfaction is a momentary judgment and a stable personality characteristic: The use of chronically accessible and stable sources. *Journal of Personality, 70*, 345–384. doi:10.1111/1467-6494.05008

Seligman, M. E. P., & Csikszentmihalyi, M. (2000). Positive psychology: An introduction. *American Psychologist, 55*, 5–14. doi:10.1037/0003-066X.55.1.5

Shao, J., Zhang, D., Wang, J., & Yi, Q. (2010). An experimental study on enhancing pupils' difficulties in emotion regulation in Chinese teaching. *Psychological Development and Education, 26*, 390–394.

Shao, Y. (2009). Research on the influence of positive psychology on psychological education in schools. *Journal of Teaching and Management, 5*, 36–38.

Shi, G., & Tian, L. (2009). The reliability and validity of The Trait Hope Scale (TTHS) in middle school students. *Studies of Psychology and Behavior, 7*, 203–206.

Shi, G., & Yang, M. (2006). Subjective well-being of middle school students. *China Journal of Health Psychology, 20*, 238–241.

Shi, G., & Zhu, W. (2008). The intervention of gratitude and subjective well-being for junior middle school students. *Psychological Exploration, 28*(3), 63–66.

Sun, B. (2008). Positive expectation: Application of positive psychology to sports teaching in elementary school. *China School Physical Education, 10*, 44–45.

Sun, S., Fan, F., Zheng, Y., Zhu, Q., Chen, S., Zhang, L., & Tan, Y. (2012). Mediating effect of resilience between parenting styles and PTSD symptoms in adolescents. *Chinese Journal of Clinical Psychology, 20*, 502–505.

Tang, H., & Guo, F. (2011). Enlightenment of positive psychology on cultivating students' creativity. *Innovation and Entrepreneurship Education, 2*(1), 31–33.

Tao, F., Sun, Y., Feng, E., Su, P., & Zhu, P. (2005). Development of school life satisfaction rating questionnaire for adolescents and its reliability and validity. *Chinese Journal of School Health, 26*, 987–989.

Tian, L. (2008). Developing scale for school well-being in adolescents. *Psychological Development and Education, 24*(3), 100–106.

Tian, L. (2010). Experience of school life in senior high school students: Based on the day reconstruction method. *Psychological Development and Education, 26*, 473–481.

Tian, L., & Liu, W. (2005). Test of the Chinese version of Multidimensional Students' Life Satisfaction Scale. *Chinese Mental Health Journal, 19*, 301–303.

Tian, L., Liu, W., & Gilman, R. (2005). A cross-cultural comparison study of middle school students' life satisfaction. *Chinese Journal of Applied Psychology, 11*(1), 21–26.

Wang, C., & Zhang, D. (2007). Experimental research on the effect of psychological education to middle school students, academic self-efficacy in the teaching of mathematics. *Psychological Development and Education, 3,* 62–67.

Wang, J., Zhang, H., Xu, J., Gao, M., Wang, M., & Wu, Z. (2008). Relationship between resilience and social support of primary school students in Hefei. *Chinese Mental Health Journal, 21*(3), 162–164.

Wang, P., & Zhang, S. (2011). Relationship between life events, resilience, and learning burnout in junior school students. *Science of Social Psychology, 26*(8), 95–98.

Wang, R., & Zou, H. (2008). The influencing effect of personality to immigrant children's subjective well-being. *Psychological Exploration, 28*(3), 82–87.

Wang, R., & Zou, H. (2010). Subjective well-being of immigrant children in Beijing. *Chinese Mental Health Journal, 24,* 131–134.

Wang, X., & Zhang, D. (2012a). The change of junior middle school students' life satisfaction and the prospective effect of resilience: A two-year longitudinal study. *Psychological Development and Education, 1*(6), 91–98.

Wang, X., & Zhang, D. (2012b). The criticism and amendment for the dual-factor model of mental health: From Chinese psychological suzhi research perspectives. *International Journal of Clinical Medicine, 1,* 7–13. doi:10.4236/ijcm.2012.35063

Wei, Z. (2010). Blending positive psychology with the integrity education, improving the effect of ideological education of college students. *Higher Education Forum, 6,* 4–7.

Wen, C., Zhang, W., Li, D., Yu, C., & Dai, W. (2010). Relationship between junior students' gratitude and academic achievement: With academic engagement as the mediator. *Psychological Development and Education, 26,* 598–605.

Weng, J., Yang, G., & Xu, Y. (2006). Conceptual analysis of Chinese multiple self-esteem and scale development. In Y. G & L. L (Eds.), *Chinese self-esteem: Analysis psychology* (pp. 356–398). Chongqing, P.R. China: Chongqing University Press.

Wu, Z., & Ma, Z. (2008). Positive psychology and its education enlightenment. *Shanghai Research on Education, 6,* 30–32.

Xi, J., Sang, B., & Zuo, Z. (2011). A study of stress/adversity perception of resilient children. *Psychological Science, 34*(1), 102–107.

Yan, B., Zheng, X., & Qiu, L. (2003). A comparison of SWB in college students of Chinese mainland, Hong Kong and USA. *Psychological Exploration, 23*(2), 59–62.

Yang, W. (2003). Research on subject well-being of primary and secondary school teachers. *Journal of Health Psychology, 11,* 243–244.

Yin, X., Gu, G., & Zhao, X. (2010). Relationships among life events, coping pattern and subjective well-being in senior three students. *China Journal of Health Psychology, 18,* 1113–1115.

Yu, C., Zhang, W., Li, D., & Xiao, J. (2010). Gratitude and its relationship with well-being. *Advances in Psychological Science, 18,* 1110–1121.

Yu, Y., & Zhang, F. (2010). Study on the subjective well-being of "Left-at-home children" and the affecting factors. *China Journal of Health Psychology, 18,* 738–741.

Yue, S., Zhang, W., Huang, H., & Li, D. (2006). The adolescent's subjective well-being and mental health and relationships with stress coping. *Psychological Development and Education, 22*(3), 93–98.

Zeng, S., & Li, Q. (2003). Review of the development of children's mental flexibility. *Psychological Science, 26,* 1091–1094.

Zeng, T., Jiang, Q., & Zhang, D. (2007). The problem of the mental quality education embody to subject teaching and countermeasures. *Journal of Zhangzhou Normal University (Philosophy & Social Sciences), 21*(4), 160–164.

Zhang, D. (2010). Psychological suzhi and its structure. *Advances in Psychology Research, 70,* 239–250.

Zhang, D. (2012). Research on the integration of adolescent mental health and psychological suzhi cultivating. *Psychological Science, 35,* 530–536.

Zhang, D., Liu, Y., & Guo, C. (2004). A research of the relationship between elementary school students' mental quality and their academic achievement. *Psychological Development and Education, 20*(1), 64–69.

Zhang, D., & Wang, X. (2012). An analysis of the relationship between mental health and psychological suzhi: From perspective of connotation and structure. *Journal of Southwest University (Social Science Edition), 38*(3), 69–74.

Zhang, D., Wang, J., & Yu, L. (2011). *Methods and implementary strategies on cultivating students' psychological suzhi.* New York, NY: Nova Science.

Zhang, H. (2011). Application of positive psychology. *Intelligence, 29*, 107.

Zhang, J. (2011). Exploration of positive psychology in the teaching practice. *Journal of Campus Life and Mental Health, 9*(3), 174–176.

Zhang, J., Shi, Z., Zhao, P., & Wang, L. (2012). Posttraumatic growth and related factors in junior middle school students after the Wenchuan earthquake. *Chinese Mental Health Journal, 26*, 357–362.

Zhang, L., Shen, J., Wong, S., & Luo, M. (2011). Left-home children's belief in a just world: Its characteristic and relationship with well-being with different duration of left time. *Psychological Development and Education, 27*, 484–490.

Zhang, Q., & Tian, L. (2011). Effective construction of classroom teaching based on the theory of positive psychology. *Basic Education Research, 5*, 44–45.

Zhang, X., He, L., & Jia, L. (2007). The structural relationship among big five personality, demography variable and SWB. *Psychological Development and Education, 23*(1), 46–53.

Zhang, X., He, L., & Zheng, X. (2004). Adolescent students' life satisfaction: Its construct and scale development. *Psychological Science, 27*, 1257–1260.

Zhang, X., & Zheng, X. (2005). The relationship between big five personality and subjective well-being of adolescent students. *Psychological Development and Education, 21*(2), 98–103.

Zhao, G., & Chen, X. (2006). A study on the gratitude dimensions of middle school students. *Psychological Science, 29*, 1300–1302, 1286.

Zhao, S., Cai, T., Zeng, X., & Chen, Z. (2011). Subjective well-being of senior high school students and its relationship to school-work achievement. *Chinese Journal of Clinical Psychology, 19*(1), 128–129.

Zheng, H. (2007). Constructing pressure replying tactics for college students by positive psychology education theory. *Chinese Journal of Health Education, 23*(4), 312–314.

Zheng, L., & Tao, G. (2001). Research on influence factors of life satisfaction of children. *Chinese Journal of Clinical Psychology, 9*(2), 105–107.

Zheng, Y., Fan, F., Yu, C., & Luo, T. (2011). Relationship between gratitude and symptoms of post-traumatic stress disorder among adolescents: Mediation of social support and resilience. *Psychological Development and Education, 27*, 522–528.

Zhou, B., Yang, X., & Chen, X. (2011). Development of the Adolescent School Belonging Questionnaire. *Psychological Exploration, 31*(1), 74–78.

Zhou, D. (2010). Difference between positive psychology education and traditional education on mental health. *Journal of Chifeng University (Natural Science Edition), 10*, 174–175.

Zhu, C. (2007). Shallow discussion of application of positive psychological education to classroom teaching. *Shanghai Research on Education, 8*, 50–51.

Zhu, H. (2008). Correlates of general subject well-being and social support among laid-off workers. *China Journal of Health Psychology, 16*, 802–804.

Zhu, Q., Fan, F., Zheng, Y., Sun, S., Zhang, L., & Tian, W. (2012). Moderating and mediating effects of resilience between negative life events and depression symptoms among adolescents following the 2008 Wenchuan earthquake in China. *Chinese Journal of Clinical Psychology, 20*, 514–517.

CHAPTER SUMMARY: CHINA

- Chinese scholars have not only begun paying attention to the academic studies on positive psychology, but they have also begun putting their findings into practice.
- Key research studies of youth positive psychology in China involve subjective well-being, resilience, and psychological suzhi.
- When conducting cross-national and cultural research, the commonality and comparability of research content, cultural applicability of measures, diversity of methods, and comparability of results should be taken into consideration.
- Chinese researchers should consider the validity and applicability of international scales, which must be revised before their utilization.
- Positive psychology offers Chinese educators a new perspective for daily classroom teaching and school counseling activities.

SUGGESTED READINGS: CHINA

O'Mara, E. M., Gaertner, L., Sedikides, C., Zhou, X., & Liu, Y. (2012). A longitudinal-experimental test of the pan-culturality of self-enhancement: Self-enhancement promotes psychological well-being both in the west and the east. *Journal of Research in Personality, 46,* 157–163. doi:10.1016/j.jrp.2012.01.001

Good example of cross-cultural research methodology.

Tian, L. (2008). Developing scale for school well-being in adolescents. *Psychological Development and Education, 24*(3), 100–106.

Describes the development of the Scale for School Well-Being in Adolescents.

Tian, L., & Liu, W. (2005). Test of the Chinese version of Multidimensional Students' Life Satisfaction Scale. *Chinese Mental Health Journal, 19*(5), 301–303.

Reports on the reliability and validity of Chinese Version of the Multidimensional Students' Life Satisfaction Scale (MSLSS).

Zhang, D., Wang, X., & Yu, L. (2011). *Methods and implementation strategies on cultivating students' psychological suzhi.* New York, NY: Nova Science.

Introduces the concept of psychological suzhi and its applications to schooling.

Zou, Q. (2005). A review of the research on the relation between subjective well-being and culture. *Psychological Science, 28,* 632–633, 631.

Excellent review of the research on cross-cultural studies of subjective well-being.

28

EMOTIONAL INTELLIGENCE
School-Based Research and Practice in Italy

*Annamaria Di Fabio, Department of Psychology,
University of Florence, Florence, Italy*

*Maureen E. Kenny and Kelly A. Minor, Lynch School of Education,
Department of Counseling, Developmental, and Educational
Psychology, Boston College, Chestnut Hill, MA, USA*

EMOTIONAL INTELLIGENCE AND POSITIVE PSYCHOLOGY

In contrast with the deficit approaches that have characterized much of psychology research and practice historically, positive psychology embraces a strengths-based approach to prevention and therapy, seeking to promote positive traits among individuals and the settings that support human development (Snyder & Lopez, 2002). Although somewhat distinct in emphasis, positive youth development shares with positive psychology an intention to promote optimal development so that individuals may thrive across school, work, family, community, and other settings. Positive youth development recognizes the strengths of young people and seeks to go beyond risk reduction and to enhance assets that enable full and productive participation in society (Catalano, Berglund, Ryan, Lonczak, & Hawkins, 2004).

Consistent with ecological (Bronfenbrenner, 1979) and developmental contextual theories (Lerner, 2002), efforts to enhance positive youth development seek to identify and foster those personal and contextual strengths that enable young people to be successful in navigating the varied contexts of their lives. Just as a variety of negative development outcomes, such as academic underachievement, mental health problems, substance abuse, and underemployment, are interrelated, positive developmental outcomes in the academic, social, emotional, and career domains are interconnected (Lerner, 2002). Given the interrelation of developmental outcomes across life domains, primary prevention and positive youth development programs that enhance critical developmental competencies and simultaneously foster academic, social, emotional, and career development can be cost effective and contribute to long-term benefits for individuals and the broader society (Hage et al., 2007).

Young people in Italy, as across much of the world, are facing a social and work environment characterized by rapid change and instability, with globalization and automation eliminating routine jobs that do not require advanced technical or interpersonal skills (Savickas, 2000). Under these conditions, the development of social and emotional skills is viewed as integral to psychological well-being and workforce preparation (Lapan, 2004). In response to economic and social challenge, scholars, educators, and mental health practitioners in Italy have sought to identify individual factors that contribute to resilience, positive youth development, and mental health prevention (Kenny, 2009).

Emotional intelligence (EI) represents one individual factor that has been the focus of recent attention for its relation with indices of positive development in the academic, social, behavioral, and career domains across the lifespan (Di Fabio & Kenny, 2011). Interest in EI also accrues from evidence that it is a malleable dimension of human functioning that can be taught, with positive impacts on academic, psychological, and career development factors (Di Fabio & Kenny, 2011; Di Fabio & Palazzeschi, 2009b). EI was popularized in the 1990s with the publication of Goleman's (1995) best-selling book, *Emotional Intelligence*. Concurrent and subsequent to that time, scholars have worked to refine the conceptualization and measurement of the construct, with some debate about the extent to which EI overlaps with personality factors or is best understood as a pure set of abilities.

The work of Bar-On (1997) exemplifies the mixed-model perspective that EI overlaps with personality. In contrast, Mayer, Salovey, and colleagues (Mayer & Salovey, 1997; Mayer, Salovey, & Caruso, 2002, 2008) advocate for the ability-based perspective. We now describe these models and measures, as they are the basis for the growing body of EI research and intervention in Italy and other nations.

Bar-On Mixed EI Model

Bar-On (1997) conceptualizes EI as a mixture of personality characteristics and social-emotional abilities that determine how well people understand themselves and others, how well they express their emotions, how they relate with others, and how they cope with daily challenges and stressors. Bar-On developed the Emotional Quotient Inventory (EQ-i; Bar-On, 1997) to assess EI based on a review of existing literature and his clinical experience. Originally normed on 3,381 adults in the United States and Canada, the EQ-i is now translated into more than 30 languages, with normative data available from countries across the globe (Bar-On, 2007).

The EQ-i consists of 133 self-report items for use with persons ages 17 and older, with the Bar-On Emotional Quotient-Youth Version (EQ-i:YV) designed to assess emotionally and socially intelligent behavior of children between 7 and 18 years of age (Bar-On,

2007). Both versions assess five meta-factors and 15 subfactors. The five meta-factors are *intrapersonal* (self-awareness of and the ability to express one's emotions), *interpersonal* (empathy, social responsibility, and the capacity to establish mutually satisfying relationships), *stress management* (stress tolerance and impulse control), *adaptability* (flexibility, problem solving, and validating one's feeling and thinking with reality), and *general mood* (optimism and contentment). The Emotional Quotient Inventory: Short (EQ-i:S; Bar-On, 2002) consists of 51 items and provides a total score and scores for four factors (Intrapersonal, Interpersonal, Adaptability, Stress Management).

EI as Ability Based

Mayer and colleagues (Mayer et al., 2002, 2008) are critics of the mixed model and argue that an ability-based conception of EI offers greater conceptual and measurement clarity and scientific validity. Mayer and colleagues conceive of EI as a type of intelligence that focuses on the processing of information and emphasize the interrelation of emotion and reason, including the capacity to reason about emotion and the capacity to use emotions to enhance thinking. Mayer and colleagues first developed the Multifactor Emotional Intelligence Scale (MEIS) in the middle 1990s and the Mayer-Salovey-Caruso Emotional Intelligence Test (MSCEIT) later in the decade (Mayer, Salovey, & Caruso, 2000). The 141-item MSCEIT is a performance-based ability measure and was developed for use with adults. A 180-item youth version, MSCEIT-YV (Mayer, Caruso, & Salovey, 2005) was developed for youth between 11 and 17 years of age (Rivers, Brackett, & Salovey, 2008).

The MSCEIT (Mayer et al., 2002) assesses four branches or dimensions of EI, including *Perceiving Emotions* (PE; i.e., the ability to perceive emotions in oneself and others, as well as in objects, art, stories, music, and other stimuli); *Facilitating Thought* (FT; i.e., the ability to generate, use, and feel emotions to communicate feelings or employ them in other cognitive processes); *Understanding Emotions* (UE; i.e., the ability to understand emotional information, how emotions combine and progress through relationship transitions, and to appreciate such emotional meanings); and *Managing Emotions* (ME; i.e., the ability to be open to feelings and to modulate them in oneself and others so as to promote personal understanding and growth). For perceiving emotion, the respondent is presented with photographs of people's faces and artistic designs and landscapes and is asked to identify the emotions expressed in the picture. For using emotion, respondents are asked to compare emotions with other sensory modalities and to identify the emotions that facilitate or interfere with different cognitive and behavioral activities. Understanding emotions is assessed by tasks that ask participants to identify events that bring forth certain emotional reactions and to identify feelings that are often associated with one another. Finally, with regard to managing emotions, respondents evaluate coping strategies for responding to emotional events and strategies for managing the emotions of others (Rivers et al., 2008).

Although the literature includes additional conceptualizations and measures of EI, the Bar-On (1997) and the Mayer and Salovey (1997) models have been the foundation for much of the scholarship that has been completed within the United Sates, Italy, and other nations.

MEASUREMENT CONSIDERATIONS AND ISSUES IN ITALY

Research regarding emotional intelligence in Italy has been made possible by the development of Italian versions of measures that were originally used in the United States and England. These instruments reflect the principal types of instruments and conceptualizations of EI (ability-based and self-report) that dominate the literature and debates on emotional intelligence. Although norms regarding emotional expression and regulation vary across cultures (Hoffman, 2009), research in Italy and in other Western Eurocentric cultures has found EI to be a robust construct, with little modification of measures beyond translation. Measures developed in the English language, for example, have been translated into many languages (Bar-On, 2007), with the translated measures demonstrating stable factor structure and good convergent and discriminant validity. We now provide a description of EI measures available in Italy, along with psychometric properties.

The Italian Version of the Mayer-Salovey-Caruso Emotional Intelligence Test (MSCEIT)

D'Amico and Curci (2010) developed an Italian version of the ability-based Mayer-Salovey-Caruso Emotional Intelligence Test (MSCEIT; Mayer et al., 2002). The Italian version was developed through a process of translation and back-translation of the original measure. The same process was used in developing a Spanish version of the MSCEIT (Extremera, Fernández-Berrocal, & Salovey, 2006). The Italian version consists of the same tasks and pictorial stimuli used in the original measure. Also consistent with the original measure, the Italian version provides a total score (EIQ) and four branch scores, supported by factor analysis (D'Amico & Curci, 2010).

The Italian version was developed with a large community sample of adults between 17 and 83 years of age. Split-half reliabilities for the subscale scores were .90 for PE, .77 for FT, .75 for UE, and .72 for ME (D'Amico & Curci, 2010). Di Fabio and Kenny (2012b) found comparable split-half reliabilities with Italian high school students. D'Amico and Curci (2010) report convergent validity with correlations of the EIQ with Agreeableness and with Emotional Stability of the Big Five Questionnaire (BFQ; Caprara, Barbaranelli, & Borgogni, 1993) and with the scale total of the Standard Progressive Matrices (SPM; Raven, 1941).

The Italian Version of the Emotional Quotient Inventory (EQ-i)

The Italian version (Franco & Tappatà, 2009) of the 133-item Emotional Intelligence Inventory (EQ-i; Bar-On, 1997) offers a self-report measure for assessing the mixed model of emotional intelligence. As with the original EQ-i, the Italian version provides a total score (EQ total) and scores for five separate dimensions and 15 subdimensions. Confirmatory factor analysis supports the five-scale structure (Franco & Tappatà, 2009). Construct validity is evidenced by negative correlations with the subscales of the Toronto Alexithymia Scale (TAS; Bagby, Parker, & Taylor, 1994), which assess difficulties in identifying feelings and describing emotions, and by moderate positive correlations with the Extraversion, Agreeableness, Conscientiousness, Emotional Stability, and Openness scales of the BFQ (Di Fabio & Palazzeschi, 2009a).

Internal consistency reliability for the Italian version, assessed by Cronbach's α, was .91 for the Intrapersonal dimension, .84 for the Interpersonal dimension, .81 for the Adaptability dimension, .87 for the Stress Management, .83 for the General Mood, and .95 for the QE total (Franco & Tappatà, 2009). Di Fabio and Kenny (2012a) also report good internal consistency with high school students.

Di Fabio and Palazzeschi (in press) developed an Italian version of the 51-item Emotional Quotient Inventory: Short (EQ-i:S; Bar-On, 2002) and confirmed the four-factor structure of the original version. With Italian high school students, Di Fabio and Blustein (2010) report Cronbach's α of .79 for the Intrapersonal dimension, .79 for the Interpersonal dimension, .78 for the Adaptability dimension, and .84 for the Stress Management dimension.

The Italian Version of the Emotional Intelligence Scale (EIS)

The Italian version (Di Fabio, Giannini, & Palazzeschi, 2008) of the Emotional Intelligence Scale (EIS; Schutte et al., 1998) is a 22-item self-report measure that assesses three dimensions of EI. These dimensions are based on the theoretical model developed by Salovey and Mayer (1990), which was the precursor to the Four-Branch ability-based model (Mayer & Salovey, 1997). Like the MSCEIT, the EIS focuses on the ways in which thinking about emotion and integrating emotion into thought processes might serve to enhance reasoning but does this in a self-report rather than a performance-based format.

The Italian version (Di Fabio et al., 2008) of the EIS was developed through translation and back-translation of the original measure. Factor analysis showed a three-dimensional structure. Based on the theoretical model by Salovey and Mayer (1990), the first factor was named Appraisal and Expression of Emotions, the second factor is Regulation of Emotions, and the third factor is Utilization of Emotions in Solving Problems.

This measure has demonstrated good internal consistency reliability with Italian young adults and high school students (Di Fabio et al., 2008, Di Fabio & Kenny, 2012a). Regarding concurrent validity, positive correlations emerged between the Italian version of the EIS and the Life Orientation Test–Revised (LOT-R; Scheier, Carver, & Bridges, 1994), the Italian version (Prezza, Trombaccia, & Armento, 1997) of the Self-Esteem Scale (Rosenberg, 1965) and the EQ-i:S (Bar-On, 2002), and negative correlations with the Italian version (Bressi et al., 1996) of the Toronto Alexithymia Scale (TAS; Bagby, Parker, & Taylor, 1994).

REVIEW OF KEY RESEARCH STUDIES

Interest in emotional intelligence (EI) stems from the belief that these skills contribute to successful functioning across a variety of domains, including academic success, psychological well-being, adaptive social functioning, and workplace competence. A growing body of data both within Italy and around the globe is documenting positive associations between EI and a range of adaptive developmental outcomes.

Within the United States, for example, EI as assessed by the adolescent version of the MEIS was negatively associated with tobacco and alcohol use and attitudes among middle school students (Trinidad & Johnson, 2002; Trinidad, Unger, Chou, & Johnson,

2004). Also with regard to behavioral correlates, Mayer, Perkins, Caruso, and Salovey (2001) found that gifted youth from ages 13 to 17 years with high MEIS scores were better able to resist peer pressure than those with lower MEIS scores. With regard to academic outcomes, Parker and colleagues (2004) found EQ-i scores to be positively correlated with grade point average (GPA) among high school students.

With regard to other national contexts, EI, as assessed through the MSCEIT, was negatively correlated with maladaptive behavior (Márquez, Martin, & Brackett, 2006) and positively correlated with prosocial behavior, social competence, and peer nominations among Spanish high school students (Márquez et al., 2006; Mestre, Guil, Lopes, Salovey, & Gil-Olarte, 2006). EI was also found to be associated with positive academic behaviors, such as homework completion and class attendance (Mestre et al., 2006), and with end-of-year grades, even after accounting for students' verbal skills (Márquez et al., 2006). Negative correlations were also found with internalizing and externalizing behaviors in Malaysian secondary school students (Liau, Liau, Teoh, & Liau, 2003).

Although numerous other studies worldwide can be cited to support the relation of EI with indices of positive youth development (Bar-On, 2007), we focus on key research in the Italian context, which has been advanced by Di Fabio and colleagues. Di Fabio and colleagues have pursued a programmatic research agenda, designed to evaluate the convergent and discriminant validity of the EI construct for the Italian context and to provide a basis for the development of EI interventions. Consistent with research in the United States that has sought to refine and validate the conceptualization of EI (Rivers et al., 2008), Di Fabio and colleagues have sought to establish that EI represents an ability that is (a) correlated with but distinct from general intelligence; (b) correlated with but distinct from personality; and (c) related with positive developmental outcomes across the academic, social, and career domains of development. Di Fabio and colleagues have examined these premises from the perspective of both ability-based and mixed-model conceptualizations of EI.

Italian Research: EI as a Distinct Concept

Di Fabio and Palazzeschi (2009b) examined the relation of emotional intelligence as assessed by the Italian version of the MSCEIT and the Italian version of the EQ-i:S with fluid intelligence and personality traits among male and female students completing their final 2 years of high school in Tuscany. For this sample, fluid intelligence was significantly correlated with the MSCEIT total score ($r = .23, p < .01$) but not with the EQ total ($r = .14, p > .05$). The MSCEIT was not significantly associated with personality. For the EQ-i:S, Extraversion was significantly and negatively correlated with EQ total ($r = -.20, p < .05$), Intrapersonal ($r = -.24, p < .05$), and Interpersonal ($r = -.31, p < .05$) scores on the EQ-i:S. Neuroticism was also significantly and negatively correlated with the EQ total ($r = -.25, p < .01$), Intrapersonal ($r = -.23, p < .01$), and Stress Management ($r = -.49, p < .01$) scores of the EQi:S. The small and moderate correlations support the premise that EI overlaps with but is distinct from general intelligence and personality. With regard to the two models of EI, the findings suggest that the mixed model overlaps significantly with personality and that the ability model is associated with general intelligence more than the mixed model. Since verbal measures of intelligence are expected to overlap somewhat with EI, the mixed model may demonstrate a relation with verbal intelligence that was not evidenced with the nonverbal measure of fluid intelligence used in this study.

Italian Research: EI and Academic Development

With regard to the expectation that EI should be associated with academic success, dimensions of both the MSCEIT and the Bar-On EQ-i were associated significantly and positively with student GPA. For the MSCEIT, the total score ($r = .31, p < .01$) and the Facilitating Thought ($r = .28, p < .01$), Understanding Emotions ($r = .28, p < .01$), and Managing Emotions ($r = .38, p < .01$) subscales were associated with GPA. For the EQ-i, GPA was significantly associated with the total score ($r = .22, p < .05$) and the Intrapersonal ($r = .19, p < .05$) and Adaptability subscales ($r = .24, p < .01$). These findings suggest that varied dimensions of EI may relate differently with academic success, but this deserves further investigation with larger samples.

Di Fabio and Palazzeschi (2009b) also examined whether EI explains academic performance beyond the contributions of fluid intelligence and personality. Hierarchical regression analysis revealed, as expected, that both mixed-model and ability-based EI contribute additional significant variance in explaining academic performance, as measured by student GPA. Beyond fluid intelligence and personality, the four EQ-i subscales accounted for an additional 6% variance. For the MSCEIT, the four subscales accounted for an additional 12% of the variance beyond fluid intelligence and personality. These findings are important theoretically by documenting the significance of EI beyond fluid intelligence and personality and thereby providing evidence to support the notion that interventions that enhance EI may also facilitate academic performance. Since neither fluid intelligence nor personality is highly malleable by mid to late adolescence, interventions that develop EI could be promising in contributing to academic success.

Italian Research: EI and Social Development

With regard to adaptive correlates of EI, Di Fabio and Kenny (2012a) assessed the relation of EI with social functioning for a sample of 309 Italian high school students. Di Fabio and Kenny were interested in perceived social support as an index of social functioning for high school students based upon its association with school engagement and academic motivation (Kenny, Walsh-Blair, Blustein, Bempechat, & Seltzer, 2010) and openness to adult mentoring (Larose et al., 2009). As in the Di Fabio and Palazzeschi (2009a) study, Di Fabio and Kenny also wanted to determine whether EI explained social functioning beyond the effects of personality. For this study, EI was assessed by the Italian version of the MSCEIT and the Italian version of the EIS.

Di Fabio and Kenny (2012a) found significant positive correlations between the total social support scale and the EIS total ($r = .45, p < .01$) and the MSCEIT total ($r = .30, p < .01$), as well as among the EIS and MSCEIT subscales. Hierarchical multiple regressions reveled furthermore that the five BFQ personality scales explained a significant 14% of the variance in social support, with the self-report dimensions of the EIS accounting for an additional significant 15%. The performance-based MSCEIT accounted for an additional 4% variance beyond the BFQ scales. Both EI measures were significant beyond the effects of personality traits, thereby supporting EI as distinct from personality. In comparison with the MSCEIT, however, the self-report EIS was more strongly associated with the self-report measures of social support. This may reflect the effects of common method (self-report) variance, although it also makes sense that students' level of confidence in their emotional skills might also impact their expectation of support from others. So, while actual skill in EI is relevant and related to perceived social support, self-perceptions of EI skills may matter as much and perhaps more than performance-based EI.

Italian Research: EI and Career Decision Making

Whereas research in the United States has assessed the relation of EI with workplace competence among adults (Rivers et al., 2008), the research of Di Fabio and colleagues has made a significant and unique contribution by examining the relation of EI to career decision making among high school and university students. Di Fabio and Kenny (2012b) maintain that rational models of career decision making, which have long dominated career development literature and interventions, offer a limited understanding of career decision making at a time when young people are entering an unpredictable global economy requiring multiple career transitions. Faced with a choice between one's desires and changing labor market realities, emotional skills, such as adaptability, self-awareness, and the capacity to manage ambivalence and uncertainty, are needed. Research by Di Fabio and colleagues in Italy (Di Fabio & Blustein, 2010; Di Fabio & Kenny, 2011, 2012b) is examining the relation of EI with career decision making to gain a better of understanding of how emotions relate with decision-making processes among high school students.

Paralleling research on academic success and social functioning, Di Fabio and colleagues have assessed the relation of competing models of EI with varied facets of decision making. Di Fabio and Blustein (2010), for example, examined the relation of the EQ-i:S with decisional conflict styles among 528 Italian high school students. Di Fabio and Blustein were interested in how student approaches to decisional conflict, including the adaptive use of vigilance to carefully analyze a problem, and the maladaptive styles of avoidance, procrastination, and hypervigilance were related to EI. Regression analyses revealed that the EI dimension of adaptability was the best predictor of the adaptive style of vigilance. The maladaptive styles of responding to decisional conflict were explained best by low self-awareness of one's emotions (Intrapersonal EI).

Di Fabio and Kenny (2012b) used both the Bar-On EQ-i and the MSCEIT in exploring the relations between EI and decision-making style among a sample of 206 high school students drawn from college preparatory and technical high schools in Tuscany. Five styles of decision making—rational, intuitive, dependent, avoidant, and spontaneous—were studied. Overall, the five EQ-i scales as a set predicted all five decisional styles. More specifically and consistent with the Di Fabio and Blustein (2010) findings with the EQ-i, low intrapersonal EI was associated with maladaptive approaches to decision making, including avoidance and dependence on others to make decisions. Adaptability, conceptualized as being flexible in coping with daily problems and having knowledge and insight regarding one's feelings, was associated with the adaptive rational style of decision making. Low adaptability and poor stress management were associated with a spontaneous, impulsive style of decision making. The results for the EQ-i measure with high school students in this study also replicated prior findings among Italian young adults (Di Fabio & Palazzeschi, 2008). The ability-based components of the MSCEIT were associated only with avoidant and spontaneous styles (Di Fabio & Kenny, 2012b). Hierarchical regression analyses indicated that the MSCEIT did not significantly explain decisional style beyond the effects of the EQ-i. With regard to criticism of the mixed-model conceptualization of EI as a blend of personality and emotional skills (Mayer et al., 2008), the research of Di Fabio and colleagues suggests that the mixed model may be helpful in explaining outcomes that are not exclusively explained by skills but by personality as well.

Overall, research in the Italian context has paralleled research in the United States by demonstrating that EI, although overlapping with personality and intelligence, is a distinct construct. Although the ability-based construct overlaps more with fluid intelligence and the mixed model overlaps with personality, both models are related with positive youth functioning across varied dimensions of academic, social, and career development. In addition to the work summarized above by Di Fabio and colleagues, additional research of school-aged youth and university students in Italy has documented relations between emotional intelligence and scholastic/academic success (Lanciano & Curci, 2012; Troncone, Labella, & Drammis, 2011) and psychological well-being in school contexts (Gigantesco, Carbonari, Appelgren, Del Re, & Cascavilla, 2010). The relations between EI and multiple dimensions of adaptive functioning have created interest in Italy and other nations in developing interventions that promote EI.

EDUCATIONAL APPLICATIONS AND PRACTICES

Interest is expanding in the United States and globally in the development and evaluation of interventions that attempt to increase EI and its associated outcomes. While some scholars have questioned the ability of interventions to improve EI (e.g., Zeidner, Roberts, & Matthews, 2002), others have encouraged these efforts. Buckley and colleagues (Buckley, Storino, & Saarni, 2003), for example, urged school psychologists to assess schools' needs for EI promotion and take action. Teacher training, inclusion of EI curriculum into classrooms, and individual and group counseling have been identified as means through which emotional intelligence can be improved.

Socioemotional learning (SEL) programs have been developed and tested around the United States over the past several decades. A collaborative of researchers, educators, and advocates "formed with the goal of establishing high-quality, evidence-based SEL as an essential part of preschool through high school education" (Elbertson, Brackett, & Weissberg, 2010, p. 1017) was created at the 1994 Fetzer Institute Conference. This group was named the Collaborative for Academic, Social, and Emotional Learning, or CASEL, and has played an integral role in SEL research and development since that time. CASEL advocates for the development of social-emotional competencies in five areas, including self-awareness, self-management, social awareness, relationship skills, and responsible decision making, which overlap with the EI factors identified by Bar-On (1997) and Mayer and Salovey (1997).

Many specific SEL programs have been created and evaluated, with goals of optimizing personal, social, and academic functioning and success. Promoting Alternative Thinking Strategies (PATHS) is an example of a long-standing program that teaches the vocabulary of emotions, emotion management, and comprehension of meta-cognitive aspects of emotions (e.g., cues for recognizing emotions) but is not directly tied to the EI models of either Bar-On (1997) or Mayer and Salovey (1997). PATHS has been implemented and evaluated in both national and international settings over the years and has established positive outcomes, including improvements in child social competency, reductions in behavior problems, and enhanced academic achievement (Greenberg, Kushce, Cook, & Quamma, 1995; Kelly, Longbottom, Potts, & Williamson, 2004).

Among recently developed interventions in the United States, the RULER program is based on the EI theory of Mayer and Salovey (1997) and uses a feeling words curriculum that is taught by middle school teachers within English language arts and history classes in schools. This curriculum teaches five EI skills (recognizing, understanding, labeling, expressing, and regulating emotions) and follows the social and emotional learning principles set forth by CASEL, such as linking social-emotional learning to the standard curricula, training teachers and staff, involving family, and evaluating program outcomes (Rivers & Brackett, 2011). The program is now extended for use in high schools. The RULER approach to building emotionally literate schools includes training of school leaders and school-based teams that can then provide ongoing support and training to all teachers and other stakeholders, including family members. Brackett and colleagues (Brackett, Rivers, Reyes, & Salovey, 2012) have found multiple positive results among students, including enhanced motivation and study skills, better academic performance, better relationships, fewer behavior problems, and better communication between students and families.

In the Italian context, Di Fabio (2010) developed a school-based intervention, aligned to the theoretical model of Mayer and Salovey (1997), with the aim of increasing emotional intelligence in high school students (Di Fabio & Kenny, 2011). The 10-hour training program was delivered in four 2.5-hour sessions across 4 weeks. Each session focuses on one of the domains or branches of the Mayer and Salovey (1997) model. The first session is devoted to Perceiving Emotions in oneself and others, as well as in art, stories, music, and other stimuli. The second session focuses on Facilitating Thought, including the ability to generate and use emotions to communicate feelings and to enhance thought processes. The third session emphasizes the Understanding of Emotions, including the interpretation of emotional information and the ways in which emotions can be combined and fluctuate in the course of relationships. The fourth session is devoted to Managing Emotions, including openness to emotional experience in self and others to promote personal understanding and growth and the modulation of feelings in emotionally arousing circumstances.

The evaluation of the intervention was designed to determine, first of all, whether EI could be increased as a result of this curriculum and whether the intervention was related to changes in relevant life skills. This evaluation hypothesized that EI training would positively impact decision-making skills as a result of increased access to and understanding of emotional information about oneself and the world. Students who participated in the intervention were selected through a multistage process. Four classes completing their final year of a college-preparatory high school in the Tuscany Province of Italy were randomly selected for the initial phase of the study and completed questionnaires assessing EI through the Italian version of the MSCEIT and the Italian version of the self-report EIS. With regard to decision making, 91 students completed the Italian version (Di Fabio, Busoni, & Palazzeschi, 2011) of the Indecisiveness Scale (Frost & Gross, 1993) and the Italian version (Di Fabio & Palazzeschi, 2010, 2013) of the Career Decision Difficulties Questionnaire (Gati, Krausz, & Osipow, 1996). Two classes that showed no significant differences on pretest scores on these measures were randomly assigned to intervention and comparison group status. One month following completion of the training, students in the two classes completed the four measures a second time.

Posttest results suggested that the intervention was effective in increasing both ability-based and self-reported emotional intelligence and in reducing indecisiveness and career indecision, with the effects remaining a month after the intervention (Di Fabio & Kenny, 2011). These findings, although requiring replication with a larger sample and with impact assessed with additional objective measures over a more extended time period, are promising. Students self-reported growth in EI, documented by performance assessment of their EI skills before and after intervention. Future prospective studies are needed to assess effect over time on other theoretically linked outcomes, such as academic achievement and indices of social and emotional functioning. Nevertheless, EI appears to be a mutable construct in the Italian context, as has been demonstrated in the United States (Bar-On, 1997; Mayer et al., 2008) and associated with meaningful outcomes beyond changes in EI. From a prevention and positive psychology point of view (Kenny, Horne, Orpinas & Reese, 2009; Snyder & Lopez, 2002), emotional intelligence may offer a base for success and resilience in school, work, and social contexts.

CONCLUDING THOUGHTS

In Italy, as in other parts of the world, a significant body of research supports the relations between emotional intelligence and a variety of positive youth outcomes. The economic and social challenges of contemporary life underscore the need for and value of EI skills. Academic, social, and career success are reciprocally interrelated and require social-emotional skills along with academic development. With regard to the Italian context, interest in EI is strong, and research has documented the validity of the construct and produced reliable and valid measures for assessing EI. School-based interventions are now being developed and implemented with the goals of promoting positive development across social, academic, and career domains.

Many educators, researchers, and mental health practitioners in Italy now embrace promoting EI among children and adolescents. While direct instruction of students is a primary element of these programs, it is also important to note that parents, peers, and the community play a role in the development of these skills. In order to do this, adults who interact with children also need to be proficient in EI skills. Italian research reveals that efforts to promote teacher EI are associated with self-efficacy among Italian teachers at the high school (Di Fabio & Palazzeschi, 2008) and kindergarten and primary school levels (D'Amico, 2008). We also suggest, consistent with a broad-based prevention perspective (Kenny et al., 2009), that attention needs to be given to reducing contextual barriers and enhancing contextual supports that impact the development and use of emotional intelligence in daily life.

REFERENCES

Bagby, R.M., Parker, J.D.A., & Taylor, G.J. (1994). The twenty-item Toronto Alexithymia Scale—I. Convergent, discriminant, and concurrent validity. *Journal of Psychosomatic Research, 38,* 23–32.

Bar-On, R. (1997). *The Emotional Intelligence Inventory (EQ-I): Technical manual.* Toronto, ON, Canada: Multi-Health Systems.

Bar-On, R. (2002). *Bar-On Emotional Quotient Inventory: Short (EQ-i: S): Technical manual.* Toronto, ON, Canada: Multi-Health Systems.

Bar-On, R. (2007). How important is it to educate people to be emotionally intelligent, and can it be done? In R. Bar-On, J. G. Maree, & M. J. Elias (Eds.), *Educating people to be emotionally intelligent* (pp. 1–14). Westport, CT: Praeger.

Brackett, M.A., Rivers, S.E., Reyes, M.R., & Salovey, P. (2012). Enhancing academic performance and social and emotional competence with the RULER feeling words curriculum. *Learning and Individual Differences, 22,* 218–224. doi:10.1016/j.lindif.2010.10.002

Bressi, C., Taylor, G.J., Parker, J.D.A., Bressi, S., Brambilla, V., Aguglia, E., & Invernizzi, G. (1996). Cross validation of the factor structure of the 20-item Toronto Alexithymia scale: An Italian multicenter study. *Journal of Psychometric Research, 41,* 551–559. doi:10.1016/S0022-3999(96)00228-0

Bronfenbrenner, U. (1979). *The ecology of human development: Experiments by nature and design.* Cambridge, MA: Harvard University Press.

Buckley, M., Storino, M., & Saarni, C. (2003). Promoting emotional competence in children and adolescents: Implications for school psychologists. *School Psychology Quarterly, 18,* 177–191. doi:10.1521/scpq.18.2.177.21855

Caprara, G.V., Barbaranelli, C., & Borgogni, L. (1993). *BFQ: Big Five Questionnaire. Manuale* [BFQ: Big Five Questionnaire. Manual] (2nd ed.). Firenze, Italy: Giunti O.S. Organizzazioni Speciali.

Catalano, R.F., Berglund, M.L., Ryan, J.A. M., Lonczak, H.S., & Hawkins, J.D. (2004). Positive youth development in the United States: Research findings on evaluations of positive youth development programs. *Annals of the American Academy of Political and Social Science, 591,* 98–124. doi:10.1177/0002716203260102

D'Amico, A. (2008). Conoscere il ruolo dei fattori cognitivi ed emotivo-motivazionali nell'apprendimento scolastico, per diventare un insegnante efficace [Know the role of cognitive and emotional-motivational factors in scholastic learning, for becoming an effective teacher]. In G. Zanniello (Ed.), *La formazione universitaria degli insegnanti di scuola primaria dell'infanzia [The university training of primary teachers and kindergarten teachers]* (pp. 225–259). Roma, Italy: Armando.

D'Amico, A., & Curci, A. (2010). *Mayer-Salovey-Caruso emotional intelligence test (MSCEIT).* Firenze, Italy: Giunti O.S.

Di Fabio, A. (2010). *Potenziare l'intelligenza emotiva in classe. Linee Guida per il training* [Enhancing emotional intelligence at school: Guidelines for training]. Firenze, Italy: Giunti O.S.

Di Fabio, A., & Blustein, D.L. (2010). Emotional intelligence and decisional conflict styles: Some empirical evidence among Italian high school students. *Journal of Career Assessment, 18,* 71–81. doi:10.1177/1069072709350904

Di Fabio, A., Busoni, L., & Palazzeschi, L. (2011). Indecisiveness Scale (IS): Proprietà psicometriche della versione italiana [Indecisiveness Scale (IS): Psychometric properties of the Italian version]. *Counseling. Giornale Italiano di Ricerca e Applicazioni, 4,* 13–24.

Di Fabio, A., Giannini, M., & Palazzeschi, L. (2008). Intelligenza emotiva: Proprietà psicometriche della Emotional Intelligence Scale (EIS) [Emotional intelligence: Psychometric properties of the Emotional Intelligence Scale]. *Counseling. Giornale Italiano di Ricerca e Applicazioni, 2,* 61–71.

Di Fabio, A., & Kenny, M.E. (2011). Promoting emotional intelligence and career decision making among Italian high school students. *Journal of Career Assessment, 19,* 21–34. doi:10.1177/1069072710382530

Di Fabio, A., & Kenny, M.E. (2012a). Emotional intelligence and perceived social support among Italian high school students. *Journal of Career Development, 39,* 459–473. doi:10.1177/0894845311421005

Di Fabio, A., & Kenny, M.E. (2012b). The contribution of emotional intelligence to decisional styles among Italian high school students. *Journal of Career Assessment, 20,* 404–414. doi:10.1177/1069072712448893

Di Fabio, A., & Palazzeschi, L. (2008). Indécision vocationnelle et intelligence émotionnelle: Quelques données empiriques sur un échantillon d'apprentis Italiens [Career decision difficulties and emotional intelligence:

Some empirical evidences in an Italian sample of wage-earning apprentices]. *Pratiques Psychologiques, 14,* 213–222. doi:10.1016/j.prps.2007.11.006

Di Fabio, A., & Palazzeschi, L. (2009a). Emotional intelligence, personality traits and career decision difficulties. *International Journal for Educational and Vocational Guidance, 9,* 135–146. doi:10.1007/s10775-009-9162-3

Di Fabio, A., & Palazzeschi, L. (2009b). An in-depth look at scholastic success: Fluid intelligence, personality traits or emotional intelligence? *Personality and Individual Differences, 46,* 581–585. doi:10.1016/j.paid.2008.12.012

Di Fabio, A., & Palazzeschi, L. (2010). Career Decision-Making Difficulties Questionnaire: Proprietà psicometriche nel contesto italiano [Career Decision-Making Difficulties Questionnaire: Psychometric properties in the Italian context]. *Counseling. Giornale Italiano di Ricerca e Applicazioni, 3,* 351–364.

Di Fabio, A., & Palazzeschi, L. (Eds.). (2013). *Adattamento italiano del CDDQ—Career Decision-making Difficulties Questionnaire [Italian adaptation of the CDDQ—Career Decision-making Difficulties Questionnaire].* Firenze, Italy: Giunti O.S.

Di Fabio, A., & Palazzeschi, L. (in press). Proprietà psicometriche del Bar-On Emotional Quotient Inventory: Short (Bar-On EQ-i:S) nel contesto italiano. [Psychometric properties of Bar-On Emotional Quotient Inventory: Short (Bar-On EQ-i:S) in the Italian context]. *Counseling: Giornale Italiano di Ricerca e Applicazioni.*

Elbertson, N.A., Brackett, M.A. & Weissberg, R.P. (2010). School-based social and emotional learning programming: Current perspectives. In A. Hargreaves, A. Lieberman, M. Fullan, & D. Hopkins (Eds.), *Second international handbook of educational change* (pp. 1017–1032). Dordrecht, Netherlands: Springer.

Extremera, N., Fernández-Berrocal, P., & Salovey, P. (2006). Spanish version of the Mayer-Salovey-Caruso Emotional Intelligence Test (MSCEIT). version 2.0: Reliabilities, age and gender differences. *Psicothema, 18,* 42–48.

Franco, M., & Tappatà, L. (2009). *EQ-i™ Emotional Quotient Inventory. Validazione e taratura Italiana.* Firenze, Italy: Giunti O.S.

Frost, R.O., & Gross, R.C. (1993). The hoarding of possessions. *Behaviour Research and Therapy, 31,* 367–381. doi:10.1016/0005-7967(93)90094-B

Gati, I., Krausz, M., & Osipow, S.H. (1996). A taxonomy of difficulties in career decision-making. *Journal of Counseling Psychology, 43,* 510–526. doi:10.1037/0022-0167.43.4.510

Gigantesco, A., Carbonari, P., Appelgren, E.C., Del Re, D., & Cascavilla, E. (2010). *La promozione della salute mentale, del benessere psicologico e dell'intelligenza emotiva nella scuola secondaria [Promotion of mental health, psychological well-being and emotional intelligence in high school].* Retrieved from http://www.hepatitis.iss.it/binary/publ/cont/ONLINEmaggio.pdf

Goleman, D. (1995). *Emotional intelligence.* New York, NY: Bantam Books.

Greenberg, M.T., Kusche, C.A., Cook, E.T., & Quamma, J.P. (1995). Promoting emotional competence in school-aged children: The effects of the PATHS curriculum. *Development and Psychopathology, 7,* 117–136. doi:10.1017/S0954579400006374

Hage, S.M., Romano, J.L., Conyne, R.K., Kenny, M., Matthews, C., Schwartz, J.P., & Waldo, M. (2007). Best practice guidelines on prevention practice, research, training, and social advocacy for psychologists. *The Counseling Psychologist, 35,* 493–566. doi:10.1177/0011000006291411

Hoffman, D. (2009). Reflecting on social emotional learning: A critical perspective on trends in the United States. *Review of Educational Research, 79,* 533–536. doi:10.3102/0034654308325184

Kelly, B., Longbottom, J., Potts, F., & Williamson, J. (2004). Applying emotional intelligence: Exploring the promoting alternative thinking strategies curriculum. *Educational Psychology in Practice, 20,* 221–240. doi:10.1080/0266736042000251808

Kenny, M.E. (2009). Verso l'avanzamento della prevenzione nel Counseling [Toward the advancement of prevention in counseling]. *Counseling: Giornale Itlaiano di Ricerca e applicazioni, 2,* 127–137.

Kenny, M.E., Horne, A.M., Orpinas, P., & Reese, L.E. (Eds.). (2009). *Realizing social justice: The challenge of preventive interventions.* Washington, DC: American Psychological Association.

Kenny, M.E., Walsh-Blair, L., Blustein, L., Bempechat, J., & Seltzer, J. (2010). Achievement motivation among urban adolescents: Work hope, autonomy support, and achievement-related beliefs. *Journal of Vocational Behavior, 77,* 205–212. doi:10.1016/j.jvb.2010.02.005

Lanciano, T., & Curci, A. (2012). L'Intelligenza emotiva predice il successo accademico? Uno studio su un campione universitario Italiano [Does emotional intelligence predict academic success? A study on an Italian university sample]. *Psychofenia, 26,* 55–68. doi:10.1285/i17201632vXVn26p55

Lapan, R.J. (2004). *Career development across the K–12 years: Bridging the present to satisfying and successful futures.* Alexandria, VA: American Counseling Association.

Larose, S., Cyrenne, D., Garceau, O., Harvey, M., Guay, F., & Deschenes, C. (2009). Personal and social support factors involved in students' decision to participate in formal academic mentoring. *Journal of Vocational Behavior, 74,* 108–116. doi:10.1016/j.jvb.2008.11.002

Lerner, R.M. (2002). *Concepts and theories of human development* (3rd ed.). Mahwah, NJ: Lawrence Erlbaum.

Liau, A.K., Liau, A.W.L., Teoh, G.B.S., & Liau, M.T.L. (2003). The case for emotional literacy: The influence of emotional intelligence on problem behaviours in Malaysian secondary school students. *Journal of Moral Education, 32,* 51–66. doi:10.1080/0305724022000073338

Márquez, P.G., Martín, R.P., & Brackett, M.A. (2006). Relating emotional intelligence to social competence and academic achievement in high school students. *Psicothema, 18,* 118–123.

Mayer, J.D., Caruso, D.R., & Salovey, P. (2005). *The Mayer-Salovey-Caruso Emotional Intelligence Test-Youth Version (MSCEIT-YV), Research Version.* Toronto, Canada: Multi-Health Systems.

Mayer, J.D., Perkins, D.M., Caruso, D.R., & Salovey, P. (2001). Emotional intelligence and giftedness. *Roeper Review: A Journal on Gifted Education, 23,* 131–137. doi:10.1080/02783190109554084

Mayer, J.D., & Salovey, P. (1997). What is emotional intelligence? In P. Salovey & D. Sluyter (Eds.), *Emotional development and emotional intelligence: Educational implications* (pp. 3–31). New York, NY: Basic Books.

Mayer, J.D., Salovey, P., & Caruso, D.R. (2000). Selecting a measure of emotional intelligence: The case of ability scales. In R. Bar-On & J.D. Parker (Eds.), *The handbook of emotional intelligence* (pp. 320–342). San Francisco, CA: Jossey Bass.

Mayer, J.D., Salovey, P., & Caruso, D.R. (2002). *Mayer-Salovey-Caruso Emotional Intelligence Test (MSCEIT): User's manual.* Toronto, Canada: Multi-Health Systems.

Mayer, J.D., Salovey, P., & Caruso, D.R. (2008). Emotional intelligence: New ability or eclectic traits? *American Psychologist, 63,* 503–517. doi:10.1037/0003-066X.63.6.503

Mestre, J.M., Guil, R., Lopes, P.N., Salovey, P., & Gil-Olarte, P. (2006). Emotional intelligence and social and academic adaptation to school. *Psicothema, 18,* 112–117.

Parker, J.D.A., Creque, R.E., Barnhart, D.L., Harris, J.I., Majeski, S.A., Wood, L.M., . . . Hogan, M.J. (2004). Academic achievement in high school: Does emotional intelligence matter? *Personality and Individual Differences, 37,* 1321–1330. doi:10.1016/j.paid.2004.01.002

Prezza, M., Trombaccia, F.R., & Armento, L. (1997). La scala dell'autostima di Rosenberg: Traduzione e validazione Italiana. *Bollettino Di Psicologia Applicata, 223,* 35–44.

Raven, C.J. (1941). Standardization of progressive matrices, 1938. *British Journal of Medical Psychology, 19,* 137–150.

Rivers, S., & Brackett, M. (2011). Achieving standards in the English language arts (and more) using the RULER approach to social and emotional learning. *Reading and Writing Quarterly, 27,* 75–100. doi:10.1080/1057356 9.2011.532715

Rivers, S., Brackett, M., & Salovey, P. (2008). Measuring emotional intelligence as a mental ability in children and adults. In G.J. Boyle, G. Matthews, & D.H. Saklofske (Eds.), *The SAGE handbook of personality theory and assessment. Volume 2: Personality measurement and assessment* (pp. 440–460). Los Angeles, CA: SAGE.

Rosenberg, M. (1965). *Society and adolescent self-image.* Princeton, NJ: Princeton University.

Salovey, P., & Mayer, J.D. (1990). Emotional intelligence. *Imagination, Cognition, and Personality, 9,* 185–211.

Savickas, M.L. (2000). Renovating the psychology of careers for the 21st century. In A. Collins & R.A. Young (Eds.), *The future of career* (pp. 53–68). New York, NY: Cambridge University Press.

Scheier, M.F., Carver, C.S., & Bridges, M.W. (1994). Distinguishing optimism from neuroticism (and trait anxiety, self-mastery, and self-esteem): A reevaluation of the life orientation test. *Journal of Personality and Social Psychology, 67,* 1063–1078. doi:10.1037/0022-3514.67.6.1063

Schutte, N.S., Malouff, J.M., Hall, L.E., Haggerty, D.J., Cooper, J.T., Golden, C.J., & Dornheim, L. (1998). Development and validation of a measure of emotional intelligence. *Personality and Individual Differences, 25,* 167–177. doi:10.1016/S0191-8869(98)00001-4

Snyder, C.R., & Lopez, S.J. (2002). *Handbook of positive psychology.* New York, NY: Oxford University Press.

Trinidad, D.R., & Johnson, C.A. (2002). The association between emotional intelligence and early adolescent tobacco and alcohol use. *Personality and Individual Differences, 32,* 95–105. doi:10.1016/S0191-*8869

Trinidad, D.R., Unger, J.B., Chou, C., & Johnson, C.A. (2004). The protective association of emotional intelligence with psychosocial smoking risk factors for adolescents. *Personality and Individual Differences, 36,* 945–954. doi:10.1016/S0191-8869

Troncone, A., Labella, A., & Drammis, L.M. (2011). Personalità, autostima e rendimento scolastico: quale relazione? [Personality, self-esteem and scholastic success: Which relation?]. *Psicologia Scolastica, 10,* 223–243.

Zeidner, M., Roberts, R.D., & Matthews, G. (2002). Can emotional intelligence be schooled? A critical review. *Educational Psychologist, 37,* 215–231. doi:10.1207/S15326985EP3704_2

CHAPTER SUMMARY: ITALY

- Emotional intelligence (EI) represents a malleable, individual factor that has been the focus of recent attention for its relationship with indices of positive development in the academic, social, behavioral, and career domains across the life span.
- EI research, assessment, and intervention have grown in Italy over the past decade.
- Research in Italy has assessed both the mixed model and ability-based model of EI.
- Research has documented the validity of the construct and has produced reliable measures of both mixed-model and ability-based EI in the Italian context.
- Overall, research in the Italian context has paralleled research in the United States by demonstrating that EI, although overlapping with personality and intelligence, is a distinct construct.
- Although further research is needed in Italy, EI can be increased through school-based intervention and has promise for contributing to success in school, social relationships, and career development.

SUGGESTED READINGS: ITALY

Bar-On, R. (2007). How important is it to educate people to be emotionally intelligent, and can it be done? In R. Bar-on, J.G. Maree, & M.J. Elias (Eds.), *Educating people to be emotionally intelligent* (pp. 1–14). Westport, CT: Praeger.

This chapter describes the Bar-On EQ-i scales and the relation of EI with multiple individual outcomes (e.g., subjective well-being, physical health, social interaction, and work and school performance). Additionally, the chapter reviews findings on programs designed to enhance EI.

Brackett, M.A., Rivers, S.E., Reyes, M.R., & Salovey, P. (2012). Enhancing academic performance and social and emotional competence with the RULER feeling words curriculum. *Learning and Individual Differences, 22*, 218–224. doi:10.1016/j.lindif.2010.10.002

This empirical article examines the influence of a social-emotional learning (SEL) program, the RULER Feeling Words Curriculum, on social, emotional, and academic competence. Participants included fifth- and sixth-grade students ($N = 273$) in the U.S. context. This study provides support for the notion that SEL programs can improve important student outcomes.

Di Fabio, A., & Kenny, M.E. (2011). Promoting emotional intelligence and career decision making among Italian high school students. *Journal of Career Assessment, 19*, 21–34. doi:10.1177/1069072710382530

This article reports findings from a study evaluating the efficacy of a training program based on the ability-based model of emotional intelligence (EI) in the Italian context. The article reviews relevant literature and provides a description of the intervention and evaluation of its efficacy among Italian high school students, including changes in EI and in decisional problems.

Di Fabio, A., & Kenny, M.E. (2012). Emotional intelligence and perceived social support among Italian high school students. *Journal of Career Development, 39*, 459–473. doi:10.1177/0894845311421005

This study examines the relationship of performance and self-report measures of EI and personality traits with perceived social support among Italian high school students. EI, as assessed by both self-report and performance-based assessment, explained social support beyond the contribution of personality traits.

29

HOPE IN STUDENTS

Theory, Measures, and Applications to Portuguese Schools

Susana C. Marques, Faculty of Psychology and Educational Sciences,
Porto University, Porto, Portugal

Shane J. Lopez, Gallup/Clifton Strengths School,
Omaha, Nebraska, USA

INTRODUCTION

Positive psychology is flourishing in Portugal. The organization of national and international scholarly meetings, the development of positive psychology courses at both the undergraduate and graduate levels, and the foundation of associations and research groups to study positive human functioning are providing visibility and value. In September 2010, positive psychologists from seven countries attended the First Portuguese Positive Psychology Congress in Lisbon. In addition, well-attended positive psychology courses are offered at several Portuguese universities, with a tenfold increase of applications since the inaugural course was offered in 2008. A recently opened master's program in positive psychology in the Technical University of Lisbon, with a respectful body of international and national lectures, was offered to students from several backgrounds, such as psychologists, economists, engineers, marketers, managers, sociologists, geographers, historians, and jurists, among others. Additionally, positive psychology content and principles are being incorporated into other professional domains (e.g., nursing, education, management, and human resources) through courses and master's and Ph.D. programs. Given this emerging interest in positive psychology in Portugal, a growing number research groups (e.g., Freire and colleagues from the University of Minho; Marques and colleagues from Porto University; Marujo and colleagues from Lisbon

University; and Rego and colleagues from University of Aveiro) are actively working with institutions and communities to promote flourishing and to contribute to an evidence-based practice of positive psychology.

HOPE IN THE SCHOOLS

Hope, the ideas and energy for the future, is one of the most potent predictors of students' success. Snyder and colleagues (1991) developed a psychological theory and cognitive motivational model of hope based in goal-directed thinking. Hope theory involves a person's capacity to (a) clearly conceptualize goals (goals thinking), (b) develop the specific strategies to reach those goals (pathways thinking), and (c) initiate and sustain the motivation for using those strategies (agency thinking). When a person has a robust level of hope, she or he will convey messages such as: "I'll find a way to get this done!"; "I can do this."; and "I am not going to be stopped." Pathways and agency thinking are stronger in high-hope than low-hope individuals, and it is especially evident when the goals are important and when people are confronted with challenges or obstacles.

Over the last 20 years, researchers have gained a clearer understanding of the relations between hope and important aspects of students' lives. About 5 years ago, a group of researchers (Marques, Pais-Ribeiro, & Lopez, 2009) initiated the study of hope among Portuguese students. They found that more hopeful students do better in school and life (better scores in school and psychological indicators) than less hopeful students, which appears to be true across countries; findings from Portuguese students are consistent with expectations for the most part (e.g., Ciarrochi, Heaven, & Davies, 2007, with Australian youths; Gilman, Dooley, & Florell, 2006, with North American youths; Merkas & Brajsa-Zganec, 2011, with Croatian children). Some of these findings are discussed in the following section (for detailed hope research with students from different countries, see Marques, Lopez, Rose, & Robinson, this volume).

Hope and Academic Indicators

Hope is positively related to academic achievement among Portuguese children and adolescents (Marques, Pais-Ribeiro, & Lopez, 2009) and predicts performance in the core subjects (i.e., Portuguese, English, and French languages, history, geography, mathematics, physics-chemistry, and natural sciences) and all subjects (core subjects plus musical, physical, visual, and technological education) as much as 2 years later (Marques, Pais-Ribeiro, & Lopez, 2011). Conversely, satisfaction with life and self-worth did not predict variance in academic achievement over and above that accounted for by hope. Furthermore, recent research suggests that very-high-hope Portuguese youths (top 10%) reported significantly higher academic achievement and school engagement (Marques, Lopez, Fontaine, Coimbra & Mitchell, in press) than youths in the average (middle 25%) and very-low-hope (bottom 10%) groups.

Based on the initial findings of Marques, Lopez, Fontaine, Coimbra, and Mitchell (2013a), students with high levels of hope at the mean age of 12 years were at a reduced risk of developing school difficulties (i.e., low levels of school engagement) at the mean age of 17. These associations remained significant after controlling for age, gender, and preexisting difficulties in school engagement at the mean age of 12. Early adolescents with lower levels of hope who experienced several stressful events had a superior risk of developing difficulties of engagement at school during early adulthood, while those with higher levels of hope and life satisfaction were not exposed to this vulnerability. Findings support that hope operates as a psychological strength during early adolescence and is associated with a reduced risk of developing adverse educational outcomes.

Hope and Social-Emotional Development

Accumulating evidence suggests that hope is positively related with self-worth, life satisfaction, and mental health among Portuguese students (e.g., Marques, Lopez, & Pais-Ribeiro, 2011; Marques, Pais-Ribeiro, & Lopez, 2007a); Marques, Pais-Ribeiro, & Lopez, 2011). Extremely high-hope students (top 10%) differ from students with average (middle 25%) and extremely low hope (bottom 10%) on self-esteem and life satisfaction, with significantly higher levels on these variables for the extremely high-hope group (Marques et al., in press). Further, extremely high and average hope are associated with mental health benefits that are not found among adolescents reporting comparatively extremely low hope levels. When specifically examining the students' mental health, only the extremely low-hope students scored in the "some of the time" range when asked if during the past 4 weeks they have been "a very nervous person," they have "felt downhearted and blue," and they have "felt so down in the dumps that nothing could cheer you up." This finding suggests that mental health distress (expressed by the mean scores "some of the time" or above on the items that measure anxiety, depression, and loss of behavioral and emotional control; e.g., Means-Christensen, Arnau, Tonidandel, Bramson, & Meagher, 2005) may exist in the extremely low-hope group, but not as much in the average and extremely high-hope groups (these students responded between "a little of the time" and "none of the time" to the same items).

Hope operates as a psychological strength during early adolescence, given that high levels of hope during early adolescence are associated with a reduced risk of developing mental health problems during early adulthood (Marques et al., 2013a). That is, Portuguese students with high levels of hope at the mean age of 12 years were at a reduced risk of developing mental health problems at the mean age of 17. These associations remained significant after controlling for age, gender, and preexisting mental health problems at the mean age of 12. Early adolescents with lower levels of hope who experienced several stressful events had an increased risk of developing mental health problems during early adulthood, while those with higher levels of hope and life satisfaction were not exposed to this vulnerability.

Preliminary research suggests that hope is related to spirituality in Portuguese adolescents but shares weak relations with religious practice (connected to "attendance at a place of worship"). The magnitude of these correlations maintains for 6 months and 1 year later (Marques, Lopez, & Mitchell, 2013). Additionally, initial findings suggest no significant differences between children's hope from families that practice and do not practice religion (Santos, 2012).

Hope, Demographics, and Social Contexts

Recent research has found that hope is unrelated to the type of family structure and living situation (Santos, 2012). However, other preliminary findings suggest that students' hope is positively correlated with parents' educational level (Marques et al., 2007b; Santos, 2012). Moreover, hope is significantly lower among students from families with both parents unemployed compared to students with one or none of the parents unemployed (Santos, 2012). Hope is unrelated to gender and age among Portuguese youths between the ages of 10 and 15 years (Marques, Pais-Ribeiro, & Lopez, 2011).

Finally, although students' hope is somewhat stable over time, with moderate 1- and 2-year test–retest coefficients (Marques, Pais-Ribeiro, & Lopez, 2011), research suggests that students' hope is malleable to change through intentional efforts, and the school context seems to be an ideal place to carry out hope-based programs/interventions (e.g., Feldman & Dreher, 2011; Lopez, Bouwkamp, Edwards, & Terramoto Pedrotti, 2000; Marques, Lopez, & Pais-Ribeiro, 2011)

MEASURING HOPE IN PORTUGUESE CHILDREN AND YOUTH

Someone who knows a child well can detect hope in action. Daily conversations, letters, stories, games, poems, diaries, and journal entries are meaningful ways to evaluate an individual's hope. Additionally, self-report measures of hope can facilitate hope assessment. We describe the two most widely used, public-domain scales that measure the trait (relatively stable personality disposition) aspects of hope.

Children's Hope Scale (CHS)

The CHS developed by Snyder, Hoza, and colleagues (1997) is a trait hope measure for children ages 8 through 16 years. The scale is composed of three agency (e.g., "I am doing just as well as other kids my age") and three pathway items (e.g., "When I have a problem, I can come up with lots of ways to solve it"). The CHS has satisfactory psychometric properties when used with physically and psychologically healthy children from public schools, boys diagnosed with attention-deficit/hyperactivity disorder, children with various medical problems, children under treatment for cancer or asthma, child burn victims, adolescents with sickle-cell disease, and early adolescents exposed to violence (Snyder, Hoza et al., 1997). Besides the original version from Snyder and colleagues (1997), the CHS has been translated and validated to Portuguese (Marques et al., 2009), Serbian (Jovanović, 2013), and Spanish languages (McDermott et al., 1997). The CHS Portuguese-language version (Marques et al., 2009) shows similar psychometric properties (reliability, factorial validity, and criterion-related validity, including the concurrent and the predictive validity) to the English-language CHS, suggesting that it measures the

Table 29.1 Portuguese Version of the Children's Hope Scale

As seis questões abaixo indicadas são sobre o que as pessoas pensam acerca de si próprias e como fazem as coisas no geral. Lê cada questão com atenção. Para cada questão, pensa como és na maioria das situações. Coloca uma cruz (X) dentro do círculo (O) que melhor te descreve. Não há respostas certas nem erradas. O que interessa é a tua opinião.

O	O	O	O	O	O
Nenhuma das vezes	Poucas vezes	Às vezes	Várias vezes	Muitas vezes	Todas as vezes

1. Penso que estou a fazer bem as coisas.

2. Consigo pensar em muitas maneiras de conseguir as coisas que considero importantes.

3. Acho que faço as coisas tão bem como as pessoas da minha idade.

4. Quando tenho um problema consigo pensar em muitas maneiras de o resolver.

5. Acho que as coisas que fiz no passado vão ajudar-me no futuro.

6. Em situações em que os outros desistem, eu sei que consigo encontrar maneiras de resolver um problema.

Note. From Marques, Pais-Ribeiro, and Lopez (2009). Copyright 2009 by S. C. Marques. Users are asked to contact S. C. Marques prior to use of the scale.

same construct in the same way. The Portuguese-language version of the CHS is shown in Table 29.1.

Adult Hope Scale (AHS)

The AHS (Snyder, Harris, et al., 1991) measures the trait aspect of hope in adolescents (and adults) ages 16 and older. This scale consists of four items measuring agency (e.g., "I energetically pursue my goals"), four items measuring pathways (e.g., "There are lots of ways around any problem"), and four distracter items. This scale has been used with a wide range of samples and has exhibited acceptable psychometric properties. Besides the original version from Snyder and colleagues (1991), the AHS has been translated and validated into different languages, including Portuguese (Marques, Lopez, Fontaine, Coimbra, & Mitchell, 2013b; Marques & Pais-Ribeiro, 2007a), Dutch (Carifio & Rhodes, 2002), French (Dube, Lapierre, Bouffard, & Labelle, 2000), Slovak (Halama, 2001), Chinese (Ho, 2003), Korean (Yun, 2003), and Arabic (Abdel-Khalek, & Snyder, 2007). The Portuguese-language version of the AHS (Marques et al., 2013b) has been validated in a large sample of Portuguese high school students and shows acceptable reliability, a two-factor structure, and additional psychometric properties similar to the English-language version. Specifically, students' hope (both global hope and the two components of agency and pathways, separately) was significantly and positively correlated with life satisfaction, psychological well-being, and academic achievement (standardized school achievement test) and negative correlated with psychological distress. See Table 29.2 for the Portuguese-language version of the AHS.

Table 29.2 Portuguese Version of the Adult Hope Scale

Leia cuidadosamente cada pergunta. Utilizando a escala abaixo mencionada, por favor seleccione o número que melhor o descreve e coloque esse número em cima do traço de cada pergunta.

1 = Totalmente Falso

2 = Quase totalmente Falso

3 = Em grande parte Falso

4 = Ligeiramente Falso

5 = Ligeiramente Verdadeiro

6 = Em grande parte Verdadeiro

7 = Quase totalmente Verdadeiro

8 = Totalmente Verdadeiro

A. Consigo pensar em várias maneiras de me desenrascar.

B. Tento alcançar incansavelmente os meus objectivos.

C. Sinto-me cansado(a) a maior parte do tempo.

D. Existem vários caminhos para ultrapassar um problema.

E. Sou facilmente dominado(a)/derrotado(a) numa discussão.

F. Consigo pensar em várias maneiras de ter as coisas que acho importantes para mim.

G. Preocupo-me com a minha saúde.

H. Mesmo quando os outros se sentem desencorajados, eu sei que posso encontrar um caminho para resolver um problema.

I. A minha experiência passada preparou-me bem para o futuro.

J. Tenho sido bem sucedido(a) na vida.

K. Normalmente ando preocupado(a) com alguma coisa.

L. Alcanço os objectivos que estabeleço para mim.

Note. The Adult Hope Scale is use with adolescents ages 16 and older. See Marques, Lopez, Fontaine, and Coimbra (2013b). Users are asked to contact S. C. Marques prior to use of the scale.

CHILDREN AND ADOLESCENTS: IDEAL TARGETS FOR HOPE-BASED INTERVENTIONS

It is theorized that children are hopeful and that they report higher hope than most adults (Snyder, 1994). Although the school years should be among the most hopeful in students' lives, recent research with a large Portuguese sample of students suggests that hope declines from late childhood (ages 10–13) to adolescence (ages 14–17; Marques & Lopez, 2013). This finding seems to imply that children and adolescents are ideal targets for group and individual hope training programs.

A Case Interview Example of a Low-Hope Student

The following short interchange involves a low-hope student who is struggling with an academic transition and illustrates how a school psychologist assesses the student's hope.

Background

Carlos is a Portuguese 15-year-old high school student who has to decide the area of study (choosing between science and technology, social-economic sciences, languages and humanities, and arts areas) he would like to follow for the next 3 years of high school. In Portugal, 10th-grade students have to choose an area of study to follow in Grades 10 through 12, and the area they choose will be determine their later university course. He is having difficulties choosing his path. He came to a school psychologist on the encouragement of his parents and has been reasonably open during the course of the interview.

School Psychologist Interview Using a Hope Perspective

The school psychologist has identified low hope in Carlos's talk, implied in the following examples: "I just can't figure out how I can do it," "I can't see a way to do the math subject," and "I am blocked." Toward the end of the first interview, the school psychologist introduces the topic of Carlos's goals.

School psychologist: *Can you explain in detail the goal that you currently are pursuing?*

Carlos: *I am interested in physical education and so I have to choose the Science and Technology area.*

School psychologist: *What obstacles do you foresee to getting into Science and Technology?*

Carlos: *My major obstacle is the Math subject included in this area. I know I will be a good teacher of physical education but I am really frustrated because I can't see a way to do the math subject. I am motivated to choose this area. I just can't figure out how I can do this subject. I am blocked!*

School psychologist: *How are you thinking to get around this obstacle?*

Carlos: *Well, I have two alternatives. Follow what I want and do this subject or give up of this area and don't reach my goal.*

School psychologist: *On a scale of 1 to 10, with 1 being not much and 10 being very strong, how motivated are you to follow this area to allow you to choose physical education in the University?*

Carlos: *Probably 10.*

School psychologist: *Ok. How do you usually go about getting what you want?*

Carlos: *I usually to get what I want when I don't give up.*

School psychologist: *What strategies have you used or, do you use to do this subject so far?*

Carlos: *I have a group of friends and we study this subject together. But it is really hard for me to get good grades on it.*

School psychologist: *How easy is for you to find other/additional strategies to reach your goal?*

Carlos: *It is not very easy for me to find more strategies. . .*

School psychologist: *Ok, let's talk about additional strategies you can work to overcome this problem and reach your goal. . .*

From this interchange, we see that Carlos's problem lies in the strategies (pathways domain) and in a barrier to achieve his goal. He has the motivation (agency domain) but foresees a major obstacle, and he lacks the pathways. Interestingly, his pathways deficiency seems to be in found strategies to be successful in the math subject and not in following the area of study. This latter insight is helpful information in selecting the appropriate strategies.

BUILDING HOPE FOR THE FUTURE

Since 2000, a growing body of research is focusing on strategies, programs, and interventions to nurture hope. These initiatives (e.g., Feldman & Dreher, 2011; Lopez, Bouwkamp, Edwards, & Terramoto Pedrotti, 2000; Marques, Lopez, & Pais-Ribeiro, 2011) have demonstrated that hope can be cultivated and that students with the least hope tend to benefit most from interventions (Bouwkamp, 2001). Research shows that virtually all students raise their hope levels when taking part in school hope programs (Lopez et al., 2000; Marques, Lopez, & Pais-Ribeiro, 2011). One of these programs to foster hope in children and youth is Building Hope for the Future, a hope-based program designed and implemented with Portuguese students (Marques, Lopez, & Pais-Ribeiro, 2011). Similar to the Making Hope Happen Program (Lopez et al., 2000), this program was designed for a group format delivered over 5 weekly sessions to help students (a) conceptualize clear goals, (b) produce numerous pathways to attainment (c) summon the mental energy to maintain the goal pursuit, and (d) reframe seemingly insurmountable obstacles as challenges to be overcome.

Building Hope for the Future (BHF) is a social-ecological program that comprises direct work with students and key stakeholders such as parents, teachers, and school peers (1 hour during the first week of the students' intervention). See Table 29.3 for the BHF program topics.

A first implementation and examination of this program with Portuguese middle school students, their parents, teachers, and school peers (Marques, Lopez, & Pais-Ribeiro, 2011) revealed that students in the intervention group increased hope, life satisfaction, and self-worth for at least 1.5 years after the program. The matched comparison group demonstrated no change in hope, life satisfaction, and self-worth from baseline to post or follow-up assessments. Results suggested that an intervention designed to foster hope in middle school students, with the collaboration of key stakeholders (parents, teachers, and peers) can produce psychological benefits by increasing hope, life satisfaction, and self-worth. These findings are consistent with previous interventions to enhance goal-directed thinking. For example, the Making Hope Happen Program (Lopez et al., 2000) produced increases in hope across different school grade levels. Moreover, BHF strongly supported the application of group-based approaches for raising the hopeful thinking of all students (e.g., the curriculum and school environment for students could be arranged and improved in the direction of supporting hopeful thinking). Finally, this intervention has the potential to address issues of efficacy, accessibility (students, teachers, and parents), and sustainability (low cost to deliver in a group setting and with 5 weeks only).

Table 29.3 Content of the Building Hope for the Future Program

Session 1: Learning About Hope

The primary goal of this session is to improve students' understanding of hope theory and its relevance to the change process and to achieve positive outcomes. This session offers the participants an overview of the topic of hope, including its three components (pathways, agency, and goals). Additionally, the central role that hope plays in daily communication is addressed by learning, identifying, and practicing the vocabulary used in the model.

Session 2: Structuring Hope

A major goal of this session is for students to learn to recognize pathways and agency components of hope, and obstacles to a goal attainment. In addition, this session aims to help students build or identify personal goals (salient and attainable) they could work with for the next 4 weeks. This session encompasses three important elements: the discussion of stories and goal-oriented characters, the brainstorm of goal-oriented ideas from the past life, and the identification of present goals they would like to work.

Session 3: Creating Positive and Specific Goals

The goals of this session are to practice the model; refine personal workable goals in order to be more specific, positive, and clear; and create multiple pathways and identify agency thoughts for each personal goal. The introduction of new narratives and group activities allows the participants to reinforce and practice the model. This session also draws on the progress of personal goals, and school psychologists can collaborate with students to adjust or modify any disparities in actions or thinking that may hinder the successful achievement of the desired goals.

Session 4: Practice Makes Perfect

The goals of this session are to (a) judge, identify, and create a "hopeful talk"; (b) reinforce the hope model; and (c) review and introduce personal workable goals in a personal hope story. Hopefulness communication patterns and hopeful communication behavior are presented and supervised in role plays to help students better identify and understand hopefulness and hopeful voices. The progress of personal goals is monitored.

Session 5: Review and Apply for the Future

The primary goal of this session is to enhance exchange of personal hope stories and to plan future steps. This session proposes that students share with the group how they implement the hope theory to their unique life experiences. Process is emphasized over achievement as well as the next steps in the goal process.

Shared Considerations Across the Five Sessions

- Each session starts with a 10-minute segment dedicated to modeling and developing enthusiasm for the program and to reinforcing ideas learned in the previous session.
- The sessions are based on the theoretical and applied work of Snyder and colleagues (e.g., Lopez et al., 2000; McDermott & Snyder, 1999; Snyder, 1994; Snyder, McDermott, Cook, & Rapoff, 2002).
- The sessions integrate solution-focused, narrative, and cognitive-behavioral techniques.
- The sessions offer psychoeducational, skills training, and group-process components and include structured activities, role playing, brainstorming, and guided discussion.
- The program is managed by adult attention to promote group cohesion, social support, the discussion of hope components, sharing thoughts and feelings with peers, and engagement in session's activities.

Session With Parents and Teachers

The direct work with parents and teachers is supported by a manual designed to (a) increase parents' and teachers' awareness of the principles of hope and enhance their goal-setting behavior and (b) promote goal-setting behavior in their children/students. The manual has three sections. The first section is dedicated to "Learning About Hope" (e.g., hope concept, research on hope, how hope can be cultivated, reflection questions). The second section is the "Instilling Hope" section, and participants are first oriented to "Hope Finding" (e.g., self-evaluation with the Hope Scale from Snyder, 1991) and next to "Hope Bonding" (how to build hopeful relationships). The third section, "Increasing Hope," is dedicated to "Hope Enhancing" (this segment provides basic steps associated with hope enhancement) and "Hope Reminding" (this segment provides strategies and practical exercises to improve their own hope and in their children/students).

Note. For more information about the *Building Hope for the Future* program, see Marques, Lopez, and Pais-Ribeiro (2011).

SPREADING HOPE

Given that hope is malleable and that the hopeless can learn to be hopeful, youth need a focused effort from people who care about them and their future. Parents are the first important agents to impact children's hope because they model hope by the way they communicate ("hopeful language" in everyday life, such as "when you finish your homework we can go out" instead of "if you can finish your homework we can go out"), set goals, view challenges, and cope with problems. In the same manner, teachers play an important role in children's perceptions about their competences to achieve goals and to cope with obstacles that can arise. For example, educators should help students to develop the capacity to think about the future in complex ways, develop flexible thinking about how to attain future goals, and renew motivation when willpower is depleted. Additionally, being a high-hope parent and teacher facilitates children's hopeful thinking, and school psychologists are well positioned to facilitate this hope transmission. The chapter summary offers some suggestions on how to refine hope with teachers and parents to enhance children's hope. For more detailed information about imparting goal setting as well as pathways and agency thinking to students, parents and teachers should see McDermott and Snyder (1999, 2000), Snyder and colleagues (2002), or Lopez, Rose, Robinson, Marques, and Pais-Ribeiro (2009).

Besides parents and teachers, others can influence children's hope, such as peer groups. It is important that parents stay in touch with these influences and be active participants in their children's interests. Hope transmission through peers' interactions should also be a focus of attention in hope development. In this regard, we suggest the inclusion of peers when adults intentionally work on children's hope.

By integrating hope into curriculum or doing separate and regular hope-enhancing sessions, the school is an ideal place to work in groups and include peers. It is possible to find ways to infuse hopeful thinking into the subject matter that children are studying. For example, history is replete with high-hope people, and students may be oriented to explore their goals, the problems that had to be overcome, and the initiative and energy it took to achieve their objectives. In literature, teachers can benefit from personal narratives and can assign short stories to illustrate the hope process. In mathematics, teachers can infuse hope and at the same time may reduce math anxiety, a problem that frequently inhibits the learning of relevant skills (Snyder, 1999). For this purpose, it is important to teach the concepts in small steps and recognize the child's comprehension of each step, giving a special emphasis on their efforts in addition to their achievements. In fact, mathematics might be one of the most strategic subjects in which the steps to enhance hope described earlier produce benefits in learning and in reducing math anxiety. Physical education is also a critical area because the goals and movement toward them are more directly perceived.

CONCLUSION

An important task for Portuguese and international researchers interested in positive psychology in the schools, and more specifically in hope, is to collect and consolidate information on how to foster positive functioning in students and schools. Cross-cultural research and systematic research beyond the United States is certainly essential to reflect on the difference that hope can make in our schools and students' lives.

REFERENCES

Abdel-Khalek, A. M., & Snyder, C. R. (2007). Correlates and predictors of an Arabic translation of the Snyder Hope Scale. *Journal of Positive Psychology, 2*, 228–235. doi:10.1080/17439760701552337

Bouwkamp, J. (2001). *Making hope happen: A program for inner-city adolescents.* Master's thesis, University of Kansas, Lawrence.

Carifio, J., & Rhodes, L. (2002). Construct validities and the empirical relationships between optimism, hope, self-efficacy, and locus of control. *Journal of Prevention, Assessment, and Rehabilitation, 19*, 125–136.

Ciarrochi, J., Heaven, P.C., & Davies, F. (2007). The impact of hope, self-esteem, and attributional style on adolescents' school grades and emotional well-being: A longitudinal study. *Journal of Research in Personality, 41*, 1161–1178. doi:10.1016/j.jrp.2007.02.001

Dube, M., Lapierre, S., Bouffard, L., & Labelle, R. (2000). Psychological well-being through the management of personal goals: A group intervention for retirees. *Revue Quebecoise de Psychologie, 21*, 255–280.

Feldman, D.B., & Dreher, D.E. (2011). Can hope be changed in 90 minutes? Testing the efficacy of a single-session goal-pursuit intervention for college students. *Journal of Happiness Studies, 13*, 745–759. doi:10.1007/s10902-011-9292-4

Gallagher, M. W. & Lopez, S. J. (2009). Positive expectancies and mental health: identifying the unique contributions of hope and optimism. *Journal of Positive Psychology, 4*, 548–556. doi:10.1080/17439760903157166

Gilman, R., Dooley, J., & Florell, D. (2006). Relative levels of hope and their relationship with academic and psychological indicators among adolescents. *Journal of Social and Clinical Psychology, 25*, 166–178. doi:10.1521/jscp.2006.25.2.166

Halama, P. (2001). The Slovak version of Snyder's Hope Scale. *Ceskoslovenska Psychologie, 45*, 135–142.

Ho, S.M.Y. (2003). *Hope in Hong Kong.* Unpublished manuscript. University of Hong Kong, China.

Jovanović, V. (2013). Evaluation of the Children's Hope Scale in Serbian adolescents: Dimensionality, measurement invariance across gender, convergent and incremental validity. *Child Indicators Research.* Online first doi:10.1007/s12187-013-9195-5

Lopez, S.J., Bouwkamp, J., Edwards, L.M., & Terramoto Pedrotti, J. (2000). *Making hope happen via brief interventions.* Paper presented at the second Positive Psychology Summit, Washington, DC.

Lopez, S.J., Rose, S., Robinson, C., Marques, S.C., & Pais-Ribeiro, J.L. (2009). Measuring and promoting hope in school children. In R. Gilman, E.S. Huebner, & M.J. Furlong (Eds.), *Handbook of positive psychology in the schools* (pp. 37–51). Mahwah, NJ: Erlbaum.

Marques, S.C., & Lopez, S.J. (2013). *Age differences and short-term stability in hope: Results from a Portuguese school sample aged 8 to 17.* Manuscript submitted for publication.

Marques, S.C., Lopez, S.J., Fontaine, A. M., Coimbra, S., & Mitchell, J. (in press). *How much hope is enough? Levels of hope and students' psychological and school functioning.* Manuscript submitted from publication.

Marques, S.C., Lopez, S.J., Fontaine, A. M., Coimbra, S., & Mitchell, J. (2013a). *Psychological strengths in early adolescence and a reduced risk of developing mental health problems and educational difficulties in early adulthood.* Communication presented at the Third World Congress on Positive Psychology, LA, United States.

Marques, S.C., Lopez, S.J., Fontaine, A. M., Coimbra, S., & Mitchell, J. (2013b). *Validation of a Portuguese version of the Adult Hope Scale.* Manuscript submitted for publication.

Marques, S.C., Lopez, S.J., & Mitchell, J. (2013). The role of hope, spirituality and religious practice in adolescents' life satisfaction: Longitudinal findings. *Journal of Happiness Studies, 14*, 251–261. doi:10.1007/s10902-012-9329-3

Marques, S.C., Lopez, S.J., & Pais-Ribeiro, J.L. (2011). "Building Hope for the Future"—A program to foster strengths in middle-school students. *Journal of Happiness Studies, 12*, 139–152. doi:10.1007/s10902-009-9180-3

Marques, S.C., Lopez, S.J., Rose, S., & Robinson, C. (2014). Measuring and promoting hope in schoolchildren. In M.J. Furlong, R. Gilman, & E.S. Huebner (Eds.), *Handbook of positive psychology in the schools* (2nd ed.). New York, NY: Taylor & Francis.

Marques, S.C., Pais-Ribeiro, J.P. & Lopez, S.J. (2007a). Validation of a Portuguese version of the Students' Life Satisfaction Scale. *Applied Research in Quality of Life, 2*, 83–94.

Marques, S.C., Pais-Ribeiro, J.L., & Lopez, S.J. (2007b). *Relationship between children's hope and guardian's hope.* Paper presented at the 10th European Congress of Psychology. Prague, Czech Republic.

Marques, S.C., Pais-Ribeiro, J.L., & Lopez, S.J. (2009). Validation of a Portuguese version of the Children's Hope Scale. *School Psychology International, 30*, 538–551. doi:10.1177/0143034309107069

Marques, S.C., Pais-Ribeiro, J.L., & Lopez, S.J. (2011). The role of positive psychology constructs in predicting mental health and academic achievement in children and adolescents: A two-year longitudinal study. *Journal of Happiness Studies, 12*, 1049–1062. doi:10.1007/s10902-010-9244-4

McDermott, D., Hastings, S.L., Gariglietti, K.P., Gingerich, K., Callahan, B., & Diamond, K. (1997). *A cross-cultural investigation of hope in children and adolescents.* Lawrence, KN: Resources in Education, CG028078.

McDermott, D., & Snyder, C.R. (1999). *Making hope happen.* Oakland, CA: New Harbinger.

McDermott, D., & Snyder, C.R. (2000). *The great big book of hope: Help your children achieve their dreams.* Oakland, CA: New Harbinger.

Peterson, S.J., Byron, K. (1997). Exploring the role of hope in job performance: Results from four studies. *Journal of Organizational Behavior, 29*, 785–803. doi:10.1002/job.492

Santos (2012). *Hope, family changes, and the school context.* Unpublished master's thesis (in Portuguese).

Snyder, C.R. (1994). *The psychology of hope: You can get there from here.* New York, NY: Free Press.

Snyder, C.R. (1999). Hope, goal blocking, thought, and test-related anxieties. *Psychological Reports, 84*, 206–208. doi:10.2466/pr0.1999.84.1.206

Snyder, C.R., Harris, C., Anderson, J.R., Holleran, S.A., Irving, L.M., Sigmon, S.T., ... Harney, P. (1991). The will and the ways: Development and validation of an individual-differences measure of hope. *Journal of Personality and Social Psychology, 60*, 570–585.

Snyder, C.R., Hoza, B., Pelham, W.E., Rapoff, M., Ware, L., Danovsky, M., ... Stahl, K.J. (1997). The development and validation of the Children's Hope Scale. *Journal of Pediatric Psychology, 22*, 399–421.

Snyder, C.R., McDermott, D., Cook, W., & Rapoff, M. (2002). *Hope for the journey* (rev. ed.). Clinton Corners, NY: Percheron.

Stern, S.L., Dhanda, R., & Hazuda, H.P. (2001). Hopelessness predicts mortality in older Mexican and European Americans. *Psychosomatic Medicine, 63*, 344–351. doi:10.1016/j.jpsychores.2009.04.007

Yun, N.M. (2003). *Translating the Hope Scale into Korean.* Unpublished manuscript, Yonsei University, Seoul, Korea.

CHAPTER SUMMARY: PORTUGAL

- Let teachers and parents know that children build hope through learning to trust in the predictability and consistency of their interactions with adults.
- Explain the importance of being firm, fair, and consistent in engendering hope among children.
- Create an atmosphere of trust in which students are responsible for their actions and supported to establish growth-inducing stretch goals.
- Emphasize that children should be recognized and rewarded for both their efforts and achievements.
- Encourage teachers and parents goals that are concrete, understandable, and are broken down into subgoals.
- Work with them to focus on long-range as opposed to short-term goals.
- Emphasize the importance of preparation and planning.
- Develop an atmosphere in which students are focused on expending effort and mastering the information rather than solely on obtaining good outcomes (e.g., high grades or stellar athletic records).
- Encourage an atmosphere of hope through a give-and-take process between teachers/parents and students.
- Teachers should be encouraged to remain engaged and invested in pursuing their own important interests and life goals outside of the classroom.
- Let teachers and parents know that being a hopeful adult has many benefits. High-hope people perform better at work (Peterson & Byron, 2008), have higher well-being (Gallagher & Lopez, 2009), and live longer (Stern, Dhanda, & Hazuda, 2001).

SUGGESTED READINGS: PORTUGAL

Marques, S.C., Lopez, S.J., Fontaine, A.M., Coimbra, S., & Mitchell, J. (in press). How much hope is enough? Levels of hope and students' psychological and school functioning. *Journal of Positive Psychology.*

This study investigates the characteristics of students who report extremely high levels of hope. Taken together, the findings support the notion that extremely high hope in students is associated with adaptive psychological and school-related functioning. Overall, given the superior adjustment profile, perhaps "enough hope" should be defined as "extremely high hope."

Marques, S.C., Lopez, S.J., & Pais-Ribeiro, J.L. (2011). "Building Hope for the Future"—A program to foster strengths in middle-school students. *Journal of Happiness Studies, 12,* 139–152. doi:10.1007/s10902-009-9180-3

This study examines the effectiveness of a 5-week hope-based intervention designed to enhance hope, life satisfaction, self-worth, mental health, and academic achievement in middle school students. Results suggest that a brief hope intervention can increase psychological strengths, and participants continue to benefit up to 18 months later.

Marques, S.C., Pais-Ribeiro, J.L., & Lopez, S.J. (2009). Validation of a Portuguese version of the Children's Hope Scale. *School Psychology International, 30,* 538–551. doi:10.1177/0143034309107069

The article describes the development of the Portuguese version of the Children's Hope Scale and the examination of its psychometric properties. The validation process of the Portuguese CHS version shows psychometric properties similar to the English-language CHS, suggesting that it measures the same construct in the same way.

Marques, S.C., Pais-Ribeiro, J.L., & Lopez, S.J. (2011). The role of positive psychology constructs in predicting mental health and academic achievement in children and adolescents: A two-year longitudinal study. *Journal of Happiness Studies, 12,* 1049–1062. doi:10.1007/s10902-010-9244-4

This longitudinal study presents the first examination of the relation between positive psychology constructs, mental health, and academic achievement of students in Portugal. The variables in the study demonstrate moderate to high stability across a 1- and 2-year time frame. Hope predicts students' academic achievement, and life satisfaction was the strongest predictor of mental health over 2 years.

30

POSITIVE PSYCHOLOGICAL INTERVENTIONS IN U.S. SCHOOLS

A Public Health Approach to Internalizing and Externalizing Problems

David N. Miller, Department of Educational and Counseling Psychology, University at Albany, State University of New York, Albany, New York, USA

Amanda B. Nickerson, Graduate School of Education, Alberti Center for Bullying Abuse Prevention, University at Buffalo, State University of New York, Buffalo, New York, USA

Shane R. Jimerson, Department of Counseling, Clinical, and School Psychology, University of California at Santa Barbara, Santa Barbara, California, USA

CONCEPTUAL FOUNDATIONS AND VALUE OF POSITIVE PSYCHOLOGY AND PUBLIC HEALTH PERSPECTIVES

The contemporary zeitgeist in the field of psychology in the United States reflects both positive psychology (Gilman, Huebner, & Furlong, 2009; Linley, Joseph, Harrington, & Wood, 2006; Peterson, 2006; Snyder & Lopez, 2007) and a public health framework (Doll & Cummings, 2008; Merrell & Buchanan, 2006; Shinn & Walker, 2010; Strein, Hoagwood, & Cohn, 2003). Positive psychology emphasizes that wellness is more than the absence of disease symptoms (Huebner & Gilman, 2003; Seligman &

478

Csikszentmihalyi, 2000) and advocates a change from a preoccupation with addressing deficits to also promoting mental health and well-being (Miller, Gilman, & Martens, 2008). The public health framework emphasizes the collective well-being of populations, including the social aspects of health and preventive education (Strein et al., 2003).

Within this framework, both risk and protective factors of populations are nested within community levels and interact with individual factors to influence risk for or protection from deleterious outcomes (Strein et al., 2003). The intersect of the positive psychology and public health frameworks is reflected in the increasing focus in the United States on the promotion of health and wellness, in contrast to an exclusive focus on the reduction of disease and disorders (Mason & Linnenberg, 1999; Masten, 2001; Miller et al., 2008).

Positive Psychology and School Psychology

Following the special millennial issue of the *American Psychologist* formally introducing positive psychology (Seligman & Csikszentmihalyi, 2000), this topic has received increasing attention from a variety of applied psychological disciplines in the United States, including school psychology (e.g., Gilman et al., 2009; Huebner & Gilman, 2003; Jimerson, Sharkey, Nyborg, & Furlong, 2004; Miller & Nickerson, 2007). School psychologists have increasingly recognized alternatives to a historical deficit-based perspective regarding assessment, practice, and research (Baker, Dilly, Aupperlee, & Patil, 2003; Chafouleas & Bray, 2004; Terjesen, Jacofsky, Froh, & DiGiuseppe, 2004). There is also an increased emphasis on promoting "developmental assets," which includes a focus on the strengths of youths, families, and communities (Scales, Benson, Leffert, & Blyth, 2000). Developmental assets have been described as "the positive relationships, opportunities, competencies, values, and self-perceptions that youth need to succeed" (Scales & Leffert, 1999, p. 1).

Wieck, Rapp, Sullivan, and Kisthardt (1989) established the term "strengths perspective" as a framework to view youths and families with greater emphasis on their strengths and competencies. The use of this approach is increasing in many disciplines and practices (Rapp, 1997; Seligman, 2002a; Seligman & Csikszentmihalyi, 2000), including school psychology (e.g., Jimerson et al., 2004; Miller, 2010; Nickerson, 2007; Wellborn, Huebner, & Hills, 2012). For instance, a strength-based approach has emerged in the mental health field (e.g., constructive therapies; Hoyt, 1996), medical field (e.g., wellness vs. illness), and in the fields of prevention and education research (e.g., resilience and hardiness; see Kaplan, 1999; Rutter, 2000). Amid a growing emphasis on ecological influences on development (e.g., Bronfenbrenner, 1989), the importance of considering contextual strengths is increasingly salient.

Public Health Perspective and School Psychology

Most children in the United States begin school at an early age and attend school for approximately 12 years. Thus, there is ample opportunity for schools to facilitate students' healthy development and adjustment. Strein and colleagues (2003) delineate specific aspects of the public health model that have particular relevance to school psychology, including (a) applying scientifically derived evidence to the delivery of psychological services, (b) strengthening positive behavior versus focusing only on decreasing problem behavior, (c) placing a strong focus on prevention as well as treatment, (d) accenting community collaboration and linked services, and (e) using research strategies that may improve the knowledge base of school psychology and provide an effective framework for evaluating school psychological services.

Strein and colleagues (2003) also describe implications for practice, research, and training when applying a public health perspective to school psychology (see Table 30.1). The basic principles can be interwoven with the considerations related to positive psychology described previously and are also reflected in the development and evaluation of school-based intervention services. The adaptation of multitier public health models for developing systems of support for students is playing an increasingly important role in the provision of mental health services for

Table 30.1 Implications for Practice, Research, and Training Under a Public Health Conceptualization of School Psychology

Under Current Typical Models	Under Public Health Conceptual Model
Professional Practice and Evaluation of Services	
• Individual as client • Work focuses on individuals • Major focus on conducting individual assessments • Nearly sole focus on students in special education or who may be "nearly eligible" for special education • Intervention activity (when done at all) focused on individually referred children (indicated interventions) • Little, if any, involvement in integrated services for children and youth • Evaluation of services is case focused (either enumerative or outcome-based)	• Population (classroom, school building, school system) as "client" • Work focused at building or systems level • Greatly reduced focus on conducting individual assessments • School psychologist for the whole school • Greater focus on schoolwide interventions or interventions for "at-risk" students (universal and selective interventions) • Greater involvement collaborating with school–community agency partnerships • Greater emphasis on population parameters (e.g., schoolwide achievement, disciplinary referrals, etc.) as outcome-based evaluation
Research	
• Focus on instrument development, instrument evaluation, and clinical-personality issues • Methodological emphasis on experimental or correlational traditions	• Greater focus on large-scale data or investigating phenomena at classroom, school, or systems levels • More inclusion of nonexperimental methodologies, such as program evaluation, context-sensitive methods, qualitative methods
Professional Preparation	
• Little emphasis on organizational psychology or systems theory • Primary emphasis on skills for individual or small-group assessment and interventions • Primary emphasis on research methodology using inferential statistics and experimental design	• Greater emphasis on organizational psychology and systems theory • Greater emphasis on systems-level (classroom, school) consultation skills and program development competencies • Greater training emphasis on program evaluation methodologies

Note. From Strein and colleagues (2003), reprinted with permission from Elsevier Science.

children and youth in U.S. schools (Doll & Cummings, 2008; Merrell, Ervin, & Gimpel Peacock, 2012; Shinn & Walker, 2010), including students with internalizing (Mazza & Reynolds, 2008; Miller, 2011) and externalizing (Furlong, Jones, Lilles, & Derzon, 2010; Swearer, Espelage, Brey Love, & Kingsbury, 2008) problems.

Conceptual Heuristic for School-Based Interventions for Internalizing and Externalizing Problems

Walker and colleagues (1996) articulate the prevention and intervention planning logic within a comprehensive, multitier framework. The three overlapping tiers represent a continuum of interventions that increase in intensity (i.e., effort, individualization, specialization) to address the needs of students and promote healthy, adaptive, and prosocial behaviors. This heuristic helps to clarify that universal intervention strategies designed to promote the development of all students in a particular population (e.g., school district; school) provide a foundation for subsequent individualized strategies aimed at targeting the specific needs of a relatively small portion of the student population (see Figure 30.1). Moreover, this heuristic is consistent with a public health perspective in that it places an emphasis on schoolwide interventions as the foundation for addressing the needs of students with internalizing and/or externalizing problems. The following section provides a discussion of promoting prosocial behaviors by using positive behavior supports and social and emotional learning programs at the universal level (e.g., schoolwide). First, however, we provide a brief description of internalizing and externalizing disorders.

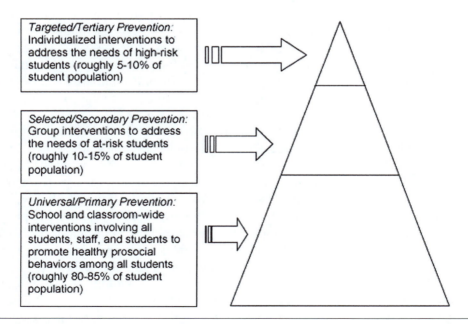

Figure 30.1 Graphic representation for considering the prevention and intervention planning logic (adapted from Walker et al., 1996).

POSITIVE PSYCHOLOGY AND UNIVERSAL PROGRAMS TO PREVENT INTERNALIZING AND EXTERNALIZING PROBLEMS

Internalizing disorders consist of problems that are based on *overcontrolled* symptoms, in the sense that individuals attempt to maintain maladaptive control or regulation of their internal emotional and cognitive states (Merrell, 2008). Characterized by a clinically significant degree of subjective distress, internalizing disorders are developed and maintained to a substantial degree within the individual. Common examples of internalizing problems include depression, anxiety, suicidal behavior, and nonsuicidal self-injury.

In contrast, externalizing disorders refer to a class of disorders that involve *undercontrolled* behavior and poor self-regulation. Examples of externalizing problems include physical aggression, antisocial behavior, bullying, and hyperactivity.

Although internalizing and externalizing problems represent two different and unique types of emotional and behavioral disorders, it is not atypical for children and adolescents to exhibit both types of problems at the same time (Merrell, 2008). Given this situation, schools are ideal venues for focused prevention and intervention efforts. However, although there is growing empirical support for the effectiveness of interventions derived from positive psychology (Seligman, Steen, Park, & Peterson, 2005), including positive psychological interventions for children and adolescents (Gilman et al., 2009), the literature on applications of positive psychology to school-based interventions is limited, particularly at the universal level.

Schoolwide Positive Behavior Support

One universal intervention that has been effectively implemented in schools is school-wide positive behavior support (SWPBS), which may be particularly useful for preventing and responding to externalizing behavior problems. SWPBS is an intervention model that clearly fits within a positive psychology framework (Carr, 2007; Sawka-Miller & Miller, 2007), especially in the area of creating psychologically healthy educational environments (Baker et al., 2003) and positive schools (Huebner, Gilman, Reschly, & Hall, 2009; Snyder & Lopez, 2007). Both positive psychology and SWPBS have a common goal: to promote optimal human functioning and enhance quality of life.

SWPBS has been defined as "a systems approach for establishing the social culture and individualized behavior supports needed for a school to be a safe and effective learning environment for all students" (Sugai & Horner, 2009, p. 309). The goal of SWPBS is to facilitate the academic achievement and healthy prosocial development of children and youth in an environment that is safe and conducive to learning (Sugai & Horner, 2009), a goal that is clearly consistent with positive psychology. SWPBS is a proactive program that emphasizes direct intervention approaches (e.g., teaching expectations, monitoring student performance, providing specific and immediate feedback) in multiple settings (e.g., classrooms, cafeteria, buses, hallways) throughout an entire school (Sprague & Horner, 2012). There are seven key features of SWPBS, including (a) define three to five schoolwide expectations for appropriate behavior, (b) actively teach the school-wide behavioral expectations to all students, (c) monitor and acknowledge students for engaging in behavioral expectations, (d) correct problem behaviors using a consistently administered continuum of behavioral consequences, (e) gather and use information about student behavior to evaluate and guide decision making, (f) obtain leadership of schoolwide practices from an administrator committed to providing adequate support and resources, and (g) procure district-level support (Sprague & Horner, 2012).

Studies have shown that SWPBS is related to reductions in problem behavior and office discipline referrals as well as improved academic performance, organizational health, and perceptions of safety (Horner, Sugai, & Anderson, 2010; Irvin, Tobin, Sprague, Sugai, & Vincent, 2004; Sprague & Horner, 2012). Moreover, research suggests that SWPBS is effective for decreasing antisocial behavior in suburban (Metzler, Biglan, Rusby, & Sprague, 2001), urban (McCurdy, Mannella, & Norris, 2003), and alternative schools (Miller, George, & Fogt, 2005), as well as in a variety of nonclassroom settings (Newcomer, Colvin, & Lewis, 2009). SWPBS may also be a useful component in preventing internalizing problems such as child and adolescent depression (Herman, Merrell, & Reinke, 2004).

For SWPBS to be effectively implemented and sustained, it is critical that strong, effective leadership occur and that leaders work with staff to develop a shared and clear vision of the need for change and how to accomplish it (George, White, & Schlaffer, 2007; McIntosh, Horner, & Sugai, 2009). A strong rationale and vision "allow for clearly articulated terminal goals, coordination among school staff to achieve the goals, standards against which to judge future success, and a plan for the dispersal of resources" (George et al., 2007, p. 47). Other issues that need to be addressed in implementing SWPBS include organizational restructuring (George et al., 2007), treatment integrity and program evaluation (Miller & Sawka-Miller, 2011), and possible barriers to implementation and how to overcome them (McIntosh et al., 2009). Patience is warranted, given that effective implementation of SWPBS requires sustained commitments and efforts of school personnel for multiple years (McIntosh et al., 2009).

Finally, although frequently not acknowledged explicitly in the SWPBS literature, the use of teachers' verbal praise of students and the subsequent enhancement of positive relationships between these two groups are critical elements in the successful implementation of SWPBS (Sawka-Miller & Miller, 2007). Maag (2001) has described how rates of verbal praise and other forms of positive reinforcement provided by teachers to students steadily decrease as children grow older. Research suggests, however, that teachers should maintain at least a 5:1 ratio between positive and negative or neutral statements toward students to create a highly disciplined, supportive, and effective classroom environment (Flora, 2000). Creating a positive school environment is a critical element in reducing the "sea of negativity" (Jenson, Olympia, Farley, & Clark, 2004, p. 67) and excessively punitive practices that may be observed in schools (Maag, 2001). This emphasis on creating stronger, healthier, more positive relationships is an integral component of SWPBS as well as an important variable for promoting positive psychology in the schools (Sawka-Miller & Miller, 2007).

Social and Emotional Learning Programs

Another universal program that has received increased attention in recent years is social and emotional learning (SEL). The term "social and emotional learning" "has been used to describe a variety of skill-based universal prevention programs that emphasize skill development in a variety of domains (e.g., self-awareness, social awareness, responsible decision making, self-management, and relationship management) to build competence in relationships, self-control, healthy values, and resistance to engagement in deviant or dangerous behaviors" (Merrell et al., 2012, p. 215). In contrast to universal applications of positive behavior support, which are particularly valuable for preventing and responding to students' externalizing problems, SEL programs may be particularly useful as a universal program for more effectively preventing and responding to internalizing problems, such as depression and anxiety (Merrell, 2008; Merrell & Gueldner, 2010a). A major premise of SEL programs is that social-emotional skills can be taught and learned, much like academic skills such as reading and math (Merrell & Gueldner, 2010a). A recent meta-analysis involving more than 270,000 students from kindergarten through high school concluded that, in comparison to controls, students in SEL programs demonstrated significantly improved social and emotional skills, attitudes, behavior, and academic performance (Durlak, Weissberg, Dymnicki, Taylor, & Schellinger, 2011).

One example of a universal SEL program is Strong Kids: a social and emotional learning curriculum designed to promote resiliency and coping skills for students in pre-kindergarten through Grade 12 (e.g., Merrell, Carrizales, Feuerborn, Gueldner, & Tran, 2007; Merrel, Parisi, & Whitcomb, 2007; Merrell, Whitcomb, & Parisi, 2009). Designed to deliver content that is sensitive to children's development, the curriculum series consists of five volumes across multiple grade levels. The Strong Kids curricula can be used with entire schools or classrooms and can be implemented without the assistance of mental health professionals such as school psychologists and school counselors. Content of the curricula is scripted to decrease preparation time, increase the ease with which the program is implemented, and ensure that foundational elements and content are delivered as intended (Merrell & Gueldner, 2010a).

Strong Kids is based on Cowen's (1994) concept of the five pathways of promoting wellness, including (a) experiencing healthy attachment, (b) developing age-appropriate competencies, (c) coping with stress, (d) having exposure to settings that promote wellness, and (e) experiencing a sense of empowerment regarding one's own fate. There is also an emphasis within Strong Kids on modifying students' irrational thoughts that may be contributing to internalizing problems such as depression and anxiety. In particular, students participate in instruction and learn emotion identification as experienced by themselves and others, are taught to understand the link between thoughts and emotions, learn to identify irrational thoughts and replace them with more appropriate and adaptive thoughts, learn relaxation techniques and ways to manage stress, and learn problem-solving and goal-setting skills (Merrell & Gueldner, 2010a).

Strong Kids is a fairly recent addition to SEL programs, and initial research on its efficacy for promoting students' mental health is promising (e.g., Merrell, 2010; Merrell, Juskelis, Tran, & Buchanan, 2008), although more research is clearly needed. For more information on Strong Kids and SEL programs, see works by Merrell and colleagues (Merrell, 2008; Merrell & Gueldner, 2010a, 2010b).

POSITIVE PSYCHOLOGY AND SELECTED AND
TARGETED INTERVENTIONS

A public health framework recognizes that even with universal interventions, selected interventions are needed for the 5 to 15% of students at risk for emotional and behavioral problems, and targeted interventions are indicated for the additional 1 to 7%

of students who experience chronic emotional and behavioral problems (Sprague & Walker, 2005). For purposes of brevity, this section describes interventions that may be used for students at both these tiers, although it should be noted that the intensity of the intervention depends on the unique needs of the student. The following section describes interventions consistent with a positive psychological framework for externalizing problems, followed by a summary of selected areas from positive psychology that can be incorporated into treatment for children and adolescents with internalizing problems.

Interventions for Externalizing Problems

Externalizing behaviors include acting-out behaviors that are aggressive, argumentative, and noncompliant (Gresham, Lane, MacMillan, & Bocian, 1999). Although the typical response to these behaviors is the application of sanctions, such as suspension, there is increased interest in more positive behavioral interventions (Chin, Dowdy, Jimerson, & Rime, 2012). An example of a positive strategy that can be used to address externalizing behavior in the classroom is the Good Behavior Game. This involves identifying target behaviors (with student input), posting rules, and dividing the class into two teams that play the game for a specified interval of instruction. The team that has the fewest fouls or, alternatively, each team that has less than a predetermined number of fouls during the interval, wins a brief activity prize. The Good Behavior Game may be used in general or special education classrooms as well as with particular groups of students and has been shown to be effective in reducing externalizing behaviors in children (Embry, 2002; McGoey, Schneider, Rezzetano, Prodan, & Tankersley, 2010) and adolescents (Kleinman & Saigh, 2011).

Because many students with emotional and behavioral disorders become disengaged from school and eventually drop out, interventions have been developed to enhance the connection that children and adolescents have with school (Cheney et al., 2009; Sinclair, Christenson, Lehr, & Anderson, 2003). For instance, Check & Connect is a comprehensive intervention designed to promote school engagement through relationship building, problem solving, and persistence by having school "monitors" work with at-risk students on these areas (Anderson, Christenson, Sinclair, & Lehr, 2004; Sinclair et al., 2003). Persistence is an essential element of the program, and monitors are involved with students for a minimum of 2 years, even if the student changes schools within the district or county (Sinclair et al., 2003). Students assigned to Check & Connect have been found to be more likely to attend school, stay on track to graduate, and be rated as more competent by teachers than students in control groups (Anderson et al., 2004; Sinclair et al., 2003).

Cheney and colleagues (2009) evaluated the effects of Check, Connect, and Expect, which combines Check & Connect with the Behavior Education Program so that students not only have a check-in with an adult but also carry a card and receive feedback from every teacher about their behavior. Results indicated that the intervention resulted in three problem behaviors returning to normative levels for the 60% of students who completed the program, although similar improvements were not found for social skills or academic achievement (Cheney et al., 2009).

Students exhibiting chronic externalizing behaviors are in need of intensive interventions that are individualized, focus on developing desirable behaviors, and maximize environmental supports. Functional behavioral assessment (FBA) and the resulting behavioral intervention plans (BIPs) are consistent with these goals. The first step in completing a BIP, which is a targeted intervention for students with the most severe behavior problems, is to conduct an FBA. An FBA involves gathering information about antecedents, behaviors, and consequences to determine the function (i.e., reason) of behavior. Once the function of behavior is identified, interventions such as manipulating antecedents, altering consequences, and teaching alternative skills using behavioral principles are implemented in a BIP (Steege & Watson, 2009). The Individuals with Disabilities Education Act (2004) recommends FBAs and BIPs for all students with severe behavior problems and requires them if a student is suspended for more than 10 days in a school year. A recent meta-analysis investigating the effectiveness of individualized positive support interventions revealed large effects in reducing students' problem behaviors and increasing their skills regardless of disability status (Goh & Bambara, 2012).

Another evidence-based intervention for children and adolescents with externalizing problems that is highly consistent with positive psychology principles is multisystemic therapy (MST; Henggeler, Schoenwald, Rowland, & Cunningham, 2002). MST works with the systems in a child's life, such as the family and peer group, to develop the relationships that potentially serve as protective factors. A critical factor in achieving long-term outcomes is empowering caregivers to serve as change agents for their children by identifying factors that interfere with their ability to provide the necessary nurturance, monitoring, and discipline for their child. The MST team then draws on the strengths of the caregiver (e.g., supportive extended family, social skills) to address these factors and facilitate the implementation of planned interventions (Henggeler et al., 2002). MST has been found to be successful in reducing problem behaviors, residential placement, and rearrest rates for students with chronic and severe behavior problems (Henggeler et al., 2002), as well as increasing family cohesion, adaptability, and interactions (Bourduin et al., 1995). For a thorough review of MST findings, see Henggeler (2011).

Interventions for Internalizing Problems

Internalizing behavior problems are characterized by subjective distress and typically inhibited responses to stimuli that may reflect social withdrawal, depression, or anxiety (Gresham et al., 1999). Although there are a number of positive psychology constructs that are applicable for school-based psychotherapy for such problems (see Miller & Nickerson, 2007), the following discusses the constructs of hope, optimism, and mindfulness due to their particular relevance for the treatment of internalizing problems in children and youth.

Hope and optimism are highly similar constructs and their overlap is considerable, although hope appears to be more emotional and optimism more purely expectational (Peterson & Seligman, 2004). Both correlate highly with mental health and happiness, cause better resistance to depression following negative or aversive events, and lead to improved physical health (Seligman, 2002b). In addition, higher levels of hope can protect against early school dropout among adolescents (Worrell & Hale, 2001) and provide a buffer against negative life events (Valle, Huebner, & Suldo, 2006).

Hope therapy attempts to help individuals conceptualize clear goals, see numerous paths to these goals, and garner the energy and commitment to reach them (Snyder, Lopez, Shorey, Rand, & Feldman, 2003). Hope has been used as an intervention with both children and adults in individual and group contexts (Snyder et al., 2003; Snyder, Rand, & Sigmon, 2002). Working with clients in therapy to enhance their hopeful thinking has been found to lead to decreased depression and anxiety as well as increased coping skills and level of well-being (Keyes & Lopez, 2002).

Similar to hope, optimism can be learned, modified, and strengthened (Seligman, 1998). People who attribute negative events to external, unstable, and specific causes are generally optimistic, whereas those who exhibit internal, stable, and global causes are generally pessimistic (Peterson & Seligman, 2004). Research has suggested that building optimism by recognizing and disputing pessimistic, irrational thoughts can reduce stress and increase satisfaction with work and play (Seligman, 2002b). However, results from a recent meta-analysis indicated that hope interventions had only limited success increasing life satisfaction and no evidence of reducing psychological distress (Weis & Speridakos, 2011).

Seligman and his colleagues (1995, 1998) have developed an approach for teaching optimism to children that has been shown to prevent depression and increase optimism, with impressive long-term outcomes. The Penn Optimism Program (POP; Shatté, Gillham, & Reivich, 2000) is a 12-week school-based group intervention curriculum that is an outgrowth of Seligman's work. The cognitive component of POP introduces participants to the relations between underlying beliefs and inaccurate ways of thinking. It also teaches children to dispute irrational beliefs and generate worst-case, best-case, and most-likely scenarios to situations, thereby expanding the arena of possible solutions for the purpose of maximizing optimism. The skills training component of POP involves teaching assertiveness and negotiation, countering procrastination, decision-making skills, and combining these skills with more optimistic thinking in a comprehensive problem-solving model (Shatté et al., 2000).

POP has been found to significantly reduce depressive symptoms and improve classroom behavior for children at risk for depression in a treatment group as compared to a control group (Jaycox, Reivich, Gillham, & Seligman, 1994). Now known as the Penn Resiliency Program (Gillham & Reivich, 2004), subsequent research has continued to support its efficacy for promoting hope and optimism (Gillham, Hamilton, Freres, Patton, & Gallop, 2006; Winder & Seligman, 2006) and reducing depressive symptoms (Brunwasser, Gillham, & Kim, 2009) in children and youth.

Another positive psychology construct that has direct relevance to treatment for children and adolescents with internalizing problems is mindfulness, or being consciously aware of and experiencing the present moment (Perticone, 2007). Mindfulness exercises have three key and interdependent elements: (a) awareness, (b) of present experience, (c) with acceptance (Germer, 2005). Segal, Williams, and Teasdale (2013) used mindfulness-based cognitive therapy as a procedure for treating adult depression for clients who initially benefited from cognitive therapy but later required further psychotherapeutic intervention to prevent relapse. One method they used was the Three-Minute Breathing Space, which involves (a) acknowledging and registering one's experience, even if it is unwelcome, (b) gently redirecting one's full attention to breathing as a method for focusing on the present moment, and (c) expanding the field of awareness around one's breathing so that it includes a sense of the body as a whole.

Mindfulness training has been used to successfully treat a variety of disorders and problems (Germer, Siegel, & Fulton, 2005), particularly adult depression (Morgan, 2005; Segal et al., 2013), anxiety (Brantley, 2003; Hayes, Follette, & Linehan, 2004), and self-injury (Walsh, 2012). Although research examining the use of mindfulness with children and adolescents is limited (Burke, 2010), it does appear to be a promising intervention. For example, results of a recent randomized trial with outpatient adolescents supported the effectiveness of mindfulness-based stress reduction in reducing internalizing symptoms and increasing psychosocial functioning (Biegel, Brown, Shapiro, & Schubert, 2009).

CONCLUSION

Interventions that focus on the full spectrum of human behavior, including both student deficits and strengths, are increasingly emerging in U.S. schools (Froh, Huebner, Youseef, & Conte, 2011). Moreover, applications of positive psychology in the schools appear to have a promising future (Miller, 2010). In this chapter, school-based positive psychological interventions for students' internalizing and externalizing problems were described within the context of a public health perspective, in which interventions are provided to students at multiple levels depending on their specific needs—a model of service delivery that is having a considerable and growing impact on schools in the United States (Merrell et al., 2012; Shinn & Walker, 2010). When evidence-based interventions are applied with appropriate levels of treatment integrity and intensity, incorporating positive psychological interventions within a public health framework can potentially lead to enhanced levels of social, emotional, and behavioral functioning for all students, including students exhibiting internalizing and externalizing problems.

REFERENCES

Anderson, A.R., Christenson, S.L., Sinclair, M.F., & Lehr, C.A. (2004). Check & Connect: The importance of relationships for promoting engagement with school. *Journal of School Psychology, 42*, 95–113. http://dx.doi.org/10.1016/j.jsp.2004.01.002

Baker, J.A., Dilly, L.J., Aupperlee, J.L., & Patil, S.A. (2003). The developmental context of school satisfaction: Schools as psychologically healthy environments. *School Psychology Quarterly, 18*, 206–221. http://dx.doi.org/10.1521/scpq.18.2.206.21861

Biegel, G.M., Brown, K.W., Shapiro, S.L., & Schubert, C.M. (2009). Mindfulness-based stress reduction for the treatment of adolescent psychiatric outpatients: A randomized clinical trial. *Journal of Consulting and Clinical Psychology, 77*, 855–866. http://dx.doi.org/10.1037/a0016241

Bourduin, C.M., Mann, B.J., Cone, L.T., Henggeler, S.W., Fucci, B.R., Blaske, D.M., & Williams, R.A. (1995). Multisystemic treatment of serious juvenile defenders: Long–term prevention of criminality and violence. *Journal of Consulting and Clinical Psychology, 63*, 569–578.

Brantley, J. (2003). *Calming your anxious mind: How mindfulness and compassion can free you from anxiety, fear, and panic.* Oakland, CA: New Harbinger.

Bronfenbrenner, U. (1989). Ecological system theories. *Annals of Child Development, 6*, 149–187.

Brunwasser, S.M., Gillham, J.E., & Kim, E.S. (2009). A meta-analytic review of the Penn Resiliency Program's effect on depressive symptoms. *Journal of Consulting and Clinical Psychology, 77*, 1042–1054. http://dx.doi.org/10.1037/a0017671

Burke, C.A. (2010). Mindfulness-based approaches with children and adolescents: A preliminary review of current research in an emergent field. *Journal of Child and Family Studies, 19*, 133–144. http://dx.doi.org/10.1007/s10826-009-9282-x

Carr, E.G. (2007). The expanding vision of positive behavior support: Research perspectives on happiness, helpfulness, hopefulness. *Journal of Positive Behavior Interventions, 9*, 3–14. http://dx.doi.org/10.1177/10983007070 090010201

Chafouleas, S.M., & Bray, M.A. (2004). Introducing positive psychology: Finding a place within school psychology. *Psychology in the Schools, 16*, 1–5. http://dx.doi.org/10.1002/pits.10133

Cheney, D.A., Stage, S.A., Hawken, L.S., Lynass, L., Mielenz, C., & Waugh, M. (2009). Two year outcome study of Check, Connect, and Expect intervention for students at risk for severe behavior problems. *Journal of Emotional and Behavioral Disorders, 17*, 226–243. http://dx.doi.org/10.1177/1063426609339186

Chin, J.K., Dowdy, E., Jimerson, S.R., & Rime, W.J. (2012). Alternatives to suspensions: Rationale and recommendations. *Journal of School Violence, 11*, 156–173. http://dx.doi.org/10.1080/15388220.2012.652912

Cowen, E.L. (1994). The enhancement of psychological wellness: Challenges and opportunities. *American Journal of Community Psychology, 22*, 149–179. http://dx.doi.org/10.1007/BF02506861

Doll, B., & Cummings, J.A. (Eds.). (2008). *Transforming school mental health services: Population-based approaches to promoting the competency and wellness of children.* Thousand Oaks, CA: Corwin Press.

Durlak, J.A., Weissberg, R.P., Dymnicki, A.B., Taylor, R.D., & Schellinger, K.B. (2011). The impact of enhancing students' social and emotional learning: A meta-analysis of school-based universal interventions. *Child Development, 82*, 405–432. http://dx.doi.org/10.1111/j.1467-8624.2010.01564.x

Embry, D.D. (2002). The Good Behavior Game: A best practice candidate as a universal behavioral vaccine. *Clinical Child and Family Psychology Review, 5*, 273–297. http://dx.doi.org/10.1023/A:1020977107086

Flora, S.R. (2000). Praise's magic reinforcement ratio: Five to one gets the job done. *The Behavior Analyst Today, 1*, 64–69.

Froh, J.J., Huebner, E.S., Youseef, A., & Conte, V. (2011). Acknowledging and appreciating the full spectrum of the human condition: School psychology's (limited) focus on positive psychological functioning. *Psychology in the Schools, 48*, 110–123. http://dx.doi.org/10.1002/pits.20530

Furlong, M.J., Jones, C., Lilles, E., & Derzon, J. (2010). Think smart, stay safe: Aligning elements within a multilevel approach to school violence prevention. In M.R. Shinn & H.M. Walker (Eds.), *Interventions for achievement and behavior problems in a three-tier model including RTI* (pp. 313–336). Bethesda, MD: National Association of School Psychologists.

George, M.P., White, G.P., & Schlaffer, J.J. (2007). Implementing school-wide behavior change: Lessons from the field. *Psychology in the Schools, 44*, 41–51. http://dx.doi.org/10.1002/pits.20204

Germer, C.K. (2005). Teaching mindfulness in therapy. In C.K. Germer, R.D. Siegel, & P.R. Fulton (Eds.), *Mindfulness in psychotherapy* (pp. 113–129). New York, NY: Guilford.

Germer, C.K., Siegel, R.D., & Fulton, P.R. (2005). *Mindfulness and psychotherapy.* New York, NY: Guilford.

Gillham, J.E., Hamilton, J., Freres, D.R., Patton, K., & Gallop, R. (2006). Preventing depression among early adolescents in the primary care setting: A randomized controlled study of the Penn Resiliency Program. *Journal of Abnormal Child Psychology, 34*, 203–219. http://dx.doi.org/10.1007/s10802-005-9014-7

Gillham, J., & Reivich, K. (2004). Cultivating optimism in childhood and adolescence. *Annals of the American Academy of Political and Social Science, 591*, 146–163. http://dx.doi.org/10.1177/0002716203260095

Gilman, R., Huebner, E.S., & Furlong, M.J. (Eds.). (2009). *Handbook of positive psychology in schools.* New York, NY: Routledge.

Goh, A.E., & Bambara, L.M. (2012). Individualized positive behavior support in school settings: A meta–analysis. *Remedial and Special Education, 33*, 271–286. http://dx.doi.org/10.1177/0741932510383990

Gresham, F.M., Lane, K.L., MacMillan, D.L., & Bocian, K.M. (1999). Social and academic profiles of externalizing and internalizing groups: Risk factors for emotional and behavioral disorders. *Behavioral Disorders, 24*, 231–245.

Hayes, S.C., Follette, V.M., & Linehan, M.M. (Eds.). (2004). *Mindfulness and acceptance: Expanding the cognitive-behavioral tradition.* New York, NY: Guilford.

Henggeler, S.W. (2011). Efficacy studies to large-scale transport: The development and validation of multisystemic therapy programs. *Annual Review of Clinical Psychology, 7*, 351–381. http://dx.doi.org/10.1146/annurev-clinpsy-032210-104615

Henggeler, S.W., Schoenwald, S.K., Rowland, M.D., & Cunningham, P.B. (2002). *Serious emotional disturbance in children and adolescents: Multisystemic therapy.* New York, NY: Guilford.

Herman, K.C., Merrell, K.W., & Reinke, W.M. (2004). The role of school psychology in preventing depression. *Psychology in the Schools, 41*, 763–775. http://dx.doi.org/10.1002/pits.20016

Horner, R.H., Sugai, G., & Anderson, C.M. (2010). Examining the evidence base for school-wide positive behavior support. *Focus on Exceptional Children, 42*, 1–16.

Hoyt, M. (1996). *Constructive therapies* (Vol. 2). New York, NY: Guilford.

Huebner, E.S., & Gilman, R. (2003). Toward a focus on positive psychology in school psychology. *School Psychology Quarterly, 18*, 99–102. http://dx.doi.org/10.1521/scpq.18.2.99.21862

Huebner, E.S., Gilman, R., Reschly, A.J., & Hall, R.W. (2009). Positive schools. In S.J. Lopez & C.R. Snyder (Eds.), *Oxford handbook of positive psychology* (2nd ed., pp. 651–658). Oxford, UK: Oxford University Press. http://dx.doi.org/10.1093/oxfordhb/9780195187243.013.0053

Individuals with Disabilities Education Act of 2004, H.R. 1350, 108th Cong. (2004) [Electronic Version].

Irvin, L.K., Tobin, T.J., Sprague, J.R., Sugai, G., & Vincent, C.G. (2004). Validity of office discipline referrals measures as indices of school-wide behavioral status and effects of school-wide behavioral interventions. *Journal of Positive Behavior Interventions, 6*, 131–147. http://dx.doi.org/10.1177/10983007040060030201

Jaycox, L.H., Reivich, K.J., Gillham, J.E., & Seligman, M.E.P. (1994). Prevention of depressive symptoms in school children. *Behaviour Research and Therapy, 32*, 801–816. http://dx.doi.org/10.1016/0005-7967(94)90160-0

Jenson, W.R., Olympia, D., Farley, M., & Clark, E. (2004). Positive psychology and externalizing students in a sea of negativity. *Psychology in the Schools, 41*, 67–79. http://dx.doi.org/10.1002/pits.10139

Jimerson, S.R., Sharkey, J., Nyborg, V., & Furlong, M. (2004). Strength-based assessment and school psychology: A summary and synthesis. *The California School Psychologist, 9*, 9–19.

Kaplan, H. (1999). Toward an understanding of resilience: A critical review of definitions and models. In M. Glantz & J. Johnson (Eds.), *Resilience and development: Positive life adaptations* (pp. 17–83). New York, NY: Plenum.

Keyes, C.L.M., & Lopez, S.J. (2002). Toward a science of mental health: Positive directions in diagnosis and interventions. In C.R. Snyder & S.J. Lopez (Eds.), *Handbook of positive psychology* (pp. 45–59). New York, NY: Oxford University Press.

Kleinman, K.E., & Saigh, P.A. (2011). The effects of the Good Behavior Game on the conduct of regular education New York City high school students. *Behavior Modification, 35*, 95–105. http://dx.doi.org/10.1177/0145445510392213

Linley, A.P., Joseph, S., Harrington, S., & Wood, A. M. (2006). Positive psychology: Past, present, and (possible) future. *Journal of Positive Psychology, 1*, 3–16. http://dx.doi.org/10.1080/17439760500372796

Maag, J.W. (2001). Rewarded by punishment: Reflections on the disuse of positive reinforcement in schools. *Exceptional Children, 67*, 173–186.

Mason, M.J., & Linnenberg, D.M. (1999). Applying public science to the counselling profession: An initial examination. *British Journal of Guidance and Counselling, 27*, 527–537.

Masten, A. (2001). Ordinary magic: Resilience process in development. *American Psychologist, 56*, 227–238. http://dx.doi.org/10.1037/0003-066X.56.3.227

Mazza, J.J., & Reynolds, W.M. (2008). School-wide approaches to prevention of and treatment for depression and suicidal behaviors. In B. Doll & J.A. Cummings (Eds.), *Transforming school mental health services: Population-based approaches to promoting the competency and wellness of children* (pp. 213–241). Thousand Oaks, CA: Corwin Press.

McCurdy, B.L., Mannella, M.C., & Norris, E. (2003). Positive behavior support in urban schools: Can we prevent the escalation of antisocial behavior? *Journal of Positive Behavior Interventions, 5*, 158–170. http://dx.doi.org/10.1177/10983007030050030501

McGoey, K.E., Schneider, D.L., Rezzetano, K.M., Prodan, T., & Tankersley, M. (2010). Classwide intervention to manage disruptive behavior in the kindergarten classroom. *Journal of Applied School Psychology, 26*, 247–261. http://dx.doi.org/10.1080/15377903.2010.495916

McIntosh, K., Horner, R.H., & Sugai, G. (2009). Sustainability of systems-level evidence-based practices in schools: Current knowledge and future directions. In W. Sailor, G. Dunlap, G. Sugai, & R. Horner (Eds.), *Handbook of positive behavior support* (pp. 327–352). New York, NY: Springer. http://dx.doi.org/10.1007/978-0-387-09632-2_14

Merrell, K.W. (2008). *Helping students overcome depression and anxiety: A practical guide* (2nd ed.). New York, NY: Guilford.

Merrell, K.W. (2010). Linking prevention science and social and emotional learning: The Oregon Resiliency Project. *Psychology in the Schools, 47*, 55–70.

Merrell, K.W., & Buchanan, R. (2006). Intervention selection in school-based practice: Using public health models to enhance systems capacity of schools. *School Psychology Review, 35*, 167–180.

Merrell, K.W., Carrizales, D., Feuerborn, L., Gueldner, B.A., & Tran, O.K. (2007). *Strong Kids: A social and emotional learning curriculum.* Baltimore, MD: Brookes.

Merrell, K.W., Ervin, R.A., & Gimpel Peacock, G. (2012). *School psychology for the 21st century: Foundations and practices* (2nd ed.). New York, NY: Guilford.

Merrell, K.W., & Gueldner, B.A. (2010a). Preventive interventions for students with internalizing disorders: Effective strategies for promoting mental health in schools. In M.R. Shinn & H.M. Walker (Eds.), *Interventions for achievement and behavior problems in a three-tier model including RTI* (pp. 799–823). Bethesda, MD: National Association of School Psychologists.

Merrell, K.W., & Gueldner, B.A. (2010b). *Social and emotional learning in the classroom: Promoting mental health and academic success.* New York, NY: Guilford.

Merrell, K.W., Juskelis, M.P., Tran, O.K., & Buchanan, R. (2008). Social and emotional learning in the classroom: Evaluation of Strong Kids and Strong Teens on students' social-emotional knowledge and symptoms. *Journal of Applied School Psychology, 24,* 209–224. http://dx.doi.org/10.1080/15377900802089981

Merrell, K.W., Parisi, D., & Whitcomb, S. (2007). *Strong Start—Grades K–2: A social and emotional learning curriculum.* Baltimore, MD: Brookes.

Merrell, K.W., Whitcomb, S., & Parisi, D. (2009). *Strong Start—Pre–K: A social and emotional learning curriculum.* Baltimore, MD: Brookes.

Metzler, C.W., Biglan, A., Rusby, J.C., & Sprague, J.R. (2001). Evaluation of a comprehensive behavior management program to improve school-wide positive behavior support. *Education and Treatment of Children, 24,* 448–479.

Miller, D.N. (2010). Assessing internalizing problems and well-being. In G. Gimpel Peacock, R.A. Ervin, E.J. Daly III, & K.W. Merrell (Eds.), *Practical handbook of school psychology: Effective practices for the 21st century* (pp. 175–191). New York, NY: Guilford.

Miller, D.N. (2011). *Child and adolescent suicidal behavior: School-based prevention, assessment, and intervention.* New York, NY: Guilford.

Miller, D.N., George, M.P., & Fogt, J.B. (2005). Establishing and sustaining research-based practices at Centennial School: A descriptive case study of systemic change. *Psychology in the Schools, 42,* 553–567. http://dx.doi.org/10.1002/pits.20091

Miller, D.N., Gilman, R., & Martens, M.P. (2008). Wellness promotion in the schools: Enhancing students' mental and physical health. *Psychology in the Schools, 45,* 5–15. http://dx.doi.org/10.1002/pits.20274

Miller, D.N., & Nickerson, A.B. (2007). Changing the past, present, and future: Potential applications of positive psychology in school-based psychotherapy with children and youth. *Journal of Applied School Psychology, 24,* 147–162. http://dx.doi.org/10.1300/J370v24n01_08

Miller, D.N., & Sawka-Miller, K.D. (2011). Beyond unproven trends: Critically evaluating school-wide programs. In T.M. Lionetti, E. Snyder, & R.W. Christner (Eds.), *A practical guide to developing competencies in school psychology* (pp. 141–154). New York, NY: Springer. http://dx.doi.org/10.1007/978-1-4419-6257-7_9

Morgan, S.P. (2005). Depression: Turning toward life. In C.K. Germer, R.D. Siegel, & P.R. Fulton (Eds.), *Mindfulness and psychotherapy* (pp. 130–151). New York, NY: Guilford.

Newcomer, L., Colvin, G., & Lewis, T.J. (2009). Behavior supports in nonclassroom settings. In W. Sailor, G. Dunlap, G. Sugai, & R. Horner (Eds.), *Handbook of positive behavior support* (pp. 497–520). New York, NY: Springer. http://dx.doi.org/10.1007/978-0-387-09632-2_21

Nickerson, A.B. (2007). The use and importance of strength-based assessment. *School Psychology Forum, 2,* 15–25.

Perticone, E.X. (2007). *The art of being better.* Springfield, IL: Charles C. Thomas.

Peterson, C. (2006). Strengths of character and happiness: Introduction to special issue. *Journal of Happiness Studies, 7,* 289–291. http://dx.doi.org/10.1007/s10902-005-3645-9

Peterson, C., & Seligman, M.E.P. (2004). *Character strengths and virtues: A handbook and classification.* Washington, DC: American Psychological Association.

Rapp, C.A. (1997). Preface. In D. Saleeby (Ed.), *The strengths perspective in social work practice* (pp. iv–x). New York, NY: Longman.

Rutter, M. (2000). Resilience reconsidered: Conceptual considerations, empirical findings, and policy implications. In J.P. Shonkoff & S.J. Meisels (Eds.), *Handbook of early childhood intervention* (pp. 651–682). New York, NY: Cambridge University Press. http://dx.doi.org/10.1017/CBO9780511529320.030

Sawka-Miller, K.D., & Miller, D.N. (2007). The third pillar: Linking positive psychology and school-wide positive behavior support. *School Psychology Forum, 1*(3), 27–39.

Scales, P.C., Benson, P.L., Leffert, N., & Blyth, D.A. (2000). Contribution of developmental assets to the prediction of thriving among adolescents. *Applied Developmental Science, 4,* 27–46. http://dx.doi.org/10.1207/S1532480XADS0401_3

Scales, P.C., & Leffert, N. (1999). *Developmental assets: A synthesis of the scientific research on adolescent development.* Minneapolis, MN: Search Institute.

Segal, Z.V., Williams, J.M.G., & Teasdale, J.D. (2013). *Mindfulness-based cognitive therapy for depression* (2nd ed.). New York, NY: Guilford.

Seligman, M.E.P. (1998). *Learned optimism.* New York, NY: Pocket Books.

Seligman, M.E.P. (2002a). Positive psychology, positive prevention, and positive therapy. In C.R. Snyder & S.J. Lopez (Eds.), *Handbook of positive psychology* (pp. 3–9). New York, NY: Oxford University Press.

Seligman, M. E. P. (2002b). *Authentic happiness: Using the new positive psychology to realize your potential for lasting fulfillment.* New York, NY: Free Press.

Seligman, M. E. P., & Csikszentmihalyi, M. (2000). Positive psychology: An introduction [Special Issue]. *American Psychologist, 55,* 5–14. http://dx.doi.org/10.1037/0003-066X.55.1.5

Seligman, M. E. P., Reivich, K., Jaycox, L., & Gillham, J. (1995). *The optimistic child.* New York, NY: Houghton Mifflin.

Seligman, M. E. P., Steen, T. A., Park, N., & Peterson, C. (2005). Positive psychology progress: Empirical validation of interventions. *American Psychologist, 60,* 410–421. http://dx.doi.org/10.1037/0003-066X.60.5.410

Shatté, A. J., Gillham, J. E., & Reivich, K. (2000). Promoting hope in children and adolescents. In J. E. Gillham (Ed.), *The science of optimism and hope* (pp. 215–234). Philadelphia, PA: Templeton Foundation Press.

Shinn, M. R., & Walker, H. M. (Eds.). (2010). *Interventions for achievement and behavior problems in a three-tier model including RTI.* Bethesda, MD: National Association of School Psychologists.

Sinclair, M. F., Christenson, S. L., Lehr, C. A., & Anderson, A. R. (2003). Facilitating student engagement: Lessons learned from Check & Connect longitudinal studies. *The California School Psychologist, 8,* 29–41.

Snyder, C. R., & Lopez, S. J. (2007). *Positive psychology: The scientific and practical explorations of human strengths.* Thousand Oaks, CA: Sage.

Snyder, C. R., Lopez, S. J., Shorey, H. S., Rand, K. L., & Feldman, D. B. (2003). Hope theory, measurements, and applications to school psychology. *School Psychology Quarterly, 18,* 122–139.

Snyder, C. R., Rand, K. L., & Sigmon, D. R. (2002). Hope theory. In C. R. Snyder & S. J. Lopez (Eds.), *Handbook of positive psychology* (pp. 257–276). New York, NY: Oxford University Press. http://dx.doi.org/10.1521/scpq.18.2.122.21854

Sprague, J. R., & Horner, R. H. (2012). School-wide positive behavioral interventions and supports. In S. R. Jimerson, A. B. Nickerson, M. J. Mayer, & M. J. Furlong (Eds.), *Handbook of school violence and school safety: International research and practice* (2nd ed., pp. 447–462). Mahwah, NJ: Erlbaum.

Sprague, J. R., & Walker, H. M. (2005). *Safe and healthy schools: Practical prevention strategies.* New York, NY: Guilford.

Steege, M. W., & Watson, T. S. (2009). *Conducting school-based functional behavioral assessments* (2nd ed.)*: A practical guide.* New York, NY: Guilford.

Strein, W., Hoagwood, K., & Cohn, A. (2003). School psychology: A public health perspective I. Prevention, populations, and, systems change. *Journal of School Psychology, 41,* 23–38. http://dx.doi.org/10.1016/S0022-4405(02)00142-5

Sugai, G., & Horner, R. H. (2009). Defining and describing schoolwide positive behavior support. In W. Sailor, G. Dunlap, G. Sugai, & R. Horner (Eds.), *Handbook of positive behavior support* (pp. 307–326). New York, NY: Springer. http://dx.doi.org/10.1007/978-0-387-09632-2_13

Swearer, S. M., Espelage, D. L., Brey Love, K., & Kingsbury, W. (2008). School-wide approaches to intervention for school aggression and bullying. In B. Doll & J. A. Cummings (Eds.), *Transforming school mental health services: Population-based approaches to promoting the competency and wellness of children* (pp. 187–212). Thousand Oaks, CA: Corwin Press.

Terjesen, M. D., Jacofsky, M., Froh, J., & DiGiuseppe, R. (2004). Integrating positive psychology into schools: Implications for practice. *Psychology in the Schools, 41,* 163–172. http://dx.doi.org/10.1002/pits.10148

Valle, M. F., Huebner, E. S., & Suldo, S. M. (2006). An analysis of hope as a psychological strength. *Journal of School Psychology, 44,* 393–406. http://dx.doi.org/10.1016/j.jsp.2006.03.005

Walker, H. M., Horner, R. H., Sugai, G., Bullis, M., Sprague, J. R., Bricker, D., & Kaufman, M. J. (1996). Integrated approaches to preventing antisocial behavior patterns among school-age children and youth. *Journal of Emotional and Behavioral Disorders, 4,* 194–209. http://dx.doi.org/10.1177/106342669600400401

Walsh, B. W. (2012). *Treating self-injury* (2nd ed.)*: A practical guide.* New York, NY: Guilford.

Weis, R., & Speridakos, E. C. (2011). A meta-analysis of hope enhancement strategies in clinical and community settings. *Psychology of Well-being: Theory, Research, and Practice, 1*:5. http://dx.doi.org/10.1186/2211-1522-1-5

Wellborn, C., Huebner, E. S., & Hills, K. J. (2012). The effects of strength-based assessment information on teachers of diverse learners. *Child Indicators Research, 5,* 357–374. http://dx.doi.org/10.1007/s12187-011-9133-3

Wieck, A., Rapp, C., Sullivan, W. P., & Kisthardt, S. (1989). A strengths perspective for social work practice. *Social Work, 34,* 350–354.

Winder, B., & Seligman, M. E. P. (2006). Depression prevention for early adolescent girls: A pilot study of all girls versus coed groups. *Journal of Early Adolescence, 26,* 110–126. http://dx.doi.org/10.1177/0272431605282655

Worrell, F. C., & Hale, R. L. (2001). The relationship of hope in the future and perceived school climate to school completion. *School Psychology Quarterly, 16,* 370–388. http://dx.doi.org/10.1521/scpq.16.4.370.19896

CHAPTER SUMMARY: UNITED STATES

- School-based prevention programs and interventions derived from positive psychology can be integrated with and correspond well to a public health framework.
- A public health approach to school-based interventions includes universal interventions for all students, selected interventions for at-risk students, and targeted interventions for students exhibiting particular internalizing (e.g., depression; anxiety) or externalizing (e.g., conduct disorder, attention-deficit hyperactivity disorder) problems. Consequently, interventions are provided to students at multiple levels based on their unique and individual needs.
- Schoolwide positive behavior support and social and emotional learning programs are positive psychological interventions that can be potentially effective universal strategies for reducing externalizing and internalizing problems, respectively.
- Positive psychological interventions for students exhibiting or at risk for externalizing problems include the Good Behavior Game, Check and Connect, and multisystemic therapy.
- Positive psychological interventions for students exhibiting or at risk for internalizing problems include the Penn Resiliency Program and mindfulness training.

SUGGESTED READINGS: UNITED STATES

Doll, B., & Cummings, J. A. (Eds.). (2008). *Transforming school mental health services: Population-based approaches to promoting the competency and wellness of children.* Thousand Oaks, CA: Corwin Press.

This book takes a public health approach to mental health services in the schools, including useful chapters addressing internalizing and externalizing problems.

Merrell, K. W., & Gueldner, B. A. (2010). *Social and emotional learning in the classroom: Promoting mental health and academic success.* New York, NY: Guilford.

This book describes how social and emotional learning programs can be effectively implemented in schools at multiple levels.

Miller, D. N., & Nickerson, A. B. (2007). Changing the past, present, and future: Potential applications of positive psychology in school-based psychotherapy with children and youth. *Journal of Applied School Psychology, 24,* 147–162. http://dx.doi.org/10.1300/J370v24n01_08

This journal article discusses several potential applications of positive psychology to a variety of internalizing and externalizing behavior problems.

Sprague, J. R., & Horner, R. H. (2012). School-wide positive behavioral interventions and supports. In S. R. Jimerson, A. B. Nickerson, M. J. Mayer, & M. J. Furlong (Eds.), *Handbook of school violence and school safety: International research and practice* (2nd ed., pp. 447–462). Mahwah, NJ: Erlbaum.

This chapter in an edited book provides a highly useful and practical overview of school-wide positive behavior support in school settings.

Strein, W., Hoagwood, K., & Cohn, A. (2003). School psychology: A public health perspective I. Prevention, populations, and, systems change. *Journal of School Psychology, 41,* 23–38. http://dx.doi.org/10.1016/S0022-4405(02)00142-5

This frequently cited journal article provides an overview and rationale for conceptualizing psychological interventions in schools from a public health perspective.

Section V

Perspective

31

POSITIVE PSYCHOLOGY IN SCHOOLS
Good Ideas Are Never Enough

Collie W. Conoley, Jane C. Conoley, Kathryn Z. Spaventa-Vancil, and Anna N. Lee, Counseling, Clinical, and School Psychology Department, Gevirtz Graduate School of Education, University of California Santa Barbara, Santa Barbara, California USA

IMPLEMENTATION OF POSITIVE PSYCHOLOGY IN SCHOOLS: GOOD IDEAS ARE NEVER ENOUGH

Twenty years of applied research in positive psychology and this volume of excellent school-based interventions could change the education system for children. Unfortunately, a chasm exists between effective positive psychology research findings and successful school-based implementation—a chasm caused not only by ignorance of new programs but also by the lack of attention to program implementation challenges. Teachers, parents, principals, consultants, and staff members must traverse the distance between the best answer and the disturbing needs armed with state-of-the-art information about positive psychology and innovation dissemination. This chapter is about helping schools implement positive psychology principles and interventions like those in this handbook. Knowing about positive psychology programs is a necessary but insufficient guarantee of success. If merely knowing about an effective program were sufficient to cause implementation, the only challenge at hand would be information dissemination. Clearly this is not the case. Better mousetraps exist. Many unused evidence-based programs are catalogued online for ease of access (e.g., What Works Clearinghouse, National Registry of Effective Programs). The bad news remains that many effective programs are not adopted.

In this chapter, we examine issues about implementation. Implementation concerns, models, examples, and suggestions are presented.

POLICY

The policies that directly relate to education in the United States are the state regulating agencies and learned society standards for teachers and school psychologists. The standards will be examined based on their implicit requirements for the skills and knowledge related to the field of positive psychology. Many of the standards require professionals to incorporate new research findings into their work, which would include keeping abreast of the research within the field of positive psychology. Such knowledge is vital because of linkages to student academic performance and well-being.

Positive psychology is concerned with studying the "conditions and processes that contribute to the flourishing and optimal functioning of people, groups and institutions" (Gable & Haidt, 2005, p. 104). The study of positive individual traits includes a focus on high talent and interpersonal skill as well as on character strengths and virtues (Seligman & Csikszentmihalyi, 2000). At the group level, it is about such things as citizenship, work ethic, and responsibility (Seligman & Csikszentmihalyi, 2000). Positive psychology can be involved in education by focusing on "encouraging and rewarding the multitude of talents and strengths a child has" (Linley, Joseph, Maltby, Harrington, & Wood, 2009, p. 39); seeking to promote students' subjective well-being and cognitive and academic competencies; establishing protective factors within the school environment; and providing "a 'wellness' focus that has the potential to expand conceptualizations of schooling, students, and educational processes" (Huebner, Gilman, Reschly, & Hall, 2009, p. 566).

The National Board for Professional Teaching Standards has five core propositions that inform all of the subsequent standards for the 25 certificate areas. These propositions are (a) teachers are committed to students and their learning, (b) teachers know the subjects they teach and how to teach those subjects to students, (c) teachers are responsible for managing and monitoring student learning, (d) teachers think systematically about their practice and learn from experience, and (e) teachers are members of learning communities (National Board for Professional Teaching Standards, 2002). The first proposition is directly related to the field of positive psychology in that National Board Certified Teachers (NBCTs) are concerned with character development and civic responsibility (National Board for Professional Teaching Standards, 2002). Additionally, the first proposition requires a concern on teachers' behalf regarding their students' self-concepts. Positive psychology skills and knowledge are more implicit in propositions 4 and 5, in which NBCTs must incorporate new findings into their practice (proposition four) and must learn how to work collaboratively with parents to engage them in their students' educational experiences (proposition 5).

The National Council for Accreditation for Teacher Education (NCATE) has unit standards, program standards, and professional development school standards. NCATE unit standards are composed of six dimensions, which help "identify the knowledge, skills, and professional dispositions expected of educational professionals" (National Council for Accreditation for Teacher Education, 2008, p. 10). The six unit standards are (a) candidate knowledge, skills, and professional dispositions; (b) assessment system and unit evaluation; (c) field experiences and clinical practice; (d) diversity; (e) faculty qualifications, performance, and development; and (f) unit governance and resources (National Council for Accreditation for Teacher Education, 2008). Each unit standard is correlated to rubrics that describe different elements and levels of the standard. Standard 1, regarding candidate knowledge, skills, and disposition, is most implicitly related to positive psychology skills and knowledge. This standard states that target (ideal) candidates "consider school, family and community contexts in connecting concepts to students' prior experience" (National Council for Accreditation for Teacher Education, 2008, p. 18). Target candidates also should have a "positive effect on learning for all students" (Standard 1d), should use research to improve learning in the classroom (Standard 1e), establish supportive learning environments (Standard 1f), and "demonstrate classroom behaviors that create caring and supportive learning environments (National Council for Accreditation for Teacher Education, 2008, pp. 19–20). Additionally, Standard 5d requires target candidates to model best practices by providing leadership at the school, state, national, and international levels. The program standards are specific to each specialized professional association (e.g., computer science, early childhood education) but reflect the six core unit standards.

The National Association of School Psychologists (NASP) has put together four documents that comprise the NASP 2010 standards. These documents include *Standards for Graduate Preparation of School Psychologists, Standards for the Credentialing of School Psychologists, Principles for Professional Ethics,* and the *Model for Comprehensive and Integrated School Psychological Services* (National Association for School Psychologists, n.d.). The Standards for Preparation of School Psychologists and for the Credentialing of School Psychologists have related elements that implicitly suggest knowledge of positive psychology and a skill set related to positive psychology would be beneficial. Both standards address the need for school psychologists to have knowledge of interventions and mental health services to develop social and life skills (Domain 2.4), knowledge of prevention, crisis intervention, and mental health (Domain 2.5 for graduate preparation and Domain 2.7 for training and credentialing), and both require school psychologists to have knowledge of how to use family strengths to create home-to-school-to-community collaborations (Domain 2.7 for graduate preparation and Domain 2.8 for training and credentialing; National Association for School Psychologists, 2000a, 2000b). These comprise the direct and indirect services component for children, families, and schools, included in the comprehensive model of school psychologist services (National Association for School Psychologists, 2010).

The policy statements of NCATE and NASP broadly support the same goals as positive psychology. Unfortunately, however, explicit calls for implementing interventions based on positive psychology do not exist in the policies.

PRESERVICE TRAINING

The amount of information and training of positive psychology in the teacher training programs can be considered an indicator of readiness for implementation. Unfortunately, explications of positive psychology are almost completely absent in the top teacher training sites in the United States or the textbooks in teacher training. We examined the curriculum and university-wide course offerings at the top rated teacher-education programs listed in the *U.S. News and World Report* 2013 website (http:// grad-schools.usnews.rankingsandreviews.com/best-graduate-schools/top-education-schools/edu-rankings) for evidence of positive psychology classes. Only one of the 20 programs listed a teacher-education requirement of a positive psychology class. Finding only one of the leading schools teaching positive psychology suggests that new teachers are unlikely candidates to lead in the implementation effort of positive psychology. A small rainbow exists in a discouragingly gloomy sky, however: 18 of the 20 universities with the top colleges of education have at least one positive psychology course at the university. The preservice teacher trainees might take a positive psychology course as an elective.

Another metric of examining the amount of exposure to positive psychology occurring in college teacher training programs relies on examining the textbooks. While positive psychology classes for teachers are rare, a possibility remains that positive psychology may be infused into the basic teacher education classes. Indeed, examining the leading texts in philosophy of education, history of education, and educational psychology, the typical core coursework for teacher training, did not reveal any mention of positive psychology. One volume of the philosophical foundations of education with a 2012 publication date contained a discussion section on the "controversial issue" of whether morality, character, or values education should be the responsibility of the school.

Our final investigation of positive psychology's acceptance into mainstream education was made by examining the program of the 2012 AERA Conference. Only one presentation dealt with positive psychology. The combination of analyses into standards, coursework, and existing textbooks suggests that a scarcity of positive psychology knowledge exists for preservice teachers in current departments of education.

Because we found no proximal indicators that widespread implementation of positive psychology interventions or philosophy was on the horizon, we turned to implementation models for schools. That is, assuming that teachers do not enter their professions proficient in applying positive psychology research findings to their practices, can they benefit from inservice programs and/or school reform approaches? The next section describes an implementation model and how it could be helpful for positive psychologists.

IMPLEMENTATION MODELS

Fortunately, models that translate, disseminate, and implement research are emerging (Elliott & Mihalic, 2004; Schoenwald & Hoagwood, 2001). Models such as the National Implementation Research Network (NIRN; Fixsen, Naoom, Blase, Friedman, & Wallace, 2005), the RE-AIM group (Glasgow, Vogt, & Boles, 1991), and the Interactive Systems Framework for Dissemination and Implementation (ISF; Wandersman et al., 2008) facilitate identification of key aspects of supporting school change in increasing detail. Our chapter uses the ISF model to present the implementation strategies of positive psychology into schools because of the systemic fit and past use of the model with schools (e.g., Moceri, Elias, Fishman, Pandina, & Reyes-Portillo, 2012). Other approaches might be as efficacious. Our view is that a systematic approach implemented with fidelity is the key to change.

The ISF (Wandersman et al., 2008) was developed for youth violence and child mal-treatment prevention to increase the implementation of evidence-based remedial and prevention programs. The model contains three systems to move research to practice; the Synthesis and Translation System, the Support System, and the Delivery System.

The Synthesis and Translation System prepares the research-generated information into a form acceptable for field implementation. Acceptability is enhanced by clarify-ing the research results and intervention procedures in language and methods useful to teachers, parents, and children. Another outcome of this process is to ascertain if the likely intervention is appropriate for the available population.

The Support System develops both the capacity of the school generally and specifi-cally to implement the positive psychology innovation. Innovation-specific capacity building is assistance developing the knowledge and skills specific to the positive psy-chology innovation. General capacity building of the school enhances the infrastructure, skills, and motivation of an organization more globally.

The Delivery System enacts the innovative positive psychology program in the school and monitors the quality of application. For the successful dissemination and imple-mentation of innovations, the ISF model specifies that each of the three systems must succeed.

Wandersman and his colleagues (2008) acknowledge the importance of the larger context of macro-policies and funding, but their model makes favorable assumptions about the context. We shall attempt to address some of the larger contextual issues in schools that affect implementation. Additionally, they acknowledge the importance of a recursive model that includes the schools informing the researchers about important issues. Unfortunately, the ISF does not address the importance of practice informing theory development.

IMPLEMENTATION EXAMPLES

The good news is that examples of positive psychology implementation in schools exist. The process can occur. While isolated classroom interventions are important, our focus is on implementation of positive psychology more broadly into a school so that the culture and identity of the school are transformed. Perhaps the best-documented implementa-tion of a positive psychology program comes from Martin Seligman's book, *Flourish* (2011), in which he describes the transformation of Geelong Grammar School, a private residential school in Australia. Geelong Grammar School engaged in a comprehensive intervention that included the teachers, support staff, and leadership to infuse current curriculum as well as develop new classes. The project involved a wealthy school invit-ing Seligman and 16 other experts to revise the curriculum. By Seligman's account, the 100 members of the faculty and skeptical headmaster were won over by a 9-day course, which initially taught the participants to use the skills in their own personal and pro-fessional lives. The course was followed by several trainers staying in residence for the year, with visiting scholars supporting the development. The curriculum has standalone courses, visiting scholar lectures, and embedded units within the regular curriculum.

The context that allowed for implementation was ideal. The resources were almost unlimited. And the charge was to implement positive psychology so that well-being was a priority for the students. Therefore, the larger context within which the school resided and the funding for positive psychology implementation provided an excellent first step.

The Synthesis and Translation group that prepared the research generated information for Geelong Grammar School from their previous research and applications was ideal as well. The group was experienced and had tested the material previously. The research in positive psychology was transformed into a curriculum acceptable to and ready for school staff, parents, and children.

The Support System team in the ISF framework develops both the capacity of the school generally and specifically to implement the positive psychology innovation. General capacity building of the school enhances the infrastructure, skills, and motivation of an organization more globally. No information was provided about the functioning of the school, but the impression was that the school was functioning well and the Geelong staff members were proud of their abilities as well as the accomplishments of the prominent private school. Perhaps, however, because the school was highly successful, the headmaster was experienced as skeptical of the positive psychology innovations that were on the horizon. Apparently, the board of directors did not include the headmaster in the decision to implement positive psychology, thus inviting at least some resistance. Accomplishing innovation-specific capacity building includes not only developing the knowledge and skills specific to the positive psychology implementation but also establishing the motivation and acceptability of the change. Alliances with headmasters or principals are mandatory for implementation. Although teachers most often are actual implementers of innovation, they require the support and encouragement of school leadership. This is vital because teachers spend the most time with children compared to all other school personnel and are relied upon to enact the curriculum, policies, and philosophy with fidelity over long periods of time.

The difficult step of motivating and forming an alliance with the headmaster and teachers was accomplished by having them experience positive psychology interventions personally. The experience of personal and professional growth via the interventions created important alliances between the implementation team and the school staff (Seligman, 2011). The 100 members of the faculty and the skeptical headmaster were won over by a 9-day course.

The Delivery System team facilitates the enactment of the curriculum and monitors the quality of application. The 9-day course was followed by a team staying in residence for the year, enhanced with visiting scholars supporting the development. The changed curriculum contained stand-alone courses, visiting scholar lectures, and embedded units within the regular curriculum. The highlighted events are the signature strength interventions, gratitude interventions, a cognitive intervention addressing adversity, using 3:1 positive communication in relationships, and embedding attention to growth or success in classroom activities.

The Geelong Grammar School Project provides an exciting example of implementation in a private school in which the policy makers could dictate and financially support change. The project provides an example of what can be done in an ideal situation. The headmaster, teachers, and other personnel were trained together on site. Trainers remaining in residence supported the initial training, which is an ideal model to maintain fidelity and motivation.

Several of the chapter authors have an experience of implementing positive psychology in an elementary school in the United States that was not under such ideal circumstances. The context was a partnership between an elementary school that was under a federal mandate to reorganize because of poor academic performance and a university. The elementary school students were more than 90% economically disadvantaged, more than 70% English Language Learners and nearly 95% ethnic minority. The implementation began with a mixture of determination, failure, threat, and hope. The sequence of change was initiated by the principal's dedication to change, willingness to raise community financial support, and her request for support from our college. The University of California Santa Barbara Gevirtz School of Education responded with cooperation by joint planning to identify goals.

The ISF model can be used to describe this successful implementation of positive psychology. Importantly, however, this change occurred in a context without an abundance of financial and training resources as well as historical prestige and high-achieving students.

The Synthesis and Translation group from the college prepared the research-generated information for elementary school. The group was experienced and had used the material previously. The research in positive psychology was transformed into a curriculum acceptable to and ready for school staff, parents, and children.

The Support System team needed to develop the general capacity of the school. Inservice training enhanced the infrastructure, skills, and motivation of the school. Many teachers were disheartened because the school had been labeled underperforming for many years, which reflected poorly upon their teaching. The experience of failure left them less flexible. The principal provided leadership and active involvement in supporting efforts for general and implementation-specific preparation. Very little time, however, was available for specific training of philosophy and skills. Most of the positive psychology skills and philosophy were communicated via consultation.

The Delivery System team facilitated the enactment of the interventions and monitored the quality of application. The team was in the school for 2 years. Enactment was noted as variable among teachers. However, students' gains on the annual standardized state assessments progressed at a rate rivaled by only one other school in the state.

Several unfortunate events followed. The principal and lead counselor of the elementary school retired. The community funding for the project disappeared. A problem with the implementation model became obvious. The sustainability of novel interventions and philosophy becomes vulnerable when the leadership changes. The larger context could not sustain change when similarly minded leadership was not available.

Excitement over examples of what could be done does not mean that positive psychology will be implemented in any large scale. None of the indicators reviewed in the first section of the chapter indicate that schools will assimilate or accommodate to positive psychology theory or interventions. Hope for implementation can be generated, however, if we have pathways and agency (Snyder et al., 2002). Reading the contributions in this volume testifies to your agency (goal-directed energy); the next section continues with suggesting pathways (routes to the goal).

IMPLEMENTATION VIA CREATING THE CONTEXT

Creating possible routes to implementation can begin the process not only of hope but also of action. As we are fond of saying at positive psychology workshops, take one idea from all those presented to apply for self-change. Systemic thinkers know the first change begins with you and grows through your interaction with others. The following are recommendation for creating a larger context to support sustainable, broadly based implementation. We hope that you the reader will identify one that you can apply.

1. Include symposia on strategies of school implementation at positive psychology conferences. Make special efforts to invite educational professionals in particular to copresent or function as discussants. Gain commitment from the audience to apply one idea to implement positive psychology in their local schools.
2. Present positive psychology interventions and philosophy at AERA and other education conferences.
3. Perform translation of positive psychology research as suggested by the ISF implementation model. Provide applicability and accessibility of interventions for schools. Write a chapter in a philosophy of education, history of education, and/or educational psychology text.
4. When doing a workshop, paper, or research project, involve a professor from a department of education. In the collaboration, the professor could become an advocate and teach the interventions and philosophy in teacher training classes. Volunteer to guest lecture in education classes.
5. Similarly, work with state education credentialing agencies. Collaboration could eventually yield policy changes and broad advocacy for positive psychology. Perhaps even funding could be developed to pilot changes in standards.
6. Include school priorities as the context for exploring your positive psychology research agenda. For example, examine interventions in the context of graduation rates for struggling minority students, increased performance on basic reading or math scores, increase interest in science, technology, engineering, and mathematics areas, or increase teacher health, persistence, or performance.
7. Write opinion columns to your local and regional newspapers presenting the interventions and philosophy of positive psychology.

CONCLUSION

The examples of successful implementations in schools do spread the knowledge of positive psychology. The examples inspire and provide models. The challenge remains that implementation remains limited, occurring in isolated sites rather than as systematic growth. Sustainability remains problematic as long as hoped-for systemic change is actually quite dependent on charismatic leadership. Charisma is not easily replaced.

With the growing number of positive psychology interventions and demonstrations of implementation, the time has come for the strategic transformation of colleges of education, parent organizations, and the school systems. A strategic movement of information into the leadership of teacher training conferences, textbooks, research journals, and the leading teacher training programs needs to occur. A parallel strategy should occur with administrator training programs, journals, texts, and conferences, as well as state, local, and national policy makers. Committing to the well-being of our children is a great virtue worthy of persistent pursuit.

REFERENCES

Elliott, D.S., & Mihalic, S. (2004). Issues in disseminating and replicating effective prevention programs. *Prevention Science, 5,* 47–52. doi:10.1023/B:PREV.0000013981.28071.52

Fixsen, D.L., Naoom, S.F., Blase, K.A., Friedman, R.M., & Wallace, F. (2005). *Implementation research: A synthesis of the literature.* Tampa, FL: University of South Florida, Louis de la Parte Florida Mental Health Institute, The National Implementation Research Network.

Gable, S.L., & Haidt, J. (2005). What (and why) is positive psychology? *Review of General Psychology, 9,* 103–110. doi:10.1037/1089-2680.9.2.103

Glasgow, R.E., Vogt, T.M., & Boles, S. (1999). Evaluating the public health impact of health promotion interventions: The RE-AIM framework. *American Journal of Public Health, 89,* 1323–1327. doi:10.2105/AJPH.89.9.1322

Huebner, E.S., Gilman, R., Reschly, A.L., & Hall, R. (2009). Positive schools. In S.J. Lopez & C.R. Snyder (Eds.), *Oxford handbook of positive psychology* (2nd ed., pp. 561–568). New York, NY: Oxford University Press.

Linley, P.A., Joseph, S., Maltby, J., Harrington, S., & Wood, A.W. (2009). Positive psychology applications. In S.J. Lopez & C.R. Snyder (Eds.), *Oxford handbook of positive psychology* (2nd ed., pp. 35–48). New York, NY: Oxford University Press.

Moceri, D.C., Elias, M.J., Fishman, D.B., Pandina, R., & Reyes-Portillo, J.A. (2012). The urgency of doing: Assessing the system of sustainable implementation model via the schools implementing towards sustainability (SITS) scale. *Journal of Community Psychology, 40,* 501–519. doi:10.1002/jcop.21477

National Association for School Psychologists. (n.d.). *NASP professional standards (adopted in 2010).* Retrieved from http://www.nasponline.org/standards/2010standards.aspx

National Association for School Psychologists. (2000a). *National Association for School Psychologists: Standards for graduate preparation of school psychologists.* Retrieved from http://www.nasponline.org/standards/2010 standards.aspx

National Association for School Psychologists. (2000b). *National Association for School Psychologists: Standards for training and field placement programs in school psychology, standards for the credentialing of school psychologists.* Retrieved from http://www.nasponline.org/standards/2010standards.aspx

National Association for School Psychologists. (2010). *Model for comprehensive and integrated school psychological services.* Retrieved from http://www.nasponline.org/standards/2010standards.aspx

National Board for Professional Teaching Standards. (2002, August). *What teachers should know and be able to do.* Retrieved from http://www.nbpts.org/five-core-propositions

National Council for Accreditation for Teacher Education. (2008, February). *Professional standards for the accreditation of teacher preparation institutions.* Retrieved from http://www.ncate.org/Standards/tabid/107/Default.aspx

Schoenwald, S.K., & Hoagwood, K. (2001). Effectiveness, transportability, and dissemination of interventions: What matters when? *Psychiatric Services, 52,* 1190–1197. doi:10.1176/appi.ps.52.9.1190

Seligman, M.E.P. (2011). *Flourish.* New York, NY: Simon & Schuster.

Seligman, M.E., & Csikszentmihalyi, M. (2000). Positive psychology: An introduction. *American Psychologist, 55,* 5–14. doi:10.1037//0003-066X.55.1.5

Snyder, C.R., Shorey, H.S., Cheavens, J., Pulvers, K.M., Adams, V.H., & Wiklund, C. (2002). Hope and academic success in college. *Journal of Educational Psychology, 94,* 820–826. doi:10.1037//0022-0663.94.4.820

U.S. News and World Report. (2013). *U.S. News & World Report; 2013* http://grad-schools.usnews.rankingsand reviews.com/best-graduate-schools/top-education-schools/edu-rankings

Wandersman, A., Duffy, J., Flaspohler, P., Noonan, R., Lubell, K., Stillman, L., . . . Saul, J. (2008). Bridging the gap between prevention research and practice: The Interactive Systems Framework for Dissemination and Implementation. *American Journal of Community Psychology, 41,* 3–4. doi:10.1007/s10464-008-9174-z

CHAPTER SUMMARY: PERSPECTIVES

- Helping schools embrace positive psychology requires significantly helpful programs and an implementation strategy with a supportive larger context. The larger supportive context presently is not adequate.
- Broad policy statements by organizations making standards influencing schools are generally supportive of positive psychology but are not specifically useful in furthering implementation.
- Positive psychology in the top teacher training sites in the United States and the textbooks used in teacher training is almost completely absent. Based on lack of exposure, we estimate that most teachers in training graduate ignorant of positive psychology and needing conversion before replacing educators in positive-psychology–oriented schools.
- Sophisticated implementation models and successful examples exist that can guide adoption of positive psychology into schools. With great skill, dedication, and effort, implementation occurs, but longevity remains dubious.
- Suggestions for how advocates for positive psychology can further the creation of a context supportive of change toward positive-psychology–informed schools are presented.

SUGGESTED READINGS: PERSPECTIVES

Donaldson, S. I., Csikszentmihalyi, M. & Nakamura, J. (2011). *Applied positive psychology: Improving everyday life, health, schools, work, and society (Applied Psychology series).* New York, NY: Taylor and Francis.

Provides summaries of the core topics in the positive psychology field by luminaries. Two chapters explicitly address positive psychology in education, giving the reader perspectives of positive psychology in education.

Fox-Eades, J. (2010). *Celebrating strengths.* Dallas, TX: CAPP Press.

A teacher-author provides engaging examples of positive psychology attitudes and interventions. The best-known chapters incorporate storytelling highlighting strengths. The author also focuses on praising effort more than results.

Seligman, M. E. P. (2011). *Flourish.* New York, NY: Simon & Schuster.

An easy-to-read book that includes examples of implementing positive psychology into schools. Also a warning that high fidelity of intervention must be accomplished for gains to occur. Research revealing how easy the intervention is to enact for gains is paramount for effective implementation.

INDEX

ABA (applied behavior analysis) 354
Abuhamdeh, S. 213
academic achievement: gender differences and 85–6; hope and 39–40; life satisfaction and 198–9; meaningful activity and 234; peer relationships and 267; predictors of 60; prosocial behaviors and 85–6; school experience and 4; self-efficacy and 119, 123; self-regulation and 104; social-emotional difficulties and 386–7; student engagement and 180, 181
academic development, EI and 456
academic dishonesty and cheating 136–7
academic efficacy 281, 283–4
academic indicators, hope and 466–7
academic intensity 217
Academic Performance Index (API) 73
academic self-concept, student engagement and 178
academic self-determination 281, 284
academic self-efficacy. *See* self-efficacy
achievement behaviors, self-efficacy and 116
achievement emotions 146–64: appraisals and goals 153–4; appraisal theories 148–51; approaches to measurement 157–9; assessment alternatives 158–9; attributional theory 148–9; autonomy, support of 159; classroom instruction 153–4; cognitive quality of instruction 159; cognitive resource theories 150–1; consequences of achievement 160; control-value theory of 149; definitions 146–8; development of 156–7; diversity and universality of 156; goal structures 160; implications for educational practice 157–60; individual and social origins 153–4; learning and performance, functions for 154–6; motivational quality of instruction 159; negative deactivating

155–6; overview 146, 160–1, 163–4; positive 154–5; research findings 152–6; resource allocation theories 150–1; self-regulated learning, support of 159; self-report measures 157–8; social origins 153–4; suggested readings 164; test anxiety 148, 150, 153–4, 157; test taking and feedback 160; theories of 148–52; three-dimensional taxonomy 147–8
Achievement Emotions Questionnaire (AEQ) 158
achievement goal orientations 132–3
Achievement Goals Scale 138
achievement goal theory 131
acquiescent response bias 442
Activating-Belief-Consequences model 424
activity checklists 290
activity emotions 150
activity participation 228. *See also* meaningful activity participation
Adams, N. E. 122
adaptive emotion regulation 107
Add Health data set 229
ADHD behavior 106–7
adolescent mental health 12–32, 416
adolescent psychological disorders 383–5
Adolescent School Belonging Questionnaire (ASBQ) 441
Adolescent's School Well-Being Scale (ASW-BS) 440
Adult Hope Scale (AHS) 469–70
adult leaders, meaningful activity and 235–6
adult outcomes 279
advance forward incrementation 167
advice-seeking strategy 102
AEQ (Achievement Emotions Questionnaire) 158
affective engagement 177